DEVELOPMENTAL PSYCHOPHYSIOLOGY

Until now, individuals interested in measuring biological signals non-invasively from typically developing children had few places to turn to find an overview of theory, methods, measures, and applications related to psychophysiology recordings in children. This volume briefly surveys the primary methods of psychophysiology that have been applied to developmental psychology research with children, what they have accomplished, and where the future lies. It outlines the practical problems that active developmental psychophysiology laboratories encounter and some solutions to deal with them. Developmental psychophysiology holds the key to forming the interface between structure and function central to psychological growth.

Louis A. Schmidt is Associate Professor of Psychology, Neuroscience and Behavior at McMaster University in Ontario, Canada. He is a Core Member of the Offord Centre for Child Studies, Division of Child Psychiatry at McMaster Children's Hospital. He received his Ph.D. from the University of Maryland, College Park. His research interests are developmental psychophysiology, human social and affective neuroscience, and the use of EEG/ERP measures to understand individual differences in temperament and affective responses in normal and special populations.

Sidney J. Segalowitz is a Professor of Psychology at Brock University, Editor of *Brain and Cognition*, and Director of the Brock Institute for Electrophysiological Research. He received his Ph.D. from Cornell University, and currently his research interests include developmental electrophysiology and psychophysiology, as they inform us about changes in cognitive and affective processing across the lifespan, especially with respect to error processing and attention, and the uses of electrophysiology to further our understanding of information processing in the brain.

Developmental Psychophysiology

Theory, Systems, and Methods

Edited by

LOUIS A. SCHMIDT

*Department of Psychology, Neuroscience & Behavior,
McMaster University*

SIDNEY J. SEGALOWITZ

Department of Psychology, Brock University

CAMBRIDGE
UNIVERSITY PRESS

CAMBRIDGE UNIVERSITY PRESS
Cambridge, New York, Melbourne, Madrid, Cape Town, Singapore, São Paulo, Delhi

Cambridge University Press
32 Avenue of the Americas, New York, NY 10013-2473, USA

www.cambridge.org
Information on this title: www.cambridge.org/9780521821063

First published 2008

Printed in the United States of America

A catalog record for this publication is available from the British Library.

Library of Congress Cataloging in Publication Data

Developmental psychophysiology : theory, systems, and methods / edited by
Louis A. Schmidt, Sidney J. Segalowitz.
    p.   ;   cm.
Includes bibliographical references and index.
ISBN 978-0-521-82106-3 (hardback)
1. Developmental psychobiology.   2. Psychophysiology.   I. Schmidt, Louis A.   II. Segalowitz,
Sidney J.
    [DNLM: 1. Child Development – physiology.   2. Psychophysiology – methods.   3. Child
Psychology.   WL 103 D4895 2008]
QP363.5.D52   2008
612.8 – dc22   2007009053

ISBN   978-0-521-82106-3 hardback

Contents

Foreword

Developmental psychophysiology is an emergent discipline that applies the technologies of psychophysiology to study developmental processes. The history of developmental psychophysiology reflects the unscripted dance of investigators moving in and out of disciplines, research questions, populations, clinical problems, physiological measures, and technologies. Developmental psychophysiology represents the products of scientific curiosity and ingenuity as investigators boldly attempt to apply new technologies to study classic problems and unanswered questions regarding the developmental trajectory of psychological processes. Unlike the psychologist, who studies both observable behaviors and subjective reports, the psychophysiologist investigates responses that do not require verbal responses or overt behaviors. Thus, the tools of psychophysiology provide developmental scientists with opportunities to expand the investigative envelope of inquiry to include the preverbal infant.

Before we can place developmental psychophysiology in perspective, we need to examine briefly the history of psychophysiology. Psychophysiology is at the crossroads of several disciplines, each with preferred models, paradigms, and measures. Unlike physiology with its focus on mechanism and structure or cardiology with its focus on clinical status, psychophysiology was driven by paradigms derived from psychology, often treating physiological parameters as if they were observable behaviors. The early psychophysiologists, defined by their use of the polygraph, applied the polygraph to "transform" unobservable psychological or mental processes into measurable physiological variables (e.g., Razran, 1961).

Early papers by Fere (1888) and Tarchanoff (1890) provide visionary statements of the paradigms that would define psychophysiology. Their papers focused on using electrodermal activity as indicators of psychological responses to a variety of stimuli. Reports of measured electrical activity generated by physiological systems piqued the interest of many psychologists during the late 1800s and early 1900s to use these signals as indices of psychological processes. The Fere and Tarchanoff papers provide examples. Others used these techniques to investigate atypical mental processes. For example, Peterson and Jung (1907) recorded electrodermal activity in normal and insane individuals seeking an objective measure of mental illness. Berger (1929) birthed human EEG research by placing electrodes on the scalp of his son and recording electrical activity via a string galvanometer and a smoked kymograph (devices long expunged from the memories of psychophysiologists). The reliability of these electrical signals and their sensitivity to psychological phenomena intrigued many scientists and provoked interest in applying these techniques to monitor mental processes.

Given the strong interest in mental processes, these early investigators had only a minor interest in the neural mechanisms mediating these responses. Ironically, the origin of modern psychophysiology is often linked to the classical conditioning of autonomic activity, which, as Pavlov (1927) demonstrated, requires the involvement of higher brain structures in the modulation of visceral responses (for a more detailed discussion of this paradox, see Porges, 2007a, b). The history of psychophysiological research with heart rate measures has a different trajectory. Heart rate entered psychophysiology from medicine and physiology. Non-invasive measurement of the electrical signal from the heart provided physicians with an opportunity to evaluate myocardial conductivity. The measurement of beat-to-beat heart rate provided physiologists with indices of neural influences. Blockade and surgical manipulations provided scientists with the ability to identify and estimate the vagal and sympathetic influences on the heart.

Developmental psychophysiology emerged with a convergence of questions from both developmental psychology and medicine. Developmental scientists found the research on classical conditioning intriguing as a possible "window" into the psychological world of young children. Most classical conditioning research (e.g., Pavlov, 1927) focused on the effect of stimulus contingencies on autonomic processes. By the 1960s, psychologists had the tools to measure the autonomic nervous system (e.g., electrodermal, heart rate) and were importing the paradigms that Soviet psychologists developed, based on the pioneering work of Pavlov, to study infants (e.g., Brackbill, Lintz, & Fitzgerald, 1968). Occurring simultaneously with these events, heart rate and heart rate variability started to be used as an index of the status of the nervous system in neonates and fetuses (e.g., Yeh, Forsythe, & Hon, 1973). Early developmental psychophysiologists (e.g., Bartoshuk, 1962; Graham, Clifton, & Hatton, 1968) studied the heart rate responses to various stimuli to index processes of orienting, attention, conditioning, and habituation. As the technologies and interests in heart rate variability emerged from both psychophysiological research with adults (e.g., Porges & Raskin, 1969) and obstetrics and neonatology (e.g., Hon & Lee, 1963), heart rate variability as a measure of individual differences and mental effort was infused into developmental paradigms (e.g., Porges, Arnold, & Forbes, 1973).

Progress in developmental psychophysiology was related to the unique opportunities of collaboration and communication that the new emergent discipline provided. Developmental psychophysiology challenged scientists with new research questions that attracted researchers with diverse skills and backgrounds. Since proximity facilitates collaboration and the integration of various scientific perspectives, a few nodes can be identified as having provided environments that nurtured developmental psychophysiology. It is possible that developmental psychophysiology owes its current success to the Fels Longitudinal Study. In the 1920s, Arthur Morgan, President of Antioch College, approached Samuel Fels, a philanthropist, to study the research question: "What makes people different?" Lester W. Sontag, the physician at Antioch College, was appointed as the first Director of the Fels Longitudinal Study in 1929. During his tenure, Sontag assembled an impressive team of scientists with interests in development, psychology, and physiology. In the 1960s, the Fels Research Institute was home to pioneering psychophysiologists John and Beatrice Lacey and discipline-defining developmental psychologists Jerome Kagan and Michael Lewis. In 1957, Frances Graham left Washington University Medical School, where she worked with very young infants suffering from hypoxia, and moved to the University of Wisconsin. At the University of Wisconsin, her developmental perspective and interest in the newborn expanded to include psychophysiological methods after her interactions with psychophysiologists such as Peter Lang, David Graham, and Rachel Keen Clifton.

Another strong influence on the roots of developmental psychophysiology came from Brown University. The Brown developmental psychologists provided an important and new emphasis on the study of young infants as an experimental science. This new subdiscipline of experimental child psychology required objective measures, even when the children were not verbal. Lewis Lipsitt and his colleagues directed their research to study early operant learning in the very young infant using the polygraph to monitor sucking and heart rate changes. A final and more personal node on this historical journey is the psychology department at the University of Illinois at Urbana-Champaign during the 1970s. This fertile node provided a unique mix in which my developmental perspective interfaced with the individual difference strategies of Michael Coles and the cognitive perspective of Emanuel Donchin. During our period together, we moved our psychophysiology laboratories to online computers, extended quantification procedures to time series models, and conducted research on the basic physiology of psychophysiological variables (e.g., Coles, Donchin, & Porges, 1986; Porges & Coles, 1976).

As we evaluate the progress of developmental psychophysiology, a discipline that is less than 50 years of age, we need to appreciate the pioneers who asked bold questions, built and designed their own equipment, carried the equipment into hospitals and clinics, and hand scored each heart beat and electrodermal response. The current volume is timely as methods have improved, paradigms have been refined, and clinical questions have been expanded. In addition, psychophysiology has moved from treating physiology as behavior to a more integrative understanding of the nervous system and the role that neurophysiological systems have in mediating behavior and psychological processes.

Stephen W. Porges, Ph.D.
Brain-Body Center
Department of Psychiatry
University of Illinois at Chicago

References

Bartoshuk, A. K. (1962). Response decrement with repeated elicitation of human neonatal cardiac acceleration to sound. *Journal of Comparative and Physiological Psychology*, *55*, 9–13.

Berger, H. (1929). Ueber das Elektroenkephalogramm des Menschen. *Archiv fuer Psychiatrie und Nervenkrankheiten, 87*, 527–570. [Reprinted in Porges, S. W., & Coles, M. G. H. (1976). *Psychophysiology*. Stroudsburg, PA: Dowden, Hutchinson & Ross.]

Brackbill, Y., Lintz, L. M., & Fitzgerald, H. E. (1968). Differences in the autonomic and somatic conditioning of infants. *Psychosomatic Medicine, 30*, 193–201.

Coles, M. G. H., Donchin, E., & Porges, S. W. (1986). (Eds.). *Psychophysiology: Systems, processes, and applications*. New York: Guilford.

Fere, C. (1888). Note on changes in electrical resistance under the effect of sensory stimulation and emotion. *Comptes Rendus des Seances de la Societe de Biologie, 5*, 217–219. [Reprinted in Porges, S. W., & Coles, M. G. H. (1976). *Psychophysiology*. Stroudsburg, PA: Dowden, Hutchinson & Ross.]

Graham, F. K., Clifton, R. K., & Hatton, H. M. (1968). Habituation of heart rate response to repeated auditory stimulation during the first five days of life. *Child Development*, *39*, 35–52.

Hon, E. H., & Lee, S. T. (1963). Electronic evaluation of the fetal heart rate. VIII. Patterns preceding fetal death, further observation. *American Journal of Obstetric Gynecology*, *87*, 814–826.

Pavlov, I. P. (1927). *Conditioned Reflexes*. London: Oxford University Press.

Peterson, F., & Jung, C. G. (1907). Psychophysical investigations with the galvanometer and pneuomograph in normal and insane individuals. *Brain, 30,* 153–218.

Porges, S. W. (2007a). The Polyvagal Perspective. *Biological Psychology. 74,* 116–143.

Porges, S. W. (2007b). A phylogenetic journey through the vagus and ambiguous Xth cranial nerve: A commentary on contemporary heart rate variability research. *Biological Psychology. 74,* 301–307.

Porges, S. W., Arnold, W. R., & Forbes, E. J. (1973). Heart rate variability: An index of attentional responsivity in human newborns. *Developmental Psychology, 8,* 85–92.

Porges, S. W., & Coles, M. G. H. (1976). *Psychophysiology*. Stroudsburg, PA: Dowden, Hutchinson & Ross.

Porges, S. W., & Raskin, D. C. (1969). Respiratory and heart rate components of attention. *Journal of Experimental Psychology, 81,* 497–503.

Razran, G. (1961). The observable unconscious and the inferable conscious in current Soviet psychophysiology: Interoceptive conditioning, semantic conditioning, and the orienting reflex. *Psychological Review, 68,* 81–147.

Tarchanoff, J. (1890). Galvanic phenomena in the human skin during stimulation of the sensory organs and during various forms of mental activity. *Pfluger's Archiv fur die Gesamte Physiologie des Menschen und der Tiere, 46,* 46–55. [Reprinted in Porges, S. W., & Coles, M. G. H. (1976). *Psychophysiology*. Stroudsburg, PA: Dowden, Hutchinson & Ross.]

Yeh, S. Y., Forsythe, A., & Hon, E. H. (1973). Quantification of fetal heart beat-to-beat interval differences. *Obstetrics and Gynecology, 41,* 355–363.

Preface

The field of cognitive and affective neuroscience has burgeoned during the last 20 years, prompting the publication of several handbooks. The allied field of psychophysiology included two such comprehensive collections over the last 7 years but, surprisingly, only one chapter in each was dedicated to issues pertaining mainly to children (Fox, Schmidt, & Henderson, 2000; Fox, Schmidt, Henderson, & Marshall, 2007) as was the case some 20 years earlier (Porges & Fox, 1986).

Today, there has been considerable research attention directed toward understanding brain-behavior relations in a developmental context. Interdisciplinary approaches to the study of behavior in which development and brain are interfaced have blossomed. We now routinely observe researchers in developmental psychology interacting with people in the fields of behavioral and cognitive neuroscience, and vice versa. This book reflects the spirit of the multidisciplinary nature of science and the dialogue of our two disparate worlds: one as a social developmental psychologist (LAS) and the other as a cognitive neuroscientist (SJS).

The seeds for this book were sown five years ago as a result of our frequent discussions of science, life, and the human condition. In addition to the friendship that quickly developed from our many talks over the years, there soon emerged the realization that, although more and more developmental child psychologists were beginning to study brain-behavior relations in a developmental context, a lack of resources in the area from which they could draw was apparent.

One purpose in compiling this book was to bring together a number of scientists into one intellectual forum that would cover most of the psychophysiological methods in our field, as well as the uses to which we put them. The book is nominally organized into four major sections. We start with a discussion of how the use of psychophysiological techniques might help us understand the complex interactions that exist in the study of human development before moving into the other chapters contained within the four major sections. Section I contains chapters that cover issues related to electrocortical measures including event-related potentials (ERPs) and continuous EEG measures across auditory, visual, cognitive, and socio-emotional processes in children. Section II presents chapters related to autonomic and peripheral psychophysiological measures including heart rate, heart rate variability, and electrodermal and electromyographic responses in children. Section III includes chapters discussing the theory and methods of non-invasive hormonal measures used to study human development. Section IV offers chapters outlining the collection of reliable psychophysiological data in basic research settings with pediatric populations.

Developmental psychophysiology is the study of psychological processes during development using physiological measures. Developmental psychophysiology essentially covers the conceptual issues and practical techniques for doing much of the exciting burgeoning research in the field of cognitive developmental neuroscience. Although development spans the period from conception to senescence, the focus of this edited volume is primarily on children and the recording of non-invasive electrical signals and non-invasive hormonal measures from birth to the adolescent years in typically developing humans. Moreover, the book was not intended to provide exhaustive coverage of all psychophysiological theory, methods, and measures. Clearly, there are other methods and measures that psychophysiologists use in their work that we have not covered here but are reviewed extensively elsewhere in other handbook volumes (see Cacioppo, Tassinary, & Berntson, 2000, 2007; Coles, Donchin, & Porges, 1986, for extensive reviews). We also did not include a discussion on the use of functional brain imaging measures (e.g., fMRI, PET). Although developmental psychophysiologists use these methods, an adequate discussion of these methods and measures was beyond the scope of this volume.

Until now, individuals interested in measuring biological signals non-invasively from typically developing children had few places to turn to find an overview of theory, methods, measures, and applications related to psychophysiology recordings in children. In this volume, we survey briefly the primary methods of psychophysiology that have been applied to developmental psychology research, what they have accomplished, and where their promise lies in the future. We also outline some of the practical problems encountered and solutions developed by active developmental psychophysiology laboratories to deal with them. Developmental psychophysiology is a rapidly growing field that holds the key, we feel, to forming the interface between structure and function necessary for the growth of developmental psychology.

With this book, we have endeavored to provide the research community with the resources to enable them to collect reliable psychophysiological signals and data from children, including the knowledge of how to avoid some of the pitfalls that many established researchers in the field have taken years to learn. Our hope is that this book will serve as a resource for researchers and students working in the areas of development psychology, developmental cognitive and affective neuroscience, clinical child psychology and psychiatry, and pediatric medicine.

Louis A. Schmidt   Sidney J. Segalowitz

Hamilton, Ontario   St. Catharines, Ontario

July 2007

References

Cacioppo, J. T., Tassinary, L. G., & Berntson, G. C. (2000). (Eds.). *Handbook of psychophysiology* (2nd ed.). New York: Cambridge University Press.

Cacioppo, J. T., Tassinary, L. G., & Berntson, G. C. (2007). (Eds.). *Handbook of psychophysiology* (3rd ed.). New York: Cambridge University Press.

Coles, M. G. H., Donchin, E., & Porges, S. W. (1986). (Eds.). *Psychophysiology: Systems, processes, & applications.* New York: Guilford.

Fox, N. A., Schmidt, L. A., & Henderson, H. A. (2000). Developmental psychophysiology: Conceptual and methodological perspectives. In J. T. Cacioppo, L. G. Tassinary, & G. C. Berntson (Eds.), *Handbook of psychophysiology* (2nd ed., pp. 665–686). New York: Cambridge University Press.

Fox, N. A., Schmidt, L. A., Henderson, H. A., & Marshall, P. J. (2007). Developmental psychophysiology: Conceptual and methodological perspectives. In J. T. Cacioppo, L. G. Tassinary, & G. C. Berntson (Eds.), *Handbook of psychophysiology* (3rd ed. pp. 453–481). New York: Cambridge University Press.

Porges, S. W., & Fox, N. A. (1986). Developmental psychophysiology. In M. G. H. Coles, E. Donchin, & S. W. Porges (Eds.), *Psychophysiology: Systems, processes, & applications* (pp. 611–625). New York: Guilford.

Acknowledgments

One does not pursue knowledge in isolation. We would like to thank our family, friends, and colleagues for their encouragement and support along the way without which this project would not have been possible. We wish to express our appreciation to the thousands of children and their parents who have contributed their time, patience, and interest to psychophysiology and developmental science. We would also like to acknowledge the Natural Sciences and Engineering Research Council of Canada and the Social Sciences and Humanities Research Council of Canada for their continued support of our work. Finally, we wish to thank Philip Laughlin, past Psychology Editor at Cambridge University Press, for his support of this project, and special thanks to Austina Reed for her help with copyediting.

Contributors

Marie T. Balaban (Ph.D., University of Wisconsin, Madison) is Professor of Psychology at Eastern Oregon University. Her research interests are early cognitive development, emotion, and psychophysiology.

Martha Ann Bell (Ph.D., University of Maryland, College Park) is Associate Professor of Psychology at Virginia Polytechnic Institute and State University. Her research interests are developmental cognitive neuroscience and frontal lobe development in infants and young children, including development of working memory, executive attention, and self-regulation.

W. Keith Berg (Ph.D., University of Wisconsin, Madison) is Professor of Psychology at the University of Florida. His research interests are psychophysiology, developmental cognitive neuroscience, and executive functioning across the lifespan.

Dana L. Byrd (Ph.D., University of Florida) is a Postdoctoral Fellow in the Department of Psychobiology, Columbia University College of Physicians and Surgeons, New York State Psychiatric Institute. Her research interests are developmental cognitive neuroscience, executive functions, future-oriented processing, planning, event-related potentials, heart rate, and functional magnetic resonance imaging.

Patricia L. Davies (Ph.D., University of Wyoming) is Associate Professor and Director of the Brainwaves Research Laboratory in the Department of Occupational Therapy and Psychology at Colorado State University. Her research interests are examining neurophysiological mechanisms that underlie cognitive, sensory, and motor behaviors in children with and without disabilities using electroencephalogram and event-related potentials.

Michelle de Haan (Ph.D., University of Minnesota) is Reader and Honorary Principal Neuropsychologist at the Institute of Child Health, University College London. Her research interests are the development and neural basis of visual recognition and long-term memory and the use of ERP and MRI measures.

Kristine Erickson (Ph.D., American University) is a Research Scientist with the Mood and Anxiety Disorders Program at the National Institute of Mental Health, Bethesda, Md. Her research interests are neural imaging and endocrine measures in mood and anxiety disorders.

Don C. Fowles (Ph.D., Harvard University) is Professor of Psychology at the University of Iowa. His research interests are psychophysiological assessment of emotional responding, using electrodermal measures.

Nathan A. Fox (Ph.D., Harvard University) is Professor of Human Development and Psychology at the Institute for Child Study, University of Maryland, College Park. His research interests are early experience and brain development and social and emotional development of infants and young children.

William J. Gavin (Ph.D., University of Miami) is a Research Scientist/Scholar III and Director of the Brainwaves Research Laboratory in the Department of Occupational Therapy at Colorado State University. His research interests are investigating the neurophysiological mechanisms that underlie the relation of perception of sensory stimuli with the development of language and cognition in children with and without disabilities using electroencephalogram and event-related potentials.

Megan R. Gunnar (Ph.D., Stanford University) is Regents Professor and Distinguished McNight University Professor of Child Development at the Institute for Child Development, University of Minnesota. Her research interests are early deprivation, stress biology, social coping, and use of hormonal measures.

J. Dee Higley (Ph.D., University of Wisconsin, Madison) is Professor of Psychology at Brigham Young University. His research interests are nonhuman primate gene-environment models of addiction, social behavior, and psychopathology.

Vasil Kolev (Ph.D., Brain Research Institute, Bulgarian Academy of Sciences) is Associate Professor of Physiology at the Institute of Neurobiology, Bulgarian Academy of Sciences. His research interests are event-related brain potentials and oscillations, methods for EEG/ERP analysis, cognitive functions, and EEG.

James Long (B.A., Oberlin College) is a computer electrical and software engineer and the owner of the James Long Company. His research interests are psychophysiology research methods.

Peter J. Marshall (Ph.D., Cambridge University) is Assistant Professor of Psychology at Temple University. His research interests are psychophysiological correlates of infant and child temperament, specifically ERP measures of sensory processing in relation to early social and emotional development.

Anita Miller (Ph.D., Vanderbilt University) is Visiting Assistant Professor of Psychology at Skidmore College and a Research Scientist with the James Long Company. Her research interests are psychophysiology, emotion, and depression.

Stephen W. Porges (Ph.D., Michigan State University) is Professor of Psychiatry in the Department of Psychiatry and Director of the Brain-Body Center in the College of Medicine at the University of Illinois at Chicago. His research focuses on describing the neural circuits that regulate social engagement behaviors and emotion in normal and atypical individuals.

Greg D. Reynolds (Ph.D., Virginia Polytechnic Institute and State University) is Assistant Professor of Psychology at the University of Tennessee. His research interests are the development of attention and memory in human infants, and the relation between behavioral and psychophysiological correlates of infant attention and memory.

John E. Richards (Ph.D., University of California, Los Angeles) is Professor of Psychology at the University of South Carolina. His research interests are developmental psychophysiology, developmental cognitive neuroscience, infant heart rate, EEG/ERP, psychophysiology, brain development, and attention development.

Louis A. Schmidt (Ph.D., University of Maryland, College Park) is Associate Professor of Psychology, Neuroscience and Behavior at McMaster University and Core Member of the Offord Centre for Child Studies, Division of Child Psychiatry at McMaster Children's Hospital. His research interests are developmental psychophysiology, human social and affective neuroscience, and the use of EEG/ERP measures to understand individual differences in temperament and affective responses in normal and special populations.

Jay Schulkin (Ph.D., University of Pennsylvania) is Research Professor in the Department of Physiology and Biophysics and Center for Brain Basis of Cognition, Georgetown University, School of Medicine, Washington, DC, and Clinical Neuroendocrinology Branch, National Institute of Mental Health, Bethesda, Md. His research interests are the neuroendocrine regulation of behavior, particularly fear and appetitive behavior.

Sidney J. Segalowitz (Ph.D., Cornell University) is Professor of Psychology at Brock University, Editor of *Brain and Cognition*, and Director of the Brock Institute for Electrophysiological Research. His research interests are developmental electrophysiology and psychophysiology, as they inform us about changes in cognitive and affective processing across the lifespan, and the uses of electrophysiology to further understanding of information processing in the human brain.

Nicole M. Talge (M.A., University of Minnesota) is a Graduate Student at the Institute of Child Development at the University of Minnesota. Her research interests are human developmental psychobiology and the impact of pre/perinatal events on subsequent psychological development.

Laurel J. Trainor (Ph.D., University of Toronto) is Professor of Psychology, Neuroscience and Behavior at McMaster University, Research Scientist at the Rotman Research Institute, and Director of the McMaster Institute for Music and the Mind. Her research interests are in the neuroscience of auditory development, the acquisition of musical knowledge, relations between music and language, and the effects of experience on developmental outcome.

Christy D. Wolfe (Ph.D., Virginia Polytechnic Institute and State University) is Visiting Assistant Professor of Psychological and Brain Sciences at the University of Louisville. Her research interests are the development of working memory and executive attention in young children and the relation to physiological processes, regulatory dimensions of temperament, and linguistic functioning.

Juliana Yordanova (Ph.D., M.D., Brain Research Institute, Bulgarian Academy of Sciences, Medical University Sofia) is Associate Professor of Psychophysiology at the Institute of Neurobiology, Bulgarian Academy of Sciences. Her research interests are event-related brain potentials and oscillations, normal and pathological development, cognitive functions, executive control, and EEG.

1 Capturing the Dynamic Endophenotype

A Developmental Psychophysiological Manifesto

Sidney J. Segalowitz and Louis A. Schmidt

WHY SHOULD DEVELOPMENTALISTS BE PARTICULARLY INTERESTED IN PSYCHOPHYSIOLOGY?

Whether we like it or not, those of us interested in psychological development can never get very far away from some form of the nature-nurture question. In general, we have become more careful about ascribing complex behavioral attributes to purely biological substrates or solely to different life experiences. However, often this care is a reflex designed to avoid arguments and not due to true insights. Yet in order to be inclusive, developmental psychologists usually now acknowledge some sources from each, a kind of nature-plus-nurture approach. Some developmental disabilities, however, have often been talked about (depending on the background of the speaker) in terms of either nature or nurture, although most people today would point to both factors. One example is developmental dyslexia, which was originally postulated to have a biological familial basis (Orton, 1937), with various models of cortical insufficiency being blamed (see Pennington 2002, for a review). These insufficiencies include a series of cortical regions noted for their anatomical relation to reading (e.g., inferior parietal lobule), functional modules related to the reading process (e.g., phonological awareness), or sometimes both, such as a model of dyslexia focusing on an anatomically underdeveloped magnocellular system leading to functional deficits that might account for reading difficulties (Stein & Walsh, 1997). Some have suggested polygenic models through twin studies and single gene etiologies through linkage studies (Ingalls & Goldstein, 1999; Meng et al., 2005). At the same time, however, there have been those who discuss poor reading in the context of poor instruction within an awkward writing system (such as English), suggesting that the problem is not one of decoding abilities but rather one of the teaching method used to link meaning to written forms (e.g., Goodman, 1973; Smith, 1977).

Another approach to the issue of nature-plus-nurture is to focus on statistical interactions of independent biological and experiential factors. An example is the developmental psychology of social/personality traits such as shyness in typical development. Evidence suggests that temperamental shyness is driven by a biological system that has various genetic and structural correlates (see Fox et al., 2001, 2005; Kagan, 1994; Schmidt & Schulkin, 1999, for reviews). Others, however, have argued from a more environmental etiology of childhood shyness linked to early attachment between mother and child (e.g., Stevenson-Hinde, 2000).

Perhaps the strongest advocate of a biological predisposition (i.e., nature) to childhood shyness is that of Kagan and his colleagues. Kagan and Snidman (1991) found that a small percentage of typically developing children (between 5 – 10%) who exhibited extreme fear and wariness in response to novelty during the first years of post-natal life were likely to be behaviorally inhibited and shy during the preschool and early school age years. These temperamentally shy children were likely to possess the short allele of the serotonin transporter (5-HTT) gene (Fox et al., 2005) and are characterized by a distinct pattern of central, autonomic, and adrenocortical activity during baseline conditions and in response to social stress (see Schmidt & Schulkin, 1999, for a review). For example, temperamentally shy children are known to exhibit greater relative right frontal EEG activity, high and stable heart rate at rest (Fox et al., 2001; Kagan et al., 1987, 1988), and high morning basal cortisol levels (Kagan et al., 1987, 1988; Schmidt et al., 1997). These patterns of psychophysiological and neuroendocrine responses are also heightened during social stress (Schmidt et al., 1999). However, only a subset of temperamentally shy children who possess these psychophysiological and neuroendocrine responses actually go on to develop shyness and social problems, suggesting that experience and context (i.e., nurture) may also be critical.

Fox and his colleagues (2005) found that among the children who possessed the short (versus long) allele of the 5-HTT gene, only those whose mothers perceived themselves low in social support actually turned out to be shy. The children with mothers who perceived themselves high in social support were less likely to be shy and behaviourally inhibited. Accordingly, the interaction of biology and context provides us with a better picture of developmental outcome (e.g., who will develop shyness).

Another recent example of typically developing shy children from our laboratory illustrates the need to examine functional interactions in human developmental science (Brunet, Mondloch, & Schmidt, 2006). Endogenously driven temperamental shyness may set up a situation in the child whereby experience may be altered, which in turn may alter the functional capacity of neural networks. For example, we noted that temperamentally shy children (nature may have wired them differently) may alter their experiences with faces such that they exhibit deficits in some aspects of face recognition. These deficits are for a specific type of face recognition known as second-order or spacing among features. Temperamentally shy children exhibit deficits in their ability to process spacing among features in faces, a pattern of deficit also observed in children who had early visual deprivation due to congenital cataract. This deficit resulting from the lack of experiences with faces may set in motion a cascade of secondary negative effects such as multiple social problems that are often observed in some shy children due to their inability to perceive accurately others' facial emotions. Thus, the dispositional feature (i.e., temperamental shyness) or main effect reveals only so much about the temperamentally shy child. Both the child and the developmental context or experience need to be considered to provide a picture of the mechanisms involved in the development of shyness.

These examples from atypical and typical development serve to illustrate that both biological and experiential factors are intrinsic to the development of skills and traits. However, current research requires more integration, and our thesis is that psychophysiology is well placed to be in the center of this integration.

WHY IS PSYCHOLOGICAL DEVELOPMENT FUNDAMENTALLY CONSTRUCTIVIST?

We think it is fair to say that developmental psychology as a field has become essentially constructivist in Piaget's (1971) sense, with the debates only focusing on the details. Most of us now see children as being highly active in the construction of their own minds, as opposed to being the passive recipients of mental structures, whether the transmission is through a genetic "blueprint" or through environmental shaping. This constructivist approach has won the day, the fundamental argument being that the child is an active player in the development of his or her own mental structures. We accept this constructivist model for reasons that go well beyond anything Piaget wrote or knew about. We now know that the constructivist model appears to be the most robust, fitting both the known facts about brain growth and about mental development. There is more than a little irony here, given that Piaget had given up on brain growth as being part of the story of psychological development (see Segalowitz, 2007, for an outline of the historical issues). We now know that the growth of neural networks is heavily dependent on prespecified growth tendencies but is sculpted by experience twice. The first time is evidenced in the role of active attention and stimulation on cortical growth; dendritic growth and synaptic proliferation are fed at least to some extent by mental activity (Diamond, 1988; Kandel, Jessell, & Sanes, 2000). The second time involves the sculpting of those networks. Considerable evidence exists that this process starts within the sensory systems very soon after birth, such as when visual experience alters the balance of connections within the visual system (Kandel et al., 2000). As far as we know, this process is the pattern for other sensory modalities and multimodal functional systems as well, such as those subserving language, spatial thinking, music, and so on. Furthermore, lack of input within one modality can dramatically alter the way the sensory systems are connected. For example, we find that in congenitally deaf or blind individuals, the linkage between sense organs and cortex is affected by deafness and blindness (Fieger et al., 2006; Stevens & Weaver, 2005). What appears to be the normal pattern of cortical networking is dependent on experience setting the stage for the unfolding of the neural plan. Such influences from experience are not confined to very early stages of development; the brain's structural and functional connections are affected by musical experience several years after birth (Elbert et al., 1995; Fujioka et al., 2006).

But all these patterns only make sense when we understand the interactions between the main effects of biological factors (genes, nutrition, prenatal, chemical, and health environment) and experience (sensory function, cognitive processes including attention and memory, social functions such as emotional interchange and communication, parenting, peers, extra-familial non-normative events, abuse, etc.). In concrete terms, development can only be understood as the growth response of the organism's particular biochemical and structural characteristics within contexts that relate to the instructions in those characteristics. The biochemical instructions built into the biological system are interpreted within the particular context in which they are found, something that has been understood in embryology for over a century and a half, but only appreciated more recently within developmental psychology. This process is also known by another meaning of the term "interaction."

WHAT IS THE MEANING OF INTERACTION?

The term interaction has come to take on more than one meaning within the developmental context, but two in particular concern us here. The first is the statistical meaning: An interaction of independent factors involves matching biological characteristics (e.g., genetic) with experiences (i.e., G × E). A classic example is the genetic combination that puts a child at risk for phenylketonuria (PKU). PKU only produces a negative outcome when a diet supplies phenylalanine. Because all natural diets produce a negative outcome, PKU appears to be a main effect "genetic" disease. However, the genotype presents a (highly likely) predisposition that then unfolds in standard environments. This example is one of the only instances for which we have virtually all the details. Another example, increasingly more common now that we have the appropriate technology for genetic typing, is when children who possessed the short versus long allele of the 5-HHT gene were compared on levels of shyness at age four years. The main effect for genotype was not significant (Schmidt et al., 2002). However, when we considered perceived social support of mothers in relation to the children's short versus long allele of the 5-HTT gene, we found a significant interaction on childhood shyness (Fox et al., 2005). Children with the short allele who had mothers low in perceived social support were likely to be more behaviorally inhibited and shy at age seven years than children either with the long allele of the 5-HTT gene or with mothers high in perceived social support.

Another complex interaction, and for which we are starting to understand the mechanisms, is illustrated by the example of how a gene that regulates the activity level of monoamine oxidase A (MAOA), which is critical for metabolizing catecholamine neurotransmitters, interacts with early stressful experiences to put the person at increased risk for antisocial behavior (Caspi et al., 2002). Now that DNA typing is possible, similar interactions are being discovered, including those for the serotonin transporter associated with affective disorders (Caspi et al., 2003; Hariri et al., 2005) and catechol-o-methyl transferase (COMT), another dopamine transporter gene, associated with a predisposition for schizophrenia (Weinberger et al., 2001). Despite these very important advances in understanding G × E interactions that influence brain function and outcome, these interactions cloud the mechanism of a different interpretation of the term "interaction."

The second meaning for the term interaction goes beyond just the genes *per se* and focuses on their function. The presence of the genes is not really the issue. It is the polypeptide mappings of the genes that are important, because these mappings lead to the chemical structures that influence the brain's structures and functions. The genetic activations that map onto these polypeptides are necessarily influenced by experience, acting through the circulating hormones. The fundamental aspect of interest then is the outcome of the genes' activation. This interaction is derived from what is called the gene-environment interplay (Rutter, Moffitt, & Caspi, 2006). Just as the child's social behavior can be mapped by following the child-parent dynamic, the child's growth of brain function can be best understood through the dynamic between biological underpinnings and experience. This dynamic helps guide the functional growth of the brain and accounts for the G × E interaction through the G × E interplay; genes influence the growth and activity of cells as a function of the context. This notion was first discovered functionally through careful observation of mother-pup social interactions that led to sex-stereotyped behavior in rats, and this effect was documented without knowledge of underlying genetic mechanisms (Moore, 1992). We now know from the seminal work of Michael Meaney and Moshe Szyf that the mechanism is one that facilitates or restricts the genome from realizing its potential options (Meaney & Szyf, 2005).

Thus, main effects themselves are interesting initial guides, but they do not really explain the variance of interest to developmental psychologists (except for the obvious outcomes that need more action than clever research, e.g., starvation is bad for everyone, light is needed for visual development, and so on). In contrast, statistical interactions point us in the appropriate direction; they imply the nature of the dynamic that explains development. However, the dynamic that this interaction implies is not at the level of the gene or environment as measured in the study; rather, it implies that the environment acts on the genome to regulate its activity in such a way that the neurodevelopmental pathway is altered. The interaction is the guide to the gene-experience interplay: interplay is the crucial component. Accordingly, the main effect of genes does not add to our understanding of developmental processes; it is the interplay (resulting in interactions) that clarifies development.

This interplay leads us to examine partial outcomes at a middle level, and the most interesting predictors that add to developmental theory are these middle-level dynamic outcomes from the genotype-environment interplay. No matter what the genetic or environmental pressures or their combination which may push the brain to be the way it is, we need to measure the state of central nervous system activity. This middle level state reflects the outcome of the G × E interplay, and the only way to examine this level in practical terms for most developmental psychologists is with psychophysiological methods. For example, researchers have hypothesized that inhibitory control networks involving various structures of the prefrontal cortex are needed to understand attention deficit hyperactivity disorder (ADHD), the development of behavioral and emotional self-regulation, and so on. This middle level of brain function is sometimes referred to as endophenotypes in order to capture the sense that they are both developmental outcomes and predictors of behavior (Castellanos & Tannock, 2002). We may also refer to them as neuropsychological and psychophysiological constructs. The study of the middle level permeates neuropsychology, with applications to psychopathology (e.g., Savitz, Solms, & Ramesar, 2005), impulsivity (Congdon & Canli, 2005), and even alcoholism (Hesselbrock et al., 2001). However, in using this middle level to understand syndromes, we must be careful not to exaggerate the explanatory value of the isolated endophenotype. For example, although those at risk for alcoholism have often been shown to have a reduction in P300 amplitude, this is not a specific marker and must be only part of the full endophenotype (Hesselbrook et al., 2001). The hope is that this neurophysiological level will help us bridge the gap between genotype and experience that will help clarify their interplay (Gottesman & Gould, 2003).

In order to bridge this gap, we may need to treat our psychophysiological measures as both predictors and outcomes, something that happens routinely in developmental psychophysiology. For example, consider the psychophysiological construct of frontal EEG asymmetry. Greater right frontal EEG activation has been used as a predictor of vulnerability to anxiety (see Davidson, 2000), and it has also been treated as a developmental outcome, reflecting the risk in emotional development for infants of depressed mothers (Field, Fox, Pickens, & Nawrocki, 2005). It would be consistent to find that the frontal EEG asymmetry is more likely in certain genotypes. In other words, psychophysiological measures reflecting this middle level may be efficient mediators between predisposition (genetic or otherwise) and outcome.

Thus, the importance of these endophenotypes for developmental psychology cannot be overstated: *It is our task as developmental psychologists to further our understanding of the dynamics of development through the interplay of function and structure, and this level of analysis must be our focus.*

HOW CAN WE MEASURE THIS ENDOPHENOTYPE LEVEL OF FUNCTION AND STRUCTURE?

Purely behavioral measures are no longer considered adequate. There was a time when most developmentalists employed only behavioral measures. Thus, researchers used complex problem-solving tasks such as the Wisconsin Card Sorting Task (WCST) or Tower of London (TOL) in order to tap into the "health" or "growth" of the prefrontal cortex (PFC). Similarly, a researcher might infer a hemisphere activation bias from a dichotic listening or a visual half-field task involving the detection or categorization of emotion. However, we now know this approach is wrong for two basic reasons. First, none of these tasks are process pure and reflect many brain functions and structures. Therefore, we cannot expect that they reflect activity of a single brain network. Second, children do not solve complex problems the same way as do the clinical adults on whom the tasks were standardized in the first place. Thus, we do not know which brain networks are reflected in good or poor performance in children.

In contrast to just one or two decades ago, the methods of choice for getting at this middle level are now available to developmental psychologists. What we need are measures that reflect the activation of specific neural systems within the context of specific tasks designed to test our hypotheses. Brain imaging systems provide some of these measures. For example, functional magnetic resonance imaging (fMRI) and positron emission tomography (PET) allow challenges to be presented to the participant while the brain is scanned for regions of specific activation. Although fMRI has some obvious benefits in its spatial resolution, the technology has some serious limitations, whether the paradigms used are event-related fMRI or blocked trials. First, fMRI is very expensive and therefore few labs can afford multiple studies with the large sample sizes needed to look for joint developmental and gender effects (not to mention the inclusion of personality or cognitive characteristics as well). Second, the demands of the machinery are relatively intrusive, making it not very friendly to young children. Third, the technology requires very limited movement and actions, in turn limiting the contexts and tasks available for use with children. Fourth, serious interpretive problems exist, owing to the nature of the non-additive factors designs typically employed (i.e., the appropriate baseline is not always clear). fMRI is one technology that requires a baseline subtraction in order to interpret individual or group differences, and it is not always clear how to go about doing this when developmental groups may differ on the baseline condition. PET is even more limited in flexibility of paradigms and is more invasive than fMRI, making it inappropriate for normative developmental studies.

The mainstays of psychophysiology are fully appropriate for the middle level of analysis: electroencephalogram (EEG), event-related potentials (ERP), electrodermal activitiy (EDA), electromyographic (EMG), and electrocardiogram (ECG) analyses all have adequate temporal resolution for studying behaviors that at least approach normal functions. They are also relatively inexpensive, are comparatively non-invasive, and can be applied to children of all ages in basic and applied or clinical research settings, as long as the children are reasonably cooperative. The methods for spatial resolution of brain function are improving for EEG and ERPs, but they probably will never achieve that of fMRI or PET. However, EEG and ERPs are increasingly interpreted as reflecting systems rather than regions of activation. Even in cases where the generator of the component seems to be well established, such as the error-related negativity associated with generators in the dorsal anterior cingulate cortex, it is also understood that this brain area is simply part of a larger network complex including other major structures in the prefrontal cortex (Devinsky, Morrell, & Vogt, 1995). These measurements are made in the order of hundredths or thousandths of a second; EEG and ERPs capture these temporal dynamics that imaging techniques cannot. Some newer technologies such as magnetoencephalography (MEG) and event-related optical signal (EROS) are promising, although they have their own limitations, especially for activity reflecting deep brain structures.

Some wide-ranging functional systems are not easily located to a single region within the nervous system. These indirect measures of brain activity include non-invasive techniques relating to heart rate and its variability, as well as to cardiac vagal tone. Still another class of structures (e.g., HPA axis, frontal cortex, and forebrain areas) is tapped by examining hormones related to the stress system (e.g., cortisol) that can be collected non-invasively in saliva.

SUMMARY AND CONCLUSIONS

Research questions in developmental psychology always come back to the nature-nurture question, but they are now better characterized as structural versus adaptational issues. In the past few years, we have grown to appreciate the middle level for its explanatory power. A middle level approach is sensitive to both structural and functional aspects of the system. This middle level is best reflected in psychophysiological measures that can measure ongoing dynamic changes in real time. These measures reflect the system's outcome of this nature-nurture interplay and can be used non-invasively with pediatric populations.

ACKNOWLEDGMENTS

The writing of this chapter was funded in part by grants from the Natural Sciences and Engineering Research Council (NSERC) of Canada awarded to SJS and the Social Sciences and Humanities Research Council (SSHRC) of Canada awarded to LAS.

References

Brunet, P. M., Mondloch, C., & Schmidt, L. A. (2006). *Shy children show deficits in some aspects of face recognition.* Manuscript submitted for publication.

Caspi, A., McClay, J., Moffitt, T. E., Mill, J., Martin, J., Craig, I. W., Taylor, A., & Poulton, R. (2002). Role of genotype in the cycle of violence in maltreated children. *Science, 29,* 851–854.

Caspi, A., Sugden, K., Moffitt, T. E., Taylor, A., Craig, I. W., Harrington, H., McClay, J., Mill, J., Martin, J., Braithwaite, A., & Poulton, R. (2003). Influence of life stress on depression: Moderation by a polymorphism in the 5-HTT gene. *Science, 301,* 386–389.

Castellanos, F. X., & Tannock, R. (2002). Neuroscience of attention-deficit/hyperactivity disorder: The search for endophenotypes. *Nature Neuroscience Reviews, 3,* 617–628.

Congdon, E., & Canli, T. (2005). The endophenotype of impulsivity: Reaching consilience through behavioral, genetic, and neuroimaging approaches. *Behavioral and Cognitive Neuroscience Reviews, 4,* 262–281.

Davidson, R. J. (2000). Affective style, psychopathology, and resilience: Brain mechanisms and plasticity. *American Psychologist, 55,* 1196–1214.

Devinsky, O., Morrell, M. J., & Vogt, B. A. (1995). Contributions of anterior cingulate cortex to behavior. *Brain, 118,* 279–306.

Diamond, M. C. (1988). *Enriching heredity: The impact of the environment on the anatomy of the brain.* New York: The Free Press.

Elbert, T., Pantev, C., Wienbruch, C., Rockstroh, B., & Taub, E. (1995). Increased cortical representation of the fingers of the left hand in string players. *Science, 270,* 305–307.

Fieger, A., Roder, B., Teder-Salejarvi, W., Hillyard, S. A., & Neville, H. J. (2006). Auditory spatial tuning in late-onset blindness in humans. *Journal of Cognitive Neuroscience, 18,* 149–157.

Field, T., Fox, N. A., Pickens, J., & Nawrocki, T. (1995). Relative right frontal EEG activation in 3- to 6-month-old infants of "depressed" mothers. *Developmental Psychology, 31,* 358–363.

Fox, N. A., Henderson, H. A., Rubin, K. H., Calkins, S. D., & Schmidt, L. A. (2001). Continuity and discontinuity of behavioral inhibition and exuberance: Psychophysiological and behavioral influences across the first four years of life. *Child Development, 72,* 1–21.

Fox, N. A., Nichols, K. E., Henderson, H., Rubin, K., Schmidt, L. A., Hamer, D., Pine, D., & Ernst, M. (2005). Evidence for a gene-environment interaction in predicting behavioral inhibition in middle childhood. *Psychological Science, 16,* 921–926.

Fujioka, T., Ross, B., Kakigi, R., Pantev, C., & Trainor, L. J. (2006). One year of musical training affects development of auditory cortical-evoked fields in young children. *Brain, 129*(Part 10), 2593–2608.

Goodman, K. S. (1973). The 13th easy way to make learning to read difficult: A reaction to Gleitman and Rozin. *Reading Research Quarterly, 8,* 484–493.

Gottesman, I. I., & Gould, T. D. (2003). The endophenotype concept in psychiatry: Etymology and strategic intentions. *American Journal of Psychiatry, 160,* 636–645.

Hariri, A. R., Drabant, E. M., Munoz, K. E., Kolachana, B. S., Mattay, V. S., Egan, M. F., & Weinberger, D. R. (2005). A susceptibility gene for affective disorders and the response of the human amygdala. *Archives of General Psychiatry, 62,* 146–152.

Hesselbrock, V., Begleiter, H., Porjesz, B., O'Connor, S., & Bauer, L. (2001). P300 event-related potential amplitude as an endophenotype of alcoholism: Evidence from the collaborative study on the genetics of alcoholism. *Journal of Biomedical Sciences, 8,* 77–82.

Ingalls, S., & Goldstein, S. (1999). Learning disabilities. In S. Goldstein & C. R. Reynolds (Eds.), *Handbook of neurodevelopmental and genetic disorders in children* (pp. 101–153). New York: Guilford.

Kagan, J. (1994). *Galen's prophecy: Temperament in human nature.* New York: Basic Books.

Kagan, J., Reznick, J. S., & Snidman, N. (1987). The physiology and psychology of behavioral inhibition in children. *Child Development, 58,* 1459–1473.

Kagan, J., Reznick, J. S., & Snidman, N. (1988). Biological basis of childhood shyness. *Science, 240,* 167–171.

Kagan, J., & Snidman, N. (1991). Infant predictors of inhibited and uninhibited profiles. *Psychological Science, 2,* 40–44.

Kandel, E. R., Jessell, T. M., & Sanes, J. R. (2000). Sensory experience and the fine-tuning of synaptic connections. In E. R. Kandel, J. H. Schwartz & T. M. Jessell (Eds.), *Principles of neural science* (pp. 1115–1130). New York: McGraw-Hill.

Meaney, M. J., & Szyf, M. (2005). Environmental programming of stress responses through DNA methylation: Life at the interface between a dynamic environment and a fixed genome. *Dialogues in Clinical Neuroscience, 7,* 103–123.

Meng, H., Smith, S. D., Hager, K., Held, M., Liu, J., Olson, R. K., et al. (2005). DCDC2 is associated with reading disability and modulates neuronal development in the brain. *Proceedings of the National Academy of Sciences U S A, 102,* 17053–17058.

Moore, C. (1992). The role of maternal stimulation in the development of sexual behavior and its neural basis. *Annals of the New York Academy of Sciences, 622,* 160–177.

Orton, S. T. (1937). *Reading, writing and speech problems in children.* New York: W.W. Norton.

Pennington, B. F. (2002). *The development of psychopathology.* New York: Guilford.

Piaget, J. (1971). *Genetic epistemology.* New York: W.W. Norton.

Rutter, M., Moffitt, T. E., & Caspi, A. (2006). Gene-environment interplay and psychopathology: Multiple varieties but real effects. *Journal of Child Psychology and Psychiatry, 47,* 226–261.

Savitz, J. B., Solms, M., & Ramesar, R. S. (2005). Neurocognitive function as an endophenotype for genetic studies of bipolar affective disorder. *Neuromolecular Medicine, 7,* 275–286.

Schmidt, L. A., Fox, N. A., Rubin, K. H., Hu, S., & Hamer, D. H. (2002). Molecular genetics of shyness and aggression in preschoolers. *Personality and Individual Differences, 33,* 227–238.

Schmidt, L. A., Fox, N. A., Rubin, K. H., Sternberg, E. M., Gold, P. W., Smith, C. C., & Schulkin, J. (1997). Behavioral and neuroendocrine responses in shy children. *Developmental Psychobiology, 30,* 127–140.

Schmidt, L. A., Fox, N. A., Schulkin, J., & Gold, P. W. (1999). Behavioral and psychophysiological correlates of self-presentation in temperamentally shy children. *Developmental Psychobiology, 35,* 119–135.

Schmidt, L. A., & Schulkin, J. (1999). *Extreme fear, shyness, and social phobia: Origins, biological mechanisms, and clinical outcomes.* New York: Oxford University Press.

Segalowitz, S. J. (2007). The role of neuroscience in historical and contemporary theories of human development. In D. Coch, K. W. Fischer, & G. Dawson (Eds.),

Human behavior and the developing brain: Typical development (2nd Edition, pp. 3–29). New York: Guilford.

Smith, F. (1977). Making sense of reading, and of reading instruction. *Harvard Educational Review, 47*, 386–395.

Stein, J., & Walsh, V. (1997). To see but not to read; the magnocellular theory of dyslexia. *Trends in Neuroscience, 20*, 147–152.

Stevens, A. A., & Weaver, K. (2005). Auditory perceptual consolidation in early-onset blindness. *Neuropsychologia, 43*, 1901–1910.

Stevenson-Hinde, J. (2000). Shyness in the context of close relationships. In W. R. Crozier (Ed.), *Shyness: Development, consolidation and change* (pp. 88–102). London: Routledge, Taylor & Francis Group.

Weinberger, D. R., Egan, M. F., Bertolino, A., Callicott, J. H., Mattay, V. S., Lipska, B. K., Berman, K. F., & Goldberg, T. E. (2001). Prefrontal neurons and the genetics of schizophrenia. *Biological Psychiatry, 50*, 825–844.

CENTRAL SYSTEM

Theory, Methods, and Measures

2 Event-Related Brain Oscillations in Normal Development

Juliana Yordanova and Vasil Kolev

CONCEPTUAL FRAMEWORK

Recently, event-related neuroelectric oscillations have provided important tools with which to study information processing in the brain and with which to enrich our knowledge of brain maturation and cognitive development. The essential advantages of this approach are the ability to (1) analyze neuroelectric responses reflecting mechanisms of stimulus information processing in comparison to electrical activity in a passive state reflecting the neurobiological maturation of the brain; (2) refine electrophysiological correlates of information processing by separating functionally different but simultaneously generated responses from different frequency ranges; and (3) reveal differential developmental dynamics of the power and synchronization of neuroelectric responses, thus providing information about independent neurophysiological mechanisms during biological and cognitive development.

In this chapter, the conceptual background of event-related oscillations will be presented with a major focus on their relevance for developmental research, followed by methods, analytic tools, and parameters for assessment of event-related oscillations. Finally, major findings on the development of the delta, theta, alpha, and gamma response systems in the brain will be described.

Event-Related Potentials

The electroencephalogram (EEG) is a time-varying signal reflecting the summated neuroelectric activity from various neural sources in the brain during rest or functional activation. An EEG response that occurs in association with an eliciting event (sensory or cognitive stimulus) is defined as an event-related potential (ERP). However, the ERP may contain EEG activity not related to specific event processing, as well as electric activity from non-neural sources. To extract the EEG response elicited specifically by the event, an averaging procedure is applied with the assumption that the stimulus-locked event-related EEG activity is invariant while the electric activity not related to the event is random. In this way, the stimulus-locked EEG signal is emphasized while random components are attenuated by the averaging (Regan, 1989; Ruchkin, 1988).

The averaged ERP is typically analyzed in the time domain. It consists of consecutive positive and negative deflections called ERP components. Time-domain ERP components are characterized by their polarity, peak latency, distribution over the scalp, and specific sensitivity to experimental variables (Picton et al., 2000; Picton & Stuss, 1980; Regan, 1989). As ERP components have been related to a variety of sensory and cognitive processes, they are commonly used in psychological and clinical research to study brain functioning (see e.g., Polich, 1998; Regan, 1989).

Event-Related EEG Oscillations

Based on the existence of oscillatory electric phenomena in the brain, ERP components have been proposed to originate from the spontaneous EEG rhythms and to reflect a superposition of oscillatory EEG responses in various frequency ranges (Basar, 1980, 1992, 1998). It has been assumed that the EEG results from the activity of generators producing rhythmic oscillations in several frequency ranges. These oscillators are usually active in an uncorrelated manner. However, by application of sensory stimulation, these generators become coupled and act together coherently. The synchronization of EEG activity gives rise to evoked or induced responses in defined frequency ranges (Basar, 1980). Experimental data have supported this model by demonstrating that after external and/or internal stimulation, oscillatory EEG potentials in different frequency bands (delta $\approx$ 0.5–4 Hz, theta $\approx$ 4–7 Hz, alpha $\approx$ 7–13 Hz, beta $\approx$ 15–30 Hz, gamma $\approx$ 30–70 Hz) can be recorded from cortical and subcortical structures in both humans and animals (Basar, 1980, 1998; Basar et al., 1997a; Kahana et al., 2001; Makeig, 2002; Pantev et al., 1994). These oscillatory potentials associated with external or internal events are called *frequency EEG responses*, or *event-related oscillations*. They can be extracted from the ERP by appropriate analytic procedures (Basar, 1998; Samar et al., 1995).

ERP components can be regarded as originating from a transition from a disordered to an ordered state of bioelectric signals in the brain, i.e., as originating from the reorganization of the ongoing EEG after sensory-cognitive input (Basar, 1980; Sayers et al., 1974). The simultaneous occurrence and superposition of various EEG frequency responses are proposed to produce the time-domain ERP components (Basar, 1992, 1998). Recently, this concept has found strong support from neuronal (Arieli et al., 1995) and EEG/ERP recordings (Basar et al., 1997b; Makeig et al., 2004). Within this framework, the most important indices of event-related reorganization of the ongoing EEG in a given frequency channel are (1) power or amplitude changes (increase or decrease) in the post-stimulus period relative to pre-stimulus EEG, and (2) phase-reordering and phase-locking in relation to a stimulus (Yordanova & Kolev, 1998a).

The Rule of Brain Response Susceptibility: Links to Developmental and Psychopathology Studies

If ERPs originate from the reorganization of the ongoing EEG activity upon application of a sensory-cognitive input (Basar, 1980), the ongoing EEG may modulate the brain's reactions to sensory-cognitive stimulation (Basar et al., 1997b). Accordingly, as indicated in the principle of 'brain response susceptibility' or 'excitability of brain tissue', if a neural population shows spontaneous activity in a given frequency range, it can be excited in the same frequency range by sensory stimuli (Basar, 1980, 1992; Basar-Eroglu et al., 1994; Kolev et al., 1994a).

The spontaneous oscillatory activity of the brain depends on several factors including the vigilance and/or cognitive state, the presence of pathology, and the participant's age. Since the age of the participant is one of the most important factors for changes in amplitude and frequency of the EEG from childhood to late adulthood (Niedermeyer, 1993, 1997), the evoked oscillatory potentials can be expected to undergo some predictable changes with increasing age.

Developmental Changes in the Spontaneous EEG Activity

Developmental changes in the spontaneous EEG in children have been previously described, with the consistent finding that age-related reduction of the spontaneous EEG activity in the slower (delta, theta) frequency bands is accompanied by an increase in the faster (alpha, beta) frequency bands (John et al., 1980; Matoušek & Petersén, 1973; Niedermeyer, 1993, 1997; Petersén & Eeg-Olofsson, 1971). In regards to slow (theta) EEG activity, measurement of spontaneous EEG (using relative power spectra) has demonstrated that theta activity is present in each age group from 6 to 17 years, but its developmental reduction is accompanied by a complementary (substituting) increase in fast alpha activity (Gasser et al., 1988). Accordingly, the developmental dynamics of the alpha activity in the spontaneous EEG include a shift of spectral alpha peak to higher frequencies from the alpha range (Niedermeyer, 1997). Spontaneous gamma EEG in 3- to 12-year-old children manifests a power increase between 3 and 4 years at all leads, especially over the frontal region, and reaches a maximum at 4 to 5 years of age (Takano & Ogawa, 1998). Thus, the power and frequency content of the spontaneous EEG undergo essential developmental alterations. According to the principle of brain response susceptibility, these alterations can be expected to affect the oscillations generated in relation with event processing.

Summary

Spontaneous EEG rhythms reflect the neurobiological background of the frequency-specific networks in the brain, whereas their reorganization is strongly modulated by the mode of event processing. Thus, analysis of both the spontaneous and event-related oscillations would indicate whether developmental changes in cognitive stimulus processing may be associated with (1) basic alterations of the neurobiological substrate mediating the development of cognitive functions, (2) processes activated only upon specific processing demands, or (3) both.

METHODOLOGICAL FRAMEWORK

Time-Domain and Time-Frequency Properties of ERPs

To study developmental EEG responses, we use an advanced conceptual and methodological framework (Yordanova et al., 2004; Yordanova & Kolev, 2004) based on the following. An EEG signal can be described in three dimensions: (1) amplitude, (2) time, and (3) frequency, although phase-relations should be also quantified for a complete signal description. Typically, developmental ERPs are analyzed in the time domain (Figure 2.1a). This analysis has shown that both the early (P1, N1) and late ERP components (P300, N400) change as a function of development (Courchesne, 1983; Ridderinkhof & van der Stelt, 2000; Rothenberger, 1982; Taylor, 1989). A classical time-domain representation of ERPs reveals the timing of underlying neural events. As illustrated in Figure 2.1a, the peak latencies of P1, N1, and P3 components can be precisely determined. However, the frequency characteristics

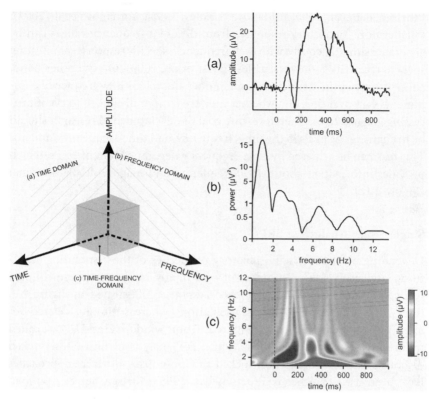

Figure 2.1. ERPs can be described in three dimensions: amplitude, time, and frequency. (a) Time domain presentation of averaged ERP. Amplitude vs. time information is present, whereas no information exists about frequency events. (b) Frequency domain presentation of the same ERP. Amplitude (power) vs. frequency information is present, whereas no information exists about time events. (c) Time-frequency representation of the same ERP by means of Wavelet transform. Events can be localized in both time and frequency domain.

of those time-domain events remain obscure, and no information can be obtained about rhythmic or oscillatory events from various frequency bands present in the signal. Figure 2.1b shows that the same ERP is characterized by peaks from the sub-delta (below 2 Hz), delta (2–4 Hz), theta (5–8 Hz), and alpha (around 10 Hz) frequency ranges. The inability of time-domain ERPs to present frequency characteristics of the signal seems to be a disadvantage because EEG activities from several frequency ranges (theta, alpha, beta, gamma) have been associated consistently with sensory, cognitive, and motor performance in both children and adults (e.g., Basar, 1998; Gevins, 1987; Klimesch et al., 1994; Klimesch, 1999; Krause et al., 1996, 2000;

Pfurtscheller et al., 2000; Yordanova & Kolev, 1998a; Yordanova et al., 2004). Furthermore, oscillatory responses from different frequency ranges can be generated simultaneously, with each frequency-specific response manifesting specific reactivity to task variables (Basar et al., 2000). On the other hand, analysis only in the frequency domain does not tell us how frequency components vary over time and whether they are temporally linked to event processing (Figure 2.1b). Therefore, one goal of developmental research should be to characterize ERPs in the time, frequency, and time-frequency domains. This task can be achieved by time-frequency decomposition of ERPs, which provides information about time, frequency, and magnitude of the signal (Figure 2.1c).

Single-Sweep Analysis of ERPs

Depending on the internal oscillatory properties of the responding structures, oscillatory EEG responses may be tightly or loosely phase-coupled to the stimulus. Tightly phase-locked responses (illustrated in Figure 2.2, time window I) are called evoked oscillations, whereas stimulus-related but loosely phase-locked responses (Figure 2.2, time windows II and III) are called induced oscillations (Galambos, 1992). For analysis of non-phase-locked or both phase-locked and non-locked EEG responses, different approaches have been used (Kalcher & Pfurtscheller, 1995; Pfurtscheller & Aranibar, 1977; Sinkkonen et al., 1995). These methods are based primarily on power (or amplitude) measurements of the EEG in the post-stimulus period. For quantification of the phase-locked activity in ERPs, the averaging procedure is usually applied because this way the phase-locked responses are enhanced and the non-phase-locked ones are attenuated, as illustrated in the bottom of Figure 2.2 (Gevins, 1987; Ruchkin, 1988). Although the phase-locked EEG activity can be extracted by means of averaging (Figure 2.2, bottom), the shapes of complex waves in the averaged ERP depend strongly not only on the time relations or phases but also on the amplitudes of single EEG trials. However, both single-sweep amplitudes and phase-relations may vary substantially and thus contribute differentially to the averaged ERP (Kolev & Yordanova, 1997; Yordanova & Kolev, 1998c). Because the phase-locking and power (amplitude) contributions cannot be separated in the averaged waveform, the averaged ERP is regarded only as a rough estimation and a first approximation of the brain response (Basar, 1980).

More important from a functional point of view are the observations that amplitude and phase-locking may reflect specific aspects of information

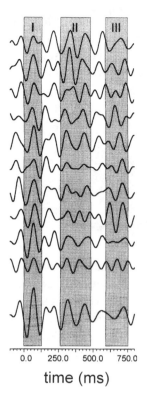

0.0   250.0   500.0   750.0

time (ms)

Figure 2.2. Effect of single-sweep phase-locking and amplitude on the averaged waveform illustrated in three time windows: ten single-sweeps (from the top) filtered in the frequency band 8–15 Hz and their averaged waveform (bottom line).
(Time window I) All single-sweeps are in congruence (strongly phase-locked). As a result, an enhanced averaged ERP is obtained.
(Time window II) Some of the single-sweeps are phase-locked, and some of them are not: the averaged amplitude is smaller in comparison to that found in time window I.
(Time window III) No phase-locking between all single-sweeps: the averaged amplitude is significantly smaller than that found in time windows I and II (with modifications from Yordanova & Kolev, 1997b).

processing; however, only a few investigations focus on the measurement of phase characteristics at the moment of, or shortly after, stimulus delivery (Brandt et al., 1991; Jervis et al., 1983; Kolev & Yordanova, 1997; Sayers et al., 1974; Tallon-Baudry & Bertrand, 1999; Yordanova & Kolev, 1996, 1998a, 1998b, 1998c). Jervis et al. (1983) have shown that the slow ERP components (theta, delta) which typically manifest an additive power effect also have a strong phase-locking effect. However, other frequency components may react with only phase-locking, without being enhanced in amplitude after stimulation (Yordanova & Kolev, 1998b). If such components are very small in amplitude relative to other frequency ERP responses, as is the case with the evoked gamma-band response, they cannot be reliably identified in the averaged potentials because they are masked by the high power components. Hence, relevant phase-locked components may be confounded by power factors. In addition, estimation of component stability at the level of single-sweep analysis has demonstrated significant differences between the variability (or stability) of exogenous and endogenous components (Michalewski et al., 1986). Specific contributions of factors like aging (Fein & Turetsky, 1989; Pfefferbaum & Ford, 1988; Smulders et al., 1994) or pathology (Ford et al., 1994; Unsal & Segalowitz, 1995) to either phase-locking or power of single responses have also been suggested (Kolev et al., 2002; Yordanova et al., 1998). Taken together, these findings imply that quantification of both aspects of single-sweep behavior might be independently informative for revealing significant information about stimulus processing (Kolev & Yordanova, 1997; Yordanova & Kolev, 1998c).

EVENT-RELATED OSCILLATIONS: ANALYSIS AND MEASUREMENT

ERP Analysis in the Time-Domain: Exogenous and Endogenous ERP Components

Averaged ERPs are most commonly used to measure the time-domain components. For time-domain analyses, single sweeps are filtered in a wide band, (e.g., 0.01–70 Hz). The number of artifact-free sweeps necessary for averaging varies in a wide range. A high number of sweeps is recommended in order to obtain a noise-free averaged ERP, but recording many trials usually requires longer recording sessions. Longer recording time introduces additional variability due to habituation, changing mental state, and so on, and is a problem of particular importance in children. For that reason, the number of sweeps used for averaging is always a matter of compromise. According to a standard procedure, time-domain ERPs are quantified by measuring latency and amplitude values of ERP components relative to a pre-stimulus baseline. Typically, early (e.g., N1, P2) and late (e.g., P300, P400–700, N400–700) components are studied (examples can be seen in Figure 2.6).

Identification of Frequency ERP Components: Analysis in the Frequency-domain

One way to verify the presence of time-locked frequency EEG responses after stimulation is to compute the amplitude-frequency characteristics (AFCs) of the averaged ERPs (see Figure 2.3a; Basar, 1980, 1998). From a theoretical point of view, AFCs describe the brain system's transfer properties, for example, excitability and susceptibility, by revealing resonant (enhanced or amplified) frequencies related to stimulus processing. Therefore, AFCs do not simply represent the spectral power density characterizing the ERP in the frequency-domain, but also the predicted behavior of the brain system that modulates defined frequencies upon stimulation. Reflecting the amplification in a given frequency channel, the AFC is expressed in relative units. Hence, the presence of a peak in the AFC reveals the resonant frequencies interpreted as the most preferred oscillations of the system in response to a stimulus (Figure 2.3a). Details of AFC computation are presented in the Appendix.

Time-Frequency Decomposition of ERPs

Digital Filtering

One approach to decomposing a signal in both time and frequency domains is to apply digital filtering (Figure 2.3a, right, see also Appendix). For ERP research, the band limits of digital filters should conform to the AFC peaks characterizing the signal in the frequency domain (Basar, 1980, 1998).

Wavelet Transform

The wavelet transform (WT) performs signal analysis in both time and frequency domains (Figures 2.3b, 2.3c). In contrast to digital filtering, the major advantage of WT decomposition is that each frequency is analyzed for time windows that are optimal in length for characterizing this frequency. In this way, the WT uses shorter effective time epochs for higher frequencies (reflecting fast and short duration processes) and longer epochs for lower frequencies (reflecting slow processes), which provides a better time localization of the frequency components of the event-related responses. Also, the WT partitions the ERP between several independent frequency components with parallel time courses, thus respecting the overlapping component structure of ERPs (Samar et al., 1995, 1999; Schiff et al., 1994).

For signal decomposition, the WT uses a single basis function (wavelet), which is a simple oscillating amplitude function of time (Figure 2.4). This basis wavelet is compared with each section of the original signal, which produces coefficients reflecting the similarity of the wavelet with the respective sections of the signal (Figure 2.3b). For analysis of low frequencies the wavelet is dilated, and for analysis of higher frequencies the wavelet is shrinked (Figure 2.4). To cover all sections of the signal, the comparison between the wavelet and the original signal is made for consecutive overlapping or non-overlapping sections (translation) (see Figure 2.4b).

If translations and dilations (scaling) are performed smoothly in small overlapping steps, the obtained transform is called continuous WT (CWT; Figure 2.3c), otherwise the WT is discrete (DWT; Figure 2.3b). Both

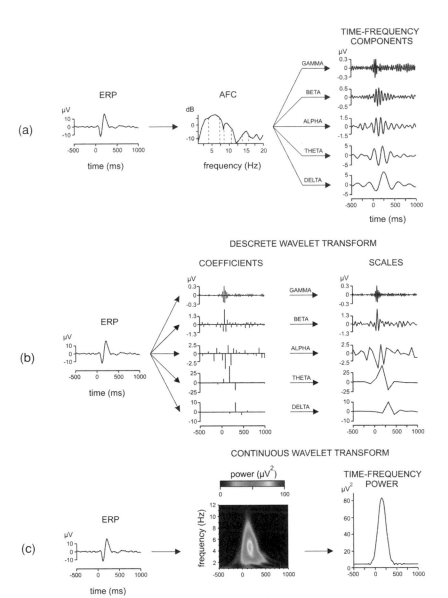

Figure 2.3. Schematic illustration of methods for time-frequency presentation and analysis. (a) ERP time-frequency components obtained by means of digital filtering. After calculating the amplitude-frequency characteristic (AFC) of the ERP, the band limits of digital filters are determined according to the maxima in the AFC. (b) The same ERP transformed to the time-frequency domain by means of discrete Wavelet transform (WT). WT coefficients for each resolution level (gamma, beta, alpha, theta, and residual delta) are obtained. By means of linear interpolation of the WT coefficients, the reconstructed time-frequency components (scales) are also obtained. (c) The same ERP transformed to the time-frequency domain by means of continuous WT. By using a complex Morlet's wavelet, the time-frequency power is calculated and presented in the middle panel. The time course of the maximal power (with central frequency of 4 Hz) is presented in the right panel.

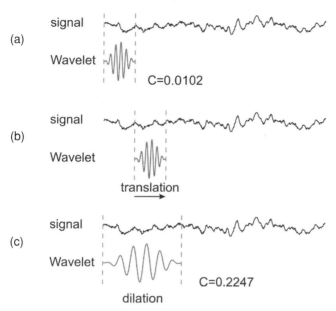

Figure 2.4. Schematic presentation of the Wavelet transform (WT) procedure. (a) The chosen wavelet is compared to a section at the start of the original signal. A number C is calculated that represents how closely correlated the wavelet is with this particular section of the signal. The higher C is, the more similarity between the wavelet and the section of the signal. (b) The wavelet is shifted to the right (translation) and step (a) is repeated until the whole signal is covered. (c) The wavelet is scaled (dilation) and steps (a) and (b) are repeated. The whole procedure is repeated for all scales.

transforms can be used for time-frequency analyses, with the CWT being most suitable for detecting unknown event-related oscillations and the DWT for decomposing the signal into previously known frequency bands (e.g., well-known EEG bands: delta, theta, and alpha). The steps of the WT and details on CWT and DWT computation are presented in the Appendix.

Event-Related Desynchronization and Synchronization

For studies of event-related oscillations, it is often relevant to assess whether and how the oscillations in the epoch during which an event is processed differ from those in a passive (reference) epoch. Event-related desynchronization (ERD) denotes power decrease, whereas event-related synchronization (ERS) denotes power increase in a given frequency band relative to a reference period (Pfurtscheller & Lopes da Silva, 1999; for details see also Appendix).

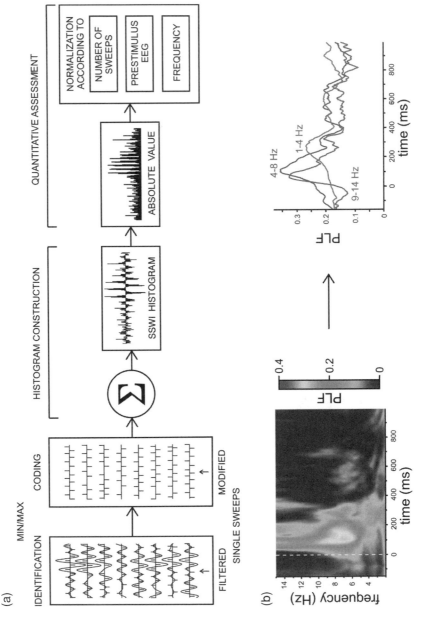

Figure 2.5. See facing page.

26

Phase-Locking Between Single Sweeps

For analysis of event-related oscillations, it is important to assess not only their amplitude variations related to event processing, but also how strongly they are synchronized with the event. To evaluate the phase-locking between single sweeps, different approaches can be used. Figure 2.5a illustrates one such approach called the single-sweep wave identification (SSWI) method (Kolev & Yordanova, 1997). This method eliminates amplitude effects by replacing amplitude values of extrema identified in the single sweeps by codes (+1 or −1 depending on the polarity). Summing thereafter the single sweeps produces a histogram, in which the information about the strength of phase-locking and polarity of phases is extracted (see Appendix).

If phase polarity is of no interest, phase-locking can be calculated on the base of the power values obtained by the Fourier transform or by the complex WT (e.g., Tallon-Baudry et al., 1997; see Figure 2.5b). Following this procedure (see Appendix), the phase-locking factor (PLF) can be calculated.

EXPERIMENTAL SETUP

Experiment 1

To evaluate developmental changes in the delta, theta, and alpha responses, a total of 50 healthy children from 6 to 10 years of age and 10 healthy young adults from 20 to 30 years were studied. The children's ages ranged between 6 and 11 years, and they were divided into 5 age groups consisting of 10 subjects (4–6 females) each. The children were free of neurological disturbances, without attentional, behavioral, or learning problems, and had normal and above IQ scores.

←———————————————————————————

Figure 2.5. Methods for evaluation of single-sweep phase-locking. (a) A flowchart of the procedure for single-sweep wave identification (SSWI). Extremes in the filtered single sweeps are identified, and corresponding single-sweeps are modified by using the values of +1 and −1 only. Modified single-sweeps are averaged so that a SSWI histogram is obtained. For measurements, the SSWI histogram is rectified (absolute values) and normalized according to the number of sweeps, pre-stimulus EEG, and frequency of the waves. (b) Phase-locking factor (PLF) is calculated after continuous wavelet transform with complex Morlet's wavelet (see Appendix) and presented in 3D on the left. Time courses of PLF for different frequency bands (layers) are shown on the right.

ERPs were elicited by auditory stimuli (intensity of 60 dB SPL, duration of 50 ms, rise/fall 10 ms, random inter-stimulus intervals 3.5–6.5 s) in two conditions: (1) *Passive* – tone bursts of 800 Hz frequency (N = 50) were presented, with participants instructed to relax silently; and (2) *Oddball* – a total of 75 high (1200 Hz) and 25 low (800 Hz) tones were delivered randomly, with the instruction given to the child to press a button as quickly and accurately as possible in response to the low tones. In both the passive and oddball conditions, the participants were instructed to keep their eyes closed.

Behavioral Data
Children's response times (RTs) to targets decreased with increasing age (group means of 6-, 7-, 8-, 9-, and 10-year-old children: 716, 702, 675, 602, and 472 ms respectively), and were significantly slower than those of adults (mean 390 ms). Error rate tended to be higher in children than in adults.

Time-Domain Averaged ERPs
Figure 2.6 illustrates time-domain ERPs from passive, target, and nontarget stimuli and shows the components obtained by means of the classical averaging method. In the time domain, ERPs of both children and adults were characterized by N1, P2, N2, and P3 (P300) components. Additionally, the children displayed a fronto-central P1 component, a frontal late negative wave N400–700, and a parietal late positive wave P400-700 identified as P3b. P400–700 occurred primarily in response to the targets and decreased in latency with increasing age in children (Yordanova et al., 1992), a finding that is commonly found in developmental ERP studies (Kurtzberg et al., 1984; Ladish & Polich, 1989).

Frequency Domain Analysis
Figure 2.7 shows the AFCs of ERPs of six representative participants from each age group. It illustrates that the AFCs of children were different from those of adults with respect to the number of identifiable peaks. The auditory AFCs of adults were characterized by a major compound response covering the range of the theta and alpha frequencies (4–12 Hz) and peaking at 6–9 Hz (Schürmann & Basar, 1994; Yordanova & Kolev, 1998a). A similar AFC pattern was observed for 10-year-old children. In younger children, distinct peaks were detected in the delta, theta, and alpha ranges. The number of separable peaks in the AFCs decreased with increasing age in children. This finding indicates that in the course of development, a specialization occurs in the resonant frequencies involved in auditory stimulus processing.

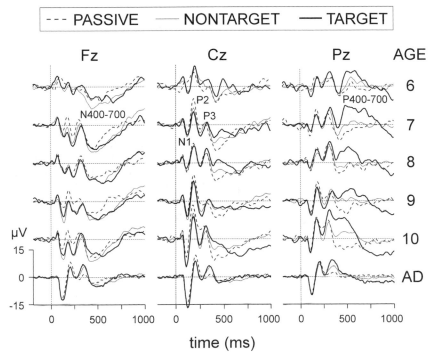

Figure 2.6. Grand average passive, nontarget, and target auditory ERPs at three electrode locations (Fz, Cz, and Pz) from different age groups: 6-year-olds, 7-year-olds, 8-year-olds, 9-year-olds, 10-year-olds, and adults (AD). Each age group consists of 10 participants (from Yordanova & Kolev, 1998b).

Time-Frequency Analysis

Time-frequency ERP components were analyzed for the midline frontal, central, and parietal electrode sites (Fz, Cz, Pz) by means of the methods described above. Single-sweep and averaged ERPs were digitally filtered in the respective frequency bands (delta, theta, and alpha).

Measurable parameters were

(1) power of the pre-stimulus EEG activity,
(2) amplitudes of averaged time-frequency ERP components calculated as the maximal peak-to-peak amplitude in a defined time window, and
(3) single-sweep parameters – amplitude, phase-locking, and enhancement relative to the pre-stimulus period. Amplitude of single-sweep responses was measured as the mean value of the maximal peak-to-peak amplitude in a defined time window. Phase-locking (between-sweep synchronization) was evaluated by means of the SSWI method

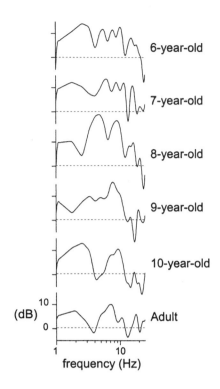

Figure 2.7. Amplitude-frequency characteristics for six representative participants at 6, 7, 8, 9, and 10 years of age, and an adult, calculated from the passive ERPs recorded at Cz. Along the x-axis – log(frequency), along the y-axis – 20log(|AFC|) (dB); (from Yordanova & Kolev, 1996).

(see Appendix). The enhancement relative to the prestimulus period was measured by calculating the so-called enhancement factor (EF; see Appendix). The EF reflects the change of the magnitude of the post-stimulus oscillations relative to the magnitude of the ongoing (pre-stimulus) EEG.

Experiment 2

In a second study, developmental gamma band responses (GBRs) were analyzed. For this study, a total of 114 children and adolescents from 9 to 16 years of age were used. They were divided into 8 age groups of 9, 10, 11, 12, 13, 14, 15, and 16 years, each comprising 12 to 17 subjects. Details on group characteristics are reported in Yordanova et al. (2002).

All children and adolescents were healthy and reported no history of neurologic, somatic, or psychiatric problems, nor did they have any learning, emotional, or other problems.

In each of the two recording conditions described below, a total of 240 auditory stimuli were used. Two stimulus types were presented randomly to the left and right ear via headphones. The stimuli were low nontarget (1000 Hz, n = 144, p = 0.6) and high target (1500 Hz, n = 96, p = 0.4) tones with a duration of 120 ms, rise/fall of 10 ms, and intensity of 85 dB SPL. Inter-stimulus intervals varied randomly from 1150 to 1550 ms. Equal numbers of each stimulus type were presented to the left and right ears. In the first condition, participants were instructed to press a button in response to the high tones (targets) presented to the right, while in the second condition the attended targets were the high tones presented to the left. Thus, there were four stimulus types in each series: target-attended (n = 48), target-unattended (n = 48), nontarget-attended (n = 72), and nontarget-unattended (n = 72).

Apart from overall developmental effects, this task permitted exploration of whether and how the functional reactivity of GBRs changed with age. The following factors which are related to cognitive stimulus processing could also be examined: attended channel (attended vs. unattended) and stimulus type relevance (target vs. nontarget). In addition, it was possible to assess whether developmental GBRs depended on the side of stimulation (left vs. right), regardless of whether left or right stimuli were attended or unattended.

To describe developmental changes in the stability and functional reactivity of auditory GBRs at specific scalp locations, these GBRs were analyzed in the time-frequency domain by means of the WT (see above section on Time-Frequency Decomposition of ERPs). The measurable parameters were (1) power of the spontaneous and pre-stimulus gamma band activity, (2) power of phase-locked GBRs, and (3) phase-locking of GBR (see above section on Phase-Locking between Single Sweeps). Age-related differences in the functional involvement of GBRs were assessed at separate scalp locations. The effects of attended channel and stimulus type relevance were examined for GBR power and phase-locking and compared among age groups.

DEVELOPMENTAL EVENT-RELATED OSCILLATIONS

Developmental Changes in Delta Responses

Functional Relevance of Delta Responses
Previous studies in adults have demonstrated that event-related delta responses (0.1–4 Hz) contribute to the generation of late endogenous ERP components such as P300 (Basar-Eroglu et al., 1992; Demiralp et al., 1999; Kolev et al., 1997; Yordanova et al., 2000a). Importantly, ERPs of children have since been known to be characterized by slow wave components, negative

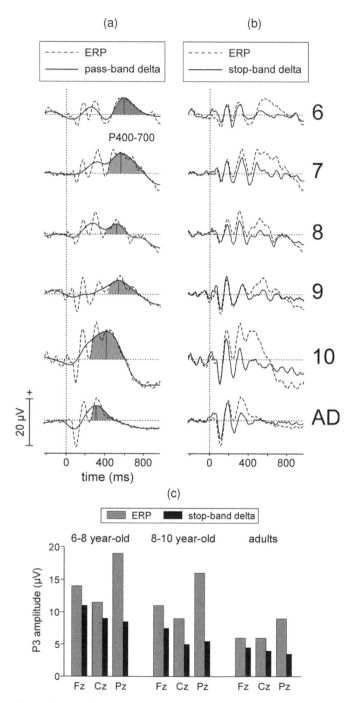

Figure 2.8. See facing page.

at frontal and positive at parietal electrodes (Courchesne, 1983; Kurtzberg et al., 1984). With this background, it is especially interesting to describe the developmental dynamics of delta responses in children, but such reports are scarce (e.g., Kolev et al., 1994b).

Delta Responses and the P300 ERP Component in Children

Because of their low frequency, delta responses are difficult to analyze in terms of oscillations in the short post-stimulus epochs of about 1 s, which are used for ERP analysis. Yet, their contribution to the expression of ERPs can still be demonstrated. Figure 2.8 shows time-domain ERPs elicited by target tones at Pz. In Figure 2.8a, averaged potentials filtered in the delta frequency band (0.1–4 Hz) are superimposed on the wide-band filtered ERPs. As shown, there is a high degree of coincidence between the wide-band slow ERP component P400–700 and event-related delta activity.

The relation between P300 and delta response in children can be examined in two ways.

(1) The peak latency of the delta response at Pz can be analyzed. It manifests a developmental decrease that follows exactly the developmental dynamics of P300 latency, which suggests a strong relation between P300 and event-related delta activity in children (Kolev et al., 1994b).

(2) The effects of event-related delta activity on P300 amplitude also can be assessed by applying a stop-band filtering procedure to ERPs (which eliminates the delta activity). P300 amplitude is measured before and after rejecting the delta frequency component from the ERPs. As shown in Figures 2.8b and 2.8c, there is a substantial amplitude reduction of the parietal P3b amplitude in both children and adults, which demonstrates that the major power of P3b comes from the delta frequency range (Kolev et al., 1994b; Kolev & Yordanova, 1995).

Figure 2.8. Time-domain averaged ERPs elicited by target tones at Pz (dashed lines) superimposed with the corresponding ERPs. (a) pass-band filtered (solid lines) in the delta frequency range (0.1–4 Hz); (b) stop-band filtered (solid lines) in the delta frequency range (0.1–4 Hz); (c) P300 amplitude measured before (ERP) and after (stop-band delta) rejecting the delta frequency component from the ERPs. A high degree of coincidence between the slow ERP component P400-700 and event-related delta activity is clearly seen in (a). Note the substantial amplitude reduction of the parietal P3b amplitude in both children and adults after stop-band filtering in the delta band. The different age groups are designated similar to those found in Figure 2.6.

Developmental Changes in the Theta Response System

Functional Relevance of EEG Theta Activity

Earlier studies have shown that higher cognitive and associative brain processes are most consistently correlated with the EEG theta (4–7 Hz) activity (Inouye et al., 1994; Lang et al., 1989; Mizuki et al., 1980, 1983). Most
recent studies strongly support the association of theta EEG activity with
higher brain processes such as memory, attention, and spatial processing
(e.g., Caplan et al., 2003; Kahana et al., 2001; Klimesch, 1997; Lisman
& Idiart, 1995). Prominent theta responses have been observed in various experimental conditions in both humans and animals and have been
assigned an important role in integrative stimulus processing (Demiralp &
Basar, 1992; Miller, 1991). For example, attended and highly relevant stimuli
in both the auditory and visual modality have produced in the first 250
ms after stimulation significantly higher theta response amplitudes than
nontarget stimuli in passive conditions (Demiralp & Basar, 1992). Furthermore, oddball ERPs have manifested larger theta and delta EEG frequency
components compared to passive ERPs (Kolev et al., 1997; Stampfer &
Basar, 1985; Yordanova & Kolev, 1998a; Yordanova et al., 2000b). Enhanced
theta responses with a prolongation up to 500 ms also have been observed
for oddball target stimuli, but not for passive stimuli (Basar-Eroglu et al.,
1992), with a similar prolongation of theta oscillations up to 800 ms found
when auditory perceptual difficulty was increased (Kolev & Schürmann,
1992). Visual stimuli inducing episodic memory processes have produced
event-related theta synchronization, which suggests a strong connection
between theta activity and memory operations (Klimesch et al., 1994, 1996).
Taken together, these findings imply that EEG theta responses in both early
and late post-stimulus epochs are functionally related to cognitive stimulus processing. Accordingly, event-related theta oscillations have been associated with the functioning of a diffuse and distributed theta system in
the brain (Basar-Eroglu et al., 1992) involving primarily the hippocampus and associative frontal cortex (Basar-Eroglu et al., 1992; Demiralp &
Basar, 1992; Klimesch et al., 1994; Miller, 1991) and generating both the
spontaneous and elicited theta oscillations (Basar, 1992). Thus, it is especially relevant to describe the developmental changes in the theta response
system of the brain, since such changes may be related to cognitive development in children. Results from such studies have been presented in detail
in several reports (Yordanova & Kolev, 1997a, 1998b) and are summarized
below.

Development of Averaged Theta Oscillations and Cognitive Stimulus Processing

Figure 2.9 illustrates averaged theta oscillations elicited by passive, target, and nontarget auditory stimuli in five groups of children and adults. It demonstrates that the amplitude of averaged theta responses does not vary substantially with age. However, the latency of the maximal theta response in averaged ERPs decreases with age. Figure 2.10a further demonstrates that the developmental decrease of maximal theta response latency is most prominent at Cz and Pz, whereas the latency differences across age is not statistically significant at the frontal site.

More interestingly, there was a high correlation between the latency of the maximal theta response and the latency of the parietal endogenous wave P3b for targets (Figure 2.10b). In a multiple step-wise regression analysis in which P3b latency was the dependent variable and maximal theta response latency and participant age were the independent variables, it was found that the latency of the maximal theta response, but not age, predicted the developmental reduction of P3b latency (Yordanova & Kolev, 1997a).

Results from the averaged theta ERPs indicate that (1) the theta response system of the brain undergoes important changes from childhood to adulthood such that the maximal theta response occurs with less delay after stimulation; and (2) there is a strong association between theta response latency and the latency of the late endogenous wave P3b of ERPs such that the developmental reduction in P3b latency can be predicted by age variations in theta response latency. These associations provide new evidence that the brain theta response is related to cognitive stimulus processing.

Developmental Reduction of Pre-Stimulus Theta Power

Figure 2.11 shows that pre-stimulus theta power decreased gradually from 6 to 10 years, with the lowest values manifested by adults. This pattern was valid for each stimulus type. These observations are consistent with previous reports on the developmental decrease of power of the spontaneous theta EEG activity (Niedermeyer, 1993). Yet, as described above, no developmental reduction was found for the magnitude of averaged theta responses, as would be expected if a relation existed between the ongoing and event-related theta activity. To explore this relation more precisely, it is necessary to consider the possibility that amplitude and phase-locking effects are confounded in the averaged waveforms (see above section on Single-Sweep Analysis of ERPs), which may have smeared relevant correlations. It is, therefore, meaningful to perform the analysis at the level of single-sweeps, which can separate

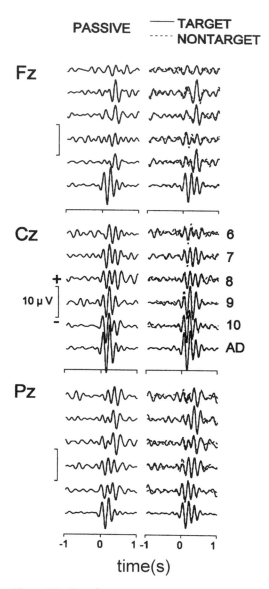

Figure 2.9. Grand average passive, target, and nontarget auditory ERPs at three electrode locations (Fz, Cz, Pz) pass-band filtered in the theta (4–7 Hz) range. The different age groups are designated similar to those found in Figure 2.6 (from Yordanova & Kolev, 1997a).

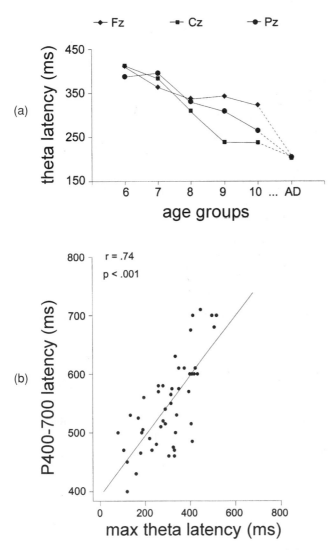

Figure 2.10. Developmental effects on the event-related theta oscillations. (a) Site ×
age effect on the latency of the maximal theta response. The age groups are designated
similar to those found in Figure 2.6. (b) Scatter plot of P400-700 latency vs. latency
of the maximal theta response for the Pz lead (with modifications from Yordanova &
Kolev, 1997a).

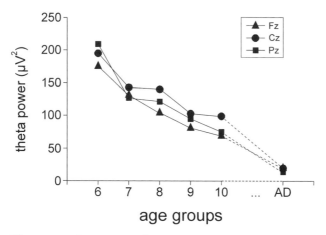

Figure 2.11. Group mean theta power (4–7 Hz) of the pre-stimulus EEG activity in passive condition at Fz, Cz, and Pz. The age groups are designated similar to those found in Figure 2.6 (from Yordanova & Kolev, 1997a).

developmental dynamics of magnitude and phase-stability of event-related theta oscillations.

Developmental Neurodynamics of Event-Related Theta Oscillations

Maximal Peak-to-Peak Theta Amplitude

Figure 2.12a illustrates that (1) adults had significantly lower single-sweep theta amplitudes than children from each group, (2) theta amplitudes declined with age in children, and (3) the developmental time-courses differed between the passive and task-related stimuli. For the target and non-target ERPs, significant developmental changes were found at 10 years of age, with adults producing significantly lower amplitudes compared to all children groups. For the passive ERPs, significant decreases were observed for the groups of 7- and 9-year-olds.

Previous studies in adults have indicated that late (later than 250–300 ms) theta oscillations might have a specific functional involvement in cognitive stimulus processing that might differ from the functional relevance of the early (0–300 ms) theta responses (Stampfer & Basar, 1985; Yordanova & Kolev, 1998a). Thus, there may be a disproportional developmental course of early versus late theta responses in different task and stimulus conditions. Figure 2.12a further illustrates that only in adults were the early theta responses larger than the late ones. For children younger than 10 years, late

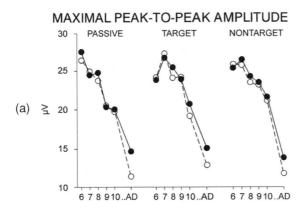

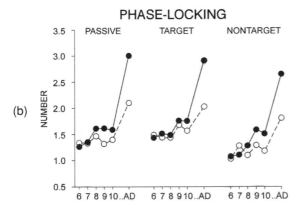

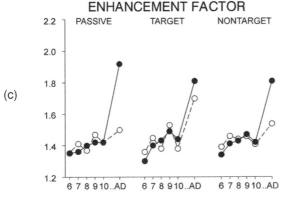

age groups

Figure 2.12. Effects of time window on the theta responses to passive, target, and nontarget stimuli. (a) Maximal peak-to-peak amplitude of the single theta responses; (b) Number of the phase-locked single theta oscillations; (c) Enhancement factor. The age groups are designated similar to those found in Figure 2.6 (with modifications from Yordanova & Kolev, 1998b).

theta responses at frontal locations were either as large as, or even larger than, the early ones.

In summary, these observations show that single theta response amplitudes decreased with age in children and were lowest in adults. The difference between early and late response amplitudes was significant only in adults.

Theta Response Phase-Locking

Figure 2.12b demonstrates that for each stimulus type (passive, target, and nontarget) the phase-locking of theta oscillations was stronger in adults than in children from each group. As also shown in Figure 2.12b, the phase-locking of the early theta responses increased at 8–9 years of age, whereas for the late theta responses no difference was found among the groups of children. The developmental increase in the phase-locking of the early theta responses was expressed mainly at Cz and was much less evident at Fz and Pz.

Thus, the phase-locking of theta responses was significantly stronger in adults than in children. A developmental increase was observed for the phase-locking of the early theta responses at the vertex location.

Enhancement Factors (EFs)

Figure 2.12c illustrates that the EFs of auditory theta responses were significantly larger in adults than in children from each age group. No significant differences in EFs were observed among the groups of children. In adults, EFs were significantly greater for the early than the late theta responses. In contrast to adults, 6- and 7-year-old children manifested significantly stronger enhancement for the late than for the early theta responses in the task-related ERPs. Unlike adults, all children groups tended to produce greater EFs for the late than for the early theta responses to task-related ERPs over the frontal brain area.

Thus, the enhancement of single theta responses relative to pre-stimulus theta activity was substantially greater in adults than in children. No increase in EFs was observed in children from 6 to 10 years. In contrast to adults, children, especially the younger (6–7-year-old) ones, tended to produce a stronger enhancement of the late theta responses to task-related stimuli at the frontal site.

Relation between Pre-Stimulus and Event-Related Theta Activity

The results obtained so far demonstrate the presence of developmental variations in the amplitude and phase-locking of the early theta responses. However, the pre-stimulus theta power also decreased with increasing age. To determine the extent to which age influenced theta response parameters due to the developmental power reduction of the pre-stimulus theta activity, step-wise multiple regression analyses were performed for the children's data from each stimulus type. The dependent variables were single theta response amplitude and phase-locking, and the predictor variables were log-transformed pre-stimulus theta power and children's age in months. The results obtained were similar for the three stimulus types.

At each electrode site, single theta response amplitude was entirely predicted by the pre-stimulus theta power, since the age variable was removed from the equations [R^2 *total* > 0.46, $F(1,47)$ > 39.6, $p < 0.001$]. In contrast, the stability of phase-locking at Cz depended only on the age factor and was not predicted by variations of the pre-stimulus theta power [R^2 *total* > 0.17, $F(1,47)$ > 3.02, $p < 0.005$]. No significant correlations were found between children's reaction times and single-sweep parameters of theta responses to oddball targets.

Auditory Theta Responses in Children have a Specific Organization

Results from single-sweep analyses help to reveal that the organization of the auditory theta response was specific for children. This pattern was evidenced by the significant differences between the single-sweep parameters of 6–10-year-old children and adults: (1) Single theta responses of children had larger absolute values, but were not enhanced compared to pre-stimulus theta levels, and they were also less synchronized than those of adults; (2) In adults, the early theta oscillations expressed higher responsiveness than the late ones, whereas in children the late responses were either more enhanced than the early ones or no reliable differences were observed between the early and late theta activity. It is noteworthy that the differences between children and adults were similar for the three stimulus types. This finding implies that (a) during auditory stimulus processing the theta response system in adults operates in a manner different from that found in 6–10-year-old children, and (b) the specific organization of the theta response in children reflects developmental variations of basic stimulus-processing mechanisms common for the different stimulus processing conditions. Yet, stimulus-dependent developmental differences such as those reflected by single-sweep amplitudes and enhancement factor indicate that event-related theta oscillations are additionally engaged in cognitive stimulus-specific evaluation.

Theta Response System Development

Single theta responses of children not only differed from those of adults, but also changed with advancing age from 6 to 10 years. For maximal theta response amplitude, a significant decrease occurred at 7 and 9 years for

passive ERPs, and at 10 years for task-related ERPs. These effects resulted
from the developmental decrease in power of the ongoing EEG theta activity.
Furthermore, the early theta responses displayed a maximum at Cz as did the
pre-stimulus theta power. This observation of the strong relation between the
pre- and post-stimulus theta amplitudes supports the concept of the diffuse
and distributed theta system in the brain subserving both the spontaneous
and stimulus-related 4–7 Hz activity (Basar, 1992). Hence, the developmental
reduction of both the ongoing and event-related EEG theta activity may
indicate a decrease in the number and/or intensity of the neuronal elements
that determine operative theta states of the brain.

In contrast to adults, single theta responses of children did not change
relative to the pre-stimulus theta activity after stimulation. The ability to
enhance the magnitude of the evoked theta component does not improve
from 6 to 10 years.

Paralleling this decrease in amplitude, an increase in the phase-locking of
early theta responses took place at about 8–9 years of age. However, for all
three types of ERPs, adults had remarkably stronger phase-locking than any
of the child groups. The stability (congruency) of theta responses to auditory
stimulation improves with development and appears to reach maturation
at developmental stages later than 10 years. Because the phase-locking in
children did not depend on the power of the pre-stimulus EEG theta activity,
theta response phase-locking reflects processes specifically activated after
stimulus presentation, and these are sensitive to age.

Major developmental differences also were revealed for the time dynamics of theta oscillations. Adults manifested clearly larger and better phase-
locked early than late theta responses, but in children younger than 9–10
years, these were similar. Furthermore, younger (6–7-year-old) children, in
contrast to older children and adults, had greater late compared to the early
theta responses, and all child groups tended to enhance the frontal late theta
responses more than the early ones. Whether the reverse pattern in children reflects a different way that processes are functionally specific to the
early and late responses compared to that in adults or a qualitatively different mode of organization of the event-related theta activity is still an open
question.

Summary
Taken together, the results demonstrate that the theta response system is
not completely developed at the age of 10 years. The age at which the adult
values of single theta response parameters are reached is not clear, but the
processes related to the theta response system obviously reach maturation at

later stages of human development. It should be emphasized that at the age of 10 years, the frontal lobes, unlike other brain structures, have not reached functional maturity with respect to their anatomical structure and input-output connections (Rothenberger, 1990). Miller (1991) has suggested that the EEG theta rhythm may reflect the fronto-hippocampal interplay during context processing. Incomplete development of theta responses at 10 years of age, as well as of the delayed enhancement of frontal theta responses in children, may be due to an association between the theta response and frontal lobe processes. Since frontal lobe functioning has been assigned a major role for the occurrence and course of psychiatric disorders in children (Rothenberger, 1990), event-related theta activity may be informative as a supplementary tool for clinical studies (e.g., Rothenberger, 1995; Yordanova et al., 1997a). It should also be noted that the developmental changes of single-sweep parameters, although occurring at different ages, were step-wise rather than gradual, which points to their possible relation with stages of cognitive development (Piaget, 1969), but the precise correlations of single theta response parameters with cognitive stage is still to be investigated.

Developmental Changes in the Alpha Response System

Functional Relevance of EEG Alpha Activity

Oscillatory activity in the alpha range in the first 250–300 ms after stimulation defines the alpha response or the alpha frequency component of the evoked or event-related brain potential. The alpha response is assumed to be the most fundamental and almost invariant component of brain neuroelectric activity, since a number of cortical and subcortical structures respond to stimuli with dampened oscillations in the alpha frequency band (Basar et al., 1997a). Cellular recordings also have demonstrated alpha responses in subcortical and cortical neurons (e.g., Llinás, 1988; Steriade et al., 1990). Alpha networks with similar design are distributed in various brain structures where they generate spontaneous and response-related alpha oscillations (Basar et al., 1997a, b; Lopes da Silva et al., 1973; Lopes da Silva, 1993). Functionally, alpha is not just a spontaneous background EEG rhythm but appears to be related to primary sensory processing (Schürmann & Basar, 1994), motor behavior (Pfurtscheller & Klimesch, 1992), memory processes (Klimesch, 1999), and anticipation (Basar et al., 1997a). Thus, the alpha frequency component of the event-related brain potentials may reflect important aspects of information processing by the brain and, accordingly, may provide knowledge about developmental and higher brain processes.

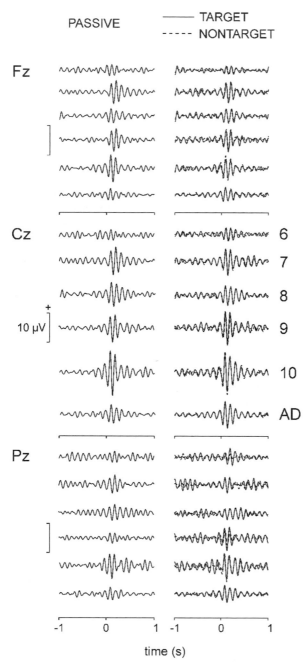

Figure 2.13. Grand average passive, target, and nontarget auditory ERPs at three electrode locations (Fz, Cz, Pz) filtered in the alpha (8–15 Hz) range. The different age
groups are designated similar to those found in Figure 2.6.

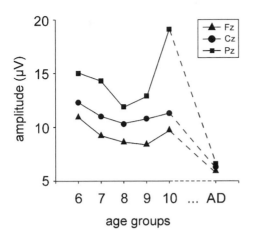

Figure 2.14. Mean group amplitude of the pre-stimulus alpha activity in the passive condition at Fz, Cz, and Pz. Age groups are designated similar to those found in Figure 2.6 (from Yordanova & Kolev, 1996).

Alpha responses were analyzed for the same groups of children and adults described above, and for the same stimulus conditions (passive, target, and nontarget). Analyses were performed for averaged and single-sweep ERPs filtered in the 8–15 Hz frequency range (details are presented in Yordanova & Kolev, 1996, 1998c).

Alpha Oscillations in Averaged ERPs

The amplitude of the average alpha responses changed significantly with age. As shown in Figure 2.13, the highest amplitudes were observed in 10–11-year-old children, with adult participants manifesting lowest values.

Age-Related Oscillations of Pre-Stimulus Alpha Activity

Figure 2.14 illustrates that the absolute band power of the pre-stimulus alpha activity was lowest in adults, with no statistically reliable differences observed among groups of children. All age groups displayed maximal alpha power over the parietal area.

Event-Related Alpha Oscillations: Neurodynamics with Age

Maximal Peak-to-Peak Alpha Amplitudes

Figure 2.15 shows that no significant differences among groups of children were found, with adult participants displaying significantly lower amplitudes

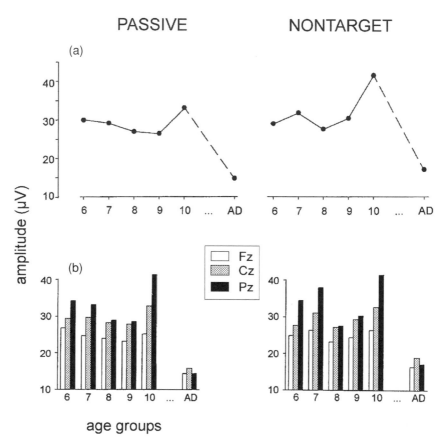

Figure 2.15. Developmental changes of the single-sweep alpha responses in passive and nontarget ERPs. (a) Group mean amplitude of single-sweep alpha responses vs. age; (b) Group mean amplitude of single-sweep alpha responses vs. age at three electrode locations (Fz, Cz, Pz). Age groups are designated similar to those in Figure 2.6 (with modifications from Yordanova & Kolev, 1996).

than each of the child groups. As illustrated in Figure 2.15b, in adults, single alpha responses were significantly higher at Cz than at Fz and Pz. Unlike adults, however, in each group of children, single alpha amplitudes were maximal at the parietal and minimal at the frontal locations.

Alpha Response Phase-Locking
As illustrated in Figure 2.16a, alpha response phase-locking increased with age. Although a developmental increase in the alpha phase-locking was

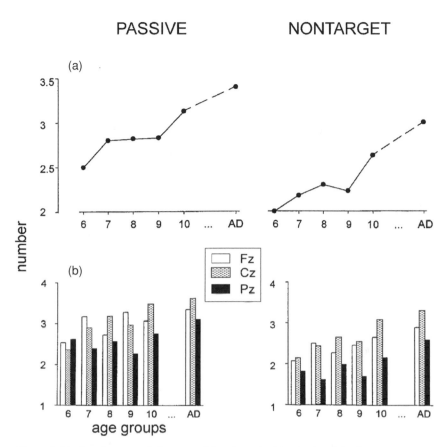

Figure 2.16. Developmental changes of the phase-locking in the alpha frequency range in passive and nontarget ERPs. (a) Group means of the number of phase-locked alpha waves as calculated from normalized SSWI-histograms vs. age; (b) Group means of the number of phase-locked alpha waves vs. age at three electrode locations (Fz, Cz, Pz). Age groups are designated similar to those found in Figure 2.6 (with modifications from Yordanova & Kolev, 1996).

evident after the age of 6–7 years, this increase was significant only for the 10–11-year-old children and adults, who did not differ significantly.

In both passive and task conditions, adults had maximal alpha response phase-locking at Cz and minimal parietally (Figure 2.16b). Exactly the same pattern was observed for 10-year-old children. The other child groups had a parietal minimum of alpha response phase-locking, but did not have the central maximum observed in adults and 10-year-old children.

Relation between Pre-Stimulus and Event-Related Alpha Activity
Pearson correlation coefficients calculated for each lead were used to evaluate
the relation between pre-stimulus and event-related alpha activity. The correlation was positive and very strong for pre-stimulus alpha band power
and single-sweep amplitude (Fz, $r = 0.90$; Cz, $r = 0.86$; Pz, $r = 0.92$;
$p < 0.001$), but negative and much weaker for pre-stimulus alpha power
and phase-locking (Fz, $r = -0.33$; Cz, $r = -0.39$; Pz, $r = -0.36$; $p < 0.02$). No
correlation was found between single alpha response amplitude and phase-
locking.

Alpha Responses in Children and Adults are Different

Alpha responses of adults are smaller in amplitude but more strongly phase-
locked with the stimulus than those of children. These differences in alpha
response amplitudes appear to result primarily from the age-related changes
in power of the ongoing alpha EEG activity, as indexed by the strong correlation between the two measures. More interestingly, in adults, but not in
children, the maximal alpha activity during auditory stimulus processing is
focused at the central scalp area despite the parietal maximum of the ongoing alpha activity. This ability to reorganize spatially and focus the maximal
alpha power to the central site appears not yet developed even in children
at 10–11 years of age, since they responded with maximal alpha amplitudes
over these areas where the pre-stimulus alpha activity was mostly expressed.

Hence, the maturation of the alpha response spatial organization appears
not yet complete at 11 years of age. However, the lack of difference between
10–11-year-olds and adults with regard to both the synchronization and
topography of phase-locked alpha waves suggests that the mature level of
alpha response phase-locking might be achieved at the age of 10–11 years.

The differences between the evoked alpha activity in children and adults
suggest that the alpha response system in 6–11-year-old children operates
differently in adults such that adults produce alpha responses lower in
amplitude, more strongly synchronized, and spatially different from the
spontaneous alpha oscillations.

Developmental Changes in the Alpha Response System
The main developmental change in the alpha response system was in the phase
stability of alpha oscillations after external (auditory) stimulation. The age-
related increase in alpha locking to the stimulus was discontinuous. The
most prominent increase in the between-sweep synchronization, occurring

at 7–8 and 10–11 years of age, corresponds to the stages at which a considerable increase in the cognitive performance of children has been observed (Piaget, 1969). Thus, production of repeatable phase-locked alpha oscillations upon stimulation may be linked to cognitive developmental stages of the brain.

Theoretical Considerations about the Alpha Response System in Children

The results from amplitude measures suggest that fewer networks, or networks of lower intensity and specific localization, may account for alpha oscillations after auditory stimulation in adults than in children (cf. Basar, 1992; Lopes da Silva, 1993). Alpha phase-locking depends on the age, topography, and pre-stimulus alpha power in a way different from that of alpha amplitude, suggesting a mechanism of phase reordering might operate independently from mechanisms regulating the spontaneous alpha power and the magnitude (instantaneous intensity) of the response. Single-sweep analysis results may reflect more specialization of the alpha mechanism in adults compared to children. In adults, fewer but selected and functionally specialized alpha networks are involved in responding to external stimuli, whereas in children there may be alpha networks more in number but less specialized.

Summary

The alpha response system appears to be involved functionally in 6–11-year-old children, but its development is not complete even at the age of 11 years. Alpha response magnitude undergoes developmental changes that are different in nature, timing, and topography from those of the alpha response phase-locking to stimulus.

Developmental Changes in the Gamma Response System

Functional Relevance of Gamma Band Activity

Recent findings from neuronal, EEG, and magnetoencephalographic (MEG) measurements indicate that fast oscillations in the gamma frequency range (30–70 Hz) are associated with basic aspects of brain functioning such as conscious perception, feature and temporal binding, attention, and memory (e.g., Basar-Eroglu et al., 1996; Gruber et al., 1999; Pantev et al., 1994; Tallon-Baudry & Bertrand, 1999; Traub et al., 1999). Neurocognitive development of children is accompanied by substantial alterations in neural substrates and higher brain functions that have been correlated with gamma band activity in adults. Hence, age differences in event-related fast frequency oscillations can be expected to occur during cognitive task processing in children. Knowledge of whether and how functional gamma oscillations may vary from childhood to adulthood is highly relevant for both basic and applied neuroscience.

In humans, different types of EEG gamma activity associated with external stimulation. Event-related gamma oscillations may be strongly or loosely phase-locked to stimulus onset, may occur early or late after stimulus presentation, and may also vary in frequency as a function of specific processing conditions (Basar, 1998; Galambos, 1992; Tallon-Baudry & Bertrand, 1999). In the auditory modality, simple tone bursts elicit transient EEG and MEG gamma band responses (GBRs) around 40 Hz, which are strongly phase-locked to the stimulus in the first 100–120 ms (Basar et al., 1987; Pantev et al., 1991, 1994). This early phase-locked 40-Hz response has been demonstrated to originate in the auditory cortex (Bertrand & Pantev, 1994; Pantev et al., 1991). Despite the modality-specific source of generation, auditory GBR power does not manifest a tonotopic organization as would be expected if it simply reflected sensory mechanisms (Pantev et al., 1991, 1994). Instead, the GBR has been correlated with vigilance and arousal because it attenuates in the course of a long-term (5-hour long) stimulation (May et al., 1994) and disappears during deep sleep (Llinás & Ribary, 1993) and anesthesia (Madler et al., 1991). Furthermore, actively processed auditory targets have been shown to enhance the early 40 Hz activity, thus pointing to the associations of the GBR with selective and focused attention (Jokeit & Makeig, 1994; Tiitinen et al., 1993; Yordanova et al., 1997b). These previous results strongly suggest that, in humans, the early phase-locked GBR is related to attentive conscious behavior in the auditory environment. Although the functional role of the GBR is not precisely known, most recent findings from the visual modality substantiate the notion that event-related gamma oscillations are associated with early attention processes (Gruber et al., 1999; Herrmann & Knight, 2001; Mueller et al., 2000). With this background, describing the development and functional reactivity of event-related gamma oscillations may highlight additional aspects of cognitive development.

Early Development of Spontaneous and Pre-Stimulus Gamma Band Activity

Yordanova et al. (2002) reported that spontaneous gamma band activity did not vary with age in children 9 to 16 years of age (Figure 2.17a), although the pre-stimulus gamma band activity decreased over this age range (Figure 2.17b). Pre-stimulus gamma power was largest at the frontal sites and decreased in the posterior direction. The anterior vs. posterior difference decreased with age indicating that the gamma band activity preceding stimuli is age-sensitive. Interestingly, in contrast to the spontaneous gamma EEG, the pre-stimulus gamma power in the selective attention task was significantly larger at the left than at the right frontal sites for each group, which points to the functional involvement of gamma oscillations in overall task performance.

Averaged Gamma Band Responses

Phase-locked GBR power did not vary significantly as a function of age from 9 to 16 years (Figure 2.17c). Across age groups, overall GBR power was larger at anterior (central-frontal) than at parietal locations. As also shown in the figure, there was a non-significant trend for the younger (9–12-year-old) children to produce larger GBRs over left-hemisphere locations. GBR power was significantly larger for left- vs. right-side stimuli, but this effect was prominent only for younger (9–12-year-old) children at central-parietal locations. Only in 9–12-year-old children, did the targets elicit larger frontal GBRs relative to the nontargets, which was observed at frontal (Fz, F4) locations (Figure 2.18a).

Phase-Locking of Gamma Band Responses

Figure 2.17d shows that GBR phase-locking did not vary significantly as a function of age. For all age groups, the GBR was more phase-locked at central sites. The figure also shows that only in 9–12-year-old children was the GBR phase-locking significantly stronger at left than at right-hemisphere sites, with this laterality difference not being present in the 13–16-year-old groups.

Figure 2.18b demonstrates that at the parietal locations the GBRs of children (9–13-year-old) were better phase-locked to unattended relative to attended stimuli, whereas in adolescents (14–16-year-old) attended stimuli produced better synchronized gamma responses than did the unattended ones.

Developmental Gamma-Band Response and Processing Strategies

These results demonstrate that (1) spontaneous gamma band power does not undergo substantial developmental changes, whereas the gamma activity generated during an auditory attention task decreases with age from 9–11 to 16 years; (2) although the power and stability of stimulus-locked gamma responses does not depend on age, the functional reactivity of auditory GBRs at specific locations changes in the course of development. In children (9–12-year-old), GBRs are sensitive to target stimulus features because the GBRs at frontal locations were larger to target than to nontarget stimulus type. Also,

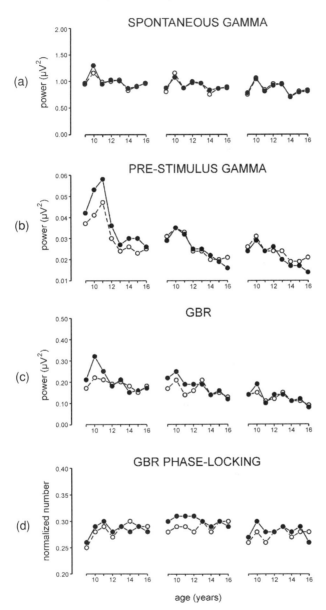

Figure 2.17. Group means of different age groups for (a) power of the spontaneous gamma band EEG activity; (b) power of the pre-stimulus gamma band activity; (c) power of the maximal phase-locked gamma band response (GBR) in the time window 0–120 ms; and (d) phase-locking of GBR as measured by normalized between-sweep synchronization. Frontal, central, and parietal electrodes are pooled together and presented in the left, middle, and right columns respectively (from Yordanova et al., 2002).

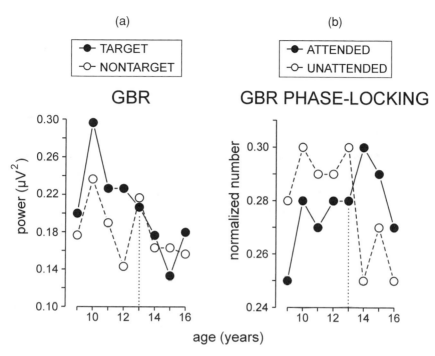

Figure 2.18. Effects of (a) stimulus type on GBR power at frontal sites and (b) attended channel on GBR phase-locking at P3 in different age groups (with modifications from Yordanova et al., 2002).

only in 9–12-year-old children are the auditory GBRs larger and better phase-synchronized over the left hemisphere locations. In contrast, in adolescents (14–16-year-old), GBRs are associated with internal focusing of attention because the phase-locked GBRs at parietal sites were synchronized by processing in the attended versus unattended channel; and (3) independently of age, enhanced phase-locked GBRs are produced at right central-parietal scalp locations by left-side stimuli.

Taken together, these results indicate that (1) specific aspects of task-stimulus processing engage distinct spatially localized gamma networks in functionally relevant areas, and (2) the neuronal substrates of gamma networks and the ability to synchronize them in relation to task-specific processes are available in both children and adolescents from 9 to 16 years of age. However, the mode and efficiency with which a particular task component can entrain functional gamma oscillations depend on the participant's age. The differential task-specific reactivity of GBRs in children and adolescents may therefore reflect developmental differences in task processing strategies, each engaging specific spatial patterns of gamma networks.

CONCLUSIONS

The results of event-related oscillations from different frequency bands yield the following general conclusions.

(1) *Event-related oscillations undergo substantial developmental changes from childhood to adulthood.* These changes are determined by both the age-dependent alterations of the spontaneous EEG activity and the modes of information processing during development. Since the spontaneous (and ongoing) EEG activity in a given frequency range is an important determinant of the magnitude of event-related neuroelectric responses in the same frequency range, spontaneous and event-related EEG oscillations may be generated by a common frequency-specific network.

(2) *Developmental changes of event-related oscillations are frequency-specific.* For example, the theta response system, as reflected by averaged theta oscillations, has not (yet) reached maturity at the age of 10–11 years in children, whereas at that age, the alpha response system manifests most of its adult-specific features. The gamma response system may be functional well before 9 years of age, but its functional reactivity to specific task demands undergoes a substantial alteration at the age of 12–13 years. These observations indicate that frequency-specific networks distributed in the brain are differentially related to brain maturation and/or cognitive development. It is of importance for future studies to establish the precise functional correlates of event-related oscillations from different frequency ranges and, accordingly, the functional roles of frequency-specific networks for cognitive development.

(3) *Developmental dynamics are different for amplitude, phase-locking, and enhancement of event-related oscillations.* These differential developmental courses may reflect sequential effects in the maturation of a common underlying mechanism subserved by a frequency-specific system. Alternatively, they may point to independent mechanisms that contribute separately to the event-related reorganization of oscillatory EEG activity in the course of development. The amplitude of oscillations during development is strongly correlated with the ongoing oscillatory activity, thus reflecting the maturation of the neurobiological substrate. The synchronization and enhancement with stimuli appear less dependent on the power of background oscillations, thus implying an association of these parameters with active processing mechanisms. Further developmental research is needed to determine the precise relation of phase-locking and enhancement of event-related oscillations with ongoing oscillatory activity and the cognitive variables and neurophysiological mechanisms involved.

(4) *The most important developmental changes in the mechanisms of stimulus information processing, as reflected by event-related oscillations, are (a) the ability to synchronize the neuroelectric oscillations with stimulus onset in a stable manner, (b) the ability to modulate the magnitude of oscillatory responses relative to ongoing activity, and (c) the ability to re-organize spatially event-related oscillations.* For oscillations from the theta and alpha frequency bands, these mechanisms appear to develop late in the course of development (later than 10–11 years), while the ability to synchronize gamma oscillations appears developed at the age of 9 and does not change thereafter. Future studies with participants from a wider age range are needed to determine when the maturation of synchronizing and enhancing abilities take place in childhood and how this maturation correlates with cognitive stages of development.

(5) *Implications.* The strong phase-locking of oscillatory responses to stimulus onset in adults compared to children suggests stable connections between neuronal elements develop quite late. The adult's phase-locking increase accompanied by a decrease in response magnitude might reflect a developmental specialization where frequency networks engage fewer but functionally more defined elements. The large enhancement factors in adults suggest that the neuronal elements in a given frequency channel can be coactivated (synchronized) simultaneously by the external stimulus, while such mechanisms are relatively absent in the earlier stages of development in children.

ACKNOWLEDGMENTS

Supported by the National Research Council by the Ministry of Education and Science, Sofia, Bulgaria (Projects L-1316/2003 and L-1501/2005).

APPENDIX

1. CALCULATION OF AMPLITUDE-FREQUENCY CHARACTERISTICS (AFCS)

To calculate the AFCs, averaged ERPs are transformed to the frequency domain by means of the one-sided Fourier transform (Laplace transform) of the following form (Basar, 1980, 1998; Solodovnikov, 1960):

$$|G(j\omega)| = \left| L\left(\frac{d\{c(t)\}}{dt} \right) \right| = \left| \int_0^\infty \frac{d\{c(t)\}}{dt} \exp(-j\omega t)\, dt \right|, \tag{1}$$

where $|G(j\omega)|$ is the complex representation of the Fourier transformed time series (i.e., the ERPs), providing the frequency characteristics of the system; $c(t)$ is the transient step response of the system (in this case, the ERP); $\omega = 2\pi f$ is the angular frequency; f is the frequency of the input signal; and $j = \sqrt{-1}$, the imaginary unit.

From the complex function $G(j\omega) = RE + jIM$, where RE and IM represent the real and imaginary part of the function respectively, the AFC can be calculated as a function of f:

$$AFC(f) = |G(j\omega)| = \sqrt{RE^2 + IM^2}, \tag{2}$$

or in a digital form:

$$AFC(f) = \sqrt{\left(\sum_{n=1}^{N}(\cos\omega t_n)\,\Delta c\,(t_n)\right)^2 + \left(\sum_{n=1}^{N}(\sin\omega t_n)\,\Delta c\,(t_n)\right)^2}, \tag{3}$$

where, $\Delta c\,(t_n)$ represents the first derivative of the transient step response of the system (in this case, the ERP) at different sampling points tn, ranging from 1 to N. Although this transform is valid only for linear systems, it can be applied to nonlinear systems (to which the brain systems are assumed to belong) as a first approximation since errors due to system nonlinearities are smaller than errors resulting from the length of measurements and rapid transitions in brain activity (Basar, 1980, 1998).

For evaluation purposes, the AFCs of the averaged ERPs can be normalized such that the amplitude ratio at 0 Hz is equal to 1 (Figure 2.3a). To enable demonstration of peaks in different frequency ranges simultaneously, a double logarithmic presentation of AFCs is often used (Figure 2.7). Similar frequency peaks can also be obtained after calculating the classical power spectra (based on the two-sided Fourier transform) of the averaged ERPs.

2. DIGITAL FILTERING

Theoretical filtering of EEG epochs or ERPs is the simplest method for time-frequency analysis. Frequency band limits of the theoretical filters can be determined according to the frequency and bandwidth of the amplitude maxima in AFCs (equation 3, Figure 2.3a – dashed lines on AFC plot). To avoid phase distortion in the result, a finite impulse response (FIR) pass-band filter with zero phase shift is commonly used (Basar, 1980, 1998), whose weights are determined as binomial coefficients (Wastell, 1979). Further, minimization of filtering artifacts is obtained if the filter bandwidth is greater than 5% from the total analyzed frequency band. More information about digital filtering can be found elsewhere (e.g., Basar, 1998).

3. WAVELET TRANSFORM

The wavelet representations provide precise measurements of when and how the frequency content of the neuroelectric waveform changes over time (Samar et al., 1995, 1999; Schiff et al., 1994).

WT permits an accurate decomposition of neuroelectric waveforms into a set of component waveforms called detail functions (Figure 2.3b). These detail functions can isolate all scales (frequencies) of the waveform structure present in the signal. WT provides flexible control over the resolution with which neuroelectric components and events can be localized. This method results in statistical waveform analyses that have increased power to detect and isolate neuroelectric events and especially oscillations.

As illustrated schematically in Figure 2.4, the WT uses a family of functions that are generated from a single basis function (wavelet) by operations of dilations and translations (Heinrich et al., 1999; Samar et al., 1995, 1999). Time-domain wavelets are simple oscillating amplitude functions of time. They have large fluctuating amplitudes during a restricted time period and very low or zero amplitude outside that range. Wavelets are band-limited, that is, they are composed of a relatively limited range of frequencies. The whole procedure of the wavelet transform can be described by the following steps:

(1) Take a wavelet and compare it to a section at the start of the original signal (Figure 2.4a).
(2) Calculate a number *C*, which represents how closely correlated the wavelet is with this section of the signal. If the signal energy and the wavelet energy are equal to one, *C* may be interpreted as a correlation coefficient.
(3) Shift the wavelet to the right (translation) and repeat steps 1 and 2 until the whole signal has been covered (Figure 2.4b).
(4) Scale (stretch) the wavelet (dilation) and repeat steps 1 through 3 (Figure 2.4c).
(5) Repeat steps 1 through 4 for all scales.

Discrete wavelet transform (DWT). For ERP decomposition by means of DWT, preferred methods include a multi-resolution logarithmic scheme with quadratic beta-spline wavelet basis functions (Ademoglu et al., 1997; Demiralp et al., 1999; Kolev et al., 1997) or cubic spline wavelet basis functions (Rosso et al., 2001). The application of a DWT to the data yields sets of discrete coefficients representing the time evolution of different frequency components (Ademoglu et al., 1997; Demiralp et al., 1999; Kolev et al., 1997). Figure 2.3b illustrates the coefficients obtained by this procedure for different scales (frequency ranges). The interpolation of the coefficients, for example, with a linear function, leads to the reconstruction of the signal in the respective frequency band (scale) and represents its time course (Figure 2.3b, right).

Continuous wavelet transform (CWT). CWT can be used for analysis of phase-locked and non-phase-locked event-related oscillations. Time-frequency representations can be calculated by Morlet's wavelets (e.g., Jensen et al., 2002; Tallon-Baudry et al., 1997, 1998; Yordanova et al., 2004) which have a Gaussian shape both in the time and frequency domain around its central frequency f and which yield power measures (Figure 2.3c). The analytical presentation of the complex Morlet wavelet $w(t, f)$ is:

$$w(t, f) = A \exp\left(-t^2/2\sigma_t^2\right) \exp(2\pi f t j), \tag{4}$$

where t is time; $2\sigma_t$ is the wavelet duration; $A = (\sigma_t \sqrt{\pi})^{-1/2}$ is a normalizing factor of the wavelet family.

For time-frequency analysis, the ratio f/σ_f should be greater than 5, where $2\sigma_f$ is the width of the Gaussian shape in the frequency domain. In case of expected slower phase-locked components, although sub-optimal, the ratio f/σ_f can be smaller than 5, but this affects the shape of the Morlet wavelet and decreases its decay. For different f, time and frequency resolutions can be calculated as $2\sigma_t$ and $2\sigma_f$, respectively (Tallon-Baudry et al., 1997), which are related by the equation $\sigma_t = 1/(2\pi\sigma_f)$.

The time-varying energy $|E(t, f)|$ of the signal in a frequency band is the square norm of the result of the convolution (complex multiplication) of the complex wavelet $w(t, f)$ with the signal $s(t)$:

$$E(t, f) = |w(t, f) \times s(t)|^2. \tag{5}$$

Convolution of the signal by a family of wavelets provides a time-frequency representation of the signal. By averaging the TF energy of each single trial, both phase-locked and non-phase-locked activities are summed. Applied to averaged ERPs, the CWT reflects phase-locked activities. In both cases, the mean TF energy of the pre-stimulus, or reference, period is to be considered as a baseline level and should be subtracted from the post-stimulus energy for each frequency band. Relevant TF components can be extracted according to the central frequency *f* in the time domain (Figure 2.3c, right) and statistically analyzed.

4. CALCULATION OF EVENT-RELATED SYNCHRONIZATION/ DESYNCHRONIZATION (ERS/ERD)

The instantaneous power in a chosen frequency range can be calculated according to the formula:

$$P(k) = \frac{1}{N} \sum_{i=1}^{N} \{x(i, k)\}^2, \tag{6}$$

where $P(k)$ is the averaged power estimation of band-pass filtered data (averaged over all single sweeps), $x(i,k)$ is the k-th sample of the i-th sweep of the band-pass filtered data, and N is the number of the single sweeps (Kalcher & Pfurtscheller, 1995). Event-related desynchronization and synchronization (ERD/ERS) is quantified as the percentage change of the averaged theta power $(P(k))$ at each sampling point relative to the average theta power (R) in a reference interval:

$$ERD/ERS(k) = \frac{P(k) - R}{P(k)} \times 100\% \tag{7}$$

In this equation, ERD is presented by the negative values and ERS by the positive values.

5. CALCULATION OF PHASE-LOCKING

5.1. Single Sweep Wave Identification (SSWI) Method

For a quantitative evaluation of the phase-locking of single sweeps, a simple method called the single-sweep wave identification (SSWI) method can be applied (Kolev & Yordanova, 1997). Figure 2.5a illustrates schematically the analysis procedure, which includes the following steps.

First, all extrema (minima and maxima) are identified in the filtered (in this example 4–7 Hz) single sweeps. Maxima are replaced with +1, minima with −1, and modified single sweeps are stored. Figure 2.5a further presents the detected points along the time axis without the signals. Second, after summing the modified single sweeps (coded extrema) across trials, a histogram of the number of phase-locked single theta waves (SSWI-histogram) can be obtained.

For quantitative evaluation of single sweep phase-locking, the SSWI-histogram is rectified and normalized by dividing the bar values by the number of single sweeps included. In addition, to control for effects related to possible changes in frequency, the number of oscillations in each time window can be measured and SSWI-histograms can be normalized by the obtained value (Yordanova & Kolev, 1998c).

5.2. Calculation of Phase-Locking Factor (PLF)

The calculation procedure for the so-called phase-locking factor (PLF) is as follows. The normalized complex time-varying energy P_i of each single trial i,

$$P_i(t, f) = \{w(t, f) \times s_i(t, f)\}/|w(t, f) \times s_i(f)|, \tag{8}$$

is averaged across single trials, leading to a complex value describing the phase distribution in the TF region centered on t and f (see equation 5 for designations). The modulus of this complex value, ranging from 0 (non-phase-locked activity) to 1 (strictly phase-locked activity), is called phase-locking factor (PLF). To test whether an activity is significantly phase-locked to the stimulus, the Rayleigh statistical test of uniformity of angle can be used (Jervis et al., 1983; Tallon-Baudry et al., 1997). An example of PLF is illustrated in Figure 2.5b.

6. CALCULATION OF ENHANCEMENT FACTOR

To analyze the relation between pre- and post-stimulus amplitudes in single-sweep responses, the so-called enhancement factor (EF) is used (Basar, 1998). For each single sweep, the post-stimulus peak-to-peak amplitude value is compared to the peak-to-peak value of the EEG activity preceding the stimulus onset (Basar, 1980; Brandt et al., 1991). The real procedure includes the calculation of the ratio of the maximal response amplitude (max) to the root-mean-square (*rms*) value of the pre-stimulus EEG amplitude in a 500-ms pre-stimulus epoch according to the formula:

$$EF = \max /(2\sqrt{2}\, rms)$$

The coefficient $2\sqrt{2}$, known as a factor equalizing rms and max amplitude measures, was used to equalize the pre-stimulus rms amplitude to an equivalent peak-to-peak value. In this way, the EF reflects the change of the post-stimulus magnitude relative to the magnitude of the ongoing EEG.

References

Ademoglu, A., Micheli-Tzanakou, E., & Istefanopulos, Y. (1997). Analysis of pattern reversal visual evoked potentials (PRVEP's) by spline wavelets. *IEEE Transactions on Biomedical Engineering, 44*, 881–890.

Arieli, A., Shoham, D., Hildesheim, R., & Grinvald, A. (1995). Coherent spatiotemporal patterns of ongoing activity revealed by real-time optical imaging coupled with single-unit recording in the cat visual cortex. *Journal of Neurophysiology, 73*, 2072–2093.

Basar, E. (1980). *EEG-brain dynamics. Relation between EEG and brain evoked potentials.* Amsterdam: Elsevier.

Basar, E. (1992). Brain natural frequencies are causal factors for resonances and induced rhythms. In E. Basar, & T. H. Bullock, (Eds.), *Induced rhythms in the brain.* (pp. 425–467). Boston: Birkhäuser.

Basar, E. (1998). Brain Function and Oscillations. In H. Haken (Ed.), *Volume I. Brain Oscillations. Principles and Approaches. Springer Series in Synergetics.* Berlin: Springer.

Basar, E., Basar-Eroglu, C., Karakas, S., & Schürmann, M. (2000). Brain oscillations in perception and memory. *International Journal of Psychophysiology, 35*, 95–124.

Basar, E., Hari, R., Lopes da Silva, F. H., & Schürmann, M. (Eds.). (1997a). Brain alpha activity – new aspects and functional correlates [Special Issue]. *International Journal of Psychophysiology, 26*.

Basar, E., Rosen, B., Basar-Eroglu, C., & Greitschus, F. (1987). The associations between 40 Hz-EEG and the middle latency response of the auditory evoked potential. *International Journal of Neuroscience, 33*, 103–117.

Basar, E., Yordanova, J., Kolev, V., & Basar-Eroglu, C. (1997b). Is the alpha rhythm a control parameter for brain responses? *Biological Cybernetics, 76*, 471–480.

Basar-Eroglu, C., Basar, E., Demiralp, T., & Schürmann, M. (1992). P300-response: possible psychophysiological correlates in delta and theta frequency channels. A review. *International Journal of Psychophysiology, 13*, 161–179.

Basar-Eroglu, C., Kolev, V., Ritter, B., Aksu, F., & Basar, E. (1994). EEG, auditory evoked potentials and evoked rhythmicities in three-year-old children. *International Journal of Neuroscience, 75*, 239–255.

Basar-Eroglu, C., Struber, D., Schürmann, M., Stadler, M., & Basar, E. (1996). Gamma-band responses in the brain: A short review of psychophysiological correlates and functional significance. *International Journal of Psychophysiology, 24*, 101–112.

Bertrand, O., & Pantev, C. (1994). Stimulus-frequency dependence of the transient oscillatory auditory evoked responses (40 Hz) studied by electric and magnetic recordings in human. In C. Pantev, T. Elbert, & B. Lütkenhöner, (Eds.), *Oscillatory event-related brain dynamics (NATO ASI Series, Vol. 271).* (pp. 231–242). New York: Plenum Press.

Brandt, M., Jansen, B., & Carbonari, J. (1991). Pre-stimulus spectral EEG patterns and the visual evoked response. *Electroencephalography and Clinical Neurophysiology, 80*, 16–20.

Caplan, J. B., Madsen, J. R., Schulze-Bonhage, A., Aschenbrenner-Scheibe, R., Newman, E. L., & Kahana, M. J. (2003). Human theta oscillations related to sensorimotor integration and spatial learning. *Journal of Neuroscience, 23*, 4726–4736.

Courchesne, E. (1983). Cognitive components of the event-related potential: Changes associated with development. In A. W. K. Gaillard, & W. Ritter, (Eds.), *Tutorials in event-related potential research: Endogenous components.* (pp. 329–344). Amsterdam: North-Holland.

Demiralp, T., & Basar, E. (1992). Theta rhythmicities following expected visual and auditory targets. *International Journal of Psychophysiology, 13*, 147–160.

Demiralp, T., Yordanova, J., Kolev, V., Ademoglu, A., Devrim, M., & Samar, V. J. (1999). Time-frequency analysis of single-sweep event-related potentials by means of fast wavelet transform. *Brain and Language, 66*, 129–145.

Fein, G., & Turetsky, B. (1989). P300 latency variability in normal elderly: Effects of paradigm and measurement technique. *Electroencephalography and Clinical Neurophysiology, 72*, 384–394.

Ford, J., White, P., Lim, K., & Pfefferbaum, A. (1994). Schizophrenics have fewer and smaller P300s: A single-trial analysis. *Biological Psychiatry, 35*, 96–103.

Galambos, R. (1992). A comparison of certain gamma band (40-Hz) brain rhythms in cat and man. In E. Basar, & T. H. Bullock, (Eds.), *Induced rhythms in the brain* (pp. 201–216). Boston: Birkhäuser.

Gasser, T., Verleger, R., Bächer, P., & Sroka, L. (1988). Development of EEG of school-age children and adolescents. I. Analysis of band power. *Electroencephalography and Clinical Neurophysiology, 69*, 91–99.

Gevins, A. (1987). Overview of computer analysis. In A. S. Gevins, & A. Rémond, (Eds.), *Methods of analysis of brain electrical and magnetic signals. EEG handbook* (revised series, Vol., pp. 31–83). Amsterdam: Elsevier.

Gruber, T., Mueller, M. M., Keil, A., & Elbert, T. (1999). Selective visual-spatial attention alters induced gamma band responses in the human EEG. *Clinical Neurophysiology, 110*, 2074–2085.

Heinrich, H., Dickhaus, H., Rothenberger, A., Heinrich, V., & Moll, G. H. (1999). Single-sweep analysis of event-related potentials by wavelet networks: Methodological basis and clinical application. *IEEE Transactions on Biomedical Engineering, 46*, 867–879.

Herrmann, C. S., & Knight, R. T. (2001). Mechanisms of human attention: Event-related potentials and oscillations. *Neuroscience and Biobehavavioral Reviews, 25*, 465–476.

Inouye, T., Shinosaki, K., Iyama, A., Matsumoto, Y., & Toi, S. (1994). Moving potential field of frontal midline theta activity during a mental task. *Cognitive Brain Research, 2*, 87–92.

Jensen, O., Gelfand, J., Kounios, J., & Lisman, J. E. (2002). Oscillations in the alpha band (9–12 Hz) increase with memory load during retention in a short-term memory task. *Cerebral Cortex, 12*, 877–882.

Jervis, B. W., Nichols, M. J., Johnson, T. E., Allen, E., & Hudson, N. R. (1983). A fundamental investigation of the composition of auditory evoked potentials. *IEEE Transactions on Biomedical Engineering, BME-30*, 43–49.

John, E. R., Ahn, H., Prichep, L., Trepetin, M., Brown, D., & Kaye, H. (1980). Developmental equations for the electroencephalogram. *Science, 210*, 1255–1258.

Jokeit, H., & Makeig, S. (1994). Different event-related patterns of gamma-band power in brain waves of fast- and slow-reacting subjects. *Proceedings of the National Academy of Sciences of the USA, 91,* 6339–6343.

Kahana, M. J., Seelig, D., & Madsen, J. R. (2001). Theta returns. *Current Opinion in Neurobiology, 11,* 739–744.

Kalcher, J., & Pfurtscheller, G. (1995). Discrimination between phase-locked and non-phase-locked event-related EEG activity. *Electroencephalography and Clinical Neurophysiology, 94,* 381–384.

Klimesch, W. (1997). EEG-alpha rhythms and memory processes. *International Journal of Psychophysiology, 26,* 319–340.

Klimesch, W. (1999). EEG alpha and theta oscillations reflect cognitive and memory performance: A review and analysis. *Brain Research Reviews, 29,* 169–195.

Klimesch, W., Doppelmayr, M., Russeger, H., & Pachinger, T. (1996). Theta band power in the human scalp EEG and the encoding of new information. *NeuroReport, 7,* 1235–1240.

Klimesch, W., Schimke, H., & Schwaiger, J. (1994). Episodic and semantic memory: An analysis in the EEG theta and alpha band. *Electroencephalography and Clinical Neurophysiology, 91,* 428–441.

Kolev, V., Basar-Eroglu, C., Aksu, F., & Basar, E. (1994a). EEG rhythmicities evoked by visual stimuli in three-year-old children. *International Journal of Neuroscience, 75,* 257–270.

Kolev, V., Demiralp, T., Yordanova, J., Ademoglu, A., & Isoglu-Alkaç, Ü. (1997). Time-frequency analysis reveals multiple functional components during oddball P300. *NeuroReport, 8,* 2061–2065.

Kolev, V., & Schürmann, M. (1992). Event-related prolongation of induced EEG rhythmicities in experiments with a cognitive task. *International Journal of Neuroscience, 67,* 199–213.

Kolev, V., & Yordanova, J. (1995). Delta responses in auditory brain potentials during passive and task conditions. In N. Elsner, & R. Menzel, (Eds.), *Proceedings of the 23rd Göttingen Neurobiology Conference 1995* (Vol. II, p. 324).

Kolev, V., & Yordanova, J. (1997). Analysis of phase-locking is informative for studying event-related EEG activity. *Biological Cybernetics, 76,* 229–235.

Kolev, V., Yordanova, J., Basar-Eroglu, C., & Basar, E. (2002). Age effects on visual EEG responses reveal distinct frontal alpha networks. *Clinical Neurophysiology, 113,* 901–910.

Kolev, V., Yordanova, J., & Silyamova, V. (1994b). The relation between the endogenous P3 wave and evoked frequency components in children. *Journal of Psychophysiology, 3,* 277.

Krause, C. M., Lang, A. H., Laine, M., Kuusisto, M., & Porn, B. (1996). Event-related EEG desynchronization and synchronization during an auditory memory task. *Electroencephalography and Clinical Neurophysiology, 98,* 319–326.

Krause, C. M., Sillanmaki, L., Koivisto, M., Saarela, C., Haggqvist, A., Laine, M., & Hamalainen, H. (2000). The effects of memory load on event-related EEG desynchronization and synchronization. *Clinical Neurophysiology, 111,* 2071–2078.

Kurtzberg, D., Vaughan, H., Jr., Courchesne, E., Friedman, D., Harter, M. R., & Putnam, L. (1984). Developmental aspects of event-related potentials. *Annals of the New York Academy of Sciences, 425,* 300–318.

Ladish, C., & Polich, J. (1989). P300 and probability in children. *Journal of Experimental Child Psychology, 48*, 212–223.

Lang, M., Lang, W., Diekmann, V., & Kornhuber, H. H. (1989). The frontal theta rhythm indicating motor and cognitive learning. In R. Johnson, Jr., J. Rohrbaugh, & R. Parasuraman, (Eds.), *Current Trends in Event-related Potential Research. Electroencephalography and Clinical Neurophysiology, Supplement 40.* Amsterdam: Elsevier.

Lisman, J. E., & Idiart, M. A. (1995). Storage of 7 +/–2 short-term memories in oscillatory subcycles. *Science, 267*, 1512–1515.

Llinás, R. (1988). The intrinsic electrophysiological properties of mammalian neurons: Insights into central nervous system function. *Science, 242*, 1654–1664.

Llinás, R., & Ribary, U. (1993). Coherent 40-Hz oscillation characterizes dream state in humans. *Proceedings of the National Academy of Sciences of the USA, 90*, 2078–2081.

Lopes da Silva, F. H. (1993). Dynamics of EEG as signals of neuronal populations: Models and theoretical considerations. In E. Niedermeyer, & F. H. Lopes da Silva, (Eds.), *Electroencephalography: Basic principles, clinical applications, and related fields* (3rd ed., pp. 63–77). Baltimore: Williams & Wilkins.

Lopes da Silva, F. H., van Lierop, T. H., Schrijerr, C. F., & Storm van Leeuwen, W. (1973). Organization of thalamic and cortical alpha rhythms: Spectra and coherences. *Electroencephalography and Clinical Neurophysiology, 35*, 627–639.

Madler, C., Keller, I., Schwender, D., & Pöppel, E. (1991). Sensory information processing during general anesthesia: Effects of isuflurane on auditory evoked neuronal oscillations. *British Journal of Anesthesia, 66*, 81–87.

Makeig, S. (2002). Response: Event-related brain dynamics – unifying brain electrophysiology. *Trends in Neurosciences, 25*, 390.

Makeig, S., Debener, S., Onton, J., & Delorme, A. (2004). Mining event-related brain dynamics. *Trends in Cognitive Sciences, 8*, 204–210.

Matoušek, M., & Petersẹn, I. (1973). Frequency analysis of the EEG in normal children and in normal adolescents. In P. Kellaway, & I. Petersẹn, (Eds.), *Automation of Clinical Electroencephalography* (pp. 75–102). New York: Raven Press.

May, P., Tiitinen, H., Sinkkonen, J., & Näätänen, R. (1994). Long-term stimulation attenuates the transient 40-Hz response. *NeuroReport, 5*, 1918–1920.

Michalewski, H. J., Prasher, D. K., & Starr, A. (1986). Latency variability and temporal interrelationships of the auditory event-related potentials (N1, P2, N2, and P3) in normal subjects. *Electroencephalography and Clinical Neurophysiology, 65*, 59–71.

Miller, R. (1991). *Cortico-hippocampal interplay and the representation of contexts in the Brain.* Berlin: Springer.

Mizuki, Y., Masotoshi, T., Isozaki, H., Nishijima, H., & Inanaga, K. (1980). Periodic appearance of theta rhythm in the frontal midline area during performance of a mental task. *Electroencephalography and Clinical Neurophysiology, 49*, 345–351.

Mizuki, Y., Takii, O., Nishijima, H., & Inanaga, K. (1983). The relationship between the appearance of frontal midline theta activity (FmTheta) and memory function. *Electroencephalography and Clinical Neurophysiology, 56*, 56–56.

Mueller, M. M., Gruber, T., & Keil, A. (2000). Modulation of induced gamma band activity in the human EEG by attention and visual information processing. *International Journal of Psychophysiology, 38*, 283–299.

Niedermeyer, E. (1993). Maturation of the EEG: Development of waking and sleep patterns. In E. Niedermeyer, & F. H. Lopes da Silva, (Eds.), *Electroencephalography: Basic principles, clinical applications and related fields* (pp. 167–191). Baltimore: Williams & Wilkins.

Niedermeyer, E. (1997). Alpha rhythms as physiological and abnormal phenomena. *International Journal of Psychophysiology, 26*, 31–49.

Pantev, C., Elbert, T., & Lütkenhöner, B. (Eds.). (1994). *Oscillatory event-related brain dynamics, NATO ASI Series.* New York: Plenum.

Pantev, C., Makeig, S., Hoke, M., Galambos, R., Hampson, S., & Gallen, C. (1991). Human auditory evoked gamma-band magnetic fields. *Proceedings of the National Academy of Sciences of the USA, 88*, 8996–9000.

Petersén, I., & Eeg-Olofsson, O. (1971). The development of the electroencephalogram in normal children from the age of 1 through 15 years. *Neuropädiatrie, 3*, 247–304.

Pfefferbaum, A., & Ford, J. M. (1988). ERPs to stimuli requiring response production and inhibition: Effects of age, probability and visual noise. *Electroencephalography and Clinical Neurophysiology, 71*, 55–63.

Pfurtscheller, G., & Aranibar, A. (1977). Event-related cortical desynchronization detected by power measurements of scalp EEG. *Electroencephalography and Clinical Neurophysiology, 42*, 817–826.

Pfurtscheller, G., & Klimesch, W. (1992). Event-related synchronization and desynchronization of alpha and beta waves in a cognitive task. In E. Basar, & T. H. Bullock, (Eds.), *Induced rhythms in the brain* (pp. 117–128). Boston: Birkhäuser.

Pfurtscheller, G., & Lopes da Silva, F. H. (1999). Event-related EEG/MEG synchronization and desynchronization: Basic principles. *Clinical Neurophysiology, 110*, 1842–1857.

Pfurtscheller, G., Neuper, C., & Krausz, G. (2000). Functional dissociation of lower and upper frequency mu rhythms in relation to voluntary limb movement. *Clinical Neurophysiology, 111*, 1873–1879.

Piaget, J. (1969). Psychology of intellect. In *Selected Studies in Psychology* (pp. 55–232). Moscow: Mir (in Russian).

Picton, T. W., Bentin, S., Berg, P., Donchin, E., Hillyard, S. A., Johnson, R., Jr., Miller, G. A., Ritter, W., Ruchkin, D. S., Rugg, M. D., & Taylor, M. J. (2000). Guidelines for using human event-related potentials to study cognition: Recording standards and publication criteria. *Psychophysiology, 37*, 127–152.

Picton, T. W., & Stuss, D. T. (1980). The component structure of the human event-related potentials. *Progress in Brain Research, 54*, 17–48.

Polich, J. (1998). P300 clinical utility and control of variability. *Journal of Clinical Neurophysiology, 15*, 14–33.

Regan, D. (1989). *Human brain electrophysiology. Evoked potentials and evoked magnetic fields in science and medicine.* Amsterdam: Elsevier.

Ridderinkhof, K. R., & van der Stelt, O. (2000). Attention and selection in the growing child: Views derived from developmental psychophysiology. *Biological Psychology, 54*, 55–106.

Rosso, O. A., Blanco, S., Yordanova, J., Kolev, V., Figliola, A., Schürmann, M., & Basar, E. (2001). Wavelet Entropy: A new tool for analysis of short time brain electrical signals. *Journal of Neuroscience Methods, 105*, 65–75.

Rothenberger, A. (Ed.). (1982). *Event-related potentials in children.* Amsterdam: Elsevier Biomedical Press.

Rothenberger, A. (1990). The role of the frontal lobes in child psychiatric disorders. In A. Rothenberger, (Ed.), *Brain and behavior in child psychiatry* (pp. 34–58). Berlin: Springer.

Rothenberger, A. (1995). Electrical brain activity in children with Hyperkinetic Syndrome: Evidence of a frontal cortical dysfunction. In J. Sergeant, (Ed.), *Eunethydis. European approaches to hyperkinetic disorder* (pp. 225–270). Zürich: Trümpi.

Ruchkin, D. (1988). Measurement of event-related potentials: Signal extraction. In T. Picton, (Ed.), *Human Event-Related Potentials. Handbook of EEG* (revised series, Vol. 3, pp. 7–43). Amsterdam: Elsevier.

Samar, V. J., Bopardikar, A., Rao, R., & Swartz, K. (1999). Wavelet analysis of neuro-electric waveforms: A conceptual tutorial. *Brain and Language, 66*, 7–60.

Samar, V. J., Swartz, K. P., & Raghuveer, M. R. (1995). Multiresolution analysis of event-related potentials by wavelet decomposition. *Brain and Cognition, 27*, 398–438.

Sayers, B. Mc A., Beagley, H. A., & Henshall, W. R. (1974). The mechanism of auditory evoked EEG responses. *Nature, 247*, 481–483.

Schiff, S. J., Aldroubi, A., Unser, M., & Sato, S. (1994). Fast wavelet transformation of EEG. *Electroencephalography and Clinical Neurophysiology, 91*, 442–455.

Schürmann, M., & Basar, E. (1994). Topography of alpha and theta oscillatory responses upon auditory and visual stimuli in humans. *Biological Cybernetics, 72*, 161–174.

Sinkkonen, J., Tiitinen, H., & Näätänen, R. (1995). Gabor filters: An informative way for analyzing event-related brain activity. *Journal of Neuroscience Methods, 56*, 99–104.

Smulders, F. T. Y., Kenemans, J. L., & Kok, A. (1994). A comparison of different methods for estimating single-trial P300 latencies. *Electroencephalography and Clinical Neurophysiology, 92*, 107–114.

Solodovnikov, V. V. (1960). *Introduction to the statistical dynamics of automatic control systems.* New York: Dover.

Stampfer, G. H., & Basar, E. (1985). Does frequency analysis lead to better understanding of human event-related potentials. *International Journal of Neuroscience, 26*, 181–196.

Steriade, M., Jones, E. G., & Llinás, R. (1990). *Thalamic oscillations and signaling.* New York: John Wiley & Sons.

Takano, T., & Ogawa, T. (1998). Characterization of developmental changes in EEG gamma-band activity during childhood using the autoregressive model. *Acta Paediatrica Japonica, 40*, 446–452.

Tallon-Baudry, C., & Bertrand, O. (1999). Oscillatory gamma activity in humans and its role in object representation. *Trends in Cognitive Sciences, 3*, 151–162.

Tallon-Baudry, C., Bertrand, O., Delpuech, C., & Permier, J. (1997). Oscillatory gamma-band (30–70 Hz) activity induced by a visual search task in humans. *Journal of Neuroscience, 17*, 722–734.

Tallon-Baudry, C., Bertrand, O., Peronnet, F., & Pernier, J. (1998). Induced gamma-band activity during the delay of a visual short-term memory task in humans. *Journal of Neuroscience, 18*, 4244–4254.

Taylor, M. J. (1989). Developmental changes in ERPs to visual language stimuli. In B. Renault, M. Kutas, M. G. H. Coles, A. W. K. Gaillard, (Eds.), *Event-related potential investigations of cognition* (pp. 321–338). Amsterdam: North-Holland.

Tiitinen, H., Sinkkonen, J., Reinikainen, K. Alho, K., Lavikainen, J., & Näätänen, R. (1993). Selective attention enhances the auditory 40-Hz transient response in humans. *Nature, 364*, 59–60.

Traub, R. D., Jefferys, J. G. R., & Whittington, M. A. (1999). *Fast oscillations in cortical circuits.* Cambridge, MA: MIT Press.

Unsal, A., & Segalowitz, S. (1995). Sources of P300 attenuation after head injury: Single-trial amplitude, latency jitter, and EEG power. *Psychophysiology, 32*, 249–256.

Wastell, D. G. (1979). The application of low-pass linear filters to evoked potential data: Filtering without phase distortion. *Electroencephalography and Clinical Neurophysiology, 46*, 355–356.

Yordanova, J., Angelov, A., Silyamova, V., & Kolev, V. (1992). Auditory event-related potentials in children under passive listening to identical stimuli. *Comptes rendus de l'Academie bulgare des Science, 45*, 81–83.

Yordanova, J., Devrim, M., Kolev, V., Ademoglu, A., & Demiralp, T. (2000b). Multiple time-frequency components account for the complex functional reactivity of P300. *NeuroReport, 11*, 1097–1103.

Yordanova. J., Dumais-Huber, C., Rothenberger, A., & Woerner, W. (1997a). Fronto-cortical activity in children with comorbidity of tic disorder and attention-deficit hyperactivity disorder. *Biological Psychiatry, 41*, 585–594.

Yordanova, J., Falkenstein, M., Hohnsbein, J., & Kolev, V. (2004). Parallel systems of error processing in the brain. *NeuroImage, 22*, 590–602.

Yordanova, J., & Kolev, V. (1996). Developmental changes in the alpha response system. *Electroencephalography and Clinical Neurophysiology, 99*, 527–538.

Yordanova, J., & Kolev, V. (1997a). Developmental changes in the event-related EEG theta response and P300. *Electroencephalography and Clinical Neurophysiology, 104*, 418–430.

Yordanova, J., & Kolev, V. (1997b). Alpha response system in children: Changes with age. *International Journal of Psychophysiology, 26*, 411–430.

Yordanova, J., & Kolev, V. (1998a). A single-sweep analysis of the theta frequency band during an auditory oddball task. *Psychophysiology, 35*, 116–126.

Yordanova, J., & Kolev, V. (1998b). Developmental changes in the theta response system: A single sweep analysis. *Journal of Psychophysiology, 12*, 113–126.

Yordanova, J., & Kolev, V. (1998c). Phase-locking of event-related EEG oscillations: Analysis and application. *Applied Signal Processing, 5*, 24–33.

Yordanova, J, & Kolev, V. (2004). Error-specific signals in the brain: Evidence from a time-frequency decomposition of event-related potentials. In M. Ullsperger, & M. Falkenstein, (Eds.), *Errors, Conflicts, and the Brain. Current Opinions on Performance Monitoring. MPI Special issue in human cognitive and brain sciences* (vol. 1., pp. 35–41). Leipzig: MPI of Cognitive Neuroscience.

Yordanova, J., Kolev, V., & Basar, E. (1998). EEG theta and frontal alpha oscillations during auditory processing change with aging. *Electroencephalography and Clinical Neurophysiology, 108*, 497–505.

Yordanova, J., Kolev, V., & Demiralp, T. (1997b). The phase-locking of auditory gamma band responses in humans is sensitive to task processing. *NeuroReport, 8*, 3999–4004.

Yordanova, J., Kolev, V., Heinrich, H., Banaschewski, T., Woerner, W., & Rothenberger, A. (2000a). Gamma band response in children is related to task-stimulus processing. *NeuroReport, 11*, 2325–2330.

Yordanova, J., Kolev, V., Heinrich, H., Woerner, W., Banaschewski, T., & Rothenberger, A. (2002). Developmental event-related gamma oscillations: Effects of auditory attention. *European Journal of Neuroscience, 16*, 2214–2224.

3 Event-Related Potential (ERP) Measures in Auditory Development Research

Laurel J. Trainor

INTRODUCTION

Between birth and 2 years of age, the human cortex undergoes tremendous development, with region-specific and layer-specific patterns of synaptic maturation, overgrowth, and pruning that are undoubtedly influenced by environmental input and complex patterns of neurotransmitter expression (e.g., Huttenlocher & Dabholkar, 1997; Moore & Guan, 2001). During this period, the newborn, who is totally dependent on caregivers for survival, turns into a walking, talking, thinking, self-aware being. These anatomical and functional changes across development should be reflected *in vivo* in the electrical brain activity that can be measured at the scalp.

In practice, collecting data from infants can be rather difficult. While studies that condition a behavioral response, such as sucking or looking, are probably the most advanced of the techniques available, there remain considerable problems in the type and amount of data that can be collected from preverbal infants with short attention spans and immature motor response systems, especially in the first months after birth. Postmortem studies of brain development can also be problematic because death in infancy is usually associated with abnormalities that may invalidate generalizations to normal development. Many of the imaging techniques available for the study of adult brain responses are difficult to apply to human infants. For example, fMRI and MEG require that the subject remain very still throughout the testing period. It is thus possible to test sleeping infants, but rather difficult to test awake infants (Anderson et al., 2001; Hattori et al., 2001; Souweidane et al., 1999). Furthermore, the loud noise of the MRI machine can be very disturbing and distracting for infants. PET requires the use of radioactive materials, making its use with normally developing infants questionable. Because of these problems, auditory event-related potentials (ERPs) derived from electroencephalogram (EEG) recordings have been the most popular choice by far for studying functional cortical development in infants (e.g., Segalowitz & Berge, 1995; Steinschneider & Dunn, 2002). However, ERP results are not always consistent from study to study, and there are still many methodological issues to work out.

One of the most surprising findings from the last decade of auditory developmental ERP research is that brain responses to sound are not fully mature until well into adolescence (Albrecht, Suchodoletz, & Uwer, 2000; Čeponiené, Rinne, & Näätänen, 2002; Johnstone, Barry, Anderson, & Coyle, 1996; Pang & Taylor, 2000; Ponton, Eggermont, Kwong, & Don, 2000; Shahin, Roberts, & Trainor, 2004; Trainor, Shahin, & Roberts, 2003). From a behavioral perspective, it has also become clear that sound processing continues to improve through this time period as well (e.g., Neijenhuis, Snik, Priester, van Kordenoordt, & van den Broek, 2002). Nonetheless, the most rapid behavioral strides occur during the first year (Werner & Marean, 1996). Hearing thresholds improve dramatically over the first months after birth, asymptoting at approximately 6 months of age (Tharpe & Ashmead, 2001). Speech processing changes qualitatively. Although infants are able to discriminate speech sounds in the first months after birth, by 10 months infants process speech according to the specific speech sound categories used in the language they are learning (e.g., Pisoni, Lively, & Logan, 1994; Werker & Tees, 1984). Sound localization abilities change from sluggish left-right discrimination in newborns to fast, accurate, within-hemifield discrimination after 4 months (Muir, Clifton, & Clarkson, 1989; Muir & Field, 1979). Nonetheless, the ability to attend to specific sounds, to understand degraded speech, and to understand speech in noise continues to improve into adolescence (Neijenhuis et al., 2002).

Recent work on the structural maturation of human auditory cortex also shows a protracted development. Although maximum synaptic density is reached at 3 months of age in auditory cortex, synaptic elimination continues until about 12 years of age (Huttenlocher & Dabholkar, 1997). Detailed work on the maturation of axonal conduction times reveals a layer-specific developmental timeline. Moore and Guan (2001) compared postmortem auditory cortical tissue from fetuses up to adults 27 years of age. They examined both the presence of cell bodies (using Nissl stain) and the maturation of neurofilaments (using an immuno stain). Immature neurofilaments are associated with small axonal diameter, a lack of myelin sheaths, and therefore slow conduction velocities, leading to sluggish communication between neurons, and precluding highly synchronized neural activity. Moore and Guan (2001) found that at birth the cell bodies are largely in place, but that only layer I contains mature neurofilaments. Layer I is larger in early infancy than in adulthood, with banding into two sub-layers, compared to the single band in adults. After 4.5 months, mature neurofilaments begin to appear in deeper layers of auditory cortex (lower III, IV, V, and VI), and reach adult levels by about 3 to 5 years of age. Neurofilaments are very late to mature in superficial layers (II and upper III), with no evidence of their presence before 5 years of age; a mature level is not reached until about 12 years of age. Interestingly, primary areas do not mature earlier than secondary and tertiary areas, the same developmental sequence being apparent in areas 41/42 and 22.

The primary input to auditory cortex from thalamus is via pyramidal neurons in lower layer III and layer IV, which develop mature neural filaments between 4.5 months and 5 years of age. Layer II and upper layer III communicate extensively with other cortical areas (Moore & Guan, 2001). Upper layer III and layer II maintain immature synapses for a protracted period, a delay that is presumably important for the development of optimal communication with other cortical areas. Other animals also follow a similar developmental trajectory. For example, in neonatal kittens, the earliest responses from auditory cortex are generated in deeper cortical layers (Konig & Marty, 1974; Konig, Pujol, & Marty, 1972; Miyata, Kawaguchi, Samejima, & Yamamoto, 1982). It is also of interest that a lack of auditory input due to deafness during childhood appears to affect the development of superficial layers to a greater extent than the development of deeper layers in both cats (Kral et al., 2000) and humans (Ponton & Eggermont, 2001).

ERPs measured at the scalp reflect extra-cellular changes in electrical field potentials with cortical depth that are associated with depolarization, hyperpolarization, and firing of neurons (e.g., Mitzdorf, 1985; Vaughan Jr. & Arezzo, 1988). Therefore, the large layer-specific changes in synaptic density and functionality with development outlined above would be expected to result in large changes in measured ERPs across age. This chapter is not intended to be an exhaustive review of the auditory developmental ERP literature, but rather an illustration of how information from different levels of analysis needs to be combined to yield a deeper understanding of developmental processes. We begin with a review of adult auditory ERPs, then examine issues in recording ERPs in infants, and end with a review of ERP development in infants and children in relation to behavioral and anatomical changes.

DEVELOPMENT OF AUDITORY EVENT-RELATED
POTENTIALS (ERPS)

What are ERPs?

The voltage difference between an electrode placed at a position of interest on the scalp and a reference electrode placed at a relatively neutral position with respect to the neural activity of interest yields an EEG, a time-varying voltage signal that reflects the activity of many neurons working in concert. Such recordings require the placement of electrodes on the scalp, either singly or embedded in a stretch cap or geodesic wire system, but are non-invasive in the sense that no large magnetic field or radioactive substance needs to be administered. If a stimulus event such as a sound is presented, some of the measured neural activity will reflect the processing of that sound event. This activity is termed the event-related potential (ERP). However, on a single trial, the neural activity not systematically related to the sound event, considered "noise," typically precludes observation of the ERP waveform of interest. Thus, multiple trials of the sound event must be given, the resulting waveforms lined up according to the onset of the sound events, each waveform baselined to a short period preceding the onset of the sound event (typically between 50 and 200 ms), and the waveforms averaged. If the "noise" from neural activity unassociated with the processing of the sound is stationary (i.e., its statistical properties do not change from trial to trial) and is not time locked to the onset of the sound, the noise will tend to average to zero. The number of trials needed to obtain a good representation of the ERP depends on the size of the signal and the size and characteristics of the noise.

An idealized auditory ERP response recorded at the vertex of the head is shown in Figure 3.1. The most common variables examined are the amplitude (in μV) and latency from stimulus onset (in ms) of each peak. During the first 10 ms, there is a series of seven small peaks, known as the auditory brain stem response (ABR). These peaks represent activity from successive subcortical areas, probably from the cochlear nucleus to the thalamus. The middle latency responses occurring during the next 50 ms represent neural activity in auditory cortex. Both the brainstem and middle latency responses require many trials averaged together because these responses are relatively small in amplitude compared to the background noise. The late ERP components follow the middle latency responses, beginning around 50 ms after stimulus onset. The same basic topography is seen whether an average or mastoid reference is used. For auditory stimuli, a P1 (first positive) component is typically seen around 50 ms, an N1b (first negative) component around

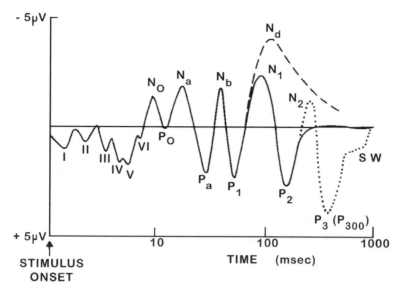

Figure 3.1. A stylized representation of the major ERP components measured at the Cz vertex of the scalp. Waves I to VI of the auditory brainstem response (ABR) occur within approximately the first 10 ms. The middle latency responses (No, Po, Na, Pa, Nb) reflect the first volley of activity into auditory cortex and occur between about 15 and 50 ms. The obligatory late auditory ERP components (P1, N1, P2) follow the middle latency responses. Task- and attention-related components may also be present (N2, P3, Nd, SW). Reprinted with permission from Hillyard and Kutus (1983).

100 ms, and a P2 component around 180 ms. If the listener is attending and performing a task related to the sound, the P2 will be followed by N2, P3, and slow wave (SW) components. A negative Nd component can overlap the N1 and P2 peaks (Figure 3.1).

The relation between ERPs measured at the scalp and their neural generators is complex (e.g., Mitzdorf, 1985; Steinschneider & Dunn, 2002; Vaughan Jr. & Arezzo, 1988). When a neuron fires, an extra-cellular sink is created by the flow of positive ions into the cell, flanked by more positive regions, termed sources. Electric fields are also created by the relatively stationary chemical depolarizations and hyperpolarizations that occur with excitatory postsynaptic potentials (EPSP) and inhibitory postsynaptic potentials (IPSP), respectively. With depolarization, an extra-cellular sink is created and the circuit will be completed with a source above or below the point of depolarization. Conversely, with hyperpolarization, a source is created, with a sink above or below. In order for these fields to be visible at the scalp, the sources and sinks must be oriented perpendicularly to the cortical surface. It is thus believed that cortical ERPs largely measure the activation of pyramidal cells, as these cells, unlike the cortical stellate cells, are largely oriented in parallel in the optimal direction.

Extra-cellular electrical field patterns depend on a number of complex factors. For example, the locations of passive source returns – the opposite charge countering the effect of the synaptic activity – depend to some extent on how the surrounding networks of cells are connected and active. The strength, timing, and spread of components measured at the scalp depend on properties of electrical field propagation through the brain and other tissue. Indeed, animal studies with multiple electrodes at various depths reveal complex sequences of sinks and sources in various layers (e.g., Fishman, Reser, Arezzo, & Steinschneider, 1998, 2000). Nonetheless, in a simple pyramidal cell model, excitatory synaptic potentials (depolarization) in deeper layers (with the passive current returns in the apical dendrites in superficial layers) will appear as a surface positivity, whereas an excitation in upper layers will appear as a surface negativity (Creutzfeldt & Houchin, 1974; Eggermont & Ponton, 2003; Fishman et al., 2000). Given the orientation of auditory cortex around the sylvian fissure, activity generated in auditory cortex typically appears at the scalp in a dipolar pattern, with fronto-central positivity accompanied by posterior negativity or fronto-central negativity accompanied by posterior positivity.

The relation between ERP components and activation in the brain is further complicated by the fact that cortical components typically reflect the activation of several temporally overlapping generators. For example, P1 is thought to be generated by activity in both primary and secondary auditory cortices (e.g., Liégeois-Chauvel et al., 1994; Ponton et al., 2000; Steinschneider & Dunn, 2002). Importantly, P1 likely represents re-entrant activation either from thalamus or from other cortical areas. N1 has been studied extensively in adults and is known to consist of several subcomponents (Näätänen & Picton, 1987). The vertex-recorded N1, or N1b, is likely generated outside of primary auditory cortex and may represent intra-cortical excitatory input to layer II and upper layer III (Eggermont & Ponton, 2002; Vaughan Jr. & Ritter, 1970). N1 is thought to be associated with conscious detection of discrete sounds and is affected by attention (Hyde, 1997; Woldorff & Hillyard, 1991). The location of the P2 generator is distinct from that of the N1b (Shahin, Bosnyak, Trainor, & Roberts, 2003), and may involve generators closer to primary auditory cortex. In addition, a T-complex can be recorded, consisting of a positivity around 100 ms followed by a negativity, N1c, at around 150 ms. The T-complex is generated in association cortex with a radial orientation, and therefore appears on the scalp at temporal sites (Scherg & von Cramon, 1986). The P1, N1, and P2 components listed above are obligatory in the

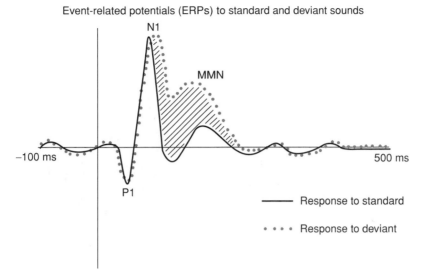

Event-related potentials (ERPs) to standard and deviant sounds

——— Response to standard

• • • • Response to deviant

Figure 3.2. A stylized representation of the Mismatch Negativity (MMN). The ERP generated by the occasional deviant stimuli is more negative than that of the standard stimuli between about 140 and 240 ms after stimulus onset.

sense that they do not require the listener to perform a task, although they can be affected by attention.

Although the subcortically generated ABR can be readily recorded in newborns, and is widely used as a screening test for hearing impairment, it is very difficult, if not impossible, to measure cortically generated middle latency responses in young infants (e.g., Stapells, Galambos, Costello, & Makeig, 1988). The amplitudes of the middle latency responses in adults are small; the immaturity of primary auditory cortex in infancy may render the amplitude too small or inconsistent to measure with current technology. Similarly, the late auditory cortical ERP components, although much larger in adults, are also very immature or absent in infancy. In this chapter, we will concentrate on the maturation of these late obligatory ERP components.

Another obligatory auditory component needs to be discussed. In adults, the mismatch negativity (MMN) component peaks between approximately 150 and 250 ms after stimulus onset, depending on the particular stimuli (Näätänen, 1992; Näätänen et al., 2001; Näätänen & Winkler, 1999; Picton et al., 2000; Schröger, 1998). The MMN component is somewhat different from the components listed above because it is only seen in an oddball paradigm in which occasional change trials (deviants or oddballs) occur in a sequence of similar trials (standards) (see Figure 3.2). MMN occurs in

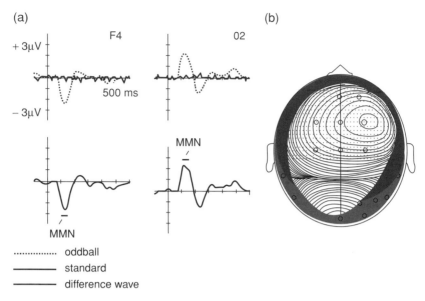

Figure 3.3. Mismatch negativity response in adults to a change in the location of a sine wave tone (1000 Hz, 50 ms; SOA = 104 ms). Standards (90% of trials) were presented in front of the listener and oddballs (10%) from 90° to the left. MMN is often illustrated by the difference wave obtained by subtracting the average ERP generated by the frequent standard stimuli from that generated by the infrequent deviant sound. (A) With the rapid presentation rate, no N1 can be seen in the standard waveforms. However, a prominent MMN is present in the difference waves. Note the reversal in polarity above (right frontal site, F4) and below (right occipital site, O2) the sylvian fissure, consistent with a source in auditory cortex. Bars represent regions of the difference waves that are significantly different from zero. (B) Isovoltage contour map of the MMN peak, showing the right focus of the MMN when the sound changes to a location 90° to the left. Data are from Sonnadara et al. (2006).

response to changes in basic sound features such as frequency, intensity, and duration, as well as to derived sound features such as pitch, timbre, and location (Näätänen et al., 2001; Picton et al., 2000). Initially, MMN was thought to reflect only basic sensory encoding. However, more recent research indicates that MMN also occurs to changes in patterns of sound (e.g., Näätänen et al., 2001; Picton et al., 2000; Trainor, McDonald, & Alain, 2002). N1 and MMN are affected differently by the rate of stimulation, with N1 diminishing in amplitude and MMN increasing in amplitude as the stimulus onset asynchrony (SOA) becomes smaller. Figure 3.3 shows MMN to a change in sound location (Sonnadara, Alain, & Trainor, 2006). The SOA is very short at 104 ms, and the standard waveforms therefore show virtually no N1 component. However, the MMN is readily apparent.

In humans, the detection of changes in different sound features appears to localize to slightly different cortical regions (e.g., Alain, Achim, & Woods, 1999; Alho et al., 1996; Takegata, Paavilainen, Näätänen, & Winkler, 1999). In monkeys, MMN in response to an intensity change is generated in the superficial layers of primary auditory cortex (Javitt et al., 1994), but it is not known whether this generalizes to humans or to other sound features. The MMN component is obligatory in the sense that it occurs regardless of whether the person is paying attention to the sounds. Interestingly, MMN appears to be less dependent on experience during a critical period than is N1b. As such, MMN readily develops in deaf patients fitted with cochlear implants whereas N1b does not (Ponton et al., 2000). These properties have made MMN of great interest to developmental researchers, the hope being that MMN will allow the investigation of auditory discrimination independent from attentional factors in infancy and childhood.

Components following the N1 and P2 are typically greatly affected by the particular task or attentional focus of the listener. For example, the N2 component, which can overlap the MMN, is very small or absent when the participant is not attending (Picton et al., 2000). The frontal P3a component is found when a salient sound in a stream of unattended sounds captures the attention of a listener (Escera, Alho, Winkler, & Näätänen, 1998; Squires, Squires, & Hillyard, 1975); thus, P3a is thought to reflect the inadvertent capture of attention. The parietal P3b component, which can peak anywhere between 300 and 600 ms depending on task difficulty, is typically only clearly present when a participant listens for and identifies a particular sound in a sequence of non-target sounds. An N4 component appears to reflect linguistic semantic mismatch, occurring in response to a sentence such as "He spread the warm bread with socks" (Kutas & Hillyard, 1980).

Researchers are interested in linking stages of processing with particular ERP components (e.g., P1 represents sensory encoding, P3 represents memory updating, N4 represents semantic encoding, etc.), but this linkage is not entirely straightforward. There are a number of reasons for this issue. First, electrical activity will only be visible in the ERP waveform if enough neurons pointing in the same direction have fired synchronously. The percentage of neural activity captured by the ERP waveform is not known, but clearly much goes on in the brain that is never seen through ERP measurement. Second, the generators of the components measured at the scalp must overlap to some extent in time, and perhaps to some extent in brain location as well, adding greatly to the complexity of identifying individual components. Obviously, one component may mask another if it is larger and occurs during the same time period. Worse, a component may be seen at the scalp that does not actually reflect the activity of any particular neural generator in the brain. For example, if two neural generators individually give rise to similar-amplitude peaks somewhat before and somewhat after 100 ms, their sum will look like a single peak at 100 ms, and a false conclusion may be drawn that there is a single neural process at 100 ms.

To some extent these problems can be overcome through the use of source modeling that takes into account not only the peaks and latencies of components at single electrodes, but also the spatial-temporal distribution of measured activity across the scalp across time (Picton et al., 1999; Scherg, 1990). If the location of a neural generator is known, the propagation of the electrical fields through the brain and skull can be modeled, and a predicted ERP potential derived. Source modeling techniques attempt to reverse this process. Starting with the measured ERP waveforms across time and scalp locations, the sources of activation that would yield that pattern of activity can be estimated. Although in theory, there is no unique solution to the number and locations of the sources giving rise to the observed activity at the scalp, simplification constraints (e.g., a limited number of generators, symmetry between hemispheres) and constraints based on prior anatomical knowledge, perhaps derived from animal studies, often yield reasonable solutions that account for most of the variance in the recorded data. However, as will be discussed below, we are not yet able to perform accurate source modeling with human infants.

ISSUES IN RECORDING ERPS IN INFANTS AND CHILDREN

Getting the Electrodes On and Keeping the Infant Still

The first challenge when recording from infants is to apply the electrodes while maintaining the infant's good mood. The next challenge is to keep the infant still, attentive, and happy during the recording. This task can be easier in younger than in older infants. Once infants reach 5 or 6 months, their behavior becomes more purposeful (e.g., they are more likely to try to remove the electrodes), and more coordinated (and hence more likely to succeed in removing the electrodes). The most challenging period in this regard is between about 1 and 2 years of age. It often works best to have one researcher devoted to keeping the infant distracted with toys, peek-a-boo games, and soap bubbles while one or two other researchers apply the electrodes and run the equipment. Beyond the newborn period, infants are often happiest when held by their mothers. If the infant is on the mother's lap, the mother can also help by holding the infant's hands.

A related issue concerns the number of electrodes that can be applied to the scalp. Obviously, the more electrodes used, the more information that can be collected, and the greater the choice of analysis procedures. However, with systems that require conducting electrogel application and impedance checking for each electrode, it is better to record from only a few electrodes in the interest of increasing signal-to-noise ratios. Because the infant will only cooperate for a short time, the more time that can be spent collecting data rather than applying the electrodes, the better. On the other hand, with high impedance systems, adequate conductivity can be obtained with nets of electrodes imbedded in sponges after the nets are simply dipped in a saline solution. In this case, 128 or even 256 electrodes can be applied in a few minutes. The use of high impedance systems allows for quick application, but such a system is more subject to electrical noise. Which system is most suitable depends on the particular application.

Choosing Reference Electrodes

EEG signals must always be referenced to something. The choice of reference has been discussed at great length in the adult literature over the past few decades (Dien, 1998), with choice locations including the ears, mastoids, nose, and base of the neck. However, as none of these locations is neutral with respect to brain activity, and with the increasing capability of recording simultaneously from many sites, a common average reference is now typical. In this case, a single site reference is used during recording (e.g., the Cz vertex), but during data analysis, the reference (or zero value) for each time point is taken as the averaged activity across all electrodes at that time. If one electrode is bad and hence excluded from the average, the homologous electrode on the other side of the head should also be excluded if hemispheric effects are to be examined. A common average reference works well if about 30 or more electrodes are used and they are spread across the scalp and face, including sites below the sylvian fissure. The activity at each site then reflects whether that site is more positive or more negative than the average. Care must be taken when using a common average reference with infants, however, because sites around the periphery of the cap or net, particularly at the back of the head, tend to be noisy. The cap may fit least well at the back, and infants sometimes flex the muscles at the back of their head because their neck control is poor. If electrodes that capture this muscle activity are included in the common average reference, the data may appear quite noisy. Bad electrodes can be interpolated and replaced, but these estimates will be worst at the periphery because there are fewer surrounding electrodes. It may be better to discard them from the common average reference calculation, although they are important for modeling the sources of the activations.

When only a few electrode sites are available, a common average reference does not work well (Dien, 1998). In this case, the choice of reference electrode may be different for different applications. For example, in adults, with a common average reference, MMN reflects activity in auditory cortex, which propagates through the brain to produce a negativity at frontal sites and a positivity at mastoid and posterior sites. Thus, if the mastoid sites are used as the reference, the MMN peak at frontal sites will be maximum. However, in this case, it will not be possible to test whether there is a reversal from negative to positive voltage across the sylvian fissure. On the other hand, if Pz (midline parietal site) is used as the reference, this reversal should be apparent.

Artifact Elimination with Children

Measured at the scalp, the electrical signals generated from muscle movement are very large compared to those generated by neurons in the brain. Adults can typically remain still, so the major artifact is usually from eye blinks and eye movements. As adults are instructed to minimize these movements, they tend to be few in number and executed quickly. With infants, verbal instructions are not possible, so other means of keeping infants still must be employed. In studies of automatic processing in which attention is not important, visual stimuli that are not time-locked to the auditory events of interest can be employed. Young infants can sometimes be mesmerized by experimenters performing peek-a-boo games and blowing soap bubbles or by bright shapes appearing and disappearing on a monitor. Older infants and children often like silent cartoons. Infants also have short attention spans, with 15 to 20 min of EEG recording typically constituting a good run, so the fewer trials lost to artifact the better.

However, enchanting the visual stimulation, infant data will likely contain substantial numbers of trials with artifact. The simplest approach is to elim-inate these trials. Rejection criteria in adults often focus on eliminating trials in which electrodes around the eyes contain large voltages, or large changes in voltage, as eye blinks and eye movements provide the vast majority of the noise. However, in infants, a wider range of electrodes for rejection may be more appropriate because considerable artifact can come from small move-ments at the back of the head. There is no simple answer to the question of how large a voltage is needed for a trial to be rejected as containing artifact. If there is a very large number of trials, a few trials with artifact will not change the average substantially. Unfortunately, with infants, there are typically few trials, and so a few noisy ones can have a large effect. Too strict a criterion, however, may result in most trials being rejected, and the remaining data will also be very noisy because there are not enough trials to average out the brain activation not due to processing the sound event. The amount of noise that can be tolerated will also depend on the size of the components of interest. The larger the component, the more noise that can be tolerated.

Given how precious every trial is in infant data, it would be helpful to develop a technique whereby artifact could be eliminated through signal processing means while keeping all, or most, trials. This procedure is possible with adult data, if ERP eye movement and eye blink responses are recorded separately in each individual subject (see Picton, Lins, & Scherg, 1995). Source models of eye movements and eye blinks can be made, and the modeled activity from these sources eliminated from the data. It is not clear, however, that taking the time to elicit and record infant eye movements and eye blinks would leave enough time for conducting the experiment of interest. Furthermore, this method does not account for artifact from the back of the head due to movement. In addition, we do not yet have a good head model for infants on which to base source modeling (see below), so at the present time, this approach is not possible. However, given how important every trial is in infant data, the development of techniques for eliminating artifact while keeping the trial should be a priority.

Averaging Infant Data

As discussed in the previous section, many similar trials must be averaged together in order to distill out the parts of the ERP waveform that are due to the sound event of interest. This process assumes that the "noise" (i.e., the rest of the brain activity) is stationary, that is, has the same mean and standard deviation statistics throughout the recording session. In adults, the stationary assumption is likely reasonable. However, infants can change their mood dramatically from the beginning to the end of the session, they may be more distracted at the end than at the beginning, they may be more sleepy at certain times than at other times, and there is probably more variance in the latency of their neural responses. All of these changes can alter the nature of the noise. To the extent that the noise is not stationary, the averaging process will be less successful at removing it. Thus, not only do we typically obtain fewer trials from infants, but eliminating noise through the averaging process is probably less effective in infants than in adults. The averaging process also assumes that the ERP generated in response to the sound is the same on every trial. In a young brain with much plasticity and much to learn quickly, the neural response to a sound event may well change over the course of the study. This point is very important because when we examine an averaged infant ERP waveform and a component appears spread out in time, we are unsure whether the infant takes a long time to perform the operation giving rise to that component, or whether there is simply a lot of noise and latency variation from trial to trial.

Individual electrodes are more likely to become bad part way through a session with infants than with adults because infants squirm. Individual electrodes can also contain artifact on particular trials that does not affect the rest of the electrodes (e.g., if one electrode is temporarily pushed). Normally, with adults, if the data from one electrode contain artifact and should be eliminated on a particular trial, the whole trial is discarded. If enough trials are bad, the electrode is eliminated entirely from the dataset. Similarly, when averaging together different adult participants, only electrodes for which data exist for all participants are included. However, these rules should probably be relaxed somewhat with infant data. First, the sources of the artifact are likely somewhat different and more independent in infants than in adults. Second, because so few trials can typically be obtained in infants, it does not make sense to throw away data from good electrodes when one isolated electrode is bad or, once averaging is complete, to not include an electrode in statistical analyses across participants because that electrode was eliminated in one individual. Additionally, it may be the case that all electrodes should be monitored for artifact, not just eye electrodes. In sum, it is particularly important with infant data to consider carefully all rules for averaging in order to obtain the cleanest signals possible.

Filtering Infant and Child Data

Filtering is important because it can clarify the components of interest and increase the signal-to-noise ratio. As with adult data, a band-pass filter is typically used with infant data. A zero-phase shift filter should be used, or different frequency components can be shifted different amounts in time, and virtually all EEG analysis packages use either a zero-phase shift FIR (finite impulse response) filter, or an IIR (infinite impulse response) filter both forward and backward in order to ensure a zero-phase shift. Adult studies examining late auditory ERP components typically use a bandpass filter of around 0.1 to 30 Hz. The steepness of the filter roll-off (related to the size of the window over which the filtering is done) is of major importance for maintaining the integrity of the data. Although a steep roll-off is desirable from the perspective of signal-to-noise ratio, very steep filters can introduce ringing artifact into the signal. Furthermore, the software associated with different EEG analysis packages specify filters in different ways, so care must be taken when comparing data collected and analyzed in different systems. For example, in some systems the cutoff frequency is specified (the frequency beyond which filtering begins), and the roll-off is expressed in dB/octave (i.e., intensity decrease per doubling of frequency). In other systems, a pass band and stop band gain are expressed in percentage (e.g., a pass band gain of 95% passes 95% of the power over the pass band frequencies; a stop band gain of 5% only passes 5% of the power over the frequencies that are almost entirely filtered out), and roll off is expressed in linear Hz units (e.g., 20 Hz to 40 Hz), which specifies the frequency region over which the signal goes from 95% to 5% power.

There are additional issues that need to be considered with respect to infant data. Infant data often contain very slow wave components. If these are of interest, the cutoff frequency for the high pass filter should be fairly low (e.g., 0.1 Hz). However, these slow waves may obscure the faster components of interest, such as MMN. The faster components will be more apparent if the high pass filter has a higher cut off (e.g., 1 or 3 Hz, depending on the speed of the component of interest; see Figure 3.4). Thus, in choosing the cutoff frequency, it is important to examine the frequency characteristics of the components that are to be analyzed.

Performing Statistics on Individual and Group Waveforms

The most common group statistical analyses of developmental ERP data use the amplitude or latency of a particular component as the dependent variable. If the question of interest is whether the component is present or not, the mean and standard deviation of the peak amplitude can be analyzed using a t-test to see whether the mean is significantly different from zero. A generalization of this procedure is to perform a t-test at every time point across the entire epoch from the onset of the sound. Although this approach is very common, it does involve a large number of t-tests (for a 500 ms epoch with a sampling rate of 500 Hz, this is 250 t-tests) and, therefore, a large probability of false positives. With this in mind, most researchers look for a series of adjacent time points surrounding a peak of interest that are all significantly different from zero before concluding that the component is reliably present. Such a procedure can be formalized through the use of Monte Carlo simulations to determine how many adjacent time points are necessary to achieve a particular significance level (e.g., $p = 0.05$ or $p = 0.01$). An alternative to the multiple t-test approach is to determine the latency of a peak in the grand average

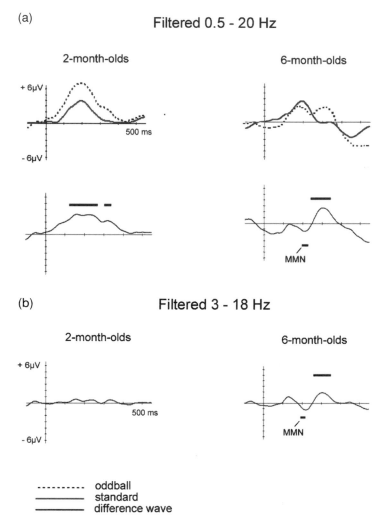

Figure 3.4. Responses from 2-month-old and 6-month-old infants at a right frontal site (F4) to standard (80%) tone pips (Gaussian-enveloped 2000 Hz sine tones) and occasional oddball (20%) tone pips (matched in overall intensity) containing short silent intervals of 12 or 16 ms. Bars represent regions of the difference waves that differ significantly from zero. (A) Standard, deviant, and difference waves are shown filtered between 0.5 and 20 Hz. Note that in 2-month-old infants, oddball waveforms are more positive than standard waveforms, whereas 6-month-olds show a significant negative difference (MMN) and the following positive difference. (B) When the data are filtered between 3 and 18 Hz no components are apparent in the difference wave at 2 months, but MMN and P3a remain at 6 months, indicating that no significant fast components are present at 2 months. Data are from Trainor, McFadden and colleagues (2003).

waveform (the average of all subjects), take a region around this peak, (e.g., 20 or 50 ms on each side), and calculate the area under the ERP waveform across this time period for each subject. These measures then form the dependent variable for a single t-test. For both approaches, Analysis of Variance (ANOVA) can be used to examine other independent variables, such as different test conditions, sex, age, and so on, although care must be taken to normalize data where appropriate. If more than one electrode is being analyzed concurrently, the electrode site may be entered as a variable in the ANOVA. However, for large numbers of electrodes, false positive errors will tend to be high. One alternative is to average several nearby sites (e.g., left frontal, right frontal, left posterior, right posterior) to reduce the number of levels in the electrode site variable. If the measure of interest is the overall strength of a component, global field power is a good approach. In this case, at every time point, the average of the square of activation across all electrodes is taken. Global field power across time is calculated by taking the square root of this value at each time point. The global field power waveform will contain only positive values, and the overall strength of a component will be reflected in the size of its peak.

One significant problem encountered by developmental researchers in analyzing infant ERP data is the large amount of variation from infant to infant. There are likely many reasons for this variation. First, infant data are inherently more noisy than adult data, as discussed above. More importantly, however, there are tremendous individual differences in the age at which infants reach various developmental milestones. For example, some infants speak in sentences soon after their first birthday, while others do not do so until three years of age. ERP waveforms change dramatically over the first year after birth (see below). Given that infants of a particular age demonstrate large differences in brain maturation, they would be expected to produce very different ERP waveforms. In some cases, the differences can be seen mainly in terms of the latencies of the components. In less severe cases, latency variation will simply result in the grand average peaks looking smaller and more spread out than in individual infants. In more severe cases, where the peaks of a component may appear to vary by 100 ms or more across infants, it is difficult to determine with certainty that the same component is present across infants, and the grand average waveform will tend to be flat with no statistically significant regions. In the worst case, different infants appear to produce completely different waveforms, with some infants showing a positivity during the same time period at which others demonstrate a negativity (Kushnerenko et al., 2002; Trainor, McFadden et al., 2003). In such cases, it is difficult to determine with certainty whether the individual waveforms represent noise, or whether they represent very different stages of cortical maturation. Several approaches to this problem are possible. One approach is to test infants multiple times. If test-retest reliability is good, then it can be assumed that the individual differences are real and reflect different cortical maturation. A second approach is to try to relate the individual differences to other variables such as performance on a behavioral test. A third approach is to conduct longitudinal studies and show that all infants go through the same stages of ERP waveform development, but do so at different ages. For the field to progress, studies are needed that outline basic ERP development and individual differences across the first years of life.

ERPs hold the potential to provide diagnostic tools for determining perceptual/cognitive problems earlier than can be determined with behavioral testing. For this possibility to become a reality, the reliability of ERP components in individual infants needs to be assessed. Statistical tests can only be performed when multiple samples are available in order to estimate the variance of the dependent variable. One approach to obtaining measures in individual infants is to use t-tests as noted above, but with individual trials within a single subject.

In sum, analysis of infant data presents a challenge because of the small number of trials, inherent noise, and large individual differences between infants. The field will not progress rapidly until these challenges are met and systematic methods of data analysis become routine.

PCA and Source Modeling with Infant Data

Because the identification of components and the association of them with brain processes are fraught with difficulties as discussed above, some researchers have taken a more atheoretic approach to the analysis of infant data. For example, Molfese and Molfese (1985) have used principal component analysis to identify factor waveforms that together account for a high percentage of the variance in the original ERP waveforms. Although each principal component waveform may not correspond to a single identifiable process in the brain, they have been used to predict, for example, which infants will have above and below average language performance at 5 years of age (Molfese & Molfese, 1997), and which infants will become dyslexic, poor, or normal readers at age 8 (Molfese, 2000).

As it becomes more common to obtain data from 128 or even 256 channels in infants, data analysis techniques that take into account spatio-temporal properties of the ERP waveforms will also become more common. In its simplest form, isovoltage contours (i.e., lines joining positions on the scalp with equal voltage amplitude taken at a particular time point such as the peak of a component) can illustrate the center and extent of activation on the scalp for different components (see Figure 3.3). Current source density contours are obtained by approximating the spatial derivative of the scalp field, and give information about the effective sources and sinks in the radial direction (see Picton et al., 1995 for a discussion). Techniques for estimating the location and direction of the sources of activation in the brain that give rise to the potentials seen at the surface of the scalp are being refined (e.g., Picton et al., 1999; Scherg, 1990), and often work quite well for adult data, especially for earlier ERP components that result from few sources of brain activation. However, at present it remains difficult to perform source analysis with infant data. Infant data do tend to be noisy, but the major limitation is that a good head model for infants is not yet available. In particular, the fontanels are still open in infants, which will have a considerable effect on how electrical fields propagate to the scalp (Flemming et al., 2005). Furthermore, as with many developmental processes, the age at which the fontanels close is variable across infants, so an individual structural MRI scan might be necessary for accurate source fitting. Despite these difficulties, it is imperative that source models be developed for infants as, to date, EEG is the main technique we have for studying the infant brain in action.

DEVELOPMENT OF ERP RESPONSES TO SOUND IN INFANCY

Basic Components of the Infant ERP Response

Auditory ERPs change dramatically across the first months after birth. The newborn response to speech sounds and tones is dominated by large, slow, positive waves, and shows little of the complex series of positive and nega-tive deflections seen in the adult waveform (Kurtzberg, Hilpert, Kreuzer, & Vaughan Jr., 1984; Kushnerenko et al., 2002b; Kushnerenko et al., 2001a; Molfese & Molfese, 1985; Novak, Kurtzberg, Kreuzer, & Vaughan Jr., 1989; Thomas & Lykins, 1995; Thomas et al., 1997). In response to a sound, new-borns show a large positivity at fronto-central sites beginning about 100 ms after stimulus onset and peaking around 250 to 300 ms. With a mid occipi-tal reference site, coincident with this positivity, mastoid and temporal sites show a small negativity (Novak et al., 1989). As age increases, the negativity between 100 and 400 ms at temporal sites becomes more positive, with virtu-ally all 3-month-old infants showing a positivity in response to sounds across frontal, central, and temporal regions. Following this widespread positivity, a negative slow wave is apparent between about 400 and 800 ms.

The positive wave is reported to dominate infant auditory ERPs between 2 and 4 months of age (Friederici, Friedrich, & Weber, 2002; Thomas et al.,

1997; Trainor, McFadden et al., 2003; Figure 3.4). However, several studies report a negative trough in the positive slow wave by 3 or 4 months of age, leading to two positive peaks. Novak et al. (1989) reported peaks at 160 and 300 ms to speech syllables; Kushnerenko et al. (2002a) reported peaks at 150 and 350 ms to complex tones; Dehaene-Lambertz and Dehaene (1994) reported peaks at 220 and 390 ms to speech syllables; and Dehaene-Lambertz (2000) reported peaks at 176 and 328 ms to tones, and at 258 and 402 ms to speech syllables. The negative trough suggests that there may be overlapping processes, although it is not clear where or in what layers these processes may be generated. The large variance in peak latency across studies is not related to the stimulus or to stimulus onset asynchrony (SOA) in any obvious way. The question also arises as to why some studies report a double peak while others do not. As discussed above, infant waveforms can be highly variable. It is possible that the variance in peak latency across individual infants obscures the presence of a double peak in some grand average waveforms. In fact, most reports only include figures of grand average waveforms, likely because individual infant data tend to be rather noisy. However, Kushnerenko et al. (2002) include both grand average and individual data, even if it is only from 4 of the 15 infants in the study. For these 4 infants, the presence of two positive peaks can be seen in the individual traces at 2 to 4 days and at 3 months, but a double peak cannot be seen in the grand averages until 6 months. In general, it is possible that much ERP development is not currently seen because latency variation obscures it in the grand average waveforms, and individual traces are too noisy.

By 6 months, there are clear faster components present (e.g., Kushnerenko et al., 2002a; Novak et al., 1989; Trainor, Samuel, Desjardins, & Sonnadara, 2001), likely reflecting the presence of more mature, faster synaptic connections (Moore & Guan, 2001). However, the waveforms still do not resemble those of adults. As will be outlined below, adult waveforms are not fully achieved until well into the teenage years.

Development of MMN in Infancy

Recent infant auditory ERP research has been dominated by studies of mismatch negativity (MMN). Because MMN reflects the brain's response to change, it appears to be an ideal component for the study of infants' perception of, encoding of, and memory for sound features. MMN also appears well suited for the study of discrimination, categorization, and learning of linguistic and musical sounds. Indeed, studies of preterm to 12-month-old infants report MMN responses to changes in duration (Friederici et al., 2002; Kushnerenko et al., 2001b; Leppänen, Pihko, Eklund, & Lyytinen, 1999;

Trainor et al., 2001; Trainor, McFadden et al., 2003), pitch (Alho et al., 1990; Čeponiené et al., 2002; Dehaene-Lambertz, 2000; Leppänen, Eklund, & Lyytinen, 1997; Morr, Shafer, Kreuzer, & Kurtzberg, 2002), and phonemic identity (Cheour et al., 1997; Cheour et al., 1998; Cheour, Leppänen, & Kraus, 2000; Dehaene-Lambertz, 2000; Dehaene-Lambertz & Baillet, 1998; Dehaene-Lambertz & Dehaene, 1994).

However, an examination of the literature indicates that very different-looking components are being labeled as MMN. Some studies report an increased negativity to occasional deviant stimuli, as is the case with adults (Alho et al., 1990; Čeponiené, Kushnerenko et al., 2002; Cheour et al., 1997; Cheour et al., 1998; He, Hotson, & Trainor, 2007; Kushnerenko et al., 2001a; Morr et al., 2002; Pang et al., 1998; Trainor et al., 2001). However, where individual data are shown, these negativities are highly variable (e.g., Cheour et al., 1998), and the presence of MMN is defined in rather different ways in different studies. For example, in a study of vowel discrimination, Cheour et al. (1998) defined MMN as "a negative deflection peaking between 200 and 500 ms in the difference waves" (p. 222). With this broad definition, individual differences were large, and it was thus impossible to perform statistics on group averages. Rather, the authors report that 9 out of 11 preterm, and 8 out of 12 full term, infants met this criterion for demonstrating MMN. On the other hand, Cheour-Luhtanen and colleagues (1995) report greater consistency across infants, with statistically significant MMN to vowel change in newborns at 200 ms. Kushnerenko and colleagues (2001a) report two negativities in the difference waves to changes in consonant duration, one at 150 ms (similar to adults) and the other at 350 ms. They report that all newborns showed at least one of the two negativities. Čeponiené and colleagues (2002b) also report two negativities in the difference waves to changes in the frequency or duration of complex tones. Kushnerenko and colleagues (2002a) defined MMN in their study of pitch change as "the largest negative deflection in the difference waveform between 80 and 300 ms after stimulus onset, greater than the average baseline voltage by 1.0 μV at any two of the four fronto-central electrodes" (p. 1844). By this definition, 10 of the 12 infants showed MMN at birth, but 3 of these infants did not have a MMN at 3 months, and another 3 infants did not have a MMN at 6 months, leading to the conclusion that MMN is inconsistent at best. With infants 6 months of age and older, the studies seem to be somewhat more consistent, with the majority reporting an MMN around 200 ms (e.g., Cheour et al., 1998; Morr et al., 2002; Pang et al., 1998; Trainor et al., 2001).

Perhaps most surprising is that a number of studies report increased positivities to occasional changes in a sequence of sounds in infants (Dehaene-Lambertz, 2000; Dehaene-Lambertz & Baillet, 1998; Dehaene-Lambertz &

Dehaene, 1994; Dehaene-Lambertz & Pena, 2001; Leppänen et al., 1997; Leppänen et al., 1999; Morr et al., 2002). For example, in a series of studies examining 4-month-olds' vowel discrimination, Dehaene-Lambertz and colleagues report that changes in a repeating vowel result in an increased positivity around 400 ms (Dehaene-Lambertz, 2000; Dehaene-Lambertz & Baillet, 1998; Dehaene-Lambertz & Dehaene, 1994). Friederici and colleagues (2002) report a significant increase in positivity between 400 and 600 ms in 2-month-olds in response to an increase in vowel duration. The increased positivity was followed by an increased negativity between 800 and 1000 ms. Trainor, McFadden and colleagues (2003) reported an increase in positivity around 150 to 400 ms in 2- to 4-month-olds to the insertion of a 16-ms silent gap in tone pips. Leppänen et al. (1999) reported a positive difference between 130 and 400 ms to a change in vowel duration in newborns and a positive difference between 250 and 350 ms to a change in pitch (Leppänen et al., 1997). He et al. (in press) also report a positive difference in the same time range to a pitch change in 2-month-olds.

How can one make sense of these seemingly contrary findings, with some studies reporting mismatch negativities and others reporting "mismatch positivities"? To answer this question, consideration needs to be given to data collection methods, analysis techniques, and the special challenges posed by infant data. Sleep state of the infant (Friedrich, Weber, & Friederici, 2004), task difficulty (Morr et al., 2002), and neurological condition of the infant (Cheour et al., 1999; Čeponiené et al., 2002; Leppänen et al., 2004; Pihko et al., 1999) have all been proposed as possible explanations; however, in a review of the literature, He, et al. (2007) found that none of these factors can explain the inconsistencies across studies. Part of the problem undoubtedly arises because infant data are so variable, and the results obtained will depend greatly on the criteria by which infants are included and excluded from the analysis. In many studies, more than half the infants tested are excluded because the data are too noisy. Obviously, this point raises questions as to how generalizable the data are, and underlines how very important it is that better testing and analysis methods for infants are developed so that cleaner individual ERP data can be obtained.

It is also possible that the positive and negative difference components represent different processes that emerge at different ages (see He et al., 2007, for a detailed discussion). As discussed above, infant data, particularly during the earliest months, are dominated by slow wave activity, which may obscure the presence of faster components of interest. To separate slower and faster components, filtering techniques can be useful. For example, by filtering their 6-month-olds' gap-detection data between 3 and 18 Hz, Trainor and colleagues

(2001) found significant MMN that resembled that of adults. When they applied the same filter to their 2-month-old gap-detection data (Trainor, McFadden et al., 2003), they were unable to see any fast negative components (Figure 3.4). Furthermore, they found that the waveforms of 3- and 4-month-olds were more variable than those of 2- or 6-month-olds. At 3 months, 31% of infants showed the 6-month pattern, whereas at 4 months, 58% of infants showed the 6-month pattern. These results suggest that both the increased positivity and the increased negativity reported in different studies may be real, but represent different neural processes that overlap in time.

A further complication is that different sound features may show different developmental trajectories, with adult-like negativities emerging at different ages for different sound features. Although fewer than half of the 3-month-olds in Trainor, McFadden et al. (2003) showed a negativity around 200 ms to a temporal deviant, He et al. (2007) found that virtually all 3-month-olds showed an MMN-like negativity to a change in pitch (Figure 3.5). Under a filter setting of 3–20 Hz, they found that MMN emerged between 2 and 4 months of age, with increases in the amplitude and decreases in the latency of the MMN with increased age (Figure 3.5). Under a filter setting of 0–3 Hz, they found that the slow positive difference wave was significant at 2 and 3, but not at 4 months of age. Interestingly, at 3 months, both the slow wave response and the MMN response were clearly present, again suggesting that these components represent different neural processes.

The neural generators of the slow positive waves seen in young infants remain unclear. However, given the immature state of neurofilament expression in all layers except layer I, and the temporal spread of the ERP response, it may be that the response reflects EPSP or IPSP rather than action potentials. According to a simple model, a surface positivity could reflect either a sink associated with an EPSP with a more superficial passive circuit-completing source, or it could reflect a superficial IPSP. Given that only layer I contains mature neurofilament expression, and that layer I is increased in thickness in early infancy (Moore & Guan, 2001), another possibility is that this response in infants involves layer I.

In monkeys, MMN involves the depolarization of apical dendrites in superficial layer II creating a sink, accompanied by a passive circuit-completing source in layer III (although an active source representing recurrent inhibition in layer III may also be involved; Javitt et al., 1994). A similar process may take place in young infants. However, the immaturity of these layers makes it difficult to see how an MMN of similar latency to that of adults could be generated. Alternatively, mature microfilaments in deeper cortical layers begin to develop after 4.5 months of age (Moore & Guan,

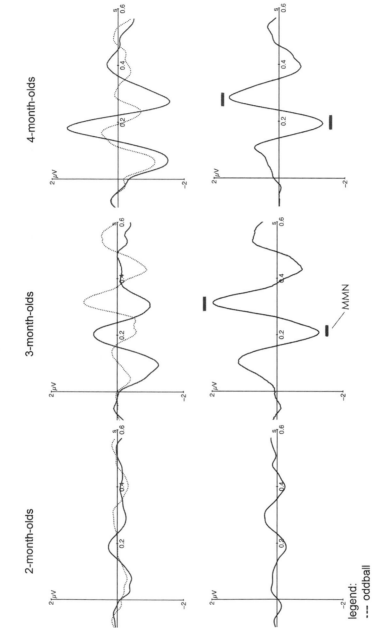

Figure 3.5. Responses from 2-, 3-, and 4-month-old infants at a central frontal site (Fz) to a piano tone with standard pitch (80%) and a deviant pitch (20%). Bars represent regions of the difference waves that differ significantly from zero (filtered between 3 and 20 Hz). Note that by 3 months of age a robust MMN is present, which gets larger and earlier by 4 months of age. Data are from He, Hotson, and Trainor (2007).

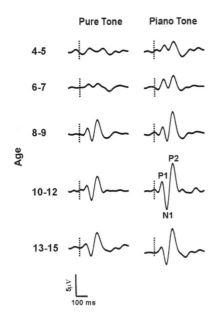

Figure 3.6. Late ERP responses of children between 4 and 15 years of age to a pure tone and piano tone. N1 and P2 emerge after 4 years of age and reach a maximum around 12 years. Responses to the spectrally rich piano tone are larger than to the sine tone. Data are from Shahin et al. (2004).

2001), so another possibility is that the infant MMN response somehow involves sources in deeper layers (Trainor, McFadden et al., 2003). It remains for future work to sort out which of these mechanisms is involved in the various MMN responses reported in the literature. Part of this process will be to test at what ages and under what specific stimulation conditions increased positivities and increased negativities are consistently seen, but developmental animal models will likely be of greatest utility.

DEVELOPMENT OF P1, N1, AND P2 RESPONSES TO SOUND IN CHILDREN

A number of studies indicate that the basic P1/N1/P2 complex continues to develop well into adolescence. Figure 3.6 shows ERP responses to musical tones between 4 and 15 years of age. In general, P1 is present early on but decreases in latency well into the teenage years (Kraus et al., 1993; McArthur & Bishop, 2002; Ponton et al., 2000; Sharma, Kraus, McGee, & Nicol, 1997; Shahin et al., 2004; Trainor, Shahin et al., 2003). The vertex N1b cannot be seen in children younger than 6 years of age unless a slow stimulation rate is used (Čeponiené et al., 2002b; Pang & Taylor, 2000; Ponton et al. 2000; Shahin et al., 2004; Trainor, Shahin et al., 2003). N1b increases in amplitude until about 10 to 12 years of age, and then decreases until adult levels are reached in the late teenage years. N1b also decreases in latency with increasing age (Johnstone et al., 1996; Kraus et al., 1993; Ponton et al., 2000; Sharma et al., 1997). The T-complex and associated N1c components, seen at temporal leads, appear to mature earlier than the N1b, and they decrease in latency and amplitude between 6 and 12 years of age (Gomes et al., 2001; Pang & Taylor, 2000). Less work has been done on the P2, but it appears to follow the development of the N1b (Johnstone et al., 1996; Shahin et al., 2004; Trainor, Shahin et al., 2003). Furthermore, as can be seen in Figure 3.6, N1 and P2 are more clearly elicited by the piano tones than the pure tones, suggesting that learning, familiarity, and/or greater spectral complexity affect this maturation.

The P1 latency decrease is likely due to its overlap with the emerging N1b, and not primarily a change in the P1 process itself. MMN also appears to change relatively little after 6 years of age (Kraus et al., 1993). Thus, the major ERP changes between 6 years and adulthood involve the N1b/P2 complex. In adults, N1b is associated with recurrent activation in the superficial layers (II and upper III; Eggermont & Ponton, 2003; Fishman et al., 2000; Mitzdorf, 1994). These layers do not begin to show mature microfilament expression until after 6 years of age, and do not reach adult levels until about 12 years of age (Moore & Guan, 2001). Therefore, the age ranges coincide over which N1 develops and layers II and upper III mature. Furthermore, the generation of N1b is associated with input from other cortical areas. As this input may be coming from regions undergoing protracted maturation, such as frontal areas, it makes sense that layers II and upper III maintain protracted plasticity. Furthermore, the N1 component is modulated by attention, an executive function that has a long developmental period. The evidence strongly suggests, then, that N1b emerges with the maturation of neurofilaments in superficial layers and allows such behaviors as sophisticated auditory attention, deciphering degraded signals, and hearing signals in noise. Interestingly, musicians show larger amplitude N1m (N1 measured with MEG) than nonmusicians, and the N1m amplitude is greater the earlier they began lessons (Pantev et al., 1998). Furthermore, the increase is specific to the timbre of their instrument of practice (Pantev et al., 2001).

Less work has been done on the P2 component. Of great interest is the fact that P2 amplitude is affected by specific experience, even in adulthood, whereas N1 amplitude appears relatively stable in adulthood (Bosnyak, Eaton, & Roberts, 2004). P2 responses to musical tones are larger in musicians than in non-musicians (Shahin et al., 2003), and frequency discrimination training in adulthood increases the P2 response for the trained frequencies (Bosnyak et al., 2004), as does speech sound discrimination training (Tremblay et al., 2001). Furthermore, children as young as 4 years of age who are beginning Suzuki music lessons show larger P2 responses than non-musician children (Shahin et al., 2004). The difference in N1b and P2 plasticity in adulthood is not yet understood. However, some studies locate N1b activity primarily in the planum temporale (secondary auditory cortex), but P2 activity closer to primary areas (see Eggermont & Ponton, 2002), and the latter areas may retain more plasticity than the former. In any case, the dramatic development of the N1/P2 complex through childhood allows for the emergence of very sophisticated auditory processing by adulthood.

SUMMARY

Although developmental ERP data are still limited by recording and analysis problems, and indeed there are some discrepancies across studies, it is clear that ERPs change from predominantly slow positive waves in the newborn to the complex series of faster components seen in the adult. Furthermore, the layer-specific maturation of cortex, with mature connections beginning in deeper layers after 4.5 months, and in superficial layers after 5 years, can be linked in a meaningful way not only to the emergence of ERP components, but also to the behavioral competencies of the child. A complete review of the developmental literature is beyond the scope of this chapter. However, ERPs are now being used to address many interesting developmental questions including how basic sound properties are encoded, how speech sounds are encoded, how attention develops, how words are learned, how foreign languages are processed, and how music is learned.

At the same time, in order for the ERP field to advance, more attention will have to be paid to how ERPs can better be recorded in infants and young children in order to maximize the number of trials obtained and minimize the artifact present. Careful attention to referencing, artifact rejection, averaging, and filtering can enhance signal-to-noise ratios. Ultimately, however, new recording and/or signal processing techniques need to be developed to ensure that results are reliable and replicable.

Finally, auditory ERPs hold great promise in the clinical diagnostic realm (e.g., Escera, Alho, Schröger, & Winkler, 2000; Hyde, 1997; Leppänen & Lyytinen, 1997). Beyond simply identifying hearing loss, ERPs recorded in newborns have been shown to predict, for example, reading competency at 8 years of age (Molfese, 2000). ERPs are of particular interest because different components in the waveform are associated with different stages of processing. Therefore, abnormalities in particular components may not only diagnose that a problem exists, but also elucidate the nature of the problem and indicate the type of remediation that is most likely to be effective. For example, Connolly, D'Arcy, Newman, and Kemps (2000) have shown that different components are associated with phonological and semantic stages of word processing. However, reliable measurement and interpretation of individual ERPs are critical issues for clinical tests. It remains difficult to distinguish between normal variation in the age at which ERP component milestones are reached and pathological conditions in which normal adult development will never be realized. Thus, much work on developmental norms needs to be done before ERP measures can become standard clinical tests. However, despite current limitations, ERPs are expanding the nature of questions that we can ask about complex developmental processes, and their use is likely to increase greatly in the future.

ACKNOWLEDGMENT

The writing of this chapter was supported by grants from the Canadian Institutes of Health Research, the Canadian Language and Literacy Research Network Centre of Excellence, and the International Music Foundation. I thank Lisa Hotson and Ranil Sonnadara for comments on an earlier draft.

References

Alain, C., Achim, A., & Woods, D. L. (1999). Separate memory-related processing for auditory frequency and patterns. *Psychophysiology, 36*, 737–744.

Albrecht, R., Suchodoletz, W., & Uwer, R. (2000). The development of auditory evoked dipole source activity from childhood to adulthood. *Clinical Neurophysiology, 111*, 2268–2276.

Alho, K., Sainio, K., Sajaniemi, N., Reinikainen, K., & Näätänen, R. (1990). Event-related brain potentials of human newborns to pitch change of an acoustic stimulus. *Electroencephalography and Clinical Neurophysiolology, 77*, 151–155.

Alho, K., Tervaniemi, M., Huotilainen, M., Lavikainen, J., Tiitinen, H., Ilmoniemi, R. J., Knuutila, J., & Näätänen, R.et al. (1996). Processing of complex sounds in the human auditory cortex as revealed by magnetic brain responses. *Psychophysiology, 33*, 369–375.

Anderson, A. W., Marois, R., Colson, E. R., Peterson, B. S., Duncan, C. C., Ehrenkranz, R. A., Schneider, M. P. H., Gore, J. C., & Ment, L. R.., et al. (2001). Neonatal auditory activation detected by functional magnetic resonance imaging. *Magnetic Resonance Imaging, 19*, 1–5.

Bosnyak, D. J., Eaton, R. A., & Roberts, L. E. (2004). Distributed auditory cortical activations are modified when nonmusicians are trained at pitch discrimination with 40-Hz amplitude modulated tones. *Cerebral Cortex, 14*, 1088–1099.

Čeponiené, R., Kushnerenko, E., Fellman, V., Renlund, M., Suominen, K., & Näätänen, R. (2002a). Event-related potential features indexing central auditory discrimination by newborns. *Brain Research: Cognitive Brain Research, 13*, 101–113.

Čeponiené, R., Rinne, T., & Näätänen, R. (2002b). Maturation of cortical sound processing as indexed by event-related potentials. *Clinical Neurophysiology, 113*, 870–882.

Cheour, M., Alho, K., Sainio, K., Reinikainen, K., Renlund, M., Aaltonen, O., Eerola, O., & Näätänen, R.., et al. (1997). The mismatch negativity to changes in speech sounds at the age of three months. *Developmental Neuropsychology, 13*, 167–174.

Cheour, M., Čeponiené, R., Hukki, J., Haapanen, M. -L., Näätänen, R., & Alho, K. (1999). Dysfunction in neonates with cleft palate revealed by the mismatch negativity. *Electroencephalography and Clinical Neurophysiology, 110*, 324–328.

Cheour, M., Čeponiené, R., Lehtokoski, A., Luuk, A., Allik, J., Alho, K., & Näätänen, R., et al. (1998). Development of language-specific phoneme representations in the infant brain. *Nature Neuroscience, 1*, 351–353.

Cheour, M., Leppänen, P. H., & Kraus, N. (2000). Mismatch negativity (MMN) as a tool for investigating auditory discrimination and sensory memory in infants and children. *Clinical Neurophysiology, 111*, 4–16.

Cheour-Luhtanen, M., Alho, K., Kujala, T., Sainio, K., Reinikainen, K., Renlund, M., Aaltonen, O., Eerola, O., & Näätänen, R., et al. (1995). Mismatch negativity indicates vowel discrimination in newborns. *Hearing Research, 82*, 53–58.

Connolly, J. F., D'Arcy, R. C., Newman, L., & Kemps, R. (2000). The application of cognitive event-related brain potentials (ERPs) in language-impaired individuals: Review and case studies. *International Journal of Psychophysiology, 38*, 55–70.

Creutzfeldt, O., & Houchin, J. (1974). Neuronal basis of EEG waves. In A. Remond, (Ed.), *Handbook of electroencephalography and clinical neurophysiology* (pp. 5–55). Amsterdam: Elsevier.

Dehaene-Lambertz, G. (2000). Cerebral specialization for speech and non-speech stimuli in infants. *Journal of Cognitive Neuroscience, 12*, 449–460.

Dehaene-Lambertz, G., & Baillet, S. (1998). A phonological representation in the infant brain. *Neuroreport, 9*, 1885–1888.

Dehaene-Lambertz, G., & Dehaene, S. (1994). Speed and cerebral correlates of syllable discrimination in infants. *Nature, 370*, 292–295.

Dehaene-Lambertz, G., & Pena, M. (2001). Electrophysiological evidence for automatic phonetic processing in neonates. *Neuroreport, 12*, 3155–3158.

Dien, J. (1998). Issues in the application of the average reference: Review, critiques, and recommendations. *Behavior Research Methods, Instruments and Computers, 30*, 34–43.

Eggermont, J. J., & Ponton, C. W. (2002). The neurophysiology of auditory perception: From single units to evoked potentials. *Audiology and Neuro-Otology, 7*, 71–99.

Eggermont, J. J., & Ponton, C. W. (2003). Auditory-evoked potential studies of cortical maturation in normal hearing and implanted children: Correlations with changes in structure and speech perception. *Acta Otolaryngologica, 123*, 249–252.

Escera, C., Alho, K., Schröger, E., & Winkler, I. (2000). Involuntary attention and distractibility as evaluated with event-related brain potentials. *Audiology and Neuro-Otology, 5*, 151–166.

Escera, C., Alho, K., Winkler, I., & Näätänen, R. (1998). Neural mechanisms of involuntary attention to acoustic novelty and change. *Journal of Cognitive Neuroscience, 10*, 590–604.

Fishman, Y. I., Reser, D. H., Arezzo, J. C., & Steinschneider, M. (1998). Pitch vs. spectral encoding of harmonic complex tones in primary auditory cortex of the awake monkey. *Brain Research, 786*, 18–30.

Fishman, Y. I., Reser, D. H., Arezzo, J. C., & Steinschneider, M. (2000). Complex tone processing in primary auditory cortex of the awake monkey. II. Pitch vs. critical band representation. *Journal of the Acoustical Society of America, 108*, 247–262.

Flemming, L., Wang, Y., Caprihan, A., Eiselt, M., Haueisen, J., & Okada, Y. (2005). Evaluation of the distortion of EEG signals caused by a hole in the skull mimicking the fontanel in the skull of human neonates. *Clinical Neurophysiology, 116*, 1141–1152.

Friederici, A. D., Friedrich, M., & Weber, C. (2002). Neural manifestation of cognitive and precognitive mismatch detection in early infancy. *Neuroreport, 13*, 1251–1254.

Friedrich, M., Weber, C., & Friederici, A. D. (2004). Electrophysiological evidence for delayed mismatch response in infants at-risk for specific language impairment. *Psychophysiology, 41*, 772–782.

Gomes, H., Dunn, M., Ritter, W., Kurtzberg, D., Brattson, A., Kreuzer, J. A., & Vaughan Jr., H. G., et al. (2001). Spatiotemporal maturation of the central and lateral N1 components to tones. *Brain Research Developmental Brain Research, 129*, 147–155.

Hattori, H., Yamano, T., Tsutada, T., Tsuyuguchi, N., Kawawaki, H., & Shimogawara, M. (2001). Magnetoencephalography in the detection of focal lesions in West syndrome. *Brain and Development, 23*, 528–532.

He, C., Hotson, L., & Trainor, L. J. (2007). Mismatch responses to pitch changes in early infancy. *Journal of Cognitive Neuroscience, 19*, 878–892.

Hillyard, S. A., & Kutas, M. (1983). Electrophysiology of cognitive processing. *Annual Review of Psychology, 34*, 33–61.

Huttenlocher, P. R., & Dabholkar, A. S. (1997). Regional differences in synaptogenesis in human cerebral cortex. *Journal of Comparative Neurology, 387*, 167–178.

Hyde, M. (1997). The N1 response and its applications. *Audiology and Neuro-Otology, 2*, 281–307.

Javitt, D. C., Steinschneider, M., Schroeder, C. E., Vaughan Jr., H. G., & Arezzo, J. C. (1994). Intracortical mechanisms of mismatch negativity (MMN) generation. *Brain Research, 667*, 192–200.

Johnstone, S. J., Barry, R. J., Anderson, J. W., & Coyle, S. F. (1996). Age-related changes in child and adolescent event-related potential component morphology, amplitude and latency to standard and target stimuli in an auditory oddball task. *International Journal of Psychophysiology, 24*, 223–238.

Konig, N., & Marty, R. (1974). On function and structure of deep layers of immature auditory cortex. *Journal of Physiology, 68*, 145–155.

Konig, N., Pujol, R., & Marty, R. (1972). A lamina study of evoked potentials and unit responses in the auditory cortex of the postnatal cat. *Brain Research, 36*, 469–493.

Kral, A., Hartmann, R., Tillein, J., Heid, S., & Klinke, R. (2000). Congenital auditory deprivation reduces synaptic activity within the auditory cortex in a layer-specific manner. *Cerebral Cortex, 10*, 714–726.

Kraus, N., McGee, T., Carrell, T., Sharma, A., Micco, A., & Nicol, T. (1993). Speech-evoked cortical potentials in children. *Journal of the American Academy of Audiology, 4*, 238–248.

Kurtzberg, D., Hilpert, P. L., Kreuzer, J. A., & Vaughan Jr., H. G. (1984). Differential maturation of cortical auditory evoked potentials to speech sounds in normal fullterm and very low-birthweight infants. *Developmental Medicine and Child Neurology, 26*, 466–475.

Kushnerenko, E., Čeponiené, R., Balan, P., Fellman, V., Huotilainen, M., & Näätänen, R. (2002a). Maturation of the auditory event-related potentials during the first year of life. *Neuroreport, 13,* 47–51.

Kushnerenko, E., Čeponiené, R., Balan, P., Fellman, V., & Näätänen, R. (2002b). Maturation of the auditory change detection response in infants: A longitudinal ERP study. *Neuroreport, 13,* 1843–1848.

Kushnerenko, E., Čeponiené, R., Fellman, V., Huotilainen, M., & Winkler, I. (2001a). Event-related potential correlates of sound duration: Similar pattern from birth to adulthood. *Neuroreport, 12,* 3777–3781.

Kushnerenko, E., Cheour, M., Čeponiené, R., Fellman, V., Renlund, M., Soininen, K., Alku, P., Koskinen, M., Sainio, K., & Näätänen, R., et al. (2001b). Central auditory processing of durational changes in complex speech patterns by newborns: An event-related brain potential study. *Developmental Neuropsychology, 19,* 83–97.

Kutas, M., & Hillyard, S. A. (1980). Reading senseless sentences: Brain potentials reflect semantic incongruity. *Science, 207,* 203–205.

Leppänen, P. H. T., Eklund, K. M., & Lyytinen, H. (1997). Event-related brain potentials to change in rapidly presented acoustic stimuli in newborns. *Developmental Neuropsychology, 13,* 175–204.

Leppänen, P. H., Guttorm, T. K., Pihko, E., Takkinnen, S., & Lyytinen, H. (2004). Maturational effects on newborn ERPs measured in the mismatch negativity paradigm. *Experimental Neurology, 190,* 91–101.

Leppänen, P. H., & Lyytinen, H. (1997). Auditory event-related potentials in the study of developmental language-related disorders. *Audiology and Neuro-Otology, 2,* 308–340.

Leppänen, P. H., Pihko, E., Eklund, K. M., & Lyytinen, H. (1999). Cortical responses of infants with and without a genetic risk for dyslexia: II. Group effects. *Neuroreport, 10,* 969–973.

Liégeois-Chauvel, C., Musolini, A., Badier, J. M., Marquis, P., & Chauvel, P. (1994). Evoked potentials recorded from the auditory cortex in man: Evaluation and topography of the middle latency components. *Electroencephalography and Clinical Neurophysiology, 92,* 204–214.

McArthur, G., & Bishop, D. (2002). Event-related potentials reflect individual differences in age-invariant auditory skills. *Neuroreport, 13,* 1079–1082.

Mitzdorf, U. (1985). Current source-density method and application in cat cerebral cortex: Investigation of evoked potentials and EEG phenomena. *Physiology Review, 65,* 37–100.

Mitzdorf, U. (1994). Properties of cortical generators of event-related potentials. *Pharmacopsychiatry, 27,* 49–52.

Miyata, H., Kawaguchi, S., Samejima, A., & Yamamoto, T. (1982). Postnatal development of evoked responses in the auditory cortex of the cat. *Japanese Journal of Physiology, 32,* 421–429.

Molfese, D. L. (2000). Predicting dyslexia at 8 years of age using neonatal brain responses. *Brain and Language, 72,* 238–245.

Molfese, D. L., & Molfese, V. J. (1985). Electrophysiological indexes of auditory-discrimination in newborn infants: The bases for predicting later language development. *Infant Behavior and Development, 8,* 197–211.

Molfese, D. L., & Molfese, V. J. (1997). Discrimination of language skills at five years of age using event-related potentials recorded at birth. *Developmental Neuropsychology, 13*, 135–156.

Moore, J. K., & Guan, Y. L. (2001). Cytoarchitectural and axonal maturation in human auditory cortex. *Journal of the Association for Research in Otolaryngology, 2*, 297–311.

Morr, M. L., Shafer, V. L., Kreuzer, J. A., & Kurtzberg, D. (2002). Maturation of mismatch negativity in typically developing infants and preschool children. *Ear and Hearing, 23*, 118–136.

Muir, D. W., Clifton, R. K., & Clarkson, M. G. (1989). The development of a human auditory localization response: A U-shaped function. *Canadian Journal of Psychology, 43*, 199–216.

Muir, D., & Field, J. (1979). Newborn infants orient to sounds. *Child Development, 50*, 431–436.

Näätänen, R. (1992). *Attention and brain function*. Hillsdale, NJ: Lawrence Erlbaum Associates.

Näätänen, R., & Picton, T. (1987). The N1 wave of the human electric and magnetic response to sound: A review and an analysis of the component structure. *Psychophysiology, 24*, 375–425.

Näätänen, R., Tervaniemi, M., Sussman, E., Paavilainen, P., & Winkler, I. (2001). 'Primitive intelligence' in the auditory cortex. *Trends in Neuroscience, 24*, 283–288.

Näätänen, R., & Winkler, I. (1999). The concept of auditory stimulus representation in cognitive neuroscience. *Psychological Bulletin, 125*, 826–859.

Neijenhuis, K., Snik, A., Priester, G., van Kordenoordt, S., & van den Broek, P. (2002). Age effects and normative data on a Dutch test battery for auditory processing disorders. *International Journal of Audiology, 41*, 334–346.

Novak, G. P., Kurtzberg, D., Kreuzer, J. A., & Vaughan Jr., H. G. (1989). Cortical responses to speech sounds and their formants in normal infants: Maturational sequence and spatiotemporal analysis. *Electroencephalography and Clinical Neurophysiology, 73*, 295–305.

Pang, E. W., Edmonds, G. E., Desjardins, R., Khan, S. C., Trainor, L. J., & Taylor, M. J. (1998). Mismatch negativity to speech stimuli in 8-month-old infants and adults. *International Journal of Psychophysiology, 29*, 227–236.

Pang, E. W., & Taylor, M. J. (2000). Tracking the development of the N1 from age 3 to adulthood: An examination of speech and non-speech stimuli. *Clinical Neurophysiology, 111*, 388–397.

Pantev, C., Oostenveld, R., Engelien, A., Ross, B., Roberts, L. E., & Hoke, M. (1998). Increased auditory cortical representation in musicians. *Nature, 392*, 811–814.

Pantev, C., Roberts, L. E., Schulz, M., Engelien, A., & Ross, B. (2001). Timbre-specific enhancement of auditory cortical representations in musicians. *Neuroreport, 12*, 169–174.

Picton, T. W., Alain, C., Otten, L., Ritter, W., & Achim, A. (2000). Mismatch negativity: Different water in the same river. *Audiology and Neuro-Otology, 5*, 111–139.

Picton, T. W., Alain, C., Woods, D., John, M. S., Scherg, M., Valdes-Sosa, P., Bosch-Bayard, J., & Trujillo, N. J. et al. (1999). Intracerebral sources of human auditory-evoked potentials. *Audiology and Neuro-Otology, 4*, 64–79.

Picton, T. W., Lins, O. G., & Scherg, M. (1995). The recording and analysis of event-related potentials. In F. Boller & J. Grafman (Eds.), *Handbook of neuropsychology* (Vol. 10, pp. 3–73). New York: Elsevier.

Pihko, E., Leppänen, P. H. T., Eklund, K. M., Cheour, M., Guttorm, T. K., & Lyytinen, H. (1999). Cortical responses of infants with and without a genetic risk for dyslexia: I. Age effects. *Neuroreport, 10*, 901–905

Pisoni, D. B., Lively, S. E., & Logan, J. S. (1994). Perceptual learning of nonnative speech contrasts: Implications for theories of speech perception. In J. C. Goodman & H. C. Nusbaum (Eds.), *The development of speech perception: The transition from speech sounds to spoken words* (pp. 121–166). Cambridge, MA: The MIT Press.

Ponton, C. W., & Eggermont, J. J. (2001). Of kittens and kids: Altered cortical maturation following profound deafness and cochlear implant use. *Audiology and Neuro-Otology, 6*, 363–380.

Ponton, C. W., Eggermont, J. J., Don, M., Waring, M. D., Kwong, B., Cunningham, J., & Trautwein, P. et al. (2000). Maturation of the mismatch negativity: Effects of profound deafness and cochlear implant use. *Audiology and Neuro-Otology, 5*, 167–185.

Ponton, C. W., Eggermont, J. J., Kwong, B., & Don, M. (2000). Maturation of human central auditory system activity: Evidence from multi-channel evoked potentials. *Clinical Neurophysiology, 111*, 220–236.

Scherg, M. (1990). Fundamentals of dipole source potential analysis. In F. Grandori, M. Hoke, & G. L. Romani (Eds.), *Auditory evoked magnetic fields and electric potentials, advances in audiology* (Vol. 5, pp. 40–69). Basel: Karger.

Scherg, M., & von Cramon, D. (1986). Psychoacoustic and electrophysiologic correlates of central hearing disorders in man. *European Archives of Psychiatry and Neurological Sciences, 236*, 56–60.

Schröger, E. (1998). Measurement and interpretation of the mismatch negativity. *Behaviour Research Methods, Instruments and Computers, 30*, 131–145.

Segalowitz, S. J., & Berge, B. E. (1995). Functional asymmetries in infancy and early childhood: A review of electrophysiologic studies and their implications. In R. J. Davidson & K. Hugdahl (Eds.), *Brain asymmetry* (pp. 579–615). Cambridge: MIT Press.

Shahin, A., Bosnyak, D. J., Trainor, L. J., & Roberts, L. E. (2003). Enhancement of neuroplastic P2 and N1c auditory evoked potentials in musicians. *Journal of Neuroscience, 23*, 5545–5552.

Shahin, A., Roberts, L. E., & Trainor, L. J. (2004). Evidence for enhancement of auditory cortical development by musical experience. *NeuroReport, 15*, 1917–1921.

Sharma, A., Kraus, N., McGee, T. J., & Nicol, T. G. (1997). Developmental changes in P1 and N1 central auditory responses elicited by consonant-vowel syllables. *Electroencephalography and Clinical Neurophysiology, 104*, 540–545.

Sonnadara, R. R., Alain, C., & Trainor, L. J. (2006). Effects of spatial separation and stimulus probability on event-related potentials elicited by occasional changes in sound location. *Brain Research, 1071*, 175–185.

Souweidane, M. M., Kim, K. H., McDowall, R., Ruge, M. I., Lis, E., Krol, G., & Hirsch, J. et al. (1999). Brain mapping in sedated infants and young children with passive-functional magnetic resonance imaging. *Pediatric Neurosurgery, 30*, 86–92.

Squires, K. C., Squires, N. K., & Hillyard, S. A. (1975). Two varieties of long latency positive waves evoked by unpredictable auditory stimuli in man. *Electroencephalography and Clinical Neurophysiology, 38*, 387–401.

Stapells, D. R., Galambos, R., Costello, J. A., & Makeig, S. (1988). Inconsistency of auditory middle latency and steady-state responses in infants. *Electroencephalography and Clinical Neurophysiology, 71*, 289–295.

Steinschneider, M., & Dunn, M. (2002). Electrophysiology in developmental neuropsychology. In S. J. Segalowitz and I. Rapin (Eds.), *Handbook of neuropsychology* (Vol. 7,
pp. 91–146). Amsterdam: Elsevier.

Takegata, R., Paavilainen, P., Näätänen, R., & Winkler, I. (1999). Independent processing
of changes in auditory single features and feature conjunctions in humans as indexed
by the mismatch negativity. *Neuroscience Letters, 266*, 109–112.

Tharpe, A. M., & Ashmead, D. H. (2001). A longitudinal investigation of infant auditory
sensitivity. *American Journal of Audiology, 10*, 104–112.

Thomas, D. G., & Lykins, S. M. (1995). Event-related potential measures of 24-hour
retention in 5-month-old infants. *Developmental Psychology, 31*, 946–957.

Thomas, D. G., Whitaker, E., Crow, C. D., Little, V., Love, L., Lykins, M. S., & Letterman,
M. et al. (1997). Event-related potential variability as a measure of information store
in infant development. *Developmental Neuropsychology, 13*, 205–232.

Trainor, L. J., McDonald, K. L., & Alain, C. (2002). Automatic and controlled processing
of melodic contour and interval information measured by electrical brain activity.
Journal of Cognitive Neuroscience, 14, 430–442.

Trainor, L., McFadden, M., Hodgson, L., Darragh, L., Barlow, J., Matsos, L., & Sonnadara, R. et al. (2003). Changes in auditory cortex and the development of mismatch
negativity between 2 and 6 months of age. *International Journal of Psychophysiology,
51*, 5–15.

Trainor, L. J., Samuel, S. S., Desjardins, R. N., & Sonnadara, R. R. (2001). Measuring
temporal resolution in infants using mismatch negativity. *Neuroreport, 12*, 2443–
2448.

Trainor, L. J., Shahin, A., & Roberts, L. E. (2003). Effects of musical training on the
auditory cortex in children. *Annals of the New York Academy of Sciences, 999*, 506–
513.

Tremblay, K., Kraus, N., McGee, T., Ponton, C., & Otis, B. (2001). Central auditory
plasticity: Changes in the N1-P2 complex after speech-sound training. *Ear and Hearing, 22*, 79–90.

Vaughan Jr., H. G., & Arezzo, J. C. (1988). The neural basis of event-related potentials. In
T. W. Picton (Ed.). *Human event-related potentials* (pp. 45–96). Amsterdam: Elsevier.

Vaughan Jr., H. G., & Ritter, W. (1970). The sources of auditory evoked responses
recorded from the human scalp. *Electroencephalography and Clinical Neurophysiology,
28*, 360–367.

Werker, J. F., & Tees, R. C. (1984). Cross language speech perception: Evidence for
perceptual reorganization during the 1st year of life. *Infant Behavior and Development,
7*, 49–63.

Werner, L. A., & Marean, G. C. (1996). *Human Auditory Development.* Boulder, CO:
Westview.

Woldorff, M., & Hillyard, S. (1991). Modulation of early auditory processing during
selective listening to rapidly presented tones. *Electroencephalography and Clinical
Neurophysiology, 79*, 170–191.

4 Event-Related Potential (ERP) Measures in Visual Development Research

Michelle de Haan

INTRODUCTION

Visual abilities undergo major transformation during infancy and childhood. Although infants arrive in the world both able to see and to learn about what they see, many aspects of vision and visual cognition continue to develop well into childhood (e.g., Chung & Thomson, 1995; Lewis & Maurer, 2005). Event-related potentials (ERPs) are a useful tool for investigating the neuro-physiological correlates of these developmental changes as they can provide information not available from behavioral measures alone. In particular, they provide precise information about the timing and some information about the spatial distribution of the brain events underlying visual process-ing. Since ERPs can be obtained in "passive" tasks, where participants simply look at visual displays without any requirement to make a verbal or behav-ioral response, they allow use of the same procedure across a wide range of age and ability levels. For example, visual ERPs have been used to study face processing in infants only a few months old (e.g., Halit, de Haan, & Johnson, 2003) and have been used to investigate aspects of visual processing in children with various developmental disorders, including autism spectrum disorder (e.g., Dawson et al., 2002; Kemner, van der Gaag, Verbaten & van Engeland, 1999), Down syndrome (e.g., Karrer et al., 1998), and attention deficit-hyperactivity disorder (reviewed in Barry, Johnstone, & Clarke, 2003). Along with these distinct advantages, however, ERPs also present challenges both in terms of experimental design and data collection, and analysis and interpretation. This chapter first provides a brief general introduction to visual ERPs, followed by a discussion of the particular challenges that can arise when applying them to developing populations. In this context, only selected studies will be highlighted to illustrate particular points. For more complete reviews of components observed in visual ERPs in infants and children see de Haan (2007), Nelson and Monk (2001), or Taylor and Baldeweg (2003).

WHAT ARE EVENT-RELATED POTENTIALS?

How ERPs Relate to VEPs and EEG

ERP and VEP

Visual ERPs are changes in the brain's electrical activity that occur in response to a discrete visual event, such as the appearance of a visual image on a computer monitor. They are typically differentiated from visual evoked potentials (VEPs), both with respect to the types of paradigms used to obtain the responses and the presumed involvement of cognitive processing. VEPs are thought to reflect basic visual functions such as resolution, color detection, and motion detection, and are typically elicited by repeated presentations of a visual stimulus that has no significant cognitive content and in the absence of a task. For example, for a typical pattern VEP, individuals are simply required to passively look at a series of high contrast black-and-white checkerboards. ERPs, on the other hand, are typically thought to reflect more complex perceptual or cognitive operations, and are elicited in contexts where stimuli do have meaningful cognitive content, and/or there is a task. For example, ERPs might be recorded to faces displaying different facial expressions of emotion, or be recorded during a task in which the participant is required to press a button each time a visual pattern repeats. Although VEPs and visual ERPs are often distinguished from one another in this manner, the two are not entirely separate, because perception and cognition are not entirely separate. Since the topic of this chapter is visual ERPs, the content will focus on studies which aim to understand more complex visual processing rather than basic visual functions (a review of the development of VEPs can be found in McCulloch, 2007).

ERP and EEG

The electroencephalogram (EEG) is the ongoing electrical activity of the brain, while the ERP is the subset of this activity that reflects processing of specific stimuli. EEG signals are typically of much larger amplitude than ERPs. Thus, in order to extract the ERP signal from the EEG, the signal is averaged over repeated presentations of a particular stimulus or stimulus condition. In this way, the part of the EEG that is random with respect to the timing of the event (and presumably unrelated to event processing) averages out to zero, while the part of the EEG that is time-locked to the stimulus (and presumably specifically relates to its processing) is retained.

ERP Waveform

The ERP waveform itself typically consists of a series of peaks and troughs called components. Components are usually characterized by the simultaneous consideration of their eliciting conditions, polarity at particular recording sites (positive or negative), timing (latency), and scalp distribution (topography). Typically components are labeled according to their polarity (P for positive, N for negative) and either their order of occurrence (e.g., P1, P2, etc.) or mean latency from stimulus onset (e.g., N170, P300), although there are exceptions (e.g., the ERN, or error-related negativity is not labeled by its order of occurrence or latency).

Sometimes, the ERP waveform also contains broad, sustained deviations from baseline called slow waves. These are usually more likely to be observed in younger individuals and/or in situations with a more prolonged recording epoch. Because they do not show prominent peaks and therefore provide less precise timing information, they are typically not labeled by their timing of occurrence but rather by their polarity and/or eliciting conditions (e.g., the CNV, or contingent negative variation).

Neurophysiological Bases

For brain electrical signals to be measurable from the scalp, they require that the activity of large numbers of neurons be summed together. It is believed that excitatory and inhibitory postsynaptic potentials likely provide the current that is detected by ERPs, as their time course is most compatible with that needed to provide sufficient summation of the signal (Allison, Woods, & McCarthy, 1986). When many neurons are activated simultaneously they summate and the activity propagates to the surface. The activity recorded at the surface is thought to be primarily from pyramidal cells of the cortex, as these cells tend to be aligned parallel to one another (which helps summation of activity) and oriented more or less perpendicular to the scalp (which helps propagation of activity to the surface).

Traditionally, ERPs are thought to be generated by stimulus-evoked brain events that are of fixed latency and polarity. In other words, each presentation of a stimulus leads to activation of specific brain areas that underlie the particular perceptual-cognitive operations involved in processing the event. A different view is that ERPs might instead reflect stimulus-induced changes in ongoing brain dynamics. In this view, each presentation of the stimulus induces a "phase resetting" of ongoing EEG rhythms, and averaging these phase-coherent rhythms produces the ERP waveform (Makeig et al., 2002; Penny, Kiebel, Kilner, & Rugg, 2002).

RECIPE FOR A DEVELOPMENTAL VISUAL ERP STUDY

Given that ERPs (a) provide precise information about the timing of brain events and some information about their spatial distribution, and (b) are relatively easy to acquire even from participants with limited verbal or motor abilities, they are a potentially attractive method for studying the development of visual functions. However, when considering applying ERPs to a question of visual development, it is important to consider not only these advantages, but also some potential limitations/challenges related to the typical methods used to acquire and analyze visual ERPs. These issues are considered in the next section, with illustrations of these points from particular visual developmental ERP experiments.

Experimental Design

As with any experiment, some careful thought is required before beginning one involving ERPs. The typical way in which ERPs are recorded places some constraints both on the types of situations or tasks that are amenable to study with ERPs and the type and amount of information that is obtainable even in a suitable paradigm.

Brief, Repeatable Events that Can Be Defined in Time

Event-related potentials are, by definition, brain activity related to a particular event that occurs at an identifiable point in time (e.g., onset of a stimulus, or execution of a behavioral response). Thus, when designing a visual ERP study, it is important to keep in mind that the experimenter must be able to precisely define, on the order of milliseconds, when the event of interest occurs. This timing places some limitations on the types of settings in which ERPs can be acquired. For example, if one wishes to examine the ERPs elicited by familiar compared to novel toys, this task would be extremely difficult to do in free-play situation as it would not be easy to document the precise moment of "onset" when the stimulus of interest came in to the infant's view (a free-play situation might be more appropriate to investigate with EEG, because it does not have the same time-locking requirements as ERPs).

Typically, this timing requirement is met by presenting images on a computer screen[1] or via slide projection with a shutter. For example, one study investigating recognition of familiar faces and toys presented 6-month-olds with images of their own toy and a novel toy or the mother's face and a stranger's face on a computer monitor. The results showed that the Nc, a fronto-centrally distributed negative component, is larger to familiar than unfamiliar items (de Haan & Nelson, 1999). In addition to documenting this basic recognition effect, the use of ERPs also provided information about the timing and spatial distribution of the brain activity related to recognition. The results showed that recognition occurred by approximately 600 milliseconds (ms) after stimulus onset and that the recognition effect was bilateral for toys but over the right hemisphere for faces. These results suggest that the right hemisphere "bias" for face processing often observed in adults may be present by 6 months of age (see de Schonen, Gil de Diaz, & Mathivet, 1986) for similar findings using a different procedure.

Usually in ERP studies, the events of interest are presented briefly because (a) when the stimulus duration is short, the time-locking is more precise because the perception is constrained to a narrow time window, and (b) the longer the stimulus presentation and recording interval, the increased likelihood of artifacts such as eye movement artifact from scanning the display or blinking. If the event that one is interested in studying is prolonged, then it is likely more suitable for EEG than ERP study.

As mentioned above, events in ERP studies are also usually presented repeatedly. This allows the time-locked response elicited by the stimulus of interest to be extracted from the ongoing EEG. Since the ERP signals are small in amplitude relative to the EEG, it is necessary to average the recorded brain activity over repeated presentations in order to extract the ERP signal from the EEG. Thus, events that are not easily repeatable are not ideal for ERP study.

Consider two examples of studies using different approaches for investigating the neurophysiological basis of sustained attention. One study (Orkeehova, Stroganova, & Posikera, 1999) investigated this question using a paradigm in which 8- to 11-month-old infants were tested in three phases: (a) sustained attention to an object, (b) anticipation of the person in a peak-a-boo game, and (c) attention to the re-appeared person in a peek-a-boo

---

[1] Note that when images are presented by computer screen there can also be issues related to timing (e.g., with respect to the time to draw the image, the uncertainty in vertical refresh, etc.)

game. These experimental conditions are not ones that are necessarily brief or easily repeatable many times, and thus are more suitable for study by EEG. Using EEG recordings, the authors of this study found that frontal theta activity was related to anticipatory attention differently depending on age but in a manner suggestive of a maturational shift in the functioning of the anterior attention system. A second study (Richards, 2003) used a different approach, and recorded heart rate as a measure of attention while 4.5-, 6-, and 7.5-month-old infants viewed briefly presented geometric patterns that were repeated or novel. As this studied employed briefly presented visual stimuli that could be repeated, it was suitable to recording ERPs. The author of this study found that the Nc was larger during periods of sustained attention, as defined by heart rate, than during periods of inattention.

The need for repeated presentations also has another implication that is particularly important for infant studies: to some extent it limits the number of different conditions that can be tested. In most infant visual ERP studies, at most 2–4 different stimulus conditions are tested (e.g., familiar vs. novel; happy vs. fearful expression), in order to maximize the likelihood that enough good (i.e., artifact-free) data can be collected in each condition before the infant stops cooperating. Although older children may be more tolerant, there still is a practical limit to how many different conditions can be tested in a session and still obtain sufficient useable data for all conditions.

Awake, Attentive Infant or Child

Although some visual brain electrical responses can be recorded from sleeping infants (e.g., flash VEPs; Apkarian, Mirmiran, & Tijssen, 1991; Shepherd, Saunders, & McCulloch, 1999), visual ERPs typically require that the child be awake, with eyes open and attending to the stimulus of interest. These requirements contrast with auditory ERPs, where components such as the mismatch negativity (MMN) can be obtained even if the participants are not attending or are asleep (Matrynova, Kirjavainen, & Cheour, 2003; Naatanen et al., 1993).

Though with older children, the required behavioral state can usually be obtained relatively easily with the instruction ("Sit as still as you can and keep your eyes on the screen") and/or by giving a task to perform during the ERP (e.g., "Press this button when you see a familiar picture"), with infants and very young children it can be more challenging. Young children may find it difficult to appropriately carry out even a relatively simple button press task in the context of an ERP experiment because, for example, they often tend to look down at their hand as they make the response and thereby introduce eye/body movement artifact.

Most visual ERP studies with infants and very young children have therefore used "passive tasks," where the only requirement is to look at the stimuli (although some studies have used different approaches due to their question of interest, such as to study EEG events related in time to the onset of responses, e.g., saccades, rather than related in time to stimulus onset, e.g., Csibra, Tucker, & Johnson, 1998; Richards, 2000). Though this task is something most infants and young children are able to do, it typically is not the case that they will continuously look at the screen for the whole series of stimuli. Typically, infants may look for a while, but then look away from the stimulus display, for example, to the ceiling or back to the caregiver on whose lap they may be sitting. Ideally, the testing area is made as uninteresting as possible to encourage sustained looking at the stimulus display (e.g., by having monochrome screens or curtains around the room, windows shut with shade, etc.). But even with these precautions, infants invariably at some point look away from the display before all the stimuli are presented. One factor that may contribute to this tendency is that stimuli are often presented for relatively brief exposures (e.g., 500 ms), followed by blank screens during inter-trial intervals that may last longer than the stimulus itself (e.g., 1000–2000 ms). From the experimenter's point of view, this opportunity allows the brief presentation to occur followed by a period where brain activity elicited by that stimulus continues to be recorded even in its absence. This period helps to ensure that brain activity returns to baseline (i.e., stimulus-elicited processing is "finished" before the next stimulus is presented). The most common solution to the problem of looking away is to present visual and/or auditory stimuli to re-attract the participant's attention to the screen. These might be colorful, small moving patterns on the screen where the stimulus is displayed and/or brief sounds from that location, or calling the infants name, and so on. Other experimenters have presented the experimental stimuli during brief streams interleaved in a more interesting children's video (Richards, 2003). In both cases, the experimenter then deletes/ignores the EEG recorded during the re-orienting stimuli or video and retains only the data from the trials in which the participant was looking appropriately at the experimental stimuli. Although these approaches are usually effective at a practical level for retaining the infant's or child's interest in the ongoing experiment, it is important to remember that the distinction between the "real" experimental stimuli and re-orienting stimuli made by the experimenter is not necessarily made by the participant. The infant or child simply observes a series of visual images, and the occasional occurrence of intervening stimuli that re-attract their attention are a part of this series and could influence their response to the "real" experimental stimuli. For example, in an oddball paradigm where one stimulus is presented frequently and the other (the oddball) presented infrequently, the occasional occurrence of the re-orienting stimuli might influence the perceived novelty or frequency of the oddball stimuli. A different approach that to some extent circumvents the disadvantage of presenting re-orienting patterns is to present stimuli without any inter-trial interval, so a stimulus is always on the screen (e.g., Gliga & Dehaene-Lambertz, 2005). However, this approach may affect the latency of the observed responses and could have other disadvantages, for example, if the presentations are brief, brain activity may not have time to return to baseline, or if presentations are longer than is typical, there may be increased likelihood of eye movement artifacts due to scanning of the visual display.

Even for infants and young children who attend well to the visual display, it is important to keep in mind that the "passive" task is in essence still a task that requires sustained attention. In order to provide useable data, the participant must be able to sustain attention to the visual display for a period of time long enough to see sufficient trials for an average ERP waveform to be extracted. It is possible that the increased ease with which participants can maintain their attention in a passive visual ERP task might contribute to the reported disappearance of the Nc component by adolescence (Courchesne, 1978), as this component is believed to reflect processes involved in orienting and/or sustaining attention.

Investigations that have related the Nc to behavioral measures of attention provide some support that it may be linked to the ability to sustain attention. For example, one study reported that the amplitude of the Nc at right frontal electrodes in toddlers correlates with their ability in a separate task to sustain visual attention on an intermittent audio-visual display (Early Childhood Vigilance Task; Goldman, Shapiro, & Nelson, 2004; see also Richards, 2003). It is possible that this study found a relation between looking time measures and the Nc because the looking time task used presents very similar attentional requirements to the typical ERP test session. Investigators who have instead attempted to correlate the size of the Nc with the length of infants' looking to novel or salient stimuli in separate behavioral tests using the visual paired comparison test have failed to find a link between the two. For example: (a) although at 6 months of age the Nc is larger for the mother's face than an unfamiliar face, infants do not look longer at the mother's face (de Haan & Nelson, 1997); (b) although infants show a larger Nc and longer looking times to fearful compared to happy faces (de Haan & Nelson, 1999; de Haan et al., 2004), there is no correlation between the amplitude of the Nc and the length of looking (de Haan et al, 2004); (c) in visual paired comparison tests of novel and standard stimuli given after two-stimuli or three-stimuli oddball tests, there is no consistent evidence that infants look longer at the novel stimuli (Karrer & Monti, 1995; Nelson & Collins, 1991, 1992) and no correlation between the Nc and the duration of looking to novelty (Karrer & Monti, 1995); and (d) although both Nc amplitude and the duration of infants' fixations decrease over a study session, the decrease in fixation appears to happen more rapidly (Nikkel & Karrer, 1994). Together, these findings suggest that there is not a close relation between Nc amplitude and length of looking to novel/salient stimuli (Nikkel & Karrer, 1994).

Adding Recording Electrodes and Requirement to Sit Still

Not only must infants and children be awake and attending to the brief, repeated events, they must do so while wearing the electrodes and sitting relatively still. Good descriptions of different systems of electrodes and their application can be found in de Boer and colleagues (2007) and Johnson and colleagues (2001). Methods in which electrodes are placed within electrode caps or nets have the advantages that inter-electrode distances are not variable and that they allow a larger number of electrodes to be placed accurately in a relatively short amount of time. The time savings is a considerable advantage, in assuring that infants and children are not so bored or tired from the electrode application procedure that they are no longer willing to cooperate with the experiment once the electrodes are placed. This issue is important as the main contributors to participant attrition tend to be failure to view sufficient trials and insufficient data due to movement artifact, both things that are likely to occur if the participant is already bored or tired from the electrode preparation period.

For infants and young children, there may be some apprehension about wearing an electrode cap or net or some urge to grab it or the electrode wires. For children, a warm-up period can help where the child has a chance to look at the net and perhaps see the mother or a favorite toy wearing it. Having an entertaining video to watch can also help the child "forget" about the net once it is in place. For infants, out of sight can be out of mind, so it can be helpful for the experimenter placing the cap or net and preparing it to work from behind while another experimenter entertains the infants with toys or blowing bubbles. Distraction with this type of entertainment also often helps calm the infant if s/he begins to cry when the cap or net is placed on the head. For infants with a tendency to grab the cap/net or wires, and if keeping these out of sight as much as possible does not help, placing infant mitts on the hands, keeping the hands occupied with toys, biscuits, or simply instructing the individual holding the child to keep control of the hands can help.

Infants and children ideally should be seated in a comfortable chair or infant seat rather than in an adult's lap. The reason is that the adult may influence how the child reacts, and also to prevent additional movement artifact (e.g., due to bouncing them on the knee or turning to look at the adult). However, for some young infants who have poor head control, this method may not be the most appropriate procedure. If infants rest their heads on the back of their seat, this position may cause artifacts in the electrodes over the back of the head (occipital area), a region that may be of particular importance in visual studies. In this case, some method for supporting the head might be needed, either with a neck support in the infant seat or with an adult holding the infant and supporting the neck.

Equal Measures of Task Performance

In cases where a task is used and different groups, such as different ages or typical versus atypical children are assessed, one consideration is whether group differences are expected in behavioral performance on the task. This issue is an important consideration for at least two reasons. First, in ERP studies with tasks, it is typically the case that only data from those trials with correct responses are included in the averages. Therefore, the task used must be one that all groups can perform at a level well enough for there to be enough correct response trials with good ERP data to create the ERP average for each subject. This issue is important to consider because often an impairment in a particular domain may be of particular interest in a study of children with developmental disorders. A second reason to consider behavioral performance is that, even if all groups are able to complete the task to some extent, the results will be more difficult to interpret if the groups differ in performance. The reason is that it is not necessarily clear in these situations to what extent any differences in the ERPs reflect developmental differences in the neural correlates of the processes being studied and to what extent they reflect more generic influences of task difficulty. This difficulty in interpretation is not solved by averaging only correct responses, as the process by which the correct answer was generated may differ for groups who find the task more versus less difficult regardless of age/stage of development.

One useful aspect of including ERPs in studies of developmental disorders is that they can reveal atypicalities even for domains in which a patient population is thought to be relatively unimpaired and behavioral performance is thus not atypical. For example, one study used ERPs to investigate face processing in individuals with the developmental disorder Williams Syndrome. Williams syndrome is a rare neurogenetic disorder in which a microdeletion on chromosome 7 is associated with physical abnormalities and a particular cognitive profile. Against the background of mild to moderate intellectual impairments, individuals with Williams syndrome often show relative strengths in verbal abilities, face recognition, and social competence, but relative weaknesses in visuo-spatial processing (Bellugi & Wang, 1998; Bellugi, Wang, & Jernigan, 1994). One study used ERPs to investigate whether the neural underpinnings of the seemingly intact face processing abilities in individuals with Williams syndrome were in fact normal (Grice et al., 2001). The study found that the response of the face-selective N170 component (Bentin et al., 1996; and see below for further discussion of N170) to turning the face upside down was atypical (absent) in the group with Williams syndrome. These results suggest that, while individuals with Williams syndrome may do well on tests of face recognition, the process by which they achieve this result may be different from typical individuals.

A similar finding of atypical neural correlates of an "intact" ability has been reported in patients with developmental amnesia following bilateral hippocampal damage sustained early in life, who are impaired on tests of recall memory but perform normally on tests of recognition (Baddeley, Vargha-Khadem, & Mishkin, 2001; Vargha-Khadem et al., 1997). Although their intact recognition abilities suggest that their recognition memory system is unaffected, event-related potentials recorded during recognition reveal otherwise. A case study of one such patient reported that the typical enhancement of the late parietal positivity to familiar items is absent while the earlier N400 effect was well preserved (Duzel, Vargha-Khadem, Heinze, & Mishkin, 2001).

Appropriate Age Range
The look of the visual ERP waveform changes dramatically with development. This finding must be taken into account when considering the age range of participants in a study. Although in studies of adults a wide age range is typically combined into one "adult" group, for studies of infants and children much narrow age ranges should be used. For example, see Figure 4.1 showing the change in response to an upright human face across the first year after birth. Clearly, combining infants into one large group over this age span would obscure important developmental changes and the resulting grand average would likely be misleading. It has been suggested for studies of children to make ERP averages over no more than 1–2 year age spans and for infants only 1–2 months (Taylor & Baldeweg, 2002).

What Spoils the Recipe: Artifacts and Attrition
Attrition rates in developmental visual ERP studies are typically higher than in behavioral studies and adult ERP studies, and also often higher in

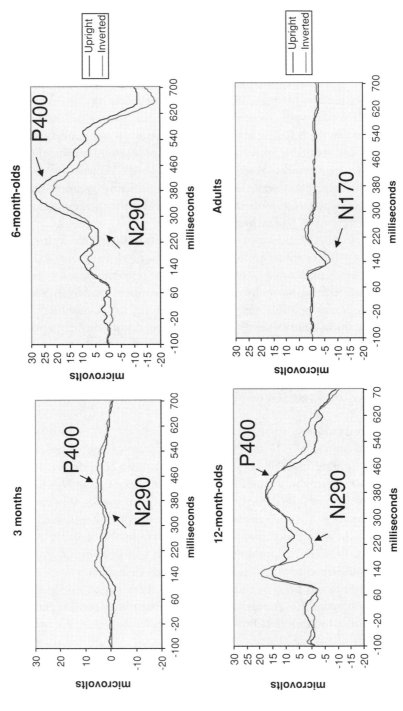

Figure 4.1. Event-related potentials to upright and inverted human faces at 3, 6, and 12 months of age and adulthood over right posterior temporal electrodes. Data from de Haan, Pascalis, and Johnson (2002) and Halit et al. (2003).

developmental visual than auditory ERP studies. For example, in infant visual ERP studies reported attrition rates range from 12.5% (Richards, 2003) to 84% (Nelson & Collins, 1991) while in infant auditory ERP studies attrition rates of 0 are not uncommon (e.g., Leppanen et al., 2004). This difference in auditory versus visual ERPs is likely in part due to the fact that auditory ERPs can be obtained when infants are sleeping, and thus less likely to create artifacts due to blinking and movement. Although the reasons for attrition vary, the most common reason for infants and children is artifacts due to eye/body movement and/or blinking. Eye movements, blinks and body movements are a problem because they typically generate fluctuations in the EEG that are much larger in amplitude than the ERP signal and thus overwhelm/obliterate it. Thus, even the participant who is willing to sit through the entire series of stimuli may not provide good data if s/he has been moving, or blinking frequently during the recording. For infants, failure to view sufficient trials to obtain reliable averages is also common reason for attrition.

The relatively high attrition rates, particularly in infant studies, are important to consider when planning studies. The likely rate of attrition should be taken into account when calculating the number of participants that need to be recruited. This issue can be particularly important when dealing with special populations whose numbers may be limited, when considering whether an ERP study is feasible.

Reporting Results

Once the challenges of experimental design and data collection have been met, the experimenter is left with what is often a large amount of data to be analyzed and interpreted. The aim of this section is to focus mainly on issues of data analysis and interpretation of particular relevance to developmental and visual ERP studies, rather than to provide a more general overview to the analysis of ERPs (for those interested in a more general treatment of this subject, see de Boer et al., 2007).

Identifying Components and Quantifying ERP Waveforms
Components are usually characterized by the simultaneous consideration of their eliciting conditions, polarity (positive or negative), timing (latency), and scalp distribution (topography). Using these characteristics helps the experimenter to relate the components observed in his/her experiment to those observed in other experiments.

ERPs are typically quantified by their peak latency (i.e., the time in milliseconds from stimulus onset until the deflection reaches its maximum or minimum amplitude) and amplitude (often defined as the most positive or negative value in microvolts relative to a pre-stimulus baseline). A factor to consider in developmental studies is that components can sometimes be broader (i.e., not show a sharp, well-defined peak but rather a peak over a more prolonged time course) and slow wave activity (a sustained deflection from baseline without any prominent peak) can be more common. Under these circumstances, it may be difficult to accurately identify a peak latency or a peak amplitude. When this occurs, a more reliable and representative measure of amplitude may be to average amplitude over the time window in which the deflection occurs rather than to sample amplitude only at single (peak) time point. A measure producing similar results is an "area score" in which the area under the deflection is computed.

Reference

ERPs are measured as the difference in voltage between a particular (active) electrode and a reference electrode. Ideally, the reference electrode should be "neutral" in that it should not affect the characteristics of interest in the ERP such as the amplitude, latency or topography of components. The question of the ideal reference is not unique to developmental or visual ERP research and a full discussion is beyond the scope of this chapter (instead see Dien, 1998 or Yao et al., 2005). The issue of reference will be briefly mentioned here because the choice of reference can influence the look of the ERP waveform and the ability to identify the component of interest. Common locations for the reference electrodes in visual research are earlobes or mastoids; with the increase use of high-density arrays, use of the average reference (a type of reference mathematically computed off-line) is increasing in developmental research. If a scalp electrode is used as reference, rather than an average reference, it should be chosen so it is distant from the presumed active brain regions. For example, if one is interested in visual ERPs, locating the reference over occipital scalp is not ideal. This is because the component itself will be picked up by the reference electrode and be subtracted out of the signal being recorded. Choice of reference is also important to consider when comparing results among studies, as use of different references can result in different-looking waveforms or pattern of results even in similar tasks. See Figure 4.2 for an example of the influence of different references on the Nc component.

What do the ERP Waveforms Mean?

ERP components in infants and children are often interpreted with reference to their presumed counterparts in the adult ERP. In studies of adults, ERP

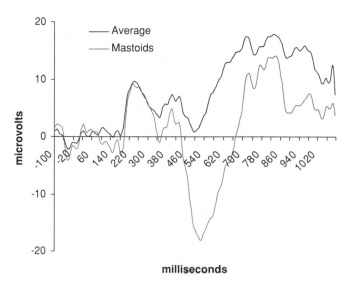

Figure 4.2. Comparing event-related to potentials to an upright human face in 7-month-old infant at Fz with averaged mastoid and average reference. Data are from de Haan et al. (2004).

components can be identified by examining their peak latencies, morphology, and spatial distribution. However, this type of interpretation can sometimes be easier said than done. Identifying the infant equivalents of such components is not simply a matter of applying the same criteria to the younger age group (a target-elicited P300 might be described as a positive component peaking between 300–500 ms with a parietal maximum) as investigations of ERPs during childhood and old age have clearly shown that timing and topography and even polarity of components can change across the lifespan (e.g., Taylor & Pang, 1999). One basic approach to identifying the infant and child equivalents of adult ERP components has been a functional one: test younger and older participants under the same conditions and look for ERP components that show similar stimulus or task-related modulations across age. Although this approach has proved useful in practice, it is important to keep in mind that it makes the assumption that there will be no change in functionality with age.

For example, this functional approach has been used to study the developmental trajectory of the N170 a component that has been termed "face-sensitive" because the presence of a face causes systematic changes in its amplitude and/or latency compared to a wide range of other classes of object. For example, although N170s of varying amplitudes can be elicited by non-face objects (Rossion et al., 2000), the response to human faces is consistently of larger amplitude and often shorter latency than that to any other object category tested (Bentin et al., 1996; Rossion et al., 2000). In addition, rotating the face 180 degrees, a manipulation known to interfere with face recognition, prolongs the latency and often increases the amplitude of the N170 for faces but not for other objects (Eimer, 2000a, b, c; Rossion et al., 2000). Developmental studies through childhood have identified the N170 as a negative deflection over posterior temporal scalp regions that is, like the adult N170, larger in amplitude and often shorter in latency for faces compared to other objects (Taylor, McCarthy, Saliba, Degiovanni, 1999). These studies show that the peak latency of the N170 decreases with age into adolescence, and that the peak amplitude over the right hemisphere increases over this time (Taylor et al., 1999, 2001).

Studies in children have identified an N170 in participants as young as 4 years, but is it observable even earlier? In infants, two components have been identified as potential precursors to the N170 based on their response properties. The N290 component is similar to the N170 in that it shows an adult-like effect of face inversion on amplitude by 12 months of age, and shows a relatively similar timing and polarity (Halit et al., 2003; see Figure 4.1). The basic question of whether the N290 differs for faces versus objects (a defining characteristic of the adult N170) remains to be tested, although a recent study did show that the N290 is larger for faces than 'noise' patterns by 3 months of age (Halit et al., 2002). The P400 is like the N170 in that it is of shorter latency for faces than objects (de Haan & Nelson, 1999), and shows an adult-like effect of face inversion on peak latency by 12 months of age (Halit et al., 2003). With respect to spatial distribution, like the N170, it shows a more lateral distribution. However, the P400 differs in latency and polarity from the N170. Overall, these findings suggest that both the N290 and P400 reflect processes that in the adult may become integrated in time in the N170 component. In other words, the structural encoding of faces may be spread out over a longer time of processing in infants than adults. It is possible that, as they become more automated, the processes involved in face processing are carried out more quickly and/or in a parallel rather than serial fashion. Currently, there is a gap between those studies that have examined face-related ERPs up to 12 months, and studies of older children that begin at 60 months, which prevents a firm conclusion. However, studies of 4- to 5-year-old children suggest that the child N170 may be double-peaked at this age, becoming a single prominent peak only later (Taylor, Batty, Itier, 2004). This pattern is consistent with the infant data suggesting two sources contributing to the N170.

What Causes ERPs to Change with Age?

The neurophysiological mechanisms underlying developmental changes in the amplitude and latency of ERP components are not precisely known but could include numerous factors such as myelination, synaptic density, and other characteristics of synapses, refractory periods, and the response variability of the generators. With respect to amplitude, the most commonly given mechanism is changes in synaptic density (Courchesne 1990; Vaughan & Kurtzberg, 1992). These investigators have noted that developmental changes in synaptic density appear to parallel developmental changes in amplitude of some ERP components, with both showing a U-shaped function of rapid increase in infancy followed by more gradual decline over childhood.

Developmental changes in ERP latency have typically been linked to changes in synaptic efficacy and/or changes in brain myelination (Eggermont, 1998; Ponton, Moore, Eggermont, 1999). For example, decreases in latency of the Nc component have been related to the myelination of the non-specific thalamic radiation that occurs during the first 7 years (Courchesne, 1990) and the rapid decrease in latency of the N1a of the flash VEP around the time of birth has been attributed to the initiation of myelination of the optic radiation (Tsuneishi & Casaer, 2000). Although the temporal coincidence of these changes is notable, there is little direct evidence for a developmental connection in humans between degree of myelination and ERP component latency. However, combining brain imaging techniques with ERPs may provide some more direct support for this view.

Thus, changes in various aspects of the neural circuitry in the brain regions responsible for generating a particular component may underlie developmental changes in its amplitude, latency, and topography. At a more functional level, changes in the efficiency of processing or strategies used in a particular task may also contribute to the changes observed.

Summary
Visual ERP studies can provide a useful insight into the development of visual processing. However, as the typical visual ERP study involves presentation of brief, precisely timed and repeated visual stimuli, some thought is required when planning such studies as to how the question of interest can be investigated given these requirements and how infants' and young children's attention can be kept on the stimuli under these conditions. Once the data are collected and analyzed, interpretation of the results can also present a challenge – what do any differences mean? To answer this question, it is helpful to be able to relate the components observed with other studies of

the same or different ages, and thus it is important to be aware of how the look of the ERP waveform can change with age and also with variations in recording/analysis procedures.

VISUAL ERPs AND ATYPICAL DEVELOPMENT

A question of interest to many researchers is how useful ERPs and EEGs are for studying atypical development, either with respect to describing an existing impairment or identifying those at risk for later developing impairments. The fact that EEGs and ERPs can be obtained passively and do not require an overt behavioural response, and indeed for some measures do not require active attention at all, makes them especially appealing both for studying potentially delayed infants and also for longitudinal study as the same response could be measured over a wide frame of development.

VEPs are clinically useful to detect, quantify, and monitor dysfunction of the developing visual system. They have many applications, including evaluation of the state of maturation of the visual system, determining visual acuity, detecting and monitoring the treatment of amblyopia, and detecting cerebral visual impairment (reviewed in McCulloch, 2007).

Compared with VEPs, use of visual ERPs to detect and quantify cognitive impairment is less developed or well established in terms of clinical use. There is, however, a relatively large and increasing body of literature examining the neural correlates of various aspects of visual cognition in children with different developmental disorders (e.g., for reviews for autism, see: Dawson, Webb, & McPartland, 2005; for attention deficit-hyperactivity disorder, see: Barry, Johnstone, & Clarke, 2003). For example, one study investigated recognition of faces and objects in 3- to 4-year-old children with autism (Dawson et al., 2002). The results showed that already by this age children with autism show atypical processing of faces: although typically developing children showed differences for familiar compared to novel items at the Nc and P400 components, those with autism showed the recognition effects only for objects. This result did not appear to reflect a general developmental delay, as a separate group mental-age matched controls did show ERP evidence of recognition of both faces and objects.

Other researchers have used visual ERPs to evaluate the effects of interventions. For example, one study examined the influence of iron supplementation on the ERPs of 8- to 10-year-old children with iron deficiency (Otero et al., 2004). Since a decrease in iron concentration is accompanied by alterations in neurotransmitters involved in brain attentional and memory systems, it was hypothesised that the children would show an abnormal P300 response in a standard oddball paradigm (in which one stimulus is presented frequently and the other "oddball" infrequently). The study reported that the iron-deficient children showed a severely reduced P300 to the oddball over central-parietal regions. Following treatment, the component increased in amplitude although still remained smaller than that seen in control children over the parietal region.

There is also an increased interest in the use of ERPs as a method for earlier identification of infants who are at risk for developmental delay. For example, one study examined infants of diabetic mothers who are believed to be at risk for memory disorders, due to the adverse fetal environment that occurs in this condition, including chronic hypoxia, reactive hypoglycemia, and iron deficiency. All of these factors may particularly affect a structure known to be critical for normal memory, the hippocampus (see discussion in Nelson et al., 2001 for further discussion). In this study, 6-month-old infants who had been born to diabetic mothers as well as control infants were tested with the mother's face and a stranger's face. The results with the control infants largely replicated prior findings showing a larger Nc to the mother's face at right hemisphere electrodes and a larger positive slow wave to the stranger's face (Nelson et al., 2001). By contrast, the infants of diabetic mothers did show an Nc and positive slow wave[2] but did not show differentiation between the two faces. In spite of these differences detected with ERPs, the two groups did not differ on a test of general ability level (Bayley Scales of Infant Development) or in a behavioral test of memory using the visual paired comparison procedure. These results illustrate the potential sensitivity ERPs in detecting atypical development at the group level, although the extent to which they can be interpreted as reflecting specifically hippocampal abnormality in this population is unclear (e.g., infants performed normally on the visual paired comparison test, which is believed to be sensitive to hippocampal damage; reviewed in Pascalis & de Haan, 2003; Nelson, 1995). Although this study and others indicate that visual ERPs may be useful in detecting early delays or atypicalities in visual cognition, there is little information about whether these measures taken in infancy predict later abilities. This question of using infant ERPs to predict later abilities has been investigated more extensively using auditory, rather than visual, ERPs (e.g., see Molfese, 2000; Molfese, Molfese, & Modgline, 2001).

These examples illustrate the potential usefulness of visual ERPs for studying atypical development. However, there are cautions when interpreting results showing differences between typical and atypical or at-risk groups.

---

[2] Nelson et al. (2000) state that the positive slow wave was 'absent or diminished' in the infants of diabetic mothers, but there was no main effect of Group on amplitude, and they reported no other direct statistical comparison of amplitude between groups.

Various aspects of the ERP procedure and data processing can affect the amplitude or latency of components other than true differences in cognitive processing between groups. For example, one study showed that the amplitude of the Nc differed for infants who saw a different total number of trials in the recording procedure (even when there were no differences in number of trials used to create averages; e.g., Snyder et al., 2003). Thus, if typical and atypical groups see different total numbers of trials (which can happen as the length of sessions is often determined by the extent of infants' cooperation), differences may be detected that are related to this procedural difference but might be interpreted as reflecting delayed or deviant development in the atypical group. Another consideration, discussed above, is how to interpret differences in ERPs in active tasks when differences in behavioral performance are observed for typical and atypical groups. In spite of these difficulties, ERPs, if used carefully, can potentially provide a very useful tool for assessing early cognitive processing.

Summary

Event-related potentials are a useful tool for studying the neurophysiological correlates of visual development. They can be particularly useful in young infants and children or those with low abilities, as they can be obtained in simple procedures where the individual need only look at the stimulus display without making any other response. Although the nature by which they are recorded and analyzed places some constraints on the types of situations that can be directly studied with ERPs, the growing body of literature in this field is testament to researchers' abilities to adapt their questions to these challenges.

There are several future directions that will help move the area forward. One is an increase in the number of longitudinal studies, or even cross-sectional studies that systematically test a wide age range under the same parameters. This is important for understanding what the developmental precursors of mature components are, and also is important for interpreting results of studies of atypical populations (determining if their responses are delayed or clearly deviant). A second direction is an increased integration of other imaging methods with ERP in developing studies, which will help to provide further data on interesting questions such as the contribution of myelination to developmental changes in ERP components. This advance includes more sophisticated analyses of EEG and ERPs that mathematically derive presumed generator sources within the brain for components of interest, as well as analyses that can relate structural or functional imaging data from other modalities with ERPs.

References

Allison, T., Wood, C. C., & McCarthy, G. (1986). The central nervous system. In M. G. H. Coles, E. Donchin, & S. W. Porges (Eds). *Psychophysiology: Systems, processes and applications* (pp. 5–25). New York: Guilford Press.

Apkarian, P., Mirmiran, M., & Tijssen R. (1991). Effects of behavioral state on visual processing in neonates. *Neuropediatrics, 22,* 85–91.

Baddelely, A., Vargha-Khadem, F., & Mishkin, M. (2001). Preserved recognition in a case of developmental amnesia: Implications for semantic memory? *Journal of Cognitive Neuroscience, 13,* 357–369.

Barry, R. J., Johnstone, S. J., & Clarke, A. R. (2003). A review of electrophysiology in attention-deficit/hyperactivity disorder: II Event-related potentials. *Clinical Neurophysiology, 114,* 184–198.

Bellugi, U., & Wang., P. P. (1998). Williams syndrome: From cognition to brain to gene. In G. Edelman & B. H. Smith (Eds.), *Encyclopedia of neuroscience.* Amsterdam: Elsevier.

Bellugi, U., Wang, P. P., & Jernigan, T. L. (1994). Williams syndrome: An unusual neuropsychological profile. In S. H. Broman & J. Grafman (Eds.), *Atypical cognitive deficits in developmental disorders* (pp. 23–56) Hillsdale, NJ: Erlbaum.

Bentin, S., Allison, T., Puce, A., Perez, E. et al. (1996). Electrophysiological studies of face perception in humans. *Journal of Cognitive Neuroscience, 8,* 551–65.

Chung, M. S., & Thomson, D. M. (1985). Development of face recognition. *British Journal of Psychology, 86,* 55–87.

Courchesne, E. (1978). Neurophysiological correlates of cognitive development: Changes in long-latency event-related potentials from childhood to adulthood. *Electroencephalography and Clinical Neurophysiology, 45,* 468–482.

Csibra, G., Tucker, L. A., & Johnson, M. H. (1998). Neural correlates of saccade planning in infants: A high density ERP study. *International Journal of Psychophysiology, 29,* 201–215.

Dawson, G., Carver, L., Meltzoff, A. N., Panagiotides, H., McPartland, J., & Webb, S. J. (2002). Neural correlates of face and object recognition in young children with autism spectrum disorder, developmental delay and typical development. *Child Development, 73,* 700–717.

Dawson, G., Webb, S. J., & McPartland, J. (2005). Understanding the nature of face processing impairment in autism: Insights from behavioural and electrophysiological studies. *Developmental Neuropsychology, 27,* 403–424.

de Boer, T., Scott, L. S., & Nelson, C. A. (2007). Methods for acquiring and analysing infant event-related potentials. In M. de Haan (Ed.), *Infant EEG and Event-Related Potentials.* (pp. 5–37). Hove, UK: Psychology Press.

de Haan, M. (2007). Visual attention and recognition memory in infancy. In M. de Haan (Ed.), *Infant EEG and event-related potentials.* (pp. 101–143). Hove, UK: Psychology Press.

de Haan, M., Belsky, J., Reid, V., Volein, A., & Johnson, M. H. (2004). Maternal personality and infants' neural and visual responsivity to facial expressions of emotion. *Journal of Child Psychology & Psychiatry, 45,* 1209–1218.

de Haan, M., & Nelson, C. A. (1997). Recognition of the mother's face by 6-month-old infants: A neurobehavioral study. *Child Development, 68,* 187–210 de Haan, M., & Nelson, C. A. (1999). Brain activity differentiates face and object processing in 6-month-old infants. *Developmental Psychology, 35*, 1113–1121.

de Haan, M., Pascalis, O., & Johnson, M. H. (2002). Specialization of neural mechanisms underlying face recognition in human infants. *Journal of Cognitive Neuroscience, 14*, 199–209

de Schonen, S., Gil de Diaz, M. & Mathivet, E. (1986). Hemispheric asymmetry in face processing in infancy. In H. D. Ellis, M. A. Jeeves, F. Newcombe, & A. Young (Eds), *Aspects of face processing* (pp. 199–208). Dordrecht: Nijhoff.

Dien, J. (1998). Issues in the application of the average reference: Review, critiques, and recommendations. *Behavior, Research Methods, Instrumentation & Computers, 30*, 34–43.

Duzel, E., Vargha-Khadem, F., Heinze, H. J., & Mishkin, M. (2001). Brain activity evidence for recognition without recollection after early hippocampal damage. *Proceedings of the National Academy of Sciences USA, 98*, 8101–8106.

Eggermont, J. J. (1998). On the rate of maturation of sensory evoked potentials. *Electroencephalography and Clinical Neurophysiology, 70*, 293–305.

Eimer, M. (2000a). The face-specific N170 component reflects late stages in the structural encoding of faces. *Neuroreport, 11*, 2319–24.

Eimer, M. (2000b). Event-related brain potentials distinguish processing stages involved in face perception and recognition. *Clinical Neurophysiology, 111*, 694–705.

Eimer, M. (2000c). Effects of face inversion on the structural encoding and recognition of faces. Evidence from event-related brain potentials. *Brain Research, Cognitive Brain Research, 10*, 145–158.

Gliga, T., & Dehaene-Lambertz, G. (2005). Structural encoding of body and face in human infants and adults. *Journal of Cognitive Neuroscience, 17*, 1328–1340.

Goldman, D. Z., Shapiro, E. G., & Nelson, C. A. (2004). Measurement of vigilance in 2-year-old children. *Developmental Neuropsychology, 25*, 227–250.

Grice, S. J., Spratling, M. W., Karmiloff-Smith, A., Halit, H., Csibra, G., de Haan, M., & Johnson, M. H. (2001). Disordered visual processing and oscillatory brain activity in autism and Williams syndrome. *NeuroReport, 12*, 2697–2700.

Halit, H., de Haan, M., & Johnson, M. H. (2003). Cortical specialisation for face processing: Face-sensitive event-related potential components in 3 and 12 month old infants. *Neuroimage, 19*, 1180–1193

Johnson, M. H., de Haan, M., Hatzakis, H., Oliver, A., Smith, W., Tucker, L. A., & Csibra, G. (2001). Recording and analyzing high density event-related potentials with infants using the Geodesic Sensor Net. *Developmental Neuropsychology, 19*, 295–323.

Karrer, J. H., Karrer, R., Bloom, D., Chaney, L., & Davis, R. (1998). Event-related brain potentials during an extended visual recognition memory task depict delayed development of cerebral inhibitory processes among 6-month-old infants with Down syndrome. *International Journal of Psychophysiology, 29*, 167–200.

Karrer, R., & Monti, L. A. (1995). Event-related potentials of 4–7-week-old infants in a visual recognition memory task. *Electroencephalography and Clinical Neurophysiology, 94*, 414–424.

Kemner, C., van der Gaag, R. J., Verbaten, M., & van Engeland, H. (1999). ERP differences among subtypes of pervasive developmental disorders. *Biological Psychiatry, 46*, 781–789.

Leppanen, P. H., Guttorm, T. K., Pihko, E., Takkinen, S., Eklund, K. M., & Lyytinen, H. (2004). Maturational effects on newborn ERPs measured in the mismatch negativity paradigm. *Experimental Neurology, 190* Suppl 1: S91–101.

Lewis, T. L., & Maurer, D. (2005). Multiple sensitive periods in human visual development: Evidence from visually deprived children. *Developmental Psychobiology, 46*, 163–183.

Makeig, S., Westerfield, M., Jung, T. P., Enghoff, S., Townsend, J., Courchesne, E., & Senjowski, T. J. (2002). Dynamic brain sources of visual evoked responses. *Science, 295*, 690–694.

Martynova, O., Kirjavainen, J., & Cheour, M. (2003). Mismatch negativity and late discriminative negativity in sleeping human newborns. *Neuroscience Letters, 340*, 75–78.

McCulloch, D. M. (2007). Visual evoked potentials in infants. In M. de Haan (Ed.) *Infant EEG and event-related potentials.* (pp. 39–76). Hove, UK: Psychology Press.

Molfese, D. L. (2000). Predicting dyslexia at 8 years of age using neonatal response. *Brain and Language, 72*, 238–245.

Molfese, V. J., Molfese, D. L., & Modgline, A. A. (2001). Newborn and preschool predictors of second-grade reading scores: An evaluation of categorical and continuous scores. *Journal of Learning Disabilities, 34*, 545–554.

Naatanen, R., Paavilainen, P., Tiitinen, H., Jiang, D., & Alho, K. (1993). Attention and mismatch negativity. *Psychophysiology, 30*, 436–450.

Nelson, C. A., & Collins, P. F. (1991). Event-related potentials and looking-time analysis of infants' responses to familiar and novel events: Implications for recognition memory. *Developmental Psychology, 27*, 50–58.

Nelson, C. A. & Collins, P. F. (1992). Neural and behavioural correlates of recognition memory in 4- and 8-month-old infants. *Brain & Cognition, 19*, 105–121.

Nelson, C. A., & Monk, C. S. (2001). The use of event-related potentials in the study of cognitive development. In C. A. Nelson & M. Luciana (Eds.), *Handbook of developmental cognitive neuroscience* (pp. 125–136). Cambridge, MA: MIT Press.

Nikkel, L., & Karrer, R. (1994). Differential effects of experience on the ERP and behaviour of 6-month-old infants: Trend during repeated stimulus presentations. *Developmental Neuropsychology, 10*, 1–11.

Orekhova, E. V., Stroganova, T. A., & Posikera, I. N. (1999). Theta synchronization during sustained anticipatory attention in infants over the second half of the first year of life. *International Journal of Psychophysiology, 32*, 151–172.

Otero, G. A., Pliego-Rivero, F. B., Contreras, G., Ricardo, J., & Fernandez, T. (2004). Iron supplementation brings up a lacking P300 in iron deficient children. *Clinical Neurophysiology, 115*, 2259–2266.

Penny, W. D., Kiebel, S. J., Kilner, J. M., & Rugg, M. D. (2002). Event-related brain dynamics. *Trends in Neurosciences, 25*, 387–389.

Ponton, C. W., Moore, J. K., & Eggermont, J. J. (1999). Prolonged deafness limits auditory system developmental plasticity: Evidence from an evoked potentials study in children with cochlear implants. *Scandinavian Auditory Suppl, 51*, 13–22.

Richards, J. E. (2000). Localizing the development of covert attention in infants with scalp event-related potentials. *Developmental Psychology, 36*, 91–108.

Richards, J. E. (2003). Attention affects the recognition of briefly presented stimuli in infants: An ERP study. *Developmental Science, 6*, 312–328.

Rossion, B., Gauthier, I., Tarr, M. J., Despland, P., Bruyer, R., Linotte, S. & Crommelink, M. (2000). The N170 occipito-temporal component is delayed and enhanced to inverted faces but not to inverted objects: An electrophysiological account of face-specific processes in the human brain. *NeuroReport, 11,* 69–74.

Shepherd, A. J., Saunders, K. J., & McCulloch, D. L. (1999). Effect of sleep state on the flash visual evoked potential – A case study. *Doc. Ophthalmology, 98,* 47–256.

Snyder, K., Webb, S., & Nelson, C. A. (2002). Theoretical and methodological implications of variability in infant brain response during a recognition memory paradigm. *Infant Behavior & Development, 25,* 466–494.

Taylor, M. J., & Baldeweg, T. (2002). Application of EEG, ERP and intracranial recordings to the investigation of cognitive function in children. *Developmental Science, 5,* 318–334.

Taylor, M. J., Batty, M., & Itier, R. J. (2004). The faces of development: A review of early face processing over childhood. *Journal of Cognitive Neuroscience, 16,* 1426–1442.

Taylor, M. J., Itier, R. J., Allison, T., & Edmonds, G. E. (2001). Direction of gaze effects on early face processing: eyes-only versus full faces. *Brain Research, Cognitive Brain Research, 10,* 333–40.

Taylor, M. J., McCarthy, G., Saliba, E., & Degiovanni, E. (1999). ERP evidence of developmental changes in processing of faces. *Clinical Neurophysiology, 110,* 910–915.

Taylor, M. J., & Pang, E. W. (1999). Developmental changes in early cognitive processes. *Electroencephalography and Clinical Neurophysiology Suppl., 49,* 145–153.

Tsuneishi, S., & Casaer, J. (2000). Effects of preterm extrauterine visual experience on the development of the human visual system: A flash VEP study. *Developmental Medicine and Child Neurology, 42,* 663.

Vargha-Khadem, F., Gadian, D. G., Watkins, K. E., Connelly, A., & Van Paesschen, W. (1997). Differential effects of early hippocampal pathology on episodic and semantic memory. *Science, 277,* 376–380.

Vaughan, H. G., Jr, & Kurtzberg, D. (1992). Electrophysiologic indices of human brain maturation and cognitive development. In M. R. Gunnar & C. A. Nelson (Eds.), *Minnesota Symposia on Child Psychology* (Vol. 24, pp. 1–36). Hillsdale, NJ: Lawrence Erlbaum Associates.

Yao, D., Wang, L., Oostenveld, R., Neilsen, K. D., Arendt-Nielsen, L., & Chen, C. A. N. (2005). A comparative study of different references for EEG spectral mapping: The issue of neutral reference and the use of the infinity reference. *Physiological Measurement, 26,* 173–184.

5 Electrophysiological Measures in Research on Social and Emotional Development

Peter J. Marshall and Nathan A. Fox

INTRODUCTION

The study of social and emotional development presents multiple complexities to the researcher. For instance, infants and young children cannot provide verbal report of their feeling states or moods, and researchers often rely on questionnaire measures given to parents or caregivers regarding the social or emotional behavior of the child. In addition, stimuli that elicit emotions in infants and young children are often age specific and the potency of these stimuli depends upon the context in which they are presented. The ability to present still pictures or video stimuli designed to elicit emotion (as is often done in adult studies) is compromised by the infant or young child's ability to attend to the stimulus, and more particularly by their ability to interpret or understand the nature of the stimuli. Finally, infants and young children display a good deal of motor behavior in response to events that elicit emotion. Such motor activity is particularly problematic for the recording of physiological responses, which are often subject to motor artifact. These issues are certainly not specific to the study of social and emotional development, and are also faced by researchers interested in cognitive as well as social and emotional development. Lack of verbal report, interpretation of stimulus characteristics, importance of context, variations in state and motor reactivity are all general problems faced in the study of infants and young children. However, the past two decades of research have demonstrated that it is possible to utilize electrophysiological recordings to examine both cognitive and social and emotional development in infants and young children. In this chapter, we begin with a discussion of recording and analysis techniques that are especially relevant to the use of EEG techniques in the study of social and emotional development. We then give a brief overview of recent research examining individual differences in certain aspects of the EEG in relation to variations in social and emotional behavior in infants and children. We also discuss a growing literature that explores the use of event-related potentials (ERP) in exploring the interactions among emotion, cognition, and sensory processing in early development. Finally, we summarize some recent advances in EEG and ERP analysis techniques that have rarely been applied to developmental data but which hold a good degree of promise for developmental researchers.

Many of the general technical issues surrounding the collection and analysis of scalp signals across a wide age range have been addressed elsewhere, for both EEG (Davidson, Jackson, & Larson, 2000; Pivik et al., 1993; Stern, 2003) and ERP techniques (Fabiani, 2000; Molfese, Molfese, & Kelly, 2001; Picton et al., 2000b). In this chapter, we aim to focus on issues that are specifically pertinent to EEG and ERP research with infants and children in the domain of social and emotional development (see also Fox, Schmidt, & Henderson, 2000; Marshall & Fox, 2001).

RECORDING CONSIDERATIONS IN DEVELOPMENTAL EEG RESEARCH

The scalp EEG signal reflects the summation of post-synaptic potentials generated in specific layers of cortical pyramidal cells that are perpendicular to the cortical surface. As the EEG signal, these summated potentials may be picked up using electrode arrays that are pre-mounted on some kind of headgear such as a lycra cap (e.g., an Electro-cap as manufactured by Electro-Cap International) or elasticated webbing (e.g., the Geodesic Sensor Net or GSN from Electrical Geodesics, Inc.). There are a number of alternative manufacturers, although the two examples given exemplify somewhat alternative collection strategies. Recordings made with Electro-Caps typically use up to around 30 electrodes in positions based on a modification of the original 10/20 configuration (see Nuwer et al., 1998), whereas the GSN provides a high-density array containing 64 or 128 and more recently 256 electrodes. As discussed later in this chapter, high-density electrode arrays allow the use of specific analysis techniques, but in terms of collecting EEG from infants or children, there are advantages and disadvantages to each method. For instance, the GSN is easier to apply but toddlers are apt to grab at and pull the webbing (Johnson et al., 2001), whereas an Electro-Cap is more time-consuming to apply but the construction of the cap makes it more difficult for children to physically interfere with the electrodes.

One issue related to the use of large numbers of electrodes is that of preparation of the scalp sites for recording. Electrodes placed directly on the head without any prior preparation of the scalp typically have very high impedance, with the EEG signal being effectively swamped by externally generated electromagnetic interference (EMI). EMI occurs mainly at the AC main frequency (e.g., 60 Hz in North America, 50 Hz in Europe) and at its harmonics, and is generated either as line noise that is propagated through cables and connectors or radiated noise, which is generated by electrical devices in the vicinity of the EEG collection room. For a full discussion of the identification and reduction of noise in electrophysiological recordings, see Cutmore and James (1999).

Collection of a suitable EEG signal requires that electrode impedances are reduced to a level at which the magnitude of the EEG signal is large relative to that of the background noise. To facilitate the reduction of electrode impedance, the scalp site below each electrode requires some degree of preparation. This procedure is commonly done using a mild abrasive gel in combination with a smoother conducting gel. With smaller numbers of electrodes, each site can be individually abraded and prepared to ensure that impedance levels have been reduced to satisfactory levels (e.g., below 5 or 10 kilohms). The larger the number of electrodes, the less feasible it is to individually prepare each scalp site to the same extent as with smaller numbers of electrodes. Scalp preparation for dense electrode arrays is often minimal, consisting of wetting the electrode array and the scalp with a conductive solution. The minimal level of preparation used with such dense arrays necessitates increased tolerance of EMI, although recent developments in bioamplifier technology have aided researchers in this respect. The susceptibility of bioelectric signals to electromagnetic interference is much reduced by high bioamplifier input impedances, which are now in the gigohm range for hardware from certain manufacturers. Added to this are improvements in the common mode rejection capabilities of bioamplifiers, which allows some electromagnetic interference to be removed from the signal prior to amplification. These developments essentially allow researchers to tolerate higher electrode impedances without a corresponding loss in signal quality, which in turn reduces the time needed for electrode preparation.

Research involving EEG and ERP with infants and young children involves the risk of attrition or data loss due to motor movement or state change. Some infants, toddlers, or preschoolers object to the placement of a cap on their heads and such distress usually leads to abandoning the experimental session. Alternatively, some infant participants tolerate cap placement, but will change state and become fussier over the course of the experimental session, causing early termination of data collection. It should also be noted that unlike studies with older children or adults, infants and young children often display exaggerated motor activity associated with positive affect as well as during the display of negative affect. Individual variation in the expression of both positive and negative affect may lead to differential attrition. In other words, the temperament of the infant or young child may be a factor in the threshold and intensity of the expression of emotion, possibly leading to differential attrition as a function of these individual differences.

The actual amount of time required to prepare the electrodes (i.e., to establish a low enough impedance and to correct any issues with electrode placement) is more of an issue with infants and young children, and less of an issue with older children, who are more likely to cooperate for a longer time. The duration of electrode preparation depends on a combination of efficiency on the part of the experimenter and on the number of electrodes and the impedance threshold that are being used. The GSN is faster to place and prepare than a conventional Electro-Cap, although its use with very young children may be restricted due to the physical nature of the apparatus: Johnson and colleagues (2001) state that the GSN is good for infants between 3 and 12 months of age, whereas toddlers tend to pull at the elastic webbing. The Electro-Cap, while being more time consuming to prepare, has wiring that is almost entirely under the cap fabric, so it is more difficult for toddlers to pull on, although it is certainly not impossible to dislodge.

Regardless of the method of EEG collection, a "distractor" is vitally important during cap placement. While the cap is being placed and the electrodes prepared by one experimenter, another experimenter engages the infant and attempts to focus his or her attention on toys or other playthings that have been placed in front of the child. Initial presentation of the EEG environment to children is made easier by use of props and decorations along a specific theme, for example, we have successfully employed an "astronaut" theme involving a special chair and room decorations (Fox et al., 1995). We have also framed photos of children in EEG caps and placed these around the lab for incoming families to see, which has proved especially useful when earlier visits in a longitudinal study do not include EEG collection. Note that such photographs were taken and used with written parental permission given specifically for this purpose.

TECHNIQUES FOR EEG PROCESSING AND ANALYSIS

Preprocessing: Referencing and Artifact Detection

The EEG signal from each electrode is usually recorded in reference to a scalp site (e.g., the vertex at Cz), with separate channels being recorded from other potential reference points, such as nosetip, mastoids, or earlobes. The preferred reference configuration can then be derived offline. Issues related to the choice of reference configuration have been debated elsewhere (e.g., Hagemann, Naumann, & Thayer, 2001), although developmental aspects of this choice have not generally been considered.

Before the EEG signal is analyzed, epochs containing artifact must be identified. This includes the detection of artifact related to eye movement (the contamination of the EEG by ocular activity) and artifact from muscle activity and gross motor movements. In terms of artifact detection, there have been a variety of approaches in the adult EEG literature including manual editing of artifact (Lawson et al., 2003), fully automated procedures (Moretti et al., 2003), or a combination of the two. The use of large numbers of electrodes increases the potential number of channels that are contaminated by artifact, and data from dense arrays may need specific techniques for pre-processing. For example, statistical methods have been proposed for dealing with the potentially larger number of channels that are contaminated by artifact in dense arrays (Junghofer, Elbert, Tucker, & Rockstroh, 2000), and for the identification of electrolyte bridges between channels (Tenke & Kayser, 2001).

The electrical activity associated with eyeblinks propagates across the scalp and may therefore become part of the scalp potentials picked up by EEG electrodes, particularly at frontal sites. Ocular activity is routinely recorded during EEG acquisition by means of the electrooculogram (EOG). Various approaches exist for dealing with the transmission of EOG activity to frontal electrode sites. Epochs containing EOG activity can be excluded from further analysis, or correction algorithms may be employed in an attempt to remove EOG contamination from the EEG channels (Berg & Scherg, 1994; Gratton, Coles, & Donchin, 1983). Developmental considerations relating to the application of correction techniques have rarely been discussed. However, in EEG data from children aged between 5 and 12 years, Somsen and van Beek (1998) concluded that for EEG analysis in children aged 5–12 years, rejection from further analysis of epochs containing eyeblinks is preferable to the use of correction algorithms. This conclusion was based on the observation that in addition to removing EOG contamination, EOG correction also appeared to remove non-artifactual EEG at low frequencies, particularly from frontal electrode sites. In adults, it has been suggested that control of eye movements may not be necessary for correlational analyses involving frontal EEG asymmetry (Hagemann & Naumann, 2001), although this more liberal approach has not yet been utilized in developmental studies.

In ERP analyses, it may be necessary to use correction algorithms rather than rejection of eyeblink artifact because of the need to maximize the number of trials collected. Developmental ERP protocols are frequently shorter than similar protocols in adults, because infants and children will generally not tolerate the same experimental durations and numbers of trials as adults. In addition, more data tend to be lost due to motor artifact in developmental studies, hence the need to maximize the number of trials through blink correction rather than rejection. However, the ability to effectively regress blinks out of the EEG depends on the collection of a clean vertical EOG signal, which can be difficult with older infants and toddlers since they tend to pull at any electrodes that are placed on their face.

Gross motor movement is a significant source of artifact in the EEG from young children. Detection of such artifact may be done manually, or it may be done in software via the imposition of a fixed threshold. If the EEG at a specific time point goes out of this range, this time point is excluded from further analysis. Since the absolute amplitude of the EEG declines over infancy and childhood, the magnitude of this threshold is partly dependent on the age of the participants.

EEG Analysis of Band Power

The main approach to analyzing EEG is through the decomposition of the signal into component frequency bands, through the use of spectral analysis techniques. Approximate frequency ranges for EEG bands in adults are delta (1–3 Hz), theta (4–7 Hz), alpha (8–12 Hz), beta (13–30 Hz), and gamma (30–50 Hz), with the boundaries of corresponding bands being generally lower in infants and children (Marshall, Bar-Haim, & Fox, 2002). In work on social and emotional development in infants and children, most research has focused on the alpha band, since activity in this band is prominent from early infancy onwards, and its magnitude has been assumed to be inversely proportional to cortical activity. This pattern is based on the principle that high amplitude alpha reflects "idling" of sensory cortex. For this reason, alpha wave activity has been commonly used as a measure of regional brain activity, with decreased alpha power corresponding to increased neuronal activity (Davidson et al., 2000). Alpha rhythm is most pronounced at occipital and parietal recording sites, but can be recorded in a weaker form at other locations on the scalp, and is stronger when the eyes are closed and is desynchronized (blocked) when the eyes are opened.

There is some debate over the precise boundaries of the alpha band and how it changes over infancy and childhood. Some studies examining the developmental course of the EEG have extrapolated the commonly accepted adult frequency bands back to infancy and childhood in order to calculate the developmental trajectories of power in these conventional bands (e.g., John et al., 1980; Matousek & Petersen, 1973). However, given clear developmental changes in alpha peak frequency, it is likely that alternative frequency bands are needed for developmental work (Marshall et al., 2002). To aid in the selection of such frequency bands, there is a rich history of examining the development of the EEG of infants and young children (for reviews see Bell, 1998; Schmidt & Fox, 1998). In general, early studies such as those of Smith (1938), Lindsley (1938), and Henry (1944) focused on the development of the occipital alpha rhythm over infancy and childhood. Using visual quantification techniques, these authors noted the emergence of a 3–5 Hz occipital rhythm at around 3 months of age. The frequency range in which this oscillation occurred was seen to increase to around 6–7 Hz by the end of the first year. The oscillations in early infancy were labeled as "alpha" by these original authors because of a visual resemblance to the classical adult alpha rhythm. Lindsley (1938) observed that the infant alpha rhythm was blocked by visual stimulation even in infants a few months of age, suggesting a functional as well as a visual similarity between infant alpha at posterior sites and the adult alpha rhythm. Drawing in part on this early work, we showed that the 6–9 Hz band appears to be a suitable alpha band for use in developmental EEG research from the end of the first postnatal year into early childhood (Marshall et al., 2002). The functional meaning and interpretation of this band depends on age and the scalp region of interest, but the 6–9 Hz band in infants and young children appears to correspond to sensory rhythms in the alpha frequency range in adults. Orekhova and colleagues used a frequency band of 6.4–10.0 Hz as the "alpha range" in a sample of infants aged 7–12 months. They conceptualized this band as encompassing both posterior alpha rhythms (the classical alpha rhythm) and sensorimotor rhythms such as the "mu" rhythm, which is an alpha-range rhythm prominent at central electrode sites in infants (Orekhova, Stroganova, & Posikera, 2001). In adults, the classical mu rhythm occurs in the 7–13 Hz range, is maximal over central sensorimotor areas and is attenuated by voluntary movement and somatosensory stimulation (Gastaut, Dongier, & Courtois, 1954). It is also minimally affected by changes in visual stimulation and is considered to be a somatosensory alpha rhythm that is sensitive to somatic afferent input (Kuhlman, 1978). Although little research has addressed the development of the mu rhythm, there appears to be a functional relation between the 6–9 Hz oscillation at central sites in infancy and early childhood with the adult mu rhythm (Galkina & Boravova, 1996; Stroganova, Orekhova, & Posikera, 1999). In a longitudinal sample, Marshall et al. (2002) found that the relative contribution of 6–9 Hz power at central sites peaked at around 14–24 months of age, before declining into early childhood. This pattern suggests a decrease in the saliency of the central sensorimotor rhythm from infancy into early childhood, which may not be coincidental given that the second year after birth is a time of such intense development of locomotor ability.

Although researchers of social and emotional development have primarily considered alpha activity in their analyses of the EEG, other rhythms been examined in various contexts in the domains of social, emotional, and cognitive development. Theta rhythms have usually been considered in the context of cognitive development: for example, in learning disorders in older children (Chabot, di Michele, Prichep, & John, 2001), joint attention (Mundy, Card, & Fox, 2000), voluntary attention (Orekhova, Stroganova, & Posikera, 1999), and working memory processes in infants (Bell, 2002). Although phasic increases in theta activity during visual attention have been found to be positively correlated with positive affect (Orekhova, Stroganova, Posikera, & Malykh, 2003), high levels of tonic theta activity have been associated with developmental disorders of learning and attention (Barry, Clarke, & Johnstone, 2003). Tonically high levels of theta activity (especially the relative amount of theta in the power spectrum) have also been associated with environmental adversity such as early institutionalization (Marshall, Fox, & the BEIP Core Group, 2004) or sociocultural risk factors (Harmony et al., 1988). The finding of high relative theta is often accompanied by (and may be a result of) reductions in the amount of power in higher frequency bands (e.g., alpha and beta). Since the amount of low-frequency power (e.g., delta and theta power) in the EEG decreases with age, and the amount of higher-frequency power (e.g., alpha and beta) increases with age (Matousek & Petersen, 1973), this EEG pattern has been suggested to indicate a maturational lag in the development of the EEG (Matsuura et al., 1993). Alternatively, an excess of low-frequency power and a deficit in higher-frequency power has been proposed as an indicator of a state of chronic underarousal (Satterfield, Cantwell, & Satterfield, 1974). Both models have been subject to criticism, and distinguishing between these two possibilities is challenging, although recent work has shown promise in this respect (for review see Barry et al., 2003).

The beta frequency band has not generally been considered in work on social and emotional development, with a few exceptions (Marshall et al., 2004; McManis, Kagan, Snidman, & Woodward, 2002). Likewise, gamma activity has received little consideration, although infant gamma has been studied in relation to visual processing in both typically developing and developmentally disordered populations (Csibra, Davis, Spratling, & Johnson, 2000; Grice et al., 2001).

EEG FINDINGS IN THE STUDY OF SOCIAL AND EMOTIONAL DEVELOPMENT

EEG Asymmetry and Approach/Withdrawal Tendencies

Most developmental research examining EEG correlates of social or emotional behavior has focused on fear of the unfamiliar and approach/withdrawal tendencies in infancy and childhood. This research has been part of an integrative approach to understanding brain-behavior relations in emotional development that began in the 1980s and reached more sophistication in the 1990s (Kopp & Neufeld, 2003). Exemplifying this trend was the work of Davidson and Fox, who stressed the primacy of approach and withdrawal tendencies in developmental affective research and who developed a model for examining the brain substrates of such tendencies (Fox & Davidson, 1984). This model is based on the association of asymmetries in the frontal cortical region with the regulation of motivational responses to appetitive or aversive stimuli (Fox, 1991). Several studies have related individual differences in approach or withdrawal behaviors in infancy and childhood to patterns of asymmetrical activation (as indexed by asymmetries in EEG alpha band activity) over frontal electrode sites. Fox (1991, 1994) has argued that the functional significance of such frontal EEG asymmetry may be conceptualized in terms of motivational systems of approach and withdrawal. In this perspective, the left frontal region promotes appetitive, approach-directed emotional responses, while the right frontal region promotes withdrawal-directed responses to perceived aversive stimuli. Individual differences in frontal asymmetry may therefore serve as an index of relative approach and withdrawal motivations. At the present time, the precise neurophysiological basis of frontal EEG asymmetry has not been ascertained: Asymmetries in frontal EEG activation may be a function of asymmetries in projections from subcortical structures, or may be generated within the cortex itself (Davidson, 1998).

With infants and young children, a number of studies of frontal EEG asymmetry have focused on the tendency to approach or withdraw from novel situations or stimuli. A set of programmatic studies by Fox and Davidson first provided evidence for the relation between patterns of EEG recorded over left and right prefrontal regions and social and emotional behavior. For example, Davidson and Fox (1982) reported that 10-month-old infants watching a video of an actress crying or smiling displayed differential EEG patterns (greater right frontal EEG activation during the crying segments as reflected in lower alpha power on the right side). Fox and Davidson (1987) went on to show that 10-month-olds presented with approach of an unfamiliar adult displayed greater right frontal EEG activation and that the pattern of left/right asymmetry could be indexed to the type of facial expression of emotion that the infant displayed. In a subsequent study, Davidson and Fox (1989) reported that infant baseline EEG patterns at 10 months of age predicted their subsequent response to maternal separation. This study was the first to find individual differences in baseline EEG asymmetry in infants related to individual differences in social and emotional behavior.

In subsequent research, Fox and colleagues have expanded upon this work. In infants and toddlers, this research has focused on the electrophysiological correlates of behavioral inhibition to the unfamiliar (BI), which has mainly been assessed in laboratory paradigms that expose an infant or toddler to unfamiliar people, objects, and contexts. Infants who displayed a stable pattern of greater right frontal activation at baseline (resting) assessments across the first two years tended to be more inhibited at both 14 and 24 months of age compared with infants who exhibited a pattern of stable greater left frontal activation (Fox, Calkins, & Bell, 1994). We found that infants who went on to be consistently inhibited up to 4 years of age exhibited stronger right frontal activation asymmetry at 9 and 14 months of age than infants who were to become less inhibited (Fox et al., 2001). The latter group of infants exhibited weak right frontal activation at 9 months of age and greater left frontal activation at 14 months of age. Davidson reported similar findings in a selected group of 3-year-olds who were high, middle, or low on laboratory measures of behavioral inhibition (Davidson, 1994). The high BI group showed greater right frontal activation, while the low BI group showed greater left frontal activation. The middle BI group showed an asymmetry level that was intermediate between the two extreme groups.

Studies have also shown relations between high negative reactivity in early infancy, right frontal activation, and BI in later infancy. Infants who were selected at 4 months of age for high frequencies of motor behavior and negative affect tended to show greater right frontal activation at 9 months of age, and were more behaviorally inhibited at 14 months of age compared with infants who showed either high positive affect or low general levels of positive and negative reactivity at 4 months of age (Calkins, Fox, & Marshall, 1996).

Other recent work has provided more insights into the correlates of frontal EEG asymmetry in infants and older children. In 6-month-olds, higher cortisol levels were associated with greater right activation, and infants showing such a pattern showed higher levels of sadness during the approach of a stranger (Buss et al., 2003). Another study examined EEG asymmetry in a sample of 10–12 year olds who had been followed since 4 months of age. Children who had exhibited high levels of behavioral inhibition to the unfamiliar in laboratory assessments at 14 and 21 months and who had shown high levels of emotional and motor reactivity at 4 months of age were more likely to show greater right frontal activation in the late childhood assessment (McManis et al., 2002). A study in slightly younger children found that 8- and 11-year-old girls with anxiety disorders showed greater right frontal activation, while non-anxious girls showed no frontal asymmetry at 8 years of age, and left frontal activation at 11 years (Baving, Laucht, & Schmidt, 2002). This study points to the importance of examining sex differences in the relation of EEG asymmetries with behavior: Boys showed almost reversed patterns compared to girls, with healthy boys having a significantly greater right than left frontal activation, and anxious boys showing no frontal asymmetry at the age of 8 and greater left than right frontal activation at the age of 11.

We have examined EEG asymmetries in two different forms of non-social behavior in preschoolers: Social reticence and solitary-passive behavior, as assessed in laboratory playgroups of four children who were unfamiliar to each other. In contrast to solitary-passive children, who occupy themselves with solitary exploratory and constructive activities such as drawing and working on puzzles, reticent children remain visually focused and oriented towards the other children in the play group, yet do not join them in their activities. We replicated previous findings of an association between right frontal activation and social reticence in preschoolers, and we extended these findings to include solitary-passive play (Henderson, Marshall, Fox, & Rubin, 2004). Both socially reticent and solitary-passive children showed a pattern of resting greater right frontal activation suggesting that these different forms of solitude may share a common withdrawal motivation. These findings are consistent with models of frontal EEG asymmetry as an index of basic approach/withdrawal motivation. In addition, the asymmetry findings paralleled the pattern of group differences seen in concurrent maternal reports of shyness for these groups of children, in which reticent and solitary-passive children were both rated as being high in shyness. However, other EEG and autonomic evidence from this study suggested that while reticent children and solitary-passive children share a common withdrawal motivation, reticence is associated with a more aroused, vigilant physiological profile compared to solitary-passive behavior (see below).

Much of the work described above has focused on individual differences in EEG asymmetry in relation to temperamental variation in approach and withdrawal behaviors in infancy and childhood. Work from Geraldine Dawson's laboratory finding greater right frontal activation in infants of depressed mothers also suggests a role for the influence of the social environ-ment as well as temperament in EEG asymmetry (Dawson et al., 1999). In adults, Hagemann and colleagues carried out an elegant state-trait analysis of EEG asymmetry, concluding that there is indeed a state component to EEG asymmetry that may be empirically quantified (Hagemann, Naumann, Thayer, & Bartussek, 2002).

Although the work reviewed above has typically focused on the behav-ioral correlates of individual differences in frontal EEG asymmetries, it is important to note and that asymmetries in the EEG also occur in normative development. In our own laboratory, we find that among typically develop-ing infants and young children, there is a tendency for individuals to show greater left frontal activation in infancy and early childhood, and a slight right frontal activation advantage in middle childhood.

EEG Band Power and Affective Development

As well as asymmetries in the EEG signal, certain researchers have also exam-ined EEG band power in research on social and emotional development. Although EEG asymmetry has been associated with the tendency to approach or withdraw, it has also been proposed that generalized EEG activation (as indexed by reduced alpha power) across both hemispheres may be associ-ated with the intensity of arousal accompanying different motivational states (Dawson, 1994). Generalized EEG activation is considered a marker of a vig-ilant state, reflecting an increased readiness to detect incoming stimuli. In addition to displaying a pattern of relative right frontal EEG activation, tod-dlers displaying high levels of behavioral inhibition also displayed a pattern of increased EEG activation (decreased alpha activity) across the frontal regions of both hemispheres (Calkins et al., 1996). For inhibited toddlers or reticent preschoolers, a high level of generalized EEG activation may reflect elevated cortical arousal associated with increased social monitoring and vigilance in novel social situations.

In our work examining reticence and solitary passive behavior in pre-schoolers (see above), we found that although separate groups of reticent and solitary-passive groups both displayed a pattern of greater resting right frontal EEG activation, only the reticent group showed a pattern of reduced alpha power in the EEG across all measured scalp regions compared to the other children (Henderson et al., 2004). This finding was interpreted as reflecting elevated tonic arousal levels in reticent children, an interpretation that is consistent with Eysenck's model of adult personality in which he attributed individual differences in introversion to lowered thresholds for cortical arousal (Eysenck & Eysenck, 1985). It is also consistent with animal studies showing that generalized cortical activation can reflect activity in the central nucleus of the amygdala (Kapp, William, & Whalen, 1994), which is a key component in current neurobiological models of fear (Davis, 1997; LeDoux, 2000). These findings are consistent with a conceptualization of social reticence in preschool children as a reflection of hyper-vigilance in the face of novelty: Along with evidence from autonomic and behavioral assessments, the EEG findings in this study suggest that solitary-passive and reticent children share a common withdrawal motivation but that in reticent children, this style is accompanied by signs of a vigilant, anxious state in the face of novelty.

EVENT-RELATED POTENTIALS AND AFFECTIVE DEVELOPMENT

Event-related potentials (ERPs) are averaged EEG responses that are time-locked to specific events, such as the onset of discrete stimuli or a participant's reaction to a task demand. In ERP analysis, the variables that are typically of interest are amplitude and latency of specific components in the ERP waveform. Approaches to interpretation of ERP (e.g., amplitude or latency differences between trial types) typically come from the perspective of cognitive neuroscience (see Fabiani et al., 2000). However, in recent years there has been increasing interest in applying such models to the study of affect and the interaction among cognition, emotion, and sensory processing. Developmental aspects of this approach are being explored, and this promises to be a very fertile intersection of cognitive neuroscience with affective development. In the following section, we will describe some recent work carried out with auditory and visual ERPs in the domain of emotional development.

In the literature on neurobiological models of behavioral inhibition to the unfamiliar, one potentially important, but relatively uninvestigated area, is the relation of individual differences in initial stages of sensory processing to the expression of inhibited behavior in childhood (Marshall & Stevenson-Hinde, 2001). We examined the mismatch negativity (MMN) in the auditory ERP of socially withdrawn and control children aged 7–12 years (Bar-Haim et al., 2003). The MMN indexes a change-detection mechanism in primary auditory cortex, and it is elicited using auditory "oddball" paradigms without specific task demands (Picton et al., 2000a). In such paradigms, the presentation of frequent, repetitive stimulus (the "standard" stimulus) is interspersed with the occasional presentation of a less frequent "deviant" stimulus, which differs from the standard in its physical makeup, for example, the deviant may have a different duration or pitch frequency than the standard. The MMN is usually derived from a comparison of the ERPs to the deviant and standard stimuli, specifically by the computation of a difference waveform in which the ERP to the standard stimulus is subtracted from the ERP to the deviant stimulus. The MMN is often taken as the most negative point in this difference waveform within a given latency range, although its characteristics in terms of morphology and latency vary over infancy and childhood (Cheour et al., 1998; Gomot et al., 2000; Morr, Shafer, Kreuzer, & Kurtzberg, 2002; Shafer, Morr, Kreuzer, & Kurtzberg, 2000). We found that socially withdrawn children have reduced MMN amplitude compared with the more outgoing control children. Interestingly, socially withdrawn and control children did not differ on P50 gating, an earlier measure of sensory gating in the mid-latency auditory ERP (Marshall, Bar-Haim, & Fox, 2004). This finding may indicate that individual differences in the processing of novelty at the cortical level are more salient than the gating of irrelevant repetitive stimuli for understanding variations in approach and withdrawal tendencies. We are currently using a modified MMN paradigm with infants to assess whether temperamentally different infants show corresponding variability in the processing of discrete changes in the auditory environment. Such individual differences in sensory processing could either be a consequence of "top-down" influences by higher affective centers, or may reflect "bottom-up" differences in early processing that may feed forward to affect the later processing and evaluation of sensory information.

Although passive paradigms such as an MMN protocol are suitable for use with infants and young children, many ERP paradigms with older children take advantage of older children's capability to perform tasks that require a behavioral response. For example, the P3b component of the auditory and visual ERP is a component that has been widely studied in both adults and children. Tasks examining the P3b require the participant to respond when he or she recognizes a target stimulus that is embedded in a train of nontarget stimuli. In terms of social and emotional development, Pollak and colleagues have examined the processing of emotion information by maltreated and control children using ERPs collected during a visual oddball paradigm in which the target and nontarget stimuli were facial displays of anger, fear, or happiness (Pollak, Klorman, Thatcher, & Cicchetti, 2001). Compared with control children, maltreated children showed larger P3b amplitude when angry faces appeared as targets, but the two groups did not differ when targets were either happy or fearful facial expressions. Given that angry faces may be especially salient to maltreated children, Pollak and colleagues (2001) interpreted the results as indicating that aberrant emotional experiences associated with maltreatment may alter the allocation of attention and sensitivity that children develop to process specific emotion information.

One ERP component that has become of much interest to researchers examining the intersection of cognitive and emotional development is the error-related negativity (ERN), which peaks 80–100 ms after the execution of an incorrect response on speeded reaction time tasks (Falkenstein, Hoormann, Christ, & Hohnsbein, 2000). The ERN is thought to be an electrophysiological correlate of self-monitoring, or the output of an internal system for monitoring behavior. In this view, the appearance of the ERN represents a conflict between current actions and established standards, which alerts response systems that attempt to correct the error on future responses. From an individual difference perspective in adults, Luu, Collins, and Tucker (2000) examined the behavioral and electrophysiological responses on a flanker task of adults according to their level of self-reported negative affect. Adults high in negative affect tended to slow down after making mistakes on the flanker task. The increased self-monitoring signaled by this slowing was also reflected in an increased amplitude of the ERN in the first block of the protocol. Some contemporary models of the ERN stress the importance of the ERN as being a combination of self-monitoring and the emotional aspects of making an error. The ERN amplitude is reduced if speed is emphasized over accuracy in the task, and ERN amplitude is increased if accuracy is emphasized over speed. In other words, the salience of making an error affects the ERN amplitude. Various research groups are currently studying the ERN developmentally. For example, Henderson (2003) has shown that children showing high withdrawal motivations show increased amplitude of the ERN in the first block of a flanker task, and they also tended to show increasing slowing of reaction time following errors. In many ways, this parallels the findings of Luu et al. (2000) with adults high in negative affect, and points the way to further work in exploring the relation of the ERN to affective development.

ADVANCED TECHNIQUES FOR EEG AND ERP ANALYSIS: A DEVELOPMENTAL PERSPECTIVE

One particular area of interest to developmental researchers using scalp electrophysiology is the opportunity presented by recent developments in analysis techniques for EEG and ERP data. Johnson et al. (2001) discuss examples of such approaches to analyzing EEG and ERP data from infants, with a particular emphasis on high-density (64-channel) recordings. They outline two specific analysis techniques, independent component analysis (ICA), and source localization, both of which we will consider in more detail below.

ICA attempts to separate the EEG into mutually independent scalp maps, or components. The electrical activity in the EEG and the ERP signal arises from several sources, such as separate neural clusters, and includes artifact such as that generated by eye movement. Each source projects a unique electrophysiological pattern onto the scalp, with the EEG being the result of many of these patterns being superimposed on the scalp. ICA aims to identify components both temporally and spatially by examining covariation of the signals from different electrodes across time (Makeig et al., 1997). Two important clarifications are that ICA does not model the location of dipole generators within the head, and that the networks creating such independent components may be distributed brain networks rather than discrete regions of the cortex. ICA is one of a family of multivariate techniques that have been used for analyzing EEG and ERP datasets. For example, principal components analysis (PCA) separates up to second-order statistics, whereas ICA separates data using higher-order statistics. PCA has been employed in developmental ERP studies (Molfese et al., 2001), but use of ICA with infants and children is still in its very beginning stages. One methodological consideration of ICA is that electrode arrays with fewer than 32 electrodes are usually considered too sparse for practical use of ICA with EEG or ERP data.

The second technique described by Johnson et al. (2001) is that of source localization, which aims to identify the location of dipoles that are responsible for the generation of ERP components or of the EEG signal in a specific frequency band. Source localization can potentially be combined with the use of ICA, for example, a temporally stable ERP component can be derived from ICA and then the brain source of this component modeled using source localization. One approach to source localization is Brain Electrical Source Analysis (Scherg & Berg, 1996; Scherg & Picton, 1991), which has been used to a limited extent in developmental work, including the application to auditory ERP components in infants (Dehaene-Lambertz & Baillet, 1998). Other tomographical approaches include Low-Resolution Electrical Tomographic Analysis, or LORETA (Pascual-Marqui, Esslen, Kochi, & Lehmann, 2002), which has been also only utilized in a very small number of developmental studies. For example, a recent paper employed LORETA to localize the mismatch negativity component in the auditory ERP to a source generator in the temporal lobe for both children and adults (Maurer, Bucher, Brem, & Brandeis, 2003). Although dense electrode arrays (64, 128, or 256 sites) are usually considered to be optimal or even essential for the application of source localization to EEG and ERP date, LORETA has been successfully used with relatively sparse electrode arrays in adults (e.g., 28 sites, Pizzagalli et al., 2001).

There are a number of major caveats about applying localization techniques to developmental EEG or ERP data. One fundamental limitation of scalp EEG measurement is that even with a very large number of electrodes, a specific patterning of the scalp EEG signal could be explained by many different distributions of generators within the brain. This example is commonly referred to as the "inverse problem." Methods such as BESA and LORETA employ sophisticated algorithms to take a "best guess" at underlying dipoles, but the precision of localization does not rival other techniques, such as fMRI. There are also many rather complex assumptions (e.g., about the physical parameters of the head) used in source localization that need to be clearly understood by the developmental researcher, who must also be aware that such assumptions may not necessarily translate well from adult work (where source localization techniques were developed) to data from infants and children. In addition, source localization may be supplementary to the questions of interest, which may involve simply asking whether different experimental conditions or groups of individuals differ with respect to EEG power spectral amplitude over specific scalp locations, or with respect to ERP amplitudes or latencies. Conventional EEG and ERP analyses in social and emotional development typically consider data from a relatively small number of electrode sites, and examine individual differences in EEG spectral power or amplitude/latency of ERP components to different trial types. It may not be the task of researchers in social and emotional development to localize specific electrophysiological phenomena in the cortex. Instead, these researchers may draw on related work in the cognitive neurosciences that uses multiple methodologies (e.g., fMRI, MEG) to localize specific electrophysiological and behavioral phenomena in the brain. Using this knowledge, developmental researchers can focus their questions more clearly by the consideration of known cognitive correlates and neurophysiological underpinnings of the measure that they are studying. That said, there is a good deal of work to be done on both sides of this integration, including the application of advanced analysis techniques and multi-method approaches to electrophysiological measures in early development.

CONCLUDING COMMENTS

Use of EEG and ERP measures in the study of affective development continues to provide a vital source of information to accompany observational and self/parent-reported measures of infant and child behavior. In this chapter, we have attempted to introduce the reader to some of the particular challenges faced by researchers using EEG and ERP measures in the study of social and emotional development in infancy and childhood. We have documented a number of salient research findings in this area, mostly drawn from work on EEG frontal asymmetry, EEG power, and certain components of the auditory and visual ERP. The temporal precision of EEG and ERP techniques is unparalleled, and their lack of spatial resolution has not been a major impediment in addressing a variety of research questions in the area of social and emotional development. In addition, with fMRI as a feasible tool for examining brain dynamics in older children, the integration of electrophysiological techniques with functional neuroimaging is an exciting possibility for developmental researchers (de Haan & Thomas, 2002).

References

Bar-Haim, Y., Marshall, P. J., Fox, N. A., Schorr, E. A., & Gordon-Salant, S. (2003). Mismatch negativity in socially withdrawn children. *Biological Psychiatry, 54,* 17–24.

Barry, R. J., Clarke, A. R., & Johnstone, S. J. (2003). A review of electrophysiology in attention-deficit/hyperactivity disorder: I. Qualitative and quantitative electroencephalography. *Clinical Neurophysiology, 114,* 171–183.

Baving, L., Laucht, M., & Schmidt, M. H. (2002). Frontal brain activation in anxious school children. *Journal of Child Psychology and Psychiatry, 43,* 265–274.

Bell, M. A. (1998). The ontogeny of the EEG during infancy and childhood: Implications for cognitive development. In B. Barreau (Ed.), *Neuroimaging in child developmental disorders* (pp. 97–111). Berlin: Springer.

Bell, M. A. (2002). Power changes in infant EEG frequency bands during a spatial working memory task. *Psychophysiology, 39,* 450–458.

Berg, P., & Scherg, M. (1994). A multiple source approach to the correction of eye artifacts. *Electroencephalography and Clinical Neurophysiology, 90,* 229–241.

Buss, K. A., Schumacher, J. R., Dolski, I., Kalin, N. H., Goldsmith, H. H., & Davidson, R. J. (2003). Right frontal brain activity, cortisol, and withdrawal behavior in 6-month-old infants. *Behavioral Neuroscience, 117,* 11–20.

Calkins, S. D., Fox, N. A., & Marshall, T. R. (1996). Behavioral and physiological antecedents of inhibited and uninhibited behavior. *Child Development, 67,* 523–540.

Chabot, R. J., di Michele, F., Prichep, L., & John, E. R. (2001). The clinical role of computerized EEG in the evaluation and treatment of learning and attention disorders in children and adolescents. *Journal of Neuropsychiatry and Clinical Neuroscience, 13,* 171–186.

Cheour, M., Alho, K., Ceponiene, R., Reinikainen, K., Sainio, K., Pohjavuori, M., Aaltonen, O., & Naatanen, R. (1998). Maturation of mismatch negativity in infants. *International Journal of Psychophysiology, 29,* 217–226.

Csibra, G., Davis, G., Spratling, M. W., & Johnson, M. H. (2000). Gamma oscillations and object processing in the infant brain. *Science, 290,* 1582–1585.

Cutmore, T. R., & James, D. A. (1999). Identifying and reducing noise in psychophysiological recordings. *International Journal of Psychophysiology, 32,* 129–150.

Davidson, R. J. (1994). Temperament, affective style, and frontal lobe asymmetry. In G. Dawson & K. W. Fischer (Eds.), *Human behavior and the developing brain* (pp. 518–536). New York: Guilford.

Davidson, R. J. (1998). Anterior electrophysiological asymmetries, emotion, and depression: Conceptual and methodological conundrums. *Psychophysiology, 35,* 607–614.

Davidson, R. J., & Fox, N. A. (1982). Asymmetrical brain activity discriminates between positive and negative affective stimuli in human infants. *Science, 218,* 1235–1237.

Davidson, R. J., & Fox, N. A. (1989). Frontal brain asymmetry predicts infants' response to maternal separation. *Journal of Abnormal Psychology, 98,* 127–131.

Davidson, R. J., Jackson, D. C., & Larson, C. L. (2000). Human electroencephalography. In J. T. Cacioppo & L. G. Tassinary (Eds.), *Handbook of psychophysiology* (2nd ed., pp. 27–52). New York: Cambridge University Press.

Davis, M. (1997). Neurobiology of fear responses: The role of the amygdala. *Journal of Neuropsychiatry and Clinical Neuroscience, 9,* 382–402.

Dawson, G. (1994). Frontal electroencephalographic correlates of individual differences in emotion expression in infants: A brain systems perspective on emotion. *Monographs of the Society for Research in Child Development, 59,* 135–151.

Dawson, G., Frey, K., Self, J., Panagiotides, H., Hessl, D., Yamada, E., & Rinaldi, J. (1999). Frontal brain electrical activity in infants of depressed and nondepressed mothers: Relation to variations in infant behavior. *Developmental and Psychopathology, 11,* 589–605.

De Haan, M., & Thomas, K. M. (2002). Applications of ERP and fMRI techniques to developmental science. *Developmental Science, 5,* 335–343.

Dehaene-Lambertz, G., & Baillet, S. (1998). A phonological representation in the infant brain. *Neuroreport, 9,* 1885–1888.

Eysenck, H. J., & Eysenck, M. W. (1985). *Personality and individual differences: A natural science approach.* New York: Plenum.

Fabiani, M., Gratton, G., & Coles, M. G. H. (2000). Event-related brain potentials. In J. T. Cacioppo & L. G. Tassinary (Eds.), *Handbook of psychophysiology* (2nd ed., pp. 53–84). New York: Cambridge University Press.

Falkenstein, M., Hoormann, J., Christ, S., & Hohnsbein, J. (2000). ERP components on reaction errors and their functional significance: A tutorial. *Biological Psychology, 51,* 87–107.

Fox, N. A. (1991). If it's not left, it's right: Electroencephalograph asymmetry and the development of emotion. *American Psychologist, 46,* 863–872.

Fox, N. A. (1994). Dynamic cerebral processes underlying emotion regulation. *Monographs of the Society for Research in Child Development, 59,* 152–166.

Fox, N. A., Calkins, S. D., & Bell, M. A. (1994). Neural plasticity and development in the first two years of life: Evidence from cognitive and socioemotional domains of research. *Development and Psychopathology, 6,* 677–696.

Fox, N. A., & Davidson, R. J. (1984). Hemispheric substates of affect: A developmental approach. In N. A. Fox & R. J. Davidson (Eds.), *The psychobiology of affective development* (pp. 353–381). Hillsdale, NJ: Lawrence Erlbaum Associates

Fox, N. A., & Davidson, R. J. (1987). Electroencephalogram asymmetry in response to the approach of a stranger and maternal separation in 10-month-old infants. *Developmental Psychology, 23,* 233–240.

Fox, N. A., Henderson, H. A., Rubin, K. H., Calkins, S. D., & Schmidt, L. A. (2001). Continuity and discontinuity of behavioral inhibition and exuberance: Psychophysiological and behavioral influences across the first four years of life. *Child Development, 72,* 1–21.

Fox, N. A., Rubin, K. H., Calkins, S. D., Marshall, T. R., Coplan, R. J., Porges, S. W., Long, J. M., & Stewart, S. (1995). Frontal activation asymmetry and social competence at four years of age. *Child Development, 66,* 1770–1784.

Fox, N. A., Schmidt, L. A., & Henderson, H. A. (2000). Developmental psychophysiology: Conceptual and methodological perspectives. In J. T. Cacioppo & L. G. Tassinary (Eds.), *Handbook of psychophysiology* (2nd ed., pp. 665–686). New York: Cambridge University Press

Galkina, N. S., & Boravova, A. I. (1996). Formation of electroencephalographic mu- and alpha-rhythms in children during the second to third years of life. *Human Physiology,* 540–545.

Gastaut, H., Dongier, M., & Courtois, G. (1954). On the significance of "wicket rhythms" in psychosomatic medicine. *Electroencephalography and Clinical Neurophysiology, 6,* 687.

Gomot, M., Giard, M. H., Roux, S., Barthelemy, C., & Bruneau, N. (2000). Maturation of frontal and temporal components of mismatch negativity (MMN) in children. *Neuroreport, 11,* 3109–3112.

Gratton, G., Coles, M. G., & Donchin, E. (1983). A new method for off-line removal of ocular artifact. *Electroencephalography and Clinical Neurophysiology, 55,* 468–484.

Grice, S. J., Spratling, M. W., Karmiloff-Smith, A., Halit, H., Csibra, G., de Haan, M., & Johnson, M. H. (2001). Disordered visual processing and oscillatory brain activity in autism and Williams syndrome. *Neuroreport, 12,* 2697–2700.

Hagemann, D., & Naumann, E. (2001). The effects of ocular artifacts on (lateralized) broadband power in the EEG. *Clinical Neurophysiology, 112,* 215–231.

Hagemann, D., Naumann, E., & Thayer, J. F. (2001). The quest for the EEG reference revisited: A glance from brain asymmetry research. *Psychophysiology, 38,* 847–857.

Hagemann, D., Naumann, E., Thayer, J. F., & Bartussek, D. (2002). Does resting electroencephalograph asymmetry reflect a trait? An application of latent state-trait theory. *Journal of Personality and Social Psychology, 82,* 619–641.

Harmony, T., Alvarez, A., Pascual, R., Ramos, A., Marosi, E., Diaz de Leon, A. E., Valdes, P., & Becker, J. (1988). EEG maturation on children with different economic and psychosocial characteristics. *International Journal of Neuroscience, 41,* 103–113.

Henderson, H. A. (2003). *Temperamental contributions to problem solving: Affective and cognitive processes.* Paper presented at the Biennial Meeting of the Society for Research in Child Development, Tampa, FL.

Henderson, H. A., Marshall, P. J., Fox, N. A., & Rubin, K. H. (2004). Psychophysiological and behavioral evidence for varying forms and functions of nonsocial behavior in preschoolers. *Child Development, 75,* 251–263.

Henry, J. R. (1944). Electroencephalograms of normal children. *Monographs of the Society for Research in Child Development, 9.*

John, E. R., Ahn, H., Prichep, L., Trepetin, M., Brown, D., & Kaye, H. (1980). Developmental equations for the electroencephalogram. *Science, 210,* 1255–1258.

Johnson, M. H., de Haan, M., Oliver, A., Smith, W., Hatzakis, H., Tucker, L. A., et al. (2001). Recording and analyzing high–density event-related potentials with infants. Using the Geodesic sensor net. *Developmental Neuropsychology, 19,* 295–323.

Junghofer, M., Elbert, T., Tucker, D. M., & Rockstroh, B. (2000). Statistical control of artifacts in dense array EEG/MEG studies. *Psychophysiology, 37,* 523–532.

Kapp, B. S. S., William F. & Whalen, P. J. (1994). Effects of electrical stimulation of the amygdaloid central nucleus on neocortical arousal in the rabbit. *Behavioral Neuroscience, 108*, 81–93.

Kopp, C. B., & Neufeld, S. J. (2003). Emotional development during infancy. In R. J. Davidson, K. R. Scherer & H. H. Goldsmith (Eds.), *Handbook of affective sciences* (pp. 347–374). New York: Oxford University Press.

Kuhlman, W. N. (1978). Functional topography of the human mu rhythm. *Electroencephalography and Clinical Neurophysiology, 44*, 83–93.

Lawson, J. S., Galin, H., Adams, S. J., Brunet, D. G., Criollo, M., & MacCrimmon, D. J. (2003). Artifacting reliability in QEEG topographic maps. *Clinical Neurophysiology, 114*, 883–888.

LeDoux, J. E. (2000). Emotion circuits in the brain. *Annual Review of Neuroscience, 23*, 155–184.

Lindsley, D. B. (1938). Electrical potentials of the brain in children and adults. *Journal of Genetic Psychology, 19*, 285–306.

Luu, P., Collins, P., & Tucker, D. M. (2000). Mood, personality, and self-monitoring: Negative affect and emotionality in relation to frontal lobe mechanisms of error monitoring. *Journal of Experimental Psychology: General, 129*, 43–60.

Makeig, S., Jung, T. P., Bell, A. J., Ghahremani, D., & Sejnowski, T. J. (1997). Blind separation of auditory event-related brain responses into independent components. *Proceedings of the National Academy of Sciences, 94*, 10979–10984.

Marshall, D. H., & Fox, N. A. (2001). Electroencephalographic assessment and human brain maturation: A window into emotional and cognitive development in infancy. In L. T. Singer & P. S. Zeskind (Eds.), *Biobehavioral assessment of the infant* (pp. 341–360). New York: Guilford Press.

Marshall, P. J., Bar-Haim, Y., & Fox, N. A. (2002). Development of the EEG from 5 months to 4 years of age. *Clinical Neurophysiology, 113*, 1199–1208.

Marshall, P. J., Bar-Haim, Y., & Fox, N. A. (2004). The development of P50 gating in the auditory event-related potential. *International Journal of Psychophysiology, 51*, 135–141.

Marshall, P. J., Fox, N. A., & The BEIP Core Group. (2004). A comparison of the electroencephalogram (EEG) between institutionalized and community children in Romania. *Journal of Cognitive Neuroscience, 16*, 1327–1338. See also erratum in *Journal of Cognitive Neuroscience, 19*, 173–174.

Marshall, P. J., & Stevenson-Hinde, J. (2001). Behavioral inhibition: Physiological correlates. In W. R. Crozier & L. E. Alden, (Eds.), *International Handbook of Social Anxiety* (pp. 53–76). Chicester: John Wiley.

Matousek, M., & Petersen, I. (1973). Automatic evaluation of EEG background activity by means of age-dependent EEG quotients. *Electroencephalography and Clinical Neurophysiology, 35*, 603–612.

Matsuura, M., Okubo, Y., Toru, M., Kojima, T., He, Y., Hou, Y., Shen, Y., & Lee, C. K. (1993). A cross-national EEG study of children with emotional and behavioral problems: A WHO collaborative study in the Western Pacific Region. *Biological Psychiatry, 34*, 59–65.

Maurer, U., Bucher, K., Brem, S., & Brandeis, D. (2003). Development of the automatic mismatch response: From frontal positivity in kindergarten children to the mismatch negativity. *Clinical Neurophysiology, 114*, 808–817.

McManis, M. H., Kagan, J., Snidman, N. C., & Woodward, S. A. (2002). EEG asymmetry, power, and temperament in children. *Developmental Psychobiology, 41,* 169–177.

Molfese, D. L., Molfese, V. J., & Kelly, S. (2001). The use of brain electrophysiology techniques to study language: A basic guide for the beginning consumer of electrophysiology information. *Learning Disability Quarterly, 24,* 177–188.

Moretti, D. V., Babiloni, F., Carducci, F., Cincotti, F., Remondini, E., Rossini, P. M., Salinari, S., & Babiloni, C. (2003). Computerized processing of EEG-EOG-EMG artifacts for multi-centric studies in EEG oscillations and event-related potentials. *International Journal of Psychophysiology, 47,* 199–216.

Morr, M. L., Shafer, V. L., Kreuzer, J. A., & Kurtzberg, D. (2002). Maturation of mismatch negativity in typically developing infants and preschool children. *Ear and Hearing, 23,* 118–136.

Mundy, P., Card, J., & Fox, N. (2000). EEG correlates of the development of infant joint attention skills. *Developmental Psychobiology, 36,* 325–338.

Nuwer, M. R., Comi, G., Emerson, R., Fuglsang-Frederiksen, A., Guerit, J. M., Hinrichs, H., et al. (1998). IFCN standards for digital recording of clinical EEG: International Federation of Clinical Neurophysiology. *Electroencephalography and Clinical Neurophysiology, 106,* 259–261.

Orekhova, E. V., Stroganova, T. A., & Posikera, I. N. (1999). Theta synchronization during sustained anticipatory attention in infants over the second half of the first year of life. *International Journal of Psychophysiology, 32,* 151–172.

Orekhova, E. V., Stroganova, T. A., & Posikera, I. N. (2001). Alpha activity as an index of cortical inhibition during sustained internally controlled attention in infants. *Clinical Neurophysiology, 112,* 740–749.

Orekhova, E. V., Stroganova, T. A., Posikera, I. N., & Malykh, S. B. (2003). Heritability and "environmentability" of electroencephalogram in infants: The twin study. *Psychophysiology, 40,* 727–741.

Pascual-Marqui, R. D., Esslen, M., Kochi, K., & Lehmann, D. (2002). Functional imaging with low-resolution brain electromagnetic tomography (LORETA): A review. *Methods and Findings in Experimental and Clinical Pharmacology, 24 Suppl C,* 91–95.

Picton, T. W., Alain, C., Otten, L., Ritter, W., & Achim, A. (2000a). Mismatch negativity: Different water in the same river. *Audiology and Neurootology, 5,* 111–139.

Picton, T. W., Bentin, S., Berg, P., Donchin, E., Hillyard, S. A., Johnson, R., Jr., Miller, G. A., Ritter, W., Ruchkin, D. S., Rugg, M. D., & Taylor, M. J. (2000b). Guidelines for using human event-related potentials to study cognition: Recording standards and publication criteria. *Psychophysiology, 37,* 127–152.

Pivik, R. T., Broughton, R. J., Coppola, R., Davidson, R. J., Fox, N., & Nuwer, M. R. (1993). Guidelines for the recording and quantitative analysis of electroencephalographic activity in research contexts. *Psychophysiology, 30,* 547–558.

Pizzagalli, D., Pascual-Marqui, R. D., Nitschke, J. B., Oakes, T. R., Larson, C. L., Abercrombie, H. C., Schaefer, S. M., Koger, J. V., Benca, R. M., & Davidson, R. J. (2001). Anterior cingulate activity as a predictor of degree of treatment response in major depression: Evidence from brain electrical tomography analysis. *American Journal of Psychiatry, 158,* 405–415.

Pollak, S. D., Klorman, R., Thatcher, J. E., & Cicchetti, D. (2001). P3b reflects maltreated children's reactions to facial displays of emotion. *Psychophysiology, 38,* 267–274.

Satterfield, J. H., Cantwell, D. P., & Satterfield, B. T. (1974). Pathophysiology of the hyperactive child syndrome. *Archives of General Psychiatry, 31*, 839–844.

Scherg, M., & Berg, P. (1996). New concepts of brain source imaging and localization. *Electroencephalography and Clinical Neurophysiology, 46*, 127–137.

Scherg, M., & Picton, T. W. (1991). Separation and identification of event-related potential components by brain electric source analysis. *Electroencephalography and Clinical Neurophysiology, 42*, 24–37.

Schmidt, L. A., & Fox, N. A. (1998). Electrophysiological studies I: Quantitative electroencephalography. In C. E. Coffey & R. A. Brumback (Eds.), *Textbook of pediatric neuropsychiatry: Section II. Neuropsychiatric assessment of the child and adolescent* (pp. 315–329). Washington, DC: American Psychiatric Press.

Shafer, V. L., Morr, M. L., Kreuzer, J. A., & Kurtzberg, D. (2000). Maturation of mismatch negativity in school-age children. *Ear and Hearing, 21*, 242–251.

Smith, J. R. (1938). The electroencephalogram during normal infancy and childhood: The nature and growth of the alpha waves. *Electroencephalography and Clinical Neurophysiology, 53*, 455–469.

Somsen, R. J., & van Beek, B. (1998). Ocular artifacts in children's EEG: Selection is better than correction. *Biological Psychology, 48*, 281–300.

Stern, R. M., Ray, W. J., & Quigley, K. S. (2003). *Psychophysiological recording*. New York: Oxford University Press.

Stroganova, T. A., Orekhova, E. V., & Posikera, I. N. (1999). EEG alpha rhythm in infants. *Clinical Neurophysiology, 110*, 997–1012.

Tenke, C. E., & Kayser, J. (2001). A convenient method for detecting electrolyte bridges in multichannel electroencephalogram and event-related potential recordings. *Clinical Neurophysiology, 112*, 545–550.

6 The Use of the Electroencephalogram in Research on Cognitive Development

Martha Ann Bell and Christy D. Wolfe

INTRODUCTION

The field of developmental psychophysiology provides the methodology for examination of age-related changes in the functioning of the brain. The electroencephalogram (EEG) is an efficient, non-invasive, and relatively inexpensive method for studying brain development in infants and children and for relating brain development to changes in cognitive behaviors. Utilizing EEG allows for examination of these developmental changes without dramatic interference with normal ongoing behaviors. All of these characteristics make the EEG one of the more favorable methods for investigating brain-behavior relations with young populations (Casey & de Haan, 2002; Taylor & Baldeweg, 2002).

The EEG discussed in this chapter is sometimes called "quantitative EEG" and is used for basic research on brain activity during cognition or emotion and for basic research on brain maturation. Typically, quantitative EEGs used for basic research are digital records that are converted from the time domain to the frequency domain by means of spectral analysis, yielding spectral power at specific frequencies, or by means of phase coherence analysis, yielding the degree to which the EEG signals at two distinct scalp locations are in phase at a specific frequency. This quantitative methodology differs from the traditional use of the EEG in the clinical setting to localize seizures or tumors. It also differs from event-related potentials, or ERPs, which are brain electrical responses that are time locked to a specific set of stimuli. ERP methodology and research is reviewed in Chapters 2, 3, and 4 of this volume.

Thus, the purpose of this chapter is to highlight the value of the EEG for the study of cognitive development in infancy and childhood. We begin with an overview of the EEG and, then, a review of the classic EEG development literature to highlight the longstanding history of this methodology in the study of brain maturation. We then examine the recent use of the EEG in studies of infant, toddler, and child cognition by providing selective examples of research findings from the developmental psychophysiology literature that highlight our interests in working memory. It is our intent to provide the reader with basic information for synthesizing research in this exciting area of developmental science.

EEG Overview

The EEG represents spontaneous electrical activity recorded from the scalp, with the assumption that the origin of these electrical signals is in the brain itself. Although once thought to be the product of action potentials, there now is general agreement among psychophysiologists that the scalp signal is the summation of postsynaptic potentials (Nelson & Monk, 2001). Although the EEG signal is spontaneous, it also is context-related, with the signal generated during quiet rest very different from that generated during mental activity. The EEG signal has excellent temporal resolution, potentially on the order of hundreds of milliseconds or better, depending on the frequency examined. Thus, postsynaptic changes are reflected rapidly in the EEG, making this methodology outstanding for tracking rapid shifts in behavior.

Limitations of EEG

Although EEG is one of the more favorable brain imaging methods for use with infants and children, there are some drawbacks to this methodology. We note these limitations early in this chapter so that the reader can keep them in mind as we review the classic infant/child EEG development literature and some of the most current EEG developmental research. Although the EEG signal has excellent temporal resolution, it has poor spatial resolution. There are at least three reasons for this shortcoming (Davidson, Jackson, & Larson, 2000). First, even with multiple electrodes, there are gaps between electrodes on the scalp. These gaps disallow a complete electrical mapping of the scalp. Second, the skull behaves like a low-pass filter and distorts the underlying brain electrical activity over a large area of the scalp. Finally, scalp potentials are likely generated by multiple groupings of cortical and subcortical generators spread across a relatively wide area. Thus, an electrode is likely detecting electrical activity generated from non-local groups of neurons.

Another drawback is that the EEG is prone to some distortion because of motor movement. Artifact may result from such gross motor activity as motion of the arms and legs, or from motor activity as fine as a simple eye

movement. Although adult research participants are generally cooperative
when requested to sit without moving, young children often have difficulty
in refraining from gross motor movements. Researchers must ensure that
their expectations for the behavior of young children in EEG paradigms
are developmentally appropriate. Researchers who conduct EEG research
with infants must take special care in designing cognitive tasks that result in
behavioral stilling for the infants.

EEG Rhythms

There is a rhythmic quality to the EEG signal, although there is some disagreement as to the source of this rhythmicity. Some researchers view the
EEG rhythms as driven by the thalamus, whereas others propose that the
drivers reside in the pyramidal cells in the cortex (Davidson et al., 2000).
In adults, the EEG rhythmicities are reliably observed and are defined in
terms of the number of cycles per second (frequency) and size of the signal
(amplitude).

The *alpha rhythm* is the predominant frequency band and is readily observable during quiet rest, especially when the eyes are closed. This signal cycles
at 8–13 Hz and has a relatively large amplitude. When an adult is engaged in
cognitive activity, the alpha rhythm is no longer visible, especially at specific
electrode sites. These sites are dependent upon the nature of the cognitive
task. For example, engagement in a verbal task tends to be associated with
the attenuation of alpha activity in frontal and central areas of the left hemisphere, whereas engagement in a spatial task tends to be associated with
attenuation of alpha activity in parietal areas of the right hemisphere (e.g.,
Bell & Fox, 2003; Davidson, Chapman, Chapman, & Henriques, 1990).

During adult cognition and the attenuation of the alpha rhythm, it appears
that alpha activity is replaced by the *beta rhythm*, which cycles at 18–30 Hz
and has smaller amplitude than alpha. Beta activity signifies alertness or
attentiveness. Brain electrical activity in the 30–70 Hz range or higher is designated as *gamma rhythm*. Gamma activity in adults appears to be associated
with the integration of stimuli into a logical whole, with gamma activity differentiating between important and inconsequential stimuli (Stern, Ray, &
Quigley, 2001).

Theta rhythms cycle at 4–8 Hz and also figure prominently in cognitive
activity. Adults tend to exhibit increases in theta activity during memory and
attention tasks, with these increases even greater for correct as opposed to
incorrect responses (e.g., Burgess & Gruzelier, 2000; Klimesch, Doppelmayr,
Schimke, & Ripper, 1997). Interestingly, theta also is associated with drowsiness or sleep onset. These disparate findings have led to the suggestion that

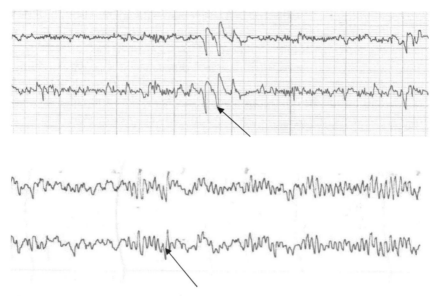

Figure 6.1. Adult (top) and infant (bottom) EEG tracings from scalp electrodes placed on the forehead (Fp1, Fp2). Arrows point out an eye blink in each record.

there are two different types of theta activity (Schacter, 1977). One type of theta associated with drowsiness and the other is associated with attention and active cognitive processing, leading to the possibility that these two types of theta activity have different sources.

Delta rhythm is of low frequency (1–4 Hz) and is associated with sleep in adults, especially deep sleep. Of interest is that this particular frequency range is the prominent frequency in infants during the first few months of postnatal life, gradually developing into the adult-like frequency patterns over time (Bell, 1998a). We trace the development of the EEG in the sections below. First, we summarize the classic infant and child EEG literature and then we report on current work on EEG and cognitive development in infancy and childhood.

Classic EEG Development Literature

By placing electrodes on the scalp, Berger (1929) was the first to demonstrate that the EEG was related to brain activity rather than other physiological processes. It was Berger's (1932) publication highlighting EEG differences among infants, children, and adults that began the interest in developmental aspects of these scalp recordings. These differences are readily observable in EEG tracings from our research lab (see Figure 6.1). Infant EEG has much greater amplitude, as evidenced by the eye blinks highlighted in these two tracings. Infant EEG also cycles at a lower frequency than adult EEG, with the average adult frequency being 10 Hz and the average infant frequency ranging from 3 Hz to 7 Hz, depending upon the infant's age. From Berger's time, researchers have assumed that EEG differences among infants, children, and adults reflect differences in brain maturation. Working with paper tracings and keen eyesight, these early researchers studied EEG developmental changes across the scalp.

Developmental Changes in the EEG During Infancy

We have completed a comprehensive review of the classic longitudinal and cross-sectional studies that are the basis of our current knowledge of EEG development during infancy and childhood (for these details, see Bell, 1998a). There have been four longitudinal samples of EEG recorded from awake infants in the classic EEG literature. Two of these were accomplished in the 1930s and appear to have been a result of Berger's (1932) publication examining EEG differences between children and adults. The EEG samples collected by Smith (1938a, 1938b, 1939, 1941) and by Lindsley (1939; later republished by Henry, 1944) were examined by visual analysis and give us identical information as to the developmental changes associated with the EEG. Both noted the emergence of a rhythm over the occipital area around 3 months of age and termed this rhythm "alpha" because its waveform is visually similar to the adult 8–13 Hz alpha wave. Measured by hand, Smith and Lindsley reported that this waveform oscillated at 3–5 Hz. Each speculated as to the significance of the appearance of this oscillation and agreed that it was associated with visual capacities of the occipital cortex (Lindsley, 1939; Smith, 1938b). The Lindsley (1939) and Smith (1938b, 1939, 1941) EEG data also showed that this occipital activity gradually increased to 6–7 Hz by 12 months of age. In addition to the occipital rhythm, Smith (1941) noted the emergence of a 7 Hz signal at central scalp locations around 3 months of age and hypothesized links between the appearance of this rhythm, the disappearance of primitive reflexes, and the emergence of voluntary muscular control associated with reaching. This central activity remained stable for several months, not increasing in frequency until 10 months of age (Smith, 1941).

With the aid of technological advancements, the other two longitudinal samples of EEG in awake infants were measured mechanically in terms of frequency and amplitude. The EEG data collected by Hagne (1968, 1972) and Mizuno (Mizuno, Yamaguchi, Iinuma, & Arakawa, 1970) were accomplished via frequency analysis that divided the EEG into preselected frequency bands, but these researchers gave an account of EEG frequency development during the first postnatal year that was consistent with the reports of Smith and Lindsley. Hagne (1968, 1972) reported a decrease in amplitude at 1.5–3.5 Hz, with a corresponding increase in amplitude at 3.5–7.5 Hz during the first year at central, temporal, parietal, and occipital locations. Reporting on EEG recorded at the right occipital scalp location, Mizuno and colleagues (1970) showed a predominance of 2.0–4.15 Hz activity at 3 months and 3.5–8.6 Hz activity at 12 months. Interestingly, Hagne (1968) made note of individual differences in amplitude in same-age EEG recordings. She also stated that these individual differences persisted throughout the first year.

Mizuno and colleagues (1970) made detailed observations of each infant's physical development, noting weight, height, head and chest circumference, and physical milestones (e.g., holding up head, sitting, standing, walking) at each EEG recording session. No attempt was made, however, to relate physical development with EEG maturation. Hagne (1972), on the other hand, did neurological and developmental assessments on each infant in association with each EEG recording. She reported correlations between peak frequency (frequency where the infant displayed the greatest amplitude) at parietal/occipital scalp locations and total score on the Griffiths Scale of Mental Development at 4 months, and between peak frequency at central scalp locations and Griffiths score at 10 months of age. Hagne also reported a correlation between 4-month EEG activity at 1.5–7.5 Hz, temporal and central locations, and total score on the Griffiths Scale.

Developmental Changes in the EEG During Childhood

The early infant longitudinal studies of Smith, Lindsley, and Henry were remarkable in that they also contained longitudinal samples of children. Smith (1938a, 1938b, 1939, 1941) continued to obtain EEG recordings from many in his infant sample until they were 4.5 years of age. There were also 95 children from ages 3 to 16 years from whom he made single EEG recordings (Smith, 1941). Using visual inspection, Smith noted that the occipital EEG had a frequency of almost 8 Hz by 30 months of age. This period of rapid EEG development during infancy and early childhood was followed by a more gradual change in EEG during childhood (Smith, 1941). EEG frequency of 9 Hz at occipital locations was not obtained until 8 years of age (Smith, 1938b), while the adult mean of 10 Hz at occipital scalp locations was not seen until 16 years of age (Smith, 1941). Smith made note that Lindsley's data showed 10 Hz occipital EEG in some 12-year-old children (Smith, 1941), although Lindsley's (1939) data tables revealed that 10 Hz activity was displayed by some children as early as 6 years of age. These early data sets appear to demonstrate a range of individual differences in EEG development.

The child EEG reported by Smith, Lindsley, and Henry may appear to be inconsistent with the work by Mizuno and colleagues (1970) summarized earlier, who reported that by 12 months of age infants already were exhibiting 3.5–8.6 Hz EEG activity. The apparent inconsistency is due to research methodology, however. The early EEG work by Smith, Lindsley, and Henry was accomplished with visual analysis of paper EEG tracings and the variable of interest was *peak frequency*, or the fastest individual rhythm (i.e., of 1 Hz width) exhibited by infants of a certain age. The work by Mizuno was accomplished with a frequency analyzer using preselected frequency bands that summed EEG activity across multiple frequencies. Thus, the variable of interest was *power*, or the amount of electrical activity (in microvolts) at a specific frequency interval. The report of infants of 12 months exhibiting EEG activity within a 3.5–8.6 Hz range does not tell us the peak frequency exhibited by the infants, exemplifying why caution must be taken when comparing EEG findings across different analysis methodologies.

One of the most informative EEG data sets is the one begun by Lindsley (1939) and reanalyzed by Henry (1944). This valuable data set included 95 infants and children ranging in age from 3 months to 19 years. Each child contributed a minimum of 5 recordings, collected over a minimum of 5 years, to the data set. Until 1 year of age, recordings were made every 3 months. From ages 1 to 5, recordings were done every 6 months and then every year thereafter. Recordings were made from occipital and central sites and analyzed using visual inspection. Lindsley (1939) reported that occipital amplitude began to decrease after 12 months of age, with the sharpest decline occurring near the 2nd birthday. He suggested that sharp decline around 2 years of age was due to the closing of the fontanelle because the drop in amplitude was not accompanied by a change in frequency. Lindsley (1939) further suggested that the continued drop in amplitude evident throughout childhood was associated with maturational increases in skull thickness.

Henry (1944) reported some sudden frequency changes at occipital recordings sites prior to age 4, but after age 6 most children exhibited an occipital EEG in the 9–11 Hz range. Henry also noted that individual differences in the maturation of the adult-like EEG frequency were evident in his visual analysis of the EEG data. Some children appeared to reach this mature frequency at a young age, while others showed slow increases in frequency throughout childhood. Individual differences in dominant frequency tended to be stable. Children with faster dominant frequencies (>11 Hz), and those with slower dominant frequencies (<9 Hz), tended to be at the maximum and minimum levels of the group mean throughout their participation in the longitudinal study (Henry, 1944). Thus, individual differences between the children in the Henry data set and those in the Smith data set appear to be the reason that the Smith children did not demonstrate 9 Hz occipital EEG until 8 years of age. Individual differences in EEG power values have been the focus of our research program on cognitive development that we report in a later section of this chapter.

One of the best-known data sets of EEG development in children and adolescents was published by Matousek and Petersen (1973). Originally, Petersen and Eeg-Olofsson used visual analysis to report on EEG development in children from 1 to 15 years of age (Petersen & Eeg-Olofsson, 1971) and in adolescents from 16 to 21 years of age (Eeg-Olofsson, 1971). Recordings were made from frontal, central, temporal, parietal, and occipital scalp locations. Later, the EEG data were submitted for a frequency analysis by Matousek and Petersen. This work confirmed earlier cross-sectional reports by Petersen and Eeg-Olofsson (1971) of decreases in 1.5–3.5 Hz activity with age and increases in 9.5–12.5 Hz activity with age. Matousek and Petersen (1973) reported that EEG development occurred more quickly at posterior scalp locations than central ones. They also noted that age-related EEG changes were linear during childhood and logarithmic during adolescence.

John and colleagues (John et al., 1980) compared a data set of 306 children, aged 6 to 16 years with the Matousek and Petersen's data set of 324 children, aged 6 to 16, and confirmed the notion of linear changes in the EEG as age increases. Again, EEG activity in the 1.5–7.5 Hz frequency band decreased with age, while EEG activity greater than 7.5 Hz increased with age.

These earlier notions of linear changes in EEG development were questioned with a graphical display of the EEG data by Epstein (1980). Examining EEG activity reported longitudinally by Smith (1938b), Lindsley (1939), and Henry (1944), and cross-sectionally by Matousek and Petersen (1973), Epstein recalculated the EEG changes across age to reflect biennial increments in 8–13 Hz activity. Epstein reported that this reconfiguration of the data revealed 5 stages of EEG development that correlated with the stages of brain growth with respect to gross weight of the brain.

With these classic EEG data sets, we have a great deal of information concerning the ontogeny of the EEG during infancy and childhood. What these data sets do not tell us, however, is whether there is functional significance to these age-related EEG changes. It was assumed by these researchers that age-related changes in EEG were associated with changes in cognition, but this assumption was never tested except by Hagne (1972). More recently, a correspondence between Piaget's stages of cognitive development and stage-like patterns of brain development has been posited by Fischer (Fischer & Rose, 1994). Fischer has noted the need for precise and simultaneous brain-behavior assessments to detect correlations between brain maturation and cognitive development during childhood (Fischer & Rose, 1994). Current EEG work is heeding that call.

Perhaps one of the biggest contributions of these early researchers is the acknowledgment of individual differences in EEG development. Interestingly, there was no speculation regarding the implications of these individual differences, except for Henry (1944). He examined correlations between EEG peak frequency and IQ and reported low to moderate correlations. Current infant and child basic EEG research is incorporating cognitive and emotion behaviors into the EEG recording sessions. Although most of this work is focused on age-related effects, there is a growing trend toward the examination of individual differences in EEG and corresponding behavioral correlates.

Next we turn to an examination of infant EEG frequency bands. If work is to progress on brain-behavior development, researchers need to have precise EEG definitions with which to work.

Infant EEG Frequency Bands

Psychophysiologists working with child, adolescent, and adult populations examine the theta (4–8 Hz), alpha (8–13 Hz), and beta (13–20 Hz) rhythms and note their associations with cognitive behaviors (e.g., Davidson et al., 1990; Klimesch, Doppelmayr, Schimke, & Ripper; 1997; Roberts & Bell, 2002). In the infant psychophysiology literature, however, there is no standardization of EEG rhythms as found in adult EEG work (Pivik et al., 1993). As a result, we know little concerning the associations of specific frequencies with cognitive behaviors during infancy.

In a set of recommendations for recording and analyzing EEG in research contexts, Pivik et al. (1993) noted that traditional frequency bands used with adults may not apply to studies of infant EEG. Two approaches were suggested. In the first, EEG analyses can be accomplished on a wide frequency band that includes all frequencies in which there is evidence of power. This approach has been used in some studies of infant emotion, where differences in baseline frontal EEG asymmetries in the 3–12 Hz band have been reported between infants with depressed mothers and infants with non-depressed mothers (e.g., Field, Fox, Pickens, & Nawrocki, 1995; Jones et al., 1998). The wide band method, however, is not commonly used in infant research. Given the rapid changes in EEG development during the first postnatal year, the wide frequency band may not be very informative.

In the second approach to infant EEG frequency bands noted by Pivik and colleagues (1993), individual spectra are examined and frequency bands are determined that center around the peaks in the spectrum. We have used this second approach with our infant EEG data. In a longitudinal study examining relations between frontal brain electrical activity and cognitive development from 7 to 12 months of age, we began by doing spectral plots of each EEG lead for each longitudinal participant for every monthly testing session. The plots generally revealed a dominant frequency for most infants in the data set in all leads at all ages at 6–9 Hz (Bell & Fox, 1992). There were individual differences in this peak, however. Figure 6.2 (top) shows the spectral plots for F3 and F4 for one infant who exhibited a sharp peak at 5–9 Hz at 8 months of age. This pattern is contrasted with another 8-month-old infant who does not exhibit this peak (Figure 6.2, middle). These two infants exhibited these same patterns monthly through 12 months of age.

We verified this peak at 6–9 Hz by performing spectral analysis on a different data set which included the EEG recordings of a group of 74 eight-month-old infants (Bell & Fox, 1997). The group mean spectral plot for F3 is shown in Figure 6.2 (bottom). Although the peak at 6–9 Hz is evident, it is much smaller in amplitude than the peak exhibited by the infant in Figure 6.2 (top), yet much larger in amplitude than the non-peak exhibited by the infant in Figure 6.2 (middle), demonstrating that group data can obfuscate individual differences in the EEG. Thus, within any infant EEG data set, researchers can expect a wide range of individual differences in spectral power among same-age infants.

The spectral-plot approach was also used by Marshall with a longitudinal data set that included resting baseline EEG from a group of children at 5, 10, 14, 24, and 51 months of age (Marshall, Bar-Haim, & Fox, 2002). Marshall and colleagues reported a peak in the spectra in the 6–9 Hz frequency band that emerged across multiple scalp locations. This frequency range was consistent across all scalp locations by 10 months of age and continued to be the predominant frequency band through 51 months of age. The earliest EEG recordings at 5 months of age showed 6–9 Hz to be prominent at central scalp locations, with the lower 4–6 Hz band more prominent at posterior locations. For individual infants, there was an increase in the peak frequency across the four-year study reminiscent of the data reported in the classic infant EEG research reports.

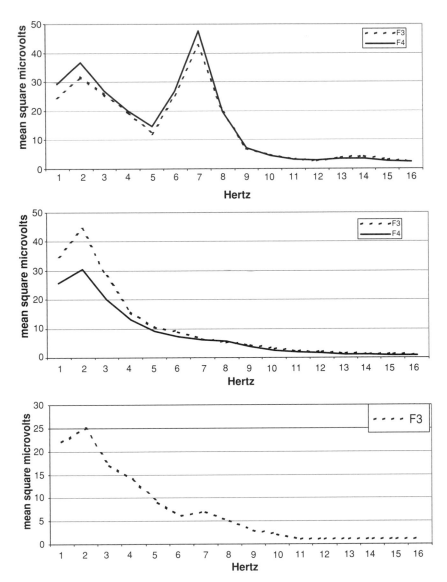

Figure 6.2. Spectral plots of frontal EEG for 8-month-old infants demonstrating individual differences in infant EEG and group means. (top) One infant with a well-defined peak frequency band between 5 and 9 Hz (Bell & Fox, 1992, data set). (middle) One infant without a peak frequency band between 5 and 9 Hz (Bell & Fox, 1992, data set). (bottom) Group mean data for 74 infants (Bell & Fox, 1997, data set).

Infant EEG and Cognitive Development

Working Memory and Inhibitory Control Tasks

The 6–9 Hz frequency band is of little intrinsic value unless it can be shown to be correlated with behavior. Based on the individual spectral plots in our own data set, we focused on the 6–9 Hz band and noted that changes in resting baseline frontal EEG power values from 7 to 12 months of age were associated with changes in performance on a classic infant cognitive task which requires the infant to search manually for a hidden toy in one of two hiding sites (Bell & Fox, 1992). It has been proposed that spatial working memory and inhibitory control, among other cognitive behaviors, are essential for performance on this type of task (Diamond, Prevor, Callender, & Druin, 1997; Nelson, 1995). Many of these cognitive behaviors are associated with the dorsolateral prefrontal cortex (Diamond et al., 1997), although the EEG cannot be that specific with respect to brain location.

Next, we assessed a group of same-age infants and found that individual differences in 6–9 Hz baseline frontal EEG at 8 months of age were related to differences in performance on the classic reaching spatial working memory task (Bell & Fox, 1997). Higher levels of performance were associated with greater baseline EEG power values at both frontal and occipital scalp locations. We then designed an infant looking task that was similar to the classic infant reaching task so that we could record EEG *during* task performance. On this looking task, infant performance at 8 months of age was associated with EEG activity at 6–9 Hz (Bell, 2001). Infants with high levels of performance on the visual spatial working memory task exhibited task-related EEG power values at 6–9 Hz which were higher than their baseline power values. Infants with low levels of performance had task-related EEG power values that were similar to their baseline values.

Thus, in our studies of infant cognition, increases in EEG power values at 6–9 Hz have been associated with higher levels of performance on cognitive tasks. In the adult EEG literature, researchers have long focused on the 8–13 Hz peak in the adult spectrum. As previously noted, it is commonly reported that alpha activity (8–13 Hz) exhibits decreased power values during increased cortical processing, although there are some reports of alpha increased power values during long-term memory tasks (Klimesch, Doppelmayr, Schwaiger, Auinger, & Winkler, 1999). Recently, researchers have noted that adult theta activity (4–7 Hz) exhibits increases in power during memory and attention tasks (e.g., Burgess & Gruzelier, 2000; Klimesch et al., 1997). Thus, for the mature EEG signal, specific patterns of fluctuations in power levels at the defined frequency bands are associated with different

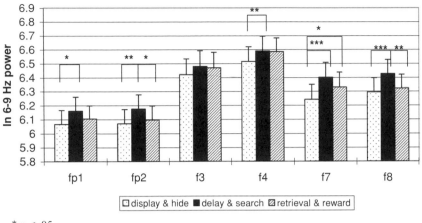

* p < .05
** p < .01
*** p < .001

Figure 6.3. EEG power values at 6–9 Hz for the frontal scalp electrodes during different cognitive processing stages of the infant spatial working memory task. Adapted from Bell (2002).

types of cognitive processing. This type of information is lacking with respect to infant EEG.

Based on the spectral plots we had done in the past, and based on factor analysis of one of our infant EEG data sets (Bell, 1998b), we decided to compare the task-related EEG activity at 6–9 Hz with activity at both 3–5 Hz and 10–12 Hz (Bell, 2002). After a baseline EEG recording, a group of 8-month-old infants performed our spatial working memory looking task while we continued to record EEG. Thus, we had both baseline and task-related EEG data. Our first analysis was a comparison of baseline and task EEG at each of the three frequency bands. All three bands (3–5 Hz, 6–9 Hz, 10–12 Hz) discriminated between baseline and task activation at all electrode locations. At each frequency band, power values were higher during the memory task than during baseline.

Next, we analyzed the three frequency bands during the different processing stages of the cognitive task. We proposed that the processing stages involved an attention component, a working memory and inhibitory control component, and an emotion component associated with a task reward. Both the 3–5 Hz and the 6–9 Hz bands differentiated among various processing stages at specific electrode sites (see Figure 6.3). The 10–12 Hz band did not.

Perhaps the most intriguing results involved comparisons of the EEG during correct and incorrect responses. Only the 6–9 Hz band made this distinction. Power values were greater during correct responses than during incorrect responses. Thus, the 6–9 Hz band appears to be most informative concerning spatial working memory during infancy. With this band, there were differences between baseline and task EEG data, variations in power among the processing stages of the task, and power value differences between correct and incorrect responses (Bell, 2002).

Attention Tasks

Similar results have been reported by other researchers who specialize in infant EEG and cognitive development. Infants between 8 and 11 months of age exhibited a peak in 6.0–8.8 Hz EEG at frontal scalp locations during sustained visual attention to an interesting stimulus (Stroganova, et al., & Posikera, 1999). Similarly, infants between 8 and 11 months with longer anticipatory attention spans had higher 6.8 Hz alpha amplitude values (EEG was divided into 0.4 Hz bins) at posterior scalp locations than infants with shorter anticipatory attention spans (Orekhova, Stroganova, & Posikera, 2001). Those EEG data were recorded while infants were in a state of internally controlled attention; that is, they were waiting or anticipating the reappearance of a social stimulus.

Other infant EEG studies have focused on the 4–6 Hz frequency band, suggested by Marshall to be more appropriate for younger infants (Marshall et al., 2002). Increases in power at 4–6 Hz during internally controlled or anticipatory attention were evident in both 7–8-month-old (Stroganova, Orekhova, & Posikera, 1998) and 8–11-month-old infants (Orekhova, Stroganova, & Posikera, 1999). In both of these reports, it is the EEG data at frontal scalp locations that were most associated with the attention condition.

These studies may begin to form the foundation for defining EEG frequency bands that are appropriate for use with infants and for understanding the function of these EEG frequency bands during cognitive activities. It is also crucial to the field of developmental psychophysiology to know whether the infant frequency bands are appropriate for use with young children and with what age it is expedient to begin to use adult-defined EEG frequencies.

It is also crucial to determine the ontogeny of the 6–9 Hz frequency band. During infant cognitive professing, this frequency band performs as theta (4–7 Hz) does during adult cognition. It is intriguing to note that the 6–9 Hz band during infancy also behaves similarly to adult alpha (8–13 Hz) during eyes closed (or "lights off" for infant research participants). Stroganova and colleagues (Stroganova et al., 1999) have reported that in 8- and 11-month-old infants, the amplitude of occipital EEG at 5.2–9.6 Hz increases during total darkness. Thus, the functional significance of the infant 6–9 Hz frequency band encompasses characteristics of both adult theta and adult alpha. Whether this infant 6–9 Hz oscillation has different generators depending on if it behaves like adult theta or adult alpha is unknown, but perhaps source analysis can eventually be used to differentiate these two different functions. One of the more intriguing research agendas will be to sort out the ontogeny of infant EEG and trace the transition from infant EEG to child and then adult-like brain activity patterns.

Toddler EEG and Cognitive Development

The field of developmental psychophysiology is lacking with respect to EEG data from children during the second year after birth. Although children of this age are well known for having an independent spirit that might not translate into cooperation during an EEG laboratory session, these data are crucial for bridging the infant and early childhood EEG literatures. The longitudinal resting baseline 6–9 Hz EEG data from 5 months to 4 years reported by Marshall and colleagues (2002) contain EEG at the 14-month time point, making this a valuable and unique EEG data set.

Resting EEG data have been utilized in an examination of the joint attention skills of 14-month-old toddlers. Joint attention refers to the coordination of attention between two social partners. The developmental literature focuses on infant and toddler attempts to initiate joint attention as well as respond to the attention bids of others. The tendency for the toddlers to initiate joint attention bids with the experimenter was associated with left frontal EEG power values (Mundy, Card, & Fox, 2000).

Currently, we are collecting baseline and task-related EEG with a group of 24- to 25-month-old children. These children are members of a longitudinal data set that we have assessed on spatial working memory tasks twice when they were infants. As toddlers, they are participating in both spatial and verbal working memory assessments. As would be expected, each toddler is participating in the spatial working memory task, where we are seeing individual differences in task performance. Participation in the verbal working memory task is possible only if the toddler has sufficient spoken language. Our first examination of the data will involve the 6–9 Hz frequency band, as per the findings of Marshall and colleagues (2002). We anticipate that these task-related EEG data will be an important addition to the brain-behavior developmental literature.

Early Childhood EEG and Cognitive Development

During the early childhood years, significant changes in attention, executive, and self-control processes are clearly identifiable (e.g., Diamond et al., 1997; Posner & Rothbart, 2000). These changes are inarguably associated with transformations in cortical function and organization. It has been suggested that the most salient changes in brain anatomy (i.e., growth in brain weight, increased myelination, glucose utilization, and synaptic growth) take place in the first four years (Van Baal, De Geus, & Boomsma, 1996). There are few EEG studies of cognition in early childhood, however. This void is particularly surprising because early childhood is a time when many advances are being made in cognitive and related behavioral skills, particularly in the executive function domain. The paucity of EEG literature is further intriguing as EEG is one of the more favorable methodologies for brain imaging investigations with this age population (Casey & de Haan, 2002).

In our research lab, we are attempting to provide a systematic, developmental view of the cognitive skills of working memory and inhibitory control and their associated electrophysiology by extending our infant work on spatial working memory (e.g., Bell, 2001, 2002) to the preschool years. From the work of Diamond, we know that many advances are being made in certain executive function skills during the early childhood years (Diamond et al., 1997). For example, children are unable to successfully perform working memory and inhibitory control tasks, such as the day-night Stroop-like task, at 3.5 years. By age 4, however, performance has increased to competent levels (Diamond et al., 1997).

Recently, we have investigated the EEG correlates of working memory and inhibitory control in 4.5-year-old children (Wolfe & Bell, 2004). As did Marshall and colleagues (Marshall et al., 2002), we found the 6–9 Hz frequency band to be informative with this age group. The children with higher performance on the day-night Stroop-like task of working memory and inhibitory control had higher baseline and task-related EEG power values at frontal scalp locations than did children with lower performance on the task. This finding is similar to our infant EEG results and highlights the value of individual differences research within the field of developmental psychophysiology.

Middle/Late Childhood EEG and Cognitive Development

There is an extensive developmental psychophysiology literature focusing on cognitive development in middle and late childhood. Most of this work focuses on associations between EEG and constructs such as intelligence and school-related skills (e.g., Roberts & Kraft, 1990; Schmid, Tirsch, & Scherb, 2002), although there is some focus on specific cognitive skills such as mental rotation (e.g., Roberts & Bell, 2000, 2002). These studies tend to utilize adult EEG frequency band definitions of alpha, theta, and beta. In our own work, we have demonstrated the alpha frequency band to be appropriate for 8-year-old children, although the power values of this age children are greater than the power values of adults (Roberts & Bell, 2000, 2002).

Working memory performance also has been associated with adult-like EEG frequencies in children 8–10 years of age. EEG power values at 8–9.5 Hz were higher at frontal scalp locations for correct responses on a verbal working memory task than they were for incorrect responses (Fernandez et al., 1998). In another study, the 10–12 Hz EEG associated with short-term memory performance of 12-year-old children did not differ from the EEG of adults completing the same task, suggesting that brain-behavior memory systems might be fully developed by age 12 (Krause, Salminen, Sillanmaki, & Holopainen, 2001).

Conclusion

In this chapter, we have highlighted the value of the EEG for the study of cognitive development in infancy and childhood by focusing on research on working memory. These studies suggest that not only does cognition change dramatically during this time period, but also the EEG is undergoing major developmental changes. We have focused on the need to combine brain-behavior measures in developmental research and have proposed that the EEG is the ideal methodology for this purpose.

We have also highlighted two areas of the developmental psychophysiology literature that deserve more attention. First, continued work on defining standardized EEG frequency bands that are developmentally appropriate for infants and young children is essential to interpreting any EEG research results. Second, the paucity of EEG research with toddlers and young preschool-age children severely limits our knowledge of EEG development during this crucial phase of brain-behavior development. Most valuable would be longitudinal studies that encompass the infancy to childhood time periods and examine changes in task-related EEG.

Developmental psychophysiologists have a wide variety of research methods available for the study of age-related changes in the functioning of the brain and associated cognitive behaviors. The EEG remains one of the most efficient and relative inexpensive methodologies for examining developmental change.

ACKNOWLEDGMENTS

Much of the research reported in this chapter was funded by grants from the College of Arts & Sciences at Virginia Tech and from the Office of Sponsored Programs and Research at the University of South Carolina.

References

Bell, M. A. (1998a). The ontogeny of the EEG during infancy and childhood: Implications for cognitive development. In B. Barreau (Ed.), *Neuroimaging in child neuropsychiatric disorders* (pp. 97–111).Berlin: Springer-Verlag.

Bell, M. A. (1998b). *Search for valid infant EEG rhythms: Factor analysis of power data.* Poster presented at the Annual Meeting of the Society for Psychophysiological Research, Denver.

Bell, M. A. (2001). Brain electrical activity associated with cognitive processing during a looking version of the A-not-B task. *Infancy, 2*, 311–330.

Bell, M. A. (2002). Power changes in infant EEG frequency bands during a spatial working memory task. *Psychophysiology, 39*, 450–458.

Bell, M. A., & Fox, N. A. (1992). The relations between frontal brain electrical activity and cognitive development during infancy. *Child Development, 63*, 1142–1163.

Bell, M. A., & Fox, N. A. (1997). Individual differences in object permanence performance at 8 months: Locomotor experience and brain electrical activity. *Developmental Psychobiology, 31*, 287–297.

Bell, M. A., & Fox, N. A. (2003). Cognition and affective style: Individual differences in brain electrical activity during spatial and verbal tasks. *Brain and Cognition, 53*, 441–451.

Berger, H. (1929). On the electroencephalogram of man. I. *Arch. Psychiatr. Nervenkr, 87*, 527–570.

Berger, H. (1932). On the electroencephalogram of man. V. *Arch. Psychiatr. Nervenkr, 98*, 231–254.

Burgess, A. P., & Gruzelier, J. H. (2000). Short duration power changes in the EEG during recognition memory for words and faces. *Psychophysiology, 37*, 596–606.

Casey, B. J., & de Hann, M. (2002). Introduction: New methods in developmental science. *Developmental Science, 5*, 265–267.

Davidson, R. J., Chapman, J. P., Chapman, L. J., & Henriques, J. B. (1990). Asymmetrical brain electrical activity discriminates between psychometrically-matched verbal and spatial cognitive tasks. *Psychophysiology, 27*, 528–543.

Davidson, R. J., Jackson, D. C., & Larson, C. L. (2000). Human electroencephalography. In J. T. Cacioppo, L. G. Tassinary, & G. G. Berntson (Eds.), *Handbook of psychophysiology* (2nd ed., pp. 27–52). Cambridge: Cambridge University Press.

Diamond, A., Prevor, M. B., Callender, G., & Druin, D. P. (1997). Prefrontal cortex cognitive deficits in children treated early and continuously for PKU. *Monographs of the Society for Research in Child Development, 62* (4, Serial No. 252).

Eeg-Olofsson, O. (1971). The development of the EEG in normal young persons from the age of 16 through 21 years. *Neuropadiatrie, 3*, 11–45.

Epstein, H. T. (1980). EEG developmental stages. *Developmental Psychobiology, 13*, 629–631.

Fernandez, T., Harmony, T., Silva, J., Galan, L., Diaz-Comas, L., Bosch, J., Rodriguez, M., Fernandez-Bouzas, A., Yanez, G., Otero, G., & Marosi, E. (1998). Relationship of specific EEG frequencies at specific brain areas with performance. *NeuroReport, 9,* 3681–3687.

Field, T., Fox, N. A., Pickens, J., & Nawrocki, T. (1995). Relative right frontal EEG activation in 3- to 6-month-old infants of "depressed" mothers. *Developmental Psychology, 31,* 358–363.

Fischer, K. W., & Rose, S. P. (1994) Dynamic development of coordination ofcomponents in brain and behavior: A framework for theory and research. In G. Dawson & K. W. Fischer (Eds.), *Human behavior and the developing brain* (pp. 3–45). New York: Guilford.

Hagne, I. (1968). Development of the waking EEG in normal infants during the first year of life. In P. Kellaway & I. Petersen (Eds.), *Clinical electroencephalography of children* (pp. 97–118). New York: Grune & Stratton.

Hagne, I. (1972). Development of the EEG in normal infants during the first year of life. *Acta Pediatrica Scandinavia, Supplement 232,* 25–53.

Henry, J. R. (1944). Electroencephalograms of normal children. *Monographs of the Society for Research in Child Development, 9,* (3, Serial No. 39).

John, E. R., Ahn, H., Prichep, L., Trepetin, M., Brown, D., & Kaye, H. (1980). Developmental equations for the electroencephalogram. *Science, 210,* 1255–1258.

Jones, N. A., Field, T., Fox, N. A., Davalos, M., Lundy, B., & Hart, S. (1998). Newborns of mothers with depressive symptoms are physiologically less developed. *Infant Behavior & Development, 21,* 537–541.

Klimesch, W., Doppelmayr, M., Schimke, H., & Ripper, B. (1997). Theta synchronization and alpha desynchronization in a memory task. *Psychophysiology, 34,* 169–176.

Klimesch, W., Doppelmayr, M., Schwaiger, J., Auinger, P., & Winkler, T. (1999). "Paradoxical" alpha synchronization in a memory task. *Cognitive Brain Research, 7,* 493–501.

Krause, C. M., Salminen, P. A., Sillanmaki, L., & Holopainen, I. E. (2001). Event-related desynchronization and synchronization during a memory task in children. *Clinical Neurophysiology, 112,* 2233–2240.

Lindsley, D. B. (1939). A longitudinal study of the occipital alpha rhythm in normal children: Frequency and amplitude standards. *Journal of Genetic Psychology, 55,* 197–213.

Marshall, P. J., Bar-Haim, Y., & Fox, N. A. (2002). Development of the EEG from 5 months to 4 years of age. *Clinical Neurophysiology, 113,* 1199–1208.

Matousek, M., & Petersen, I. (1973). Automatic evaluation of EEG background activity by means of age-dependent EEG quotients. *Electroencephalography and Clinical Neurophysiology, 55,* 603–612.

Mizuno, T., Yamaguchi, N., Iinuma, K., & Arakawa, T. (1970). Maturation of patterns of EEG: Basic waves of healthy infants under 12 months of age. *Tohoku Journal of Experimental Medicine, 102,* 91–98.

Mundy, P. Card, J., & Fox, N. A. (2000). EEG correlates of the development of infant joint attention skills. *Developmental Psychobiology, 36,* 325–338.

Nelson, C. A. (1995). The ontogeny of human memory: A cognitive neuroscience perspective. *Developmental Psychology, 31,* 723–738.

Nelson, C. A., & Monk, C. S. (2001). The use of the event-related potentials in the study of cognitive development. In C. A. Nelson & M. Luciana (Eds.), *Handbook of developmental cognitive neuroscience* (pp. 125–136). Cambridge: MIT Press.

Orekhova, E. V., Stroganova, T. A., & Posikera, I. N. (1999). Theta synchronization during sustained anticipatory attention in infants over the second half of the first year of life. *International Journal of Psychophysiology, 32*, 151–172.

Orekhova, E. V., Stroganova, T. A., & Posikera, I. N. (2001). Alpha activity as an index of cortical inhibition during sustained internally controlled attention in infants. *Clinical Neurophysiology, 112*, 740–749.

Petersen, I., & Eeg-Olofsson, O. (1971). The development of the electroencephalogram in normal children from the age of 1 through 15 years: Non-paroxysmal activity. *Neuropediatric, 2*, 247–301.

Pivik, R. T., Broughton, R. J., Coppola, R., Davidson, R. J., Fox, N. A., & Nuwer, M. R. (1993). Guidelines for the recording and quantitative analysis of electroencephalographic activity in research contexts. *Psychophysiology, 30*, 547–558.

Posner, M. I., & Rothbart, M. K. (2000). Developing mechanisms of self-regulation. *Development and Psychopathology, 12*, 427–441.

Roberts, J. E., & Bell, M. A. (2000). Sex differences on a mental rotation task: Variations in EEG hemispheric activation between children and college students. *Developmental Neuropsychology, 17*, 199–223.

Roberts, J. E., & Bell, M. A. (2002). The effects of age and sex on mental rotation performance, verbal performance, and brain electrical activity. *Developmental Psychobiology, 40*, 391–407.

Roberts, T. A., & Kraft, R. H. (1990). Developmental differences in the relationship between reading comprehension and hemispheric alpha patterns: An EEG study. *Journal of Educational Psychology, 81*, 322–328.

Schacter, D. L. (1977). EEG theta waves and psychological phenomena: A review and analysis. *Biological Psychology, 5*, 47–82.

Schmid, R. G., Tirsch, W. S., & Scherb, H. (2002). Correlation between spectral EEG parameters and intelligence test variables in school-age children. *Clinical Neurophysiology, 113*, 1647–1656.

Smith, J. R. (1938a). The electroencephalogram during normal infancy and childhood: I. Rhythmic activities present in the neonate and their subsequent development. *Journal of Genetic Psychology, 53*, 431–453.

Smith, J. R. (1938b). The electroencephalogram during normal infancy and childhood: II. The nature and growth of the alpha waves. *Journal of Genetic Psychology, 53*, 455–469.

Smith, J. R. (1939). The "occipital" and "pre-central" alpha rhythms during the first two years. *Journal of Psychology, 7*, 223–226.

Smith, J. R. (1941). The frequency growth of the human alpha rhythms during normal infancy and childhood. *Journal of Psychology, 11*, 177–198.

Stern, R. M., Ray, W. J., & Quigley, K. S. (2001). *Psychological recording* (2nd ed.). Oxford University Press.

Stroganova, T. A., Orekhova, E. V., & Posikera, I. N. (1998). Externally and internally controlled attention in infants: An EEG study. *International Journal of Psychophysiology, 30*, 339–351.

Stroganova, T. A., Orekhova, E. V., & Posikera, I. N. (1999). EEG alpha rhythm in infants. *Clinical Neurophysiology, 110*, 997–1012.

Taylor, M. J., & Baldeweg, T. (2002). Application of EEG, ERP, and intracranial recordings to the investigation of cognitive functions in children. *Developmental Science, 5*, 318–334.

Van Baal, G. C. M., De Geus, E. J. C., & Boomsma, D. I. (1996). Genetic architecture of EEG power spectra in early life. *Electroencephalography and Clinical Neurophysiology, 98*, 502–514.

Wolfe, C. D., & Bell, M. A. (2004). Working memory and inhibitory control in early childhood: Contributions from electrophysiology, temperament, and language. *Developmental Psychobiology, 44*, 68–83.

AUTONOMIC AND PERIPHERAL SYSTEMS

Theory, Methods, and Measures

7   Infant Heart Rate

A Developmental Psychophysiological Perspective

Greg D. Reynolds and John E. Richards

INTRODUCTION

Psychophysiology is the study of the relation between psychological events and biological processes in human participants. The electrocardiogram (ECG) and heart rate (HR) have been commonly used measures throughout the history of psychophysiological research. Early studies found that stimuli eliciting differing emotional responses in adults also elicited HR responses differing in magnitude and direction of change from baseline (e.g., Darrow, 1929; Graham & Clifton, 1966; Lacey, 1959). Vast improvements in methods of measuring ECG and knowledge regarding the relation between HR and cognitive activity have occurred.

Heart rate has been particularly useful in developmental psychophysiological research. Researchers interested in early cognitive and perceptual development have utilized HR as a window into cognitive activity for infants before they are capable of demonstrating complex behaviors or providing verbal responses. Also, the relation between brain control of HR and the behavior of HR during psychological activity has helped work in developmental cognitive neuroscience. In this chapter, we address the use of the ECG and HR in research on infants. We review three ways in which HR has been used in psychophysiological research: HR changes, attention phases defined by HR, and HR variability (particularly respiratory sinus arrhythmia). Topics we focus on are the areas of the brain that are indexed with these measures, developmental changes associated with these measures, and the relation of these measures to psychological processes. Before covering research with infants, we briefly review background information on the heart, the ECG and HR, and its relation to psychophysiology.

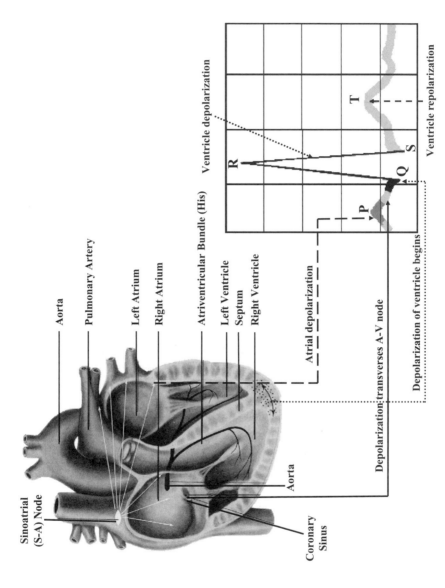

Figure 7.1. Schematic representation of the heart and the areas involved in the heart beat (upper portion). Lines from structures in the upper portion to points on the ECG waveform (lower portion) represent sources of the electrical impulses produced on the ECG (adapted from Andreassi, 1989).

The Heart, the Electrocardiogram and Heart Rate, and Heart Rate Psychophysiology

The heart, which is the strongest muscle in the human body, is composed of three layers of tissue. The outermost layer of tissue is the epicardium. This layer contains coronary vessels and the cardiac autonomic nerves. The middle layer of tissue, known as the myocardium, is composed of layers of muscle tissue. The endocardium lines the inner walls of the heart chambers. Cells of the endocardium are smooth, offering little resistance to circulation. The four chambers that compose the heart are the left and right atria, which serve as reservoirs for incoming blood, and the left and right ventricles, which together provide the majority of pumping force for the heart (Hassett & Danforth, 1982).

The heart muscle contracts at regular intervals, that is, the heart beat. Figure 7.1 shows a schematic illustration of the heart and the areas involved in the heart beat (Andreassi, 1989). The beat occurs by the spread of spontaneously originating electrical activity through the sinoatrial (SA) node, atrial bundles, the atrioventricular (AV) node, the bundle of His, and the Purkinje networks. Cells within these specialized conduction tissues spontaneously depolarize and generate an action potential. The SA node is made up of a small group of cells within the walls of the right atrium. These cells have a resting membrane potential that is lower than other cardiac pacemaker cells. The cells of the SA node depolarize and repolarize at a faster discharge rate than other cardiac cells because of this lower resting membrane potential. Thus, the SA node normally serves as the location of the cardiac pacemaker.

The ECG is a record of the electrical activity produced as action potentials are generated in the SA node of the right atrium. Figure 7.1 shows a representation of the heart and how the components of the ECG are related to the events in the heart beat. A single cardiac cycle is represented in the ECG as a characteristic waveform comprised of four waves and three primary intervals (Brownley, Hurwitz, & Schneiderman, 2000). The P-wave represents atrial depolarization beginning at the SA node and spreading in all directions over the atrial muscle. Ventricular depolarization is conducted from the endocardial tissue to the epicardial tissue of the left ventricle and is represented in the ECG by the R-wave. Further depolarization of the right ventricle occurs at the S wave. Finally, the T-wave represents the completion of depolarization and the beginning of repolarization (Smith & Kampine, 1984). The three intervals are identified by the waves in between that they occur. The P–R interval signifies the passage of the action potential from the atrium to the ventricular muscle. The early part of this interval (from the P-wave to the Q-wave) represents the spread of the cardiac impulse through the AV node. The Q–T interval reflects the process of ventricular depolarization and repolarization.

Einthoven pioneered the use of the ECG for recording cardiac potentials in the early part of the twentieth century. The ECG is recorded by placing electrodes on two surface points (bipolar recording) of the body tissue surrounding the heart. Because body tissues conduct electricity, a constant fraction of the cardiac potential will be picked up between these two electrodes. The ECG is the sum of all the action potentials that occur during depolarization of the myocardial tissue of the heart. This potential is then amplified and recorded. Depolarization toward an electrode produces positive potentials and depolarization away from an electrode produces negative potentials in the ECG recording. The classic method of measuring ECG is to record from three electrodes placed on three extremities of the body. The most common placement of electrodes is the left and right arms and the left or right leg (which is used as a reference electrode). Use of this three-lead configuration is based upon Einthoven's equilateral triangle (Einthoven, Fahr, & de Waart, 1913), a configuration of leads that records the activity of the heart within a 2D geometric figure (Brownley, Hurwitz, & Schneiderman, 2000). This configuration records the primary waves of the ECG waveform as positive potentials.

The classic three-lead configuration is modified in infants by placing electrodes on the right and left chest area and the right abdomen (used as a reference electrode). Figure 7.2 shows an infant with the chest leads and electrooculogram (EOG) recording (Richards, 1998, 2000). This method provides good ECG recordings and is less sensitive to movement artifact produced by movement of the arms and legs. An alternative configuration is to place the two active electrodes on the chest and back. Either configuration serves to provide good ECG recordings, and both are less sensitive to movement artifact than placement on the limbs. The reference lead may also be placed in the center of the chest between the right and left chest leads for use with infants.

Quantification of Heart Rate

The ECG is the electrical signal produced by the heart and represents the events occurring during the cardiac cycle. However, psychophysiological use of the ECG itself is rare. Rather, some measure of the length of the cardiac cycle is derived from the ECG and used in psychophysiological research.

The length of the cardiac cycle is often expressed as "interbeat-interval" (IBI, in ms units) and is termed "heart period," that is, the period of the cardiac cycle. The IBI can be determined by measuring each occurrence of a

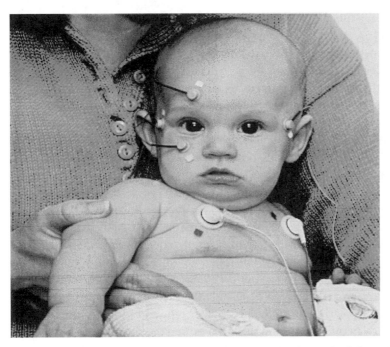

Figure 7.2. Picture of an infant with HR and EOG leads. The two leads located on the chest, along with an additional reference lead placed on the right abdomen area (not seen in picture), are used for ECG recording. The leads located in the facial area are used for EOG recording (Richards, 1998, 2000).

specific component of the ECG waveform. The most common point of the cardiac cycle used when measuring heart period is the peak of the R-wave. The R-wave is most commonly used to calculate the time between cardiac cycles because it is manifested as a sharp positive peak followed by a negative deflection in the ECG waveform. The peak of the R-wave is normally greater in amplitude than all other peaks, making it easily discriminable from other components of the cardiac cycle. Thus, IBI is often defined as the duration between successive R-waves (R-R interval).

Heart rate is the number of beats in a given time period, and its units are beats-per-minute (BPM). Heart rate can be calculated by counting the beats in some period of time. However, it is most conveniently calculated as the inverse of the IBI (60000/IBI ms). Most early work with "cardiac cycle length" used HR as the measure of quantification. Some methodological issues suggest that IBI is a better quantification than HR for psychophysiological research. There has been some discussion about the use of time or beats as the appropriate domain for quantification. Typical analysis quantifies the data as a function of time rather than beats. We use the term "heart rate" in this chapter synonymously for HR or IBI [i.e., changes in cardiac cycle length whether they are decreased HR (longer IBIs) or increased HR (shorter IBIs)]. The direction of the cardiac cycle length is the underlying biological process that is changing, when using either the IBI or HR terminology.

Brain Influences on Heart Rate

The influence of the central nervous system upon HR is mediated by the sympathetic and parasympathetic nervous systems. Sympathetic nervous system impulses increase HR through a pressor effect triggered by the release of adrenalin (Hassett & Danforth, 1982). The sympathetic innervation of the heart originates through axons in the intermediolateral cell column of the spinal cord. Activity in the sympathetic nervous system increases the rate of depolarization in the pacemaker cells, shortens the interval between beats, and results in increased HR. The parasympathetic innervation of the heart comes from neurons in the 10th cranial nerve, the vagus. Activity in the parasympathetic nervous system releases acetylcholine on the SA node, slows the depolarization of the pacemaker cells and increases the length of the interval between the T and the P waves, and thus results in HR decreases. The ventrolateral medulla, dorsal motor nucleus of the vagus nerve, and the nucleus ambiguus are primarily responsible for the parasympathetic nervous system influence on HR. The bidirectional nature of HR does not necessarily lead to correct inferences about whether parasympathetic or sympathetic activity is causing HR change. Slowing of HR may be caused by activation of the parasympathetic system or by withdrawal of the sympathetic system. Increases in HR may be caused by parasympathetic withdrawal or sympathetic system activity.

The impact of the cerebral cortex on HR is of particular interest for psychophysiological research. This interest is due to the role of the cerebral cortex in processing sensory information and cognitive information, which in turn influences autonomic functioning. Structures within the central nervous system that impact the cardiovascular system can be found within the spinal cord, hindbrain, and forebrain. The hypothalamus and cerebral cortex (forebrain structures) influence HR (Brownley et al., 2000).

One particularly interesting CNS influence is a cardio-inhibitory system found in the frontal cortex, limbic system, and the mesencephalic reticular activating system. Stimulation of the reticular activating system evokes low-voltage, high-frequency, desynchronized electrical activity throughout the cortex that is associated with alert wakefulness and vigilance (Moruzzi & Magoun, 1949; Starzl, Taylor, & Magoun, 1951). Other components of this system are involved in auditory and visual perception and attention (Posner, 1995; Posner & Petersen, 1990). Richards (2001) shows how this system is linked to a general arousal system involving the mesencephalic reticular activating system (Heilman, Watson, Valenstein, & Goldberg, 1987; Mesulam, 1983) and the neurochemical systems controlling arousal (Richards, 2001; Robbins & Everitt, 1995). This general arousal system has an ascending influence on cortical areas and enhances processing and arousal. This same system has a descending influence on HR through a parasympathetic outflow. Activation of this system decreases HR in infants and children, or decreases HR variability in adults. Thus, extended HR slowing is an index of a state of general arousal in the brain. Further research is needed to determine at what age activation of the general arousal system no longer elicits HR decelerations but instead leads to decreased HR variability.

A much-studied variability in HR, called respiratory sinus arrhythmia (RSA), has a well-known nervous system control. Respiratory sinus arrhythmia is variability in HR that is coincident with respiration. It is an "arrhythmia" because it disrupts the constant rate of the sinus rhythm caused by the pacemaker cells in the SA node. Accelerations and decelerations in HR occurring in this frequency band occur at the same rate of respiration inhalations and exhalations (Porter, Bryan, & Hsu, 1995; Richards & Casey, 1992). The respiratory control centers in the brainstem and midbrain alternately inhibit and disinhibit the nucleus ambiguus of the vagus nerve (Anrep, Pascual, & Rossler, 1935; Berntson, Cacioppo, & Quigley, 1993; Katona & Jih, 1975; Porges, McCabe, & Yongue, 1982; Reed, Ohel, David, & Porges, 1999). This activity results in a cyclical outflow of acetylcholine to the SA node, alternatively accelerating (during inspiration and vagal inhibition) and decelerating (during expiration and vagal disinhibition) HR. The parasympathetic nervous system thus solely mediates RSA activity.

Heart Rate in Psychophysiology

As has been the case for many areas of psychophysiological research, infant HR studies emerged out of a history of research utilizing ECG in adult populations. Darrow (1929) was one of the first researchers to utilize HR in psychophysiological research. Darrow concluded that HR and blood pressure change associated with stimulus exposure was due to associative processes linked with emotion. Other early adult studies focused on the HR response as a component of Sokolov's (1963) orienting reflex (Davis, Buchwald, & Frankmann, 1955; Zeaman, Deane, & Wegner, 1954). The orienting reflex is the first response of an organism to a stimulus. The orienting response is composed of specific behavioral reactions, as well as changes in central and autonomic nervous system activity, that reflect alterations in the organism's general level of arousal. These alterations in arousal level are associated with attending to an environmental stimulus. Sokolov argued that these physiological responses amplify or reduce the effects of sensory stimulation by acting directly on sensory receptors and indirectly through feedback to central mechanisms. The orienting reflex ultimately has major effects on learning and perceptual processes. Sokolov differentiated the orienting reflex from the defensive reflex. The orienting reflex is associated with a decrease in sensory thresholds, whereas the defensive reflex is a generalized response system associated with an increase in sensory thresholds. In Sokolov's view, increased sympathetic activity had a facilitating effect on information processing by maintaining cortical activation. While Sokolov's own work with the orienting reflex did not focus on HR as a component of the response, it was assumed that the HR component of the orienting reflex would take the form of an acceleratory response.

Lacey (1959) was involved with HR research and developed the concept of "directional fractionation" to replace contemporary views of arousal as a global phenomenon. Directional fractionation refers to Lacey's findings that different fractions of the total somatic response pattern may respond in different directions. Thus, although cortical areas may become activated, HR may decelerate. In fact, Lacey and Lacey (1958) proposed an "intake-rejection" hypothesis stating that increased HR was associated with inhibition of cortical activity. The authors proposed that this physiological response was likely to occur in situations where stimulation is unpleasant or painful, thus facilitating a "rejection" of environmental information. However, in situations where attention is called for, decreases in HR associated with increased sensitivity to stimulation are found to occur (Lacey, 1959; Lacey, Kagan, Lacey, & Moss, 1962). In other words, decreased HR is associated with a decrease in sensory thresholds, and increased HR is associated with an increase in sensory thresholds.

Graham and Clifton (1966) noted that Sokolov's hypothesis regarding the orienting reflex and the Laceys' intake-rejection hypothesis were consistent with one another except in the interpretation of the role of HR changes. Recall that Sokolov assumed that the orienting reflex was associated with HR accelerations. Graham and Clifton (1966) proposed that two possibilities could explain the contrasting interpretations of HR changes: (1) HR acceleration is a phasic component and HR deceleration is a tonic component of the orienting reflex, or (2) HR acceleration is part of the defense reflex and HR deceleration is a part of the orienting reflex. After reviewing the literature and focusing on studies that utilized simple stimuli appropriate for eliciting an orienting reflex, Graham and Clifton (1966) concluded that HR deceleration is a component of the orienting reflex and HR acceleration is a component of the defense reflex.

Infant Heart Rate Studies

Much of the early research utilizing infant HR focused on the ability of infants of differing ages to demonstrate the orienting reflex. Several studies utilizing 75 dB auditory stimulation revealed acceleratory HR responses in newborns (Chase, 1965; Keen, Chase, & Graham, 1965). Davis, Crowell, and Chun (1965) found that newborns responded with HR accelerations to tactile and olfactory stimulation in addition to auditory stimulation. In a longitudinal analysis conducted by Lipton and Steinschneider (1964), infants who demonstrated an acceleratory response at birth showed decelerations in HR to the same stimuli at 2, 4, and 5 months of age. These findings led researchers at the time to conclude that newborns were unable to demonstrate the orienting reflex and responded solely with the defense reflex or startle responses. However, Graham and Jackson (1970) noted that the stimuli used in prior newborn studies were not appropriate for eliciting orienting responses in newborns. Abrupt onsets had been utilized with intense stimuli in many cases. Additionally, the behavioral state of the infants had not been controlled during testing procedures. Subsequent research revealed that the direction and magnitude of HR change were dependent, in part, upon the behavioral state of the infant. For example, stimuli that evoke HR decreases in awake newborns have been found to evoke HR accelerations during sleep (Clifton & Nelson, 1976; Pomerleau & Malcuit, 1981; Pomerleau-Malcuit & Clifton, 1973). Only newborns in the awake state have been found to exhibit sustained HR decreases (Graham, Anthony, & Zeigler, 1983). Furthermore, stimulus complexity and intensity appear to interact in determining the direction of HR responses in newborns. Simple auditory stimuli presented at 75–80 dB elicit HR decelerations, while complex auditory stimuli of equivalent intensity elicit HR accelerations (Clarkson & Berg, 1983; Fox, 1979). Newborns also show larger and longer HR decelerations following presentations of stimuli they visually prefer (e.g., horizontal versus vertical grating, novel versus familiar stimuli; Lewis, Kagan, Campbell, & Kalafat, 1965; McCall & Kagan, 1967).

Heart rate responses have been found to change with age. Infants are more likely to display HR decelerations following stimulus exposure as age increases during the first year of postnatal development. While newborns demonstrate HR accelerations following exposure to air puff streams, HR

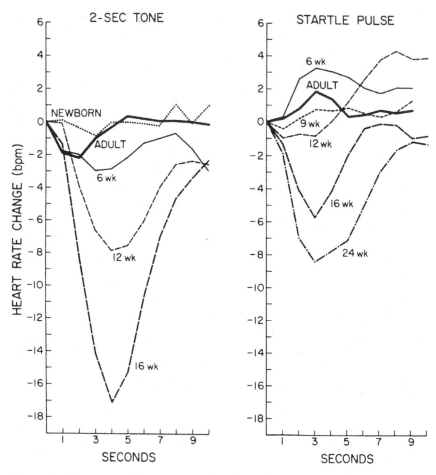

Figure 7.3. Changes in HR response as a function of age to a 2-s 75-dB, 1000 Hz tone (left panel; Graham et al., 1970). HR response as a function of age to a 50-ms white noise startle pulse at 104 dB for adults and 109 dB for infants (right panel; Graham et al., 1981, 1983).

decelerations are consistently found for 2.5-month-olds following air stream exposure (Berg & Berg, 1979; Davis et al., 1965). Similarly, the magnitude of HR decelerations to a 75 dB, 1000 Hz tone increases with age from birth to 10 months (Berg, 1975; Graham et al., 1970). Figure 7.3 shows a graph of HR responses to a 2 s tone and HR responses to a startle pulse of white noise as a function of age (Graham et al., 1970; Graham, Strock, & Zeigler, 1981; Graham et al., 1983). Infants' heart rate response to a 2 s tone of moderate intensity (75 dB) takes the form of the orienting reflex (Figure 7.3, left panel) that increases in magnitude from birth to 16 weeks of age. In contrast, HR responses to a more intense (109 dB) auditory stimulus (Figure 7.3, right panel) take the form of the defensive reflex in 6-week-olds but shifts to a heart rate deceleration (orienting reflex) of increasing magnitude from 12 to 24 weeks of age. Adults demonstrate heart rate responses of much lesser magnitude than infants regardless of the direction of the response.

Many of the early studies of infant HR responses utilized brief stimuli. These types of stimulus presentations elicit relatively short duration responses. Berg and Berg (1979) noted the importance of discriminating between brief and sustained HR decelerations. Brief decelerations may reflect an immature, subcortically mediated orienting reflex or an automatic interrupt component of orienting (Graham, 1979). If this is the case, then information processing associated with orienting and attention would be expected to occur during periods of sustained decreases in HR. Research has expanded upon the relation between HR and various components of attention and information processing in infants.

One line of work showing extended changes in HR to stimuli has been the study of children's attention to television programs (Richards & Cronise, 2000; Richards & Gibson, 1997; Richards & Turner, 2001). Rather than brief stimuli, infants and young children from 3 months to 2 years of age were presented with recordings of a "Sesame Street" movie, computer-generated geometric patterns, and similar visual stimuli. These presentations were accompanied by sound. One visual response to such stimuli is extended fixations, lasting for some occurrences up to 2 min in length. It has been hypothesized that during such long looks there is an increase in attention engagement over the course of the look (Richards & Anderson, 2004). Heart rate changes have been used in adult participants to index attentiveness to television programs (e.g., Lang, 1990). The studies of infants' and children's extended television viewing showed a typical HR deceleration as if the orienting response occurred (see, for example, Figure 7.3). Figure 7.4 shows the heart rate changes that occur in children from 6 months to 2 years of age during extended viewing (Richards & Cronise, 2000). The extended looks were accompanied by increasingly deep heart rate changes. These changes in heart rate are also associated with an increasing resistance to distraction by a peripheral stimulus (Richards & Turner, 2001). The extended slowing of HR accompanying these extended looks implies that there is an increase over the course of such looks in the extent of attentional engagement (Richards & Anderson, 2004).

Resting HR decreases with age during infancy (Bar-Haim, Marshall, & Fox, 2000; Izard et al., 1991). Heart rate also shows consistent individual

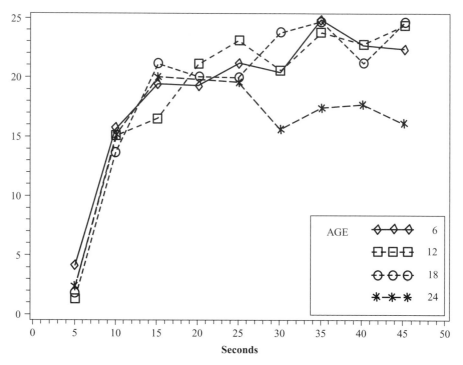

Figure 7.4. The change in IBI length (mean 5-s IBI – average prestimulus IBI) as a function of the duration of the fixation for the four testing ages, averaged across all look length categories. This figure is combined for the "Sesame Street" movie and the mixed-stimuli session. The last 5 s of the look were not included in these averages (Richards & Cronise, 2000).

differences in early development. Bar-Haim and colleagues (2000) found that resting HR at 4 months of age was significantly correlated with HR at 14, 24, and 48 months of age. However, there are specific time periods during the first year that appear to be periods of transition in which instability is found in HR measures. The first of these periods is around 6 weeks of age. It is more difficult to elicit HR deceleration at this age than at earlier and later ages (Figure 7.3; Brown, Leavitt, & Graham, 1977; Graham et al., 1983). This period of instability may reflect a shift from a predominance of subcortical to cortical control of orienting (Field et al., 1980). Beginning at around 4 months of age and lasting for several months, infants show reliable increases in HR orienting (HR deceleration) and decreases in resting HR. However, Bar-Haim and colleagues (2000) found that HR at 9 months of age was not correlated with HR at any other age measured. The developmental trend of decreasing HR begins to slow around 9 months of age, this finding may

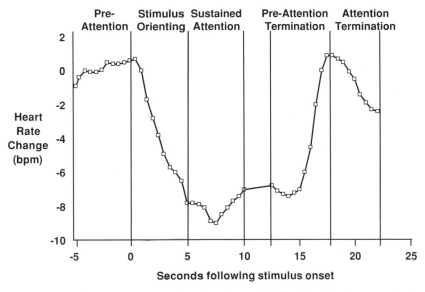

Figure 7.5. Average HR change as a function of seconds following stimulus onset during the HR-defined attention phases (Richards & Casey, 1992).

explain the lack of correlation between 9-month HR and HR measured at earlier and later ages. A cognitive transition may also be occurring at this time. Areas of frontal cortex (e.g., dorsolateral frontal cortex, orbito-frontal cortex) are becoming more functionally mature at this time, which is reflected by gains in performance on tasks measuring attention and memory (e.g., Bell, 1998; Diamond, Cruttenden, & Neiderman, 1994; Diamond, Prevor, Callender, & Druin, 1997).

Attention Phases Defined by Infant HR

Several researchers have proposed that HR measures can be used to index four phases of information processing (Courage, Reynolds, & Richards, 2006; Graham, 1979; Graham et al., 1983; Porges, 1976, 1980; Richards, 1988a, 2001; Richards & Casey, 1992; Richards & Hunter, 1998). These phases are the automatic interrupt, stimulus orienting, sustained attention, and attention termination. Changes in HR that are linked with visual fixation may be used as a means of determining which phase of attention an infant is engaged. The HR changes associated with the latter three phases of attention are depicted in Figure 7.5 for young infants. The pre-attention period depicts the time before the presentation of the visual stimulus. The pre-attention termination period is an artifact of operational definitions of attention termination (cf. Richards & Casey, 1992).

The automatic interrupt phase is the first of the information processing phases (Graham, 1979). During this phase, the infant is involved in detecting transient changes in environmental stimulation. This phase may or may not be followed by further processing of the novel information provided by the transient changes in the environment. A brief bi-phasic HR response (deceleration-acceleration) occurs in cases in which information processing is terminated. In these cases, the automatic interrupt system is manifested as a startle reflex. The automatic interrupt system is obligatory and is under the control of short-latency nervous system pathways (Richards & Casey, 1992).

Stimulus orienting is the second HR phase of attention. This phase is controlled by long-latency pathways within the nervous system. Stimulus orienting is activated by the automatic interrupt phase and is identical to the orienting reflex studied by Sokolov (1963; cf. Graham & Clifton, 1966). The stimulus orienting system is similar to the automatic interrupt system in that both are reflexive and follow the same time course regardless of subsequent input. A large deceleration in HR lasting about 5 seconds is indicative of activation of the stimulus orienting system. Stimulus orienting is an early phase of information processing in which the infant evaluates stimulus novelty, processes preliminary stimulus information, and decides whether to allocate further mental resources (Kahneman, 1973). The magnitude of HR deceleration is related to the novelty of the stimulus being processed by the infant.

Sustained attention is the third HR phase of attention (Courage et al., 2006; Porges, 1976, 1980; Richards, 1987, 1988a, 2001; Richards & Casey, 1992; Richards & Hunter, 1998). In contrast to the preceding phases, sustained attention involves voluntary, participant-controlled cognitive processing. Heart rate shows a sustained decrease from baseline, has decreased levels of variability, and is accompanied by decreased respiration amplitude, inhibition of body movements, and other bodily changes during sustained attention (Jennings, 1986). Sustained attention begins 4 to 5 seconds after visual fixation. The duration of this phase depends on the behavioral state of the infant, the relative novelty of the stimulus, stimulus complexity, and characteristics of the participant. Sustained attention may last from 2 or 3 seconds to 20 seconds or longer. This phase of attention is the phase in which the majority of information processing occurs.

The final HR attention phase is attention termination (Richards, 1988a, 1988b; Richards & Casey, 1992; Richards & Hunter, 1998). Heart rate returns to baseline levels and variability. Behaviorally, the infant continues to fixate on the stimulus during attention termination. However, the infant is no longer processing information provided by the stimulus. Attention termination lasts for approximately 6 seconds (Casey & Richards, 1991; Richards & Casey, 1991).

These attention phases are probably controlled by a variety of brain areas. The initial deceleration of HR during stimulus orienting is mediated by the parasympathetic nervous system. The CNS areas that control such changes are likely areas of the brain involved in sudden arousal or orienting such as the mesencephalic reticular activating system (Heilman et al., 1987; Mesulam, 1983). If such an orienting in the CNS leads to continued processing of the stimulus, sustained attention begins and a second CNS system is engaged. This system is a general arousal system associated with alertness and vigilance. The arousal system in the CNS is mediated by neurochemical systems that energize cortical systems (Richards, 2001; Robbins & Everitt, 1995). The neural basis for attention termination is unknown. Perhaps there is a refractory period in the attentional system that inhibits its engagement for a short period of time following sustained attention (Casey & Richards, 1991). Alternatively, it may simply be that at the end of sustained attention it takes some measurable amount of time for a new HR deceleration to occur. In this case, attention termination would simply be the cessation of the brain's arousal state before attention was yet engaged.

Relation Between Heart Rate and Behaviorally Defined Attention Phases

Differing types of attention in young infants have been found using behavioral measures of attention engagement. "Focused attention" is a period of time when infants are actively examining objects (Oakes, Madole, & Cohen, 1991). Ruff (1986) defined attentive fixation as looking combined with fingering or turning the object about with an intent facial expression. "Casual attention" is a period of time when fixation is directed toward a stimulus or object, but the infant is not actively examining the stimulus. As with the attention phases defined by HR, these attention phases occur within the course of a single look towards a stimulus, or an episode of play with a toy.

The implications for information processing of focused and casual attention are similar to those of sustained attention and attention termination. Focused attention and casual attention are behaviorally defined periods of attention and inattention. Sustained attention and attention termination are HR-defined periods of attention and inattention. Infants take longer to disengage from a central stimulus and shift attention to a distractor stimulus during focused attention than during casual attention (Oakes & Tellinghuisen, 1994; Ruff, Capozzoli, & Saltarelli, 1996; Tellinghuisen & Oakes, 1997). Similarly, infants demonstrate longer distraction latency to a peripheral stimulus presented during sustained attention than during attention termination (Casey & Richards, 1988; Hunter & Richards, 2003; Richards, 1987, 1997b). Sustained attention and focused attention are operationally defined phases of attention that represent periods when the infant is actively engaged in information processing. Distraction latencies are longer when infants are engaged in these phases of attention because infants are processing information provided by a central stimulus. During casual attention or attention termination, infants respond more rapidly to peripheral stimuli because they are no longer engaged in attention to the central stimulus.

Lansink and Richards (1997) conducted a study aimed at establishing a link between behaviorally defined and HR defined phases of attention. Infants of 6, 9, and 12 months of age were tested. Infants were seated on a parent's lap at a table. A TV monitor was located 45° to the right of the infant. The infant was allowed to play freely with a toy secured to the top of the table with suction cups. At various times during play sessions, dynamic computer-generated patterns were presented on the TV monitor as a distractor stimulus. Once the infant localized the distractor, the monitor was turned off, marking the end of the trial. For each distractor, either HR or behavior was used to determine if the infant was attentive (HR: sustained attention; behavior: focused attention) or inattentive (HR: attention termination; behavior: casual attention).

There were several interesting findings. Figure 7.6 shows the distraction latencies for infants when attentive or inattentive defined by behavior, HR, or a combination of the two. Infants had longer distraction latencies during focused attention than during casual attention. Infants also demonstrated longer distraction latencies during sustained attention than during attention termination. These findings replicate several studies (Casey & Richards, 1988; Oakes & Tellinghuisen, 1994; Richards, 1987; Ruff et al. 1996). When HR and behavioral measures were concordant for attentiveness, the infants showed the longest distraction latencies. Infants showed the shortest distraction latencies when HR and behavioral measures were concordant for inattentiveness (Figure 7.6, right panel). In addition to the distraction latencies, the HR decelerations on the focused attention trials were larger than on the casual attention trials (Figure 7.7, left panel). These findings show a large overlap between attentional status defined by HR changes and attentional status defined by behavioral indices.

Heart Rate Phases and Distractibility

Developmental psychophysiologists have investigated peripheral stimulus localization in infants for several decades. Early research in this area used

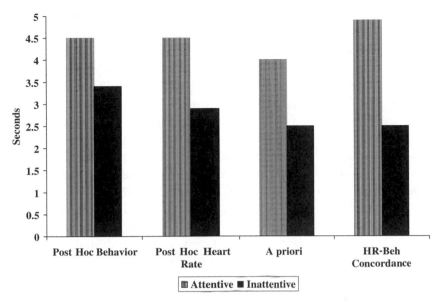

Figure 7.6. Distraction latency for engaged (shaded bars) and unengaged (solid bars) trials. This finding is shown separately for the trials defined online with HR or behavior ("a priori"), for trials defined post hoc with behavior, post hoc with HR, or post hoc when HR and behavior indices were in concordance (Lansink & Richards, 1997).

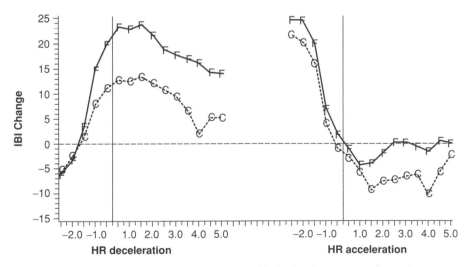

Figure 7.7. Changes in IBI when heart rate and behavioral measures of attention are congruent and incongruent. Heart rate 2.5 s before through 5 s after the heart rate deceleration and heart rate acceleration criteria were met (C: Casual attention behavioral rating; F: Focused attention behavioral rating (Lansink & Richards, 1997)).

peripheral stimulus localization as a means of determining the effective visual field of infants of varying ages (Aslin & Salapatek, 1975; de Schonen McKenzie, Maury, & Bresson, 1978; Harris & MacFarlane, 1974; MacFarlane, Harris, & Barnes, 1976; Tronick, 1972). As age increases in early development, infants will demonstrate fixation shifts of increasing eccentricity from a central stimulus to a peripheral stimulus. This increase in the eccentricity at which an infant will shift fixation from a central to peripheral stimulus was interpreted as an increase in the size of the effective visual field. Subsequent research has utilized peripheral stimulus localization as a measure of infant attention to a central stimulus (Atkinson, Hood, Braddick, & Wattam-Bell, 1988; Atkinson, Hood, Wattam-Bell, & Braddick, 1992; Hood & Atkinson, 1993; Richards, 1987, 1994; Richards & Casey, 1992). The logic behind this approach is partially based on the finding that infants demonstrate greater localization eccentricities to peripheral stimuli when no central stimulus is used, or the central stimulus is turned off, than in competitive situations when the central stimulus remains on after presentation of the peripheral stimulus (Harris & MacFarlane, 1974). Furthermore, infants demonstrate longer latencies to localize peripheral stimuli if a central stimulus is present (Aslin & Salapatek, 1975). These findings have been interpreted as an effect of attention to the central stimulus (Finlay & Ivinskis, 1984; Harris & MacFarlane, 1974; Richards, 1987). A lack of responsiveness to a peripheral stimulus is indicative of an enhanced level of attention directed toward the central stimulus, and responsiveness to a peripheral stimulus indicates distractibility due to a lack of attention toward the central stimulus.

Several studies have used the HR-defined attention phases to study infant distractibility (Casey & Richards, 1988; Hicks & Richards, 1998; Hunter & Richards, 2003; Lansink & Richards, 1997; Richards, 1987, 1997b; Richards & Hunter, 1997; Richards & Turner, 2001; see review in Richards & Lansink, 1998). These studies have several things in common. First, the infant's attention is attracted to a central stimulus (i.e., a stimulus located in the center of the infant's visual field). Examples of central stimuli used are computer-generated visual patterns, audiovisual patterns, movies and television programs such as "Sesame Street," and objects and small toys. Second, HR is recorded during the presentations and computer algorithms are used to evaluate the HR online. When a significant deceleration in HR occurs, or when HR returns to its prestimulus level, a stimulus is presented in the periphery. Examples of the peripheral stimuli that have been used are: small lights, a presentation of a large stimulus on another television, a small peripheral square, or dynamic stimulus presented in the periphery. Third, consistent findings have been found in each of these studies. When a peripheral stimulus is presented contingent upon the deceleration of HR (i.e., sustained attention is occurring), a localization to the peripheral stimulus does not occur, or takes a long time. Alternatively, when the peripheral stimulus is presented contingent upon the return of HR to its prestimulus level (i.e., attention termination), peripheral stimulus localization occurs more frequently and rapidly. These findings imply that it is not simply the presence of a central stimulus that attenuates peripheral stimulus localization. Rather, increased attentiveness to the central stimulus blocks or attenuates the localization of the peripheral stimulus. If the infant is looking at the central stimulus but not attentive, the response to the peripheral stimulus occurs at nearly normal levels (see Richards & Lansink, 1998, for further details).

An example of these studies is that of Richards (1997b). This study examined the impact of infant attention to a central stimulus on peripheral stimulus localization. A cross-sectional design was utilized with infants of 14, 20, and 26 weeks of age. Infants were seated in a parent's lap facing the inner edges of two TV monitors. A central stimulus (e.g., computer-generated patterns or a Sesame Street program) was presented on one monitor, and a peripheral stimulus (e.g., a white square traveling from top to bottom) was presented on the other monitor. The onset of peripheral stimulus presentations was determined online by HR changes or by predetermined time delays. The heart rate-defined delays were HR deceleration, HR deceleration plus 2 seconds, HR acceleration, and HR acceleration plus 2 seconds. The HR deceleration delays represented periods in which the infant was engaged in sustained attention, and the HR acceleration delays represented attention termination. The time-defined delays were 0, 2, 4, 6, 8, 10, and 12 seconds. For the time-defined delays, the level of HR change at the onset of the peripheral stimulus was measured.

Figure 7.8 shows the percentages of peripheral stimulus localization as a function of the HR changes occurring during the presentations. The detection of the peripheral stimulus when no central stimulus was present (Prestim in Figure 7.8) was about 80%, and was close to that when the HR had returned to its prestimulus level (HRAcc in Figure 7.8; attention termination). Conversely, shortly after stimulus presentation (Immed in Figure 7.8) or during HR deceleration (HRDec; sustained attention), peripheral stimulus localization dropped to about 35%. The small levels of peripheral stimulus localization during sustained attention indicate an enhanced level of attention directed toward the central stimulus. The increased levels of response to the peripheral stimulus in the prestimulus or attention termination periods indicate inattentiveness toward the central stimulus.

In addition to measuring the percentage of peripheral stimulus localizations following these delays, the epochs of peripheral stimulus localization trials were classified into four categories for signal detection analysis:

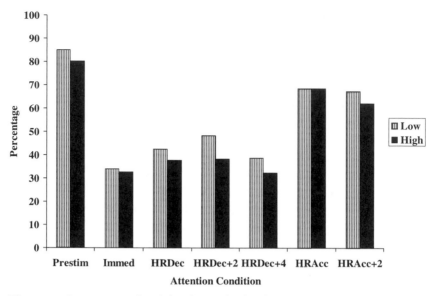

Figure 7.8. Percentages of peripheral stimulus localization as a function of the HR changes occurring during distractor presentations. No central stimulus was present during the prestimulus period (Prestim). The immediate period (Immed) refers to stimulus onset. Sustained attention coincides with all of the HR deceleration periods (HRDec), and attention termination is represented by HR accelerations (HRAcc) (adapted from Richards, 1997b).

localization (hit), nonlocalization (miss), correct rejection, and false alarm (also see Hicks & Richards, 1998). The latter two categories applied to control trials in which no peripheral stimulus was presented. A false alarm occurred when the infant performed a saccade toward the peripheral screen on trials when no peripheral stimulus was presented. The purpose of this analysis was to determine whether attention affected stimulus discriminability or response bias. The results of the signal detection analysis provide insight into a possible mechanism behind the impact of attention on peripheral stimulus localization. Stimulus discriminability was equivalent for the sustained attention and attention termination epochs, but localization was more probable during attention termination than during sustained attention. In addition, the false alarm percentage during attention termination was significantly higher than during sustained attention indicating, a low response bias against localizing the peripheral stimulus during periods of inattention. The bias against responding to the peripheral stimulus was much higher during sustained attention. These findings demonstrate that the effect of attention on peripheral stimulus localization is due to an increased bias to maintain fixation toward the central stimulus during sustained attention. Attentional processes do not affect perceptual sensitivity toward peripheral distractors; instead, infant-controlled decision processes to maintain attention toward the central stimulus explain lower percentages of peripheral stimulus localization during sustained attention.

Attention and Recognition Memory

Another construct of interest to developmental psychophysiologists is recognition memory. The paired-comparison procedure is a behavioral measure often utilized in recognition memory studies. This procedure entails familiarizing the infant with an individual visual stimulus. Following the familiarization procedure, the infant is presented simultaneously with two stimuli. One stimulus is the previously seen familiar stimulus; the other stimulus is a novel stimulus. Look duration toward each stimulus is the dependent variable. A novelty preference indicates recognition of the familiar stimulus because infants naturally prefer to look at novel stimuli. A familiarity preference indicates partial processing of the previously seen stimulus during the familiarization phase (Hunter, Ross, & Ames, 1982; Rose, Gottfried, Melloy-Carminar, & Bridger, 1982; Wagner & Sakovits, 1986). Past research indicates that older infants require less exposure time during the familiarization phase than younger infants to demonstrate a novelty preference (Colombo, Mitchell, & Horowitz, 1988; Rose, 1983; Rose et al., 1982). Rose et al. (1982) found that 3- and 6-month-olds demonstrated familiarity preferences following familiarization exposure times of 5 or 10 seconds. Three-month-olds required 30 seconds of familiarization to demonstrate novelty preferences, while 6-month-olds required only 15 seconds of familiarization. It is clear that older infants process the familiar stimulus more efficiently than younger infants. One possible explanation for this age effect is that older infants are more attentive during familiarization than younger infants.

Richards (1997a) investigated the role of attention in the paired-comparison recognition memory paradigm. A Sesame Street video was shown to infants 14, 20, and 26 weeks of age in order to elicit the various phases of attention. After a delay, infants were exposed to a visual pattern for 2.5 or 5 seconds. The visual pattern was presented while the infant was engaged in sustained attention, attention termination, or 5 seconds following attention termination. It was hypothesized that each of these conditions would be associated with differential amounts of processing of the familiar stimulus. Exposure during sustained attention should be associated with enhanced processing compared to exposure during attention termination. The last condition was used because following the process of attention termination infants should be receptive to the presentation of a novel stimulus.

In contrast to Rose and colleagues' (1982) finding that 6-month-olds require 15 seconds of exposure to demonstrate a novelty preference, in the sustained attention and the attention termination plus 5 seconds delay conditions, 20- and 26-week-olds (i.e., 4.5- and 6-month-olds) preferred the novel stimulus after only 5 seconds of familiarization. These age groups demonstrated familiarity preferences with 5 seconds of familiarization during the attention termination delay condition. Moreover, a post-hoc analysis of the attention termination plus 5 seconds delay condition revealed that exposure to the familiarization phase during sustained attention was positively correlated with novelty preferences during the test phase. This finding indicates that infants demonstrating a novelty preference in this condition had cycled out of attention termination and were once again engaged in sustained attention. Thus, determining stimulus presentation based on visual fixation and HR measures of attention provides greater control over the attentional status of the infant during exposure and may lead to an increased effect size than when stimulus presentation is based on visual fixation alone.

Individual differences in look duration and the amount of time spent in various HR phases of attention related to performance in the paired comparison paradigm have been investigated (Colombo et al., 2001). Longer duration of looking during a pretest phase and the familiarization phase was positively associated with more time spent in sustained attention and attention termination. Interestingly, individual differences in the overall amount of time spent in sustained attention did not account for a significant amount of variance in recognition memory performance, but individual differences in attention termination did account for a significant amount of variance in performance. However, amount of time spent in attention termination was negatively correlated with novelty preferences. The greater the amount of time spent in attention termination the less likely the infant demonstrated a novelty preference.

Several studies of infant recognition memory development have used the electroencephalogram (EEG) to measure event-related potentials (ERPs) related to recognition memory. ERPs are voltage oscillations recorded on the scalp that are time-locked with a specific physical or mental event (Fabiani, Gratton, & Coles, 2000; Picton et al., 2000). Nelson and Collins (1991, 1992) designed a modified oddball procedure for measuring ERP correlates of recognition memory in infants. First, infants are exposed to repeated presentations of two different stimuli. Then, the participants are exposed to one of the familiar stimuli on 60% of the trials (frequent familiar), the other familiar stimulus on 20% of the trials (infrequent familiar), and novel stimulus presentations on the remaining 20% of the trials (infrequent novel). Infants tested using the modified oddball procedure demonstrate a large negative ERP component occurring about 400–800 ms after stimulus onset located primarily in the frontal and central EEG leads. This pattern has been labeled the "Negative central" (Nc) component (Courchesne, 1977, 1978). Nelson and Collins (1991, 1992) found no differences in the Nc component for any of the stimulus presentation conditions for 4-, 6-, and 8-month-old infants. The authors concluded that the Nc is indicative of a general orienting response. Later components of the ERP did differ between presentation conditions for older infants. Older infants demonstrated a negative slow wave following novel stimulus presentations and a positive slow wave following infrequent familiar stimulus presentations. The positive slow wave is likely a response associated with an updating of working memory following presentation of a familiar yet only partially encoded stimulus, whereas the negative slow wave represents the initial processing of new information provided by a novel stimulus. Thus, it is plausible that the late slow wave ERP components reflect processes associated with recognition memory, while the Nc component reflects general orienting and attention.

The close association of attention and the Nc component was addressed in a study by Richards (2003). Infants were tested at 4.5, 6, or 7.5 months of age. During the modified oddball procedure, a recording of Sesame Street was presented between the brief stimulus presentations. Heart rate changes elicited by the Sesame Street presentation were used to distinguish periods of time before attention was engaged (before heart rate deceleration), during sustained attentiveness (during heart rate deceleration), and inattentiveness after sustained attention (after heart rate deceleration). The ERP components occurring during sustained attention were compared to those occurring during periods of inattentiveness. There were several findings of interest. First, the Nc did not differ for the three stimulus types (frequent familiar, infrequent familiar, infrequent novel), but the Nc amplitude was significantly larger during periods of attention (i.e., stimulus orienting and sustained attention) than during periods of inattentiveness (see Figure 7.9). The Nc component during sustained attention also increased in amplitude with age. Second, late slow waves were found at about 1 to 2 s following stimulus onset. During attention, 4.5-month-olds demonstrated a positive late slow wave that was similar for familiar and novel presentations. The older infants (6- and 7.5-month-olds) displayed a negative late slow wave following presentations of the novel stimulus, which stood in contrast to the positive slow wave these groups displayed following infrequent familiar stimulus

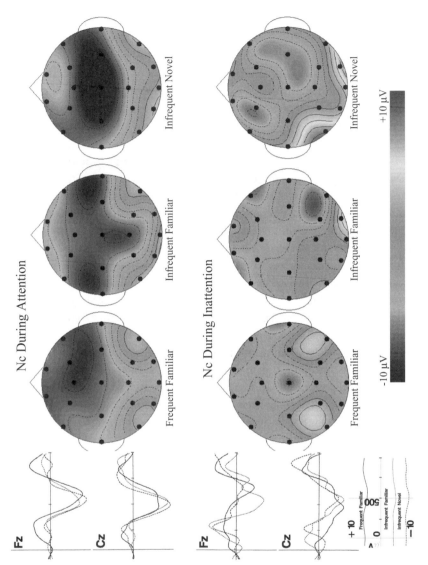

Figure 7.9. See facing page.

presentations. The age differences suggest that (during sustained attention) the older two age groups were sensitive to stimulus novelty and probability, whereas the younger infants were sensitive only to stimulus probability. The stimulus presentations occurring during inattention did not show the slow wave differences among the three presentation procedures.

Reynolds and Richards (2005) conducted an investigation of the relation between attention and ERP correlates of recognition memory in infants utilizing high-density (124 channel) EEG recordings and HR. The studies discussed in the preceding paragraphs utilized small numbers of electrodes when recording EEG (<30). The data obtained using relatively small numbers of electrodes can only yield limited conclusions regarding the electrical activity measured at the scalp, and cannot be used to accurately estimate the cortical sources of this electrical activity. High-density EEG recordings provide sufficient data for estimating the cortical sources of ERP components. Equivalent current dipole analysis is used to determine source localization (Richards & Hunter, 2002). Findings indicated that the cortical source of the Nc component occurs in regions of the prefrontal cortex including the anterior cingulate. The anterior cingulate is part of the cingulate cortex, a paralimbic region of the brain that shares reciprocal connections with several subcortical, cortical, and limbic regions (Cohen, 1993). Studies have shown that the anterior cingulate is involved in visual target detection and the control or direction of attention (Casey et al., 1997; Goldman-Rakic, 1988). The Nc component was greater in magnitude during sustained attention than during periods of inattention following novel stimulus presentations. Additionally, infants demonstrated Nc of greater magnitude following novel stimulus presentations than familiar stimulus presentations. The interaction between HR attention phases and stimulus type on the magnitude of the Nc component combined with cortical source localization of Nc in the anterior cingulate suggests that the Nc component represents a general orienting response more closely associated with attention than with recognition memory (Nelson & Collins, 1991, 1992; Richards, 2003).

Figure 7.9. The Nc component during attention and inattention. The ERP recording from 100 ms prior to stimulus onset through 1 s following stimulus onset is shown for the Fz and Cz electrodes for attentive (top figures) and inattentive (bottom figures) periods, combined over the three testing ages. The topographical scalp potential maps show the distribution of this component for the three memory stimulus types in attention and inattention. The topographical maps represent an 80-ms average of the ERP for the Nc component at the maximum point of the ERP response. The data are plotted with a cubic spline interpolation algorithm and represent absolute amplitude of the ERP (Richards, 2003).

Moreover, the use of HR as a means of controlling for attentiveness during stimulus presentation may serve to increase effect sizes found in studies utilizing EEG recordings (similar to increased effect sizes found in behavioral studies).

Heart Rate Variability

Resting HR shows variability in normal, healthy humans. The pacemaker cells in the SA node spontaneously depolarize at a constant rate. Thus, left unaided, resting HR would be a continuous unvarying level. However, several sources of variability occur in HR due to the central and autonomic nervous systems. Blood pressure regulation, homeostatic control for activity needs, and respiration all act to modify the pacemaker cells depolarization, and thus keep resting HR variable. Thus, variability in HR is assumed to reflect continuous feedback between the central nervous system and peripheral autonomic receptors.

A well-known variability in HR is called respiratory sinus arrhythmia (RSA). Variability in HR has been found to oscillate at three frequencies (Berntson et al., 1997; Porges, 1992; Porter, 2001). The highest frequency oscillation in HR ranges from 0.3 to 1.5 Hz. Accelerations and decelerations in HR occurring in this frequency band occur at the same rate of respiration inhalations and exhalations (Porter et al., 1995; Richards & Casey, 1992), thus giving the term "respiratory" to RSA. As presented in the first section, the brain areas controlling RSA are well known. This rhythmic activity is controlled by brain stem respiratory centers modulating the parasympathetic influence over HR via the vagus nerve. Because of its close association with the level of vagal activity, RSA is often labeled "vagal tone" (Porges, 2001).

Porges (1985, 1992; Porges & Bohrer, 1990) has developed a method for quantifying RSA. This method involves four steps: (1) detection of the IBIs, (2) time sampling of the heart period data, (3) detrending the heart period time series with the use of a moving band-pass filter, and (4) extracting and logarithmically transforming the variance in the frequency band associated with respiration. Other methods of obtaining variability measures at the frequency of RSA include spectral analysis and peak-to-trough filters (Askelrod et al., 1985; Berntson et al., 1997; Harper, Scalabassi, & Estrin, 1976; Richards, 1986; Womack, 1971; Schectman, Kluge, & Harper, 1981). Richards (1995b) has evaluated the reliability of RSA for each method of quantification in infants and found that the use of moving band-pass filters is more reliable in some cases than peak-to-trough filters. Additionally, spectral analysis

TABLE 7.1. (A) Heart rate changes in attention phases from 2 to 6 months of age. (B) Heart rate changes in attention phases for high and low RSA infants. (C) Baseline HR and RSA in full-term infants from 3 to 6 months of age (adapted from Richards, 1995a)

1A. Heart rate changes in attention phases from 2 to 6 months

	8 weeks	14 weeks	20 weeks	26 weeks
Stimulus orienting	−3.7	−4.2	−5.2	−4.7
Sustained attention	−6.9	−6.9	−8.5	−11.0
Attention termination	−1.7	−2.8	0.3	0.3

1B. Heart rate changes in attention phases for high and low RSA infants

	Low RSA	High RSA
Stimulus orienting	−4.8	−5.2
Sustained attention	−7.9	−11.5
Attention termination	−1.3	−0.5

1C. Baseline HR and RSA in full-term infants from 3 to 6 months of age

	14 weeks	20 weeks	26 weeks
Baseline HR	152	148	142
Baseline RSA	0.78	0.86	0.92

techniques require longer sampling durations to demonstrate reliability than the other methods. Furthermore, utilizing a fixed high-frequency band corresponding to RSA frequency (0.333–1.250 Hz) produced results equivalent to those obtained using the observed respiration frequency found from measuring actual respiration with a pneumatic chest cuff. This finding indicates that the measurement of HR along with filtering techniques is adequate for the measurement of RSA in infants, and measuring the actual respiration of infants to determine their specific respiration frequency is not necessary for obtaining reliable, valid data.

Infant Heart Rate Variability Studies

Many studies have shown a relation between resting levels of HR variability, particularly RSA, and infant attention and social behavior. Individual differences in HR responding are shown by the strong relation between changes in sustained attention and RSA in early development. Heart rate change during sustained attention increases from 8 weeks to 6 months of age (Richards, 1985a; see Table 7.1a). From 3 to 6 months of age, the HR response during sustained attention is larger for infants with high levels of RSA than those with low RSA (Table 7.1b). Overall, RSA is stable over this age range

(Izard et al., 1991; Richards, 1989, 1994). The relation between RSA and sustained attention appears to be due to developmental change in RSA during this time period (Table 7.1c). RSA increases over the first postnatal year and HR decreases (Bar-Haim et al., 2000; Frick & Richards, 2001; Harper et al., 1978; Katona, Frasz, & Egbert, 1980; Richards, 1985b, 1987; Richards & Casey, 1991; Watanabe, Iwase, & Hara, 1973). Increases in RSA most likely account for developmental decreases in resting HR and increases in HR responding during sustained attention.

The reason that HR changes during attention and RSA are correlated is likely due to their common control by the parasympathetic nervous system. The HR deceleration occurring during attention, indicating the onset of stimulus orienting and sustained attention, is caused by a large efferent discharge of vagal activity. Similarly, the rhythmic aspect of RSA is controlled by the brainstem respiratory centers, but the changes in HR are mediated by the vagal innervation of the heart. The relation between these two systems suggests that individual differences in RSA level do reflect a tonic difference in resting vagal activity (i.e., vagal tone; Porges, 2001). Thus, heart rate variability manifested in vagal tone (RSA level) is correlated with sustained attention because both are mediated through activity of the same network of structures within the central nervous system.

Other measures of HR variability during testing have been found to be related to individual differences in looking time in the visual habituation paradigm (Maikranz, Colombo, Richman, & Frick, 2000). In the visual habituation paradigm, infants receive multiple exposures to a visual stimulus. The duration of looks toward the stimulus declines across repeated presentations as the stimulus is more fully processed. Look duration is measured as an indicator of attention and information processing during habituation. The duration of looks reflects the efficiency of information processing in an individual infant (Cohen, 1988; Colombo & Mitchell, 1990). Look duration is moderately stable across the first year of postnatal life and may reflect individual differences in cognitive functioning (Bornstein, Pecheux, & Lecuyer, 1988; Byrne, Clark-Tousenard, Hondas, & Smith, 1985; Colombo, 1993; Colombo & Mitchell, 1990). From this perspective, infants demonstrating shorter look durations (short-lookers) during habituation are posited as more efficient information processors than infants demonstrating longer look durations (long-lookers). In support of this hypothesis, short-looking infants achieve novelty preferences in the paired-comparison paradigm with comparatively shorter familiarization exposure times than long-looking infants (Colombo, Freeseman, Coldren, & Frick, 1995; Colombo, Mitchell, Coldren, & Freeseman, 1991; Frick & Colombo, 1996; Jankowski & Rose, 1997). Maikranz et al. (2000) found that at 4 months of age, short-looking infants demonstrate greater HR variability than long-looking infants across habituation sessions. Additionally, long-looking infants displayed greater acceleration in HR following stimulus onset than short-looking infants. This finding may indicate that long-looking infants are more physiologically reactive during testing procedures than short-looking infants. Thus, the long-lookers may have actually reacted with a startle response to stimulus onsets. In a study conducted by Bornstein and Suess (2000), infants with higher baseline RSA at 2 and 5 months of age demonstrated shorter looking times in an infant-controlled habituation task than lower baseline RSA infants. Greater suppression of RSA during habituation was associated with more efficient habituation. Richards and Casey (1991) found that RSA decreases during sustained attention. Thus, infants demonstrating suppression of RSA during habituation were likely engaged in sustained attention.

Frick and Richards (2001) investigated the relation between baseline RSA, attention, and performance on the paired-comparison paradigm in 14-, 20-, and 26-week-olds. Baseline RSA was measured, and the paired-comparison procedure was administered with familiarization exposure presented during periods of attention or inattention as indicated by HR phases. Older infants (i.e., 20- and 26-week-olds) and infants with higher RSA showed more evidence of recognition memory than the 14-week-olds and the low RSA infants. Additionally, familiarization exposure during sustained attention was associated with greater novelty preferences than familiarization exposure during periods when HR indicated inattention (replicating Richards, 1997a). Infants from 14 to 26 weeks of age with high baseline RSA have larger and more sustained HR responses in sustained attention than do low RSA infants (Casey & Richards, 1988; Richards, 1985b, 1987, 1989). Heart rate changes in sustained attention correlate with RSA, whereas heart rate changes in stimulus orienting and attention termination do not correlate with RSA (Richards, 1985b).

Variability in HR has been found to correlate with behavioral measures of temperament. In particular, behavioral inhibition is a personality style associated with temperament in which the child is reluctant to display approach behaviors in unfamiliar conditions. Low RSA is associated with behavioral inhibition in children across cultures (e.g., Kagan, Kearsley, & Zelazo, 1978; Garcia-Koll, Kagan, & Reznick, 1984). Kagan has posited that this finding may be due to a decrease in RSA associated with increased mental work load for behaviorally inhibited children in unfamiliar situations. This significant increase in processing of information in unfamiliar situations may not occur in uninhibited children.

Research conducted by Fox (1989) indicates that greater RSA in the first year of life is associated with greater cardiovascular and behavioral reactivity to environmental stimulation. Infants with higher RSA at birth demonstrate more self-regulatory behaviors in response to arm restraint at 5 months. Five-month-old infants with high RSA also display more negative expressions during arm restraint than low RSA infants (Stifter & Fox, 1990). Additionally, infants with greater RSA demonstrate longer durations of interest expression in face-to-face interactions with their mothers (Fox & Gelles, 1984). Feldman, Greenbaum, and Yirmiya (1999) noted that face-to-face interactions begin around 2 months of age, and these interactions expose the infant to high levels of cognitive and social information. The coordination of affective expressions (termed mother-infant affect synchrony) during face-to-face interactions is believed to facilitate transition from mutual-regulation to self-regulation. Self-regulation develops in the context of mutual regulation between parent and infant. Maternal-infant affect synchrony at 3 months of age is negatively correlated with infant negative affect during maternal-infant interactions. Maternal-infant affect synchrony in interaction at 3 months of age is positively related to self-control at 9 months of age, and both are negatively correlated with difficult temperament. Thus, although high RSA is associated with behavioral reactivity, infants with high RSA may be more responsive during maternal-infant interactions associated with the development of enhanced self-regulatory capacities. Thus, depending on early social experience with a primary caregiver, infants with high RSA may or may not develop behaviors consistent with maladaptive temperament categories (e.g., behavioral reactivity). The relation between RSA and temperament measures is not clear at this point and may change over time with development.

Summary and Conclusion

The use of the HR in developmental psychophysiological research has been reviewed focusing on three measures obtained from HR data. These measures are HR changes, phases of attention indexed by HR, and HR variability. The research in this area has provided valuable insight into cognitive functioning in infants before they are able to provide verbal responses or engage in complex behavioral tasks. These HR measures are all associated with activity in similar and dissimilar brain areas. A common brain area for HR change is the sympathetic or parasympathetic innervation of the heart, since all CNS control influences HR via these systems. However, phasic HR changes during stimulus orienting, the extended slowing of HR during sustained attention, and the rhythmic variability found in RSA are controlled by different brain systems. We believe that research with infants using HR has provided not only an interesting set of findings concerning infants' psychological processes but also an understanding of the cognitive neuroscience processes influencing such behaviors.

Developmental change has been documented in HR responses throughout the first year of postnatal life. For example, resting HR decreases (Bar-Haim et al., 2000; Izard et al., 1991), and HR responses to stimulus presentations change in direction and/or magnitude with age during infancy (e.g., Berg, 1975; Berg & Berg, 1979; Graham et al., 1970; Graham et al., 1983; Harper et al., 1976, 1978; Katona et al., 1980; Watanabe et al., 1973). The level of HR change during sustained attention increases from 8 to 26 weeks of age. This change in sustained attention parallels the increasing ability of infants to acquire familiarity with stimulus characteristics (e.g., Frick & Richards, 2001; Richards, 1997a). This increased ability to process information occurs primarily during sustained attention rather than the other attention phases. Sustained attention is the HR phase indicative of intensive cognitive processing. RSA increases during this time period, and this increase most likely accounts for the developmental changes found in sustained attention (Bar-Haim et al., 2000; Frick & Richards, 2001; Harper et al., 1978; Katona et al., 1980; Richards, 1985b, 1987; Richards & Casey, 1991; Watanabe et al., 1973).

Changes in RSA and sustained attention reflect further development of a "general arousal attention system" composed of reciprocal connections in the frontal cortex, the limbic system, and the mesencephalic reticular activating system (Heilman et al., 1987; Mesulam, 1983; Richards, 2001; Richards & Casey, 1992; Richards & Hunter, 1998). Developmental changes in sustained attention and RSA throughout infancy are a result of this system developing, the development of this system's role in invigorating neural systems involved in attention, and the increasing level of integration between this general arousal system and attention systems that specifically enhance cognitive operations. Sustained attention thus correlates with behavioral measures of attention and information processing. High RSA infants demonstrate greater HR responses during sustained attention (Richards, 1995a). Baseline measures of RSA are indicative of individual differences in the capacity of infants to demonstrate sustained attention. Heart rate measures can thus be used as an immediate measure of cognitive processing in infants, and as a measure of an individual infant's capacity to demonstrate attentional responses. The insight obtained from heart rate measures provides developmental psychophysiologists with an invaluable tool for investigating cognitive development in infancy.

ACKNOWLEDGMENTS

This research was supported by a grant to JER from the National Institute of Child Health and Human Development (R01-HD18942).

References

Akselrod, S., Gordon, D., Madwed, J. B., Snidman, N. C., Shannon, D. C., & Cohen, R. J. (1985). Hemodynamic regulation: Investigation by spectral analysis. *American Journal of Physiology, 249*, H867–H875.

Andreassi, J. L. (1989). *Psychophysiology: Human behavior and physiological response.* Hillsdale, NJ: Lawrence Erlbaum Associates.

Anrep, G. W., Pascual, W., & Rossler, R. (1935). Respiratory variations of the heart rate. I. The reflex mechanism of the respiratory arrhythmia. *Royal Society of London Proceedings, Series B, 119*, 191–217.

Aslin, R. N., & Salapatek, P. (1975). Saccadic localization of visual targets by the very young human infant. *Perception and Psychophysics, 17*, 293–302.

Atkinson, J., Hood, B., Braddick, O. J., & Wattam-Bell, J. (1988). Infants' control of fixation shifts with single and competing targets: Mechanisms for shifting attention. *Perception, 17*, 367–368.

Atkinson, J., Hood, B., Wattam-Bell, J., & Braddick, O. J. (1992). Changes in infants' ability to switch visual attention in the first three months of life. *Perception, 21*, 643–653.

Bar-Haim, Y., Marshall, P. J., & Fox, N. A. (2000). Developmental changes in heart period and high-frequency heart period variability from 4 months to 4 years of age. *Developmental Psychobiology, 37*, 44–56.

Bell, M. A. (1998). Frontal lobe function during infancy: Implications for the development of cognition and attention. In J. E. Richards (Ed.), *Cognitive neuroscience of attention: A developmental perspective* (pp. 287–316). Hillsdale, NJ: Lawrence Erlbaum Associates.

Berg, W. K. (1975). Cardiac components of the defense response in infants. *Psychophysiology, 12*, 244.

Berg, W. K., & Berg, K. M. (1979). Psychophysiological development in infancy: State, sensory function, and attention. In J. Osofsky (Ed.), *Handbook of infant development* (pp. 283–343). New York: Wiley.

Berntson, G. G., Bigger, J. T., Eckberg, D. L., Grossman, P., Kaufmann, P. G., Malik, M., Nagaraja, H. N., Porges, S. W., Saul, J. P., Stone, P. H., & van der Molen, M. W. (1997). Heart rate variability: Origins, methods, and interpretive caveats. *Psychophysiology, 34*, 623–648.

Berntson, G. G., Cacioppo, J. T., & Quigley, K. S. (1993). Respiratory sinus arrhythmia: Autonomic origins, physiological mechanisms, and psychophysiological implications. *Psychophysiology, 30*, 183–196.

Bornstein, M. H., Pecheux, M. G., & Lecuyer, R. (1988). Visual habituation in human infants: Development and rearing circumstances. *Psychological Research, 50*, 130–133.

Bornstein, M. H., & Suess, P. E. (2000). Physiological self-regulation and information processing in infancy: Cardiac vagal tone and habituation. *Child Development, 71,* 273–287.

Brown, J. W., Leavitt, L. A., & Graham, F. K. (1977). Response to auditory stimuli in 12-week-old infants. *Developmental Psychobiology, 10,* 255–266.

Brownley, K. A., Hurwitz, B. E., & Schneiderman, N. (2000). Cardiovascular psychophysiology. In J. T. Cacioppo, L. G. Tassinary, & G. G. Berntson (Eds.), *Handbook of psychophysiology* (pp. 224–264). Cambridge, UK: Cambridge University Press.

Byrne, J. M., Clark-Tousenard, M. E., Hondas, B. J., & Smith, I. M. (1985). *Stability of individual differences in infant visual attention.* Unpublished paper presented at the Biennial Meeting of the Society for Research in Child Development, Toronto, Canada.

Casey, B. J., & Richards, J. E. (1988). Sustained visual attention measured with an adapted version of the visual preference paradigm. *Child Development, 59,* 1514–1521.

Casey, B. J., & Richards, J. E. (1991). A refractory period for the heart rate response in infant visual attention. *Developmental Psychobiology, 24,* 327–340.

Casey, B. J., Trainor, R., Giedd, J., Vauss, Y., Vaituzis, C. K., Hamburger, S., Kozuch, P., & Rapoport, J. L. (1997). The role of anterior cingulate in automatic and controlled processes: A developmental neuroanatomical study. *Developmental Psychobiology, 30,* 61–69.

Chase, H. H. (1965). *Habituation of an acceleratory cardiac response in neonates.* Unpublished Master's Thesis, University of Wisconsin.

Clarkson, M. G., & Berg, W. K. (1983). Cardiac orienting and vowel discrimination in newborns: Crucial stimulus parameters of acoustic stimuli. *Child Development, 54,* 162–171.

Clifton, R. K., & Nelson, M. N. (1976). Developmental study of habituation in infants: The importance of paradigm, response system and state. In T. J Tighe & R. N. Leaton (Eds.), *Habituation: Perspectives from child development, animal behavior, and neurophysiology* (pp. 159–206). Hillsdale, NJ: Lawrence Erlbaum Associates.

Cohen, L. B. (1988). The relationship between infant habituation and infant information processing. *European Bulletin of Cognitive Psychology/Cahiers de Psychologie Cognitive, 8,* 442–444.

Cohen, R. A. (1993). *The neuropsychology of attention.* New York, NY: Plenum Press.

Colombo, J. (1993). *Infant cognition: Predicting later intellectual functioning.* Newbury Park, CA: Sage.

Colombo, J., Freeseman, L. J., Coldren, J. T., & Frick, J. E. (1995). Individual differences in infant visual fixation: Dominance of global and local stimulus properties. *Cognitive Development, 10,* 271–285.

Colombo, J., & Mitchell, D. W. (1990). Individual and developmental differences in infant visual attention. In J. Colombo & J. W. Fagan (Eds.), *Individual differences in infancy* (pp. 193–227). Hillsdale, NJ: Lawrence Erlbaum Associates.

Colombo, J., Mitchell, D. W., Coldren, J. T., & Freeseman, L. J. (1991). Individual differences in infant visual attention: Are short lookers faster processors or feature processors? *Child Development, 62,* 1247–1257.

Colombo, J., Mitchell, D. W., & Horowitz, F. D. (1988). Infant visual behavior in the paired-comparison paradigm. *Child Development, 59,* 1198–1210.

Colombo, J., Richman, W. A., Shaddy, D. J., Greenhoot, A. F., & Maikranz, J. M. (2001). Heart rate-defined phases of attention, look duration, and infant performance in the paired-comparison paradigm. *Child Development, 72,* 1605–1616.

Courage, M. L., Reynolds, G. D., & Richards, J. E. (2006). Infants' visual attention to patterned stimuli: Developmental change from 3- to 12-months of age. *Child Development, 77,* 680–695.

Courchesne, E. (1977). Event-related brain potentials: Comparison between children and adults. *Science, 197,* 589–592.

Courchesne, E. (1978). Neurophysiological correlates of cognitive development: Changes in long-latency event-related potentials from childhood to adulthood. *Electroencephalography and Clinical Neurophysiology, 45,* 468–482.

Darrow, C. W. (1929). Differences in the physiological reactions to sensory and ideational stimuli. *Psychological Bulletin, 26,* 185–201.

Davis, R. C., Buchwald, A. M., & Frankmann, R. W. (1955). Autonomic and muscular responses and their relation to simple stimuli. *Psychological Monographs, 69,* 1–71.

Davis, C. M., Crowell, D. H., & Chun, B. J. (1965). Monophasic heart rate accelerations in human infants to peripheral stimulation. *American Psychologist, 20,* 478.

de Schonen, S., McKenzie, B., Maury, L., & Bresson, F. (1978). Central and peripheral object distances as determinants of the effective visual field in early infancy. *Perception, 7,* 499–506.

Diamond, A., Cruttenden, L., & Neiderman, D. (1994). AB with multiple wells: 1. Why are multiple wells sometimes easier than two wells? 2. Memory or memory + inhibition. *Developmental Psychology, 30,* 192–205.

Diamond, A., Prevor, M. B., Callender, G., & Druin, D. P. (1997). Prefrontal cortex cognitive deficits in children treated early and continuously for PKU. *Monographs of the Society for Research in Child Development, 62,* 4.

Einthoven, W., Fahr, G., & de Waart, A. (1913). Uber die richtung und die manifeste grosse der pontetialshwankungen in menchlichen herzen und uber den einfluss der herzlage auf die for des elecktrokardiogram. *Archives of Physiology, 150,* 275–315.

Fabiani, M., Gratton, G., & Coles, M. G. H. (2000). Event-related brain potentials: Methods, theory, and applications. In J. T. Cacioppo, L. G. Tassinary, & G. G. Berntson (Eds.), *Handbook of psychophysiology* (pp. 53–84). New York: Cambridge University Press.

Feldman, R., Greenbaum, C. W., & Yirmiya, N. (1999). Mother-infant affect synchrony as an antecedent of the emergence of self-control. *Developmental Psychology, 35,* 223–231.

Field, J., Muir, D., Pilon, R., Sinclair, M., & Dodwell, P. (1980). Infants' orientation to lateral sounds from birth to three months. *Child Development, 51,* 295–298.

Finlay, D., & Ivinskis, A. (1984). Cardiac and visual responses to moving stimuli presented either successively or simultaneously to the central and peripheral visual fields in 4-month-old infants. *Developmental Psychology, 20,* 29–36.

Fox, N. A. (1979). *Cardiac responses to two types of auditory stimuli in preterm infants.* Paper presented at the Annual meeting of the Society for Psychophysiological Research, Cincinnati, Ohio.

Fox, N. A. (1989). Psychophysiological correlates of emotional reactivity during the first year of life. *Developmental Psychology, 25,* 364–372.

Fox, N. A., & Gelles, M. (1984). Face-to-face interaction in term and preterm infants. *Infant Mental Health Journal, 5,* 192–205.

Frick, J. E., & Colombo, J. (1996). Individual differences in infant visual attention: Recognition of degraded visual forms by 4-month-olds. *Child Development, 67,* 188–204.

Frick, J. E., & Richards, J. E. (2001). Individual differences in recognition of briefly presented stimuli. *Infancy, 2,* 331–352.

Garcia-Koll, C., Kagan, J., & Reznick, J. S. (1984). Behavioral inhibition in young children. *Child Development, 55,* 1005–1019.

Goldman-Rakic, P. S. (1988). Topography of cognition: Parallel distributed networks in primate association cortex. *Annual Review of Neuroscience, 11,* 137–156.

Graham, F. K. (1979). Distinguishing among orienting, defense, and startle reflexes. In H. D. Kimmel, E. H. van Olst, & J. F. Orlebeke (Eds.), *The orienting reflex in humans* (pp. 137–167). Hillsdale, NJ: Lawrence Erlbaum Associates.

Graham, F. K., Anthony, B. J., & Zeigler, B. L. (1983). The orienting response and developmental processes. In D. Siddle (Ed.), *Orienting and habituation: Perspectives in human research* (pp. 371–430). Sussex, UK: Wiley.

Graham, F. K., Berg, K. M., Berg, W. K., Jackson, J. C., Hatton, H. M., & Kantowitz, S. R. (1970). Cardiac orienting response as a function of age. *Psychonomic Science, 19,* 363–365.

Graham, F. K., & Clifton, R. K. (1966). Heart-rate change as a component of the orienting response. *Psychological Bulletin, 65,* 305–320.

Graham, F. K., & Jackson, J. C. (1970). Arousal systems and infant heart rate responses. In H. W. Reese & L. P. Lipsitt (Eds.), *Advances in child development and behavior.* (Vol. 5, pp. 59–117). New York: Academic Press.

Graham, F. K., Strock, B. D., & Zeigler, B. L. (1981). Excitatory and inhibitory influences on reflex responsiveness. In W. A. Collins (Ed.), *Aspects of the development of competence* (pp. 1–38). Hillsdale, NJ: Lawrence Erlbaum Associates.

Harper, R. M., Hoppenbrouwers, T., Sterman, M. B., McGinty, D. J., & Hodgman, J. (1976). Polygraphic studies of normal infants during the first six months of life. I. Heart rate and variability as a function of state. *Pediatric Research, 10,* 945–961.

Harper, R. M., Scalabassi, R. J., & Estrin, T. (1976). Time series analysis and sleep research. *IEEE Transactions and Autonomic Control, AC-19,* 932–943.

Harper, R. M., Walter, D. O., Leake, B., Hoffman, H. J., Sieck, G. C., Sterman, M. B., Hoppenbrouwers, T., & Hodgman, J. (1978). Development of sinus arrhythmia during sleeping and waking states in normal infants. *Sleep, 1,* 33–48.

Harris, P., & MacFarlane, A. (1974). The growth of the effective visual field from birth to seven weeks. *Journal of Experimental Child Psychology, 18,* 340–348.

Hassett, J., & Danforth, D. (1982). Introduction to the cardiovascular system. In J. T. Cacioppo & R. E. Petty (Eds.), *Perspectives in cardiovascular psychophysiology* (pp. 4–18). New York: Guilford Press.

Heilman, K. M., Watson, R. T., Valenstein, E., & Goldberg, M. E. (1987). Attention: Behavior and neural mechanisms. In V. B. Mountcastle, F. Plum, & S. R. Geiger

(Eds.), _Handbook of physiology, Section 1: The nervous system_ (Vol. V, pp. 461–481). Bethesda, MD: American Physiological Society.

Hicks, J. M., & Richards, J. E. (1998). The effects of stimulus movement and attention on peripheral stimulus localization by 8- to 26-week-old infants. _Infant Behavior and Development, 21,_ 571–589.

Hood, B. M., & Atkinson, J. (1993). Disengaging visual attention in the infant and adult. _Infant Behavior and Development, 16,_ 405–422.

Hunter, S. K., & Richards, J. E. (2003). Peripheral stimulus localization by 5- to 14-week-old infants during phases of attention. _Infancy, 4,_ 1–25.

Hunter, M. A., Ross, H. S., & Ames, E. W. (1982). Preferences for familiar or novel toys: Effect of familiarization time in 1-year-olds. _Developmental Psychology, 18,_ 519–529.

Izard, C. E., Porges, S. W., Simons, R. F., Haynes, O. M., Hyde, C., Parisi, M., & Cohen, B. (1991). Infant cardiac activity: Developmental changes and relations with attachment. _Developmental Psychology, 27,_ 432–439.

Jankowksi, J. J., & Rose, S. A. (1997). The distribution of attention in infants. _Journal of Experimental Child Psychology, 65,_ 127–140.

Jennings, J. R. (1986). Bodily changes during attention. In M. G. H. Coles, E. Donchin, & S. W. Porges (Eds.), _Psychophysiology: Systems, processes, and applications_ (pp. 268–289). New York: Guilford Press.

Kagan, J., Kearsley, R., & Zelazo, P. (1978). _Infancy._ Cambridge, MA: Harvard University Press.

Kahneman, D. (1973). _Attention and effort._ Englewood Cliffs, NJ: Prentice-Hall.

Katona, P. G., Frasz, A., & Egbert, J. R. (1980). Maturation of cardiac control in full-term and preterm infants during sleep. _Early Human Development, 4,_ 145–159.

Katona, P. G., & Jih, F. (1975). Respiratory sinus arrhythmia: Noninvasive measure of parasympathetic control. _Journal of Applied Physiology, 39,_ 801–805.

Keen, R. E., Chase, H. H., & Graham, F. K. (1965). Twenty-four hour retention by neonates of an habituated heart rate response. _Psychonomic Science, 2,_ 265–266.

Lacey, J. I. (1959). Psychophysiological approaches to the evaluation of psychotherapeutic process and outcome. In E. A. Rubinstein & M. B. Parloff (Eds.), _Research in psychotherapy_ (pp. 160–208). Washington, DC: American Psychological Association.

Lacey, J. I., Kagan, J., Lacey, B. C., & Moss, M. A. (1962). The visceral level: Situational determinants and behavioral correlates of autonomic response patterns. In P. Knapp (Ed.), _Expression of the emotions in man_ (pp. 161–196). New York: International Universities Press.

Lacey, J. I., & Lacey, B. C. (1958). The relationship of resting autonomic activity to motor impulsivity. In _The brain and human behavior_ (Proceedings of the Association for Research in Nervous and Mental Disease, pp. 1257–1290). Baltimore, MD: Williams & Wilkins.

Lang, A. (1990). Involuntary attention and physiological arousal evoked by structural features and emotional content in TV commercials. _Communication Research, 17,_ 275–299.

Lansink, J. M., & Richards, J. E. (1997). Heart rate and behavioral measures of attention in 6-, 9-, and 12-month-old infants during object exploration. _Child Development, 68,_ 610–620.

Lewis, M., Kagan, K., Campbell, H., & Kalafat, J. (1965). The cardiac response as a correlate of attention in infants. [Abstract]. _American Psychologist, 20,_ 478.

Lipton, E. L., & Steinschneider, A. (1964). Studies on the psychophysiology of infancy. *Merrill-Palmer Quarterly, 10,* 103–177.

Maikranz, J. M., Colombo, J., Richman, W. A., & Frick, J. E. (2000). Autonomic correlates of individual differences in sensitization and look duration during infancy. *Infant Behavior and Development, 23,* 137–151.

MacFarlane, A., Harris, P., & Barnes, I. (1976). Central and peripheral vision in early infancy. *Journal of Experimental Child Psychology, 21,* 532–538.

McCall, R. B., & Kagan, J. (1967). Stimulus-schema discrepancy and attention in the infant. *Journal of Experimental Child Psychology, 5,* 381–390.

Mesulam, M. M. (1983). The functional anatomy and hemispheric specialization for directed attention. *Trends in Neuroscience, 6,* 384–387.

Moruzzi, G., & Magoun, H. W. (1949). Brain stem reticular formation and activation of the EEG. *Electroencephalography and Clinical Neurophysiology, 1,* 455–473.

Nelson, C. A., & Collins, P. F. (1991). Event-related potential and looking-time analysis of infants' responses to familiar and novel events: Implications for visual recognition memory. *Developmental Psychology, 27,* 50–58.

Nelson, C. A., & Collins, P. F. (1992). Neural and behavioral correlates of visual recognition memory in 4- and 8-month-old infants. *Brain and Cognition, 19,* 105–121.

Oakes, L. A., Madole, K. L., & Cohen, L. B. (1991). Infant object examining: Habituation and categorization. *Cognitive Development, 6,* 377–392.

Oakes, L. M., & Tellinghuisen, D. J. (1994). Examining in infancy: Does it reflect active processing? *Developmental Psychology, 30,* 748–756.

Picton, T. W., Bentin, S., Berg, P., Donchin, E., Hillyard, S. A., Johnson, R. Jr., Miller, G. A., Ritter, W., Ruchkin, D. S., Rugg, M. D., & Taylor, M. J. (2000). Guidelines for using human event-related potentials to study cognition: Recording standards and publication criteria. *Psychophysiology, 37,* 127–152.

Pomerleau, A., & Malcuit, G. (1981). State effects on concomitant cardiac and behavioral responses to a rocking stimulus in human newborns. *Infant Behavior and Development, 4,* 163–174.

Pomerleau-Malcuit, A., & Clifton, R. K. (1973). Neonatal heart-rate response to tactile, auditory and vestibular stimulation in different states. *Child Development, 44,* 485–496.

Porges, S. W. (1976). Peripheral and neurochemical parallels of psychopathology: A psychophysiological model relating autonomic imbalance in hyperactivity, psychopathology, and autism. In H. Reese (Ed.), *Advances in Child Development and Behavior* (Vol. 11, pp. 35–65). New York: Academic Press.

Porges, S. W. (1980). Individual differences in attention: A possible physiological substrate. In *Advances in Special Education* (Vol. 2, pp. 111–134).Greenwich, CT: JAI Press.

Porges, S. W. (1985). Spontaneous oscillations in heart rate: Potential index of stress. In P. G. Mogberg (Ed.), *Animal stress: New directions in defining and evaluating the effects of stress.* Bethesda, MD: American Physiological Society.

Porges, S. W. (1992). Autonomic regulation and attention. In B. A. Campbell, H. Hayne, R. Richardson (Eds.), *Attention and information processing in infants and adults: Perspectives from human and animal research* (pp. 201–223). Hillsdale, NJ: Lawrence Erlbaum Associates.

Porges, S. W. (2001). The polyvagal theory: Phylogenetic substrates of a social nervous system. *International Journal of Psychophysiology, 42*, 123–146.

Porges, S. W., & Bohrer, R. E. (1990). Analyses of periodic processes in psychophysiological research. In J. T. Cacioppo & I. G. Tassinary (Eds.), *Principles of psychophysiology: Physical, social, and inferential elements* (pp. 708–753). New York: Cambridge University Press.

Porges, S. W., McCabe, P. M., & Yongue, B. G. (1982). Respiratory-heart rate interactions: Psychophysiological implications for pathophysiology and behavior. In J. T. Cacioppo & R. Petty (Eds.), *Perspectives in cardiovascular psychophysiology* (pp. 223–264). New York: Guilford Press.

Porter, F. L. (2001). Vagal tone. In L. Singer & P. Zeskind (Eds.), *Biobehavioral assessment of the infant* (pp. 100–124). New York: Guilford Press.

Porter, C. L., Bryan, Y., & Hsu, H. (1995). Physiological markers in early infancy: Stability of 1-to 6-month vagal tone. *Infant Behavior and Development, 18*, 363–367.

Posner, M. I. (1995). Attention in cognitive neuroscience: An overview. In M. S. Gazzaniga, (Ed.), *Cognitive neurosciences* (pp. 615–624). Cambridge, MA: MIT Press.

Posner, M. I., & Petersen, S. E. (1990). The attention system of the human brain. *Annual Review of Neuroscience, 13*, 25–42.

Reed, S. F., Ohel, G., David, R., & Porges, S. W. (1999). A neural explanation of fetal heart rate patterns: A test of the polyvagal theory. *Developmental Psychobiology, 35*, 108–118.

Reynolds, G. D., & Richards, J. E. (2005). Familiarization, attention, and recognition memory in infancy: An ERP and cortical source localization study. *Developmental Psychology, 41*, 598–615.

Richards, J. E. (1985a). The development of sustained attention in infants from 14 to 26 weeks of age. *Psychophysiology, 22*, 409–416.

Richards, J. E. (1985b). Respiratory sinus arrhythmia predicts heart rate and visual responses during visual attention in 14- and 20-week-old infants. *Psychophysiology, 22*, 101–109.

Richards, J. E. (1986). Power spectral analysis quantification of respiratory sinus arrhythmia. *Psychophysiology, 23*, 414.

Richards, J. E. (1987). Infant visual sustained attention and respiratory sinus arrhythmia. *Child Development, 58*, 488–496.

Richards, J. E. (1988a). Heart rate changes and heart rate rhythms, and infant visual sustained attention. In P. K. Ackles, J. R. Jennings, & M. G. H. Coles (Eds.), *Advances in psychophysiology* (Vol. 3, pp. 189–221). Greenwich, CT: JAI Press,

Richards, J. E. (1988b). Heart rate offset responses to visual stimuli in infants from 14 to 26 weeks of age. *Psychophysiology, 25*, 278–291.

Richards, J. E. (1989). Development and stability of HR-defined, visual sustained attention in 14, 20, and 26 week old infants. *Psychophysiology, 26*, 422–430.

Richards, J. E. (1994). Baseline respiratory sinus arrhythmia and heart rate responses during sustained visual attention in preterm infants from 3 to 6 months of age. *Psychophysiology, 31*, 235–243.

Richards, J. E. (1995a). Infant cognitive psychophysiology: Normal development and implications for abnormal developmental outcomes. In T. H. Ollendick & R. J. Prinz (Eds.), *Advances in Clinical Child Psychology* (Vol. 17, pp. 77–107). New York: Plenum Press.

Richards, J. E. (1995b). Reliability of respiratory sinus arrhythmia in R-R intervals, in 14-, 20-, and 26-week-old infants. *Infant Behavior and Development, 18,* 155–161.

Richards, J. E. (1997a). Effects of attention on infants' preference for briefly exposed visual stimuli in the paired-comparison recognition-memory paradigm. *Developmental Psychology, 33,* 22–31.

Richards, J. E. (1997b). Peripheral stimulus localization by infants: Attention, age and individual differences in heart rate variability. *Journal of Experimental Psychology: Human Perception and Performance, 23,* 667–680.

Richards, J. E. (1998). Focusing on visual attention. *Early Development and Parenting, 7,* 153–158.

Richards, J. E. (2000). Development of multimodal attention in young infants: Modification of the startle reflex by attention. *Psychophysiology, 37,* 65–75.

Richards, J. E. (2001). Attention in young infants: A developmental psychophysiological perspective. In C. A. Nelson & M. Luciana (Eds.), *Handbook of developmental cognitive neuroscience* (pp. 321–338). Cambridge, MA: MIT Press.

Richards, J. E. (2003). Attention affects the recognition of briefly presented visual stimuli in infants: An ERP study. *Developmental Science, 6,* 312–328.

Richards, J. E., & Anderson, D. R. (2004). Attentional inertia in children's extended looking at television. *Advances in Child Development and Behavior, 32,* 163–212.

Richards, J. E., & Casey, B. J. (1991). Heart rate variability during attention phases in young infants. *Psychophysiology, 28,* 43–53.

Richards, J. E., & Casey, B. J. (1992). Development of sustained visual attention in the human infant. In B. A. Campbell, H. Hayne, & R. Richardson (Eds.), *Attention and information processing in infants and adults: Perspectives from human and animal research* (pp. 30–60). Hillsdale, NJ: Lawrence Erlbaum Associates.

Richards, J. E., & Cronise, K. (2000). Extended visual fixation in the early preschool years: Look duration, heart rate changes, and attentional inertia. *Child Development, 71,* 602–620.

Richards, J. E., & Gibson, T. L. (1997). Extended visual fixation in young infants: Look distribution, heart rate changes, and attention. *Child Development, 68,* 1041–1056.

Richards, J. E., & Hunter, S. K. (1997). Peripheral stimulus localization by infants with eye and head movements during visual attention. *Vision Research, 37,* 3021–3035.

Richards, J. E., & Hunter, S. K. (1998). Attention and eye movement in young infants: Neural control and development. In J. E. Richards (Ed.), *Cognitive neuroscience of attention: A developmental perspective.* Hillsdale, NJ: Lawrence Erlbaum Associates.

Richards, J. E., & Hunter, S. K. (2002). Testing neural models of the development of infant visual attention. *Developmental Psychobiology, 40,* 226–236.

Richards, J. E., & Lansink, J. M. (1998). Distractibility during visual fixation in young infants: The selectivity of attention. In C. Rovee-Collier (Ed.), *Advances in Infancy Research* (Vol. 13, pp. 407–444). Norwood, NJ: Ablex Publishing Co.

Richards, J. E., & Turner, E. D. (2001). Distractibility during extended viewing of television in the early preschool years. *Child Development, 72,* 963–972.

Robbins, T. W., & Everitt, B. J. (1995). Arousal systems and attention. In M. S. Gazzaniga, (Ed.), *Cognitive neurosciences* (pp. 703–720). Cambridge, MA: MIT Press.

Rose, S. A. (1983). Differential rates of visual information processing in full-term and preterm infants. *Child Development, 54,* 1189–1198.

Rose, S. A., Gottfried, A. W., Melloy-Carminar, P., & Bridger, W. H. (1982). Familiarity and novelty preferences in infant recognition memory: Implications for information processing. *Developmental Psychology, 18,* 704–713.

Ruff, H. A. (1986). Components of attention during infants' manipulative exploration. *Child Development, 57,* 105–114.

Ruff, H. A., Capozzoli, M., & Saltarelli, L. M. (1996). Focused visual attention and distractibility in 10-month old infants. *Infant Behavior and Development, 19,* 281–293.

Schectman, V. L., Kluge, K. A., & Harper, R. M. (1988). Time-domain system for assessing variation in heart rate. *Medical and Biological Engineering and Computing, 26,* 367–373.

Smith, J. J., & Kampine, J. P. (1984). *Circulatory physiology: The essentials.* Baltimore, MD: Williams & Wilkins.

Sokolov, E. N. (1963). *Perception and the conditioned reflex.* New York: Macmillan.

Starzl, T. E., Taylor, C. W., & Magoun, H. W. (1951). Ascending conduction in reticular activating system, with special reference to the dienchephalon. *Journal of Neurophysiology, 14,* 461–477.

Stifter, C. A., & Fox, N. A. (1990). Infant reactivity: Physiological correlates of newborn and five-month temperament. *Developmental Psychology, 26,* 582–588.

Tellinghuisen, D. J. & Oakes, L. M. (1997). Distractibility in infancy: The effects of distractor characteristics and type of attention. *Journal of Experimental Child Psychology, 64,* 232– 254.

Tronick, E. (1972). Stimulus control and growth of the infants' effective visual field. *Perception and Psychophysics, 11,* 373–376.

Wagner, S. H., & Sakovits, L. J. (1986). A process analysis in infant visual and cross-modal recognition memory: Implications for an amodal code. *Advances in Infancy Research, 4,* 195–217.

Watanabe, K., Iwase, K., & Hara, K. (1973). Heart rate variability during sleep and wakefulness in low-birthweight infants. *Biology of the Neonate, 22,* 87–98.

Womack, B. F. (1971). The analysis of respiratory sinus arrhythmia using spectral analysis and digital filtering. *IEEE Transactions on Bio-Medical Engineering, 18,* 399–409.

Zeaman, D., Deane, G., & Wegner, N. (1954). Amplitude and latency characteristics of the conditioned heart response. *Journal of Psychology, 37,* 235–250.

Examining Cognitive Development Using
Psychophysiological Correlates

Evidence of a Hierarchy of Future-Oriented Processes
Across Measures

W. Keith Berg and Dana L. Byrd

INTRODUCTION

In order to effectively function in the world, it is critical that we be able to prepare for future events. The "future" event can be anything from events that will happen in a few seconds to events that will happen in days, weeks, or months. A very general term that has been applied to such abilities or activities is "future-oriented processes" (Haith, Benson, Roberts, & Pennington, 1994). Often we are aware that an event is going to take place in the future due to a warning event. Information inherent in the warning event itself or information from our past experience with that warning event can inform us about both the nature and the timing of the upcoming event. For example, when the traffic light turns yellow, from past experience we know it soon will turn red and approximately how long this will take. In cases when we have knowledge about or experience with the future event we can not only tailor our anticipation or preparation regarding the nature of the upcoming event, but we can also time them so to be optimally ready when the event occurs, and not too early or too late to be effective.

Among the most pervasive and effective paradigms used in the investigations of these future-oriented processes is the simple paired-stimulus or S1-S2 paradigm. In the typical use of this paradigm an initial stimulus or event with minimal inherent significance is followed after a fixed duration by a more significant stimulus or event. In the classical conditioning paradigm, for example, the conditioned stimulus (CS) precedes the unconditioned stimulus (US) by a short period. With continued pairing of these stimuli, a conditioned response (CR) develops, typically during the CS-US interval. Often, this anticipatory response serves a protective function. Similarly, with fixed-foreperiod reaction time studies, the initial stimulus is usually identified as a warning stimulus and the subsequent stimulus is usually defined as the go stimulus to which the participant performs an imperative response. Studies of infant anticipation may also make use of the paradigm, except here the warning stimulus is frequently followed by a novel, highly engaging event rather than a go stimulus for a speeded response. The engaging event would typically elicit covert and overt attentive responses. This same paradigm can work well with children and adults, of course. The recent expansion of the study of prospective memory (e.g., Bradimonte, Einstein, & McDaniel, 1996) also includes a variant of this basic design with a much wider range of inter-stimulation durations. In this approach, an initial memory cue, such as "Remember to pick up bread at the grocery store," is followed at some future time by our passing by the grocery store, which would elicit our stopping to purchase bread provided the prospective memory is effective. The basic S1-S2 paradigm historically has been and continues to be in widespread use. What is remarkable about these examples is that, though they all use essentially the same paradigm, they study what could be argued to be very different psychological phenomena (conditioning, foreperiod effects, anticipation, and prospective memory).

The S1-S2 paradigm, in several of its guises, has been especially attractive to psychophysiologists in part because they allow us to enhance substantially our knowledge about the covert cognitive events occurring within the S1-S2 anticipation/preparation period. Exclusively behavioral research using the S1-S2 paradigm often focuses on what happens *after* the S1-S2 interval – that is, what behavior happens in response to the imperative S2. With this behavioral approach, inferences about the effects of the anticipation or preparation during the S1-S2 interval must be made backward in time. In contrast, the psychophysiologist can expand upon this behavioral approach significantly by measuring ongoing, continuous physiological responses *throughout* the S1-S2 interval, as the anticipatory and preparatory cognitive events are actually unfolding. With this continuous measurement, psychophysiologists can bolster hypotheses based solely on the behavior data, and, more importantly, can be the source of information to generate new concepts about future-oriented cognitive events and their temporal nature.

A wide variety of psychophysiological measures have been employed in this regard, including beat-by-beat heart rate patterns (e.g., Bohlin & Kjellberg, 1979), startle blink modulation (Putnam, 1990), and event-related potentials including the contingent negative variation (CNV; Brunia & van Boxtel, 2001). The vast majority of this body of research has assessed the future-oriented processes and physiological correlates of these processes in adults.

However, this paradigm and the measures are also effective with infants and children, allowing for insight into the ontogeny of the cognitive processes engaged by variations on the S1-S2 paradigm.

In this chapter, we first review some of the physiological measures of future-oriented processes evoked in the S1-S2 paradigm, focusing on the practical issues concerning the measurement of these responses with infants, children, and adults. This description is followed by a discussion of how the task requirements in the S1-S2 paradigm affect these physiological correlates of future-oriented processing in adults. We then review the developmental data using this paradigm and propose a new way to understand the development of active future-oriented processes. Finally, we propose a number of lines of research that would provide direct tests of our hypothesized organization of future-oriented processes and the ontogeny of these processes.

PHYSIOLOGICAL CORRELATES OF FUTURE-ORIENTED PROCESSES: PRACTICAL ADVICE FOR THE RECORDING AND ANALYSIS OF THESE MEASURES IN ADULTS, CHILDREN, AND INFANTS

A number of different physiological measures have been utilized with the S1-S2 interval. These not only provide a variety of additional "tools" available to study the future-oriented processing during this interval, but more importantly can provide information not readily available with typical behaviorally oriented measures, particularly with infants and children. As beneficial as physiological measures are in young adults, they are even more beneficial when working with younger and also older populations. Many common behavioral events cannot be readily recorded from the very young and the very old. For example, the common foreperiod reaction time paradigm does not work well prior to about the age of 4 years or so, and can be compromised in its validity with older adults who have a motor-control-compromising conditions such as arthritis or Parkinson's Disease. Of course, other paradigms can be substituted in many cases, such as looking or head turns (e.g., Donohue & Berg, 1991; Garner, 1993; Garner & Berg, 1993), but this makes comparisons across age groups much more problematic. In most cases, physiological measures can be used across the entire developmental spectrum. Given the benefits of physiological recording in examining future-oriented processes, it is useful to consider the specific measurement issues involved in some of the more common measures.

In this section, we briefly examine three frequently used physiological correlates of future-oriented processes that we have employed in our exploration of the development of future-oriented processes. These include one measure each from the autonomic nervous system, the motor system, and the central nervous system: (1) the triphasic heart rate response, (2) the startle blink modulation, and (3) the contingent negative variation or CNV. For each measure, we first will address generally how the measure can be utilized to assess future-oriented processing, and then we will discuss relevant methodological issues. Because excellent methodological papers have already been published providing details on how to utilize each of these measures with adults (e.g., Blumenthal et al., 2005; Jennings et al., 1981; Picton et al., 2000), we will focus on issues related to their use with infants and children.

General Testing Issues with Infants and Children

Before focusing on specific measures, there are several critical factors that affect psychophysiological recording with infants and children that transcend the particular type of recording.

State

One such factor for successful data collection in infants and children is their state at test time. For infants, the concern is that testing usually needs to be done during an awake, alert period. Infants, especially the youngest infants, are in this testable state for relatively short periods of their 24-hour cycle. With neonates, for example, the periods of uninterrupted awake, alert time are very short indeed, perhaps about 10 minutes or so (Berg, Adkinson, & Strock, 1973), and only gradually do these periods lengthen. The arousal state affects all studies with infants, but the problem is exacerbated when recording psychophysiological measures because a significant amount of this precious testing time can be taken up with positioning electrodes and checking that the measures are being recorded well. Thus, it is critical that test personnel be very well practiced at this process so that it can occur both quickly and accurately, otherwise the infant participants will soon grow uncooperative. Generally, it is best if infants can be scheduled for testing around their normal nap times allowing for electrodes to be placed during the sleepy period and testing to take place during the subsequent awake period. It is also best if older children can be scheduled for testing earlier in the day rather than in the evening in order to minimize problems with sleepiness that often occur when children are asked to stay relatively or completely still. State problems can be worsened by another issue: hunger. Data collection for infants and children should not be scheduled during regular meal times as they may be distracted and uncooperative. We suggest that researchers encourage the parents of infants to bring formula or milk to the laboratory. For older children, we keep some light snacks (such as peanut butter and crackers, animal crackers, and raisins) and bottled water in the lab and offer these snacks to any child who is becoming increasingly uncooperative and who may have missed a meal. Of course, check first with parents for any food allergies.

Because of the equipment necessary for physiological measurement, certain issues of state can be exacerbated. By as young as 6 or 7 months of age, infants start becoming wary of strangers, and by preschool years also may be very wary of the strange-appearing laboratory surroundings. When you combine strangers performing the testing in strange surroundings with attempts to place strange objects on the child's body, you have a recipe for producing a very fearful child. This issue may be especially true if the participant has had any recent painful medical experiences such as shots or surgery. At the very least, this situation may compromise your test conditions and measures, physiological or behavioral, and at worst may result in a child refusing to participate.

Several steps can be taken to reduce these difficulties. One is for laboratory personnel to spend time building rapport with the young participants. This process can begin before the participant even comes to the building. Sending pictures of the setting and the personnel used in testing or making them available on a website may make older children feel they know what they are going to experience and whom they will meet. Also, when the child arrives, either locate recording equipment where the child will not see it, or provide colorful or child-themed curtains to hide equipment. Having a separate "play" room for the parent and child with books, coloring materials, and the like can make the initial introduction to the testing environment more comfortable. Electrode application can occur in this comfortable room as well. Of course, always avoid the white lab coat or "scrubs," which are too reminiscent of the doctor's office. Use of cartoons or television programs to keep children's minds off the setting during electrode set up can be very helpful in this regard. We have found that shorter video programs with many different times where the program can be stopped without upsetting the children are best (e.g., cartoons, sing-a-long tapes, etc.).

Rapport can also be built by beginning the testing session with a simple task unrelated to the experimental task, such as coloring together for a few minutes. When the child seems comfortable, provide a brief explanation of the events that will occur in the study and show them the electrodes (call them "sensors") and demonstrate how and where they will be placed on the body, using an assistant, a doll, or if possible, a willing parent. If children are interested in why these electrodes are being placed, they can be described easily as microphones or telephones that listen to the body. If possible, let the child handle a no-longer-used electrode. The sensors' functions can be related to the children's interests, such as indicating something like, "it's like the astronauts wear when they fly into space." Once the child is comfortable with this procedure, begin electrode application, explaining what you are doing at each step and reminding them they have seen this process before with the doll or parent.

Movement/Motor Artifact

A second general issue that can make recording any physiological activity difficult with infants or children is their uncontrolled movements, which are likely to produce artifacts in physiological recordings. These movement artifacts can occur with any participant, but are commonly much more of an issue with infants and children because in most cases only minimal instructional control can be achieved until about the age of 3 years or so, and even from 3 to about 10 years instructions to minimize movements will be considerably less effective than with adults. With neonates and very young infants, swaddling may be used to reduce movements, but past the age of 1 or 2 months this technique does not work and may even induce struggling.

Movement artifacts can arise from two sources. The first source is internal in origin, the large electrical signal that can be generated by muscles located near the electrodes. Of course, this issue is an artifact only when the researcher is not trying to record muscle activity, but even here muscle artifact can occur when a muscle other than the muscle of interest produces a signal of sufficient magnitude that it alters the recording of the signal from the muscle of interest. When muscle activity is not the activity of interest, the muscle artifact is always a concern. The second source of movement artifact is external in origin, the movement of the electrodes against the skin and the movement of the electrode wires through the air.

The first type of artifact, internal muscular artifact, sometimes can be minimized by placing electrodes in areas with minimal underlying muscle. Other times the use of smaller electrodes can help by allowing more exact placement of the recording surface. The second type of movement artifact, due to electrode and wire movement, can be reduced using two techniques. The first involves carefully taping the electrodes to the skin, and where possible bringing wires up behind the back out of reach. This latter suggestion is especially important with infants and young children because it not only reduces lead movement but it puts the leads out of the participants' grasp. The second technique involves lightly twisting together the length of lead wires that will leave the body and go to the amplifier. This procedure will allow this group of wires to move as one. Because of the differential nature of the biological amplifiers, having them move together means that voltages that may be created as the wires move in the air will tend to be equalized between the two active leads and thus be cancelled out by the amplifier. Both techniques are valuable even with adults, of course, but are particularly critical with the more frequent movement that occurs with infants and children. Removal of any remaining artifact by appropriate filtering of the data during or following the recording session may also be possible, depending upon the measure of interest.

Measure-Specific Methodological Suggestions

Although there are many aspects of methodology that generalize across measures, there are certainly more aspects that are specific to the physiological response of interest. These measure-specific methodological issues are described here for heart rate, startle blink electromyogram (EMG), and brain slow potentials (contingent negative variation or CNV).

Heart Rate Response

This section addresses methodological issues of particular relevance to development of the S1-S2 paradigm, but interested readers are encouraged to see the Jennings and colleagues (1981) methodological report for more general information.

Measurement of cardiac rate activity can take many forms. At one extreme, one can simply record the number of beats in a fixed time, such as is done when exercising. This is generally too crude a measure for most research purposes, preventing a view of important fluctuating activity during the interval of interest. To provide much more detail, one can record the time between each beat, usually recorded as the time between R-wave signals of the electrocardiogram (ECG – Figure 8.1). There is a very large developmental literature with this beat-by-beat, evoked heart rate pattern (e.g., Berg & Berg, 1987; Byrd & Berg, 2002). Other research has focused on measurements of the variability in beat-to-beat timing over a longer period of time (see Berntson et al., 1997), but we will focus here only on the beat-to-beat timing, which is often converted into the changes in each second and used to examine relatively short periods such as an S1-S2 interval on the order of seconds.

During the S1-S2 interval, beat-by-beat recordings in a host of studies reveal consistent patterns of heart rate change during the S1-S2 interval. The heart rate responding in this paradigm was first reviewed by Bohlin and Kjellberg in 1979 and, for over three decades, this measure has continued

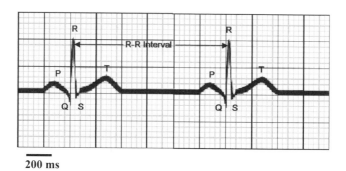

Figure 8.1. Typical ECG signal showing the basic components, P, Q, R, S, and T, and the R-R interval measured between beats. The contraction of the heart, the "beat," occurs shortly following each R-wave.

to offer fruitful information about future-oriented processes. The recording of heart rate in these studies, most often measured from young adults, has been guided by clearly established experimental methods and forms of analysis established for adult research. The reader is encouraged to examine Jennings and colleagues (1981) for basic guidelines in recording adult heart rate. Developmental heart rate work offers unique challenges due to a number of factors involved in working with children and infants.

Earlier it was noted that movement artifact can be minimized by locating electrodes over areas with minimal muscle. Classic electrode placements in adults would place the two active electrodes on the right arm and left leg, the standard type II positioning for clinical recording. This type II positioning usually maximizes the signal of the R-wave relative to the other cardiographic components and therefore allows the best detection of the "beat" (see Figure 8.1). In the case of infants and children, however, placing electrodes on the limbs typically results in very significant movement artifact. A more optimal placement of electrodes on infants, one that achieves good R-wave delineation, results from positioning the active leads at the top and bottom of the sternum, one on either side of the heart. In this placement, electrodes are not located over large muscle groups and shift much less during body movements than they do with limb placements. The ground electrode can be placed conveniently off to either side of the chest. Note that the ground electrode achieves its purpose so long as it makes good contact with the skin anywhere on the body. It does not need to be near the organ of interest. Heart rate electrodes placed on the chest are usually well tolerated by the infants, and the ECG is usually able to be recorded without being riddled with artifact from movements.

With children, this placement of electrodes on the sternum underneath clothes often makes children and parents uncomfortable. In this case, we suggest instead a modified limb placement of the electrodes, which can somewhat reduce motor artifact. One lead can be placed on the bony area of the ankle (avoiding areas above muscle or skin that stretches during ankle flexion), another on the collarbone, and a ground placed behind the ear (on the mastoid). This placement, combined with a child-sized seat where the children's feet are solidly on the floor (to minimize leg swinging) can also decrease motor artifact. This modified position of electrodes on children also keeps all electrodes out of the children's sight, decreasing the likelihood that the participants will chose to investigate the electrodes and remove them instead of performing the desired task.

Because artifacts can be caused by movement in any age participant – infant, child, or adult – all heart rate records should be examined off line after the session. Artifacts can result in both a missed R-wave as well as artifacts that are detected as additional R-waves. Procedures for correction are described in Jennings and colleagues (1981).

Statistical problems also arise when trying to examine and compare heart rate responding across developmental groups. The problem arises because of large differences in the resting level of heart rate for infants, children of different ages, and young adults. Generally speaking, from infancy to young adulthood resting heart rates decrease, though there is a rise in heart rate from the neonatal period, with rates of about 120 beats-per-minute (bpm), to about 135 bpm by 2–4 months or so. This pattern slows to about 80–85 bpm in the preschool years, with a gradual decline thereafter to about 70 bpm for young adults (e.g., Bar-Haim, Marshall, & Fox, 2000). These large resting level differences become a problem when comparing heart rate responses across age to the extent that the responses to discrete stimuli or events of interest depend on the resting heart rate level. Typically, not only does resting heart rate differ across age, so too does the typical magnitude of the heart rate response. Thus, a decelerative response of a 4-month-old infant to a very engaging stimulus might be as much as 15 or 20 bpm, whereas with an adult the response is not commonly more than 5 to 8 bpm, if that. In this case, the question would be, is the larger response by the infant indicative of a greater cognitive reaction, or could it be simply due to the higher resting heart rate level or other physiological phenomenon? The answer to this is not fully clear and a discussion of it is well beyond the scope of this chapter. However, it is safe to say that it would be very risky to make inferences about differing cognitive processes based solely on differences between heart rate response magnitude across age, at least where age groups differed widely or resting heart rate differed significantly (Byrd & Berg, 2002).

We suggest an alternative approach to the problem, one in which the researcher examines the effect an interaction of age on some other variable using not only the amplitude information, but the pattern of heart rate change as well. Patterns, as well as amplitude of many physiological responses, can be effectively assessed using orthogonal trend analysis. For example, to determine the effects of increasing stimulus complexity on age-related changes in beat-per-minute heart rate, we would examine the second-by-second heart rate patterns as beats-per-minute relative to the pre-S1 baseline second. The heart rate patterns could then be analyzed by looking at the effects of complexity on orthogonal trend contrasts of the second-by-second heart rate activity with follow-up t-tests on particular seconds of interest. If the basic response pattern here was a simple deceleration, then, for example, the changes in the trends with complexity could be reflected in the effect of complexity variable on the quadratic trend associated with the deceleration, and the effect would differ across age. Statistically, we would be looking for an interaction of complexity by age on the quadratic trend in this example. The quadratic trend would be affected not only by simple amplitude changes but also by pattern changes, such as shifts away from a quadratic response. The emphasis would be on how age changes the effect of complexity (or some other variable of interest) on the pattern and amplitude. Such an approach does not eliminate the problem of baseline heart rate differences, but when changes are seen in the pattern of response, it becomes less likely that baseline differences are the explanation. This statistical approach can readily be accomplished with standard statistical software in the context of an analysis of variance (ANOVA).

Additionally, because of issues with state and movement, we encourage the video taping of all sessions, with children and infants especially, to allow for off-line analysis of participants' state, movements, and engagement with the task. All of these factors can be significant contributors to differences in resting heart rate as well as response magnitude.

Startle Blink Modulation

Another useful measure of future-oriented processing that has revealed a great deal concerning the development of psychological processes is the modulation of the startle blink reflex. In general, startle responses are elicited by any abrupt, strong stimulation, though auditory stimulation is generally the most common and convenient (see, Berg & Balaban, 1999, for a detailed explanation of this response and the eliciting stimuli). There are many response components of startle, but in humans the blink component is the one most readily elicited and usually the slowest to habituate. Startle blink modulation refers to modifications of the startle magnitude, probability, or latency by non-startling stimuli or conditions. The S1-S2 paradigm has proven to be a very useful way to evaluate startle blink modulation (e.g., Dawson, Schell, & Böhmelt, 1999).

The combination of S1-S2 paradigm and the technique of eliciting the startle reflex during the S1-S2 interval has proved a valuable method for answering questions about attentional shifts that occur during this anticipation/preparation interval. Interest in this measure has continued to increase across almost three decades and detailed information on measure procedures in adults is available (Berg & Balaban, 1999; Blumenthal et al., 2005). Details of measurement issues with infants and children will not be reviewed here since they can be found in the Balaban and Berg, Chapter 9 in this volume.

Contingent Negative Variation

Event-related potentials (ERPs) recorded from the scalp may also provide us with evidence concerning future-oriented processing during a fixed interval, and provide a more direct measure of brain activity than startle or heart rate. ERPs may provide us information concerning possible neural areas engaged during future-oriented processing in an S1-S2 paradigm, especially when combined with source localization analyses, and can provide this information on a millisecond-by-millisecond basis. The recording and analysis of scalp potentials is a long-used technique. However, the development of high-density recordings, recordings that can involve 32 to 256 electrodes, has resulted in this area of work burgeoning even more in recent years. Fortunately, a relatively recent guidelines article describing ERP recording methods is available (Picton et al., 2000).

One type of ERP that may inform us about future-oriented processing during the S1-S2 interval is the Contingent Negative Variation or CNV. The CNV is a much slower changing potential than other commonly evaluated ERP components and occurs with the repeated presentation of S1-S2 pairings, most markedly when a response is required to S2. This waveform can be seen during S1-S2 intervals as short as 0.5 s to as long as 8 s (Brunia & van Boxtel, 2001; Weerts & Lang, 1973). Shorter periods, such as 0.5 or 1 s, generate a single, simple CNV waveform. However, as illustrated in Figure 8.2, longer S1-S2 periods can result in two components to the CNV wave, an initial shorter negative component, the O-wave (for Orienting), and a typically longer lasting component, the E-wave (for Expectancy). The O-wave, not always seen (e.g., Rohrbaugh et al., 1997), has been hypothesized to result

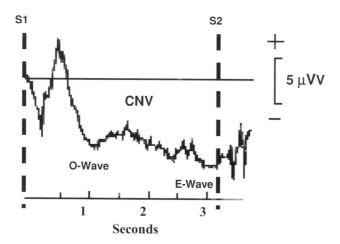

Figure 8.2. Representative CNV from the Pz lead with O- and E-wave components indicated. The typical short-latency ERP precedes the CNV wave. The O-wave is not always seen. Data drawn from Rohrbaugh et al. (1997).

from the orienting to the first stimulus. The E-wave has been hypothesized to result from motor preparation for a response signaled by S2 (Brunia & van Boxtel, 2001), attentional focus shifts during the interval (Ritter, Rotkin, & Vaughn, 1980), or processing during the interval (Ruchkin et al., 1997).

Although electrodes for recording ERPs and CNV can be placed and attached individually on the scalp, increasingly, there is use of various kinds of caps and nets that hold multiple electrodes, and allow for far quicker placement and, with care, more accurate positioning of the electrodes. The speed of application is especially important with infants and children. However, infants' and children's tolerance of scalp electrodes differs greatly among participants. Some are very averse to having anything placed on their head. For these participants, you can request that parents train the children to tolerate caps by having the child wear a cap daily for a period of time leading up to testing. For children who are especially fearful of novelty, sending home a mock cap for the parent to use (e.g., a no longer usable cap) may allow for habituation to the cap prior to the child arriving for testing. For older children who are less fearful of caps and novelty, sending home a picture of the cap and happy children wearing it may also increase likelihood of a successful testing experience. In preparation for a test session, if the child seems weary of the cap then having a parent wear a similar cap may also help the child feel that the cap is a safe and innocuous part of testing.

Even among infants and children who are comfortable having electrodes placed on their heads, a consistent problem has been the time required for the correct placement of multiple leads with low electrical impedances. Although the use of a cap or net is almost certainly faster than the placement of separate electrodes, the application time can still be substantial with the larger numbers of electrodes inherent in high-density EEG setups. New technologies, such as rapid apply nets and high-impedance amplifiers have had an invigorating effect on the field of developmental neuroscience, providing new opportunities for multi-lead research with infants and children. However, these nets, which are more susceptible to slipping out of alignment and electrical bridging across electrodes, may result in methodological concerns of their own.

When recording ERPs, it is necessary to also record electrical activity associated with eyeblinks and other eye movements because these may contaminate the measured brain activity. As a result, the measurement of ERPs from children shares some of its challenges with the measurement of startle blinks. As with startle, the placement of the eye electrodes and measurements of clean blinks (a necessity for the use of eye blink removal techniques) may be challenging. Also, the blinks of infants and children may be more frequent and often differ in shape, sometimes appearing as multi-blink complexes, making the artifacts they generate harder to remove using algorithms such as Independent Components Analysis (Anderson, Byrd, & Berg, in preparation). Specifically, increased frequency of eye movements and multi-blink complexes in children may require the removal of additional components of the blink artifact from the ERP waveform. Proper measurement of blink and successful removal of these artifacts are especially important in achieving usable ERP from infants and children, particularly with long, multisecond epochs such as those that are of interest with the S1-S2 interval CNV. Movement artifacts are also a concern in the ERP record, and as discussed before, reducing this to a minimum may be challenging with infants and children.

TASK-RELATED CHANGES IN PHYSIOLOGICAL CORRELATES OF FUTURE-ORIENTED PROCESSING IN ADULTS

As described in the introduction, future-oriented processes elicited by the S1-S2 paradigm are modulated by the nature of the S1 and S2 and the nature of the task required of the participants. Physiological measures of future-oriented processing including the triphasic heart rate response, startle blink modulation, and CNV, all appear to be sensitive to the type and complexity of the cognitive process required by the participant. There is a considerable body of literature for all three measures in the S1-S2 paradigm with young adult participants, but the developmental literature in this area is sparse. This void is surprising because the paradigm and the response measures are readily adapted to studying participants of all ages. Here we will briefly review the adult research to serve as a developmental anchor for our following review of the ontogeny of future-oriented processes.

The Triphasic Heart Rate Response

Bohlin and Kjellberg (1979) reviewed a large set of adult heart rate studies making use of the paired-stimulus paradigm (referred to as the two-stimulus paradigm by these authors). In the review they examined the well-documented heart rate pattern that typically occurs during the inter-stimulus interval (ISI) between the paired stimuli: an initial deceleration, the D1, occurring immediately after the initial stimulus, the S1; a subsequent acceleration, the A component, that sometimes extends well above baseline; and a final deceleration, the D2, that typically peaks just at the point of the second stimulus, the S2. Bohlin and Kjellberg interpreted the D1 and D2 in terms of orienting responses, relying heavily on the work of Sokolov (1963) and of Graham and Clifton (1966) to bolster their argument. The D1 component is rather small and has proven to be inconsistently present across conditions and experiments whereas the D2 is very robust.

The A component, a component whose magnitude varies strongly with conditions, was more problematic to interpret than the two decelerative components. Bohlin and Kjellberg (1979) suggest this component has been interpreted variously as reflecting (a) a defensive response or, similarly, an active coping response engaged to deal with an aversive event; (b) information processing; (c) reactive attention to a meaningful stimulus (1976); or (d) the physical response demands of the upcoming stimulus.

Of these various interpretations, Bohlin and Kjellberg (1979) suggest there is the least support for the physical response demand hypothesis because one can get a clear A component when the S2 requires no response. Bohlin and Kjellberg do find better support for each of the other views, but argue that none were entirely satisfactory. Nonetheless, they conclude generally that cognitive processes associated with response requirements of the S2 appear to be a particularly powerful elicitor of the accelerative response.

Since the publication of the Bohlin and Kjellberg (1979) review, additional research has suggested still other manipulations in the task requirements during the S1-S2 interval that appear to affect the A component of the triphasic pattern. For example, within this fixed-foreperiod reaction time paradigm, Hatayama, Yamaguchi, and Ohyama (1981) found that the certainty of the S2 as a speeded response cue affects the acceleratory component of the heart rate pattern. In this study, participants were given varying certainty levels wherein over a block of trials there was a 100% or a 25% probability that one of four reaction time go signals would follow the warning signal. In the 100% condition the particular go signal was always the same whereas in the 25% condition the participant was uncertain which of the four responses would be required. The mapping of the type of response signal on the type of response to be made was somewhat complex and required, in the 25% condition only, that this mapping be remembered. In the 100% probability task, which corresponds to the typical foreperiod reaction time condition in other studies, an acceleration above baseline was followed by a late deceleration response. However, in the 25% probability task, the acceleration component of the response was even larger than the 100% probability condition.[1] The authors interpreted the enhanced acceleration in the 25% probability condition as being due to the increased significance of the S2 to the participants. Whether this acceleration is due to increased significance of the S2 or perhaps the anticipation of a more demanding auditory discrimination that was not required in the 100% condition is difficult to discern on the basis of these data.

Other data suggest that the acceleratory component appears to vary depending upon the amount of processing required during the interval. Dennis and Mulcahy (1980) used the S1-S2 paradigm wherein the S1 was a list of six numbers, and the S2 was a single number. The participants were instructed to judge if the S1 digit sequence contained the number presented as S2. This task had three levels of difficulty. In the easiest condition, all six numbers in the span were the same (i.e., 222222), in the medium difficulty condition, three numbers in the span differed (i.e., 512512), and in the difficult condition all six numbers in the span differed (i.e., 514986). Larger amounts of acceleration above baseline were seen with increasing difficulty. The authors believed this increasing acceleration was due to rehearsal during the inter-stimulus interval.

Taken together, the evidence from these two studies demonstrates that task differences affect the heart rate response during the S1-S2 interval, suggesting that this psychophysiological correlate may index more than just anticipation or simple motor or orienting preparation, but may also provide information about more complex cognitive processes occurring during the

---

[1] There was no initial decelerative component to the responses in this study. Also, what was described as a 0% condition was also evaluated wherein no warning stimulus (S1) was used at all. For this condition, essentially a control condition, a near flat heart rate pattern was evident during the period corresponding to a foreperiod preceding the response stimulus.

S1-S2 interval. Specifically, the acceleration component appears to be sensitive to the certainty and processing requirements of a task. Clearly, this acceleratory component should be studied more thoroughly in a number of task contexts. Also, the possible sensitivity of this acceleratory component to the type and extent of cognitive processing suggests that developmental differences in response to task demands should be explored. Later, we will further develop and explore these issues.

Startle Blink Modulation

Startle blink modulation has been used within the S1-S2 paradigm in a number of ways. In some studies, the startle blink eliciting stimulus (e.g., a strong, abrupt auditory stimulus) follows an S1 warning stimulus, often referred to as a prepulse, and the startle-eliciting stimulus serves as the S2 itself. In others, startle blinks instead are elicited at various points during the ISI between S1 and S2, neither of which are startle stimuli. In either paradigm, the startle blinks during the ISI or at the end of the ISI are compared to startle blinks elicited outside of the ISI. This comparison is critical to determining whether the startle blink is being modulated as a result of the anticipation, preparation, or other processes occurring during the S1-S2 interval. The exploration of the modulation of the startle reflex has been investigated by systematically varying the elements of the procedure (e.g., the qualitative aspects of S1 and S2, the timing of startle probes, and the duration of ISIs). It is these manipulations of the elements of the procedure that afford the study of different intervals and foci of anticipation.

Frances Graham (e.g., Graham, Putnam, & Leavitt, 1975) pioneered the examination of modulation of the startle reflex in humans, utilizing the S1-S2 paradigm with varying duration ISIs with S1 as a tone and S2 as an auditory startle probe. This method demonstrated a facilitation of startle when the S2-startle probe was both 1400 and 2000 ms after the onset of S1. Greater facilitation was seen at the 2000 ms lead interval as compared to 1400 ms. Larger facilitation was also seen when S1 was a tone that continued through the interval until S2, as compared to a transient S1. Graham concluded that this facilitation of startle at long lead intervals could be resulting from attentional processes during the interval. This increase in facilitation of the startle over the course of the ISI could be explained by increasing attention to the stimulus or overall arousal during the anticipatory interval.

Putnam (1990) refined this hypothesis and suggested that if startle probes were to be presented during the S1-S2 interval, they could be used to determine the selectivity of the anticipatory set occurring during the interval. That is, the startle might not only be facilitated by a more general attentional set, but might be differentially modulated by more specific attentional sets. Putnam suggested that when the S2 event was, for instance, an auditory event, anticipation of this should facilitate startle blinks elicited by auditory stimuli. This response would occur because the anticipatory set for audition (developed as the result of an auditory S2) would match that of the startle-eliciting stimuli. This prediction was based on a theory of perception by Hochberg (1970, cited in Putnam, 1990), which proposed that there were perceptual schemas that shifted perceptual sets to be biased towards similar modalities. A number of studies were conducted by Putnam and colleagues (Putnam, 1990) exploring this possibility. The paradigm, developed by Anthony, Butler, and Putnam (1978) and reviewed in detail by Putnam, 1990, employed a 6-second ISI and included a motor task at S2. In the initial three studies in the series, visual or tactile stimuli were employed with onset of the stimulus serving as the S1 and offset serving as the S2. Acoustic stimulation probes were used to elicit startle during the ISI – that is, during the visual or tactile stimulus. Probes were presented at 2000, 3000, 4000, 5000, and 5500 ms after S1 onset.

This methodology yielded findings congruent with the Hochberg's (1970) theory. The auditory startle response was increasingly inhibited during the course of the ISI when non-auditory stimuli were being anticipated. This result was found for both types of the non-auditory stimuli (Anthony et al., 1978). By contrast, in the fourth study of the series when participants were placed in the same conditions with a 6-second tactile S1 that was terminated coincident with a strong auditory S2, and no task required, the auditory startle probes occurring prior to S2 were increasingly facilitated as the S1-S2 interval continued. These findings support the theory that when the participants' attention was shifted away from the auditory modality by an expected termination of a non-auditory S2, either the visual or tactile, then auditory startle responses to the probes were inhibited. When attention was shifted toward the auditory modality by the expectation of a strong auditory stimulus, startle responses to the probes were facilitated. Putnam (1990) did not find such selectivity for the triphasic heart rate response during the S1-S2 interval, though it did reflect a more general attentional set such as orienting.

It is important to note that some of the research that followed Putnam's work has suggested alternative explanations to some of the selective attention findings on startle modulation, and other work has failed to replicate the effects. For example, Bradley, Cuthbert, and Lang (1990, 1999) suggested the facilitation effect reported in the Anthony and colleagues (1978) study could also be due to negative emotional effects arising from the anticipation of the unpleasant S2. Lang and colleagues (e.g., Lang, 1995) and others have reported extensively on the facilitative effects on startle blinks of negative stimuli. Other attempts to replicate the selective attention effects, such as that by Lipp and colleagues (Lipp, 2002; Lipp, Siddle, & Dall, 1998), have not been successful, finding that startle was facilitated both early and late in the interval regardless of probe and task modalities. Lipp (2002) suggests that a fixed-foreperiod reaction-time paradigm with a second stimulus requiring difficult discrimination and resulting in immediate feedback may be necessary to produce the modality-specific selective attention effects seen in Putnam's work. Putnam agrees that modality specific attention effects may occur only under very specific circumstances (Putnam, personal communication).

In general, the data suggest that startle modulation does seem to occur during preparation for an upcoming event. Whether this modulation is selective and whether it results from a cognitive or emotional appraisal of the events to come very likely depends on the specific parameters of testing, and further research is needed to clarify the issues involved.

Contingent Negative Variation

As noted earlier, the CNV, like the moment-to-moment heart rate response, has multiple components that occur during the S1-S2 interval. Given a sufficiently long interval, an O-wave occurs earlier in the interval followed later by an E-wave, which typically peaks at the end of the S1-S2 interval (see Figure 8.2). A number of studies have shown that aspects of the stimuli and tasks involved in the S1-S2 paradigm independently can modulate the two CNV components. Multiple repetitions of S1-S2 stimulus pairs in a reaction time paradigm result in habituation of the O-wave but not the E wave (Weerts & Lang, 1973). More complex manipulations, such as maintenance of information, appear to change the E-wave. For example, memory rehearsal for numbers results in increasing frontal negativity of the E-wave with increasing memory load (Ruchkin, Johnson, Canoune, & Ritter, 1991). Changes in the aspect of the stimulus maintained in the visuospatial sketchpad (for example, object or location) result in slightly different morphologies and different topographies of activation of the E-wave over frontal areas of the scalp (Ruchkin, Johnson, Grafman, Canoune, & Ritter, 1997). Because these studies employed tasks that likely require involvement of executive functioning, they suggest that manipulations of executive functioning during the S1-S2 interval are likely to specifically impact the E-wave component of the CNV.

A number of studies have tested the neurological sources of the E-wave. Intra-cranial recordings directly from the basal ganglia of candidates for temporal lobe epilepsy surgery provide evidence of the importance of the basal ganglia as part of a cortico-basal ganglia-thalamo-cortical circuit generating the ramp-shaped waveform (Bareš & Rektor, 2001). The authors admit that it is difficult to determine to what extent this deep structure results in the waveform at the scalp, but the timing suggests that these activations may play a role in the activation circuit resulting in the scalp waveform. Recent work employing high-density recording of the CNV suggests that the waveforms at the maximal point of the E-wave have a frontal source (Brodmann's Areas 9 and 10, Basile, Callester, de Castro, & Gattaz, 2002). This again suggests that executive functioning could be one of the important factors in producing E-waves because these areas of the frontal lobe are important in executive functioning (e.g., Casey et al., 1997). The neural source of the O-wave was not explored using these high-density recordings. Although the number of explorations of the O-wave of the CNV are minimal at best, the research on the E-wave does suggest this component is reflective of complex cognitive processes involved in future oriented behavior.

HIERARCHY OF S1-S2 FUTURE-ORIENTED PROCESSES: A HYPOTHESIS

As noted earlier, the S1-S2 paradigm and the physiological correlates that are evoked in this type of paradigm have been utilized within a wide variety of guises to study fixed-foreperiod, future-oriented processing. These studies have typically been classified by the specific concept being explored using that paradigm, such as classical conditioning, foreperiod reaction time, or expectancy, and sometimes by the specific manipulation used with a particular paradigm, such as amount of information processed or uncertainty levels proposed for foreperiod reaction time results. We argue here that that many, if not all, of the wide variety of cognitive concepts that have been suggested to occur during the S1-S2 interval could be subsumed under an overarching construct of future-oriented executive functioning.

Executive functions are cognitive abilities that require control over one's own cognition and behavioral responses. At one time these functions were, and sometimes still are, referred to as "frontal lobe functions" (Luria, 1966) even though other areas of brain are now known also to be involved. These executive functions include inhibition, manipulation, and updating of information, as well as planning, and attentional set shifting. Such abilities typically display systematic patterns of deficits in children and in frontally

TABLE 8.1. Characteristics of the Proposed Hierarchy of Development of
Anticipatory Processes. It is hypothesized that movement through the hierarchy is
related to development of executive functioning

Level	Cognitive processes	Age Range	S1-S2 Heart Rate
1	Simple Association – Non-Anticipatory	Prior to 4 Months	Deceleration after S2 Omission
2	Passive Anticipation – Non-Preparatory	4 months to Early Preschool	D1 and D2, no A during S1-S2
3	Under-Developed Active Preparation	Early Preschool to Early Adolescence	D1, A, D2 during S1-S2
4	Fully-Developed Active Preparation	Early Adolescence through Middle Adulthood	D1, A, D2 during S1-S2

lesioned adults (Luria, 1966). In some circumstances, future-oriented processes may require one or more types of active processing such as: (1) focusing of attention for the upcoming event; (2) analysis or retention of the
cues at the warning and their implications for the response to be given at
or before the upcoming event; (3) processing of information from cues and
the environment; and/or (4) inhibition of prepotent responses until the Go
signal. In short, the S1-S2 paradigm, depending on task requirements, frequently require different amounts of engagement of what neuropsychologists
call controlled cognitive functions (Casey, Durston, & Fosella, 2001), frontal
lobe functions (Luria, 1966), or executive functions (Baddeley, 1998). These,
we believe, can usefully be organized into a hierarchical structure.

In our hierarchy, we organize future-oriented processes by the extent to
which they engage or require executive functioning. Also, we suggest that
the ontogeny of future-oriented processing develops in a hierarchical progression. We pose this organization with discrete levels for didactic reasons,
but are fully aware that the underlying processes may well change in a more
gradual, continuous manner. There are four levels to the proposed hierarchy (see Table 8.1). The first level is the non-anticipatory level where only a
simple association is formed between the first and second stimulus, but no
anticipatory processes occur between S1 and S2. This type of processing may
dominate the responding of very young infants when presented this S1-S2
paradigm. The second level is a basic anticipatory level where anticipation
does occur in the S1-S2 interval, but it is only a low level, *passive* anticipation
of an upcoming second stimulus. This type of processing may develop a few
months into infancy and may remain dominant during the infant period. At

the third level, some cognitive and behavioral control is exerted to actively prepare for the upcoming event, but is as yet inefficient or incomplete due to underdevelopment of higher-level cognitive functioning. The fourth level, the fully functional active preparatory level, is reached when the cognitive processes underlying active future-oriented processes, executive functions, or cognitive control processes, are fully developed. This development allows for the cognitive and behavioral control used for active anticipation, preparation, and planning for the upcoming event.

Although the strongest support for our proposal comes from the studies of beat-by-beat heart rate patterns, we also explore the extent to which the other physiological correlates evoked by this paradigm, startle blink modulation and event-related potentials, appear to support this hypothesis. The data to support this approach from our own and others' laboratories are presented below for each of the hierarchical levels in turn.

Level 1: Simple Association – Non-Anticipatory

At this level of processing, participants are not yet able to demonstrate active future-oriented processes, but can readily develop a simple association between S1-S2 with repeated pairings. That is, we propose that no responses during the S1-S2 period reflect an anticipation or preparation for the arrival of S2. Nonetheless, there is evidence of this important precursor to anticipation, simple association, in early infancy from beat-by-beat heart rate patterns during the S1-S2 interval.

This first level of future-oriented processing is well illustrated by Clifton's (1974) study of classical conditioning in neonates. In this study, trials consisted of an 8-second tone (CS, S1) paired with a 10-second presentation of glucose (UCS, S2) through a nipple. The UCS was initiated 6 seconds after onset of the CS and second-by-second heart rate was recorded. Both CS and UCS onsets initiated heart rate decelerations on initial trials, but on later trials heart rate change was not evident during the CS-UCS (that is, S1-S2) interval. The results suggested neither anticipatory response during the interval nor, indeed, any other evidence of conditioning. However, on the initial extinction trial when the CS-alone condition was first presented, a very marked and abrupt heart rate deceleration occurred at 6 seconds after UCS onset, just at the point when the UCS had previously appeared. Thus, despite the lack of any evidence of S1-S2 interval responding, the clear response to UCS omission indicates an association between CS and UCS had occurred during pairing.

Berg and colleagues (in Berg & Richards, 1997; Bosswell, Garner, & Berg, 1994) identified this same process in 2-month-olds when a warning tone

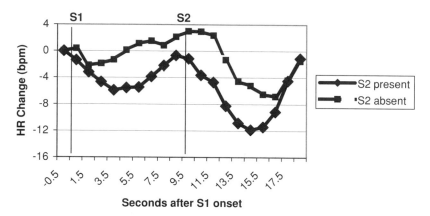

Figure 8.3. Heart rate responding of 2-month-olds during and following an S1-S2 interval. Note that the large deceleration following the S2 indicator is as great when S2 was presented as on the following trial when S2 was omitted. S1 was the same in both cases.

was paired with an interesting video event in a 10-second ISI. They report that onset of S1 reliably elicited an initial deceleration (the D1 response) but neither a subsequent A nor an anticipatory D2 response was seen. However, when S2 was omitted after just five pairings, a deceleration occurred at the point where S2 previously had occurred, and this deceleration was nearly indistinguishable in size or latency from that seen in the prior trial in response to a presented S2 (see Figure 8.3). That is, in this study *lack* of an expected stimulus was as powerful an elicitor of deceleration as was presence of an actual stimulus. This result again occurred in the absence of either an A or a D2 component during the pairing or the omission trial. Thus, these data for 2-month-olds bear a strong similarity to what Clifton (1974) found for neonates despite the very different stimulus types and timing employed in the two studies. Both studies suggest the young infants developed an association between the paired stimuli that included their temporal relation, but the infants did not yet evidence anticipatory responding to S2. Such a capability would be a necessary condition for anticipation to later develop. It is clear that lack of the A and D2 components in this situation cannot be accounted for by immaturity of the heart rate control system since both accelerative and decelerative responding are readily elicited in infants 2 months and younger.

This circumstance, when no evidence of anticipation is apparent during the S1-S2 interval, but an association between the two can be demonstrated by the response to an omitted S2, is what we propose to identify here as the non-anticipatory S1-S2 processing level of the hierarchy. At this level, an association between S1 and S2 is developed and information regarding the time interval between them is retained. There is no evidence, however, of future-oriented processes in the S1-S2 interval. In Clifton's clever terms, in this situation the infant develops a "What happened?" response, but not a "Here it comes!" response (Clifton, 1974). The "What happened?" response shown by the young infants may reflect more *automatic* association processes whereas the "Here it comes" may require more elaborate stimulus processing needed for anticipation to occur.

Other evidence for this first level of future-oriented processing, automatic associative pairing of stimuli by neonates, comes from the reports of temporal conditioning of heart rate responses in neonates (e.g., Stamps, 1977). In its most simple form, this version of the S1-S2 paradigm, temporal conditioning, involves presenting a potent stimulus at regular intervals. Each stimulus serves as both an S2 (UCS) and an S1 (CS) for the subsequent stimulus. For a small subset of trials, a stimulus in the sequence is omitted, and if temporal conditioning has occurred, a response is evident at, and not before, the point of omission. A study of this type was conducted in our laboratory by Davies (1985) who presented 1- to 2-month-old infants with stimuli that cycled on and off at 20-second intervals. Thus, every 20 seconds a stimulus transition, either onset or offset, occurred with occasional omissions of one or the other. Infants displayed a heart rate deceleration at the point of the omission of the first two stimulus transitions indicating these young infants had retained information about when a stimulus transition should occur and reacted when it failed to do so. Once again, this pattern suggests that at a young age (1 to 2 months in this study), there is a simple temporal association of the stimuli changes that can develop even when stimuli are as much as 20 seconds apart. However, because there was no evidence in these data of anticipation or preparation in the heart rate, it exemplifies our level 1 behavior. At this level, what we suggest is absent is the more complex processing of the regularly spaced stimuli necessary to be able to anticipate an upcoming stimulus.

Level 2: Passive Anticipation – Non-Preparatory

Though benefits to an individual derive from simple level 1 associations, an organism can gain immeasurably from being able to anticipate an event *prior* to its arrival. Yet the more elaborate anticipatory cognitive processes required to achieve that benefit may be expressed in more than one form. We here propose a distinction between two types of anticipatory processing: one that would require little or no active, effortful, or controlled processing as it occurs, and another that would require these types of more sophisticated processing to regulate the flow of information, cognition, and action. Only the latter would involve what we know as executive processing. We suggest that the former, the basic, passive anticipatory level II process, occurs in the absence of active cognitive or behavioral control and therefore does not involve executive functioning. Further, we suggest that the more basic level of anticipation will not be accompanied by an accelerative heart rate component during the S1-S2 interval. Only later, at the next developmental level when the more active and elaborative anticipatory processing becomes possible, will that accelerative component of the heart rate response in the S1-S2 interval be produced. During both of these levels the D1 and D2 heart rate components can occur. The late deceleration, the D2, occurring just prior to S2 onset would signal anticipation, but not distinguish between the two types of anticipation we propose. In short, though we make a distinction between the two levels of anticipatory processing at a conceptual level, we suggest that this difference may be more objectively signaled physiologically by the pattern of heart rate activity during the period when anticipation would develop, the S1-S2 interval.

Brooks and Berg (1976) first alluded to these types of passive anticipatory, future-oriented processes in 4-month-olds, but results were not unequivocal. Subsequently, Donohue and Berg (1991) tested 7-month-old infants using a noise stimulus as an S1 followed by a dancing, music-playing toy bear as an S2. During the 10-second interval from S1 to S2 onset, there was a clear initial deceleratory (D1) response at S1 onset on the first pairing and a clear, anticipatory deceleration (D2) that developed over pairings. A small and non-significant acceleratory component above baseline was present on early trials but not evident on later trials when the anticipatory D2 developed.

Berg (cited in Berg & Richards, 1997) reported that 4-month-olds tested with a tone-bull's-eye combination as an S1 followed by an animated video as an S2 also showed the two deceleratory components, D1 and D2, but without any evidence of acceleration above baseline. This pattern was the same study reported above that found with 2-month-olds, an orienting D1 but no anticipatory D2 response, the automatic association of level 1 (see Figure 8.4). Similar anticipatory decelerations for infants of 7 months (Donohue, 1991) and of 14 months (Garner, 1998) have also been reported by our laboratory. What we suggest here is that the infants of at least 4 months are demonstrating with their anticipatory decelerations evidence that they know when a stimulus is arriving, and are responding to that upcoming event prior to its arrival, clearly putting them above level 1.

But what are we to make of the absence of accelerative responding during the S1-S2 interval? One possibility is that infants are physiologically incapable

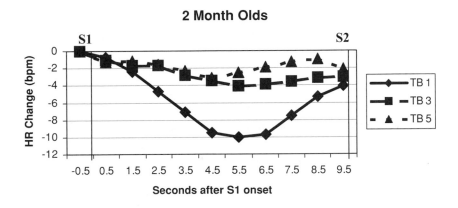

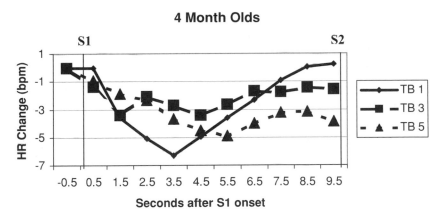

Figure 8.4. Heart rate responding of 2- and 4-month-old as they await an interesting visual event. Note simple habituation of the initial deceleration for the younger infants (upper panel), and the growth of a late deceleration for the older infants (lower panel).

of accelerative responses. This hypothesis is readily dispelled because during fussing or crying, infants elicit very large increases in heart rate. Also, even neonates can show clear accelerative responses to single stimulus presentations (e.g., Keen, Chase, & Graham, 1965). Thus, it seems clear infants are physiologically capable of producing such acceleratory responses from birth. We propose here that the reason for the lack of such accelerations in the S1-S2 paradigms is that, at least under test conditions explored thus far, infants in the first year either are not able to produce the active information processing and stimulus elaboration that otherwise might go on while awaiting such an engaging stimulus, or that the engaging S2 did not require any active information processing prior to its arrival. Neurophysiological evidence would favor the first of these propositions because the frontal lobes that are critical to executive functions likely to be involved in such active processing are not well developed by this age (e.g., Durston et al., 2001). Currently, there is no direct empirical evidence to allow us to choose between these possible explanations for the absence of the accelerative component at this age. However, either explanation would be consistent with our working hypothesis: we propose the lack of acceleration in the S1-S2 pattern evident in the infants' heart rate responses during the S1-S2 interval may be explained by lack of active executive processing, and we present evidence below in support of that view.

Level 3: Under-Developed Active Preparation

It can be reasonably presumed that a principal evolutionary benefit of being able to anticipate significant future events would be to provide the opportunity to actively prepare for those events and thus maximize beneficial effects of upcoming events and minimize detrimental effects. This hypothesis would mean that frequently it is not enough to know that something significant is about to occur, but that one must also select among a set of potential actions or procedures to engage when that event does occur. Functionally, therefore, it is not usually sufficient to only anticipate future events. Rather, there is also a need to control our cognition and behavior to plan and prepare for those future events. The need for control and the need for active engagement during this higher level of anticipation, are hallmarks of a central executive, of what we understand to be executive processing (e.g., Baddeley, 1998). Thus, we propose to conceive of these actions during this higher level of anticipation in terms of the engagement of executive functioning. However, we would also suggest that during this third level these executive processes are as yet underdeveloped and not fully functioning. The result is that during this level increased effort for successful performance in future-oriented S1-S2 paradigms is required, even if not always entirely effective. If, as we propose, the heart rate accelerative component during the S1-S2 interval indexes this effort, then we should see the component when this higher level of anticipation and the executive processes required are engaged. As executive functioning involves a variety of different cognitive processes, we shall illustrate this third level with several types of studies involving S1-S2 paradigms. The studies incorporate response inhibition, working memory, and planning, all important components of executive functioning.

Inhibition of a Response During the S1–S2 Interval

Fixed-foreperiod reaction time studies require a speeded response to the second stimulus. In this paradigm, participants must actively prepare to produce the required motor action while also inhibiting an early response. As with executive functions, generally children gradually develop in their ability to successfully inhibit a motor response over childhood, due to development of frontal areas and the pathways connecting frontal and posterior regions through control circuits (Casey et al., 2001; Diamond, 2000). If, as we hypothesize, acceleration in the triphasic heart rate response indexes engagement of executive control, we would suggest that efforts toward inhibiting a response would result in acceleration during the delay period of the foreperiod reaction time paradigm in children as a result of their increased executive functioning effort required. In other words, we suggest that, depending on the task demands, children may have to put forth more effort to successfully inhibit making an early response in a simple S1–S2, fixed-foreperiod reaction time task than adults, and as a result should exhibit a larger or at least different acceleratory component.

A number of studies from our laboratory and others support this hypothesis. These studies, which presented school-age children with short 5- or 6-second preparatory ISIs, found that children displayed the triphasic heart rate pattern (Anthony & Putnam, 1985; Garner, 1993; Jennings & Matthews, 1984; Klorman & Lang, 1972; Lawler, Obrist, & Lawler, 1978). However, this pattern appeared to have a slightly different morphology in children from that in adults. The individual components of the triphasic response were larger in 5- and 11-year-old children than in adults (Anthony & Putnam, 1985; Lawler et al., 1978) with the acceleration component slightly delayed as compared to adults (Anthony & Putnam, 1985).

Research from our laboratory examining a wider age range of children concurs with this pattern. In Byrd and Berg (2002), we compared the children, adolescents, and adults in this situation while recording beat-by-beat heart rate patterns. The two younger age groups showed the classic triphasic heart rate response (Figure 8.5), including an accelerative component that exceeds pre-S1 baseline. However, the acceleration was larger for children, than adolescents, and essentially absent for adults, as would be predicted if inhibition were most difficult to manage for younger participants. The acceleration also appeared delayed in the youngest group. The behavioral results indicated the percent of early (pre S2) responses were greatest for children, consistent with the suggestion that inhibition was more difficult for younger participants. The larger accelerative component could be indicative

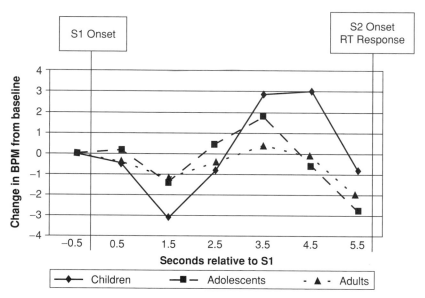

Figure 8.5. Heart rate responding during the foreperiod of a speeded reaction time task.
Note the lack of an above-baseline heart rate acceleration component for adults, but
presence of this for adolescents and children, larger for the latter. All three groups show
the initial deceleration (D1) and late deceleration (D2).

of an active engagement, though not necessarily optimal results. This pattern
would be characteristic of the limitation of this level.

One strong test of the hypothesis that the acceleration can be evoked by
the need to inhibit an upcoming response would be an experiment where the
need to inhibit is removed but the S1-S2 paradigm otherwise retained. In this
circumstance, we would hypothesize that the accelerative component, and
only the accelerative component, should be absent from the response during
the delay. Garner (1993, Garner & Berg, 1993) tested 5-year-old children in
one of two conditions: the typical fixed-foreperiod reaction time paradigm
with a 10-second S1-S2 interval and an equivalent condition where the child
was not required to respond to the S2 signal but rather only waited to watch
a short, very engaging video clip. No explicit response was required in the
latter condition. Thus, in both conditions the S2, the response signal and
the video, was relevant to the child, but only in the former circumstance
was response inhibition needed. What can be seen in Figure 8.6 is that in
both conditions an initial deceleration as well as a late, anticipatory deceleration is present, and these components are similar in magnitude across the
test conditions. The above-baseline acceleration component is only present,

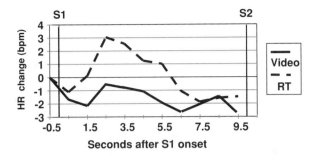

Figure 8.6. Heart rate responding by 5-year-old children as they await either a signal to press a button as quickly as possible (RT) or await a brief, interesting video clip (Video), with no explicit response required. The inhibition required to avoid making an early response to the signal is proposed to produce the accelerative component seen only in the RT group.

however, in the reaction time condition, where response inhibition was required.

Although we have thus far focused on heart rate components in our psychophysiological differentiation of our hierarchical levels, other psychophysiological response systems may also provide valuable information. For example, modulation of startle blink responses may also provide us information about the development of active preparation and inhibition during an interval, providing information about arousal and attentional modulation. Anthony and Putnam (1985) compared 5-year-olds to adults using the S1-S2 paradigm with a 6-second ISI and probing at 3000, 4000, 5000, and 5500 ms. In order to search for the differences in selective attention shifts, the S1 was the onset of a vibrotactile stimulus to the hand, and the S2 was the offset of that vibrotactile stimulus. This offset-S2 was also an imperative stimulus for a reaction time task. An interesting pattern of results emerged from this study. The adults showed the expected increasing startle inhibition as the interval proceeded; however, the 5-year-olds showed increasing startle facilitation as the interval progressed. The authors' interpreted this finding as being due to the children producing a general, not selective, increase in attention. The adult findings were explained as showing the same modality specific, selective attention shifts as seen in past research. It could be concluded from these findings that the ability to selectively attend to one modality increases with age somewhere between 5 years and adulthood. This study suggests that in early childhood attention may be less selective and more general in timed preparation for a S2 perhaps due to less active cognitive control over attention. In our terms, this result might suggest something more akin to our level

II responding for this paradigm for children, but a higher, more controlled level for adults.

The CNV can also provide important information about differences in neural activation during future-oriented processing of different varieties. As discussed in a prior section, subcranial recordings and high-density scalp source localization suggest that the CNV waveform may be generated by a network including the basal ganglia (Bareš & Rektor, 2001), and that the last part of the CNV prior to the S2, may originate from pre-frontal areas (Basile et al., 2002). Across a number of studies, these two areas have been found to show a particularly prolonged developmental trajectory (see review by Durston et al., 2001). Therefore, it is not surprising that the few studies examining children's CNV in an S1-S2 paradigm have found developmental differences.

The majority of the CNV studies conducted with children have been during simple fixed-foreperiod reaction time tasks with relatively short ISIs (1 to 1.5 seconds), preventing the analysis of the O-wave and E-wave separately. In these short ISIs, adult-like CNVs are most commonly reported in late childhood and early adolescence. Low, Borda, Frost, and Kellaway (1966) describe adult-like CNVs only in children 12-years-old and older, with younger children's CNVs being slower to emerge over repetitions and elongated in form. Low and Stoilen (1973) used a 1-second ISI and found inconsistent and sometimes positive CNVs in children 7 and younger, but all children over 10 years old showed consistently negative CNVs. Cohen (1973) examined the CNV in a 1.5-second ISI paradigm, finding that by 10 years old, the CNV appeared normal in morphology and that adult-sized CNV responses were seen by age 15. The topography of the CNV also appears to develop. Cohen found that the CNV was more parietally centrally peaked in adults and more parietally peaked in children.

Our research also suggests that young children also differ in their CNV in longer-duration fixed-foreperiod reaction time paradigms (Austin, Berg, & Fields, 1996; Byrd, Austin, & Berg, 1997). In this research, we presented a speeded foreperiod reaction time task to 20 adults and 16 6-year-olds using a 6-second foreperiod. CNV was recorded from Cz referenced to linked mastoids. Resulting ERPs showed typical negative CNVs in adults, but positive CNVs in many of the children (11 positive responses, 3, with little or no slow change, and 2 with negative change). The participants were asked not to blink, which may have affected the CNV by adding an additional inhibitory task during the interval. This study suggests that neural processing during a highly motivated speeded fixed-foreperiod reaction time task differs in children possibly due to inefficient control over the inhibition of response during preparation, and executive function.

Two studies from other laboratories have also examined developmental differences in the CNV over a longer ISI, though the developmental differences were only compared across adolescence and early adulthood, and did not include younger children. Klorman (1975) examined developmental differences among 10-, 14-, and 19-year-old's CNV occurring in a traditional S1-S2 reaction time paradigm with a 5-second ISI. At Cz, a two-component waveform, O- and E-wave, was found in all three age groups. In 10-year-olds, the E-wave amplitudes were smaller, and actually not significantly different from baseline. Even though the 14- and 19-year-old groups did have E-wave amplitudes significantly different from baseline, none of the three age groups had amplitudes of their initial O-wave that were significantly different from baseline.

A more recent study of the developmental differences in the CNV waveform (Segalowitz, Unsal, & Dywan, 1992) also examined potential differences in this waveform of 12-year-old children and adults, and also the relation between the CNV and executive functioning measures (standardized neuropsychological tests). As compared to the adults, the CNV of the children appeared to be smaller during both the O-wave and the E-wave, but only significantly so for the O-wave. In the child group, this early component (but not the later component) significantly correlated with inappropriate set perseveration (a measure of attentional set-shifting), non-verbal intelligence, mazes (a measure of planning), and trails A and B (also a measure of planning), such that better performance was correlated with larger O-wave amplitudes. This evidence supports the hypothesis that the functioning of neurological regions underlying executive functions may be related to functioning of neurological regions underlying the CNV.

In summary, the development of the morphology of CNV in appears to remain fairly constant when ISIs are brief, but for longer ISIs the development of the amplitude is quite prolonged, reaching full maturity in late elementary school and early middle school ages (e.g., Low et al., 1966). At the longer ISIs, where executive functioning may be more challenged, there are suggestions of differences in CNV morphology and localization as well as amplitude. These findings as a whole suggest that the neural activity underlying simple anticipation and preparation is not fully developed until adolescence. The studies necessary to explore if there is a executive component of active preparation (e.g., attentional control, inhibitory control of early responses) related to a specific aspect of CNV have yet to be conducted.

Working Memory During Future-Oriented Processing

When a substantial accelerative component was found in the heart rate foreperiod studies from our laboratory described above, some sort of an explicit speeded response was required at S2. In all three of those studies, participants were engaged in a speeded foreperiod reaction time paradigm, and therefore their response needed to be inhibited prior to S2. However, because our proposal argues that executive processing generally should elicit an accelerative component during the S1-S2 interval, we should expect executive processes other than inhibition should also have this effect. One such executive process is working memory, which involves retaining in memory a small number of items for a short time as well as manipulation of these items (Baddeley, 1998). One example of this process might be mentally reorganizing a small set of objects to imagine how they might appear when rearranged. In the Dennis and Mulcahy (1980) study described earlier, the increased acceleratory component that occurred as adults were retaining increasingly complex digit sequences, the results could readily be interpreted as being due to the increased working memory demands of the task during rehearsal.

The findings of Griffin, Davis, Berg, and Garner (1995) also suggest the heart rate acceleration component of the S1-S2 paradigm occurs for executive processes other than inhibition. In a study of anticipation, 18 3-year-old and 16 5-year-old children were presented with a small container holding a variety of Halloween masks, interesting hats and other items they might place on their heads or faces (all with unobstructed eyeholes). Before to each trial, the child selected a single item of their choice, placed it on his or her head, and awaited a warning stimulus (S1), a simple bull's-eye appearing on a small monitor in front of them. Ten seconds following onset of this S1, a much larger monitor with a live video feed of their own face appeared, the S2, for 5 seconds. The children were required only to sit quietly and await the "TV picture" of themselves with their adornment. At S1 onset, the typical child sat attentively watching the monitor where their image would appear. No overt response to the live video was required and typically spontaneous responding was limited to a positive facial expressions. Our original intent with this paradigm was simply to produce an interesting S2 stimulus and our expectation was that we might see something like the D1 and D2 responses we found for infants and 5-year-olds awaiting a recorded video (see Garner study above). There was no expectation of an acceleration component. However, the participants produced a triphasic heart rate response dominated by an accelerative component (see Figure 8.7), especially in participants who judged

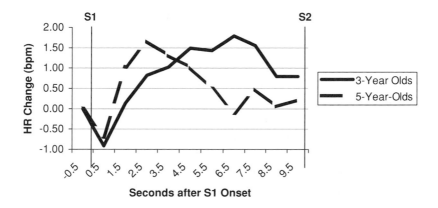

Figure 8.7. Heart rate responding as 3- and 5-year-olds await a brief live video of themselves wearing an interesting mask or other headwear. A prominent acceleration is present in both groups, and peaks earlier in the older group. Note the similarity of the 5 year olds' response to the RT group in Figure 8.4. The acceleration for this study is proposed to occur because of the working memory involvement in trying to imagine one's appearance prior to the video showing.

to show the strongest behavioral interest in the S2. A D1 was consistently evident, but the D2 did not consistently go below baseline.

Clearly, even when no overt response is required, and there is no necessity for response inhibition, a prominent accelerative component can be seen. This result is markedly different from what the Garner (1993, Garner & Berg, 1993) study described above found for a seemingly similar situation. In the Garner study children who were cued to an interesting video (see Figure 8.7) showed the two decelerative components, but no accelerative component. This result suggests an anticipatory response to the upcoming video. But, in the Griffin and colleagues (1995) study, when children awaited not just an interesting video, but one in which they would see themselves with masks, the marked acceleration occurred, just as it did when children awaited making a speeded response. We suggest what differs between these studies, and what results in an accelerative component, is the presence of executive functioning and the active processing of the anticipated stimulus. We propose that for the Griffin and colleagues (1995) study working memory was engaged during the S1-S2 interval as the children were trying to imagine how the mask they selected would look when it was placed on their own head. This situation would involve remembering what the item looked like in their hand and manipulating this view to imagine what it might look like on their own face or head. Such a task for a young child would likely require considerable working memory effort.

Of course, a simpler explanation for the accelerative response might be that the children were excited as they awaited either the reaction time stimulus or the video image of themselves with a mask. If so, one would need to require that there be no excitement, or at least substantially less so, for an interesting video, a video to which they were very attentive. In any case, we are aware of no evidence that clearly demonstrates that excitement, a concept not easily defined, is accompanied by acceleration when not also accompanied by active motor activity. Children in this study sat surprisingly still as they awaited their video image to appear. Still, studies could be and should be carried out that would attempt to separate these possible interpretations.

Planning as an Active Future-Oriented Process

Planning is another future-oriented process requiring active control over cognition and behavior, and an important aspect of executive functioning. Planning has been found to be related to both inhibition and working memory abilities in adults (Welsh, Satterlee-Cartmell, & Stine, 1999). Thus, as part of our hypothesis, we expect that the increased cognitive and behavioral control required during planning would result in modulation of the physiological responses during the fixed foreperiod of planning. Also, we expect this cognitive and behavioral control to be more difficult for children, resulting in developmental differences in physiological responses over the ISI when they are planning.

Byrd and Berg (2002) examined this issue by assessing adults and children 6 to 9 years old on the Tower of London task, a well-known neuropsychological planning task. In this task, a set of three differently colored balls sitting on pegs must be rearranged to match their positions on the "goal" set in both position and color. For the version of the task used in this study, adult and child participants were required to wait for a period of 9 seconds prior to moving the balls. During this time, one of two conditions was tested. In one, the plan condition, participants could see the balls in the starting position as well as the goal set but could not move them, and thus had an opportunity to plan but not make their moves. In the control condition participants could see only a blank set of pegs with no balls, wherein no planning or moves could take place. At the end of the 9 seconds, the balls appeared if not already present and the participants could begin moving balls at their own pace to try to reach a solution. In this situation, the onset of the 9-second period prior to ball movement constituted the S1, and the presentation of the opportunity to move the balls constituted S2.

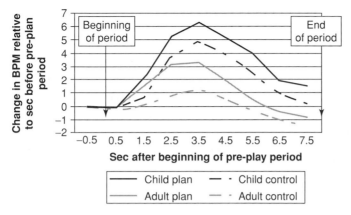

Figure 8.8. Heart rate responding of 6- to 9-year-old children and adults as they await the opportunity to move ("play") the balls in the Tower of London task. In the Plan condition they could see but not move the balls they needed to plan their solutions, but in the Control condition only the empty pegs were visible. Note the larger accelerative components for children than adults, and for planning than control.

Second-by-second heart rate showed a significant acceleration in all conditions (Figure 8.8). Acceleration was larger in children than adults, and both children and adults showed increased acceleration when planning as compared to waiting. Perhaps the child group had to exert more effort for cognitive and behavioral control in both conditions, resulting in the age group differences in acceleration. Because the resting heart rate of children was higher than that of adults, it is unlikely the age difference in acceleration could be attributed to this difference. Normally, higher resting heart rate should, if anything, mitigate against greater acceleration. Additionally, both children and adults may have had to increase cognitive control during planning, further increasing acceleration in that condition.

Level 4: Fully-Developed Active Preparation

In this fourth level of development of future-oriented processing, adult-like anticipation/preparation for S2 is achieved. Frontal lobe development as well as development of the circuitry connecting these frontal association areas has been estimated to continue into late adolescence and early adulthood (Durston et al., 2001). Likewise, executive functioning performance on measures requiring preparation for an action, such as inhibition and planning, also appear to reach adult performance levels only by the late teens and early twenties (De Luca et al., 2003). In the previous section, we reviewed the physiological evidence of this adult level of future-oriented functioning as part of our introduction to the task-related modulation of the physiological measures used in the S1-S2 paradigm.

We are aware that this fourth level might be simply viewed as the end point of level 3, which it surely is. However, we mark it tentatively as a distinct level because a great deal of maturation of the executive functioning must occur over such a long period of time that young adulthood has the appearance of a very different form of future-oriented functioning. Also, we can well imagine that as we begin to better understand the process of development of executive functioning and of the nature of executive functions themselves (e.g., Baddeley, 1998), we may well find that during that long period there is not a gradual development of one integrated set of executive functions, but rather uneven development of several different component abilities that make up executive functioning (Byrd, in preparation). As such, the point at which each component reaches optimal maturity in young adulthood would appear to be an important milestone.

We wish to emphasize that this fourth level should be considered a young adult performance level, and is not an end point to life-span development of future-oriented processes. This executive functioning theory regarding S1-S2 processes could be easily expanded to examine the declines in future-oriented processing that occur in later adulthood as the frontal areas show typical age-related neural changes (e.g., Pruel, Gabrieli, & Bunge, 2000) and executive functions show typical developmental declines (e.g., West, 1996). Because our expertise falls primarily within child development of future-oriented processes, for now we limit our proposal to the four levels that end in early adulthood. However, life-span development of future-oriented processes is clearly a fruitful area to pursue.

Overview of Proposed Hierarchy

Based on our review of the developmental research using the S1-S2 paradigm from our own laboratory and others' laboratories, we have proposed that the results may be viewed from a neuropsychological perspective, in which we analyze future-oriented processes by the component processing requirements in the tasks (Welsh et al., 1999). We have attempted here to explore a hypothesis that this far-ranging literature might be organized, with at least a heuristic value, by considering the processes that can occur within the S1-S2 interval as a hierarchy of anticipatory capabilities. We propose that this hierarchy can be followed as a developmental trajectory from infancy into young adulthood.

In early infancy, simple associations between the first and second stimuli can be made, accompanied by information on the timing of the delay between S1 and S2. At this developmental point, no active future-oriented processes occur, nor is there active preparation or processing for the second event. After a few months, the infant begins to show evidence of being able to anticipate the onset of S2. This suggests the emergence of active, future-oriented processes that accompany simple association. This level 2 can be viewed as an intermediate stage in which some basic responses occur prior to S2 onset. These are, however, typically limited to reflexive or autonomic responses. What is still absent at this level is the controlled, active, or more complex cognitive processing needed to provide effective preparation for the upcoming S2.

To reach this complex processing level, there needs to be sufficient neurological development of frontal brain areas and associated neural circuits capable of coordinating these complex cognitive processes. As the necessary brain development occurs, the third level of future-oriented processing begins to be possible, one in which participants, during the interval between S1 and S2, can involve conscious control of cognition and behavior using executive functions. This level has a very protracted development, presumably because of the gradual development of the frontal lobes and other brain areas involved in executive functioning. As noted earlier, it may well be that some executive functioning components take longer to develop than others, making this clearly a fruitful area for research. If so, with additional data, this third level could be refined or broken into additional milestones and sublevels.

In late adolescence/early adulthood, with the full maturation of the frontal areas, adult-like executive functioning allows for adolescents/young adults to reach the fourth stage of future-oriented processing. At this developmental level, we propose that: (1) responses can be successfully inhibited over the delay interval, and that these responses are given correctly and quickly at the S2 with minimal effort; (2) participants can encode stimuli in order to plan multiple steps ahead to give a response at S2; and (3) arousal and attention are consistently modulated over the anticipatory/preparatory interval for better and quicker performance of the response at S2. At this fourth stage, fully developed future-oriented processing, the most demanding form of processing, is achieved.

Throughout the levels of development, we find that psychophysiological measures, especially second-by-second heart rate, play an important role in delineating and evaluating the progress and processes being expressed. Startle responding may provide further information, but it is perhaps CNV and other neurological measures that hold the most promise for furthering this research.

We reiterate here that though we have presented this theory as discrete "levels" it is much more likely that these developmental changes are closer to a continuum. For example, there may be greater or lesser levels of the simple level 2 anticipation, just as there may be greater or lesser use of executive functions as development occurs over level 3, partially functional anticipation, prior to level 4, fully functional anticipation thereafter. Further, we can well imagine that there may be instances in which one may function at higher levels in one circumstance than in another. Yet, we argue there is some value in viewing this development as a progression of increasing competence in handling future-oriented requirements, and these involve qualitative as well as quantitative changes.

Future Directions with the Hierarchy

The value of the hypothesis of a hierarchy of future-oriented processes – and it should be seen as only as a hypothesis at this time – could be assessed by a number of areas of future research. We see four areas of research that could evaluate components of this hypothesis.

1. A first group of studies would examine our hypothesis that different types of executive functions affect these physiological correlates in similar ways due to the engagement of the Central Executive (Baddeley, 1998). One could test this hypothesis by examining multiple physiological measures during preparation for tasks requiring different executive functions. These different executive functions could include preparation for inhibition (such as the Stroop task), planning for a multi-step problem-solving task (such as the Tower of London task), or preparing for attentional set shifting (such as the Wisconsin Card Sorting Task). In order to best test this hypothesis, varying levels of difficulty for each of these tasks would need to be included. These tasks would also need to be carefully controlled for the complexity of the stimuli and the type of behavioral responses required in order to prevent confounds. Again, it is crucial that this work be conducted with a variety of age groups to determine if our developmental progression results in expected developmental differences due to the executive functioning requirements of these different tasks. This test would be especially so if there is the possibility of differential rates of development of the abilities.

2. A second fruitful area of research would examine our hypothesis that it is the executive functioning/frontal lobe nature of active preparation that affects these physiological responses. These studies would examine preparation in

an S1-S2 interval requiring different levels of executive functioning while measuring both the classic psychophysiological measures discussed in this chapter as well as correlates of brain activity using event-related potentials and/or functional MRI. The concurrence or lack of concurrence of frontal activation and changes in these physiological measures would directly assess the relation between changes in frontal requirements in future-oriented processing and changes in these autonomic and motor system physiological correlates. Again, it is important that this work be conducted developmentally so that developmental differences in frontal maturation can be related to the intensity and topography of frontal activation and the differences in these other psychophysiological correlates. Specifically, as has been found in past fMRI work, we would expect to find increased frontal activation with increased executive functioning demands in children as compared to adults (Casey et al., 1997).

3. It would also be very useful to compare future-oriented processes and physiological correlates from samples of typically developing populations with those from atypically developing populations thought to experience abnormal rates of executive functioning development. Examples of such atypically developing populations may include children and adults with Attention-Deficit/Hyperactivity Disorder, who have delayed executive functioning development (Aman, Roberts, & Pennington, 1998), and adults with Alzheimer's Disease, who have faster than typical executive declines with aging (Bondi et al., 2003). By comparing these groups to a typically developing sample, we could examine our hypothesis concerning executive functioning and physiological correlates during future-oriented processes. We would anticipate poorer executive functioning performance and evidence of increased executive functioning effort by the groups with expected executive functioning deficits. These studies could serve to expand our theory to include life-span development and include typical and atypical development. However, these studies would need to be conducted with carefully age-matched samples and also would need to include measures of non-executive cognitive functions in order to confirm that the samples are comparable on non-executive cognitive processes.

4. Our last proposed direction for future research is the exploration of the possibility that participants can move through this hierarchy of future-oriented processing, not only during the developmental process but also at any given age during the learning and mastery of a complex task. Microgenetic methods have been employed recently by developmental researchers as a way to examine progressions in performance due to learning that are similar to progressions in performance due to development by examining

participants' performance as they gain expertise with a given task across repeated exposures (McNamara, 2003; Siegler, 1996). In this research, we would test whether there are decreases in the amount of executive functioning necessary to prepare for the task with increases in experience and proficiency with the task. That is, we would expect that when faced with a new complex situation success could be achieved only with the full use of executive processes to control the circumstances. With experience, however, more and more of the task demands could become routinized and therefore not require the active processing necessary with the new task. Therefore, we could expect that adults would initially be making use of the highest levels of processing for challenging tasks, and this process would shift to at least middle level of processing as learning progressed, and to the lowest levels with highly learned tasks. For young children who might not be able to start out processing at the highest levels, we would see shifts from the middle to lowest level with increased experience on the task. In both cases, this would occur as the task became more automatic and less effortful. We would expect this shift in behavior and processing level to be reflected in a change in physiological correlates.

References

Aman, C. J., Roberts, R. J., Jr., & Pennington, B. F. (1998). A neuropsychological examination of the underlying deficit in attention deficit hyperactivity disorder: Frontal lobe versus right parietal lobe theories. *Developmental Psychology, 34,* 956–969.

Anthony, B. J., Butler, G. H. & Putnam, L. E. (1978). Probe startle inhibition during HR deceleration in a forewarned RT paradigm. [Abstract]. *Psychophysiology, 15,* 285.

Anthony, B. J. & Putnam, L. E. (1985). Cardiac and blink reflex concomitants of attentional selectivity: A comparison of adults and young children. *Psychophysiology, 22,* 508–516.

Austin, G. J., Berg, W. K., & Fields, H. (1996). Slow cortical positivity in 6-year-old children during an S1-S2 paradigm. [Abstract]. *Psychophysiology, 33,* S20.

Baddeley, A. (1998). The central executive: A concept and some misconceptions. *Journal of the International Neuropsychological Society, 4,* 523–526.

Bareš, M., & Rektor, I. (2001). Basal ganglia involvement in sensory and cognitive processing. A depth electrode CNV study in human subjects. *Clinical Neurophysiology, 112,* 2022–2030.

Bar-Haim, Y., Marshall, P. J., & Fox, N. A. (2000). Developmental changes in heart period and high frequency heart period variability from 4 months to 4 years of age. *Developmental Psychobiology, 37,* 44–56.

Basile, L. F., Ballester, G., de Castro, C. C., & Gattaz, W. F. (2002). Multifocal slow potential generation revealed by high-resolution EEG and current density reconstruction. *International Journal of Psychophysiology, 45,* 227–240.

Berg, W. K., Adkinson, C. D., & Strock, B. D. (1973). Duration and frequency of periods of alertness in neonates. *Developmental Psychology, 9,* 434.

Berg, W. K., & Balaban, M. T. (1999). Startle elicitation: Stimulus parameters, recording techniques, and quantification. In M. E. Dawson, A. M. Schell, & A. H. Böhmelt (Eds.), *Startle modification: Implications for neuroscience, cognitive science, and clinical science* (pp. 21–50). New York: Cambridge University Press.

Berg, W. K., & Berg, K. M. (1987). Psychophysiological development in infancy: State, startle and attention. In J. Osofsky (Ed.) *Handbook of Infant Development*(2nd ed., pp. 238–317). New York: John Wiley & Sons.

Berg, W. K., & Richards, J. (1997). Attention across time in infant development. In P. Lang, M. Balaban, & R. Simons (Eds.), *Attention and Orienting: Sensory and Motivational Processes* (pp.347–368). Mahwah, NJ: Lawrence Erlbaum Associates.

Berntson, G. G., Bigger, J. T., Eckberg, D. L., Grossman, P., Kaufmann, P. G., Malik, M., Nagaraja, H. N., Porges, S. W., Saul, J. P., Stone, P. H., & van der Molen, M. W. (1997). Heart rate variability: Origins, methods, and interpretive caveats. *Psychophysiology, 34*, 623–648.

Blumenthal, T. D., Cuthbert, B. N., Filion, D. L., Hackley, S., Lipp, O. V., & van Boxtel, A. (2005). Committee report: Guidelines for human startle eyeblink electromygraphic studies. *Psychophysiology, 42*, 1–15.

Bohlin, G., & Kjellberg, A. (1979). Orienting activity in two-stimulus paradigms as reflected in heart rate. In H. D. Kimmel, E. H. Von Olst, & J. E. Orlebeke (Eds.), *The orienting response in humans* (pp. 169–195). Hillsdale, NJ: Lawrence Erlbaum Associates.

Bondi, M. W., Houston, W. S., Salmon, D. P., Corey-Bloom, J., Katzman, R., Thal, L. J., & Delis, D. C. (2003). Neuropsychological deficits associated with Alzheimer's disease in the very-old: Discrepancies in raw vs. standardized scores. *Journal of the International Neuropsychological Society, 9*, 783–795.

Boswell, A., Garner, E. E., & Berg, W. K. (1994) Changes in cardiac components of anticipation in 2, 4, and 8-month infants, *Psychophysiology, 31*.

Bradley, M. M., Cuthbert, B. N., & Lang, P. J. (1990). Startle reflex modification: Emotion or Attention? *Psychophysiology, 27*, 513–522.

Bradley, M. M., Cuthbert, B. N., & Lang, P. J. (1999). Affect and the startle reflex. In M. E. Dawson, A. M. Schell, & A. H. Böhmelt (Eds.), *Startle modification: Implications for neuroscience, cognitive science, and clinical science* (pp.157–183). New York: Cambridge University Press.

Brandimonte, M., Einstein, G. O., & McDaniel, M. A. (1996). *Prospective memory: Theory and applications.* Mahwah, NJ: Lawrence Erlbaum Associates.

Brooks, P., & Berg, W. K. (1979). Do 16-week-old infants anticipate stimulus offsets? *Developmental Psychobiology, 12*, 329–334.

Brunia, C. H. M., & van Boxtel, G. J. M. (2001). Wait and see. *International Journal of Psychophysiology, 43*, 59–75.

Byrd, D. L., Austin, A. J., & Berg, W. K. (1997). Contingent negative variation: Clarifying the course of development. [Abstract]. *Psychophysiology, 34*, S26.

Byrd, D. L., & Berg, W. K. (2002). The relationship between age and the preparatory heart rate response: Childhood through adulthood. *Biological Psychology, 61*, 271–276.

Casey, B. J., Durston, S., & Fosella. J. A. (2001). Evidence of a mechanistic model of cognitive control. *Clinical Neuroscience Research, 1*, 267–282.

Casey, B. J., Trainor, R. J., Orendi, J. L., Schubert, A. B., Nystrom, L. E., Giedd, J. N., Castellanos, F. X., Haxby, J. V., Noll, D. C., Cohen, J. D., Forman, S. D., Dahl, R. E., &

Rapoport, J. L. (1997). A developmental functional MRI study of prefrontal activation during performance of a go-no-go task. *Journal of Cognitive Neuroscience, 9*, 835–847.

Clifton, R. K. (1974). Heart rate conditioning in the newborn infant. *Journal of Experimental Child Psychology, 18*, 9–21.

Cohen, J. (1973). The CNV in children with special reference to learning disabilities. *EEG and Clinical Neurophysiology, 33S*, 151–154.

Davies, M. B. (1985). *Infants' responses to temporally regular events and their omission.* Unpublished Doctoral Dissertation, University of Florida, Gainesville, FL.

Dawson, M. E., Schell, A. M., & Böhmelt, A. H. (1999). *Startle modification: Implications for neuroscience, cognitive science, and clinical science.* New York: Cambridge University Press.

De Luca, C. R., Wood, S. J., Anderson, V., Buchanan, J., Proffitt, T. M., Mahony, K., & Pantelis, C. (2003). Normative data from the Cantab. I: Development of executive function over the lifespan. *Journal of Clinical and Experimental Neuropsychology, 25*, 242–254.

Dennis, S. S, & Mulcahy, R. F. (1980). Heart-rate changes during covert rehearsal and response execution. *Perceptual and Motor Skills, 50*, 595–602.

Diamond, A. (2000). Close interrelation of motor development and cognitive development and of the cerebellum and prefrontal cortex. *Child Development, 71*, 44–56.

Donohue, R. L. (1991). *Seven-month-olds' display of anticipatory heart rate decelerations in an S1+/S1- fixed fore-period paradigm.* Unpublished Doctoral Dissertation, University of Florida, Gainesville, FL.

Donohue, R. L., & Berg, W. K. (1991). Infant heart-rate responses to temporally predictable and unpredictable events. *Developmental Psychology, 27*, 59–66.

Durston, S., Hulshoff Pol, H. E., Casey, B. J., Giedd, J. N., Buitelaar, J. K., & van Engeland, H. (2001). Anatomical MRI of the developing human brain: What have we learned? *Journal of the American Academy of Child and Adolescent Psychiatry, 40*, 1012–1020.

Garner, E. E. (1993). *Effects of a speeded motor task on cardiac and startle indices of anticipation in 5-year-old children.* Unpublished Master's Thesis, University of Florida, Gainesville, FL.

Garner, E. E. (1998). Follow your head (and your heart?): Cardiac and motor indices of anticipation in 15-month-old infants in a two- alternative, cued location memory task. *Dissertation Abstracts International: Section B: The Sciences & Engineering Univ. Microfilms International, 58*, 3944.

Garner, E. E., & Berg, W. K. (1993) Effects of speeded motor tasks on cardiac and startle indices of anticipation in 5-year-old children. [Absract]. *Psychophysiology, 30*, S29.

Graham, F. K., & Clifton, R. K. (1966). Heart-rate change as a component of the orienting response. *Psychological Bulletin, 65*, 305–320.

Graham, F. K., Putnam, L. E. & Leavitt, L. A. (1975). Lead-stimulation effects on human cardiac orienting and blink reflexes. *Journal of Experimental Psychology: Human Perception and Performance, 204*, 161–169.

Griffin, C. J., Davis, L. J., Berg, W. K., & Garner, E. E. (1995). *Anticipation in 3 and 5-yr-old children: Cardiac responses while awaiting a cued, interesting event.* Paper presented at the Biennial Meeting of the Society for Research in Child Development. Indianapolis, IN.

Haith, M. M., Benson, J. B., Roberts, R. J., Jr., & Pennington, B. F. (1994). *The development of future-oriented processes.* Chicago, IL: University of Chicago Press.

Hatayama, T., Yamaguchi, H., & Ohyama, M. (1981) Cardiac response patterns during a foreperiod in reaction time tasks. *Tohoku Psychologica Folia, 40,* 137–145.

Jennings, J. R., Berg, W. K., Obrist, P., Hutcheson, J. H., Porges, S. & Turpin, G. (1981). Publication guidelines for heart rate studies in man. *Psychophysiology, 18,* 226–231.

Jennings, J. R., & Matthews, K. A. (1984). The impatience of youth: Phasic cardiovascular response in Type A and Type B elementary school-aged boys. *Psychosomatic Medicine, 46,* 498–511.

Keen, R. E., Chase, H. H., & Graham, F. K. (1965). Twenty-four hour retention by neonates of an habituated heart rate response. *Psychonomic Science, 2,* 265–266.

Klorman, R. (1975). Contingent negative variation and cardiac deceleration in a long preparatory interval: A developmental study. *Psychophysiology, 12,* 609–617.

Klorman, R., & Lang, P. J. (1972). Cardiac responses to signal and nonsignal tasks in 9-year-olds. *Psychonomic Science, 28,* 299–300.

Lang, P. J. (1995). The emotion probe: Studies of motivation and attention. *American Psychologist, 50,* 372–385.

Lawler, K. A., Obrist, P. A., & Lawler, J. E. (1978). Cardiac and somatic response patterns during a reaction time task in children and adults. *Psychophysiology, 13,* 448–455.

Lipp, O. V. (2002). Anticipation of a non-aversive reaction time task facilitates the blink startle reflex. *Biological Psychology, 59,* 147–162.

Lipp, O. V., Siddle, D. A. T., & Dall, P. J. (1998). Effects of stimulus modality and task condition on blink startle modification and on electrodermal responses. *Psychophysiology, 35,* 542–461.

Low, M. D., Borda, R. P., Frost Jr., J. D., & Kellaway, P. (1966). Surface-negative, slow potential shift associated with conditioning in man. *Neurology, 16,* 771–782.

Low, M. D., & Stoilen, L. (1973). CNV and EEG in children: Maturational characteristics and findings in the MCD syndrome. *EEG and Clinical Neurophysiology, 33S,* 139–143.

Luria, A. R. (1966). *Higher cortical functions in man.* New York: Basic Books.

McNamara, J. P. H. (2003). *Preschoolers' use of a holding peg strategy on the Tower of London.* Unpublished Master's Thesis, University of Florida, Gainesville, FL.

Picton, T. W., Bentin, S., Berg, P., Donchin, E., Hillyard, S. A., Johnson, R., Jr., Miller, G. A., Ritter, W., Ruchkin, D. S., Rugg, M. D., & Taylor, M. J. (2000). Guidelines for using human event-related potentials to study cognition: Recording standards and publication criteria. *Psychophysiology, 37,* 127–152.

Pruel, M. W., Gabrieli, J. K. E., & Bunge, S. A. (2000). Age-related changes in memory: A cognitive neuroscience perspective. In F. I. M. Craik, & T. Salthouse (Eds.), *The handbook on aging and cognition* (2nd ed.). Mahwah, NJ: Lawrence Erlbaum Associates.

Putnam, L. E. (1990). Great expectations: Anticipatory responses of the heart and brain. In J. W. Rohrbaugh, & R. Parasuraman (Eds.), *Event-related brain potentials: Basic issues and applications* (pp. 109–129). New York: Oxford University Press.

Rohrbaugh, J. W., Dunham, D. N., Stewart, P. A., Bauer, L. O., Kuperman, S., Conner, S. J., Porjesz, B., & Henri Begleiter, H. (1997). Slow brain potentials in a visual-spatial memory task: Topographic distribution and inter-laboratory consistency. *International Journal of Psychophysiology, 25,* 111–122.

Ruchkin, D. S., Johnson, R. Jr., Canoune, H., & Ritter, W. (1991). Event-related potentials during arithmetical and mental rotation. *Electroencephalography and Clinical Neurophysiology, 79,* 473–487.

Ruchkin, D. S., Johnson, R. Jr., Grafman J., Canoune, H., & Ritter, W. (1997). Multiple visiuospatial working memory buffers: Evidence from spaiotemporal patterns of brain activity. *Neuropsychologia, 35*, 195–209.

Segalowitz, S. J., Unsal, A., & Dywan, J. (1992). Cleverness and wisdom in 12-year-olds: Electrophysiological evidence for late maturation of the frontal lobe. *Developmental Neuropsychology, 8*, 279–298.

Siegler, R. S. (1996). *Emerging minds: The process of change in children's thinking.* New York: Oxford University Press.

Sokolov, Y. N. (1963). *Perception and the conditioned reflex.* New York: Pergamon Press.

Stamps, L. E. (1977). Temporal conditioning of heart rate responses in newborn infants. *Developmental Psychology, 13*, 624–629.

Weerts, T. C., & Lang, P. J. (1973). The effects of eye fixation and stimulus response location on the contingent negative variation (CNV). *Biological Psychology, 1*, 1–19.

Welsh, M. C., Satterlee-Cartmell, T., & Stine, M. (1999). Towers of Hanoi and London: Contribution of working memory and inhibition to performance. *Brain and Cognition, 41*, 231–242.

West, R. L. (1996). An application of prefrontal cortex function theory to cognitive aging. *Psychological Bulletin, 120*, 272–292.

9 Measuring the Electromyographic Startle Response

Developmental Issues and Findings

Marie T. Balaban and W. Keith Berg

INTRODUCTION

A sudden noise occurs while you are concentrating and you respond quickly and automatically – your body muscles flex, your eyes blink, and your facial expression registers a grimace of surprise. You have just experienced a startle reflex. The startle reflex (or startle response) is commonly measured in research studies by a blink response in humans, elicited by some startling stimulus such as a loud noise. The blink response is an early and reliable component of startle in humans. It occurs to stimuli in various sensory modalities (e.g., auditory, visual, cutaneous) and often begins within 30 ms after the onset of a sudden and intense stimulus.

The word "reflex" often seems to bring to mind a stable, simple, and unchanging response elicited under specific circumstances. But in the case of the startle reflex, this view is overly simplistic. Though this reflex can be reliably elicited, it turns out to also be highly modifiable by an extensive variety of stimuli, circumstances, and clinical conditions. The wide range of studies examining this process of modification is generally referred to as startle modification research. Fundamentally, the paradigms employed in this research involve situations in which the startle reflex is modulated or modified in amplitude, latency, or probability by another non-startling variable of interest. The remarkably wide range of factors that can modify startle is what has generated such a broad interest in its study. Detailed research in animals on the neural pathways underlying startle and startle modulatory effects undergirds the interest in startle modification in humans (e.g., Davis, 1984; 1997; Koch, 1999).

Although the modern research on the modulation of the startle reflex is more than 35 years old, there has been a real explosion of this research in the last 15 years. A search of psychological and medical literature for "startle response," "prepulse inhibition," "fear potentiated startle," and the like during this period easily produces over 1000 articles. The versatility and sensitivity of the technique is unquestionable. The range of topics studied with this technology is truly astounding, from studies of numerous medical disorders and personality and emotion issues to work on basic cognitive processes. We selected the following two topic areas, and an illustrative study within each area, from startle modification research in human adults as examples to illustrate the usefulness of the startle modification approach for discovery in psychology.

One robust modulatory effect, prepulse inhibition, occurs when an onset, offset, or sudden change in a prestimulus occurs slightly before the onset of a startle-eliciting stimulus. For example, a relatively weak (60 dB) and brief (30 ms) tone might occur 120 ms prior to a startle-eliciting 50-ms 100 dB burst of white noise. The result is a marked reduction in the size of the startle blink response to the noise burst in studies of human adult control (that is, non-clinical) populations. Yet this inhibitory effect is not robust in schizophrenia patients (Cadenhead & Braff, 1999). In one study, patients with schizophrenia, relatives of patients with schizophrenia, and participants with schizotypal personality disorder were compared on prepulse inhibition to a startle-eliciting white noise burst preceded by a brief, lower intensity, white noise prepulse (Cadenhead et al., 2000). The results indicated considerable overlap in the range of prepulse inhibition across the control and clinical and familial groups (see their Figure 9.2). Nevertheless, analyses confirmed that prepulse inhibition of startle, measured from the muscle surrounding the right eye, was reduced in schizophrenic patients, their non-schizophrenic relatives, and patients with schizotypal personality disorder, compared to the control participants. The authors concluded that "prepulse inhibition distinguishes an intermediate phenotype that is present in schizophrenia spectrum disorders" (Cadenhead et al., 2000, p. 1666). Conceptually, the relative lack of prepulse inhibition in schizophrenia implies "a preattentive filtering dysfunction of schizophrenia patients, which could lead to information overload and cognitive disruption" (Cadenhead & Braff, 1999, p. 234). These authors speculated that deficient gating of incoming sensory stimulation leads to thought disorders due to cognitive flooding. In this case, a simple reflex modification measure provides links between psychopathology, an underlying neural mechanism for sensory or attentional gating, and cognitive dysfunction.

Another burgeoning area of startle modification research involves fear-potentiated startle, which refers to the finding that the startle reflex is facilitated by fear in humans and other animals (e.g., Davis, 1997; Grillon & Davis, 1997). This finding is similar to results of investigations of startle modification due to affective valence, that is, startle blink magnitude is facilitated while participants imagine or view images with negative emotional content and diminished while participants imagine or view images with positive emotional content (e.g., Cook, Hawk, Davis, & Stevenson, 1991; Vrana, Spence, & Lang, 1988). For example, one study examined blink measures of startle modification and other responses during affective imagery in control participants as well as in participants with fear-related disorders such as phobias (Cuthbert et al., 2003). In this task, participants were instructed to attempt vivid images based on the content of memorized sentences that were either neutral and scripted (common for all participants), fear-related and scripted, or fear-related and personal to the participant. During the imagery periods, acoustic startle-eliciting stimuli were presented. For control participants and for participants with specific phobias and social phobias, blink responses were significantly potentiated during imagery of fear sentences compared to imagery of neutral sentences. In this study, the potentiation of startle by fear imagery was less robust for participants with post-traumatic stress disorder and was not found for participants with panic disorder. Based on the startle potentiation data as well as other physiological responses and subjective ratings, the authors concluded that "the overall results are consistent with the view that reactions to fear memory cues differ significantly among the anxiety disorders" (Cuthbert et al., 2003, p. 416) and that comparison studies such as this one are a start for discerning whether these differences in responses to fear imagery "reflect variations in attentional patterns, language processing, associative learning, efferent inhibition, or some interaction of all these factors with the dynamics of memory retrieval" (p. 420). This study illustrates the basic phenomenon of fear-potentiated startle in human adults and extends the usefulness of this type of startle modification measure as a means of examining the responses of different diagnostic groups. Later in this chapter we review evidence of this phenomenon in infants and children.

Dawson, Schell, and Bohmelt (1999) asserted that "startle modification . . . promises to bridge human and infrahuman research; cognitive, motivational, and affective processes; and concepts drawn from neuroscience, cognitive science, and clinical science" (p. 16–17). In light of the widespread success of this method in studying both animal and adult human populations, the number of studies of startle modulation in human infants and children is surprisingly small. In the past 10 years or so fewer than 20 articles have appeared with this age group. This void is all the more surprising because some of the earliest work on startle modulation in humans by Frances Graham's and Howard Hoffman's laboratories was carried out with infants (e.g., Anthony & Graham, 1983; Marsh, Hoffman, & Stitt, 1979). Because startle can be elicited in infants, startle modification is an appropriate model system for investigating the development of psychological processes, including attention, emotion, and individual differences. Why then has so little attention been paid to using startle with developmental populations?

There are several reasons for this, but one important one is simply that few developmental psychologists are provided with the training and information needed to utilize this procedure. On the other hand, investigators who are trained with using the necessary procedures with adults may find that transferring the technology to the testing of children and infants can lead to some serious roadblocks. Detailed reviews of startle recording and modulation procedures oriented toward adults are available (e.g., Berg & Balaban, 1999; Blumenthal et al., 2005), but such information that is focused on the procedures needed for using the paradigm with infants and children is lacking. Therefore, the function of the current chapter is to review procedures for measuring startle and startle modulation with particular focus on the techniques needed to make it work effectively with infants and young children.

To this end, we will attempt to provide a concise but reasonably comprehensive review of the techniques for producing, recording, and scoring startle in infants and children. We will start by reviewing a number of procedures that can be used to elicit startle blink reflexes and follow this discussion with techniques for recording the most commonly used form of the response, electromyography, in young populations. Special problems with eliciting and scoring responses in younger participants will be assessed in these sections. Finally, we will provide a sampling of some of the successful applications of startle modulation procedures in the study of infants, children, and adolescents.

STARTLE PRODUCTION: ELICITING STARTLE RESPONSES

Startle blinks can be elicited by sudden, fast rise time stimuli in various sensory modalities. The rise time of a stimulus refers to the change in stimulus intensity over time as the stimulus reaches its maximum intensity, and a rapid rise time is necessary for eliciting startle. Stimulus intensity and duration are also important parameters to consider in choosing startle-eliciting stimuli. We will review basic characteristics of eliciting startle in auditory, visual, and cutaneous modalities, with a focus on whether and how eliciting startle in these modalities with infants and children differs from eliciting startle in adults.

The choice of stimulus modality will depend upon the intent of the study. For example, selective attention studies typically direct attention toward one sensory modality and then compare the resulting effects on reflex blinks elicited with stimuli in this attended modality and in another, unattended modality (e.g., Anthony & Graham, 1983; Richards, 1998). Several reviews of the underlying sensory, neural, and motor pathways for reflex blinks are available (e.g., Balaban, 1996; Berg & Balaban, 1999; Blumenthal et al., 2005 – this latter article is a committee report on measuring startle for the Society for Psychophysiological Research).

Eliciting startle blinks with auditory stimulation is a common technique in developmental and adult studies of startle modulation. In the auditory modality, a typical startle-eliciting stimulus for suprathreshold responses is a sudden, brief, and loud burst of white noise. Although startle can also be elicited by narrow-band noise or tones of a single frequency, white noise is typically a more reliable and effective eliciting stimulus (Blumenthal & Berg, 1986) except when using very short duration stimuli near startle threshold (Berg, 1973). Threshold studies for adult startle indicate that the integrated stimulus intensity during the first 10–12 ms of the stimulus is a key characteristic (Berg, 1973), and the latency of the adult acoustic blink response is about 25 to 50 ms. For adults, 50-ms white noise bursts with rapid rise times can elicit startle at threshold intensities of about 84 to 87 dB(A) (Berg, 1973).

In developmental populations, auditory stimuli are convenient and effective in eliciting blink responses, and as a result are a popular choice for research. The reflex blinks to acoustic stimuli have been measured in preterm infants (Yamada, 1984), although they have a higher threshold than adults (by about 10 to 30 dB; Graham, Anthony, & Zeigler, 1983), and the onset latency of the blink is longer in infants than adults (Anthony, Zeigler, & Graham, 1987). Ornitz and colleagues reported that blink latencies to a white-noise suprathreshold stimulus decreased with age in children of 4, 5, and 8 years (e.g., Ornitz, Guthrie, Sadeghpur, & Sugiyama, 1991).

Although some developmental studies have presented auditory stimuli through speakers, head movements can result in shifts in stimulus loudness and in the binaural characteristics of the stimulus. Therefore, it is preferable to use headphones that fit snugly over the ears if such a procedure can work effectively for the developmental population being studied. If speakers are used, it may be advantageous to have observers rate whether the infant's or child's head was positioned directly between the speakers on each startle trial. When calibrating sound intensity, some researchers produce the sound continuously in order to calibrate steady-state intensity. When sounds with rapid rise times are presented via speakers or headphones, however, intensity of transients within the stimulus can exceed steady-state intensity (Blumenthal & Goode, 1991), and thus the peak intensity of the actual eliciting stimulus presented through headphones or speakers should be measured if possible. It is also important to consider the safety standards for presentation of noise delineated by the Occupational Safety and Health Act (OSHA). The OSHA maximum for impulse noise (the kind typically used to elicit startle, for example) is set at 140 dB sound pressure level (OSHA, 2005, section 1926.52(e)), although OSHA standards were developed for adults, not children.

Visual startle can be elicited by sudden flashes of light. A typical stimulus might be a flash from two photo flash units, approximately 10^3 mL in intensity and less than 500 µs in nominal duration (Balaban, Anthony, & Graham 1985). This photic blink response is distinct from another type of visual startle to threatening or looming stimuli (see Balaban, 1996 or Blumenthal et al., 2005 for further review). Responses in infants and children seem especially prolonged for the photic blink. Whereas adult onset latencies for suprathreshold visual startle blinks are in the 40 to 70 ms range, infant onset latencies may be as long as 185 ms (Anthony et al., 1987). Visual blink latency decreased with age from preterm infants to full-term infants to children, with 9-year-olds approximating adult response latencies (Yasuhara, Hori, & Kobayashi, 1989). Two components of the visual blink can occur, with the early component latency at about 50 ms in adults, and the later component latency at about 80 ms (Blumenthal et al., 2005; Hackley & Boelhouwer, 1997). Compared to acoustically elicited blinks, visual blinks are typically smaller and slower in adults and infants (Anthony et al., 1987; Hackley & Johnson, 1996), although the durations of the eliciting stimulus and the integration of stimulus energy over time may differ across modalities. Many factors influence the effectiveness of a stimulus in eliciting the visual blink, and Blumenthal and colleagues (2005) stipulated that researchers should report "peak intensity (luminance), duration, rise/fall time, predominant wavelength (if the light is not white), size and position relative to fixation (in degrees of arc...) as well as ambient viewing conditions (p. 5)."

Startle can also be elicited through cutaneous stimulation, including electrical pulses or magnetic stimulation of areas on the face, mechanical taps to the glabella (forehead area), and mechanical puffs of air directed toward the face. (See Bischoff et al., 1993, for information on eliciting blinks via a magnetic coil). The cutaneous blink has an early ipsilateral (R1) and a late bilateral (R2) component; the R2 component is associated with the lid closure in the reflex blink. One system for presenting glabellar tap stimuli used successfully with infants involved a mechanical tapper with intensity controlled by a solenoid (Marsh et al., 1979). In general, however, electrical, magnetic, and, to some extent, airpuff stimuli allow greater control of stimulus parameters, particularly duration, than does the mechanical tapper. Although electrical and magnetic stimulation may give the most consistency and control, the negative aspects of being "shocked" in a psychological study, particularly on facial areas, may be reason to warrant the use of mechanical airpuff stimuli in developmental studies. In a recent study of adults, airpuffs were as effective in eliciting blink responses as acoustic stimuli (white noise bursts) and were judged by participants to be less intense and aversive than acoustic stimuli (Lissek et al., 2005). Airpuffs are typically delivered through a tube aimed toward the nasal bridge or the forehead near (but not directly at) the eye. A system of compressed air passing through control valves is employed (more details on this system were presented by Berg & Balaban, 1999; Haerich, 1998). The researcher must check and attempt to minimize both electrical and auditory artifacts that can accompany the control valve so that the blink elicitation and recording is not contaminated. A typical airpuff stimulus is exemplified in the Lissek et al. (2005) study, which used a 40 ms, 3 psi puff of air presented to the center of the forehead. They report that this stimulus elicited reflex blinks that were comparable to acoustic blinks elicited by a 120 dB, 40 ms white noise burst stimulus. Participants wore headphones to attenuate the acoustic click from the solenoid valve when the airpuff was triggered. Researchers might also consider the use of noise-canceling earphones in order to minimize any acoustic artifact. The delay between triggering the solenoid valve that releases the air from the source and the actual airpuff's arrival at the skin will depend upon the length of the tube through which the airpuff is delivered. This event should be measured. Blumenthal and colleagues (2005) suggest that researchers measure the onset, duration, and rise time of the stimulus with a microphone placed at the opening in the tube. Their recommendation for monitoring stimulus presentation and timing can be extended to all stimulus modalities: "By sampling and recording the stimulus output as if it were an input line during data collection, a researcher can be certain of the timing of stimulus onset relative to response onset." (p. 4). Of course, transduction characteristics of the measuring device (photocell, microphone, etc.) must also be considered.

Developmental studies have measured cutaneous blinks in infancy using mechanical, electrical, and airpuff stimulation. The early (R1) response appears to mature early in infancy, whereas the amplitude and latency of the late (R2) response, particularly the contralateral response, continues to mature in later childhood (Hatanaka, Yasuhara, & Kobayashi, 1990). These researchers noted that the latency of the late (R2) response was quite variable in infants and children.

This overview has demonstrated that stimuli in auditory, visual, and cutaneous modalities can be used successfully in developmental studies of startle modification. Once the stimulus modality and characteristics for an experiment have been chosen and calibrated in order to reliably elicit startle blink responses, the next step involves recording and quantifying the size and speed of the blink responses.

RECORDING, PROCESSING, AND SCORING OF STARTLE RESPONSES

Obtaining the Startle Blink Data

Issues in Recording

Startle blinks can be recorded in a variety of ways, but we focus here on what is currently the most commonly used method, recording of the muscle activity (electromyogram or EMG) near the eye. Many of the basic issues of startle blink measurement, analysis, and interpretation in adults are unchanged when studying children. However, there are additional issues that arise when utilizing startle blink to study future-oriented processes or other psychological processes with children. We will briefly review the basic recording process but direct the interested reader to previous work for details (e.g., Berg & Balaban, 1999; Blumenthal et al., 2005). Our discussion will focus on the modifications to the adult procedures needed to record this response effectively from infants and children.

The EMG activity is recorded primarily from the orbicularis oculi, the muscle that surrounds the eye and is activated when startle blinks are elicited (see Berg & Balaban, 1999 for information on recording startle by other methods). The optimal recording electrodes are small (e.g., 5 mm) silver/silver chloride cup electrodes made by companies such as Sensor Medics. The electrodes are filled with any of a variety of recording gels and typically attached to the skin surface with a self-adhesive collar. In adults and older children, the skin is typically prepared prior to electrode attachment by cleaning and very gently abrading the skin sites with a substance such as Omniprep (D. O. Weaver and Co.). With children and infants, avoid using cleaning agents that irritate the eyes, such as isopropyl alcohol. Because this skin area is very sensitive and thin, very little abrasion is needed, and with infants little or none. However, abrasion can lower the skin resistance substantially, thus greatly reducing recording noise (see following sections).

The EMG activity from the orbital portion of the orbicularis oculi does not record the eyelid movement per se, but rather an associated muscle activation that normally precedes and accompanies a startle blink. The orbital portion of the muscle is far easier to record from than the tiny palpebral muscles that overlay and directly move the eyelid. In the awake adult, EMG of the orbicularis oculi closely correlates with more direct measurements of eyelid closure (Flaten, 1993; Gehricke, Ornitz, & Siddarth, 2002; Schmidt, Fox, & Long, 1998). Further, the muscles of the orbicularis oculi respond to startling stimuli even when the eyes are closed at stimulus onset, such as in sleep. As well, EMG activity can be recorded for small muscle contractions, when little or no observable lid movement occurs. Thus, in many regards the response can be seen as more effective than direct recording of the blink, especially in the often-sleeping infant. A large number of studies have shown that the orbital EMG response is very sensitive to a wide array of startle modulation procedures (e.g., Dawson et al., 1999).

To obtain this measure in older children and adults, one electrode is normally placed at or just below the margin of the bony orbit, centered between the corners of the eye, and a second electrode about 1 cm lateral to this. With older infants and children other cautions are necessary. Children are usually more fearful of objects being affixed to their face, especially near the eye. We have found that distracting the child, or even adult, with a video allows us to approach the eye region by moving the electrode up the face from the child's cheek so that it can be placed under the eye without eliciting the flinch that would likely otherwise occur. Also with children, as with adults, it is helpful to avoid indicating that the sensor will be placed "near the eye" but rather noting that it will be placed by the "ear," "cheek," "forehead," or "temple" (Haerich, 1994). The term "sensor" is much preferable to the possibly frightening "electrode" when working with adults or children. With both infants and children, it is important to place these electrodes quickly while avoiding unnecessary re-application. For this reason, it is critical that personnel become well practiced with cooperative adults before testing children or infants. In studies with children, the physiological recording and the experiment itself are often presented in the context of a challenge or game. For example, Hawk, Pelham, and Yartz (2002) asked each of their 9- to 12-year-old male participants to "pretend that he was an astronaut on a mission to decode a message from outer space (p. 334)."

Also, because infants' and children's faces are smaller, the electrode distance must be reduced proportionately. In infants, it can be quite difficult to move the electrode close enough to the eye to position it over the orbicularis muscle without modification of the usual procedure. We have found that the portion of the adhesive collar that is closest to the eyelid should be trimmed or folded back to allow the electrode itself to be moved closer to the eye. The electrode can be held in place sufficiently securely by the remaining portion of the adhesive collar and some adhesive tape (Figure 9.1). We also have found

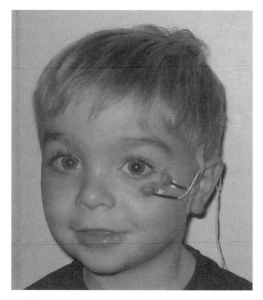

Figure 9.1. Photo indicating the placement and method of attaching electrodes for measuring orbicularis oculi EMG in younger children and infants.

that the use of a thick and sticky electrode paste (such as Elefix paste) can help adhere the electrode while also reducing electrical impedances. However, care must be taken not to allow excess paste to bridge the two electrodes placed on the recording sites of the orbicularis oculi muscle. Preventing of the bridging with gel or paste also can be difficult because the eye region is so much smaller in young children and infants.

The small muscle and face size of children may also make it difficult to locate the electrode so as to minimize contributions from other facial muscles. This issue causes additional concern because children in reaction time tasks often show associated movements or motor overflow prior to a speeded response at S2 (e.g., Cohen, Taft, Mahadeviah, & Birch, 1967; Lazarus & Todor, 1987; 1991). This overflow often appears as a grimace that can cause motor artifact in the eye electrodes. Also, the startle blink is less reliable in children, and the electrical record often has more poorly defined peaks or includes multiple peaks, making the blink more difficult to score. For this reason, a peak-detection algorithm designed for adults will need modification (discussed in a later section). Because of these issues, we encourage researchers to manually check and correct the results of any blink-scoring algorithm.

Computer Sampling of the EMG Blink Response

Virtually all current methods of recording the EMG response involve computerized sampling (digitizing) of an analog signal, and a variety of hardware and software products are available for this purpose. In acquiring and digitizing the blink EMG signal, several major considerations arise: when to sample, how frequently to sample, and how to filter the signal prior to sampling. Details and some recommendations are provided in Blumenthal and colleagues (2005). Sampling can either be done continuously during the recording session, with segments involving startle blinks extracted subsequently off line, or by sampling in brief bursts beginning just prior to the blink eliciting stimulus and for a short time thereafter. The latter is more efficient in that only the data needed are extracted, but the former allows a more complete record and, importantly, allows greater flexibility in determining how data are processed.

Regardless of which sampling procedure is used, the next consideration is at what rate samples are gathered, and this issue will depend on the fastest frequency in the signal. Based on van Boxtel, Boelhouwer, and Bos (1998), nearly all of the activity in the blink EMG signal is below 500 Hz in frequency, but to insure this, the low-pass filter should be set at between 400 and 500 Hz. However, the majority of the power of the blink EMG signal falls at 200 Hz or below and the peak power at 100 Hz or less. Thus, adequate EMG blink responses can be obtained with low pass filters set much lower. Whatever upper frequency cutoff chosen, the sample rate then should be at least twice the highest frequency remaining in the signal after this filtering. One minor benefit with lower sampling rates is smaller data file sizes, especially with continuous recording throughout the session. This method may save processing time with some scoring or off-line filtering programs. Setting the cutoff point for filtering out of low frequencies (high pass filters) may also be important since frequencies below about 20 Hz are probably artifact.

When sampling in bursts, or for off line extraction of blinks from a continuously sampled record, it is useful to extract samples for as much as 500 ms of data prior to and at least 250 ms after each startle onset. For visually elicited startle or with very young infants, the period of recording after stimulus onset might be extended to 350 to 500 ms since these conditions produce slower and more extended responses (Anthony et al., 1987; Yasuhara et al., 1989). The data prior to the stimulus are very useful for determining if the baseline was stable at onset, or whether movement or other artifacts were in progress. If excess baseline activity occurs, then responses usually cannot be scored adequately. When prepulse stimuli are used prior to the startle-eliciting stimulus, the longer sampling prior to the startle stimulus will also allow the investigator to determine if the prepulse has elicited an unintentional startle response (See Developmental Issues section below for more on the prepulse paradigm). With infants and children an even longer pre-startle baseline may be advisable since artifacts are more common. With a continuously sampled signal, these artifacts can be more effectively evaluated than with the burst method because a complete record of all activity between stimuli is available.

Processing the EMG Response: Conditioning the Signal

Once the sampled recording is obtained, it is typically necessary to process the recorded signal to allow proper scoring of the startle blink. There are two major goals in this process. One is to reduce or eliminate sources of noise, being defined as any part of a recorded signal unrelated to the blink EMG response. Such noise includes electrical signals coming from outside the body, such as 60 Hz noise, signals from muscles other than the orbicularis oculi, and movement artifacts, such as those coming from shifting of the electrode or lead wires, or from muscles other than the orbicularis oculi. The second major goal is to modify the original raw EMG signal so to make it easier to score. The latter is particularly necessary if one wishes to average blink responses together, as is typically done. The problem is that the EMG response associated with any muscle contraction is a burst of rapid negative- and positive-going waves (see Figure 9.2a). Unlike an event related EEG response, which has a somewhat consistent pattern for any given stimulus type, the EMG burst is rather random in its negative and positive peaks. As a result, averaging together a number of raw EMG signals will produce a virtually flat line. The most common solution is first to rectify the signal and then to filter the rectified signal in order to smooth it. Rectification involves reversing the polarity of either the negative or positive half of the signal (for example, the negative waves are changed to corresponding positive ones) and adding this inverted portion to the remaining unmodified portion. The result is that the entire signal is all negative or all positive (Figure 9.2b). This rectified wave is then typically smoothed through a filtering technique to allow easier determination of onset and peak blink activity. If done properly, the rectification and smoothing process, sometimes incorrectly called "integration," results, with appropriate filtering, in a relatively smooth response curve that at least roughly corresponds to the envelope of the original EMG burst (see Figure 9.2c). A number of companies provide software to handle filtering, rectification, and smoothing and it is either integrated through the hardware used to obtain the response or provided as a separate product.

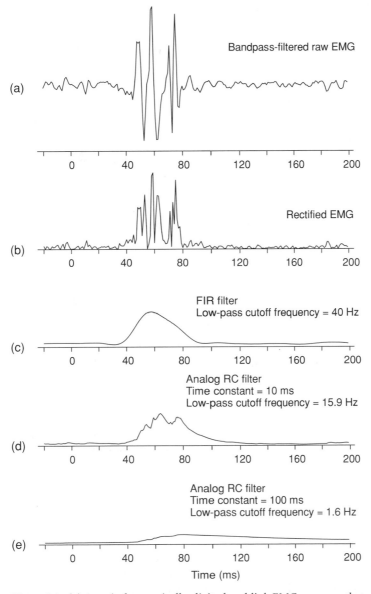

Figure 9.2. (a) A typical acoustically elicited eyeblink EMG response that was digitally filtered (28–500 Hz passband) and sampled at 1000 Hz. The eliciting stimulus (presented at 0 ms) was a 95 dB(A), 50 ms duration broadband noise burst with a rise/fall time shorter than 1 ms, presented via headphones (AKG, Model K100). In (b), EMG was rectified. This signal was then smoothed, either with (c) a variable-weight FIR filter (101 coefficients, low-pass cutoff frequency 40 Hz), or (d and e) a digital implementation of an analog resistor-capacitor (RC) filter (time constant 10 ms or 100 ms). Caption and Figure reprinted from Blumenthal et al. (2005) with permission of the Society for Psychophysiological Research and Blackwell Publishers.

It is, however, important to understand the procedure even when software automates the process. A complete review and the important details of these signal conditioning processes are beyond the scope of the present chapter, but can be found in Blumenthal and colleagues (2005).

The rectification process is straightforward. The only choice is whether to convert all negative portions of the raw EMG signal to corresponding positive ones or the reverse. The decision is essentially arbitrary because polarity carries no useful information and depends upon which sensor is in the positive and the negative amplifier input (this is typically not controlled). Further, the terms "negative" and "positive" are not defined by absolute electrical levels relative to ground, but by whether the portion of the wave is more or less negative relative to the pre-response baseline. Therefore, the process normally involves obtaining a stable baseline value prior to each startle stimulus by, for example, averaging the baseline period, subtracting this value from every data point for the blink period, and calculating the absolute value for the resulting data. The most important part of this is first determining if the baseline was relatively unchanging and, if not, excluding the data for that startle trial.

In contrast to this straightforward process, the process of smoothing the rectified signal allows for a large number of possibilities. Blumenthal and colleagues (2005) have outlined some of these, but essentially any digital signal filtering process that takes out high frequency changes from the rectified signal and leaves in the smooth low frequency ones can work. One of the most common methods is known as low pass, infinite impulse response (IIR) filtering, which simulates hardware filters commonly used in older hardware filters, but many others are possible, some of which are probably better, such as finite impulse response (FIR) filtering. The latter has the advantage of not phase shifting (e.g., not shifting the peak latency) of the filtered output. See Figure 9.2 (c, d, e) for examples of the effects of different filters on the EMG signal.

Regardless of the *type* of filter chosen, one must also consider the *extent* of filtering. The extent of filtering will be determined by the cut-off frequency of the filter, sometimes expressed as a time constant and sometimes in terms of a frequency. For a low pass, smoothing filter (see Figure 9.2c), longer time constants and lower frequency cut-offs indicate greater filtering. This increased filtering has two effects, one desirable and one not: they produce greater smoothing and make scoring easier, but also can substantially decrease the resulting amplitude, which may be a problem (Blumenthal, 1994). A more critical question in any filtering, however, is the signal-to-noise ratio. How much does the filter reduce the noise or distort the signal relative to the undistorted signal? Older research tended to use time constants of about 100 ms, but most researchers have moved to shorter time constants (less filtering). Blumenthal (1994) suggested 10 ms, but this was with an IIR filter. With other filter types, more filtering and better smoothing (less distortion of the signal) may be possible and desirable.

One consideration in the smoothing process is that the blinks of children and infants tend to be slower and more extended. This method might allow one to use more extensive filtering with less distortion of the response shape. This procedure could be important because younger children and infants also have startle responses that are much more variable in shape than those of older children and adults. As such, more extensive smoothing may help determine whether EMG activity is blink-related or not (see later section on scoring).

Other Methods of Obtaining Startle Blink Responses

The focus of this chapter has been on obtaining the startle blink response through recording of the EMG response of the orbicularis oculi muscle. We will here mention two other methods that are of continued interest, and Berg and Balaban (1999) have reviewed others.

The electrooculogram (EOG) measures the electrical potentials corresponding to eye movements. Standard placement of pairs of EOG electrodes monitors both vertical and horizontal eye movements. These signals are often recorded in conjunction with studies of brain wave activity (electroencephalogram, or EEG) in order to determine whether the EEG measures are affected by artifacts from eye movements. The EOG recording can also be used to measure blink responses when orbicularis oculi EMG is not recorded (Simons & Zelson, 1985; see comparison of measures in Schmidt et al., 1998); however, reflex-elicited blinks must be distinguished from other eye movement activity. The vertical EOG has also been used to distinguish reflex from spontaneous blinks in children because reflex blinks, but not spontaneous blinks, showed a pattern of EMG activity occurring before the onset of EOG activity (Gehricke et al., 2002). The addition of the EOG measure enabled these researchers to exclude some likely spontaneous blinks that might have been included in reflex blink averages if selection was based on EMG recordings alone.

Another alternate method of recording startle blink is illustrated in a recent study examining the feasibility of measuring blink magnitude from video recordings. Essex and colleagues compared blink EMG measures with video-scored measures (Essex et al., 2003) in a group of 31 children ranging in age from 3 to 7 years. The video measure used a specified 7-point scale with each step defined. For example, scores of 3 indicated that the eyelid closed to about

25% of maximal closure. The temporal resolution of the video measure (at 33.3 ms per frame) was much less precise than the EMG measure, so response latencies were not assessed. Interestingly, computer-automated scoring of EMG was successful for 77% of trials whereas video scores were obtained for 95% of trials. This pattern likely reflects the EMG scoring procedure, which rejects trials when activity is detected during the prestimulus, baseline period. In this study, the EMG and video-scored blink magnitudes were positively correlated for all but one participant, and the researchers suggested that the video measure is a plausible alternative when studies are done outside the laboratory or when recording of EMG is not feasible.

Blink Scoring

In this section, we focus on how startle responses are scored from rectified, smoothed EMG recordings in adults and we present, when information is available, related developmental issues. Computer scoring allows precise definition of how startle blinks are identified and quantified. Berg and Balaban (1999) explained the distinction between computer-automated and computer-assisted scoring. Some research groups rely on computer-automated systems but allow trained researchers to override scores for anomalous cases. Researchers who are new to the startle blink domain may be surprised that there is no universally agreed-upon standard for identifying and scoring startle blinks. Computer scoring procedures for measuring the size and speed of blink responses have been developed by several laboratories, and there are also commercially available systems. In developmental studies, where blink responses may be quite variable in onset latency, peak latency, duration, and magnitude, researchers should inspect the results of computer scoring algorithms and compare the scores with the recorded EMG signals. The goal in scoring is, of course, to be as accurate and reliable as possible in selecting and scoring actual blink responses while ignoring background noise and electromyographic activity that is not part of the elicited reflex response. Typical attributes of startle blinks that are scored are onset latency, peak latency, and peak amplitude or magnitude. Some studies also measure the duration, area, or probability of the response (e.g., Blumenthal, 1988).

In order to measure response characteristics, the scoring procedure must first identify the response to be scored. Because there can be background EMG activity, eye movement artifacts, spontaneously occurring blink responses, and other "noise," a defined window of response is often used in order to detect a response and determine whether it should be considered a reflex response. The time windows will differ depending on the characteristics of the eliciting stimulus (including, importantly, stimulus modality) and on the characteristics of the participants (including age). The onset window is the time during which the initial change in response must be detected in order to meet the criteria for a reflex response and to be scored. The peak window is the time during which the response must reach its maximum and begin to return to baseline in order to meet the criteria for a reflex response and to be scored. For example, in a computer-automated scoring program developed in Frances Graham's laboratory, the recommended window for scoring the onset of an adult response from integrated EMG recordings was 21–120 ms for acoustic blinks and 21–145 ms for visual blinks (Balaban, Losito, Simons, & Graham, 1986a,b); the respective windows for infants were 21–170 and 21–350 ms. The window for the peak of the response was recommended to be 21–150 ms for acoustic and 21–175 ms for visual blinks for adults; for infants the values were 21–200 and 21–450 ms. Blumenthal and colleagues (2005) more recently suggested that a narrower window be adopted in order to reduce the inclusion of non-reflex responses (for example, they suggest 21–80 ms as an onset latency window for adult acoustic startle), but note that this suggestion was based on adult data. Recordings for infants and young children would almost certainly need to be longer. Scoring parameters for cutaneous startle blinks (R2 component) are often comparable to scoring for acoustic startle blinks. The windows selected for onset and peak latency detection may also depend upon the extent of the filtering and smoothing that is done to the EMG signal, as discussed in a previous section of this chapter.

Scoring of the onset of a response is based on some measure of change from baseline levels of EMG activity. Various measures of baseline activity have been used (see Berg & Balaban, 1999; Blumenthal et al., 2005), including the average activity during the first 20 ms after stimulus onset (Balaban et al., 1986a,b). Change from baseline has been identified in various ways, including a change in slope of the smoothed EMG waveform, or identifying the time of the first sample to exceed the baseline by some amount (see Blumenthal et al., 2005). Once a response onset is detected during the specified onset window, then the peak of the response must be identified. The peak is often identified simply as the maximum response amplitude within the peak response window. The smoothed EMG response may not always have the unipolar shape depicted in Figure 9.2c, and thus there should be some specification for how multiple peaks are handled by the scoring procedure. This issue may be especially necessary in developmental studies where the response shape is more variable.

The identification of the peak of the response is important for reporting peak latency, that is, the time at which the peak occurs, and for the quantification of response size. The convention in startle blink research is that the

term *amplitude* is typically used when referring to the size of a single identifiable response or to the average of scores of the sizes of all non-zero blink
responses. The term *magnitude* is typically used when averages of response
size include both zero and non-zero responses, or when the scoring is based
on EMG recordings that have been averaged over trials. The size of a response
is typically measured as the difference between the amplitude of the smoothed
EMG signal at the peak and the average amplitude of the pre-response baseline, or as the difference between the amplitude of the smoothed EMG signal
at peak and the amplitude at response onset.

Although raw, rectified, and smoothed blink magnitudes are often
reported in arbitrary analog-to-digital units, we (Berg & Balaban, 1999)
and Blumenthal et al. (2005) argued that it is preferable to report response
amplitude/magnitude in microvolts (microvolt-seconds for smoothed signal) in order to support direct comparisons across laboratories. It should be
noted that such comparisons need to account for differences in the extent of
filtering and smoothing done since these can have very marked effects on the
reported amplitudes.

Computerized scoring procedures typically exclude trials that have excessive activity during the prestimulus baseline period. Such activity might
indicate that the participant's eyes were moving, that they were squinting
or grimacing, or that they were in the midst of a spontaneous blink. The
criteria used to exclude trials, and the number of trials excluded, should be
reported.

There is considerable inter-individual variation in blink magnitude in
adult and in developmental studies (e.g., Blumenthal et al., 2005; Ornitz,
1999), leading some researchers to standardize or otherwise transform magnitudes (see Berg & Balaban, 1999 or Blumenthal et al., 2005 for further
discussion). In addition, many studies test some participants who do not
react to the startle-eliciting stimuli with measurable responses; these non-
responding participants are sometimes excluded from further data analysis.
Blumenthal et al. (2005) suggested that this may be true for 5–10% of adult
participants, and that this rate may be higher for children, older adults, and
some clinical groups.

The result of these exclusions is that attrition rates may be particularly
high in developmental studies with infants and very young children. As examples, consider two recent infant studies. Schmidt and Fox (1998) tested 73
9-month-old infants and excluded 50 of those participants for the following reasons: "(a) equipment failure ($n = 4$); (b) the infant did not have at
least two identifiable EMG trials during the stranger approach ($n = 13$); (c)
electrode(s) became detached ($n = 9$); (d) the infant became too distracted

and/or fussy during the session, terminating the session ($n = 8$); (e) the EMG signal was noisy (n = 12); and (f) the infant had no scoreable baseline trials ($n = 4$)" (p. 117). Richards (1998) measured both acoustically and visually elicited blinks and included 160 infants in his analysis, 40 each in age groups of 8, 14, 20, and 26 weeks. In addition, he tested but excluded 50 infants for the following reasons: "... they did not have at least two identifiable blinks in the prestimulus condition ($N = 5$), did not show at least one identifiable blink in each testing condition ($N = 22$), or did not complete all of the testing sessions due to fussiness or crying ($N = 23$)" (p. 46). Researchers who are planning to extend startle modification studies to infants should note that these attrition rates are typical. Studies that focus on older children typically report lower attrition rates, but sometimes children do ask to stop the study prior to completion. In addition to reporting attrition rates, researchers should publish the criteria used for exclusion of participants from data analysis.

DEVELOPMENTAL ISSUES

Our focus in this chapter thus far has been methodological; however, in this section we select several examples of how and why the startle blink has been studied developmentally in order to provide a sampling of current research. Modification of the startle response is useful as a developmental tool because the automatic, simple blink reflex connects maturing psychological processes at various levels of analysis: for example, at neural, sensory, cognitive, and emotional levels. Our intention is not to provide a complete summary, but rather to give some idea of the breadth of the applications of startle modification in developmental psychology, and also to indicate some of the complexities in extending adult findings to developmental populations.

One area of startle research focuses on the effects of lead stimulation, that is, other stimuli that temporally precede the presentation of the startle-eliciting stimulus, on subsequently evoked startle blinks, and on the implications of such stimulation effects for psychological processing. Ornitz (1999) reviewed the developmental research on these modulatory effects on startle. One phenomenon within this domain is prepulse inhibition of startle, discussed in the introduction of this chapter in relation to sensory and cognitive processes in schizophrenia. A change in stimulation in a weak prestimulus that occurs shortly (e.g., 30–250 ms) before a startle-eliciting stimulus typically causes a striking inhibition of the response to the startle-eliciting stimulus in adults (Graham, 1975). Related interpretations of the psychological significance of the prepulse inhibition effect include sensory gating, which is the filtering of stimuli and inhibited response to stimuli that occur within a short temporal window after another stimulus, and automatic protection of preattentive processing for the initial prestimulus (Cadenhead & Braff, 1999; Graham, 1975; see Blumenthal, 1999, for further discussion). On these accounts, processing of the prestimulus change constrains sensory input for a brief period of time.

It is intriguing that this fundamental and, to some extent, automatic process has a protracted course of maturation. The prepulse inhibition effect is weak or absent in newborns and, when it does occur, it requires much longer stimulus intervals (Hoffman, Cohen, & Anday, 1987). Inhibition comparable to adults does not occur until about age 8 years (Ornitz, 1999). Balaban, Anthony, and Graham (1985) suggested that this pattern reflects "slow development of structures mediating extrinsic inhibition or of structures processing transient information, or of both" (p. 455). Ornitz (1999) suggested that this developmental trajectory coincides with the maturation of neural processes of inhibition. Thus, the findings of weak prepulse inhibition in young children may indicate immature sensory/attentional gating processes, and this measure of reflex modification can be used to assess normal as well as atypical maturation of such gating processes.

The basic phenomenon of prepulse inhibition also offers an interesting paradigm for investigating higher-level cognitive processes. For example, when adults' attention is directed toward the prepulse, then inhibition of the startle response is greater. This effect was examined developmentally in 9- to 12-year-old boys who were instructed to distinguish longer 8-s tones from shorter 5-s tones of a pitch designated as "attended" and to ignore tones of another pitch (Hawk et al., 2002). During this attentional task, startle-eliciting noise bursts occurred at select intervals following the tones, and participants were instructed to ignore those. Significant prepulse inhibition occurred to the noise bursts that followed the prestimulus by 120 ms, and this inhibition was greater following attended than ignored tones in the initial session of a two-part study. Thus, children exhibited the same attentional effects on prepulse inhibition as did adults. While some parametric developmental studies of prepulse inhibition have been done, there is room for further exploration of the maturation of prepulse inhibition and its relation to preattentive processes or sensory and attentional gating.

Related to research on effects of actively directed attention to a prepulse have been investigations of the influences of attention to the modality of the startle-eliciting stimuli. For example, attracting 4-month-old infants' attention to a particular sensory modality was shown to enhance their responses to startle-eliciting stimuli in that same modality and to decrease their responses to startle-eliciting stimuli in other modalities by Anthony and Graham (1983). In their study, infants either viewed visual "foreground" stimuli that were low in salience (blank slides) and high in salience (smiling adults faces) or they heard auditory "foreground" stimuli that were low in salience (constant tone) and high in salience (melody). Responses to visual startle-eliciting stimuli were greater when elicited during visual than auditory foreground stimuli, and this effect was pronounced during the salient visual foregrounds (faces). Likewise, responses to acoustic startle-eliciting stimuli were greater during auditory than visual foregrounds, and more pronounced with the salient auditory foregrounds (melodies). Thus, the infants' engagement in, and selective attention toward, a stimulus modified their intake of other sensory stimuli. Richards (1998) demonstrated that this effect increased developmentally: 8-week-old infants did not show significant attentional modulation, and the effect increased from 14 to 26 weeks. Unlike the prolonged maturation of prepulse inhibition, these modality-selective attentional processes are present early in life. In this area of startle modification research, the automatic and low-level blink reflex response functions as a probe to reveal influences of higher levels of selective attentional processing.

Startle can also probe emotional processing. Examples of fear potentiation of startle in adults were described in the introduction of this chapter. Many studies (e.g., Greenwald, Cook, & Lang, 1989) have demonstrated that acoustic startle magnitude in adults is facilitated during viewing of pictures with negative affective content, relative to viewing of pictures with positive affective content. Extension of this approach to children has yielded varying results (see Ornitz, 1999, for an earlier review). For a recent example, in a study of children and adolescents, girls showed the typical pattern of affective modulation of acoustic blinks to negative, compared to positive, pictures, but boys did not show this effect (McManis et al., 2001). The authors suggested that perhaps "boys, more so than girls, react with interest and attention to moderately arousing aversive stimuli, such as images of war, violence, and aggression, whereas girls respond more defensively" (McManis et al., 2001, p. 230).

In a study of anxious and non-anxious children, blink responses to a white-noise burst presented early in the viewing of affective pictures (60 ms following picture onset) produced affective modulation across both groups of children (Waters, Lipp, & Spence, 2004). That is, blinks were larger during negative pictures, smaller during positive pictures, and intermediate during neutral pictures. Also, blink amplitude at the 60-ms interval was facilitated more across all picture conditions for anxious than for non-anxious children. The affective modulation effect is surprising because it suggests that emotional processes can have a very rapid influence on the intake of other sensory stimuli. The authors suggested that this "accords with cognitive theories to the extent that anxiety-related biases are thought to occur early, during preattentional and attentional stages, rather than during the later stages of information processing" (Waters et al., 2004, p. 277).

A multi-site study investigated emotional modulation in a different manner, by using threat (of an unpleasant airpuff stimulus) and darkness to elicit fear-potentiated startle in adolescents (Grillon et al., 1999). In the threat condition, one of two colored lights indicated the possibility of an aversive airpuff directed toward the participant's larynx. In the darkness condition, the room illumination varied between light and darkness. This study found significant potentiation of startle for both the threat and darkness conditions in adolescents and did not find significant gender differences.

In an attempt to extend the investigation of affective modulation of startle to young ages, Balaban (1995) found that 5-month-old infants showed potentiated startle during the viewing of photographic slides of angry, compared to happy, adult faces, even though the infants' other behaviors did not indicate greater distress during viewing of the angry faces.

These examples of research extending the fear potentiation or affective modulation of startle to developmental populations illustrate some promising directions; however, inconsistencies in whether such modulation effects are found, and in gender differences, point to the need for further research in this domain of startle modification.

Although the focus of the developmental work described thus far has been primarily on normal developmental processes, the startle modification paradigms are also useful probes of cognitive and emotional processing in special populations. For example, Schmidt and Fox (1998) found greater fear-potentiated startle to white-noise bursts during the approach of a stranger in 9-month-old infants who had been classified as temperamentally negative at 4 months compared to infants who had been classified as temperamentally positive. In the latter group, startle magnitude was actually smaller during stranger approach than during baseline. In this study, the startle response probed early individual differences in temperamental reactivity. The authors' conclusions illustrate how startle modification allows inferences from neural to psychological processing. They suggest that "there may be a subset of infants who are biologically predisposed to a low threshold for arousal in forebrain limbic structures that regulate negative affect" causing "withdrawal from situations which they perceive as threatening" (Schmidt & Fox, 1998, p. 119).

In another study of fear-potentiated startle, gender differences were found in startle responses of adolescents whose parents had a history of anxiety disorders (Grillon, Dierker, & Merikangas, 1998). Participants included low-risk adolescents, who had no parental histories of psychological disorders, and high-risk adolescents, whose parents had anxiety disorders. The experiment used a procedure similar to that described earlier (Grillon et al., 1999), where colored lights indicated safe or threat signals for the occurrence of an aversive airpuff and the startle-eliciting stimulus was a loud white-noise burst. The high-risk female participants had greater overall startle magnitudes than female controls, but the high-risk male participants did not show that effect. They did, however, show greater fear-potentiation of startle during a "threat" period than did male controls. The authors concluded that "vulnerability to anxiety disorders might be associated with certain types of aversive stimuli more than with others (explicit versus contextual stimuli) and that this relation might be affected by gender" (Grillon et al., 1998, p. 996). Using a similar technique, Grillon and colleagues (2005) tested children and grandchildren of parents at high or low risk for major depressive disorder. For the second generation (children), both high- and low-risk groups demonstrated fear-potentiated startle, but overall startle magnitude was greater for the high-risk than the low-risk group. For the third generation (grandchildren), both high- and low-risk groups demonstrated fear-potentiated startle, but overall startle magnitude was greater for high-risk girls than for low-risk girls, and boys did not show this group difference. The authors discussed the potential links between depressive and anxiety disorders, and suggested that "high-risk individuals exhibit enhanced anxious apprehension in stressful contexts [leading to increased startle magnitude overall], while displaying appropriate responses to imminent threat [that is, fear-potentiation of startle]" (Grillon et al., 2005, p. 959). The need for longitudinal follow-up for the development of depressive disorders was emphasized.

Other studies have used the startle reflex alone, that is, presented in the absence of other stimulation, as a potential marker for psychological disorders. For example, Grillon, Dierker, and Merikangas (1997) found that children and adolescents whose parents had anxiety disorders showed larger magnitude startle responses to white-noise bursts than did control participants. They suggested that the exaggerated blink responses in this group could either be indicative of a "trait-related" and "tonic characteristic" or of a "phasic state related change (i.e., fear-potentiated startle)" (Grillon et al., 1997, p. 930). This study also revealed that children and adolescents whose parents had a history of alcoholism showed less habituation of the startle response over trials and showed less prepulse inhibition. The authors suggested that the latter effect might be linked to personality attributes previously linked to alcoholism, namely, those "characterized by impulsivity, disinhibition, and undercontrolled behavior" (Grillon et al., 1997, p. 930). The authors commented on the need for longitudinal research to investigate whether startle modulation differences like the ones they noted in children and adolescents in this study will translate into greater risk of later anxiety disorders and alcoholism.

Although by no means exhaustive, this overview provides evidence that startle modification is a promising approach for investigating developmental processes. It also reveals that there are many questions to be explored, including further elaboration of the gender differences and other individual differences in startle reactivity, and the emergence of those differences during development from infancy through adolescence.

RECOMMENDATIONS AND CONCLUSIONS

This review has indicated that, although the basic techniques for eliciting, recording, and scoring startle-elicited blinks in infants and children are similar to those used with adults, there are a number of important issues that need adaptation or special attention. Our specific recommendations can be summarized as follows:

- Application of electrodes to infants and children requires more care to adapt the placements to their smaller facial structure and their greater concerns over having the electrodes placed near their eyes.
- Startle blinks can be elicited in children of all ages, but these responses will be more variable both within and between individuals than with adults. This variability will result in more problems and greater care needed in scoring the blinks, and a larger loss of data than would occur with adults.
- Stimulus intensities necessary to elicit a response need to be at least as intense as for adults, and perhaps more so, to increase the likelihood of responses at the younger ages. More intense stimuli may cause concern for parents or Institutional Review Boards. Generally, with typical intensities and duration (e.g., 100 dB, 50 ms duration), the startle stimuli are easily within the range of sounds that infants experience in their everyday life. This intensity is well below OSHA standard maximum of 140 dB for impulse noise in adults.
- Response latencies both to onset and peak response are generally going to be longer with children and infants than adults, and scoring criteria should be adjusted to handle this difference.

These modifications to the adult procedures are readily managed. The result is that, although startle research with infants and children is more

Essex, M. J., Goldsmith, H. H., Smider, N. A., Dolski, I., Sutton, S., & Davidson, R. J. (2003). Comparison of video – and EMG-based evaluations of the magnitude of children's emotion-modulated startle response. *Behavior Research Methods, Instruments, and Computers, 35*, 590–598.

Flaten, M. A. (1993). A comparison of electromyographic and photoelectric techniques in the study of classical eyeblink conditioning and startle reflex modification. *Journal of Psychophysiology, 7*, 230–237.

Gehricke, J., Ornitz, E. M., & Siddarth, P. (2002). Differentiating between reflex and spontaneous blinks using simultaneous recording of the orbicularis oculi electromyogram and the electro-oculogram in startle research. *International Journal of Psychophysiology, 44*, 261–268.

Graham, F. K. (1975). The more or less startling effects of weak prestimulation. *Psychophysiology, 12*, 238–248.

Graham, F. K., Anthony, B. J., & Zeigler, B. L. (1983). The orienting response and developmental processes. In D. Siddle (Ed.), *Orienting and habituation: Perspectives in human research* (pp. 371–430). New York: John Wiley and Sons.

Greenwald, M. K., Cook, E. W., & Lang, P. J. (1989). Affective judgment and psychophysiological response: Dimensional covariation in the evaluation of pictorial stimuli. *Journal of Psychophysiology, 3*, 51–64.

Grillon, C., & Davis, M. (1997). Fear-potentiated startle conditioning in humans: Explicit and contextual cue conditioning following paired versus unpaired training. *Psychophysiology, 34*, 451–458.

Grillon, C. Dierker, L. & Merikangas, K. R. (1997). Startle modulation in children at risk for anxiety disorders and/or alcoholism. *Journal of the American Academy of Child and Adolescent Psychiatry, 36*, 925–932.

Grillon, C. Dierker, L. & Merikangas, K. R. (1998). Fear-potentiated startle in adolescent offspring of parents with anxiety disorders. *Biological Psychiatry, 44*, 990–997.

Grillon, C., Merikangas, K. R., Dierker, L., Snidman, N. Arriaga, R. I., Kagan, J., Donzella, B., Dikel, T., & Nelson, C. (1999). Startle potentiation by threat of aversive stimuli and darkness in adolescents: A multi-site study. *International Journal of Psychophysiology, 32*, 63–73.

Grillon, C., Warner, V., Hille, J., Merikangas, K. R., Bruder, G. E., Tenke, C. E., Nomura, Y., Leite, P., & Weissman, M. M. (2005). Families at high and low risk for depression: A three-generation startle study. *Biological Psychiatry, 57*, 953–960.

Hackley, S. A., & Boelhouwer, A. J. W. (1997). The more or less startling effects of weak prestimulation – revisited: Prepulse modulation of multicomponent blink reflexes. In P. J. Lang, R. F. Simons, & M. T. Balaban (Eds.), *Attention and orienting: Sensory and motivational processes* (pp. 205–227). Hillsdale, NJ: Lawrence Erlbaum Associates.

Hackley, S. A. & Johnson, L. N. (1996). Distinct early and late components of the photic blink reflex: Response characteristics in patients with retrogeniculate lesions. *Psychophysiology, 33*, 239–251.

Haerich, P. (1994). Startle reflex modification: Effects of attention vary with emotional valence. *Psychological Science, 5*, 407–410.

Haerich, P. (1998). Using airpuffs to elicit the human blink reflex. *Behavior Research Methods, Instruments, & Computers, 30*, 661–666.

challenging than with adults, it is definitely feasible. In fact, exactly the same technology that has been developed and widely utilized to assess detailed event-related brain potentials (ERP) in infants and children (e.g., Richards, 2005; Thierry, 2005) can be used to assess startle responding; that is, the same amplifiers and electrodes that record EEG activity can be utilized for startle. In fact, the combined use of both ERP and startle is a fruitful area to explore with infants and children, just as it has been examined with adults (e.g., Dawson, Oray, Lu, & Schell, 2004).

The literature briefly reviewed in this chapter makes it clear that the study of startle responding and modulation in younger participants can and has yielded valuable results. But the paucity of such developmental research to date indicates that startle modification is a technology that is being under utilized. The fact that both cognitive and emotional issues can be addressed with startle modulation techniques argues for the expansion of the developmental research using this approach.

References

Anthony, B. J., & Graham, F. K. (1983). Evidence for sensory-selective set in young infants. *Science, 220*, 742–744.

Anthony, B. J., Zeigler, B. L., & Graham, F. K. (1987). Stimulus duration as an age-dependent factor in reflex blinking. *Developmental Psychobiology, 20*, 285–297.

Balaban, M. T. (1995). Affective influences on startle in five-month-old infants: Reactions to facial expressions of emotion. *Child Development, 66*, 28–36.

Balaban, M. T. (1996). Probing basic mechanisms of sensory, attentional, and emotional development: Modulation of the infant blink response. In C. Rovee-Collier & L. P. Lipsitt (Eds.), *Advances in infancy research* (Vol. 10, pp. 219–256). Norwood, NJ: Ablex.

Balaban, M. T., Anthony, B. J., & Graham, F. K. (1985). Modality-repetition and attentional effects on reflex blinking in infants and adults. *Infant Behavior & Development, 8*, 443–457.

Balaban, M. T., Losito, B. D. G., Simons, R. F., & Graham, F. K. (1986a). Offline latency and amplitude scoring of the human reflex eyeblink with Fortran IV [computer program abstract]. *Psychophysiology, 23*, 612.

Balaban, M. T., Losito, B. D. G., Simons, R. F., & Graham, F. K. (1986b). *Offline latency and amplitude scoring of the human reflex eyeblink with Fortran IV*. Unpublished user's guide.

Berg, K. M. (1973). Elicitation of acoustic startle in the human (Doctoral dissertation, University of Wisconsin, 1973). *Dissertation Abstracts International, 34*, 5217B–5218B.

Berg, W. K., & Balaban, M. T. (1999). Startle elicitation: Stimulus parameters, recording techniques, and quantification. In M. E. Dawson, A. M. Schell, & A. M. Böhmelt (Eds.), *Startle modification: Implications for neuroscience, cognitive science, and clinical science* (pp. 21–50). Cambridge: Cambridge University Press.

Bischoff, C., Liscic, R., Meyer, B. U., Machetanz, J., & Conrad, B. (1993). Magnetically elicited blink reflex: An alternative to conventional electrical stimulation. *Electromyography and Clinical Neurophysiology, 33*, 265–269.

Blumenthal, T. D. (1988). The startle response to acoustic stimuli near startle threshold: Effects of stimulus rise and fall time, duration, and intensity. *Psychophysiology, 25*, 607–611.

Blumenthal, T. D. (1994). Signal attenuation as a function of integrator time constant and signal duration. *Psychophysiology, 31*, 201–203.

Blumenthal, T. D. (1999). Short lead interval startle modification. In M. E. Dawson, A. M. Schell, & A. M. Böhmelt (Eds.), *Startle modification: Implications for neuroscience, cognitive science, and clinical science* (pp. 51–71). Cambridge: Cambridge University Press.

Blumenthal, T. D. & Berg, W. K. (1986). Stimulus rise time, intensity, and bandwidth effects on acoustic startle amplitude and probability. *Psychophysiology, 23*, 635–641.

Blumenthal, T. D., Cuthbert, B. N., Filion, D. L., Hackley, S., Lipp, O. V., & Boxtel, A. V. (2005). Committee report: Guidelines for human startle eyeblink electromyographic studies. *Psychophysiology, 42*, 1–15.

Blumenthal, T. D., & Goode, C. T. (1991). The startle eyeblink response to low intensity acoustic stimuli. *Psychophysiology, 28*, 296–306.

Cadenhead, K. S. & Braff, D. L. (1999). Schizophrenia spectrum disorders. In M. E. Dawson, A. M. Schell, & A. M. Böhmelt (Eds.), *Startle modification: Implications for neuroscience, cognitive science, and clinical science* (pp. 231–244). Cambridge: Cambridge University Press.

Cadenhead, K. S., Swerdlow, N. R., Shafer, K. M., Diaz, M., & Braff, D. L. (2000). Modulation of the startle response and startle laterality in relatives of schizophrenic patients and in subjects with schizotypal personality disorder: Evidence of inhibitory deficits. *American Journal of Psychiatry, 157*, 1660–1668.

Cohen, H. J., Taft, L. T., Mahadeviah, M. S., & Birch, H. G. (1967). Developmental changes in overflow in normal and aberrantly functioning children. *Journal of Pediatrics, 71*, 39–47.

Cook, E. W., Hawk, L. W., Davis, T. L., & Stevenson, V. E. (1991). Affective individual differences and startle reflex modulation. *Journal of Abnormal Psychology, 100*, 5–13.

Cuthbert, B. N., Lang, P. J., Strauss, C., Drobes, D., Patrick, C. J., & Bradley, M. M. (2003). The psychophysiology of anxiety disorder: Fear memory imagery. *Psychophysiology, 40*, 407–422.

Davis, M. (1984). The mammalian startle response. In T. C. Eaton (Eds.), *Neural mechanisms of startle behavior* (pp. 287–351). New York: Plenum.

Davis, M. (1997). The neurophysiological basis of acoustic startle modulation: Research on fear motivation and sensory gating. In P. J. Lang, R. F. Simons, & M. T. Balaban (Eds.), *Attention and orienting: Sensory and motivational processes* (pp. 69–96). Hillsdale, NJ: Lawrence Erlbaum Associates.

Dawson, M. E., Oray, S., Lu, Z.-L., & Schell, A. M. (2004). Prepulse inhibition of event-related brain potentials and startle eyeblink. In S. P. Sholov (Ed.), *Advances in psychology research* (Vol. 29, pp. 57–70). Hauppauge, NY: Nova Science Publishers.

Dawson, M. E., Schell, A. M. & Böhmelt, A. H. (1999). *Startle modification: Implications for neuroscience, cognitive science, and clinical science.* New York: Cambridge University Press.

Hatanaka, T. Yasuhara, A., & Kobayashi, Y. (1990). Electrically and mechanically elicited blink reflexes in infants and children: Maturation and recovery curves of blink reflexes. *Electroencephalography and Clinical Neurophysiology, 76*, 39–46.

Hawk, L. W., Jr., Pelham, W. E., Jr., & Yartz, A. R. (2002). Attentional modification of short-lead prepulse inhibition and long-lead prepulse facilitation of acoustic startle among preadolescent boys. *Psychophysiology, 39*, 333–339.

Hoffman, H. S., Cohen, M. E., & Anday, E. (1987). Inhibition of the eyeblink reflex in the human infant. *Developmental Psychobiology, 20*, 277–283.

Koch, M. (1999). The neurobiology of startle. *Progress in Neurobiology, 59*, 107–128.

Lazarus, J. C. & Todor, J. I. (1987). Age differences in the magnitude of associated movement. *Developmental Medicine & Child Neurology, 29*, 726–733.

Lazarus, J. C. & Todor, J. I. (1991). The role of attention in the regulation of associated movement in children. *Developmental Medicine & Child Neurology, 33*, 32–39.

Lissek, S., Baas, J. M. P., Pine, D. S., Orne, K., Dvir, S., Nugent, M., Rosenberger, E., Rawson, E., & Grillon, C. (2005). Airpuff startle probes: An efficacious and less aversive alternative to white-noise. *Biological Psychology, 68*, 283–297.

Marsh, R. R., Hoffman, H. S., & Stitt, C. L. (1979). Eyeblink elicitation and measurement in the human infant. *Acta Otolaryngolica, 85*, 336–341.

McManis, M. H., Bradley, M. M., Berg, W. K., Cuthbert, B. N., & Lang, P. J. (2001). Emotional reactions in children: Verbal, physiological and behavioral responses to affective pictures. *Psychophysiology, 38*, 222–231.

Ornitz, E. M. (1999). Startle modification in children and developmental effects. In M. E. Dawson, A. M. Schell, & A. M. Böhmelt (Eds.), *Startle modification: Implications for neuroscience, cognitive science, and clinical science* (pp. 245–266). Cambridge: Cambridge University Press.

Ornitz, E. M., Guthrie, D., Sadeghpur, M. & Sugiyama, T. (1991). Maturation of prestimulation-induced startle modulation in girls. *Psychophysiology, 28*, 11–20.

OSHA (2005). OSHA regulations (standards). Retrieved October 31, 2005, from http://www.osha.gov/index.html.

Richards, J. E. (1998). Development of selective attention in young infants: Enhancement and attenuation of startle reflex by attention. *Developmental Science, 1*, 45–51.

Richards, J. E. (2005). Localizing cortical sources of event-related potentials in infants' covert orienting. *Developmental Science, 8*, 255–278.

Schmidt, L. A., & Fox, N. A. (1998). Fear-potentiated startle responses in temperamentally different human infants. *Developmental Psychobiology, 32*, 113–120.

Schmidt, L. A., Fox, N. A., & Long, J. M. (1998). Acoustic startle electromyographic (EMG) activity indexed from an electroencephalographic (EOG) electrode placement: A methodological note. *International Journal of Neuroscience, 93*, 185–188.

Simons, R. F., & Zelson, M. F. (1985). Engaging visual stimuli and blink modification, *Psychophysiology, 22*, 44–49.

Thierry, G. (2005). The use of event-related potentials in the study of early cognitive development. *Infant & Child Development, 14*, 85–94.

van Boxtel, A., Boelhouwer, A. J. W., & Bos, A. R. (1998). Optimal EMG signal bandwidth and interelectrode distance for the recording of acoustic, electrocutaneous, and photic blink reflexes. *Psychophysiology, 35*, 690–697.

Vrana, S. R., Spence, E. L., & Lang, P. J. (1988). The startle probe response: A new measure of emotion? *Journal of Abnormal Psychology, 97*, 487–491.

Waters, A. M., Lipp, O. V., & Spence, S. H. (2004). The effects of affective picture stimuli on blink modulation in adults and children. *Biological Psychology, 68*, 257–281.

Yamada, A. (1984). Blink reflex elicited by auditory stimulation: Clinical study in newborn infants. *Brain & Development, 6*, 45–53.

Yasuhara, A., Hori, A., & Kobayashi, Y. (1989). Photo-evoked eyelid microvibration in newborn infants and children: Reflex arc and maturational change. *Electromyography and Clinical Neurophysiology, 29*, 439–444.

10   The Measurement of Electrodermal Activity in Children

Don C. Fowles

INTRODUCTION

The measurement of electrodermal activity (EDA) or palmar sweat gland activity in children involves many of the same issues as in adults. There are, however, some special problems that can arise with children, all of which are inversely proportional to age. The most fundamental problem has to do with possible differences in which stimuli elicit electrodermal responses. This topic has not been well researched, but infants and toddlers appear to respond to a more restricted range of stimuli and children may not respond to some stimuli as well as adults do. The second problem has to do with difficulties in timing the presentation of stimuli, especially in toddlers and very young children for whom compliance with experimental instructions is substantially less than for older children and adults. A third problem, also related to problems with compliance, is managing the stress associated with attaching electrodes in a strange laboratory setting. This chapter will begin with the nature and measurement of the electrodermal effector system, followed by the problems specific to children.

For readers interested in a more thorough coverage of this topic than is provided by the present chapter, there are a number of reference sources. Introductions to psychophysiology, including EDA, are available in the texts by Stern, Ray, and Quigley (2001) and Hugdahl (1995). Consensus recommendations for how to record EDA are offered by Fowles and colleagues (1981). Fowles (1986) summarizes the nature of the skin (or epidermis) and sweat glands and discusses mechanisms by which sweat gland responses are transformed into electrical changes across the skin, and Edelberg (1993) presents an important revision of theories of the mechanisms of EDA. Boucsein (1992) comprehensively reviews all aspects of EDA, including methods of data collection and quantification. It serves as an invaluable, high-level reference source. Margerison, Binnie, and Venables (1967) provide advanced coverage of the rudiments of electricity, magnetism, and electronics in the context of psychophysiological research. The book edited by Roy, Boucsein, Fowles, and Gruzelier (1993) contains useful overviews of many areas of EDA research. Finally, the chapter by Dawson, Schell, and Filion (2000) contains a recent and excellent overview of the literature, including the psychological inferences to be drawn from measurements of EDA. The summaries below of electrodermal mechanisms and recording methodology are from Fowles (1986) and Fowles et al. (1981), respectively, which can be consulted for more technical coverage. In addition to this chapter, the new investigator is strongly urged to read one or both of the introductory texts, the overview by Dawson et al. (2000), and the consensus recommendations of Fowles et al. (1981). After mastering these sources, Boucsein's (1992) book can be used as an additional reference source.

TERMINOLOGY AND THE ELECTRODERMAL EFFECTOR SYSTEM

Terminology

The terminology used in this field can be confusing, especially because of multiple terms for overlapping phenomena. The starting point is to understand that the phenomenon of interest is the response of the eccrine sweat glands (usually on the palms) but that the process of measurement is influenced by properties of the skin. Thus, one fundamental distinction is between tonic and phasic aspects of electrodermal measurement. "Tonic" refers to the stable, relatively unchanging or, more often, slowly changing component. "Phasic" refers to more rapid changes over a time period of a few seconds, which reflect sweat gland responses. Phasic responses often are of more interest to psychologists, especially when they represent a response to a discrete stimulus. By tradition, amplitudes of responses to discrete stimuli are the quantification of choice. In some instances, one might count the number of responses (exceeding a given minimal threshold) during a time period without any discrete stimuli – for example, during a rest period or during a period when shock is threatened (but not delivered). In that case, the amplitudes often are ignored. Tonic levels may reflect characteristics of the skin unrelated to sweat gland activity (so-called non-sudorific aspects), but they are also believed to be affected by the extent to which sweat gland ducts are filled with sweat (see below) and by hydration of the skin, which increases its electrical conductivity. Thus, secretion of sweat not only produces a phasic response, but it also fills the duct and hydrates the skin around the sweat gland duct. As a result, *changes* in levels can be of psychological interest.

A second distinction is between "endosomatic" and "exosomatic" measures of electrodermal activity. Endosomatic refers to measurements of an endogenous potential across the skin, obtained by placing one electrode on the skin surface and the other at a site that has been abraded. The abrasion eliminates the barrier layer in the skin, in effect placing the electrode in contact with the conductive interstitial fluid beneath the skin. Fortunately, for the sake of simplicity, this measurement is seldom used because of its complexity and can be ignored by most investigators. Exosomatic refers to measurements of the electrical properties of the skin obtained by applying an external voltage, which causes current to flow through the skin (between the electrodes). As explained in the following section, depending on how this circuit is arranged, the resulting measurements will be in units of skin conductance (SC) or skin resistance (SR).

The tonic measure, then, is called skin conductance level (SCL) or skin resistance level (SRL), and the corresponding response is the skin conductance response (SCR) or skin resistance response (SRR). For technical reasons, conductance measures are preferred. For that reason, most studies in the literature report SCLs and SCRs. It is convenient to use the terms EDA to refer to any or all measures, electrodermal response (EDR) to refer to phasic changes without regard to units of measurement, and SCL and SCR to refer to specific measures. Although not often used by experts in the field, historically the terms psychogalvanic response (PGR) and galvanic skin response (GSR) were used to refer to the phasic responses. These terms largely are of historic interest only, but they sometimes may be found in secondary sources, such as introductory psychology texts.

The Eccrine Sweat Gland

The physiological response of interest is the secretion of sweat on the palms of the hands or the plantar surfaces of the feet. These sweat glands are innervated solely by the sympathetic nervous system. However, in contrast to most sympathetic innervation, the neurotransmitter is acetylcholine – a characteristic of all exocrine glands (exocrine glands secrete their substances onto an external or internal body surface, often via a duct).

The sweat glands found on the general surfaces of the human body are known as eccrine sweat glands. These glands secrete an aqueous solution containing salts, especially sodium chloride (NaCl), which has a concentration comparable to that of plasma when initially secreted. As shown in Figure 10.1, these glands are divided into a secretory portion lying in a coil well below the

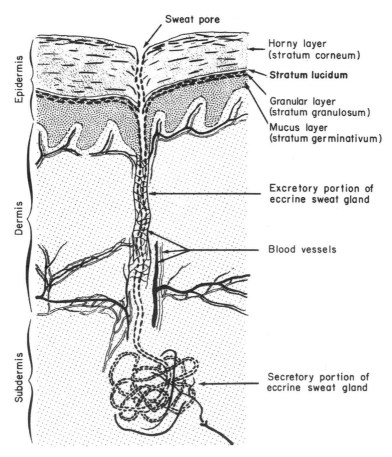

Figure 10.1. Schematic drawing of a sweat gland.

skin and a ductal portion that begins in the coiled portion of the gland and then rises to and passes through the skin. Loss of salt through sweating serves no purpose and in warm climates can result in salt depletion. To reduce this loss, a portion of the NaCl in the sweat is reabsorbed back into the body by the ductal portion of the gland.

The outer layer of the skin consists of compact, dead cells known as the stratum corneum. These cells provide a protective barrier between the body and the outside world. Importantly in the present context, they create a high resistance barrier to the passage of electrical current. As a result, the skin has high resistance or low conductivity in the absence of sweat gland activity. When sweat fills the duct in the stratum corneum portion of the skin, the sweat provides a highly conductive pathway through the skin, causing the EDR.

The stratum corneum is said to be hydrophilic, meaning that it readily absorbs water. In most of the body, thermoregulation is the primary purpose of sweating. To that end, it is important to hold the water on the surface of the skin, allowing it to evaporate and cool the body (heat is lost from the body in the process of converting H_2O from liquid to vapor). As the duct passes to the skin surface, it follows a corkscrew path (not shown in the figure) that increases the surface area in contact with the corneum and thus facilitates diffusion of sweat into the corneum, where it is held until it evaporates. On the palms of the hands and plantar surfaces of the feet, the corneum is much thicker than in other parts of the body, probably to provide greater protection against abrasion and other mechanical assaults. At the same time, hydration is required in order to keep the skin pliable, thereby promoting tactile sensitivity and good frictional contact with objects. It is at least partly for this reason that sweat glands on the palms and soles are not exclusively thermoregulatory and are relatively responsive to other stimuli.

Hydration of the skin is important for electrodermal measurements because the hydrated corneum conducts electricity better than the dry corneum. Almost all electrode pastes used to promote contact with the skin will slowly diffuse into the corneum over the course of an experimental session, causing a slow increase in SCL. At the same time, sweat gland responses are thought to hydrate the lower portions of the corneum as the sweat passes to the skin surface, causing an increase in conductance that is beyond experimental control. Hydration of the skin by electrode paste is highly desirable because it provides improved electrical contact with the sweat gland ducts, but it is impossible to keep this effect stable throughout a recording session. For this reason, one should try to standardize the duration of contact between the skin and electrode paste for all participants, or at least make it comparable across experimental conditions. For example, delays in progressing through the experiment for less compliant children may result in greater hydration for those children during given experimental procedures. As a result, variations in compliance would be confounded with the degree of hydration. Similarly, experimental conditions that are confounded with time may be differentially affected by hydration. Counterbalancing will eliminate this confound. If counterbalancing is not possible, comparisons between conditions should be considered with some caution. Although systematic differences in hydration should be avoided if possible, any such effects on SC measurements should be small, that is, after approximately 15 minutes hydration by the electrode paste or cream becomes a minor source of variation.

If participants have few or no sweat gland responses during a 10- to 15-minute rest period, one sees a steady decline in SCL, possibly at a decreasing rate, with the passage of time. With the introduction of stimulation (e.g., experimental instructions) at the end of that time, usually there will be one or more SCRs that have the effect of raising the SCL. Such responses have been termed slow recovery SCRs – referring to the time constant (the recovery time required from the peak of the response to 37% of the amplitude) of the recovery limb. In contrast, once the participant has responded with several SCRs and the SCL has increased substantially, additional SCRs often show a quite rapid recovery to the initial level and thus are termed rapid recovery SCRs. The literature on electrodermal mechanisms generally has assumed that two different mechanisms or effectors are responsible for these differences in recovery level, and much speculation has centered on the nature of these mechanisms.

The most attractive explanation for the slow recovery responses, as well as the decline in SCL in the absence of SCRs, attributes these responses to duct filling and emptying, respectively. If the ducts are empty at the beginning of stimulation (e.g., after a rest period), the filling of the duct in connection with secretion of sweat produces a rapid increase in transepidermal conductivity. Depending on the amount of sweat secreted, a near-maximum SCL might be reached in one response or, more typically, in several responses. Duct emptying proceeds by diffusion of sweat into the corneum and a slower process of reabsorption of sweat through the duct wall below the corneum, producing a concomitant decline in SCL. It should be noted that slow recovery SCRs precede the appearance of sweat on the skin surface and can be observed in the absence of any surface sweating. That is, they are assumed to reflect changes in duct filling without necessarily resulting in surface sweat.

The mechanism for the rapid recovery SCRs has been the subject of much debate over the years. Investigators agree that these SCRs are associated with higher levels of within-participant SCL and the appearance of sweat droplets on the surface of the skin (therefore suggesting that the ducts are relatively full). A discussion of the history of different theories is not relevant for the present chapter, but it may be of interest to mention the last proposal by Robert Edelberg (1993), a physiologist who devoted much of his career to this question. Two key considerations are that the (swollen) hydrated corneum under the electrode exerts pressure that tends to collapse the sweat pore and the adjacent portion of the sweat duct. Sweat secretion produces high intraductal pressure that greatly augments the movement of sweat into the lower, less hydrated portion of the corneum. If the intraductal pressure becomes great enough, it overcomes the opposing pressure from the corneum, producing a transient opening of the pore and movement of sweat to the skin surface with a concomitant rapid increase in conductance (an SCR). The discharge of sweat to the surface reduces intraductal pressure, and the pore and terminal duct collapse again, producing a rapid fall in conductance, that is, the rapid recovery SCR.

Although these arcane theories of mechanisms of increases in epidermal conductivity need not be mastered by investigators using the measure for psychological research, it is useful for investigators to be aware of the phenomena of rapid and slow recovery SCRs and to understand that they may reflect different mechanisms and thus may not be comparable. Given that the magnitude of the sympathetic nervous system stimulation of the sweat glands is the phenomenon of psychological interest, investigators should realize that, for these reasons and others, the transduction of SNS activity into a SCR amplitude contains a great deal of uncorrectable noise. As a result, one must expect to average across responses and participants to increase the signal-to-noise ratio and expose psychological phenomena of interest.

ELECTRICAL ASPECTS OF THE SKIN AND RECORDING APPARATUS

Electrical Circuits

In order to understand recording methodology, it is necessary to have a rudimentary knowledge of the simplest electrical circuits. The starting point for this knowledge is Ohm's Law:

$$I = E/R$$

where I is the current in amperes (A), E is the electromotive force or voltage in volts (V), and R is the resistance in ohms (Ω). For example, if the voltage is 6 V and the resistance is 3 Ω, the current will be $6/3 = 2$ A. The next point to understand is that resistances in *series* are additive and that the voltage in the circuit is divided in proportion to the resistance. Thus, if (as in Figure 10.2) a resistor of 2 Ω (R_1) is wired in series with one of 4 Ω (R_2) and connected to a 6 V battery (E), the formula becomes $I = E/(R_1 + R_2) = 6/(2 + 4) = 1$ A. The total resistance in the circuit (R_T) equals $R_1 + R_2$, and $I = V/R_T = 6/6 = 1$ A. The 6 volts in the circuit are distributed into a 2 V drop across the 2 Ω resistor and a 4 V drop across the 4 Ω resistor. For resistors in series, the 1 A current in this example must of necessity flow fully through each resistor. Thus, the distribution of voltage in the circuit can be calculated by an arithmetic transformation of Ohm's Law:

$$E = I \times R$$

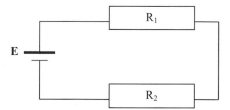

Figure 10.2. Sample circuit showing resistors (R_1 and R_2) connected in series with a battery (E).

Given that we have calculated that the current through each resistor is 1 A, we can calculate the voltage drop across each resistor. For the 4 Ω resistor, it is 4 Ω × 1 A = 4 V. Similarly, for the 2 Ω resistor, it is 2 Ω × 1 A = 2 V. That is, the total 6 V is distributed across the two resistors in proportion to their resistances.

Next, consider the same resistors wired in parallel, rather than in series, with the same 6 V battery as portrayed in Figure 10.3. The 6 V is applied across both resistors, and the total current equals the sum of the currents through each resistor, which can be calculated with Ohm's Law: $I_1 = E/R_1 = 6/2 = 3$ A and $I_2 = E/R_2 = 6/4 = 1.5$ A. The total current flow (I_T) is $I_1 + I_2 = 3 + 1.5 = 4.5$ A. Combine these calculations into a single equation:

$$E/R_T = I_T = I_1 + I_2 = E/R_1 + E/R_2 = E \times (1/R_1 + 1/R_2)$$

where R_T is the total resistance of the circuit. Dividing both sides of the equation by E yields $1/R_T = 1/R_1 + 1/R_2$.

At this point, the value of the concept of conductance can be appreciated. Conductance (abbreviated G for total or a single conductance and g for individual conductance when there is more than one conductance under discussion) is simply the reciprocal of resistance (G = 1/R). Historically, the

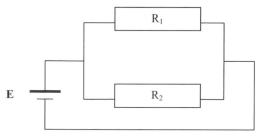

Figure 10.3. Sample circuit showing resistors (R_1 and R_2) connected in parallel with a battery (E).

unit of conductance was the mho (ohm spelled backward), but the mho has been replaced by the Siemen (S), where $1/1 \ \Omega = 1$ S. The equation above $(1/R_T = 1/R_1 + 1/R_2)$ can be transformed into $G_T = g_1 + g_2$, where $g_1 = 1/R_1$ and $g_2 = 1/R_2$. That is, in parallel circuits, conductances are additive. Ohm's law becomes $I = E \times G$.

Skin resistances are very large, requiring units of scale different from the examples above. Instead of ohms, one speaks of kilohms (1,000 ohms or $1 \ k\Omega$) or megohms (1,000,000 ohms or $1 \ M\Omega$). Skin conductances are small and measured in units of microsiemens. A microsiemen (μS) is the conductance of 1 megohm or $1/1,000,000$ ohms, and there are 10^6 (i.e., 1 million) μS for $1 \ \Omega$ of resistance. If the skin resistance is $50 \ k\Omega$, then the conductance is $1/50,000 \ \Omega = 0.00002$ S or $0.00002 \times 10^6 = 20 \ \mu$S. The arithmetic is more convenient if microsiemens are calculated directly by dividing 1,000 by the resistance in $k\Omega$, that is, in this example $1,000/50 \ k\Omega = 20 \ \mu$S.

With this information, one can take the first step toward understanding how SC is measured. Although the range of SRL values will vary with recording site and size of electrode (larger contact area should yield lower resistance), a rough figure is $25 \ k\Omega$ to $1 \ M\Omega$. Consider a simple circuit with a 0.5 V source and a $1 \ k\Omega$ resistor in series with the skin, where SC is measured by monitoring the voltage drop across the $1 \ k\Omega$ series resistor. (In this and all other examples, 1% resistors should be used – i.e., resistors whose nominal resistance is accurate within $\pm$ 1%.) The current through this circuit will be the voltage divided by the sum of the skin resistance (R_s) and $1 \ k\Omega$. With the simplifying assumption that the $1 \ k\Omega$ series resistance is negligible compared to the skin resistance, the current flow through the circuit becomes $I = 0.5$ V/R_s, with skin resistance in ohms.

Since conductance is the reciprocal of resistance, the participant's SC (G_s) can be substituted for $1.0/R_s$, converting the formula to $I = 0.5$ V $\times \ G_s$. Thus, the current flow through the skin and series resistance is proportional to the SC. As shown above, the voltage drop across the $1 \ k\Omega$ series resistor is $E = 1,000 \ \Omega \times I = 1,000 \ \Omega \times 0.5$ V x $G_s = 500 \times G_s$. For example, if the SC is $1/100 \ k\Omega$ (or $10 \ \mu$S), then $E = 500/100,000 \ \Omega = .005$ V or 5 millivolts (mV). Alternatively, one could calculate the voltage drop in terms of conductance: $E = 500 \times 10 \ \mu$S $= 500 \times 10/10^6 = .005$ V $= 5$ mV. From this calculation, it is clear that the voltage across the series resistor yields 5 mV for $10 \ \mu$S of conductance or 0.5 mV/μS throughout the range of SC. One can then set the amplifier gain for the appropriate sensitivity. For example, if one wanted an output of 0.5 V/μS, one would set the amplifier to $\times$ 1000 (1000×0.5 mV $= 0.5$ V). This example illustrates the principle that when a constant voltage is applied to the skin, the millivoltage measurements obtained across the series resistor are proportional to SC. Fowles and colleagues (1981) suggest using 0.5 V as the applied voltage, which will be used in all examples in this chapter. It should be noted, however, that 1.0 V is quite acceptable for the bipolar recordings assumed here in which both electrodes are placed on an active site (as opposed to having one electrode as a reference electrode at an abraded site with very low resistance on the forearm; Venables & Christie, 1980).

It is obvious from the arithmetic that the larger the series resistor, the larger the mV per μS. At the same time, the larger the resistor, the less negligible it is. A 500 ohm resistor is a good choice, but a 1 kΩ resistor is acceptable.

If a constant current were applied to the skin and the voltage drop across the skin monitored, then the equation $E = I \times R$ would involve a constant for the current and E would be proportional to skin resistance. That is, a constant current measurement system yields millivoltage measurements across the skin that are proportional to skin resistance. However, because there are several advantages to constant voltage circuits with conductance as the unit of measurement, constant voltage has become standard methodology.

Displaying SCRs and Balancing SCL: The Wheatstone Bridge

One problem faced in electrodermal recording is that the SCRs are super-imposed on SCL and are small relative to the range of SCL: for example, a small SCR (e.g., 0.1 μS) might be superimposed on a 15 μS SCL. With paper and pen recording techniques of the past, 5 cm might be allowed for the SC channel. If the investigator wanted to cover a range from 0 to 40 μS in order to cover a broad range of SCL, the sensitivity of the amplifier output would have to be adjusted to yield 8 μS/cm. As a result, a 0.1 μS response would cause a pen deflection of only $0.1/8 = 0.0125$ cm or 0.125 mm, which is too small to score. Similar problems are encountered with computer monitor displays. The solution is to display only a part of the full range of SCL. If one displays only 5 μS in the 5 cm SC channel, then the sensitivity would be increased eightfold to a 1.0 mm deflection for a 0.1 μS SCR, which can then be scored reliably.

The Wheatstone bridge, which can be used to cancel out or balance part of the range, is a common method to display only part of the full SCL range. If one keeps track of the amount cancelled or balanced, the data can be corrected offline later by adding in the amount balanced. In the case of paper and pen recordings, one just makes a note on the polygraph paper. With experience one can often predict large increases in SCL and adjust the Wheatstone bridge balance in advance. For example, at the end of a rest period, the balance adjustment can be used to move the current SCL to the

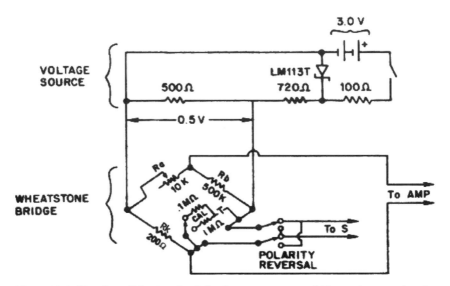

Figure 10.4. Signal conditioning circuit for the measurement of skin conductance (modified with permission from Fowles et al., 1981).

bottom part of the displayed range in anticipation of a large increase due to experimental instructions. For unusually reactive or labile subjects, the gain or amplification can be reduced, again making note of when and to what extent this change was made.

The specifications for constructing a Wheatstone bridge can be found in Fowles et al. (1981), reproduced in Figure 10.4 (an alternative method employing operational amplifiers is described by Boucsein, 1992, pp. 83–88). Note that the upper part is nothing more than circuitry to generate the 0.5 V to be applied across the skin, using two flashlight batteries (e.g., D cells) in series as the original voltage source. Although nominally 1.5 volts, the actual voltage from such batteries starts high and then declines as a result of use or the passage of time. To address this problem, an LM113T precision low voltage reference diode drops the voltage and maintains it at a constant 1.22 V (our instrumentation engineer has replaced this diode with a newer, LM385Z-1.2 precision low reference diode that also maintains a constant 1.22 V). This voltage is divided by the two series resistors (500 Ω and 720 Ω) into 0.5 V and 0.72 V, according to the principles discussed above. The 0.5 V drop across the 500 Ω resistor provides the voltage for the bridge. Although not shown in the figure, connections should be added to the box enclosing the bridge that permit separate testing of the voltages of the two batteries in order to detect when their voltage has dropped enough that they need to be replaced.

Also not shown in the figure, two capacitors in parallel with each other should be connected across the outputs from the low voltage reference diode in order to reduce electrical noise. One should be a 0.1 µF nonelectrolytic capacitor to filter out high-frequency noise and the other a 10 µF electrolytic capacitor to filter out low-frequency noise. Any instrumentation engineer should be familiar with this practice.

This methodology is somewhat primitive by current standards. If an instrumentation engineer is consulted, s/he will likely want to employ a different approach. If so, be sure that the resultant circuit delivers a constant 0.5 V to the bridge.

The Wheatstone bridge consists of four resistors arranged into two "arms" each with two resistors in series. One arm contains the circuitry already described: the participant's skin resistance (R_s) in series with a known resistance (R_k), in this case 200 Ω. The other arm has a fixed resistor (R_b) equal to 500 kΩ in series with a calibrated variable resistor in the form of a 10-turn potentiometer with a maximum resistance of 10 kΩ, that is, each complete turn of the dial equals 1 kΩ, with smaller units indicated by the calibrations as the dial is turned. Note that the output to the amplifier is taken from the midpoints of each of the arms of the bridge. The Wheatstone bridge originally was designed to measure unknown (static) resistances, which was accomplished by varying the potentiometer's resistance so as to produce a zero potential difference to the voltmeter or, in this case, the amplifier for recording conductance. When that condition is met, the 0.5 V across the two arms of the bridge is said to be in balance. The voltage drop across R_b is identical to that across R_s; similarly, the voltage drop across R_a equals that across R_k. Under these conditions, the following equation is true:

$$R_s/R_k = R_b/R_a \text{ or } R_s = R_k \times R_b/R_a = 200 \times 500{,}000/R_a = 100{,}000{,}000/R_a$$

Thus, if $R_a = 1{,}000\ \Omega$ (one complete turn of the potentiometer), $R_s = 100{,}000\ \Omega$ or 10 µS in conductance units. That is, 10 µS are balanced for each turn of the potentiometer.

Of course, human SC varies constantly, making it impossible to keep the bridge perfectly balanced. As a result, the total SC can be resolved into balanced and unbalanced components. The conductance balanced by the bridge is indicated by the potentiometer reading as just discussed. The unbalanced conductance produces an "imbalance" voltage across the two midpoints on the arms of the bridge that is read by the amplifier. Fortunately, the imbalance voltage in this circuit is proportional to conductance, as noted above (see Edelberg, 1967, for actual calculations for a Wheatstone bridge). In this case, with a 200 Ω series resistor, the imbalance voltage equals 0.1 mV per µS (i.e., 20% of the voltage calculated above for a 1,000 Ω series resistor; Fowles et al., 1981).

There are two more components to the circuit in Figure 10.4, a polarity reversal switch and two calibration resistors. The former is just a switch connected to the wires from the participant to the bridge, permitting a reversal of polarity of the voltage applied across the participant. As described in the following section, the polarity reversal permits a check on polarization of electrodes. The two calibration resistors are wired in parallel with the participant. Resistors in parallel often are better viewed as conductors in parallel, because conductances in parallel add. For example, a 1.0 MΩ calibration resistor has a conductance of 1.0 µS. When added to the circuit, this resistor increases conductance by 1.0 µS. The second calibration resistor in Figure 10.4 has a value of 0.1 MΩ and increases conductance by 10 µS. A simple switch allows selection of one or the other calibration resistor and a push button switch allows the experimenter (E) to briefly insert the calibration conductance. Such "cal pulses" are valuable for testing equipment in various ways.

Displaying SCRs: Capacitance Coupling

In addition to the standard Direct Current or DC output from the Wheatstone bridge that preserves a true reading of SC, it is useful to add a second output (in parallel) that filters out the standing level of SCL and allows only SCRs to pass. This output is then amplified to yield a second a-d channel with greater sensitivity. For example, the input voltage to the a-d board might be adjusted to yield a range of 5 µS, that is, four times more sensitive than the SCL channel (see below). This filtering can be achieved with what is known as capacitance coupling or resistor-capacitance (R-C) coupling. A capacitor allows alternating current to pass but blocks direct current. The capacitance is specified in units of Farads (F) or, more likely, millionths of a Farad known as microfarads (µF).

An important property of capacitance coupling is its time constant (see above). All R-C coupled outputs will filter out standing voltages, but they will filter out low-frequency components to varying degrees. Long-time constants allow low frequencies to pass, whereas short-time constants filter out low frequencies. The ideal time constant is long enough to avoid attenuating the

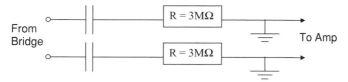

Figure 10.5. Capacitance coupling for eliminating the DC component of SC measurements. See text for discussion.

SCR amplitude and short enough to keep the output at zero baseline between SCRs. Fowles and colleagues (1981) cite Edelberg (1967) in recommending a time constant of 6 seconds for accurate SCR amplitudes. The time constant T (in sec) $=$ R (in ohms or Ω) $\times$ C (in farads or F). For example, if a 2 µF capacitor is used with 3 MΩ resistors, the time constant would be 3,000,000 Ω $\times$.000002 F $=$ 6 seconds. The calculation is simplified if the above equation is transformed to T (in sec) $=$ R (in megohms or MΩ) x C (in microfarads or µF), which changes the above example to $T=$ 3 MΩ $\times$ 2 µF $=$ 6 seconds.

Separate capacitors are connected to each of the outputs from the Wheatstone bridge between that output and the input to the DC amplifier (the outputs connected directly to the amplifier in Figure 10.4). Additionally, a resistor is connected to ground between each capacitor and the input to the DC amplifier (see Figure 10.5). As indicated above, convenient values for the capacitors and resistors are 2 µF and 3 MΩ, respectively. The capacitors should be nonelectrolytic capacitors with $\pm$ 5% accuracy. Assuming the input impedance of the DC amplifier is at least ten times larger than the 3 MΩ value of the resistor to ground, it is generally ignored. In modern amplifiers, the input impedance usually is 100 MΩ or higher, making the 3 MΩ resistance negligible in the calculations of the time constant.

It is helpful to relate the time constant to the attenuation of specific frequencies. The equation $T = 1/(2\pi f)$, where π refers to the value pi or 3.14159, can be used to calculate the value of the frequency (f) that is attenuated by the circuit to 70% of the input amplitude (Geddes & Baker, 1975, p. 592). Thus, $T = 1/(2 \times 3.14 \times f) = 1/(6.28 \times f)$ or $f = 1/(6.28 \times T)$. If T has the value of 6 sec as in the above recommendation, then f $= 1/(6.28 \times 6) =$ $1/37.68 = 0.0265 \approx 0.03$ Hz. That is, a R-C coupling with a time constant of 6 seconds will cause a 30% attenuation of the amplitude of a sine wave with a frequency of 0.03 Hz. The attenuation will be greater for frequencies below 0.03 Hz and lesser for frequencies above 0.03 Hz.

Filtering Electrical Noise

Most of the time electrodermal recordings will be troubled by unwanted electrical noise, especially the 60 Hz frequency used in the United States for electrical power and by fluorescent lamps. The power lines generate an alternating electromagnetic field in the air that induces current flow (i.e., noise) in wires connecting the participant to the equipment. This electrical noise can be reduced by twisting the wires from the two electrodes together, attempting to ensure that the same voltage is induced in both wires and possibly otherwise reducing the induced voltages. Balanced input amplifiers (as opposed to single-ended) only amplify voltage differences between the input wires (called common mode rejection; Edelberg, 1967; Margerison et al., 1967), thereby eliminating electrical noise that is the same in both wires. Fluorescent lamps generate electrostatic noise through capacitive coupling, which can be reduced through the use of shielded cables with the shield connected to ground. Equipment including the Wheatstone bridge can be grounded.

Finally, since the SCR contains only low-frequency components, low-pass filters allow the SCR to pass while strongly attenuating the 60 Hz noise. Edelberg (1967) found that, although rare SCRs may contain frequency components up to 2 Hz, passing frequencies up to 1 Hz without attenuation "is adequate for faithful recording" (p. 35) of amplitudes. Thus, one avoids attenuation at 1 Hz. Filters are specified in terms of a cutoff frequency, which is the frequency at which the output from the filter is attenuated by 3 dB – a reduction to 70% of the input amplitude.

Computerized Data Collection

The old paper and pen recording techniques seem primitive today, although they do have the important virtue of technological simplicity (and a new investigator can conduct a study with relatively modest technical support). Almost all psychophysiology laboratories use computers for data acquisition with a laboratory interface board that provides analog-to-digital (a-d) conversion. Analog-to-digital conversion means that the continuously variable physiological signal, in this case SC, is sampled at a constant frequency and the value stored in digital form. With SC, a sampling rate of 20/sec is recommended. Thus, the computer will read the value of the SC every 50 msec and store that value digitally. An a-d board with 12-bit input, which can count from 0 to 4,095 in decimal (2^{12} in binary), will suffice. If the input voltage to the a-d board is adjusted to represent a range of 20 μS, the resolution will be adequate to detect even small SCRs (E. W. Cook, personal communication,

August 14, 2002). In principle, the resolution would be 20 μS/4,095 $\sim$ 0.005 μS. Although noise in the recording might preclude such precision, one certainly should be able to score SCRs $\geq$ 0.05 μS – a common convention for the smallest SCRs to be counted (Dawson, Schell, & Filion, 2000). The range from 0 to 20 μS will accommodate most subjects, requiring adjustment by means of the Wheatstone bridge or decreased amplification on relatively few occasions.

Sophisticated software will be needed to handle both data acquisition and data reduction. Unless the user is technically sophisticated, technical support is crucial. The author uses a general-purpose psychophysiological data collection and stimulus control program called VPM (Cook, 2003; Cook, Atkinson, & Lang, 1987). VPM is a powerful program that is ideal for a psychophysiology laboratory, but the technical support is limited and assumes sophistication regarding computer use in psychophysiology. Perhaps the best recommendation is to find another laboratory using a program that will do what is needed, arrange for technical support, and adopt that laboratory's software.

MAKING CONTACT WITH THE SKIN: ELECTRODES AND ELECTROLYTES

Electrodes

Electrodes are needed to make contact with the skin and sweat glands. As a result of two potential problems with electrodes, silver-silver chloride (Ag-AgCl) electrodes have become the standard. The first problem has to do with a possible voltage difference between the electrode pair, called a bias potential. An electrode in contact with a salt solution has what is called a half-cell potential. If the half-cell potentials for two electrodes are not matched, as is intentionally the case with differently constructed electrodes in a battery, there is a potential difference between them. Even when the electrodes are ostensibly identical (i.e., both are Ag-AgCl), there can be bias potentials due to subtle differences. Consequently, the construction and care of electrodes should be as similar as possible.

Often bias potentials can be reduced by shorting the electrodes together and placing them in a beaker of salt solution comparable to that used in the electrolyte (see below) for several days. In effect, any bias potential will cause current to flow, producing electrochemical reactions at the Ag-AgCl interface that may reduce the bias potential between electrodes. Assuming sodium chloride (NaCl) is used in the electrolyte, such a solution can be obtained by purchasing physiological saline (also called isotonic saline) from a university chemistry store and mixing it with two parts distilled water. Alternatively, the same solution is produced by adding 8.7 grams of reagent grade (or better) NaCl to 1.0 liter of distilled water. The electrodes should be tested by storing them (not shorted together) overnight in the salt solution and measuring the bias potential the next day without moving the container (any movement of the salt solution will cause the bias potentials to drift). Pairs of electrodes should be selected to have no more than 3 mV initially and monitored to ensure that the bias potential does not exceed 5 mV once in use. When not in use (i.e., between experiments), electrodes should be stored dry after careful cleaning. Note that if a 5 mV bias potential is in the same direction as the 0.5 V applied voltage from a battery, the effective applied voltage is 0.505 V. If it is in the opposing direction, the effective applied voltage is 0.495 V – i.e., an error of $\pm 1\%$.

The second problem has to do with what is called a counter electromotive force (emf). The counter emf refers to the development of a voltage difference between electrodes (as a result of current flow) that acts like a battery to oppose the applied voltage. When current is passed through metal electrodes in contact with a salt solution, an electrochemical reaction takes place that creates this counter emf. In many cases, the counter emf can be quite large and reduces the flow of current, which gives the appearance of high resistance or low conductance. Using an electrode consisting of a metal (e.g., Ag) in contact with a solution of its own ions (e.g., Ag^+ as part of Ag^+ and Cl^-), called nonpolarizable or reversible electrodes, can eliminate these problems. The flow of current either adds to (chlorides) or subtracts from (dechlorides) the AgCl deposit on the silver electrodes, depending on the direction of the current. Within fairly broad limits, this reaction does not create a significant counter emf, which is an important reason for using Ag-AgCl electrodes. If connected for a long enough time, however, the electrode that is being dechlorided could lose its AgCl coating and become polarized. For this reason, when being used for experiments, a given electrode should be attached to the positive pole of the bridge roughly half the time and the negative pole the other half to average out the chloriding and dechloriding. Most investigators assume that such reversal will occur due to chance as a result of randomly connecting electrodes for each experimental session.

Electrodes should be checked for polarization. The first step is to make electrical contact between the electrodes (by placing them in a beaker of salt solution or taping them together with electrode paste making the contact between them) and connect them to the Wheatstone bridge with a resistor of known value inserted between one of the electrodes and the bridge.

This procedure uses the resistor as an artificial participant. For example, if a 50 kΩ resistor is used, the conductance should be 20 μS. If the output of the amplifier yields a conductance significantly less than 20 μS, one of the electrodes may be polarized.

The second step in checking polarization is to reverse the polarity of the applied voltage by throwing the polarity reversal switch described above for the bridge. For example, if the applied voltage is 0.5 V and polarization has created a counter emf of 0.1 V, the effective applied voltage has been reduced to 0.4 V, with a subsequent reduction in current flow and, therefore, of apparent conductance. When polarity is switched suddenly, the counter emf initially adds to the applied voltage, making it 0.6 V in this example. The amplified output of the Wheatstone bridge will appear to show a sudden increase in conductance, which will dissipate as the counter emf declines and then builds up again in a direction to oppose the applied voltage. Fowles et al. (1981) suggest allowing current to flow for the period of time corresponding to an experiment (e.g., 45 minutes) and then testing for polarization. Ideally, the equipment should show a value of 20 μS (if a 50 kΩ resistor is used) both at the beginning and end of this time period with only a modest effect of reversing polarity. This procedure represents an extreme test, inasmuch as it is rare to average 20 μS throughout a session, and thus the current flow is higher than would be expected. When new electrodes are purchased, testing them will both permit detection of any problematic electrodes and provide E with experience in recognizing how much polarization is outside the normal range to be expected even with good electrodes.

Polarization can be checked *in vivo* by reversing polarity during an experiment when data are not being collected (e.g., during inter-trial intervals). Because the skin itself polarizes, more polarization will be observed with an actual participant than with a resistor used in lieu of a participant, but with a little practice it is possible to know the difference between a bad electrode and polarization in the skin. If this procedure can be done several times within the experiment (e.g., every 10 or 15 min), it has the added advantage of reversing the process of chloriding and dechloriding the electrodes that takes place during the experiment, that is, of making systematic an averaging of the direction of current flow that otherwise is assumed to happen through random connection of electrodes to the Wheatstone bridge (see comment above).

When bipolar recordings are used, there is no need to abrade the skin or otherwise to compromise the integrity of the skin. As a result, concerns about possible infections are minimal. Nevertheless, it is a good precaution to sterilize electrodes between uses, as recommended by Putnam, Johnson, and Roth (1992).

Electrode Paste

In order to be reversible, Ag-AgCl electrodes must be used with either potassium chloride (KCl) or NaCl (Fowles et al., 1981). Typically, NaCl is used because it is the major salt in sweat and thus is unlikely to affect the skin or sweat glands. Another consideration is that the half-cell potential for the electrodes is strongly influenced by the concentration of Cl^- in the electrolyte, making it important to have the same concentration at both electrodes in order to avoid generating a bias potential between them. NaCl concentrations in the range of 0.050–0.075 molar, similar to that found in sweat, are used. Given this similarity, the diffusion of surface sweat into the electrolyte is unlikely to change the NaCl concentration appreciably and is especially unlikely to alter differentially the NaCl concentration at the two electrodes.

Most commercial electrode pastes (creams or jells) are designed to reduce skin resistance as much as possible, often doing so with extremely high salt concentrations. As a result, such pastes are unsuitable for electrodermal recording. For many years, it was possible to make one's own electrode paste by purchasing a neutral ointment cream marketed by Parke-Davis under the trade name Unibase. This method, originally recommended by Lykken and Venables (1971) and later by Fowles and colleagues (1981), became a standard. When a 1-pound jar was mixed thoroughly with 230 ml of physiological saline, the resultant mixture had an NaCl concentration of about 0.050 molar. An anti-mold ingredient in Unibase contributed to an almost unlimited shelf life.

Unfortunately, Unibase is no longer available, and no clear consensus has emerged concerning its substitute. Edelberg (1967) recommended the use of K-Y Jelly, which is inexpensive and available at any pharmacy. Furthermore, the major psychophysiological research program headed by Peter Lang and Margaret Bradley used K-Y Jelly for skin conductance measurements with good results for many years. Based on the criterion of not changing its viscosity, Edelberg (personal communication, August 12, 2005) found a shelf life at least two years. Assuming that the completion of a study requires no more than a few months, purchasing a new tube at the beginning of each study may suffice. On the other hand, Edelberg (personal communication, August 11, 2005) suspects that the composition of K-Y Jelly has been changed and no longer is sure that it is satisfactory. Thus, K-Y jelly has much to recommend it, but there is some uncertainty about it.

Probably a more attractive option is Discount Disposables TD 246 skin resistance-skin conductance electrode paste (formerly sold by Med Associates), which is advertised as 0.5% saline in a neutral base that meets the recommendations of Lykken and Venables (1971). It is advertised with a "virtually unlimited" shelf life, which a sales representative said should be interpreted as 4 years on the shelf or one year once opened. Both Dawson (personal communication, April 4, 2004) and Edelberg (personal communication, August 9, 2005) currently recommend its use.

The AgCl coating on electrodes is easily damaged and should not be cleaned by rubbing. The best approach is to wash away the electrode paste with a jet of tap water – from a tap or water bottle or other source of pressurized flow such as an oral cleaning system (e.g., Waterpik). After cleaning, the electrode should be rinsed with distilled water to preclude leaving salt deposits from the evaporated tap water.

Placement and Attachment of Electrodes

Electrodes can be placed either on the medial (middle section of the finger) or distal (fingertip) phalanges of the fingers or on the fleshy areas of the palms known as the thenar and hypothenar eminences (adjacent to the wrist, the thenar eminence being at the base of the thumb) – in all cases on the same hand. For finger placements, the index and middle fingers often are recommended. Diagrams of these placements can be found in Boucsein (1992, p. 97), Dawson and colleagues (2000, p. 205), Hugdahl (1995, p. 115), and Stern and colleagues (2001, p. 212). If experimental procedures preclude palmar recordings, a medial site on the side of the foot will serve well (see Boucsein, 1992, pp. 98–99).

Boucsein (1992, pp. 97–98) cited evidence that SCR amplitudes from the distal phalanges of the fingers are 3.5 times larger than from the medial phalanges, but that the thenar and hypothenar eminences may yield responses as large or even larger than the fingers. Because of the greater responsivity of the distal phalanges, they represent an ideal site so long as the fingers are not too small to attach the electrodes. For either finger location, encircling the finger and electrode with tape (the author uses 3M micropore tape) – in addition to the double-sided adhesive collars described below – is a simple way to ensure that electrodes stay in place even with sweaty palms. The thenar and hypothenar eminences provide larger surface areas for attachment of electrodes, which may be important with young children. It may be necessary to wrap tape around the hands in several directions in order to keep the electrodes firmly attached, especially if the electrode collar does not stick well. The additional taping is somewhat awkward but, nevertheless, is possible and necessary in some cases. Although in adults it may be possible to put both electrodes on the thenar eminence or both on the hypothenar eminence (taking care to avoid electrical contact between electrodes via electrode paste), children's small hands may dictate that one electrode be placed on the thenar and one on the hypothenar eminence (of the same hand). Overall, finger tips are both responsive and permit secure attachments if they are large enough for the electrode, but the thenar and hypothenar eminences provide an attractive alternative, especially in children.

Although the relation is less than perfect, in principle SC and SCR amplitudes will be proportional to the area of contact with the skin. Electrodes usually are attached to the skin with double-sided adhesive disks with a hole punched in them appropriate to the size of the electrode. If used properly, the size of the hole in the disk defines the area of contact. The area is calculated from the formula for the area of a circle πr^2 or more conveniently $\pi d^2/4$, where the value of pi is 3.1416 and r and d stand for the radius and diameter, respectively. Seepage of the electrode paste beneath the adhesive tape is a source of error that varies with contact area. For example, if the seepage increases the radius by 1 mm, the increased area of contact will be a larger percentage of the nominal contact area for small than for large electrodes. An area of 1.0 cm^2 (i.e., diameter equal to 1.13 cm) is recommended by Fowles and colleagues (1981) when possible, but even in adults that size works best on the thenar and hypothenar eminences. In small children, the contact area must be smaller. Care should be taken to minimize seepage of the electrode paste, and the area of contact should be reported.

There is little consensus regarding how to prepare the skin before applying electrodes. Because of findings that SC is significantly lowered by washing with soap and water, Venables and Christie (1980) recommend having all subjects wash their hands. They reasoned that some participants will have washed their hands prior to appearing in the laboratory and that having all participants wash their hands will standardize this effect. If this practice is adopted, use a hand soap that is as neutral as possible (e.g., Johnson's baby soap, Ivory soap) and certainly avoid any soap with detergent additives. Dawson and colleagues (2000) cite this recommendation, apparently sympathetically, and warn against the use of alcohol. On the other hand, Boucsein (1992, p. 100) suggests that allowing a period of time for the electrode paste to penetrate the skin will offset the effects of washing hands, making it unnecessary to standardize by having all participants wash their hands. Boucsein suggests cleaning the skin surface with alcohol for participants whose oily skin prevents good adhesion of the adhesive disks used to attach electrodes. Venables and Christie do not mention alcohol but do say that they found no differences in the effect on SC from washing the skin with acetone, ether, or distilled water. Distilled water would seem to be the least invasive method of cleaning, whereas acetone seems fairly harsh, as it is an organic solvent that removes oil from the skin. Edelberg (personal communication, August 9, 2005) has employed washing hands and alcohol at different times but suggests that it may be adequate just to have participants rinse their hands with water to initiate hydration.

This question of differences in the conductivity of the outer layers of the corneum as a result of hydration by the applied paste or of treatment of the skin is quite important. Recall that the duct filling component of the SCR takes place without reaching the skin. This duct filling component of the SCR can be conceptualized as a variable resistor in series with a relatively fixed (or slowly changing) resistor due to the resistance of the corneum separating the sweat-filled duct from the electrode paste. This series resistor in the corneum not only reduces the measured conductance, but also the measured amplitude of the underlying SCR (Edelberg, 1967). That is, for equal increases in conductance associated with duct filling, the measured change in conductance across the skin will be smaller when the corneal resistance is high than when it is low. Thus, variations in corneal resistance associated with washing with soap (increased resistance) or hydration of the skin by the applied paste (decreased resistance) will affect the apparent amplitude of SCRs associated with changes in duct filling.

The author has typically followed the Venables and Christie recommendations to have all participants wash their hands but does entertain some doubt as to the wisdom of employing a procedure known to reduce SC for all participants – one requiring exposure to electrode paste for a significant time to reverse. This consideration may be especially relevant to children, whose intolerance of long rest periods makes extensive hydration by the electrode paste problematic. Too little data are available for resolution of this problem on empirical grounds. The author is inclined not to recommend hand washing for all participants, especially with young children. Perhaps the best solution in the face of this uncertainty is to have all participants rinse their hands with water only, and suggested by Edelberg, and to use alcohol only when needed because of oily skin, as recommended by Boucsein.

QUANTIFICATION AND INTERPRETATION OF ELECTRODERMAL DATA

A comprehensive coverage of various methods of quantifying electrodermal data and of the types of theoretical inferences that may be drawn is beyond the scope of this chapter. An excellent summary of these issues is provided by Dawson et al. (2000) from which the following summary is taken, unless otherwise specified. As is the case for most topics, Boucsein (1992) provides an outstanding, comprehensive coverage, although one that requires substantial effort for the novice because of the comprehensiveness itself.

Quantification

The prototypical EDA study consists of presenting discrete stimuli and assessing one or more aspects of the SCRs elicited by each stimulus – known as "specific" SCRs. Most often the amplitude of the response is scored, which is the value at the peak of the SCR minus the initial level. Additional components that may be scored are the latency, rise time, and half recovery time. Latency is the time from stimulus presentation to onset of the response, and rise time is the time from onset to peak of the response. Half recovery time refers to the recovery limb following the peak of the response and is the time from peak to the point at which half the amplitude has been recovered. It correlates highly with the time constant of the recovery limb. As Dawson and colleagues note, the relation of latency, rise time, and half recovery time to psychophysiological processes is not well known. Unless there is a clear reason to score these components, amplitude is the measure of choice.

Although less common than presentation of discrete stimuli, a considerable literature assesses EDA during prolonged stimulation such as threat of shock or performance of an ongoing task. Because an SCR during these periods is not associated with discrete stimuli, it is called a "spontaneous" or "nonspecific" SCR and abbreviated NS-SCR. These responses traditionally have been counted without reference to the amplitude and reported as number of SCRs per minute. A minimum amplitude must be specified as the threshold for the SCR to be counted. Dating from the era of paper recordings, 0.05 μS has commonly been used. Even though computer scoring of digitized SCRs can detect smaller SCRs than 0.05 μS, use of the 0.05 μS criterion is to be preferred because it has the advantage of relating to a large literature.

An alternative to counting NS-SCRs during periods of prolonged stimulation is to compute SCL during these periods. Since sweat gland responses affect SCL, SCL can be used as an index of sweat gland activity during prolonged stimulation. One issue that arises with this approach is how to deal with SCRs. With computerized a-d sampling at 20 per second it is easy to compute a mean SCL over a time period appropriate for the overall period of stimulation – for example, second by second for short time periods or blocks of 10, 20, or 30 seconds for longer time periods – in order to track changes over time. This method ignores any distinction between SCRs and SCL. An alternative would be to sample the SCL at a given interval such as every second or every five seconds, but to avoid sampling during an SCR, perhaps using the initial level at the onset of the SCR as a substitute for any sample that comes during the SCR. This method obviously is cumbersome for automated data analysis, and most investigators would ignore the SCRs. On the other hand, if the period of prolonged stimulation consists of a series of stimuli to which SCRs are being recorded, scoring these SCRs will necessarily require a reading of the initial SCL before the onset of the response. These initial values can serve as a convenient way to monitor changes in SCL over the period.

The possible occurrence of NS-SCRs creates a small problem in the scoring of specific SCRs: how to distinguish between the SCR to the discrete stimulus and one that is spontaneous but happens by chance to occur at a time near the presentation of the stimulus. Based on the distribution of latencies to effective discrete stimuli, it is commonly assumed that the latency of a specific SCR has a minimum of 1 second and a maximum of 3 or 4 seconds. This latency window is used to identify specific SCRs and to exclude other SCRs as reflecting NS-SCRs. Dawson and colleagues (2000) suggest applying a latency window possibly even shorter than 1–3 seconds. It should be kept in mind, however, that these latencies are based on simple stimuli that do not require cognitive processing. If one has a paradigm requiring such processing that might delay the response, it is advisable to look at the distribution of latencies before setting a latency criterion.

Dawson and colleagues (2000) view the study of individual differences as a third type of study employing EDA. They mention the importance of test-retest reliability when attempting to view electrodermal responding as a trait. One should also add the caveat that psychometric principles apply to psychophysiological measures just as they do to other forms of assessment. For example, to use the amplitude of the SCR to a single stimulus as an index of some hypothetical trait is comparable to developing a single-item questionnaire.

One final issue in the quantification of electrodermal activity is whether to use a "range correction" (Lykken, 1972, 1975; Lykken, Rose, Luther, & Maley, 1966). The rationale for this approach is simple: both SCL and SCRs vary across individuals for reasons having nothing to do with psychological influences, and it makes sense to quantify a given SCL or SCR measurement in the context of a person's own range of responding. Doing so requires a measurement of the maximum and minimum values for each person. Noting that participants are most responsive at the beginning of the session and most relaxed at the end when told there is only a rest period left, Lykken (e.g., 1975) suggested obtaining the maximum SCL and the maximum SCR at the beginning of the experiment and the minimum SCL during an end-of-session rest period. He elicited the maximum SCL by asking the participant to blow up a balloon until it burst and the maximum SCR by presenting one strong, standard stimulus. Any given SCR is computed as a proportion of the maximum SCR (e.g., 0.63 μS/1.43 μS = 0.44, where 1.43 μS is the SCR_{max}). Similarly, an SCL measurement is computed as a proportion of the range: $(8.72–3.17 \mu S)/(10.41–3.17 \mu S) = 5.55/7.24 = 0.77$, where 8.72 is the SCL of interest, 3.17 is SCL_{min}, and 10.41 is SCL_{max}. Lykken (1975) suggests that if the experimental procedures include enough stimulation to elicit SCL values near the maximum and minimum, then it is unnecessary to add the balloon task and the end-of-session rest period.

Lykken (1975) noted that a within-participants ANOVA will also eliminate the irrelevant individual differences. However, the ANOVA will be influenced by the magnitude of the scores, in which case the more responsive participants will have a greater impact. In contrast, the range correction attempts to weight the data from less responsive participants equally to that of more responsive participants. Both approaches are to be found in the literature. One other consideration: when electrodermal responding is to be correlated with other variables (e.g., a correlation between the SCR to an aversive picture and the subjective rating of the aversiveness of the picture), the range correction may be especially helpful, because the within-participants ANOVA does not work for this comparison.

Dawson and colleagues (2000) note two limitations of the range correction procedure. First, it obviously does not work when comparing groups differing in psychological processes that produce differences in range. If one group is psychologically less responsive than the other, using the range correction will eliminate meaningful individual differences in reactivity. Second, the estimates of maximum and minimum values can be unreliable, undermining the effectiveness of the range correction. One author (Ben-Shakhar, 1985) suggested that the within-participants mean and standard deviation are more reliable statistics and can be used to compute standardized scores. To these concerns might be added the special difficulty of presenting very strong stimuli to children. Overall, a range correction can be valuable under the right conditions. An experimenter should take into account the experimental context and the questions being asked to see if the range-correction should be employed for any given study.

Interpretation of EDA

It is important to understand that an electrodermal response does not inherently represent any single psychological process. As Dawson and colleagues

(2000) comment, the SCR responds to stimuli that "include stimulus novelty, surprisingness, intensity, emotional content, and significance" (p. 212). The psychological interpretation depends on the experimental paradigm being employed and the degree of experimental control over competing explanations for the response. These authors describe the use of the SCR amplitude to discrete stimuli in paradigms involving lie detection, response to faces of famous people, and discrimination classical conditioning. They cite two related theoretical approaches converging on the suggestion that attentional processes play a crucial role in eliciting the SCR to discrete stimuli. In one theory, when preattentive mechanisms identify a stimulus as novel or as significant, their call for additional controlled processing elicits the SCR. In the second theory, it is the actual allocation of controlled processing resources to stimulus processing that elicits the SCR. With regard to chronic stimulation, Dawson and colleagues review increases in NS-SCRs or SCL in paradigms involving performance of various tasks or social interactions. The increases in EDA have variously been attributed to (a) increases in tonic arousal, energy regulation or mobilization, (b) attentional and information processing, or (c) stress and affect. The investigator interested in measuring EDA in a given experimental paradigm or in a specific theoretical context should consult the relevant literature to ascertain the best current methodologies and experimental designs.

PROBLEMS SPECIFIC TO CHILDREN

Participant Compliance

There are two major issues with infants and very young children regarding compliance: (a) attaching the electrodes and keeping them attached by controlling the stressfulness of the situation, and (b) coordinating stimulus presentation with the child's attention to the task. With respect to the first point, infants and young children are unaccustomed to having wires attached and to attempts to keep their spontaneous activity to a minimum. While many are not bothered by these attempts, some infants and children find it stressful. For example, Scarpa, Raine, Venables, and Mednick (1997) reported that 42% of a large sample of 3-year-old children cried during presentation of a series of 75 dB tones, in spite of being tested while sitting in their mother's lap.

In an effort to address this problem with 4-year-olds, Fowles and colleagues (2000) employed the commonly adopted strategy of decorating the laboratory with astronaut themes and telling the child it was an astronaut training laboratory. The mother stayed in the room, remaining neutral and completing questionnaires. In spite of these procedures, a small number of children were distressed. If attempts to soothe the child failed, the mother would be seated next to the child or, in extreme cases, would sit in the experimental chair with the child in her lap. These measures sufficed for all but one or two children, who were then rescheduled for another time. A small number of children continued to express distress initially but quickly calmed down as the experiment proceeded, although a number of children asked several times when they could remove the electrodes. The obvious cost in terms of less standardized conditions as a result of having the mother closer to the child in some cases than others is clearly justified. Without these procedural adaptations, some children either would not participate at all or their recordings would be influenced by their distress.

Social interactions with young children in the laboratory are more complex than with adult participants. The author was advised by his collaborator (Grazyna Kochanska), a prominent researcher in the area of social development, that only female experimenters should be used to interact with toddlers and young children. The obvious rationale for this policy is that, by and large, most caretakers of young children are female, and thus females are a more normative social stimulus – males potentially being seen by the child as more threatening. Additionally, there are differences in social interactional style with young children as a function of the adult's gender. Even among potential female experimenters, the skill with which they handle and sooth children is likely to vary and should be considered.

Ensuring that the child attends to stimulus presentation and other aspects of the procedures presents some difficulties, especially if computerized program control and data acquisition are involved. With adult subjects, it is possible to program stimulus presentation, inter-trial intervals, and the timing of data collection in a rigid format, assuming that participants will comply with instructions and attend to the demands of the experiment. In contrast, young children are to some extent "free-responding" organisms who are incompletely compliant with experimental demands. Additionally, it is likely that an experimenter will be in the room with the child and will initiate some or all tasks. It should be possible to program pauses in the data acquisition programs that initiate data collection when the experimenter presses a key on the computer. For example, if the computer controls presentation of a loud noise, the computer operator could watch the child through a TV monitor and initiate the SC data collection and presentation of the noise when the child is not engaged in some distracting activity. The situation is more complex if the stimulus presentation or task is initiated by the experimenter in the room with the child because the computer operator may not be able to anticipate the onset. The experimenter needs to signal the computer operator or have some way of initiating the computer data acquisition (e.g., pressing a key).

In other cases, it may be even more difficult to anticipate the onset of the task. For example, Fowles and colleagues (2000) demonstrated a toy with a plunger that made a newspaper pop (cf. popping a paper bag). Then the child was asked to make it pop. The initiation of this effort was under the child's control, making it impossible to accurately time the data collection. Because of the impossibility of controlling task onset in this case and the general difficulty of doing so in other cases, one of the experimenters (Kathleen Murray) wrote a data acquisition program that allowed the computer operator to press different keys to indicate the onset of different activities (e.g., "n" for newspaper, "b" for breath, etc.). Thus, data collection was continuous, and the interaction between the experimenter and the child was unencumbered by having to signal task onset. However, the experimenter also had to write programs to find the task onset and to read the subsequent data, accordingly. These special purpose programs, while desirable in many respects, require an unusual degree of sophistication in writing data acquisition programs.

The special-purpose programs are described here not so much to suggest a solution as to underscore the nature of the problem of controlling stimulus presentation with young children. It might be noted that, with the old pen-and-paper polygraph recordings, it is relatively easy to note such events on the chart during recording and to adapt hand scoring to the timing indicated by the notations. That is, the "problem" is, to a large extent, due to the rigidity of computerized experimental control and data acquisition.

Developmental Changes in Electrodermal Responsiveness

Although systematic information is not available, it is clear that from birth to adulthood there is an increase in the range of stimuli to which the electrodermal system responds. Fowles and colleagues (2000) summarized a number of findings for infants and very young children. Some of the basic findings include the following. EDRs were smaller and less easily elicited in infants 3 to 11 months old than in older children, with startle (e.g., mildly painful shock, loud sounds, sudden withdrawal of support) or frustration (e.g., removal of the bottle when nursing) being the most effective stimuli for the infants. Furthermore, infants required higher stimulus intensities than adults to produce a response. No EDRs were observed to visual stimuli, pleasant stimuli, and conditions producing relief. Children from age 2 to 4 years showed the greatest responses to loud sounds (doorbell, Klaxon) and the threat of loss of balance (chair tipping), smaller EDRs to turning lights on or off, and minimal EDRs to verbal stimuli (e.g., "look there" and "you are a brave boy"). EDRs to stimuli in a reaction time paradigm have been reported in children as young as age 6.

In their own study of 92 children with a mean age of 52 months, Fowles and colleagues (2000) found SCRs or increases in SCL to a fairly wide range of stimuli. Large SCRs were observed to breaths and to all abrupt onset, mildly startling stimuli, including some that presumably were affectively positive. Smaller SCRs were elicited by a mild positive stimulus of turning off the lights so the child could see glow-in-the-dark planets and stars, as well as by affectively negative pictures. SCRs were not elicited by neutral and affectively positive pictures, two emotion conflict tasks, or periods of eager anticipation while waiting for a Jack-in-the-box to pop up. Similarly, the children did not respond electrodermally to affectively positive and negative popular film clips in spite of apparently rapt attention and facial expressions of negative affect for the latter. Thus, a number of more psychological stimuli failed to elicit SCRs. There was, however, one interesting exception. When children watched a "Mickey Mouse clock" while the second hand ticked off 60 seconds and told E when the minute was up, they showed the expected decline in SC during the first three-quarters of the period followed by an anticipatory increase in SC as the end of the period approached.

Although children 6 and above appear to respond more than younger children to an adult-like range of stimuli, Fowles, Furuseth, and Beeghly (1991) reported differences between 8–10 year-old and 11–14 year-old normal children. Using a word association task (WAT) paradigm in which E presented words reflecting fear-related (e.g., snake), drug-related (e.g., cigarettes), attachment-related (e.g., Mom), and neutral (e.g., table) words, 11–14 year-old children responded with the expected larger SCRs to the three categories of "signal" words relative to the neutral words. Surprisingly, the 8–10 year-old children did not, that is, they produced similar and small SCRs to all categories of stimuli. Following up that result, Furuseth (1993) was able to elicit larger SCRs to positively and negatively valenced pictures compared to neutral pictures in 8–10 year-olds. It appears, therefore, that 8–10 year-old children show differential SC responding to affectively charged or significant visual stimuli but not to words.

One other issue deserves comment. Investigators traditionally have been concerned that motor activity will produce SCRs, and they often try to note any unexpected movements in order to discard concomitant SCRs. In the Fowles and colleagues (2000) study, it quickly became obvious that (a) children engage in too much spontaneous speech and motor activity (pointing, moving limbs, squirming in the seat) to record and (b) such activity seldom was associated with SCRs. The authors tentatively concluded that motor activity per se had little effect on SCRs. Similarly, Latzman, Knutson, and Fowles (2007) recorded SC in 8–12 year-old children while pressing keys on a computer terminal and observed no SCRs to the movement *per se.* These observations are important because of the difficulty of eliminating motor activity in younger children.

The important conclusion from this brief review is that an investigator interested in using EDA to study emotional or cognitive processes in children cannot assume that children will respond as adults do. S/he should examine the current literature with children of a similar age to see whether the experimental procedure in question has been found to be effective. If such literature does not exist, it will be essential to collect pilot data to determine the appropriateness of the procedure and the theoretical inferences to be drawn.

ACKNOWLEDGEMENTS

The author wishes to thank Robert Edelberg for his many helpful suggestions that have improved the manuscript. Similarly, the author wishes to thank Mr. Lloyd Frei, instrumentation engineer in the Department of Psychology at the University of Iowa, for expert consultation on the R-C coupling circuit in Figure 10.5, time constant calculations, and several other technical aspects of the chapter.

References

Ben-Shakhar, G. (1985). Standardization within individuals: Simple method to neutralize individual differences in skin conductance. *Psychophysiology, 22,* 292–299.

Boucsein, W. (1992). *Electrodermal activity.* New York & London: Plenum Press.

Cook, E. W., III (2003). *VPM reference manual.* Birmingham: Author.

Cook, E. W., III., Atkinson, L. S., & Lang, K. G. (1987). Stimulus control and data acquisition for IBM PCs and compatibles. *Psychophysiology, 24,* 726–727.

Dawson, M. E., Schell, A. M., & Filion, D. L. (2000). The electrodermal system. In J. T. Cacioppo, L. G. Tassinary, & G. G. Berntson (Eds.), *Handbook of psychophysiology* (2nd ed., pp. 200–223). Cambridge, England: Cambridge University Press.

Edelberg, R. (1967). Electrical properties of the skin. In C. C. Brown (Ed.), *Methods in psychophysiology* (pp. 1–53). Baltimore: Williams & Wilkins.

Edelberg, R. (1993). Electrodermal mechanisms: A critique of the two-effector hypothesis and a proposed replacement. In J. C. Roy, W. Boucsein, D. Fowles, & J. Gruzelier (Eds.), *Progress in electrodermal research* (pp. 7–29). London: Plenum Press.

Fowles, D. (1986). The eccrine system and electrodermal activity. In M. G. H. Coles, S. W. Porges, & E. Donchin (Eds.), *Psychophysiology: Systems, processes, and applications* (Vol 1., pp. 51–96). New York: Guilford Press.

Fowles, D., Christie, M., Edelberg, R., Grings, W., Lykken, D., & Venables, P. (1981). Publication recommendations for electrodermal measurements. *Psychophysiology, 18*, 232–239.

Fowles, D. C., Furuseth, A. M., & Beeghly, J. (1991, June). *The signal-orienting response in externalizing disorders.* Paper presented at the Annual Meeting of the Society for Research in Child and Adolescent Psychopathology, Zandvoort, Holland.

Fowles, D. C., Kochanska, G., & Murray, K. (2000). Electrodermal activity and temperament in preschool children. *Psychophysiology, 37*, 777–787.

Furuseth, A. (1993). *Children's orienting responses to relatively permanent sets of significant stimuli.* Unpublished doctoral dissertation, University of Iowa, Iowa City.

Geddes, L. A., & Baker, L. E. (1975). *Principles of applied biomedical instrumentation* (2nd Ed). New York: John Wiley and Sons.

Hugdahl, K. (1995). *Psychophysiology: The mind-body perspective.* Cambridge, MA: Harvard University Press.

Latzman, R. D., Knutson, J. F., & Fowles, D. C. (2007). Schedule-induced electrodermal responding in children. *Psychophysiology, 43*, 623–632.

Lykken, D. T. (1972). Range correction applied to heart rate and GSR data. *Psychophysiology, 9*, 373–379.

Lykken, D. T. (1975). The role of individual differences in psychophysiological research. In P. H. Venables & M. J. Christie (Eds.), *Research in psychophysiology* (pp. 3–16). New York: John Wiley and Sons.

Lykken, D. T., Rose, R. J., Luther, B., & Maley, M. (1966). Correcting psychophysiological measures for individual differences in range. *Psychological Bulletin, 66*, 481–484.

Lykken, D. T., & Venables, P. H. (1971). Direct measurement of skin conductance: A proposal for standardization. *Psychophysiology, 8*, 656–672.

Margerison, J. H., Binnie, C. D., & Venables, P. H. (1967). Basic physical principles. In P. H. Venables & I. Martin (Eds.), *A manual of psychophysiological methods* (pp. 1–52). Amsterdam: North-Holland.

Putnam, L. E., Johnson, R., & Roth, W. T. (1992). Guidelines for reducing the risks of disease transmission in the psychophysiology laboratory. *Psychophysiology, 29*, 127–141.

Roy, J.-C., Boucsein, W., Fowles, D., & Gruzelier, J. (Eds). (1993). *Progress in electrodermal Research.* London: Plenum Press.

Scarpa, A., Raine, A., Venables, P. H., & Mednick, S. A. (1997). Heart rate and skin conductance in behaviorally inhibited Mauritian children. *Journal of Abnormal Psychology, 106*, 182–190.

Stern, R. M., Ray, W. J., & Quigley, K. S. (2001). *Psychophysiological recording* (2nd Ed). New York: Oxford University Press.

Venables, P. H., & Christie, M. J. (1980). Electrodermal activity. In I. Martin & P. H. Venables (Eds.), *Techniques in psychophysiology* (pp. 3–67). New York: John Wiley and Sons.

NEUROENDOCRINE SYSTEM

Theory, Methods, and Measures

11 Emotion, Temperament, Vulnerability, and Development

Evidence from Nonhuman Primate Models

Kristine Erickson, J. Dee Higley, and Jay Schulkin

INTRODUCTION

Nonhuman primates provide the opportunity to study the development of emotional behavior, temperament, and vulnerability to psychiatric disorders under controlled conditions. Like humans, these animals display temperamental variability (Byrne & Suomi, 2002; Higley & Suomi, 1989). Manipulation of prenatal and early life environments influence behavioral, cognitive/ emotional, and physiological variables in monkeys and environmental variables continue to affect these domains in adulthood. This finding has implications for vulnerability to conditions such as anxiety disorders, depression, and alcoholism in humans. Alterations in early life experience, subsequent behavioral patterns, and neuroendocrine activity are associated with anatomical and functional changes in brain regions implicated in emotional behavior and psychopathology. Linking variables observed during early development with long-term mental health outcomes in adulthood is an area of research in which nonhuman primate studies can contribute important knowledge.

A great advantage of nonhuman primate research is the ability to investigate developmental hypotheses that cannot be studied in human children. First, the ability to manipulate the environment and tightly control that environment is an advantage of nonhuman primate research. Also, procedures are possible with nonhuman primates that are too invasive and therefore anxiety-provoking or even dangerous for human children. For example, measuring plasma concentrations of substances like cortisol requires blood samples; measurement of neuropeptide or neurotransmitter metabolite concentrations requires a lumbar puncture in order to extract cerebral spinal fluid (CSF) samples. Therefore, nonhuman primates provide a way of investigating environmental effects on these types of biological variables.

Cortisol and Corticotropin-Releasing Hormone

Actions of the glucocorticoid system contribute to the pathophysiology of mood and anxiety disorders. Cortisol (corticosterone in rats) is a glucocorticoid hormone secreted by the adrenal gland, which may differentially affect certain neurotransmitter systems in various brain regions. Cortisol contributes to a wide range of regulatory functions, including glucose metabolism (Khani & Tayek, 2001) and various behavioral and cognitive functions (for review, see Lupien & McEwen, 1998). Glucocorticoid secretion by the hypothalamic-pituitary-adrenal (HPA) axis is counter-regulated through negative feedback inhibition at the level of the pituitary and hypothalamus (for review, see Arborelius et al., 1999). In contrast, outside the HPA axis, glucocorticoids and corticotrophin-releasing hormone (CRH) comprise a positive feedback system in areas such as the amygdala (see Figure 11.1), and are implicated in the stress response and in cognitive-emotional appraisal (Makino et al., 1994a; Makino et al., 1994b; Watts & Sanchez-Watts, 1995).

A potential mechanism by which glucocorticoids may influence emotional behavior is via their effects on the neurophysiological activity of the amygdala and prefrontal cortical structures known to participate in emotional processing (Cahill et al., 1996; McGaugh, 2000; Roozendaal et al., 2001). Human imaging studies indicate that amygdala, ventral medial prefrontal, and other prefrontal cortical areas are activated during tasks requiring processing of affective stimuli (Fischer et al., 2000; Iidaka et al., 2001). These data converge with lesion analysis and electrophysiological studies performed in humans or experimental animals, indicating these structures participate in brain circuits important for processing emotional information (Davis & Whalen, 2001; Drevets et al., 1996). These brain structures contain dense concentrations of glucocorticoid (GR) and mineralocorticoid (MR) receptors (Brooke, de Haas-Johnson et al., 1994; Leverenz, Wilkinson et al., 2001; Patel, Lopez et al., 2000; Sanchez, Young et al., 2000; Seckl, Dickson et al., 1991). Both experimental animal studies (Goldstein et al., 1996; Makino et al., 1994a) and human studies (Drevets et al., 1997; Drevets et al., 2002) suggest that increased glucocorticoids potentiate activation of the amygdala and influence processing of emotionally-laden stimuli.

Role of Cortisol and CRH in Emotional Behaviors

Glucocorticoids bind to both GR and MR receptors, which are distributed within the amygdala, hippocampus, and prefrontal cortex (Sanchez et al., 1999). In rodents, the GRs and MRs to which glucocorticoids bind are

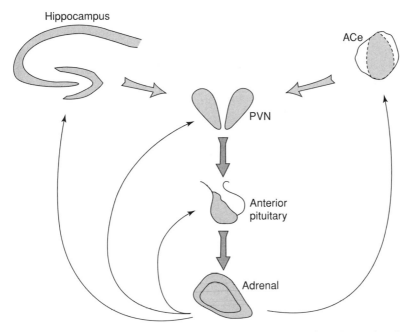

Figure 11.1. The neuroendocrine inter-related, stress-activated corticotropin releasing hormone(CRH) loops. Stress-conveying signals rapidly activate immediate early genes in CRH-expressing neurons of the central nucleus of the amygdala (ACe). Rapid CRH release in the ACe is thought to activate CRH expressing neurons in the hypothalamic paraventricular nucleus (PVN) to secrete CRH into the hypothalamo-pituitary portal system, inducing ACTH and glucocorticoid secretion from the pituitary and adrenal, respectively. In response to stress, CRH expression is also activated rapidly in these neurons. Glucocorticoids exert a negative feedback on PVN (directly and via hippocampus), yet activate CRH gene expression in the amygdala, potentially promoting further CRH release in this region. (From Brunson et al., 2001).

primarily located in the hippocampus, PVN, and septum (Fuxe et al., 1985; Price, 1999; Reul & de Kloet, 1985). However, distribution of MRs and GRs in primates have been described in the amygdala, hippocampus, medial prefrontal and orbitofrontal cortical areas (Leverenz et al., 2001; Sanchez et al., 2000; Sarrieau et al., 1986; Sarrieau et al., 1988; Seckl et al., 1991). These same regions underlie the perception, memory, and experience of emotional events. Cortisol can be elevated in a number of contexts that may or may not be "stressful", but rather arousing. These include attachment behaviors, food intake, territorial and predatory behaviors, focused attention, social presentation, sustained effort, and effortful thought (Dallman et al., 1993; Schulkin, 1999; Wingfield & Grimm, 1977). Therefore, cortisol's effects may be viewed as important in modulating cognitive appraisal mechanisms. The effects of cortisol on neurotransmitters and neuropeptides within various functional circuits can influence perception of, attention toward, and memory for environmental events.

Behaviorally, evidence for an association between glucocorticoids and mood exists. Because cortisol has a role in the stress response, elevated concentrations are often viewed as an adverse state of affairs. However, although some studies of glucocorticoid administration report depressive effects on mood, others report euphoric or hypomanic effects in humans. For example, exogenously administered prednisone (a glucocorticoid agonist) and ACTH caused euphoria in individuals with non-psychiatric medical disorders (Cameron et al., 1985). In healthy humans, either cortisol or dexamethasone injections can result in feelings of euphoria (Plihal et al., 1996; Schmidt et al., 1999a), and some individuals reported mood elevation following chronic prednisone treatment (Wolkowitz et al., 1990).

This evidence suggests that elevated cortisol is not in itself a negative condition. Cortisol release is inhibited during sleep (Plihal & Born, 1999) and increased after waking in the morning (Dallman et al., 1993). Children described as bold and energetic had increased cortisol levels compared to other children (Granger et al., 1994; Gunnar, 1994). Also, acute glucocorticoid elevations may enhance focused attention toward emotionally arousing stimuli (Corodimas et al., 1994; Jones et al., 1988). This evidence suggests that elevated cortisol concentrations may be important in a number of contexts involving readiness to respond to environmental events. The brief acute elevations experienced during a normal day appear adaptive and allow the individual to attend and respond to important events.

Plasma concentrations of cortisol are increased in the presence of stress, fear and anxiety, and chronic administration of glucocorticoids can lead to mood changes in humans (Plihal et al., 1996). When experiencing chronic long-term stress, plasma cortisol concentrations are usually elevated. Cortisol exhibits restraint on CRH in regions such as the paraventricular nucleus of the hypothalamus (PVN; Sawchenko et al., 1993; Swanson & Simmons, 1989), while potentiating CRH expression in other brain regions such as the amygdala (Makino et al., 1994a; Swanson & Simmons, 1989; Watts & Sanchez-Watts, 1995). Concentrations of CRH in cerebrospinal fluid and CRH expression in the central nucleus of the amygdala (ACe) are associated with mood and behavioral states such as depression, fear, and anxiety. Figure 11.2 shows the behavioral withdrawal in a rhesus macaque following CRH infusions into the CSF (Strome et al., 2002). CRH antagonists were shown to decrease anxious and depressive behaviors in rhesus macaques (Habib et al.,

Figure 11.2. The behavioral effects of ICV CRH in an adult male rhesus monkey when housed in his normal social group. Note the brown nylon jacket the animal is wearing, which contains the pump used to infuse CRH. The animal has withdrawn from his peers and is exhibiting huddling wall-facing behavior, one of the depressive-like behaviors induced by ICV CRH in socially housed monkeys. (From Strome et al., 2002).

2000), suggesting that CRH activity is important to understanding mood and anxiety disorders.

The facilitory effects of chronic glucocorticoid administration on aversively motivated behaviors are thought to be a consequence of increased expression of CRH in the amygdala and/or bed nucleus of the stria terminalis (Makino et al., 1994a; Makino et al., 1994b; Shepard & Barron, 2000; Swanson & Simmons, 1989; Watts & Sanchez-Watts, 1995). Chronic glucocorticoid administration increases CRH mRNA expression in both the ACe and the bed nucleus of the stria terminalis. Both of these extrahypothalamic sites have been linked to the enhanced behavioral effects of CRH on fear or anxiety-related measures and to stress-induced drug relapse in rats (Kalin et al., 1994; Koob, 1999; Lee & Davis, 1997).

Glucocorticoids affect neurotransmitter and neuropeptides and neurotransmitters other than CRH, and these systems also contribute to the expression of mood and anxiety disorders. For example, cortisol activity is associated with the monoamine serotonin, which is implicated in the neuropharmacology of depression, aggression, anxiety, and alcoholism (Fumagalli et al., 1996). Similarly, dopamine transmission, important for hedonic response, is influenced by glucocorticoids (Patterson et al., 1997). Norepinephrine, critical for consolidating emotional memories, is also influenced by glucocorticoid activity (Quirarte et al., 1997). Acetylcholine (Bouzat & Barrantes, 1996), and glutamate (Moghaddam et al., 1994) are likewise regulated by glucocorticoids. Neuropeptide Y, regulated by glucocorticoids, may be an anxiolytic that works in opposition to CRH during positive and negative emotional events. These effects of glucocorticoid activation have implications for the development of normal emotional processes and psychopathology that are subserved by these neuropharmacological systems.

Nonhuman Primates and Behavioral Characteristics

Among captive nonhuman primates, a wide range of behaviors can be observed in various experimental situations. Within models of psychopathology and normal fearful/anxious or depressive responses, changes in the duration or frequency of certain behaviors indicate the amount of distress experienced by the animal in response to stress. Behaviors that tend to increase during stress paradigms include vocalizations, withdrawal, freezing, and locomotion about the cage, while decreases in social behaviors (e.g., grooming) also are observed. Using these ethologically valid behaviors, primate samples can be described in terms of normal temperamental continuums or as categories of high or low psychopathological behavior.

Experimental manipulations employed to invoke chronic stress in primate research include maternal deprivation and peer-rearing, variable foraging conditions, and periodic modification of the primate social or family group. Invocation of acute stress includes maternal separation, social separation in cases of peer-reared primates, and introduction of a stranger to the home cage. In cases of maternal deprivation, infants are separated from their mothers within a day or two of birth, and raised in a nursery. "Peer-reared" infants are then introduced to and housed with a social group of other juvenile monkeys. The acute stress of maternal separation can be performed in several ways. One method is the removal of the juvenile monkey from the home cage and placement in an isolated cage. Another is the removal of the mother from the home cage, leaving the juvenile with the other remaining primate group members of the home cage. In cases of peer-reared animals, social separation can be performed by introducing a barrier in the home cage, physically separating the animal from its peers in the home cage.

Responses to acute stress by primates reared under normal conditions can be used to characterize temperament and to investigate neurobiological responses to stress. Maternal separation in nonhuman primates elicits fear- and anxiety-related behaviors such as increased distress vocalizations and locomotion about the cage (Suomi, 1991). Withdrawal responses in macaques can also be defined by time spent motionless or freezing in response to a human entering the cage or in response to maternal separation (Kalin et al., 1998a; Kalin et al., 1998b).

Exposure to chronic stress alone or coupling a chronic early life stressor with an acute stressor allows study of the potential roles of these environmental situations and events on the development of psychopathology. For example, when presented with an acute stressor such as parental separation, some nonhuman primates demonstrate behavioral and physiological reactions suggestive of clinical depression (McKinney, 1984). Additionally, parental deprivation and peer-rearing can be viewed as a chronic stressor that places a developing primate at risk for more severe responses to social separation stress and increased risk for despair during a social separation (Mineka & Suomi, 1978). Longitudinal studies that follow primates subjected to early life stress through adolescence and adulthood allow observation of how diseases such as alcoholism and anxiety disorders develop.

Maternal deprivation, a chronic early life stressor, has multiple effects on behavior. Increased frequency and duration of behaviors suggestive of anxiety is one effect. Also, monkeys subjected to maternal deprivation and peer-rearing tend to show characteristics of type II alcoholism, a form of alcoholism associated with impulsive behavior and sensation-seeking. Monkeys experiencing maternal deprivation in the form or peer rearing are more likely to display antisocial personality traits and to drink alcohol chronically to excess when alcohol is freely available (Higley et al., 1991). The higher rates of diminished social competence among peer-reared compared to mother-reared animals, characterized by impulsive aggression and lower social dominance ranking suggest that early experience aggravates antisocial tendencies and contributes to the development of alcoholism in a subgroup of individuals (Higley et al., 1996a).

High levels of withdrawal behaviors may be a relatively stable characteristic among nonhuman primates throughout development. For example, we found that when two different criteria (a baseline and a stress-elicited criteria) for rating withdrawal were used with mother-reared nonhuman primates none of the primates that were highly withdrawn during baseline conditions were categorized as having low withdrawal during the stress-elicited condition. This finding is consistent with observations that this characteristic is stable over time in human children only in cases of extreme behavioral inhibition (Kagan et al., 1988; Kagan et al., 1998). Behaviorally, elevated durations of withdrawal in nonhuman primates vacillated between periods of withdrawal and high activity. To the extent that locomotion represents increased arousal and agitation, the greater increase in locomotion by the highly withdrawn group during acute separation also supports the hypothesis that these animals are less able to cope skillfully with the stressful separation procedures.

For example, in addition to displaying agitation, they were less likely to seek arousal-reducing social grooming. As behaviorally inhibited children are at risk for developing anxiety disorders in adulthood (Rosenbaum et al., 1993), longitudinal studies of nonhuman primates with similar characteristics may contribute to understanding how to reduce risk in these children.

Linking Environment, Behavior, and Neuropharmacology in Nonhuman Primates

Manipulating the environments of nonhuman primates facilitates the study of relations among experience, subsequent behavior, and neuropharmacology. For example, early life events have long-term consequences on both the brain and behavior and alter CRH expression in the brain (Rots et al., 1996). Maternally-deprived rats were more likely to develop helpless behavior in the presence of negative events, suggesting that these rats were excessively stressed or fearful. Systemic levels of glucocorticoids as adults were not different from normal rats, but the exaggerated fearful reactions induced by the early experience were long lasting (Caldji et al., 1998; Levine, 2001; Plotsky & Meaney, 1993). These rats were deprived of maternal closeness for 3 hours a day for a 2-week period as pups, and subsequently had higher levels of CRH mRNA expression in the PVN, ACe and the lateral bed nucleus of the stria terminalis as adults than those rats who were separated only 15 minutes a day (Barna et al., 2003; Meaney et al., 1996).

In nonhuman primates, separation from the mother increases an infant's time spent freezing, and the duration of freezing behavior is correlated with increased cortisol concentrations (Kalin et al., 1998b). In addition, cortisol levels increase in rhesus infants when they are separated from their mothers and peers (Higley et al., 1992; Shannon et al., 1998). Primates characterized as inhibited or fearful based on behavioral characteristics have higher cortisol reactivity (Byrne & Suomi, 2002). Concentrations of neurotransmitter metabolites of serotonin (Higley et al., 1996b), dopamine (Brake et al., 1997; Higley et al., 1991), and norepinephrine (Higley & Linnoila, 1997b; Schneider et al., 1998) change in response to various types of stressors or stressful situations, including social separation (Bayart et al., 1990; Breese et al., 1973).

Early life environments influence behavior and neuropharmacology. The chronic stress of maternal deprivation results in long-lasting alterations in neuropharmacological profiles. Evidence is accumulating from both human (Heim et al., 1997) and nonhuman primate studies (Suomi et al., 1975) that early life trauma can produce long-lasting alterations in neurobiological systems that may predispose one to behavioral disorders later in adulthood. Long-term effects of early experience on neurobiology include significantly

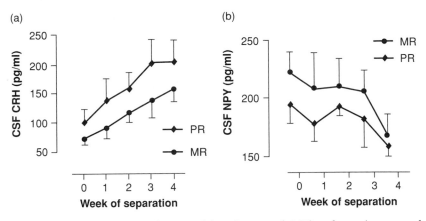

Figure 11.3. Effect of repeated maternal (mother reared; MR) and peer (peer reared; PR) separation of 6-month-old infant rhesus macaques on their (a) CSF concentrations of corticotropin-releasing hormone (CRH) and (b) neuropeptide Y (NPY).

increased CRH immunoreactivity in the cerebrospinal fluid (CSF) of bonnet macaques whose mothers had been exposed to variable foraging demands several months after exposure to psychosocial instability (Coplan et al., 1996). Increased CSF CRH is associated with increased fearful behaviors (Kalin et al., 2000) that are reduced with the administration of CRH receptor antagonists (Habib et al., 2000).

In contrast to CRH, neuropeptide Y (NPY) may be an anxiolytic brain peptide (Heilig et al., 1993) that undergoes reciprocal changes in relation to CRH in the rat (Heilig et al., 1994). Concentrations of NPY also can be influenced by environmental factors during development. Peer-reared animals, when compared to mother-reared animals, have significantly higher CSF CRH immunoreactivities, while NPY tends to be lower in peer-reared animals (see Figure 11.3; Gabry et al., unpublished). Taken together, the evidence suggests that increased CRH activity is associated with negative, adverse events, while increased NPY is associated with positive central states, and early life experiences can chronically influence the central expression of these neuropeptides and the expression of behaviors associated with them.

Nonhuman primate studies of type II-like alcohol consumption patterns indicated that for a subset of individuals these behaviors are preceded by early maternal deprivation and associated with low serotonergic function (Higley et al., 1996b). As noted earlier in the chapter, increased rates of baseline alcohol consumption were associated with impulsive aggression, and appear to fit the model of type II alcoholism. In these animals, high baseline rates of alcohol consumption, impulsivity, and aggression are associated with low CSF concentrations of the serotonin metabolite 5-HIAA and increased levels of cortisol in both peer-reared and mother-reared animals; these characteristics are more frequent in peer-reared animals (Higley & Bennett, 1999; Higley et al., 1991). In primates who imbibe excessive amounts of alcohol under baseline conditions, consumption can be reduced by administering a serotonin reuptake inhibitor (Higley et al., 1998). This treatment also reduces aggressive and anxious behaviors in these animals in baseline non-stressed conditions. The evidence suggests that a genetic tendency towards type II alcoholism and antisocial behaviors can be aggravated by early life events, and are associated with specific neurobiological characteristics, specifically serotonergic activity.

Elevated glucocorticoid concentrations are associated not only with type II alcoholism, but also have a role in cases of so-called type I alcoholism. Mother-reared animals, when exposed to stress and express behaviors suggestive of high anxiety, had increased cortisol concentrations and were more likely to consume alcohol, when it is available, under conditions of stress than during baseline conditions (Higley & Linnoila, 1997b). In addition, in cases of type II alcoholism treated with serotonin reuptake inhibitors, this treatment is ineffective under conditions of stress such as peer separation when cortisol concentrations increase (Higley et al., 1998).

Evidence is accumulating that suggests a labile cortisol system is preferable. Rhesus monkeys characterized as having relatively low levels of anxiety showed reductions in anticipatory cortisol concentrations across several maternal separation episodes (see Figure 11.4). Such habituation is seen as evidence for reduced anxiety and better coping (Clarke, 1993; Eriksen et al., 1999); this finding suggests that these animals may be able to cope more effectively with the expectation of social separation than animals who express high levels of anxiety. Our study revealed that the initial cortisol concentrations during the social stressor are at least as high in the low anxious animals as in the high anxious animals. The substantial reduction in cortisol seen in the low anxious animals was observed following the initial separation procedure. Reduced social behaviors and sustained cortisol response of the high anxious animals during acute separations suggest reduced coping mechanisms.

Both low and high glucocorticoid levels are associated with deficits in memory performance, indicating that glucocorticoid effects on this cognitive domain follows the "inverted U-shaped" curve such that sufficient concentrations of cortisol are necessary for optimal memory consolidation (de Quervain et al., 1998; McGaugh, 2000; Michiels & Cluydts, 2001; Roozendaal & McGaugh, 1997; Starkman et al., 2001). However, chronically elevated cortisol is associated with fear and anxiety. Failure in reducing cortisol concentrations seen in the highly anxious animals not only may

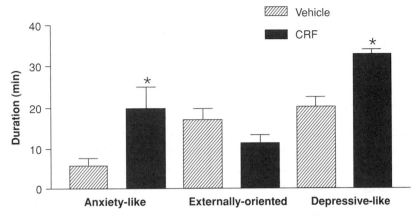

Figure 11.4. Duration of time spent performing anxiety-like, externally oriented, or depressive-like behaviors during ICV infusion of vehicle or CRF in eight animals tested in a social group. Data are mean ± standard error; *$P < 0.05$. (From Strome et al., 2002).

reflect suboptimal coping strategies but may also lead to enhanced memory of the aversive events. The cortisol concentrations of the low anxious animals are diminished over multiple separations, suggesting the intriguing possibility that the aversive memories may be reduced in these animals and, therefore, less pervasive.

In the animals showing high frequencies of anxious behaviors, CSF 5-HIAA concentrations also were higher than in the low anxious animals. Previously, impaired central nervous system serotonin functioning, as measured by low 5-HIAA levels, have been linked to impulsive behaviors (Higley & Linnoila, 1997a), whereas anxiety disorders show a more complex relationship with the serotonergic system (for review see, Charney & Drevets, 2002), and variations in the serotonin transporter gene have been associated with extreme shy temperament in children (Arbelle et al., 2003). The link between behavioral inhibition and impulsive temperament, and the hypothesized relation to serotonin systems, has not received much attention. However, the data presented above suggest a common serotonin link between these seemingly two polar extremes. Perhaps increased serotonin activity in highly inhibited macaques contributes to the observed behavioral manifestations of increased withdrawal behaviors and decreased social behaviors.

Studies of monkeys with low levels of CSF 5-HIAA and increased cortisol show that they exhibit impulsive behaviors, violence, increased alcohol consumption and reduced social interactions, and when low 5-HIAA is present in maternally-deprived animals, these animals are more likely to engage in inept social and aggressive behaviors than mother-reared animals (Higley et al., 1996b). In contrast, high CSF 5-HIAA concentrations coupled with attenuated cortisol response may be associated with anxiety and increased risk of developing anxious psychopathology.

Behavior, Psychopathology, and Brain

Alterations in behavior, early life experiences, and vulnerability to psychopathology are associated with altered anatomy and function of brain regions implicated in emotional behavior and psychopathology. Because patients with psychiatric disorders have a higher incidence of negative early life events and trauma, systems that are altered by negative environmental events are potentially important in the development of these disorders. The structure and functional integrity of these brain regions, as well as the expression and availability of neurotransmitters and their receptors, are affected by stress and glucocorticoids, and primate studies help illustrate these effects on neurobiology and behavior. Brain regions that are implicated in stress-induced changes of neuropeptide and neurotransmitter systems include the hippocampus, striatum, hypothalamus, and amygdala, and these regions are also implicated in the pathophysiology of mood and anxiety disorders. Prefrontal cortical regions, particularly medial and orbitofrontal areas important for emotional cognition and behavior, may also be affected by stress-induced or innate chronic cortisol elevations. Taken together, this suggests that neuropeptide and neurotransmitter systems are of importance.

Multiple examples of affected neurotransmitter and peptide systems exist. The reciprocity of NPY and CRH, described previously in rodents (Heilig et al., 1994), has implications for the role of early life experience in the development of psychiatric diagnoses. NPY activity may be negatively correlated with the CRH system, operating as an anxiolytic brain peptide (Heilig et al., 1993; Heilig et al., 1994). Reductions in NPY have been reported in depressed patients (Westrin et al., 1999; Widdowson et al., 1992), and lithium treatment can increase experimentally reduced NPY concentrations in rats (Husum & Mathe, 2002). We reported a similar relation between CRH and NPY in both mother-reared and peer-reared nonhuman primates (Gabry et al., unpublished).

Chronically elevated cortisol concentrations, such as that demonstrated in highly anxious animals and in some extremely behaviorally inhibited children, can lead to changes in physiology, neurobiology, and cognition (Sapolsky, 2000). These effects can include fatigue, depression, apathy, and impaired concentration (Schmidt et al., 1999a; Starkman & Schteingart, 1981; Wolkowitz et al., 1990). Within the context of repeated stress, long-term

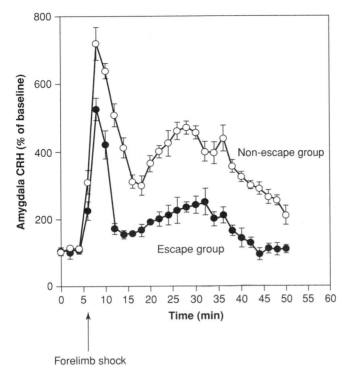

Figure 11.5. Effects of a forelimb shock on amygdala CRH in escape group (black symbols) and the nonescape group (white symbols) animals. Data are exhibited as percent change (mean ± SE) from baseline. Baseline CRH were 63.8 ± 14.9 and 89.5 ± 19.4 pg/ml for the escape and nonescape groups, respectively. (From Cook, 2002).

consequences include neural atrophy in the hippocampus (McEwen, 1998; Sapolsky et al., 1990b) and medial prefrontal cortex (Wellman, 2001), and compromised immune system function (Sapolsky, 2000).

Much evidence suggests that the amygdala is the primary neural site of action for the facilatory effects of glucocorticoids (McGaugh, 2000; Roozendaal et al., 2001), and numerous studies illustrate the importance of the amygdala on emotional cognition and emotional behavior. For example, glucocorticoids implanted into the amygdala facilitate anxiety responses in rats (Shepard & Barron, 2000), while stimulation of the amygdala produces freezing behavior in animals, and feelings of fear and anxiety in humans (Chapman et al., 1954; Gloor, 1992; LeDoux, 1996). Experience shapes the expression of neuropeptides in the amygdala (see Figure 11.5).

Human PET and fMRI imaging studies show that neural responses to facial expressions of sadness and fear involve the amygdala, and selective attention to a negative facial expression results in cortisol elevation, when compared to perception of neutral facial expressions (van Honk et al., 2000; van Honk et al., 2002). Amygdala lesions result in impaired processing of emotionally expressive faces (Adolphs et al., 1994).

Consequences of dendritic reshaping in the hippocampus and medial prefrontal cortex (Leverenz et al., 1999; Sapolsky et al., 1990a; Wellman, 2001), changes in 5-HT1A receptor mRNA expression (Meijer & de Kloet, 1994), and altered CRH mRNA expression in the amygdala (Makino et al., 1994a; Watts & Sanchez-Watts, 1995) as a result of chronically elevated glucocorticoid concentrations have implications for emotional perception, memory, and behavior. Therefore, those individuals who spend more time in heightened anxious and fearful states, such as behaviorally inhibited children, may be at risk for altered neural development, which may contribute to their higher risk for developing anxiety disorders. This outcome is further suggested by a recent study of adults who were categorized as behaviorally inhibited during infancy, who had greater hemodynamic responses in amygdala bilaterally when viewing novel stimuli when compared to amygdala responses of those who were behaviorally categorized as uninhibited in infancy (Schwartz et al., 2003).

In healthy humans, memory for emotional scenes rated as "intense" correlated positively with amygdala activation (Canli et al., 2000). The mechanism through which glucocorticoids facilitate emotional memory consolidation and attention toward emotional information (Buchanan & Lovallo, 2001; McGaugh, 2000) is through an interaction between the basolateral amygdala, basal ganglia, and hippocampus (Roozendaal, 2000). Norepinephrine also contributes, and acts in concert with glucocorticoids within the amygdala during this process (Cahill et al., 1994; McGaugh, 2000; Quirarte et al., 1997).

The amygdala is functionally connected to prefrontal cortical areas, and nonhuman primate studies have linked prefrontal activation, CSF CRH concentrations, and temperament. This finding is important for those interested in the development of psychopathology because it ties together findings from experimental rat studies and developmental human studies of anxious temperament. In rats, altered CRH expression in the amygdala results from stress and early life deprivation, and is associated with anxious or fearful behaviors (Caldji et al., 1998; Levine, 2001). In humans, extremely shy and socially wary children exhibited elevated morning salivary cortisol (Schmidt et al., 1997) and, at baseline, greater relative right frontal EEG activation compared with other non-shy children (Fox et al., 1995). These temperamentally shy children also exhibited a greater increase in right, but not left, frontal EEG activity and heart rate in response to social challenge and displayed a relative lower decrease from baseline levels on salivary cortisol reactivity measures (Schmidt et al., 1999b). A nonhuman primate study linked these and similar findings by showing CSF CRH concentrations are elevated and stable over time in

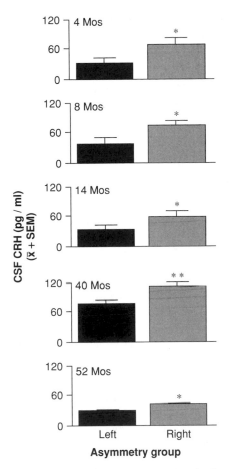

Figure 11.6. CSF CRH concentrations in the extreme left compared to the extreme right frontal animals at 4, 8, 14, 40, and 52 months of age. $**p < 0.01$, $*p < 0.05$. (From Kalin et al., 2000).

monkeys with extreme right frontal activation (see Figure 11.6; Kalin et al., 2000). In addition, greater right frontal electrical activity is a stable character-istic in nonhuman primates, is associated with increased freezing responses, and is correlated with elevated cortisol concentrations (Kalin et al., 1998).

CONCLUSION

These findings suggest that neural systems associated with emotional percep-tion, memory, and regulation are implicated in anxious temperament. The findings associated with this temperamental characteristic implicate the neu-roendocrine system, the amygdala in particular, and monoamine systems, as well as prefrontal cortical functioning. Individuals who spend an inordinate time in heightened anxious states may be at risk for altered neural development in limbic and cortical regions, which may contribute to a higher risk for developing anxiety disorders in adulthood (Biederman et al., 2001; Rosenbaum et al., 2000; Van Ameringen et al., 1998). Temperamental shyness is more likely to manifest in children whose parents are diagnosed with social phobia and depression (Rosenbaum et al., 2000).

References

Adolphs, R., Tranel, D., Damasio, H., & Damasio, A. (1994). Impaired recognition of emotion in facial expressions following bilateral damage to the human amygdala. *Nature, 372,* 669–672.

Arbelle, S., Benjamin, J., Golin, M., Kremer, I., Belmaker, R. H., & Ebstein, R. P. (2003). Relation of shyness in grade school children to the genotype for the long form of the serotonin transporter promoter region polymorphism. *American Journal of Psychiatry, 160,* 671–676.

Arborelius, L., Owens, M. J., Plotsky, P. M., & Nemeroff, C. B. (1999). The role of corticotropin-releasing factor in depression and anxiety disorders. *Journal of Endocrinology, 160,* 1–12.

Barna, I., Balint, E., Baranyi, J., Bakos, N., Makara, G. B., & Haller, J. (2003). Gender-specific effect of maternal deprivation on anxiety and corticotropin-releasing hormone mRNA expression in rats. *Brain Research Bulletin, 62,* 85–91.

Bayart, F., Hayashi, K. T., Faull, K. F., Barchas, J. D., & Levine, S. (1990). Influence of maternal proximity on behavioral and physiological responses to separation in infant rhesus monkeys (Macaca mulatta). *Behavioral Neuroscience, 104,* 98–107.

Biederman, J., Hirshfeld-Becker, D. R., Rosenbaum, J. F., Herot, C., Friedman, D., Snidman, N., Kagan, J., & Faraone, S. V. (2001). Further evidence of association between behavioral inhibition and social anxiety in children. *American Journal of Psychiatry, 158,* 1673–1679.

Bouzat, C., & Barrantes, F. J. (1996). Modulation of muscle nicotinic acetylcholine receptors by the glucocorticoid hydrocortisone: Possible allosteric mechanism of channel blockade. *Journal of Biological Chemistry, 271,* 25835–25841.

Brake, W. G., Noel, M. B., Boksa, P., & Gratton, A. (1997). Influence of perinatal factors on the nucleus accumbens dopamine response to repeated stress during adulthood: An electrochemical study in the rat. *Neuroscience, 77,* 1067–1076.

Breese, G. R., Smith, R. D., Mueller, R. A., Howard, J. L., Prange, A. J., Jr., Lipton, M. A., Young, L. D., McKinney, W. T., & Lewis, J. K. (1973). Induction of adrenal catecholamine synthesizing enzymes following mother-infant separation. *Nature, New Biology, 246,* 94–96.

Brooke, S. M., de Haas-Johnson, A. M., Kaplan, J. R., & Sapolsky, R. M. (1994). Characterization of mineralocorticoid and glucocorticoid receptors in primate brain. *Brain Research, 637,* 303–307.

Brunson, K. L., Avishai-Eliner, S., Hatalski, C. G., & Baram, T. Z. (2001). Neurobiology of the stress response early in life: Evolution of a concept and the role of corticotropin releasing hormone. *Molecular Psychiatry, 6,* 647–656.

Buchanan, T. W., & Lovallo, W. R. (2001). Enhanced memory for emotional material following stress-level cortisol treatment in humans. *Psychoneuroendocrinology 26*, 307–317.

Byrne, G., & Suomi, S. (2002). Cortisol reactivity and its relation to homecage behavior and personality ratings in tufted capuchin (Cebus apella) juveniles from birth to six years of age. *Psychoneuroendocrinology, 27*, 139–154.

Cahill, L., Haier, R. J., Fallon, J., Alkire, M. T., Tang, C., Keator, D., Wu, J., & McGaugh J. L. (1996). Amygdala activity at encoding correlated with long-term, free recall of emotional information. *Proceedings of the National Academy of Sciences of the United States of America, 93*, 8016–8021.

Cahill, L., Prins, B., Weber, M., & McGaugh J. L. (1994). Beta-adrenergic activation and memory for emotional events. *Nature, 371*, 702–704.

Caldji, C., Tannenbaum, B., Sharma, S., Francis, D., Plotsky, P. M., & Meaney M. J. (1998). Maternal care during infancy regulates the development of neural systems mediating the expression of fearfulness in the rat. *Proceedings of the National Academy of Sciences of the United States of America, 95*, 5335–5340.

Cameron, O. G., Addy, R. O., & Malitz, D. (1985). Effects of ACTH and prednisone on mood, incidence and time of onset. *International Journal Psychiatry in Medicine, 15*, 213–223.

Canli, T., Zhao, Z., Brewer, J., Gabrieli, J. D., & Cahill, L. (2000). Event-related activation in the human amygdala associates with later memory for individual emotional experience. *Journal of Neuroscience, 20*, RC99.

Chapman, W., Schroeder, H., Guyer, G., Brazier, M., Fager, C., Poppen, J., Solomon, H., & Yakolev, P. (1954). Physiological evidence concerning the importance of the amygdaloid nuclear region in the integration of circulating function and emotion in man. *Science, 129*, 949–950.

Charney, D., & Drevets, W. (2002). The neurobiological basis of anxiety disorders. In K. Davis, D. Charney, J. Coyle, & C. Nemeroff (Eds.), *Psychopharmacology: The fifth generation of progress* (pp. 901–930). New York: Lippincott, Williams & Wilkins.

Clarke, A. S. (1993). Social rearing effects on HPA axis activity over early development and in response to stress in rhesus monkeys. *Developmental Psychobiology, 26*, 433–446.

Cook, C. J. (2002). Glucocorticoid feedback increases the sensitivity of the limbic system to stress. *Physiology and Behavior, 75*, 455–464.

Coplan, J. D., Andrews, M. W., Rosenblum, L. A., Owens, M. J., Friedman, S., Gorman, J. M., & Nemeroff, C. B. (1996). Persistent elevations of cerebrospinal fluid concentrations of corticotropin-releasing factor in adult nonhuman primates exposed to early-life stressors: Implications for the pathophysiology of mood and anxiety disorders. *Proceedings of the National Academy of Sciences of the United States of America, 93*, 1619–1623.

Corodimas, K. P., LeDoux, J. E., Gold, P. W., & Schulkin, J. (1994). Corticosterone potentiation of conditioned fear in rats. *Annals of the New York Academy of Sciences, 746*, 392–393.

Dallman, M. F., Strack, A. M., Akana, S. F., Bradbury, M. J., Hanson, E. S., Scribner, K. A., & Smith, M. (1993). Feast and famine: Critical role of glucocorticoids with insulin in daily energy flow. *Frontiers in Neuroendocrinology, 14*, 303–347.

Davis, M., & Whalen, P. J. (2001). The amygdala, vigilance and emotion. *Molecular Psychiatry, 6*, 13–34.

de Quervain, D. J., Roozendaal, B., & McGaugh, J. L. (1998). Stress and glucocorticoids impair retrieval of long-term spatial memory. *Nature, 394*, 787–790.

Drevets, W. C., Price, J. L., Bardgett, M. E., Reich, T., Todd, R. D., & Raichle, M. E. (2002). Glucose metabolism in the amygdala in depression: Relationship to diagnostic subtype and plasma cortisol levels. *Pharmacology, Biochemistry and Behavior, 71*, 431–447.

Drevets, W. C., Price, J., Simpson, J., Todd, R., Reich, T., & Raichle, M. (1996). State- and trait-like neuroimaging abnormalities in depression: Effects of antidepressant treatment. *Society for Neuroscience Abstract, 22*, 266.

Drevets, W. C., Price, J. L., Simpson, J. R., Todd, R. D., Reich, T., Bardgett, M. E., & Raichle, M. E. (1997). Amygdala hypermetabolism in unipolar and bipolar depression with plasma cortisol. *Society for Neuroscience Abstract, 23*, 1407.

Eriksen, H. R., Olff, M., Murison, R., & Ursin, H. (1999). The time dimension in stress responses: Relevance for survival and health. *Psychiatry Research, 85*, 39–50.

Fischer, H., Andersson, J. L., Furmark, T., & Fredrikson, M. (2000). Fear conditioning and brain activity: A positron emission tomography study in humans. *Behavioral Neuroscience, 114*, 671–680.

Fox, N. A., Rubin, K. H., Calkins, S. D., Marshall, T. R., Coplan, R. J., Porges, S. W., Long, J. M. & Stewart, S. (1995). Frontal activation asymmetry and social competence at four years of age. *Child Development, 66*, 1770–1784.

Fumagalli, F., Jones, S. R., Caron, M. G., Seidler, F. J., & Slotkin, T. A. (1996). Expression of mRNA coding for the serotonin transporter in aged vs. young rat brain: Differential effects of glucocorticoids. *Brain Research, 719*, 225–228.

Fuxe, K., Wikstrom, A., Okret, S., Agnati, L., Harfstrand, A., Yu, Z., Granholm, L., Zoli, M., Vale, W., & Gustafsson, J. (1985). Mapping of glucocorticoid receptor immunoreactive neurons in the rat tel- and diencephalon using a monoclonal antibody against rat liver glucocorticoid receptor. *Endocrinology, 117*, 1803–1812.

Gabry, K. E., Erickson, K., Champoux, M., Chrousos, G. P., Schulkin, J., Gold, P. W. & Higley, J. D. (unpublished data). *Increased CSF corticotropin-releasing hormone and decreased neuropeptide Y concentrations in response to psychosocial stress.*

Gloor, P. (1992). Role of the amygdala in temporal lobe epilepsy. J. Aggleton. (Ed.), *The amygdala: Neurobiological aspects of emotion, memory and mental dysfunction.* (pp. 339–352). New York: Wiley-Liss.

Goldstein, L. E., Rasmusson, A. M., Bunney, B. S., & Roth, R. H. (1996). Role of the amygdala in the coordination of behavioral, neuroendocrine, and prefrontal cortical monoamine responses to psychological stress in the rat. *Journal of Neuroscience, 16*, 4787–4798.

Granger, D. A., Weisz, J. R., & Kauneckis D. (1994). Neuroendocrine reactivity, internalizing behavior problems, and control-related cognitions in clinic-referred children and adolescents. *Journal of Abnormal Psychology, 103*, 267–276.

Gunnar, M. (1994). Psychoendocrine studies of temperament and stress in early childhood: Expanding current models. In T. Wachs (Ed.), *Temperament: Individual differences at the interface of biology and behavior* (pp. 175–198). Washington, DC: American Psychological Association.

Habib, K. E., Weld, K. P., Rice, K. C., Pushkas, J., Champoux, M., Listwak, S., Webster, E. L., Atkinson, A. J., Schulkin, J., Contoreggi, C., Chrousos, G. P., McCann,

S. M., Suomi, S. J., Higley, J. D., & Gold, P. W. (2000). Oral administration of a corticotropin-releasing hormone receptor antagonist significantly attenuates behavioral, neuroendocrine, and autonomic responses to stress in primates. *Proceedings of the National Academy of Sciences of the United States of America, 97*, 6079–6084.

Heilig, M., Koob, G. F., Ekman, R., & Britton, K. T. (1994). Corticotropin-releasing factor and neuropeptide Y: role in emotional integration. *Trends in Neuroscience, 17*, 80–85.

Heilig, M., McLeod, S., Brot, M., Heinrichs, S. C., Menzaghi, F., Koob, G. F., & Britton, K. T. (1993). Anxiolytic-like action of neuropeptide Y: Mediation by Y1 receptors in amygdala, and dissociation from food intake effects. *Neuropsychopharmacology, 8*, 357–363.

Heim, C., Owens, M. J., Plotsky, P. M., & Nemeroff, C. B. (1997). Persistent changes in corticotropin-releasing factor systems due to early life stress: Relationship to the pathophysiology of major depression and post-traumatic stress disorder. *Psychopharmacology Bulletin, 33*, 185–192.

Higley, J. D., & Bennett, A. J. (1999). Central nervous system serotonin and personality as variables contributing to excessive alcohol consumption in non-human primates. *Alcohol and Alcoholism, 34*, 402–418.

Higley, J. D., Hasert, M. F., Suomi, S. J., & Linnoila, M. (1991). Nonhuman primate model of alcohol abuse: Effects of early experience, personality, and stress on alcohol consumption. *Proceedings of the National Academy of Sciences of the United States of America, 88*, 7261–7265.

Higley, J. D., Hasert, M., Suomi, S., & Linnoila, M. (1998). The serotonin reuptake inhibitor sertraline reduces excessive alcohol consumption in nonhuman primates: Effect of stress. *Neuropsychopharmacology, 18*, 431–443.

Higley, J. D., & Linnoila, M. (1997a). Low central nervous system serotonergic activity is traitlike and correlates with impulsive behavior. A nonhuman primate model investigating genetic and environmental influences on neurotransmission. *Annals of the New York Academy of Sciences, 836*, 39–56.

Higley, J. D., & Linnoila, M. (1997b). A nonhuman primate model of excessive alcohol intake: Personality and neurobiological parallels of type I- and type II-like alcoholism. *Recent Developments in Alcoholism, 13*, 191–219.

Higley, J. D., & Suomi, S. J. (1989). Temperamental reactivity in non-human primates. In G. A. Kohnstamm, J. E. Bates & M. K. Rothbart (eds.), *Temperament in childhood* (pp. 153–167). New York: John Wiley & Sons.

Higley, J. D., Suomi, S. J., & Linnoila, M. (1992). A longitudinal assessment of CSF monoamine metabolite and plasma cortisol concentrations in young rhesus monkeys. *Biological Psychiatry, 32*, 127–145.

Higley, J. D., Suomi, S. J., & Linnoila M. (1996a). A nonhuman primate model of type II alcoholism? Part 2. Diminished social competence and excessive aggression correlates with low cerebrospinal fluid 5-hydroxyindoleacetic acid concentrations. *Alcoholism: Clinical and Experimental Research, 20*, 643–650.

Higley, J. D., Suomi, S. J., & Linnoila M. (1996b). A nonhuman primate model of type II excessive alcohol consumption? Part 1. Low cerebrospinal fluid 5-hydroxyindoleacetic acid concentrations and diminished social competence correlate with excessive alcohol consumption. *Alcoholism: Clinical and Experimental Research, 20*, 629–642.

Husum, H., & Mathe, A. A. (2002). Early life stress changes concentrations of neuropeptide Y and corticotropin-releasing hormone in adult rat brain: Lithium treatment modifies these changes. *Neuropsychopharmacology, 27*, 756–764.

Iidaka, T., Omori, M., Murata, T., Kosaka, H., Yonekura, Y., Okada, T., & Sadato, N. (2001). Neural interaction of the amygdala with the prefrontal and temporal cortices in the processing of facial expressions as revealed by fMRI. *Journal of Cognitive Neuroscience, 13*, 1035–1047.

Jones, R., Beuving, G., & Blokhuis, H. (1988). Tonic immobility and heterophil/lymphocyte responses of the domestic fowl to corticosterone infusion. *Physiology and Behavior, 42*, 249–253.

Kagan, J., Reznick, J. S., & Snidman, N. (1988). Biological bases of childhood shyness. *Science, 240*, 167–171.

Kagan, J., Snidman, N., & Arcus, D. (1998). Childhood derivatives of high and low reactivity in infancy. *Child Development, 69*, 1483–1493.

Kalin, N. H., Larson, C., Shelton, S. E., & Davidson, R. J. (1998a). Asymmetric frontal brain activity, cortisol, and behavior associated with fearful temperament in rhesus monkeys. *Behavioral Neuroscience, 112*, 286–292.

Kalin, N. H., Shelton, S. E., & Davidson, R. J. (2000). Cerebrospinal fluid corticotropin-releasing hormone levels are elevated in monkeys with patterns of brain activity associated with fearful temperament. *Biological Psychiatry, 47*, 579–585.

Kalin, N. H., Shelton, S. E., Rickman, M., & Davidson, R. J. (1998b). Individual differences in freezing and cortisol in infant and mother rhesus monkeys. *Behavioral Neuroscience, 112*, 251–254.

Kalin, N. H., Takahashi, L. K., & Chen, F. L. (1994). Restraint stress increases corticotropin-releasing hormone mRNA content in the amygdala and paraventricular nucleus. *Brain Research, 656*, 182–186.

Khani, S., & Tayek, J. (2001). Cortisol increases gluconeogenesis in humans: Its role in the metabolic syndrome. *Clinical Science (London), 101*, 739–747.

Koob, G. F. (1999). Stress, corticotropin-releasing factor, and drug addiction. *Annals of the New York Academy of Sciences, 897*, 27–45.

LeDoux, J. (1996). *The emotional brain.* New York: Simon & Schuster.

Lee, Y., & Davis, M. (1997). Role of the hippocampus, the bed nucleus of the stria terminalis, & the amygdala in the excitatory effect of corticotropin-releasing hormone on the acoustic startle reflex. *Journal of Neuroscience, 17*, 6434–6446.

Leverenz, J., Wilkinson, C., Raskind, M., & Peskind, E. (2001). Immunihistochemical localization of glucocorticoid and mineralocorticoid receptors in the primate hippocampus and amygdala. *Society for Neuroscience Abstract*, 708.

Leverenz, J. B., Wilkinson, C. W., Wamble, M., Corbin, S., Grabber, J. E., Raskind, M. A., & Peskind, E. R. (1999). Effect of chronic high-dose exogenous cortisol on hippocampal neuronal number in aged nonhuman primates. *Journal of Neuroscience, 19*, 2356–2361.

Levine, S. (2001). Primary social relationships influence the development of the hypothalamic–pituitary–adrenal axis in the rat. *Physiology and Behavior, 73*, 255–260.

Lupien, S., & McEwen, B. (1998). The acute effects of corticosteroids on cognition, integration of animal and human model studies. *Brain Research Reviews, 24*, 1–27.

Makino, S., Gold, P. W., & Schulkin, J. (1994a). Corticosterone effects on corticotropin-releasing hormone mRNA in the central nucleus of the amygdala and the parvocellular region of the paraventricular nucleus of the hypothalamus. *Brain Research, 640,* 105–112.

Makino, S., Gold, P. W., & Schulkin, J. (1994b). Effects of corticosterone on CRH mRNA and content in the bed nucleus of the stria terminalis: Comparison with the effects in the central nucleus of the amygdala and the paraventricular nucleus of the hypothalamus. *Brain Research, 657,* 141–149.

McEwen, B. (1998). Protective and damaging effects of stress mediators. *New England Journal of Medicine, 338,* 171–179.

McGaugh, J. L. (2000). Memory–a century of consolidation. *Science, 287,* 248–251.

McKinney, W. T. (1984). Animal models of depression: An overview. *Psychiatric Developments, 2,* 77–96.

Meaney, M. J., Diorio, J., Francis, D., Widdowson, J., LaPlante, P., Caldji, C., Sharma, S., Seckl, J. R., & Plotsky, P. M. (1996). Early environmental regulation of forebrain glucocorticoid receptor gene expression: Implications for adrenocortical responses to stress. *Developmental Neuroscience, 18,* 49–72.

Meijer, O. C., & de Kloet, E. R. (1994). Corticosterone suppresses the expression of 5-HT1A receptor mRNA in rat dentate gyrus. *European Journal of Pharmacology, 266,* 255–61.

Michiels, V., & Cluydts, R. (2001). Neuropsychological functioning in chronic fatigue syndrome: A review. *Acta Psychiatrica Scandinavica, 103,* 84–93.

Mineka, S., & Suomi, S. J. (1978). Social separation in monkeys. *Psychological Bulletin 85,* 1376–1400.

Moghaddam, B., Bolinao, M. L., Stein-Behrens, B., & Sapolsky, R. (1994). Glucocorticoids mediate the stress-induced extracellular accumulation of glutamate. *Brain Research, 655,* 251–254.

Patel, P. D., Lopez, J. F., Lyons, D. M., Burke, S., Wallace, M., & Schatzberg, A. F. (2000). Glucocorticoid and mineralocorticoid receptor mRNA expression in squirrel monkey brain. *Journal of Psychiatric Research, 34,* 383–392.

Patterson, T., Zavosh, A., Schenk, J., Wilkinson, C., & Figlewicz, D. (1997). Acute corticosterone incubation in vitro inhibits the function of the dopamine transporter in nucleus accumbens but not striatum of the rat brain. *Society for Neuroscience Abstract. 23,* 693.

Plihal, W., & Born, J. (1999). Memory consolidation in human sleep depends on inhibition of glucocorticoid release. *Neuroreport, 10,* 2741–2747.

Plihal, W., Krug, R., Pietrowsky, R., Fehm, H. L., & Born, J. (1996). Corticosteroid receptor mediated effects on mood in humans. *Psychoneuroendocrinology, 21,* 515–523.

Plotsky, P. M., & Meaney, M. J. (1993). Early, postnatal experience alters hypothalamic corticotropin-releasing factor (CRF) mRNA, median eminence CRF content and stress-induced release in adult rats. *Brain Research, Molecular Brain Research 18,* 195–200.

Price, J. L. (1999). Prefrontal cortical networks related to visceral function and mood. *Annals of the New York Academy of Sciences, 877,* 383–396.

Quirarte, G. L., Roozendaal, B., & McGaugh, J. L. (1997). Glucocorticoid enhancement of memory storage involves noradrenergic activation in the basolateral amygdala. *Proceedings of the National Academy of Sciences of the United States of America, 94,* 14048–14053.

Reul, J., & de Kloet, E. (1985). Two receptor systems for corticosterone in rat brain: Microdistribution and differential occupation. *Endocrinology, 117*, 2505–2511.

Roozendaal, B. (2000). 1999 Curt P. Richter award. Glucocorticoids and the regulation of memory consolidation. *Psychoneuroendocrinology, 25*, 213–238.

Roozendaal, B., de Quervain, D. J., Ferry, B., Setlow, B., & McGaugh, J. L. (2001). Basolateral amygdala-nucleus accumbens interactions in mediating glucocorticoid enhancement of memory consolidation. *Journal of Neuroscience 21*, 2518–2525.

Roozendaal, B., & McGaugh, J. L. (1997). Glucocorticoid receptor agonist and antagonist administration into the basolateral but not central amygdala modulates memory storage. *Neurobiology of Learning and Memory, 67*, 176–179.

Rosenbaum, J. F., Biederman, J., Bolduc-Murphy, E. A., Faraone, S. V., Chaloff, J., Hirshfeld, D. R., & Kagan, J. (1993). Behavioral inhibition in childhood: A risk factor for anxiety disorders. *Harvard Review of Psychiatry, 1*, 2–16.

Rosenbaum, J. F., Biederman, J., Hirshfeld-Becker, D. R., Kagan, J., Snidman, N., Friedman, D., Nineberg, A., Gallery, D. J., & Faraone, S. V. (2000). A controlled study of behavioral inhibition in children of parents with panic disorder and depression. *American Journal of Psychiatry, 157*, 2002–2010.

Rots, N. Y., de Jong, J., Workel, J. O., Levine, S., Cools, A. R., & De Kloet, E. R. (1996). Neonatal maternally deprived rats have as adults elevated basal pituitary-adrenal activity and enhanced susceptibility to apomorphine. *Journal of Neuroendocrinology, 8*, 501–506.

Sanchez, M. M., Young, L. J., Plotsky, P. M., & Insel, T. R. (1999). Autoradiographic and in situ hybridization localization of corticotropin-releasing factor 1 and 2 receptors in nonhuman primate brain. *Journal of Comparative Neurology, 408*, 365–77.

Sanchez, M. M., Young, L. J., Plotsky, P. M., & Insel, T. R. (2000). Distribution of corticosteroid receptors in the rhesus brain: Relative absence of glucocorticoid receptors in the hippocampal formation. *Journal of Neuroscience, 20*, 4657–4668.

Sapolsky, R. M. (2000). Glucocorticoids and hippocampal atrophy in neuropsychiatric disorders. *Archives of General Psychiatry, 57*, 925–35.

Sapolsky, R. M., Uno, H., Rebert, C. S., & Finch, C. E. (1990). Hippocampal damage associated with prolonged glucocorticoid exposure in primates. *Journal of Neuroscience, 10*, 2897–2902.

Sarrieau, A., Dussaillant, M., Agid, F., Philibert, D., Agid, Y., & Rostene, W. (1986). Autoradiographic localization of glucocorticoid and progesterone binding sites in the human post-mortem brain. *Journal of Steroid Biochemistry, 25*, 717–721.

Sarrieau, A., Dussaillant, M., Sapolsky, R. M., Aitken, D. H., Olivier, A., Lal, S., Rostene, W. H., Quirion, R., & Meaney, M. J. (1988). Glucocorticoid binding sites in human temporal cortex. *Brain Research, 442*, 157–160.

Sawchenko, P. E., Imaki, T., Potter, E., Kovacs, K., Imaki, J., & Vale, W. (1993). The functional neuroanatomy of corticotropin-releasing factor. *Ciba Foundation Symposium, 172*, 5–21.

Schmidt, L. A., Fox, N. A., Goldberg, M. C., Smith, C. C., & Schulkin, J. (1999a). Effects of acute prednisone administration on memory, attention and emotion in healthy human adults. *Psychoneuroendocrinology, 24*, 461–483.

Schmidt, L. A., Fox, N. A., Rubin, K. H., Sternberg, E. M., Gold, P. W., Smith, C. C., & Schulkin, J. (1997). Behavioral and neuroendocrine responses in shy children. *Developmental Psychobiology, 30*, 127–140.

Schmidt, L. A., Fox, N. A., Schulkin, J., & Gold, P. W. (1999b). Behavioral and psychophysiological correlates of self-presentation in temperamentally shy children. *Developmental Psychobiology, 35,* 119–135.

Schneider, M. L., Clarke, A. S., Kraemer, G. W., Roughton, E. C., Lubach, G. R., Rimm-Kaufman, S., Schmidt, D., & Ebert, M. (1998). Prenatal stress alters brain biogenic amine levels in primates. *Developmental Psychobiology, 10,* 427–40.

Schulkin, J. (1999). *The neuroendocrine regulation of behavior.* New York: Cambridge University Press.

Schwartz, C. E., Wright, C. I., Shin, L. M., Kagan, J., & Rauch, S. L. (2003). Inhibited and uninhibited infants grown up: Adult amygdalar response to novelty. *Science 300,* 1952–1953.

Seckl, J. R., Dickson, K. L., Yates, C., & Fink, G. (1991). Distribution of glucocorticoid and mineralocorticoid receptor messenger RNA expression in human postmortem hippocampus. *Brain Research, 561,* 332–337.

Shannon, C., Champoux, M., & Suomi S. J. (1998). Rearing condition and plasma cortisol in rhesus monkey infants. *American Journal of Primatology, 46,* 311–321.

Shepard, J. D., & Barron, K. W. (2000). Corticosterone delivery to the amygdala increases corticotropin-releasing factor mRNA in the central amygdaloid nucleus and anxiety-like behavior. *Brain Research, 861,* 288–295.

Starkman, M. N., Giordani, B., Berent, S., Schork, M. A., & Schteingart, D. E. (2001). Elevated cortisol levels in Cushing's disease are associated with cognitive decrements. *Psychosomatic Medicine, 63,* 985–993.

Starkman, M. N., & Schteingart, D. E. (1981). Neuropsychiatric manifestations of patients with Cushing's syndrome: Relationship to cortisol and adrenocorticotropic hormone levels. *Archives of Internal Medicine, 141,* 215–219.

Strome, E. M., Wheler, G. H., Higley, J. D., Loriaux, D. L., Suomi, S. J., & Doudet, D. J. (2002). Intracerebroventricular corticotropin-releasing factor increases limbic glucose metabolism and has social context-dependent behavioral effects in nonhuman primates. *Proceedings of the National Academy of Sciences of the United States of America, 99,* 15749–15754.

Suomi, S. (1991). Primate separation models of affective disorders. In J. Madden,IV (Ed.), *Neurobiology of learning, emotion and affect.* (pp. 195–214). New York: Raven Press.

Suomi, S. J., Eisele, C. D., Grady, S. A., & Harlow, H. F. (1975). Depressive behavior in adult monkeys following separation from family environment. *Journal of Abnormal Psychology, 84,* 576–578.

Swanson, L. W., & Simmons, D. M. (1989). Differential steroid hormone and neural influences on peptide mRNA levels in CRH cells of the paraventricular nucleus: A Hybridization histochemical study in the rat. *Journal of Comparative Neurology, 285,* 413–435.

Van Ameringen, M., Mancini, C., & Oakman, J. M. (1998). The relationship of behavioral inhibition and shyness to anxiety disorder. *Journal of Nervous and Mental Disorders, 186,* 425–431.

van Honk, J., Hermans, E. J., d'Alfonso, A. A., Schutter, D. J., van Doornen, L., & de Haan, E. H. (2002). A left-prefrontal lateralized, sympathetic mechanism directs attention towards social threat in humans: Evidence from repetitive transcranial magnetic stimulation. *Neuroscience Letters, 319,* 99–102.

van Honk, J., Tuiten, A., van den Hout, M., Koppeschaar, H., Thijssen, J., de Haan, E., & Verbaten, R. (2000). Conscious and preconscious selective attention to social threat: Different neuroendocrine response patterns. *Psychoneuroendocrinology, 25*, 577–591.

Watts, A. G., & Sanchez-Watts, G. (1995). Region-specific regulation of neuropeptide mRNAs in rat limbic forebrain neurones by aldosterone and corticosterone. *Journal of Physiology, 484*, 721–736.

Wellman, C. L. (2001). Dendritic reorganization in pyramidal neurons in medial prefrontal cortex after chronic corticosterone administration. *Journal of Neurobiology, 49*, 245–253.

Westrin, A., Ekman, R., van den Hout, M., Koppeschaar, H., Thijssen, J., de Haan, E., & Verbaten, R. (1999). Alterations of corticotropin releasing hormone (CRH) and neuropeptide Y (NPY) plasma levels in mood disorder patients with a recent suicide attempt. *European Neuropsychopharmacology, 9*, 205–211.

Widdowson, P. S., Ordway, G. A., & Halaris, A. E. (1992). Reduced neuropeptide Y concentrations in suicide brain. *Journal of Neurochemistry, 59*, 73–80.

Wingfield, J. C., & Grimm, A. S. (1977). Seasonal changes in plasma cortisol, testosterone and oestradiol-17beta-in the plaice: Pleuronectes platessa L. *General and Comparative Endocrinology, 31*, 1–11.

Wolkowitz, O. M., Reus, V. I., Weingartner, H., Thompson, K., Breier, A., Doran, A., Rubinow, D., & Pickar, D. (1990). Cognitive effects of corticosteroids. *American Journal of Psychiatry, 147*, 1297–1303.

12   Neuroendocrine Measures in Developmental Research

Megan R. Gunnar and Nicole M. Talge

INTRODUCTION

Maladaptive responses to stress are components of both the etiology and expression of many psychiatric disorders (Anisman & Zacharko, 1982; Walker, Walder, & Reynolds, 2001). In addition, the neurobiological systems involved in activating and regulating stress-sensitive physiological systems are believed to contribute to individual differences in emotionality or temperament (Kagan, Reznick, & Snidman, 1988; Rothbart, Derryberry, & Posner, 1994). Finally, social regulation of stress physiology during development is hypothesized, based on animal studies, to regulate the expression of genes involved in the development of the neural substrates of stress and emotion (Meaney, 2001). This process, in turn, is expected to contribute to vulnerability stressors and thus to mental and physical health over the individual's life course (Sanchez, Ladd, & Plotsky, 2001). For all of these reasons, developmental researchers are interested in assessing the reactivity and regulation of stress biology in studies of children and adolescents.

Much of the focus of this work has been on the limbic-hypothalamic-pituitary-adrenocortical (LHPA) system, often considered one of the two major arms of the mammalian stress system. The LHPA system produces steroid hormones termed glucocorticoids (GCs). The predominant GC in humans is cortisol. The development of competitive binding assays in the 1960s allowed measurement of cortisol in urine and blood (Murphy, 1967). Soon afterwards, the first studies of cortisol in children appeared (e.g., Anders et al., 1970). However, the immense challenge of collecting urine reliably and the invasiveness of plasma sampling limited human developmental LHPA research (reviewed in Gunnar, 1986). This changed in the early 1980s when assay techniques were refined to allow the measurement of cortisol and other steroid hormones in small amounts of saliva (Peters, Walker, Riad-Fahmy, &

Hall, 1982). Salivary cortisol reflects the unbound or biologically active fraction of the hormone and is highly correlated with plasma levels (Kirschbaum & Hellhammer, 1989). Largely because of the availability of salivary cortisol assays, the number of child publications increased from fewer than a dozen in the 1970s to nearly that many each month during the last year.

The simplicity and non-invasiveness of salivary cortisol measurement belies the complexity of adequately sampling and interpreting findings using these measures. We have two goals in this chapter. The first goal is to provide researchers with some insight into the neurobiology and physiology of the LHPA system to facilitate accurate assessment and interpretation. The second goal is to provide researchers with at least a rudimentary understanding of how to sample, analyze, and interpret salivary cortisol measures in their research.

Neurobiology of the LHPA System

The LHPA is one of the two principle arms of the mammalian stress system, the other arm being the sympathetic-adrenomedullary or SAM system. Situations that threaten or are perceived to threaten our well-being set into motion cognitive, emotional, and physiological responses orchestrated to foster preservation of the physical and psychological self (Dickerson & Kemeny, 2004). Immediate responses to stressors include mobilization of energy resources, shunting of blood to the heart, muscles, and brain, and narrowing of attentional focus. These responses are supported by basal levels of GCs that are present prior to the onset of the stressor (termed permissive actions of GCs), but do not require activation of the LHPA system in order to occur. Instead, these immediate fight/flight/freeze reactions to stressors are largely orchestrated by the central nervous system (CNS) through increased activity of the locus ceruleus (LC) norepinephrine (NE) system and extra-hypothalamic CRH produced in the central nucleus of the amygdala. The LC-NE and amygdala-corticotropin-releasing hormone (CRH) system operate to orchestrate behavioral and cognitive reactions to stressors and to activate the SAM system (Chrousos & Gold, 1992; Rosen & Schulkin, 1998; Sapolsky, Romero, & Munck, 2000).

Activation and Inhibition
Increases in GCs to acute stressors are instigated by production of CRH and argentine vasopressin (AVP) by cells in the paraventricular nucleus (PVN) of the hypothalamus (see Figure 12.1). Activation of the PVN is the result of a complex interplay of both activating and inhibiting pathways

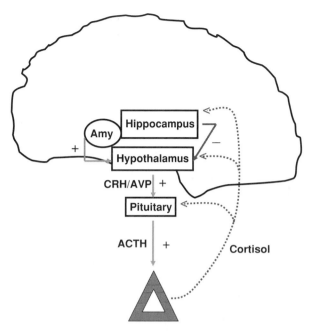

Figure 12.1. Schematic of the limbic-hypothalamic-pituitary-adrenocortical (LHPA) system. Excitatory pathways are shown in green, inhibitory in red. Cells in the paraventricular region of the hypothalamus are stimulated to secrete corticotropin releasing hormone (CRH) and aginine vasopressin (AVP). These substances stimulate cells in the anterior pituitary gland to produce adrenocorticotropic hormone (ACTH). Released into general circulation, ACTH stimulates cells in the adrenal cortex to produce glucocorticoids, primarily cortisol in humans. Pathways from the amygdala (Amy) provide excitatory and from the hippocampus provide inhibitory input to the CRH/AVP producing cells in the hypothalamus. The system is regulated through negative feedback at the level of the hippocampus, hypothalamus, and pituitary. Multiple other pathways (not shown) contribute to excitation and inhibition of the LHPA system, including pathways from the prefrontal, medial, and infralimbic cortex.

(Herman & Cullinan, 1997). Information about systemic or physical stressors (e.g., hypotension, hypoxia, infection) reaches the PVN via the brainstem through afferents originating in the dorsal roots of the autonomic system and the vagus cranial nerves. Limbic centers transmit information to the PVN about processive or psychological stressors via corticolimbic efferent pathways. These pathways converge in the fimbria/fornix, a collection of nerve bundles emanating from the hippocampus, subiculum, and cortical regions. The central amygdala and lateral bed nucleus of the stria terminalis (BNST is sometimes considered an extension of the amygdala) are centrally involved in *activating pathways*. The various nuclei of the amygdala mediate behavioral and autonomic cardiovascular responses to stress indirectly using the BNST or nucleus tractus solitaris (NTS) as relay stations with the fibers terminating two or more steps removed from the PVN. *Inhibitory influences* are mediated through limbic structures: the ventral subiculum, preoptic area, medial BNST, and cingulated, medial, and prefrontal cortex. Damage to these structures or their major outflow pathways increases PVN CRH expression and thus GC increases to processive or psychological stressors (Herman, Tasker, Ziegler, & Cullinan, 2002).

From the PVN, CRH and AVP reach cells in the anterior pituitary gland that produce adrenocorticotropic hormone (ACTH). ACTH, in turn, is released into general circulation where it stimulates cells in the cortex of the adrenal glands to produce and release GCs (cortisol in humans). From stimulation at the level of the PVN to peak cortisol levels in plasma takes between 20 and 30 minutes. GCs in circulation enter into the cytoplasm of cells throughout the body and brain where the hormone interacts with its receptors. The activated receptors then enter the nucleus of the cell where they regulate the transcription of genes with GC responsive elements (GREs) in their promoter regions (Sapolsky et al., 2000). Thus, unlike the rapid effects produced by activity of the SAM system, the impact of rising levels of GCs take minutes to hours to develop. Increases in GCs also result in increased production of another steroid hormone, dehydroepiandrosterone (DHEA). This steroid is in the androgen family and as such has anabolic effects (Kroboth et al., 1999). The effects of this steroid are often counter to those of glucocorticoids, and as such, it has been described as "anti-cortisol." There is some belief that the ratio of DHEA to cortisol may be a better index of the likely impacts of GCs on the body; however, there is as yet only a small literature on this in psychoendocrine research and no published studies of associations between behavior and DHEA/cortisol ratios in children (see, however, Granger and Kivlighan, 2003). Thus, research on DHEA will not be reviewed in this chapter.

Receptors

The effects of GCs depend on the type of GC receptor that has been activated by the hormone. There are two GC receptors: MR and GR. Both are responsive to GCs in the brain, while outside the brain, GC effects operate almost exclusively through GR. In the brain, MR have high affinity for GCs, while GR have lower affinity (de Kloet, 1991). What this difference means is that MR become occupied before GR and thus at lower concentrations of GCs in circulation. MR tend to predominate when GCs are low or in basal ranges, while GR tend to become activated (along with MRs) as GCs rise above basal levels or at the peak of the daily GC rhythm (see below). MR and GR mediate different, often opposing, functions. MR-mediated effects tend, on the whole, to promote processes that support physical and mental health, while GR-mediated effects tend to be suppressive (Sapolsky et al., 2000). For example, MR support neural plasticity, fostering learning and memory, while GR reverse the effects of MR, impairing neural plasticity and the processes involved in learning and memory. The suppressive effects of GR, however, are essential for counter-regulating acute responses to stressors. Thus, for example, as a function of immediate responses to stressors, there is an increase in glucose to the brain. GR-mediated mechanisms reduce glucose uptake by neurons. Similarly, immediate responses to stressors support the development of explicit memories of the event, while GR-mediated processes tend to reduce the processes involved in the formation of explicit memories.

Not surprisingly, given this description of the GC time course, receptors, and functions, interpretation of GC (cortisol) levels and patterns of activity is not straightforward. An increase in cortisol that is well within basal levels, and increases the MR-mediated effects of GCs, will be different from an increase in basal levels that results in significant GR activation. Low cortisol levels may be associated with impaired health and ability to respond to stressors if those levels are very low over prolonged periods, resulting in more chronic impairment in MR-mediated effects, but might be associated with good health and capacity to respond to acute stressors if they are only moderately low, resulting in adequate MR occupation. Elevations in cortisol to ranges associated with GR occupancy may be associated with healthy functioning if the stressor is acute and cortisol levels quickly return to baseline, while prolonged elevations may be associated with negative outcomes if they produce prolonged GR occupation.

Diurnal Rhythm

Levels of GCs vary throughout the day under basal or non-stressed conditions. GCs are at their peak around the time of awakening in the morning and at their nadir or lowest point soon after the onset of nighttime sleep (Daly & Evans, 1974). The pattern of early morning peak and evening nadir in GCs can be detected in human children at least as early as the 6th postnatal week, but become more reliable from day to day over the first months of life (Larson, White, Cochran, Donzella, & Gunnar, 1998; Price, Close, & Fielding, 1983). As the child's sleeping and napping pattern becomes more adult-like over the preschool years, diurnal decreases in GCs over the middle portion of the day (e.g., 10 A.M. to 4 P.M.) begin to be detected with regularity (Watamura, Donzella, Kertes, & Gunnar, 2004).

At the peak of the daily cycle, GC levels are such that in the brain both GR and MR are occupied, while at the nadir GR and MR are unoccupied. Consistent with evidence that the combination of MR and acute GR occupation is invigorating, stimulating appetite for carbohydrates and interest in exploration (de Kloet, 1991; Plihal, Krug, Pietrowsky, Fehm, & Born, 1996), the early morning peak in GCs supports the ability to enthusiastically embrace the coming day. Consistent with evidence that a healthy diurnal rhythm in GCs is disturbed by failure to achieve a nadir low enough to clear MR of GC occupation (Bradbury, Akana, & Dallman, 1994), adults with major depression often exhibit both elevations in GCs late in the day and a loss of a clear diurnal cortisol rhythm (Johnson, Kamilaris, Chrousos, & Gold, 1992).

Negative Feedback

GCs are self-regulating in the sense that elevations that stimulate GR result in inhibitory signals to the PVN that turn off production of CRH (termed negative feedback). The efficiency of negative feedback varies with the time at which a stressor occurs during the diurnal rhythm. At the peak of the rhythm, it takes smaller increases in GCs to stimulate GR-mediated negative feedback control, thus tending to result in smaller and shorter lived increases in GCs to stressors. Near the nadir of the rhythm, GC increases tend to be larger (Dallman et al., 1992; Dickerson & Kemeny, 2004). Negative feedback regulation of the GC response to acute stressors also may be linked to the robustness of an individual's diurnal pattern of GC production. Elevated GC levels near the nadir of the GC rhythm are associated, in animals, with sluggish feedback regulation of the GC stress response (Engeland et al., 1977; Jacobson et al., 1988). Conversely, a robust diurnal rhythm (larger amplitude in the cycle) appears to be associated with more rapid mobilization of both the SAM and LHPA response to acute stressors (Smyth et al., 1998).

Although studies conducted late in the day may be more capable of detecting reactivity of the system to stressors, studies of basal levels conducted earlier in the day may be more likely to detect stable and heritable trait components of the system. Several studies using latent state-trait modeling procedures on unstimulated salivary cortisol samples have shown larger trait components for samples collected early in the morning relative to those collected late in the day (Kirschbaum et al., 1990; Shirtcliff, Granger, Booth, & Johnson, 2005). Similarly, estimates of heritability are higher for samples collected at times corresponding to those when trait components have been shown to be higher (Bartels, de Geus, Kirschbaum, & Boomsma, 2003). All of these findings indicate that it is critical to carefully control time of day in research using GC measures.

Plasma, Urinary, and Salivary Cortisol Measures

Once GCs are secreted into circulation they bind to proteins. One in particular, termed cortisol-binding globulin (CBG), binds cortisol with high affinity. As a result, most GCs in circulation are bound and unable to enter cells and produce biological effects (Riad-Fahmy, Read, & Hughes, 1979). Binding globulins are low in newborns and very young infants, thus when GC levels rise, the free or biologically active fraction of the hormone increases rapidly (Hadjian, Chedin, Cochet, & Chambaz, 1975). Using small samples of blood, the total amount of cortisol in circulation (bound and free) can be estimated using available assays. However, unless extra steps are taken in the assaying procedures, one cannot differentiate bound and free fractions of the hormone. This issue is not the case for salivary cortisol as only the free fraction of the hormone can enter into saliva through the parotid gland (Riad-Fahmy, Read, Joyce, & Walker, 1981). Once in circulation, steroid hormones are broken down and excreted through the kidneys. This process also allows estimates of cortisol and its metabolites in urine (Franks, 1973).

Each of these matrixes (plasma, urine, or saliva) has its value and its problems. Plasma sampling is invasive, but it has the advantage that ACTH (or the pituitary level of the axis) can also be assayed in these samples, which is not true of salivary sampling (e.g., Wallace et al., 1991). Urinary cortisol measures have been used to examine acute responses to stressors, but to do so requires having participants void, load up on fluids, and then void again some time after the stressor (see work by Frankenhaueser and colleagues, e.g., Frankenhauser, Lundberg, & Forsman, 1978). When urinary measures are used in children, typically the researcher collects the samples whenever the child chooses to void, and then attempts to work backwards to when increases in GCs may have been produced (e.g., Lundberg, de Chateau, Winberg, & Frankenhaeuser, 1981) or collects urine over night or over 24 hours to examine total production during a specified time period (e.g., De Bellis et al., 1999).

Saliva sampling is by far the most viable method of sampling GCs in children. Because cortisol is produced by the adrenal and secreted into saliva through the parotid, salivary flow rate does not affect estimates of cortisol concentrations (Walker, Riad-Fahmy, & Read, 1978). Several reviews of the use of salivary cortisol measures in adults are available, and the reader is referred to these as when adolescents are the subject of inquiry, many concerns raised in studies of adults will apply (e.g., contraceptive use, smoking, see Kirschbaum & Hellhammer, 1989; Kirschbaum & Hellhammer, 1994). In the remainder of this paper, we will focus on methodological issues pertinent to measuring cortisol in saliva in infants and children.

Methodological Issues in Measuring Cortisol in Infants and Young Children

One challenging question researchers face in designing studies to include GC measures is how often and when to sample. The answer depends on whether the researcher is interested in state factors influencing momentary or acute GC responses to stressors or trait characteristics associated with stable individual differences in GC activity. Financial constraints related to the cost of GC assays and participant characteristics dictate feasibility.

Assessing Stress Responses

The challenges associated with the measurement and subsequent interpretation of acute cortisol responses to stress in children arise from individual differences in the latency to display peak cortisol responses, as well as the nature of the baseline levels to which cortisol response measures are compared. Although group means suggest that peak levels of salivary cortisol are reliably observed between 20 and 25 minutes following challenges, analyses of the individual data indicate notable variation in this latency measure even among infants. For example, Lewis and Ramsay (2003) recently showed that among 6 month olds, relatively equal proportions of infants peaked at 15, 20, and 25 minutes in response to inoculations, with some infants peaking even later at 30 minutes. Variability in the latency to peak cortisol levels has also been observed among 12- to 18-month-olds participating in the Strange Situation and other stressor paradigms in which children displayed peak cortisol responses as long as 40 minutes post-challenge (Goldberg et al., 2003). Although it remains unclear whether these individual differences are stable across time, such findings collectively suggest that researchers should consider collecting more than one saliva sample following a stressful event, with the specific number determined by financial considerations as well as children's compliance with the sampling procedures. Furthermore, increasing researchers' sensitivity to individual differences in peak responses may help reduce inconsistencies across laboratories regarding the relation between this response parameter and other behavioral and physiological measures.

What is Baseline?

Researchers examining children's cortisol responses to stress must also consider the nature of the sample that is used as the pre-manipulation comparison. Typically, saliva samples are collected from children when they arrive at the laboratory and are compared to samples obtained following the challenge.

Such methods, however, implicitly assume that the sample obtained at lab arrival reflects the child's typical cortisol levels at that time of day, and research from our laboratory and others suggests that this assumption is likely incorrect. Indeed, comparisons between samples obtained at lab arrival and samples obtained at home matched for the same time of day as the lab visit reveal that the initial lab sample may reflect a *response* to coming to the lab. Studies of infants and preschoolers suggest that cortisol levels decrease from home to laboratory (Goldberg et al., 2003; Gunnar, Mangelsdorf, Larson, & Hertsgaard, 1989; Larson, Gunnar, & Hertsgaard, 1991; Legendre and Trudel, 1996; Lundberg, Westermark, and Rasch, 1993). In contrast, in at least one study, we have observed increases from home to laboratory among children 9 years and older (Tottenham, Parker, & Liu, 2001). These findings raise the possibility that in laboratory studies with young children, researchers are examining cortisol responses to stressors starting from a level suppressed below typical baselines, while with older children, researchers may be starting from already elevated levels. Both findings indicate that it is helpful in interpreting cortisol reactivity to obtain home levels timed to those obtained in the laboratory and to consider employing a period of adaptation to the laboratory before introducing the stress experience (see example from van Goozen et al., 2000).

Trait vs. State

Most human developmental researchers using cortisol measures are interested in identifying stable, individual differences in activity of the LHPA axis that may related to trait characteristics of their participants and/or reflect the impact of experiences on the activity of this system. In this regard, the LHPA system is not necessarily user-friendly. Regarding *basal cortisol* assessed under ambulatory conditions, using latent state-trait modeling it has been shown that the balance of state and trait components varies over the day with generally larger trait components obtained soon after morning awakening and larger state component obtained later in the day (Kirschbaum et al., 1990; Shirtcliff et al., 2005). In contrast, state estimates are much larger later in the day, sometimes so large that latent state-trait models cannot be fit near the nadir of the rhythm (e.g., Kirschbaum et al., 1990). These findings suggest that when a single cortisol sample is taken and/or when cortisol is assessed on only one day, this may serve as a poor reflection of the individual's typical cortisol levels. Indeed, in unpublished work in our laboratory, we have examined the cortisol levels of preschool children by taking one sample each day over many days (>20 days) at the same time of day. By randomly sampling days and creating averages with increasing numbers of samples, we have sought to determine how many days of sampling we need in order to obtain stable indices of individual differences in classroom cortisol levels. Modest, but statistically significant test-retest correlations (around r = 0.3) required aggregating over at least 3 days of samples, while even with 7 days averaged these correlations still hovered around 0.7. We and others have noted, however, that when the state and experience of the child is controlled in the 30–60 minutes prior to baseline sampling, test-retest correlations between two samples tend to be in the r = 0.5 to r = 0.6 range (Goldberg et al., 2003; Gunnar et al., 1989).

Assessing the stability of the LHPA *stress* response is more complicated because the same stressor repeated a second time is less novel and thus would be expected to produce less of an activation. However, several researchers have recently reported moderate test-retest stability (e.g., *r*'s of around 0.5) in infants and toddlers (e.g., Goldberg et al., 2003; Lewis & Ramsay, 1995a). Again, aggregation tends to produce more reliable measures. For example, in one study using the Trier Social Stress Test (TSST) administered repeatedly over several days, no correlation was obtained for the cortisol area under the curve when the first day's reaction was examined relative to later trials (Pruessner, Gaab, Hellhammer, Lintz, Schommer, & Kirschbaum, 1997). However, later trials were inter-correlated and, when aggregated, substantially increased associations with personality measures.

In sum, results such as these should lead researchers to be cautious in interpreting effects or the lack thereof when cortisol measures are based on a limited set of assessments. Furthermore, such findings challenge researchers to examine the stability/reliability of their cortisol measures and take this information into account when interpreting their results. Given the general pattern of large and often unexplained state variance in estimates of cortisol levels and responses, it is likely that in many studies, researchers are quite restricted in their capacity to detect associations between LHPA activity and the outcomes in which they are interested.

Problems in Sampling and Assaying Cortisol

Cortisol Assays

In general, all the assays used to measure cortisol operate on the principle of competitive antibody-antigen binding (Verma & Marks, 1983). The two compounds of the assay are the antigen and the antibody. The antibody is the agent that binds to the ligand (antigen, in this case, cortisol). However, there are a limited number of binding sites on the antibody. When ligands (antigens) from two sources compete for binding sites, the source with more of the antigen will contribute more than the source with less antigen to bound hormone once the total solution is reaches equilibrium. If one source of the antigen or hormone has a fixed amount of antigen and if those antigens are labeled or identifiable, then working backwards, one can infer how much antigen must have been in the other source.

The first competitive binding assays used radioactive iodine as the label (radioimmune assays or RIAs). Thus, in these assays, an unlabeled antigen (participant's cortisol sample) was added to a solution with radioactive antigen (always a constant concentration of cortisol) and the two were allowed to compete for binding sites on the antibody. After reaching equilibration (termed the incubation period), the bound fraction of the hormone (both labeled and unlabeled) are then separated from the remaining solution (termed separation phase) through some process (often through use of another antibody). The amount of labeled antigen is then measured in a radioimmune assay using a gamma counter. A calibration or standard curve is set up based on testing known quantities of cortisol in solution with labeled cortisol. The unknown or participant concentrations of cortisol are then inferred by reading off the curve.

Although radioactive competitive binding assays were the first type widely used, there are now other labels in common use. In immunofluorescence assays, a fluorescent compound is used as the label and what is measured is the fluorescence of the antibody ligand. In ELISA assays, an enzyme is used that converts a colorless substrate (chromogen) to a colored product, and it is the amount of color that is read. However, in all these types of assays the underlying principles are the same.

Variability

Several issues are critical for whichever type of assay is used. First, these are biological assays and the results they yield on two identical samples are never exactly the same. Thus, researchers need to be aware of the reliability of the assay. Estimates of reliability, termed coefficients of variation (CVs), are typically provided by the laboratory that conducts the assay. If the researcher does his or her own assaying, then computing the CVs will be part of the assaying procedure. The CV is calculated by taking a large saliva sample and splitting it into a number of vials (termed aliquots). All of the aliquots of the same sample have the same amount of cortisol, but the values reported in the assay will not be identical. Alternatively, aliquots may be made up of known amounts of cortisol at different concentrations that typically reflect the high and low end of the assay's sensitivity. The CV is the mean of the values for the aliquots divided by the standard deviation and multiplied by

100. Batch refers to the fact that only a certain number of samples can be run at the same time. Reliable assays yield within batch (termed intra-assay) CVs of between 5 and 8 and between batch (termed inter-assay) CVs of lower than 12.

The second issue is the sensitivity range of the assay. Generally speaking, the ability to discriminate between samples with different amounts of cortisol (or another ligand if one is assaying a different hormone) is poor near the upper and lower detection limits of the assay. This means that at the upper and lower range of the standard curve, CVs are larger than in the midrange of the standard curve. To estimate the amount of assay error contributing to ones analyses, researchers should also try to obtain CVs for the assay that match the median range of values of their participants.

Assay variation, which can be reduced but never avoided, is one reason single measures of cortisol are an unreliable index of the individual. To reduce this assay noise, during the assay process each sample is typically split into two aliquots and both are assayed (termed duplicate assaying). The two retrieved values are then examined. If they differ from each other greatly (where this difference should be decided by the researcher), the sample is typically re-assayed until the two duplicates fall within a percentage of difference that the researcher deems tolerable. At this point, the two duplicates are averaged, and it is this average that is used in subsequent analyses. However, sometimes no matter how often a sample is assayed, the duplicates continue to differ substantially. Most researchers do not report results on samples that do not duplicate well. Sometimes the problem for poor duplicates is that there is an interfering substance in the sample as will be discussed below.

Saliva Stimulants and Collection Materials

Saliva sampling with most participants is an easy procedure. However, this is not always the case with infants and young children. Newborns and premature infants have very little saliva in their mouths, especially after events that cause them to cry. Older infants and toddlers are often quite resistant to the procedures required to obtain a saliva sample. As well, any time the researcher wants to take more than one sample from a child, unless the experience is pleasant, he or she may find resistance increases with each attempt to sample. For these reasons, many studies of infants and young children involve the use of mild stimulants to increase saliva flow and make the procedure pleasant. The best stimulants are ones that taste sweet and produce a lot of saliva. Typically, these are citric acid based and sugar sweetened. Unfortunately, these stimulants may reduce the pH of the participant's saliva and this procedure interferes with most assays, although the degree of interference varies with some assays being very affected and others more robust to this interference (Schwartz, Granger, Susman, Gunnar, & Laird, 1998).

In addition, infants and young children cannot be induced to spit into a collection device; thus, the researcher must use some technique to get the saliva from their mouths. Some researchers have tried pipetting from the mouth. This procedure can be very difficult, especially if the children are only producing a small amount of saliva. Many researchers use some kind of absorbent material that is placed in the mouth and mouthed by the participant. Sterile cotton dental rolls are often used with infants and young children as these can be purchased in lengths that allow an adult to hold onto one end while the other is in the child's mouth. With very young infants, particularly premature infants, the mouth is so small that the cotton rolls do not fit. Smaller cotton-tipped sticks have been used in some studies of prematures, as well as suction catheters, sometimes in connection with wall-suction devices. It must be noted, however, that whenever saliva is collected using any absorbent material, the material itself may introduce cortisol-like substances into the saliva that are read as cortisol by the assay or cortisol make stick to the fibers reducing the amount that gets into the saliva sample that is then assayed.

The bottom line is that there is no perfect solution for obtaining saliva samples from young children. What is critical, however, is that researchers examine the impact of their collection procedures on the assay they are using. This process can be done by collecting clear saliva from adults, pooling it, and then working aliquots from that pool through the various components of the collection and assay procedures. What the researcher is looking for is the procedure that works (gets the children to provide the needed samples without distress due to sampling), and produces the least impact on their assessment of the children's cortisol levels.

Once children have reached an age when they can be induced to spit on request, two methods are in frequent use, both of which yield good results. One method uses something termed a Salivette. This object is a collection device that includes a small cotton roll that can be removed and replaced in a capped plastic collection vial and is produced commercially by Sarstedt company (US phone number 704-465-4000). The participant removes the cotton roll or plug gently chews it for about a minute, and then replaces it in the plastic vial. The vials are later spun in a centrifuge to remove the saliva from the cotton. The other method is to chew, a piece of sugarless original flavor Trident™ for one minute after rinsing ones mouth. After a minute of chewing, the participant spits through a straw into a vial that is then sealed and saved for assay (Schwartz et al., 1998). The latter method has the advantage that children much prefer chewing gum to chewing a dry cotton plug and each sampling occasion can be seen by the child as an opportunity to get a new piece of gum. Any time any object is introduced to the mouth, however, there is the possibility of choking. As part of a research protocol, it is generally wise to have the child spit the gum out after each sample is obtained.

Interfering Substances

In addition to the problem of stimulants and collection material, researchers also need to be aware of substances that children have in their mouths that can affect cortisol results. Bovine cortisol often cross-reacts with in assays for human cortisol and bovine cortisol is found in all milk products (Pearlman, 1983). Breast milk creates a similar problem (Magnano, Diamond, & Gardner, 1989). The problem is not that the child has consumed a milk-based product, but that it is still in their mouths. Having children rinse their mouths before sampling is a good idea, as long as the water itself does not end up diluting the sample. With very young children or for participants where the more complex the procedure the more one loses samples, trying to avoid consumption of milk products in the 15–30 minutes before sampling is often the best approach. The effects of other stimulants, such as caffeine, nicotine, and birth control, are more difficult to judge as these affect results through activation of the LHPA axis (see for discussion Kirschbaum & Hellhammer, 1989, 1994; Kirschbaum et al., 1999).

Storing and Mailing

Following saliva collection, researchers typically need to store samples prior to the time when they will be assayed. Cortisol is a very stable compound, thus it is not necessary to immediately freeze to prevent the hormone from degrading. Indeed, samples can sit unfrozen for days or weeks without any problem. Sometimes, though, substances grow in the samples and this may interfere with results. Thus, it is a good idea to keep the samples refrigerated, if not frozen. The fact that they can remain unfrozen, however, also allows them to be sent through the mail without affecting results (Clements & Parker, 1998). More critical, perhaps, than freezing and refrigeration, is whether the vials used to store the saliva have a tight seal. The measurement of cortisol is based on the concentration of the hormone in its matrix (in this case, saliva). Any evaporation of the sample, thus, can have sizeable effects on measurement. We have seen problems with vials that pop open during transport or when the sample is frozen. We have also seen samples returned to us where there is liquid around the lid of the vial. Choosing which vial to use is, thus, an important issue. Consequently, researchers may want to aliquot samples from the same source into the vials they are choosing among, put the vials through the procedures that will be used in the study, and see which type of vial yields the most consistent result.

Batching

Finally, once the study has been conducted and the samples are ready to be assayed, the researcher has another set of decisions to make. Assays are conducted in batches based on the number of samples that can be managed in one run. This procedure varies by assay type, but is usually fewer than the number of samples that need to be analyzed. Because the values will differ among batches (inter-assay CV) more than within a batch (intra-assay CV), the researcher should decide where they want to introduce the most error. For example, it would be unwise to have all the samples from one sex in one batch and those from the other in another batch. If the main point of the study is to examine changes in cortisol levels within participants, then the researcher may want to organize their samples so that all of those from one participant are in the same batch for assay. If the main point of the study is between participant comparisons, then batches should be balanced across the factors that will be main effects in the analysis. Researchers may want to enter their own blind control samples into each batch so that they can calculate their own CVs. Researchers should also be aware that when a laboratory or commercial kit company gets in a new lot of antibody, the dynamics of the assay often change. Thus, it is good to know that all the samples for a study are being assayed using the same antibody lot. This process can be a challenge for longitudinal studies that are conducted and assayed over years. Whether researchers complete their own assays or send them out for analysis, it is very wise to maintain a set of vials with samples aliquoted from the same source. These control vials can be included in each assay and tracked across studies and years. This procedure allows the researcher to determine, when some studies yield lower or higher cortisol estimates than others, whether the difference is due to changes in the assay or changes in the participants or contexts of the study.

Data Analysis

Once the samples have been assayed, the researcher confronts the challenge of data analysis. The first step involves examining the data for outliers. Sometimes extreme outliers are noted that are unlikely to reflect a healthy participant's true cortisol level. Generally speaking, unless the participant is sick or exposed to an extreme, life-threatening stressor, it is highly unlikely that he or she will produce salivary cortisol concentrations that are more than 3 or 4 times peak early morning levels. Depending on the assay, the average early morning peak level is somewhere between 0.4 and 0.8 µg/dl, so levels that are 3.5 to 4.0 µg/dl or higher are suspect. We have experienced some participants with multiple samples the 5 to 25 µg/dl range. In every instance, we were able to trace the results to introduction of cortisol into the saliva sample, typically through the use of a topical corticoid cream or other medication that did not initially appear on the list of medications the participant was taking. Sometimes, however, a single sample will yield extremely high values that may duplicate reliably. There are no clear-cut rules in the psychoendocrine literature on whether to retain or delete these values; however, when they are very extreme (>4 or 5 SDs above the mean), the usual transformation of the data will not eliminate their impact on subsequent statistical analyses. Even without such extreme values, it is often the case that cortisol distributions are positively skewed, and researchers should consider using a log10 transformation to normalize the data. Assessing whether to employ a transformation, however, should be done using the measures that will be entered into the analysis. Thus, raw data should be used to compute such measures as change scores or area under the curve (AUC). The distributions of these measures should then be examined for normality. Sometimes raw data are skewed, but change scores are not.

There are no set ways to analyze salivary cortisol data. The analysis depends on the samples available and the questions under study. There are, however, a few strategies that may be useful to consider. When the researcher is interested in a participant's typical cortisol levels, as noted earlier, it is good to obtain multiple measures of the individual to reduce sampling and assay error. However, in aggregating the data, the researcher may notice that some participants are much more variable than others. This variability may be of interest. For example, Goodyer and colleagues (Goodyer, Hertbert, Tamplin, & Altham, 2000) noted that among high-risk adolescents, those with more variable morning wake up cortisol levels were more likely to develop clinical depression during the course of the study.

Most researchers are interested in the cortisol responses to stressors. One concern, as noted earlier, is that not only the magnitude, but the rate and duration of the response varies from one individual to the next. All three of these parameters may be of interest. However, with children, one is often unable to obtain enough samples to reliably determine rate, peak, and duration separately. Doing so probably requires sampling at least every few minutes from the onset of the stressor to 20 or 30 minutes after its termination. In lieu of this opportunity, many researchers summarize the response using change scores or measures of area under the curve.

Change scores are more common when only one pre- and one post-test measure have been collected. This is the situation in which the question of law of initial values (LIV) has most often been raised. Specifically, Lewis and colleagues (Ramsay & Lewis, 1994, 1995a, 1995b) have noted that when pre-test cortisol levels are high prior to the stressor, they tend to decrease over the stressor period, while when they are low at pre-test, they tend to rise. This pattern likely reflects negative feedback regulation of the LHPA axis. However, the question is what the researcher should do to deal with this problem. One common solution has significant drawbacks. This solution involves computing a delta score by subtracting the pre- from the post-test value, then correlating the delta score with the pretest value and finding a significant, negative correlation. This result is interpreted as evidence of an LIV effect. To control for the effect, some researchers then use partial correlations or regression to remove or control for the variance in delta scores due to the pretest value. The drawback to this solution is that when the researcher removes the variance due to pretest values from the delta scores, he or she has essentially undone the initial change score and then has the equivalent of the uncorrected posttest values in the analysis. The appropriate solution is to either use the delta scores (as they are already corrected for the pretest level) or to regress the posttest values on the pretest values and use the residual scores from the regression. It should be noted, however, that if the pre-test and post-test values are not significantly correlated, the regression method will have little effect.

When multiple, repeated cortisol measures are obtained in response to a stressor, the researcher has other options. The most frequently used is to analyze the area under the curve (AUC, see for method and discussion Pruessner, Kirschbaum, Meinlschmid, & Hellhammer, 2003). AUC can be calculated using either the rectangle or trapezoidal rule. The trapezoidal rule accounts for more of the area and may be preferred especially when only a few sampling periods go into the calculation. As evident in the formulas discussed in Pruessner and colleagues (2003), AUC can be calculated either controlling or not controlling for baseline or pretest levels. Baseline corrected and uncorrected scores often yield very different associations with outcome measures. The reason is easiest to understand if we consider AUC measures based on cortisol samples obtained at fixed time intervals. When cortisol is sampled at fixed intervals, without the baseline correction, the formula is essentially equivalent to the average of all of the measures. Variance due to pretest and response are reflected in the AUC measure. When corrected for baseline, the measure reflects changes in cortisol levels during the stressor period. Because some participants will exhibit decreases in cortisol over a stressor period, especially if they start with a high pretest level, calculation of AUC using baseline correction needs to allow for negative numbers.

Conclusions

The development of salivary cortisol assays has resulted in a large increase in the use of cortisol as a measure in research in child development. Despite the relative ease of collecting saliva, adequate collection, analysis, and interpretation of cortisol data requires attention to details and constraints that may be unfamiliar to many researchers. It is hoped that this chapter will help those new to the use of salivary cortisol measures to introduce these measures into their research with greater confidence and reliability.

ACKNOWLEDGMENTS

Preparation of this manuscript was supported by a National Institute of Mental Health K05 award (MH 66208) to the first author.

References

Anders, T. F., Sachar, E., Kream, J., Roffwarg, H., & Hellman, L. (1970). Behavioral state and plasma cortisol response in the human newborn. *Pediatrics, 46*, 532–537.

Anisman, H., & Zacharko, R. M. (1982). Depression: The predispositioning influence of stress. *Behavioral and Brain Sciences, 5*, 89–137.

Bartels, M., de Geus, E. J. C., Kirschbaum, C., & Boomsma, D. I. (2003). Heritability of daytime cortisol in children. *Behavioral Genetics, 33*, 421–433.

Bradbury, M. J., Akana, S. F., & Dallman, M. F. (1994). Roles of type I and II corticosteroid receptors in regulation of basal activity in the hypothalamopituitary-adrenal axis during the diurnal trough and the peak: Evidence for a nonadditive effect of combined receptor occupation. *Endocrinology, 134*, 1286–1296.

Chrousos, G. P., & Gold, P. W. (1992). The concepts of stress and stress system disorders: Overview of physical and behavioral homeostasis. *Journal of the American Medical Association, 267*, 1244–1252.

Clements, A. D., & Parker, R. C. (1998). The relationship between salivary cortisol concentrations in frozen versus mailed samples. *Psychoneuroendocrinology, 23*, 613–616.

Dallman, M., Akana, S., Scribner, K., Bradbury, M., Walker, C., Strack, A., et al. (1992). Stress, feedback and facilitation in the hypothalamo-pituitary-adrenal axis. *Journal of Neuroendocrinology, 4*, 517–526.

Daly, J. R., & Evans, J. I. (1974). Daily rhythms of steroid and associated pituitary hormones in man and their relationship to sleep. In M. H. Biggs & G. A. Christie

(Eds.), *Advances in steroid biochemistry and pharmacology* (pp. 61–109). New York: Academic Press.

De Bellis, M. D., Baum, A. S., Birmaher, B., Keshavan, M. S., Eccard, C. H., Boring, A. M., et al. (1999). Developmental traumatology, Part 1: Biological stress systems. *Biological Psychiatry, 9*, 1259–1270.

de Kloet, E. R. (1991). Brain corticosteroid receptor balance and homeostatic control. *Frontiers in Neuroendocrinology, 12*, 95–164.

Dickerson, S. S., & Kemeny, M. E. (2004). Acute stressors and cortisol responses: A theoretical integration and synthesis of laboratory research. *Psychological Bulletin, 130*, 335–391.

Engeland, W. C., Shinsako, J., Winget, C. M., Vernikos-Daniellis, J., & Dallman, M. F. (1977). Circadian patterns of stress-induced ACTH secretion are modified by corticosterone responses. *Endocrinology, 100*, 138–147.

Frankenhauser, M., Lundberg, U., & Forsman, L. (1978). Dissociation between sympathetic-adrenal and pituitary-adrenal responses to an achievement situation characterized by high controllability: Comparison between type A and type B males and females. *Biological Psychology, 10*, 79–91.

Franks, R. C. (1973). Urinary 17-Hydroxycorticosteroid and cortisol. *Journal of Clinical Endocrinology and Metabolism, 36*, 702–705.

Goldberg, S., Levitan, R., Leung, E., Masellis, M., Basile, V. S., & Nemeroff, C. B. (2003). Cortisol concentrations in 12- to 18-month-old infants: Stability over time, location, and stressor. *Biological Psychiatry, 54*, 719–726.

Goodyer, I. M., Hertbert, J., Tamplin, A., & Altham, P. M. E. (2000). Recent life events, cortisol, dehydroepiandrosterone and the onset of major depression in high-risk adolescents. *British Journal of Psychiatry, 177*, 499–504.

Granger, D., & Kivlighan, K. T. (2003). Integrating biological, behavioral, and social levels of analysis in early child development: Progress, problems, and prospects. *Child Development, 74*, 1058–1063.

Gunnar, M. R. (1986). Human developmental psychoendocrinology: A review of research on neuroendocrine responses to challenge and threat in infancy and childhood. In M. Lamb, A. Brown & B. Rogoff (Eds.), *Advances in developmental psychology* (Vol. 4, pp. 51–103). Hillsdale, NJ: Lawrence Erlbaum Associates.

Gunnar, M. R., Mangelsdorf, S., Larson, M., & Hertsgaard, L. (1989). Attachment, temperament and adrenocortical activity in infancy: A study of psychoendocrine regulation. *Developmental Psychology, 25*, 355–363.

Hadjian, A. J., Chedin, M., Cochet, C., & Chambaz, E. M. (1975). Cortisol binding to proteins in plasma in the human neonate and infant. *Pediatric Research, 9*, 40–45.

Herman, J. P., & Cullinan, W. E. (1997). Neurocircuitry of stress: Central control of the hypothalamo-pituitary-adrenocortical axis. *Trends in Neurosciences, 20*, 78–84.

Herman, J. P., Tasker, J. G., Ziegler, D. R., & Cullinan, W. E. (2002). Local circuit regulation of paraventricular nucleus stress integration glutamate-GABA connections. *Pharmacology Biochemistry and Behavior, 71*, 457–468.

Jacobson, L., Akana, S. F., Cascio, C. S., Shinsako, J., & Dallman, M. F. (1988). Circadian variations in plasma corticosterone permit normal termination of adrenocorticotropin responses to stress. *Endocrinology, 122*, 1343–1348.

Johnson, E. O., Kamilaris, T. C., Chrousos, G. P., & Gold, P. W. (1992). Mechanisms of stress: A dynamic overview of hormonal and behavioral homeostasis. *Neuroscience and Biobehavioral Reviews, 16*, 115–130.

Kagan, J., Reznick, J. S., & Snidman, N. (1988). Biological bases of childhood shyness. *Science, 240*, 167–171.

Kirschbaum, C., & Hellhammer, D. H. (1989). Salivary cortisol in psychobiological research: An overview. *Neuropsychobiology, 22*, 150–169.

Kirschbaum, C., & Hellhammer, D. H. (1994). Salivary cortisol in psychoneuroendocrine research: Recent developments and application. *Psychoneuroendocrinology, 19*, 313–333.

Kirschbaum, C., Kudielka, B. M., Gaab, J., Schommer, N. C., & Hellhammer, D. H. (1999). Impact of gender, menstrual cycle phase, and oral contraceptives on the activity of the hypothalamus-pituitary-adrenal axis. *Psychosomatic Medicine, 61*, 154–162.

Kirschbaum, C., Steyer, R., Eid, M., Patalla, U., Schwenkmezger, P., & Hellhammer, D. H. (1990). Cortisol and behavior: 2. Application of a latent state-trait model to salivary cortisol. *Psychoneuroendocrinology, 15*, 297–307.

Kroboth, P. D., Salek, F. S., Pittenger, A. L., Fabian, T. J., & Frye, R. (1999). DHEA and DHEA-S: A review. *Journal of Clinical Pharmacology, 39*, 327–348.

Larson, M. C., Gunnar, M. R., & Hertsgaard, L. (1991). The effects of morning naps, car trips, and maternal separation on adrenocortical activity in human infants. *Child Development, 62*, 362–372.

Larson, M. C., White, B. P., Cochran, A., Donzella, B., & Gunnar, M. R. (1998). Dampening of the cortisol response to handling at 3 months in human infants and its relation to sleep, circadian cortisol activity, and behavioral distress. *Developmental Psychobiology, 33*, 327–337.

Legendre, A., & Trudel, M. (1996). Cortisol and behavioral responses of young children in a group of unfamiliar peers. *Merrill-Palmer Quarterly, 42*, 554–577.

Lewis, M. & Ramsay, D. S. (1995a). Stability and change in cortisol and behavioral responses to stress during the first 18 months of life. *Developmental Psychobiology, 28*, 419–428.

Lewis, M., & Ramsay, D. S. (1995b). Developmental change in infants' responses to stress. *Child Development, 66*, 657–670.

Lewis, M. & Ramsay, D. S. (2003). Reactivity and regulation in cortisol and behavioral responses to stress. *Child Development, 74*, 456–464.

Lundberg, U., de Chateau, P., Winberg, J., & Frankenhaeuser, M. (1981). Catecholamine and cortisol excretion patterns in three-year-old children and their parents. *Journal of Human Stress, 7*, 3–11.

Lundberg, U., Westermark, O., & Rasch, B. (1993). Cardiovascular and neuroendocrine activity in preschool children: Comparison between day care and home levels. *Scandinavian Journal of Psychology, 34*, 774–779.

Magnano, C. L., Diamond, E. J., & Gardner, J. M. (1989). Use of salivary cortisol measurements in young infants: A note of caution. *Child Development, 60*, 1099–1101.

Meaney, M. J. (2001). Maternal care, gene expression, and the transmission of individual differences in stress reactivity across generations. *Annual Review of Neuroscience, 24*.

Murphy, B. E. P. (1967). Some studies of the protein binding of steroids and their application to the routine micro and ultramicro measurement of various steroids in body fluids by competitive protein-binding radioassay. *Journal of Clinical Endocrinology and Metabolism, 27*, 973–990.

Pearlman, W. H. (1983). Glucocorticoids in milk: A review. *Endocrinologia Experimentalis, 17*, 165–174.

Peters, J. R., Walker, R. F., Riad-Fahmy, D., & Hall, R. (1982). Salivary cortisol assays for assessing pituitary-adrenal reserve. *Clinical Endocrinology, 17*, 583–592.

Plihal, W., Krug, R., Pietrowsky, R., Fehm, H. L., & Born, J. (1996). Corticosteroid receptor mediated effects on mood in humans. *Psychoneuroendocrinology, 21*, 515–523.

Price, D. A., Close, G. C., & Fielding, B. A. (1983). Age of appearance of circadian rhythm in salivary cortisol values in infancy. *Archives of Disease in Childhood, 58*, 454–456.

Pruessner, J. C., Gaab, J., Hellhammer, D. H., Lintz, D., Schommer, N., & Kirschbaum, C. (1997). Increasing correlations between personality traits and cortisol stress responses obtained by data aggregation. *Psychoneuroendocrinology, 22*, 615–625.

Pruessner, J. C., Kirschbaum, C., Meinlschmid, G., & Hellhammer, D. (2003). Two formulas for computation of the area under the curve represent measures of total hormone concentration versus time-dependant change. *Psychoneuroendocrinology, 28*, 916–931.

Ramsay, D. S. & Lewis, M. (1994). Developmental change in infant cortisol and behavioral response to inoculation. *Child Development, 65*, 1491–1502.

Riad-Fahmy, D., Read, G., & Hughes, I. A. (1979). Corticosteroids. In C. H. Gray & V. H. T. James (Eds.), *Hormones in blood* (3rd ed., Vol. 3, pp. 179–262). New York: Academic Press.

Riad-Fahmy, D., Read, G. F., Joyce, B. G., & Walker, R. F. (1981). Steroid immunoassays in endocrinology. In A. Vollar, A. Bartlett & J. D. Bidwell (Eds.), *Immunoassays for the 80's*. Baltimore: MD: University Park Press.

Rosen, J. B., & Schulkin, J. (1998). From normal fear to pathological anxiety. *Psychological Review, 105*, 325–350.

Rothbart, M. K., Derryberry, D., & Posner, M. I. (1994). A psychobiological approach to the development of temperament. In J. E. Bates & T. Wachs (Eds.), *Temperament: Individual differences at the interface of biology and behavior* (pp. 83–116). Washington, DC: American Psychological Association.

Sanchez, M. M., Ladd, C. O., & Plotsky, P. M. (2001). Early adverse experience as a developmental risk factor for later psychopathology: Evidence from rodent and primate models. *Development and Psychopathology, 13*, 419–449.

Sapolsky, R. M., Romero, L. M., & Munck, A. (2000). How do glucocorticoids influence stress responses? Integrating permissive, suppressive, stimulatory and preparative actions. *Endocrine Reviews, 21*, 55–89.

Schwartz, D. B., Granger, D. A., Susman, E. J., Gunnar, M. R., & Laird, B. (1998). Assessing salivary cortisol in studies of child development. *Child Development, 69*, 1503–1513.

Shirtcliff, E., Granger, D., Booth, A., & Johnson, D. (2005). Low salivary cortisol levels and externalizing behavior problems: A latent state trait model in normally developing youth. *Development and Psychopathology, 17*, 167–184.

Smyth, J., Ockenfels, M. C., Porter, L., Kirschbaum, C., Hellhammer, D. H., & Stone, A. A. (1998). Stressors and mood measured on a momentary basis are associated with salivary cortisol secretion. *Psychoneuroendocrinology, 23*, 353–370.

Tottenham, N., Parker, S. W., & Liu, C. (April, 2001). *Individual differences in cardiac and HPA reactivity to a psychological stressor*. Paper presented at the Biennial Meeting of the Society for Research in Child Development, Minneapolis, Minnesota.

van Goozen, S. H., Matthys, W., Cohen-Kettenis, P. T., Buitelaar, J. K., & van Engeland, H. (2000). Hypothalamic-pituitary-adrenal axis and autonomic nervous system activity in disruptive children and matched controls. *Journal of the American Academy of Child and Adolescent Psychiatry, 39*, 1438–1445.

Verma, R. B., & Marks, V. (1983). Immunoassays in molecular biology: Basic principles. *Indian Journal of Pharmacology, 15*, 245–254.

Walker, E. F., Walder, D. J., & Reynolds, F. (2001). Developmental changes in cortisol secretion in normal and at-risk youth. *Development and Psychopathology, 13*, 721–732.

Walker, R. F., Riad-Fahmy, D., & Read, G. F. (1978). Adrenal status assessed by direct radioimmunoassay of cortisol in whole saliva or parotid saliva. *Clinical Chemistry, 24*, 1460–1463.

Wallace, W. H. B., Crowne, E. C., Shalet, S. M., Moore, C., Gibson, S., Littley, M. D., et al. (1991). Episodic ACTH and cortisol secretion in normal children. *Clinical Endocrinology, 34*, 215–221.

Watamura, S., Donzella, B., Kertes, D., & Gunnar, M. (2004). Developmental changes in baseline cortisol activity in early childhood: Relations with napping and effortful control. *Developmental Psychobiology, 45*, 125–133.

DATA ACQUISITION, REDUCTION, ANALYSIS, AND INTERPRETATION

Considerations and Caveats

13   Psychophysiology Principles, Pointers, and Pitfalls

Anita Miller and James Long

INTRODUCTION

Psychophysiology focuses on physiological processes associated with human sensory, motor, cognitive, emotional, and social functions. Developmental psychophysiology centers on the emergence of such processes in youngsters. Over the past several decades, technological advances have revolutionized the field. Marked progress has been made in psychology and neuroscience as well as in electrical engineering and applied mathematics. Advances in circuit boards and silicon chips have facilitated manufacturing of accurate, stable, and predictable devices for amplifying and filtering analog physiological signals, converting them to a digital format, and recording sizable datasets on personal computers. In addition, the computational efficiency and storage capacity of digital hardware have increased significantly, and software tools for signal processing have grown more sophisticated and widely available. Such technological advances have created a trend toward increased performance for a given price, and complete commercial laboratory systems have made human psychophysiology measures increasingly accessible to more investigators conducting basic and applied research.

As psychophysiology tools become widely available, needs increase for introductory tutorials for conducting psychophysiology assessments. Despite the ease of obtaining turn-key equipment and recording physiological data, fundamental challenges remain inherent to the work. For instance, most psychophysiological measures have multiple determinants. Bioelectric signals are often a composite of multiple physiological processes that co-occur or interact. For example, brain recordings contain ocular and muscle activity, and voluntary breathing influences heart rate variability. In addition, noise

367

sources can mimic physiological processes, such as the AC power frequency overlapping with physiological activity and body movements confounding skin conductance responses. Thus, one core challenge is maximizing target signals relative to extraneous ones – or ensuring technical quality and high signal-to-noise ratios.

A second major challenge relates to the fact that psychophysiology measures covary with multiple psychological and contextual factors. Individual differences in psychophysiological measures are associated with traits such as temperament, cognitive capacities, and health risks. In addition, physiological changes relate to various task demands, including sensory stimulation, response characteristics, and cognitive-emotional processes. Furthermore, physiological and psychological processes change with development. Such maturational patterns hold great potential to enrich descriptions and explanations of typical and atypical development. However, the complexity of psychophysiological phenomena demands carefully controlled and designed assessments that minimize interpretative confounds. Such complexity suggests caution with rote applications of acquisition and analysis routines. Realizing psychophysiology's scientific potential requires addressing the inherent challenges of the enterprise.

The central goal of this chapter is to introduce basic issues with regard to acquiring, analyzing, and interpreting psychophysiology data for participants of all ages. Most information in this chapter applies to participants across the lifespan, and major caveats for pediatric populations are noted. The chapter is organized as a practical guide for conducting psychophysiology research. It follows the data path, beginning with principles, pointers, and pitfalls related to laboratory setup, experimental design, and data acquisition and then turning to a discussion of data analysis and interpretation.

EXPERIMENTAL DESIGN AND DATA ACQUISITION

Setting up a laboratory and conducting psychophysiology research with children or adults begin with basic principles of laboratory safety, experimental design, data acquisition, and physiological development (see Berntson & Cacioppo, 2002; Cacioppo, Tassinary, & Berntson, 2000; Coles, Donchin, & Porges, 1986; Fox, Schmidt, & Henderson, 2000; MacGregor, 2000). The methodology synchronizes various physiological and psychological phenomena for hypothesis testing. After noting core safety issues, we introduce common physiological and psychological measures and overview conceptual fundamentals, potential confounds, and practical advice for each.

Laboratory Safety

Psychophysiology assessments provide safe and noninvasive tools for examining biological processes in human participants, if basic principles are followed. Institutional review boards typically require investigators to address risk and safety standards, which apply to laboratory supervisors, personnel, and participants (see Greene, Turetsky, & Kohler, 2000). In addition to basic emergency and evacuation issues, several points are particularly relevant to psychophysiology laboratories. In general, experienced supervisors should provide laboratory guidelines, and they should be available to address safety and ethical questions if they arise. Basic operating procedures include ensuring that buildings and apparatus are properly grounded, participants are isolated from any high-voltage power supply, equipment inputs and outputs are not interchangeable, pressurized gas is stored properly, and excitation stimuli conform to standard guidelines. Laboratory personnel should follow standard procedures for waste disposal and infectious pathogens, be vigilant for potential sensitivities and allergies (e.g., to Latex), understand conditions for terminating sessions, and ensure the anonymity of participants. Participants must give informed consent for their research participation and be free to end their session, if necessary. Participants should receive appropriate feedback, in light of the fact that most psychophysiological assessments are for scientific investigation and not for medical diagnoses or treatment. If safety issues arise, they should be addressed directly by experienced, senior-level personnel and appropriately reported to institutional review boards.

Physiological Measures

Many psychophysiological measures reflect changes in the body's electrical activity or electrical properties (for an introduction to electrical principles, see Horowitz & Hill, 1989). Investigators typically record such analog signals by attaching electrodes – wires with a metal disk and conductive gel on one end – from the body surface to a bioamplifier. Customized bioamplifiers enable researchers to collect different types of electrophysiological signals simultaneously, consistent with a multiple-measures approach to psychophysiology (see Fox & Calkins, 1993). Such bioamplifiers must meet basic technical specifications, including minimal distortion and noise, high common mode rejection, high-input impedance, and medical-grade isolated participant connections. In addition, the rolloff slopes of the bioamplifier filters

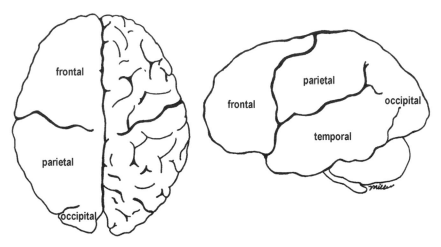

Figure 13.1. Superior and lateral brain surfaces and regional nomenclature.

must be specified, and the bioamplifier gains should be calibrated regularly. The amplified and filtered analog signal from the bioamplifier is converted to a digital format with an analog-to-digital (A/D) converter. The A/D converter must accurately resolve the entire range of each analog signal in order to preserve signal integrity.

Commonly recorded psychophysiological measures include the electroencephalogram (EEG), electrooculogram (EOG), electrocardiogram (ECG), respiration, impedance cardiogram, electromyogram (EMG), and skin conductance response (SCR). In addition, neuroendocrine measures such as cortisol level can be part of psychophysiology assessments. A wealth of information is available about anatomical and physiological contributions to such psychophysiological recordings, and the reader is encouraged to explore this literature starting with the references provided for each measure. The following discussion focuses specifically on the major issues relevant to selecting and recording the aforementioned physiological measures.

Electroencephalogram (EEG)
Electrodes placed on the scalp can pick up the sum activity of excitatory and inhibitory postsynaptic potentials from the brain (for a basic review of relevant neurophysiology and electrical principles, see Duffy, Iyer, & Surwillo, 1989; Lagercrantz, Hanson, Evrard, & Rodeck, 2002). This regional brain electrical activity is called the electroencephalogram (EEG) and typically is described in relation to the lobes of the cerebral cortex (see Figure 13.1). EEG signals are a mixture of rhythmic, sinusoidal-like fluctuations in voltage

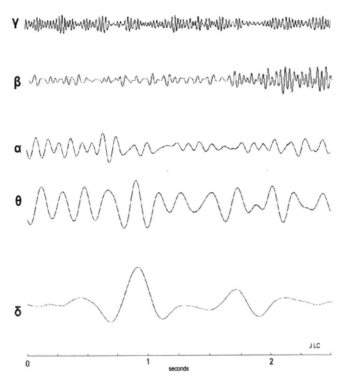

Figure 13.2. EEG spectral patterns. The sample tracings show delta (δ), theta (θ), alpha (α), beta (β), and gamma (γ) activity. Power in specific EEG frequency bands is typically quantified with Fourier analyses.

having a frequency of about 1 to 70 oscillations per second (the unit for cycles per second is hertz, abbreviated Hz).

As Hans Berger (1929) reported , the most easily recognized spontaneous brain electrical pattern, called alpha waves, has a frequency of about 8 to 12 Hz in adults. A slightly lower dominant frequency of 6 to 9 Hz is commonly observed in infants and young children (Bell & Fox, 1992; Marshall, Bar-Haim, & Fox, 2002; Niedermeyer, 1993; Yordanova & Kolev, 1996). The adult alpha rhythm is suppressed at occipital and central sites during visual or motor stimulation, respectively, consistent with the known functional specialization of these brain areas. This inverse relation between alpha power and performance supports the notion that adult alpha suppression indexes regional brain activation. In infants, power in the peak 6 to 9 Hz frequency band tends to increase during task-related brain activity (Bell, 2002). Figure 13.2 illustrates the five primary components of the EEG frequency spectrum, identified by the Greek letters delta (δ), theta (θ), alpha (α), beta (β),

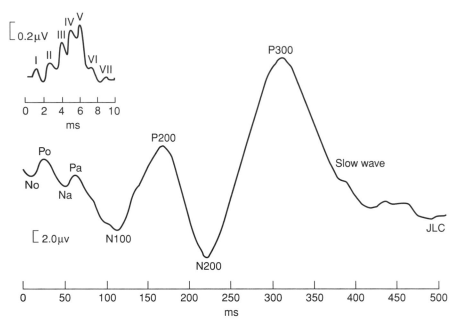

Figure 13.3. The auditory ERP, exemplifying the average waveform components elicited by infrequent auditory target stimuli. The auditory brainstem response is a series of seven small peaks during the first 10 milliseconds. The middle latency response occurs during the next 50 milliseconds. The late ERP components include the N100, P200, N200, P300, and slow wave.

and gamma (γ). The horizontal axis in the tracings reflects time, and the vertical axis represents amplitude or intensity of electrical activity.

In addition to spontaneous EEG rhythms and event-related oscillations (Baser, 1980, 1998), event-related potentials (ERPs) can be elicited in response to discrete stimuli or motor acts (Fabiani, Gratton, & Coles, 2000; Nelson & Monk, 2001). A variety of brain potentials have been observed (Brunia, 1997; Nelson, 1994; Picton et al., 2000b; Segalowitz & Davies, 2004). For example, broadband 100 µs clicks evoke brainstem auditory evoked potentials (BAEPs). Visual patterns or flashes induce visual ERPs, and warned reaction time paradigms produce motor readiness potentials. A typical auditory ERP is illustrated in Figure 13.3. Development typically brings an increase in the interdependence of brain electrical activity and an almost linear reduction of the latency of cerebral ERPs until adult values are reached during adolescence. The amplitude of brain electrical activity and ERPs follows non-linear trends characterized by sudden accelerations of change and periods of stability (Chiarenza, 1998).

Figure 13.4. Aliasing of a 40 Hz waveform as a 10 Hz fluctuation with a 50 Hz sampling rate. Aliasing occurs when a signal is digitally sampled at a frequency lower than the Nyquist frequency.

Recording brain electrical signals involves multiple steps. Selecting an appropriate EEG or ERP sampling procedure depends on the particular bioamplifier bandpass characteristics and the data frequency content. For many practical purposes, the signal can be amplified and filtered to pass electrical activity between 0.01 and 100 Hz and then digitized at a minimal sampling rate of 500 Hz (see Pivik et al., 1993). Recording brainstem ERPs requires a considerably higher bandwidth and a higher sampling rate. The sampling rate should be at least twice the highest frequency at which the filtered data have negligible power. Frequency components higher than the Nyquist frequency (i.e., $\frac{1}{2}$ the sampling frequency) are improperly recognized, and lower frequency activity can be contaminated with distortion from higher frequency components. This effect is known as "aliasing" (see Figure 13.4). No procedure compensates for aliasing after sampling, and so frequencies higher than the Nyquist frequency must be removed with analog low pass filtering. Aliasing is an essential issue for recording EEG and ERP data.

When EEG electrodes are placed on a participant, the hair and scalp surface should be clean. Scalp electrode arrays should be applied systematically relative to standard skull landmarks, including the nasion (the indentation where the nose joins the forehead), the inion (a protrusion on the backside of the skull, located by running a finger from the back of the neck toward the top of the head), and the preauricular points (located on the front of each ear, just above the tragus or the triangular cartilage that covers the ear canal opening). An electrical connection should be established using a hypertonic electrolyte gel, paste, or liquid. For systems requiring it, rubbing or abrading the skin at each site can improve the quality of the electrical interface and current flow. In doing so, care must be taken to avoid breaking the skin surface in order to minimize the risk of infection and scarring. In addition, different electrolytes and different metals should not be mixed because doing so may introduce battery potentials that overload the bioamplifier or induce perceptible shocks during impedance measurement. Furthermore, care should be taken to avoid spreading electrolyte over a wide area in order to maintain the localization capabilities of the electrode. Maintaining localization capabilities is particularly important with closely spaced, large arrays of electrodes and low viscosity electrolytes. If the electrolyte of adjacent electrodes overlaps, then a short circuit, or "salt bridge," is created and the electrodes no longer function independently but act as a large, single electrode (Duffy et al., 1989).

Electrical impedance of the electrodes (i.e., a combination of resistance and capacitive reactance) significantly affects the quality of the EEG signals. The unit for measuring impedance is the ohm (Ω). Researchers generally agree that optimal recordings are obtained when electrode impedances are less than 5 kΩ (Pivik et al., 1993), but some investigators have reported intact signals with impedances of 50 kΩ or higher (Ferree, Luu, Russell, & Tucker, 2001). In general, as long as the signal is grossly intact and marked differences do not exist among electrodes, higher impedances may be acceptable in order to reduce the manipulation and abrasion of tender skin.

Researchers who tolerate higher impedances should remain vigilant to potential signal distortions. Problems arise when output signals contain noise frequencies that are not present in the input signals. For example, coherent noise from the building AC mains (60 Hz in North America; 50 Hz in Europe and elsewhere) can be particularly problematic with high electrode impedances. The reason is that all amplifiers are vulnerable to intermodulation distortion. Intermodulation distortion is the spurious noise that is generated at frequencies that are the sum of the physiologic signal frequency and the coherent noise frequency as well as the difference between the physiologic signal and coherent noise. For example, EEG in the gamma band at 45 Hz can form a difference intermodulation signal with 60 Hz to produce a spurious signal at 15 Hz, and the amplitude of this spurious signal will be proportional to the amplitude of the 60 Hz noise. In addition, harmonic distortions of coherent noise can result in higher order harmonics aliasing down into the frequency of interest. The best way to minimize the effects of intermodulation distortion and harmonic distortion is to maximize the signal-to-coherent-noise ratio. Maximizing the target signal relative to coherent noise generally means minimizing electrode impedances. For quality control purposes, researchers should check and document electrode impedances at the beginning and end of each session and then report impedance ranges and noise levels with published data.

Investigators have a great deal of choice regarding EEG electrode arrays. Metal electrodes in plastic housing are often configured on caps made of a stretchable Lycra fabric or a string net. Although custom electrode arrays are available, many caps comprise 20, 32, 64, 128, or 256 electrodes. Figure 13.5

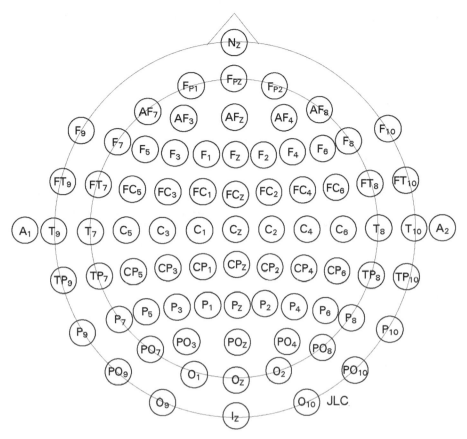

Figure 13.5. EEG electrode position nomenclature, corresponding to the Expanded International 10–20 System. Letters refer to particular brain regions (frontal, anterior, central, temporal, parietal, occipital). Single-digit numbers indicate lateral position, with odd numbers on the left and even numbers on the right. The mid-sagittal line is marked anteriorly by the nasion (the nose-forehead indentation) and posteriorly by the inion (posterior skull protrusion). The mid-coronal line is marked by the left and right preauricular points (on the front of each ear just above the tragus). The Cz electrode lies at the intersection of these two lines.

illustrates an electrode configuration based on the expanded 10–20 International System (see AEEGS, 1994). Lycra 10–20 electrode caps generally enable the user to apply electrolyte gel through a hole in the electrode housing after the cap is on the head, and they enable scalp preparation as needed to reduce impedances. Some high-density sponge electrode arrays are soaked in an electrolyte liquid prior to placement on the head, and skin abrasion at individual sites is discouraged with this system (Ferree et al., 2001). Traditional high-density electrode arrays introduce tradeoffs between data quality and time of preparation. Without electrode preparation, an experienced person can apply a large array in less than 15 minutes, but the data quality may be less than optimal. Improving the signals by reducing impedances below 5 kΩ for over 100 electrodes in a Lycra cap may take three skilled technicians 90 minutes or more with an adult or adolescent participant (e.g., Gevins et al., 1994). Active electrode technology, in which the first amplifier stage is on the electrode, can reduce preparation time and make high impedances tolerable. However, placing the first amplifier stage on the electrode precludes measuring electrode impedance. In addition, this technology requires a single-ended amplifier stage at the electrode, instead of a true differential design, with negative consequences for the common mode rejection ratio and AC mains noise at 60 or 50 Hz. Particular experimental goals influence how to balance such issues when selecting EEG electrode technologies.

Additional choices concern the reference electrode (Nuñez, 1981). Electrical potentials always reflect the voltage difference between two points in space, and the reference invariably influences the signal. Various reference options offer different geometric views of the underlying brain activity (Pivik et al., 1993). On the one hand, if the target and reference electrodes are close together, then they cancel out identical activity occurring at both sites. Methods that cancel out related activity create problems with measuring slow potentials and alpha activity, which tend to have broad fields. On the other hand, if the target and reference electrodes are far apart, then noncephalic noise and artifacts will increase. A common practice is to record EEG referenced to one site (e.g., midline central Cz, or left mastoid M1) and then algebraically re-reference the data offline. This method provides the advantage of comparing data with multiple reference montages and reporting patterns of convergence and divergence.

The average reference transformation essentially computes the difference between a target electrode and the average of all electrodes. This approach does not privilege any particular electrode, and, theoretically, the computed average potential from widely and regularly distributed electrodes should approach zero (Bertrand, Perrin, & Pernier, 1985). In practice, however, activity at a substantial number of channels (e.g., scalp muscle artifact or electrical interference) can contaminate average-referenced data. The surface Laplacian is a transform to current source density, computed from the second spatial derivative of the interpolated voltage surface (Perrin, Bertrand, & Pernier, 1987; Pernier, Perrin, & Bertrand, 1988). Laplacian transformations take the difference between a target electrode and the immediately surrounding electrodes. As such, this approach requires a large number of electrodes and emphasizes unique localized topographical changes in activity at the target electrode, which is appropriate for some but not all applications. Many investigators reference to a computed average-ears or average-mastoid (i.e., the protuberance of the temporal bone situated behind the ear). Bilateral recordings from ear or mastoid sites on separate bioamplifier channels eliminate the classic problem of impedance matching for physically linked ears (see Pivik et al., 1993). Although a unilateral ear or mastoid reference can introduce asymmetries, high-quality bilateral ear or mastoid recordings can serve as a reference that is appropriate for broad field potentials. Like many of the pointers discussed here, choosing a reference is influenced both by basic principles of psychophysiology and the specific goals of the research program. Laboratory setups that incorporate multiple approaches facilitate maximal flexibility (Dien, 1998; Yao et al., 2005).

Electrooculogram (EOG)

The voltage changes generated by eye movements (i.e., saccades) and blinks can be recorded from electrodes placed near the eyes with the electrooculogram (EOG). The eye forms an electrical potential between the cornea and the retina, and this potential's vector orientation and expressed magnitude change when the eyeball rotates and when the eyelid slides over the cornea (for anatomical and physiological descriptions, see Lins, Picton, Berg, & Scherg, 1993a, 1993b; Picton et al., 2000c). EOG signals may be of interest in themselves for investigations of saccades, and they may be used in EEG studies for ocular artifact detection or correction, given that ocular field potentials radiate across the scalp and distort EEG recordings (Croft & Barry, 2000). EOG sampling and filtering procedures should match those for EEG (particularly for ocular artifact correction procedures), but the EOG may need to be amplified at a lower gain than the EEG to avoid clipping the signal (i.e., signal loss from amplitude exceeding the bioamplifier's or A/D converter's voltage range).

Cleaning and preparing the skin with an alcohol prep pad, so that the electrode impedances are below 20 kΩ, produces a good EOG signal. Ocular activity for EEG studies with infants and young children is often recorded from bipolar electrodes placed superior and lateral to one eye. This placement minimizes the youngster pulling the electrodes off the face while still providing basic information about blinks and saccades. However, additional electrodes are required to maximize the resolution of ocular potentials, such as for ocular artifact correction routines (see later data analysis section). Eyeblinks are most robustly detected with electrodes placed directly above and

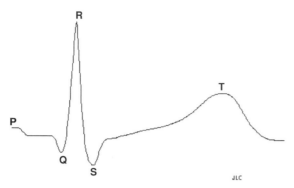

Figure 13.6. Characteristic electrocardiogram (ECG).

below the eye, with blinks producing an inverted-V pattern in the signal. This electrode placement also captures vertical saccades, which produce different signal deflections than blinks. Horizontal saccades often resemble square waves in a signal recorded from electrodes placed on the outer canthi, or laterally to each eye. Additional components can be quantified with a radial channel (e.g., computed as the sum of the supra- and infra-orbital activity minus the reference used for EEG). Ocular potentials are recorded either with a bipolar reference (e.g., the supra-orbital relative to infra-orbital voltage) or with the EEG common reference. Using the EEG common reference requires devoting one bioamplifier channel per electrode (i.e., twice as many as bipolar recordings), but this approach provides the flexibility of multiple offline algebraic computations (e.g., the supra-orbital relative to infra-orbital vertical EOG as well as the radial EOG). It is also needed for some source generator procedures, such as BESA (Scherg & Berg, 1991). Choices depend on practical constraints as well as the intended uses of the signals.

Electrocardiogram (ECG)

The electrical activity produced by the heart can be recorded with an AC differential bioamplifier as is used for EEG (for basic reviews of cardiovascular anatomy and physiology, see Artman, Mahoney, & Teitel, 2002; Berne & Levy, 2001). The ECG amplitude is in the order of one millivolt (mV). As illustrated in Figure 13.6, the ECG consists of multiple upward and downward deflections that are denoted by the letters: P, Q, R, S, and T. The most pronounced spike in ECG amplitude, reflecting the pulse or heart beat, is called the R-wave. The time duration between successive R-waves is referred to as the heart period (HP) or interbeat-interval (IBI) and is expressed in seconds or milliseconds (see Jennings et al., 1981). In addition, the heart period shows notable beat-to-beat variability, and measures of heart period variability (HPV) are often of interest in participants from infancy to adulthood. One component of HPV is respiratory sinus arrhythmia (RSA), commonly interpreted as an index of vagal or parasympathetic processes (see Akselrod et al., 1981; Attuel et al., 1986; Bar-Haim, Marshall, & Fox, 2000; El-Sheikh, 2005; Jennings & van der Molen, 2002).

Optimal measures of heart period and heart period variability are derived off-line from the digitized ECG signal using robust detection algorithms (see analysis section). This approach permits direct evaluation of the signal integrity and identification of abnormal beats (Berntson et al., 1997). The bioamplifier gain for the signal should be low (e.g., a gain of 250 to 500 into a 5 V full-scale A/D converter, in other words preferably at least 10 mV full scale) so that data are not lost during periods of movement artifact and baseline shifts. With many newer systems employing so-called digital amplifiers, this stage of setting the gain is transparent to the user. The important factor is the A/D window in millivolts. Recommended sampling rates for digitizing ECG are 500 to 1000 Hz, providing a timing resolution of 2 ms down to 1 ms (Riniolo & Porges, 1997). The ECG signal should be filtered minimally at the time of recording (e.g., 0.01 to 1000 Hz bandpass), in order to avoid signal distortion introduced by filtering and to maximize precision in R-wave onset measurement. Aliasing introduced by minimal filtering and sampling at the lower end of the recommended range (e.g., as part of a large multi-channel dataset) does not create the problems that it creates with EEG, given that ECG analyses focus on time domain analyses of the R-waves. Once the R-wave peaks are identified and converted to inter-beat-intervals, the frequency characteristics of the original ECG data become irrelevant. Filtering distorts the ECG signal, and it decreases precise R-wave detection. When IBI data are analyzed spectrally, epoch lengths of IBI data should be at least 32 to 64 s in order to obtain precise estimates of heart period variability due to RSA.

Investigators have proposed a number of ECG electrode placements. Recording from the chest maximizes the R-wave amplitude and minimizes movement and muscle artifact. For most participants, especially moving participants, an axial placement optimizes the signal quality (i.e., the two primary electrodes are attached under the armpits, on the left rib and right rib at roughly the same elevation as the heart). A bipolar reference is used, with the positive electrode on the left and the negative electrode on the right; when the two electrodes are switched, the R-wave deflection is a negative voltage. The ECG ground can be placed on the sternum or anywhere halfway between positive and negative electrodes, unless EEG is collected, in which case the ground for all sites is typically on the scalp. One can remove skin oils with an alcohol pad before placing the electrodes, but extensive skin preparation rarely is warranted for ECG, unless marked environmental noise is present and the investigator needs to increase the signal-to-noise ratio. Investigators can attach leads to disposable electrodes and label them "left" and "right," so that participants or parents can place the electrodes under their own clothing. The electrode leads can be taped to the skin using surgical tape about three inches from the electrode, with slack in the wires, so that any tugging on the leads will eliminate any force on the electrodes themselves. In addition, twisting the electrode leads together several times before attaching them to the bioamplifier reduces electrical noise pickup.

Related finger and ear pulse measures employ photoplethismography (i.e., they measure blood vessel volume with plethismography using infrared light emitting diode illumination and infrared photodetectors). For example, orienting studies may include indices of pulse amplitude constriction, which is reciprocally related to vasoconstriction. Finger and ear pulse measures have arbitrary units (unlike heart period's dimensional units). In theory, finger and ear pulse can be collected without ECG, but advantages exist for having simultaneous ECG. For example, by knowing R-wave onset time, one can measure pulse transit time (i.e., the time from the R-wave until the hemodynamic pressure wave to the peripheral vessels in the earlobe or finger tip). In addition, by time locking the finger and ear pulse measurement to the R-wave, investigators can obtain better signal detection and noise reduction. Given noise and variance issues, photoplethysmography is not recommended for quantifying heart period variability (see Berntson et al., 1997).

Respiration

Respiration refers to the process of breathing (for a review of respiratory physiology, see West, 2000). Investigators may examine breathing phenomena with a variety of measures (see Harver & Lorig, 2000; Wientjes, 1992), such as respiratory period (i.e., the time in seconds from inspiration onset to inspiration onset or from expiration onset to expiration onset) and tidal volume (i.e., the volume of air inhaled/exhaled at each breath). In addition, respiratory period is commonly used to assist with computations of heart period variability due to respiratory sinus arrhythmia (Grossman, Karemaker, & Wieling, 1991).

Multiple methods exist for quantifying respiratory activity. For example, a purely electrical method uses thoracic impedance. This method involves applying a high frequency AC excitation current across the thoracic cavity with two electrodes and then measuring the induced voltage with two separate electrodes. Less invasive approaches translate respiratory activity into an electrical signal by measuring changes in thoracic girth. Early work with girth measurement used liquid mercury strain gauges, but this approach has been abandoned due to mercury hazards. Subsequently, researchers applied elastomeric strain gauges. However, problems arise with generating a linear output from elastomeric strain gauges, and the electrical hysteresis of the elastimer can create the appearance of false breaths. An approach that does not suffer from nonlinearity or hysteresis utilizes a latex rubber pneumatic bellows attached to the chest with a metal bead chain or Velcro. The bellows approach is practical for participants of all ages, from neonates to adults.

The latex rubber pneumatic bellows connects to a solid-state pressure transducer, producing voltage changes that are linearly related to thoracic girth. Such voltage changes contain timing information quantifiable in metric units, such as for respiratory period measures. The pressure transducer does not intrinsically yield a calibrated measure of tidal volume. If necessary, tidal volume can be calibrated by simultaneously using spirometers with two girth measurements (i.e., for both the chest and the abdomen) during calibration trials. However, this approach tends to be too invasive for most studies, especially with children, and it is often not necessary because hypotheses focus specifically on respiratory period or relative tidal volume. For many applications, a single thoracic girth measurement is sufficient. Absent spirometry calibration trials, girth measured tidal volume is in arbitrary units. In this case, absolute tidal volume measures are inappropriate for comparing differences between groups, but relative measures are valid for within-session ratiometric repeated measures designs.

Several practical caveats exist with regard to recording respiratory activity with bellows and bead chains. First, the bellows and bead chain should be placed to create firm tension without inducing discomfort. If the bellows and chain are too loose, then they can slip and produce spurious results. If they are too tight, then the bellows may exceed its linear range, or breathing may be restricted. Second, young participants should be distracted from the psychophysiology apparatus (e.g., by engaging their attention in a game or activity) because respiration data are particularly sensitive to artifacts from pulling or playing with the bellows. Third, if respiratory data will be used to quantify heart period variability, then the artifact issue may influence the experimental protocol design. For example, paced breathing trials may be included with older children, adolescents, and adults (Wilhelm, Grossman, & Coyle, 2004). Finally, respiration waveforms can, in theory, take on any arbitrary shape, which makes offline artifact detection problematic. A helpful tool for detecting artifacts such as movement is via video recording synchronized with the physiology record.

Impedance Cardiogram

Thoracic impedance changes as blood ejects from the heart because blood is more electrically conductive than the surrounding tissue (for a review of relevant physiology, see Berne & Levy, 2001; Lamberts, Visser, & Zijlstra, 1984). Automated equipment is available for measuring such cardiac changes. In particular, an impedance cardiograph delivers a constant AC current (e.g., 1 mA rms at 100 kHz) and computes impedance from the measured voltage. Such computations are based on Ohm's Law. Impedance cardiographs hold current constant, and so impedance is directly proportional to voltage. The equipment commonly filters and amplifies the input signal, and it provides electrical outputs for digitizing Z_0 (basal thoracic impedance), ΔZ (time-varying thoracic impedance), and dZ/dt (the first derivative of impedance with respect to time).

Researchers typically acquire Z_0, ΔZ, dZ/dt, and ECG signals in order to quantify several essential components of the heart's activity (Sherwood et al., 1990). For example, the electromechanical systole is defined as the time interval from the start of the heart's ventricular depolarization to the completion of blood ejection. Investigators use the ECG signal to measure the onset of the heart's ventricular depolarization, and they use the impedance cardiogram to identify the completion of blood ejection from the heart. In addition, the impedance cardiogram's dZ/dt signal includes a characteristic beta (β) wave. The inflection marking the onset of change (β-point) reflects the start of the heart's left ventricular ejection of blood into the aorta (Kubicek, Patterson, & Witsoe, 1970; Martin et al., 1971). The time period from depolarization to the β-point is called the preejection period (PEP). PEP is inversely related to myocardial contractility (Ahmed, Levinson, Schwartz, & Ettinger, 1972) and is interpreted as a robust index of beta-adrenergic sympathetic influences on the heart (Berntson et al., 1994; Harris, Schoenfeld, & Weissler, 1967; McCubbin et al., 1983; Newlin & Levenson, 1979; Obrist et al., 1987; Schachinger et al., 2001).

When designing studies, investigators should recognize that time-based measures such as PEP have stronger psychometric properties than volume-based measures such as stroke volume and cardiac output (Sherwood et al., 1990). Volume-based measures, such as stroke volume and cardiac output, are sensitive to electrode distance and blood resistivity, which adversely impact reliability. Volume-based computations also require assumptions about body conductivity and heart valve integrity, included as constants in computational formulas. Constants in equations may not reflect the true variability within the sample, and the uncontrolled variability decreases reliability and validity. PEP measures are much less vulnerable to such interpretative problems.

Various electrode configurations have been proposed for impedance cardiography (see Sherwood et al., 1990). A tetrapolar band electrode system produces the most robust impedance signals. The inner two impedance bands are located circumferentially around the base of the neck and around the thorax (at the xiphisternal junction level). The outer two current bands are positioned at least 3 cm distal to each impedance band. The electrode bands consist of 2.5 cm wide disposable adhesive tape strips with a thin center strip of aluminum-coated Mylar. To determine each band length, one can wrap the tape around the participant with the backing attached, allowing an extra 6 cm to fold and attach to electrode clips. For comfort, participants should deeply inspire and fully expand the chest during band measurement and placement. After removing the tape backing, one can apply a conductive gel to the bright, aluminized surface on each band's adhesive side. Next, the bands are attached to the skin, the ends folded back, and clip electrodes affixed to the bright metal surface. One should document the distance between impedance bands on both the front and back of the participant.

Alternatively, spot electrodes can be used for impedance cardiography (see Sherwood et al., 1990). In general, time-based dZ/dt indices from four spot or band electrodes show excellent correspondence (e.g., Penney, Patwardhan, & Wheeler, 1985). However, we do not recommend spot electrodes for volume-based indices (i.e., stroke volume and cardiac output), which are particularly sensitive to electrode type, number, and location. Some investigators have used two or four spot electrodes for each of the four lead-participant contacts (connected with Y-adapters) to attempt to approximate more closely results from band electrodes. Although researchers can record impedance and ECG signals from the same electrodes, separate electrodes generally produce an ECG signal with a more distinct QRS complex.

Impedance cardiography can be measured in participants of all ages, beginning during infancy (Belik & Pelech, 1988). Studies have documented moderately high temporal stability and reliability of impedance cardiography measures during baseline and challenge tasks in school-age children (McGrath & O'Brien, 2001), adolescents (Matthews, Salomon, Kenyon, & Allen, 2002), and adults (Sherwood et al., 1990). In general, baseline measures are more stable than task-related effects, and the magnitude of stress-related responses vary by task, age, and gender (Matthews et al., 2002).

Electromyogram (EMG)

The electrical signals from reflexive and voluntary muscle activity can be recorded with the surface electromyogram (EMG; for a review of muscular physiology, see Kendall & McCreary, 1980). The signal is characterized by a frequency range from less than 1 Hz to over 500 Hz, with the vast majority of activity occurring between 20 and 250 Hz (and most for voluntary movement between 50 and 100 Hz), and with amplitudes ranging from fractions of a microvolt to millivolts. These frequency and amplitude characteristics are broader than most electrophysiological signals, overlapping both the EEG and ECG as well as external 50/60 Hz signals from most AC powered equipment (Tassinary & Cacioppo, 2000). Such signal overlap can produce confounds and artifacts (see later discussion of artifacts).

One of the most widely studied EMG phenomena is the startle blink reflex, reflecting defensive fear and orienting (Graham, 1979, 1992). A startle response to an abrupt loud noise or air puff activates the orbicularis oculi muscles surrounding the eyes. Researchers often record orbicularis oculi EMG activity with two bipolar-referenced electrodes placed closely under one eye. Early startle blink studies examined EOG amplitude changes associated with blinks (Simons & Zelson, 1985), but EOG amplitude often fails to discriminate among various subthreshold blink responses (i.e., blinks with little or no eyelid movement). Although muscle activity can be quantified from the EOG signal, direct orbicularis oculi EMG recordings produce the most sensitive startle response measures (Schmidt & Fox, 1998; Schmidt, Fox, & Long, 1998). The emotional context reliably modulates the startle blink reflex (Lang, Bradley, & Cuthbert, 1990). The startle reflex increases in an aversive context, and it decreases in a pleasant context. Investigators commonly vary the emotional context with images that evoke affective states (International Affective Picture System; Lang, Bradley, & Cuthbert, 2005). Emotional startle modulation is present across the lifespan, beginning during infancy (e.g., Balaban, 1995).

EMG recordings are often used to quantify facial movements or emotional expressions such as frowns, grimaces, and smiles (Bradley, 2000; Dimberg, 1990). Bipolar-referenced electrodes are placed over particular facial muscles or regions (see Figure 13.7). For example, muscle activity in the corrugator region can be recorded with one electrode placed directly above the brow on an imaginary vertical line that crosses through the inner eye fissure (endocanthion) and a second electrode placed along the upper border of the eyebrow one centimeter lateral to and slightly superior to the first. Muscle activity in the zygomaticus region can be recorded with one electrode placed mid-way along an imaginary line between the lip corner (cheilion) and the triangular cartilage covering the external ear canal (tragus) and the second electrode placed next to the first on the imaginary line toward the mouth one centimeter inferior and medial to the first (for additional facial EMG placement guidelines, see Fridlund & Cacioppo, 1986).

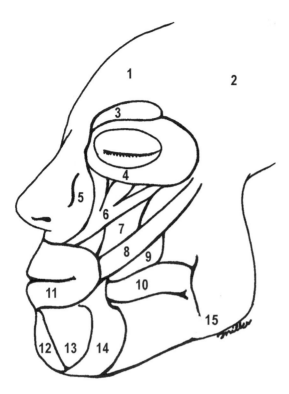

Figure 13.7. Facial musculature.

1 – *Frontalis* raises the brows.
2 – *Temporalis* closes the mouth and jaw.
3 – *Corrugator* draws the brows downward and together.
4 – *Orbicularis oculi* tightens the skin around the eye.
5 – *Nasalis* narrows the nostrils and pulls the nose downward.
6 – *Levator labii* raises the upper lip and flares the nostrils.
7 – *Levator anguli oris* raises the mouth angle.
8 – *Zygomaticus* draws the mouth upward.
9 – *Buccinator* compresses the cheek.
10 – *Risorius* retracts the lip corners.
11 – *Orbicularis oris* closes the mouth and purses the lips.
12 – *Mentalis* moves the chin.
13 – *Depressor labii inferioris* pulls the lower lip downward.
14 – *Depressor anguli oris* pulls the lip corners downward.
15 – *Masseter* provides upward traction of the lower jaw.

Recording facial EMG involves many of the aforementioned AC-signal measurement issues related to electrode impedance and lead dressing. The skin should be prepared with an alcohol pad and a hypertonic electrolyte gel so that impedances are below 20 kΩ. In addition, bipolar leads should be twisted together to minimize the inductive pickup of electromagnetic fields. Also, the leads should be strain relieved with surgical tape to minimize any pulling on the leads.

Principles informing sampling choices differ with EMG relative to other measures such as EEG, which can seriously be distorted by aliasing (see Figure 13.4). For example, recording orbicularis oculi startle EMG with a large array of EEG channels may necessitate a sampling rate as low as 512 Hz. In this case, the EEG must be band-limited well below the Nyquist frequency of 256 Hz (e.g., low pass filtered at 100 Hz) in order to avoid aliasing. Aliasing is less a problem for EMG because, unlike EEG analyses, EMG analyses examine total power or amplitude in a broad frequency range and do not require finely differentiating specific frequencies. For instance, if the EMG is low pass filtered at 240 Hz, then significant power will still be passed above this frequency, given filter roll-off characteristics. Some aliasing will occur, so EMG activity at 257 Hz through 300 Hz and beyond will not be differentiated from activity at 255 Hz down to 212 Hz and below. In this case, including EMG activity above 257 Hz simply adds to the total EMG power and does not introduce non-EMG contamination of the signal. This point is at times misunderstood (e.g., Blumenthal et al., 2005). Ultimately, experimenters should design their experiments by balancing pragmatic concerns, psychophysiology principles, and phenomena characteristics.

Skin Conductance

Sympathetic arousal activates the skin's eccrine glands, causing columns of sweat to rise through multiple skin layers to the palmar surface (for anatomy and physiology reviews, see Boucsein, 1992; Edelberg, 1972). As sweat fills the ducts, more conductive paths develop through the relatively resistant outer skin layer, the stratum corneum or horny palmar tissue (Fowles, 1986). This process generates a measurable change in the skin's electrical properties, referred to as skin conductance or electrodermal activity (see Fowles et al., 1981).

Historically, investigators measured electrodermal activity with several different methods and referred to the phenomena by multiple terms (see Hugdahl, 1995; Dawson, Schell, & Filion, 2000). We focus on skin conductance (SC), including both tonic skin conductance level (SCL) and phasic skin conductance responses (SCR). By passing an excitation voltage across a pair of electrodes, one can measure the current flow across the electrodes and then compute the skin conductance by dividing the measured current by the excitation voltage. The SC unit is siemens (S) – the International System unit of electrical conductance equal to one ampere per volt. Measuring conductance in this way has advantages over applying a current and measuring skin resistance. Direct skin conductance measures are more linearly related to the number of sweat glands and their rate of secretion than skin resistance measures because individual sweat glands are said to function like resistors in parallel, and the conductance of a parallel circuit is simply the sum of the conductances in parallel (Lykken & Venables, 1971). Thus, a given increase in the number of active sweat glands is said to create a constant increment in the total conductance of the pathway, regardless of the baseline activity level. This pattern suggests that phasic SCRs may be relatively independent of the tonic SCL. Such phasic-tonic distinctions are not observed with skin resistance measures. In addition, using AC excitation, rather than DC excitation, eliminates the risk of electrodes becoming polarized over time.

SC is typically recorded from the underside of the medial or distal phalanges on the pointer and index fingers (Scerbo et al., 1992), and results are usually reported in microseimens (μS). However, given that SC is linearly proportional to the gel-skin contact area, we recommend the unit microseimens per square centimeter (μS/cm^2). When recording SC, one should standardize the gel-skin contact area (e.g., to a 1 cm diameter circle) in order to facilitate comparability among participants and across laboratories. To control the gel-skin contact area, two double-sided adhesive collars with 1 cm diameter holes can be applied directly to clean, unabraded hands. An isotonic electrolyte gel is used (unlike the hypertonic EEG electrolyte gel). Two bipolar SC electrodes are then placed and secured with Velcro bands.

Tonic SCL varies widely among different participants (0.5–50 μS/cm^2), and SCL also drifts within participants over time (1–3 μS/cm^2). Phasic SCRs to novel stimuli are considerably smaller (0.1–1.0 μS/cm^2 over 1–3 s) and generally habituate after 2 to 8 consecutive trials (0.01–0.05 μS/cm^2 per trial). In addition, spontaneous SCRs tend to occur 1 to 3 times per minute in the absence of external stimulation. Given that phasic SCRs are a fraction of the tonic SCL, researchers face tradeoffs when selecting an appropriate SC gain. A low gain optimally captures the full SCL, but signal sensitivity is lost. A higher gain is more sensitive to small SCRs, but large SCL changes may cause the signal to go offscale.

Researchers have used various strategies to address the challenge posed by the large range of skin conductance values. We advocate a dual approach. First, we record the raw SCL signal with a low gain, which requires no manual offset adjustments. Second, we simultaneously create a second SCR signal from the original signal. SCR is then high pass filtered (e.g., 0.01 Hz single pole) and amplified (e.g., $\pm$ 2.5 μS full scale). This dual approach allows us to compute accurate mean SCL within epochs and also to resolve small SCR changes.

Multiple SC confounds exist. They include the aforementioned issues of controlling the gel-skin contact area and addressing sizeable individual differences in both skin conductance levels and magnitude of change. Using relative measures rather than absolute values in experimental designs can attenuate such problems. In addition, SC recordings are particularly vulnerable to movement artifacts and forces on the electrodes. If participants are compliant, stabilizing or restraining the hand and arm can reduce such artifacts. We recommend making a video recording that is time-locked with physiology in order to identify periods when participants move their hands, press the electrodes, or pull the leads and then eliminating such epochs from analyses. Given the variability of the SC signal and the fact that skin conductance waveforms can manifest virtually any arbitrary shape, differentiating artifacts and valid responses is almost impossible without visual observation. Another major confound is room temperature. Low temperatures (e.g., below 15°C) attenuate SC, high temperatures (e.g., above 25°C) potentiate SC, and either extreme can limit the magnitude of SCR changes. Temperature changes from lights and poor ventilation compound the problem. Thus, the participant room temperature should always be controlled, measured, and documented. Such factors impact both experimental design and data analysis (see data analysis section).

Cortisol Response

Cortisol has increasingly become part of psychophysiology studies. Traditionally, investigators have measured cortisol from blood samples, but practical, safe, and reliable techniques now exist to quantify cortisol levels in saliva specimens (Kirschbaum & Hellhammer, 1989). Cortisol is a hormone secreted in periodic pulses into the bloodstream from the adrenal gland, which is regulated by the pituitary gland, hypothalamus, and hippocampus (for anatomy and physiology discussions, see Gunnar, 2003; Jacobson & Sapolsky, 1991). In addition to its roles in glucose metabolism and diurnal rhythms, cortisol also exerts regulatory control functions during periods of stress. During stress, cortisol's secretion level and feedback sensitivity become biased, and circulating concentrations increase. This feedback process influences multiple bodily systems, including both the peripheral and central nervous systems.

Cortisol's secretatory patterns must be addressed when designing studies and collecting specimens. The blood contains both biologically active cortisol molecules (3–5%) and inactive, protein-bound molecules (95–97%). Given cortisol's role in diurnal rhythms, it shows variations related to the sleep-wake cycle, which become increasingly pronounced across development (Spangler, 1991; Watamura, Donzella, Kertes, & Gunnar, 2004). Blood levels range from a nadir of 1 µg/dl during sleep to a peak of 18 µg/dl at awakening, with minor elevations during the day related to meal times. Basal salivary cortisol concentrations are markedly lower (1–6 ng/ml), with small stress-related changes (1–2 ng/ml), because only the active, unbound fraction of the hormone reaches saliva through the parotid gland. Thus, highly sensitive detection techniques are necessary to maximize the data's signal-to-noise ratio.

Acute cortisol responses have a markedly different time course from the aforementioned electrophysiology measures, which occur in seconds or fractions of a second. Cortisol changes after a potent stressor usually peak after 10 to 15 minutes, and maximal responses after milder stressors may take 20 to 30 minutes. Individuals differ in the latency of such changes. Increased sensitivity to acute responses is achieved by repeatedly assessing each participant over several hours on multiple days. The multiple-day design enables within-participant comparisons between the "baseline day" and the "stressor day" (Lovallo & Thomas, 2000). In addition, all participant samples should be collected at the same time of day in order to control for diurnal effects. It is also prudent to collect data about other major covariates such as sleep-wake cycles, eating patterns, hormonal levels, and pubertal status.

Psychological Measures

Psychophysiology focuses on the relations of biological events to psychological phenomena across the lifespan. Thus, systematic psychological manipulations and observations – as well as physiological ones – are core to the scientific enterprise. Specific topics are manifold. For example, psychophysiologists may seek descriptive, normative, or explanatory data. Their questions may be basic or applied. They may conduct longitudinal studies across the lifespan or cross-sectional studies with specific age groups. Topics may span from basic reflexes to multidimensional cognitive, emotional, or social competencies. Electrophysiological measures are particularly well suited for examining auditory, visual, somatosensory, or olfactory processes. In addition, laboratory tasks can quantify orientation, habituation, attention, learning, memory, emotion, or sleep. Observational studies can systematically capture phenomena such as gaze, motor locomotion, human interactions, cognitive adaptation, or stress reactivity. The existing scientific literature can inform the process of generating hypotheses, operationalizing constructs, selecting indexes, and implementing protocols. Experimental design issues are particularly important when assessing differential deficits across groups (see Chapman & Chapman, 2001; Raine, 2002; Strauss, 2001). The following discussion highlights key principles and practical considerations for laboratory stimulation and observational studies.

Laboratory Stimulation

Psychophysiology laboratory stimulation may involve presenting instructions for recording baseline physiological data (e.g., "eyes open" and "eyes closed" resting conditions), or it may entail measuring physiology during specific experimental challenge tasks. When hypotheses pertain to task-dependent effects, laboratory stimulation timing must be synchronized precisely with other aspects of the protocol such as physiological or observational data, and time codes should be integrated with labels for specific task events such as stimulus onsets. Integrating epoch times and condition labels enables the investigator to record a single continuous physiology data file for each session, while preserving essential experimental details for analysis.

Psychological challenge tasks vary widely, but they generally can be described as either deterministic or non-deterministic. Deterministic protocols follow a predetermined course. Independent of the participant's responses, the same stimuli (e.g., visual images, auditory tones) are administered at specified times. Non-deterministic protocols depend upon participant behavior. For example, a protocol might advance to the next trial after a button press, give feedback based on different pushbutton responses, and vary task difficulty based on response accuracy. Deterministic protocols, and many non-deterministic ones, can be implemented with a number of commercial software tools that interface systematically with physiological recording and analysis. More complex, titrating tasks often require custom implementation with a general purpose programming language.

Many classic psychological challenge tasks are deterministic. For example, the autonomic orienting response habituation paradigm (see Graham, Anthony, & Zeigler, 1983; Sokolov, 1990) typically consists of presenting repetitive discrete stimuli (e.g., 75 dB, 1 s tones) with varying interstimulus intervals (e.g., 20–60 s). Likewise, the standard emotional startle modulation protocol involves presenting a series of pleasant, neutral, and aversive images and then eliciting orbicularis oculi startle responses with loud noises or air puff probes (Lang et al., 1990). In addition, sensory ERP paradigms include repetitive visual patterns (e.g., reversing checkerboards) or auditory stimuli (e.g., clicks or tone bursts; see Fabiani, Gratton, & Coles, 2000; John, Brown, Muir, & Picton, 2004; Picton, John, Dimitrijevic, & Purcell, 2003). Classic "oddball" paradigms involve detecting rare target stimuli in a series of frequently presented standard stimuli. Stimulus-response reaction time (RT) tasks with motor demands can elicit event-related slow potentials such as the motor readiness potential, contingent negative variation, or error-related negativity. More complex tasks can tap processes related to attention, memory, and facial processing (e.g., Taylor, McCarthy, Saliba, & Degiovanni, 1999; van der Molen & Ridderinkhof, 1998). Likewise, other cognitive and emotional processes can be examined by superimposing basic stimulus sequences on a contextual task such as reading, arithmetic, or imagery. Most of these laboratory tasks can be programmed with commercial software for implementing laboratory stimulation. The experimenter typically designs and controls specific task parameters, such as stimulus properties, response requirements, cognitive demands, and task difficulty.

Most laboratory stimulation involves varying somatosensory, visual, or auditory stimuli, and several core practical issues exist concerning stimulus quality, timing precision, and electrical noise. In general, the quality of laboratory protocols depends on delivering sensory stimuli with consistent and definable characteristics. For example, some startle protocols require controlled air puffs to the neck. The stimulation should be computer controlled, with precise timing and a consistent force. Such control can be achieved with a PC-based system that delivers pressurized air stimuli. Pressurized air puff stimulation supports delivery of stimulus forces on the order of 1 N and timing precision better than 1 ms. Such parameters are suitable for eliciting robust startle responses in adults as well as children.

In auditory protocols, sound stimuli must be administered with a well-defined and controlled sound pressure level, and decibel (dB) levels should be reported in manuscripts. Achieving well-defined acoustic stimuli can be a problem with consumer-grade audio equipment. In particular, consumer-grade headphones do not have NIST-traceable (National Institute of Standards and Technology) couplers for accurately measuring sound pressure levels, and they tend to be highly sensitive to the position on the ear and to pressure applied to the ear. In contrast, audiometry-grade headphones and insertable earphones are designed specifically to address such concerns. Audiometry headphones apply a virtually constant force across a range of head sizes and do not require careful positioning over the ear. Insertable earphones that insert into the ear canal remove placement and pressure issues altogether. Both audiometry headphones and audiometry insertable earphones have widely available NIST-traceable couplers for calibrating sound pressure levels. Furthermore, audiometry headphones and insertable earphones can be factory calibrated, obviating the need for experimenter calibration. For acoustic safety guidelines, refer to a review of the National Institute for Occupational Safety and Health Standards on the Centers for Disease Control and Prevention website (http://www.cdc.gov/niosh/noise2a.html).

Many stimulation protocols require precise timing, especially with ERP tasks and autonomic orienting response habituation paradigms. Precision is most critical for auditory brainstem protocols in which timing jitter of mere microseconds can affect peak heights. Such precision is not attainable with the Windows operating system, given that it performs background operations that interfere with predictable timing in application software. Such timing issues raise questions about whether Windows is a suitable environment for psychophysiology stimulation. Computer monitors also can introduce uncertainty with visual stimulus onset times. Timing is especially problematic with liquid crystal display (LCD) monitors because the displays update asynchronously. Traditional cathode ray tube (CRT) monitors are more predictable. They update displays in a raster fashion from upper left to the lower right. However, refresh rates vary from as long as 17 ms to as little as 5 ms. Thus, timing should be referenced to vertical refresh, or the point at which the electron beam is traversing from the bottom back up to the top of the screen. Otherwise, one faces up to 8.5 ms of stimulus onset timing uncertainty. Such uncertainty may be problematic for ERP and reaction time (RT) experiments depending on the time resolution needed and the number of trials one is averaging (Segalowitz & Graves, 1990). Early ERP components with a short rise/fall cycle are more vulnerable to such jitter than later slow components.

Another practical issue with visual stimulation concerns electrical noise from computer monitors, which interferes with EMG, EEG, and ERP signals. For example, CRT monitors generate electromagnetic signals at the horizontal sync frequency, the vertical sync frequency, and the AC mains frequency. To mitigate such interference, one can shield the monitor or move it away from the participant and the bioamplifer. The magnetic fields fall off rapidly, with the cube of distance. When selecting the distance from the participant to the monitor, one should remain cognizant of the size of the visual angle, or the angle that individual stimuli subtend at the retina. The visual angle has sizeable effects on visual ERP latencies, and needs to be standardized in such studies. Large monitors help to balance visual angle and electromagnetic interference issues.

Observational Studies

Observational data can be used to identify noncompliance during electro-physiology experiments (e.g., periods of bodily movement that confound some physiology measures), or it can be used to code responses during standardized protocols (e.g., an infant's crying when her mother poses a "still face," interactions between romantically involved couples) or behavior in naturalistic settings (e.g., a child's play in the presence of other youngsters, psychotherapy sessions). Multiple techniques exist for observing and quantifying behavior. We recommend placing vertical interval time code (VITC) on a video recording that is synchronized with tasks and physiology. The computer-readable VITC enables off-line coding and quantification of user-specified phenomena as well as documentation of coder reliability.

According to Bakeman and Gottman (1997), the two major defining characteristics of systematic observational research are (1) the use of predefined behavior codes and (2) a concern with observer reliability. The heart of the research is a coding scheme developed for a particular project. The coding scheme specifies which behaviors are selected from the passing stream and recorded for subsequent analysis. After the coding scheme is implemented, each coder's reliability should be verified against a standard protocol. Cohen's Kappa is the statistic traditionally used to assess observer reliability (Cohen, 1960, 1968). Two coders should code a subset of all experimental sessions, and the data should be Kappa assessed. In addition, a second Kappa should be computed with a time tolerance window to differentiate between coders making errors of fact versus errors of timing (see Bakeman & Gottman, 1997). The goal is to train observers to produce essentially the same codes for a given behavior stream.

A well-designed coding scheme for a particular set of phenomena is mutually exclusive and exhaustive. Thus, the scheme has a code for each possible event or interval, and only one code may apply at any instant in time. Most coding schemes can be made exhaustive simply by adding a null code (e.g., "other"). For example, an investigator may plan to code sets of independent phenomena for a set of observational sessions (e.g., two different people in a recorded interaction). Each of these two categories of phenomena, considered individually, comprises a mutually exclusive and exhaustive list of phenomena. For instance, in an interaction between a mother and her infant, "infant is still" and "mother is still" remain two separate events even if they occur at the same time. The set of codes for the infant is one variable or major code, and the set of codes for the mother is another variable or major code. Each individual code describing the state of the child is a minor code (e.g., still, crying, smiling, other). Each event can be described with a major code (infant) combined with a minor code (still). We recommend designing focused coding schemes to test specific hypotheses, not to capture everything. Coding with a clearly defined focus has practical advantages for achieving coder reliability as well as for analysis and interpretation.

DATA ANALYSIS AND INTERPRETATION

Quantifying psychophysiology data depends on basic principles of digital signal processing. Perhaps the most basic principles relate to standardized units of measurement, the SI system (Système International d'Unités), and the reader is referred to the U.S. National Institute of Standards and Technology website: http://www.physics.nist.gov/cuu/Units/index.html, as well as to a treatise about dimensional analysis (Sonin, 2001). Methods for quantifying particular psychophysiology measures include multiple steps of data reduction prior to descriptive and inferential statistical analysis. The aim of the following section is to introduce major data analysis issues and potential interpretative confounds in order to guide practical decision-making.

Epoch Selection and Artifact Elimination

In most psychophysiology studies, researchers denote data segments for analyses prior to data collection. They typically do so based on time (e.g., second-by-second) or events (i.e., selected condition epochs). To denote specific experimental conditions, protocols are set up with appropriate recording sequences, event marks, and condition labels signifying the beginning and end of each segment or epoch. Data are aggregated across multiple trials for each condition in order to resolve the signal of interest relative to background noise. Numerous trials are also needed because some data are eliminated from analyses due to artifacts (Fisch, 1991). Establishing effective and reliable procedures for minimizing artifacts, which are blind to experimental hypotheses and group membership, is an essential step in preparing for data analysis.

Artifacts can be defined as recorded signals that are not part of the target phenomenon (e.g., non-cerebral signals that occur in the EEG). Depending on their source, artifacts can be divided into one of two categories: non-physiological or physiological. First, non-physiological artifacts arise from external electrical interference (e.g., power lines, electrical equipment) or from internal electrical system malfunction (e.g., electrodes, bioamplifier, cables, computers). Such non-physiological artifacts tend to have specific defining characteristics. Artifacts from a malfunctioning system provide tangible clues for laboratory troubleshooting and diagnosis. For example, flat signals or extreme noise can reflect loose cable connections in the signal path. Isolated electrical noise (such as that generated by AC power lines, lights, dimmer switches, relays, and transformers) tends to have a narrow band, near 60 Hz in North America and 50 Hz in Europe and elsewhere. CRT computer monitors generate electrical noise specifically at the AC frequency as well as at the horizontal and vertical sync frequencies. Such narrow-band noise is particularly problematic when it overlaps with the target signal frequency, such as with EMG (Tassinary & Cacioppo, 2000). Although some investigators advocate analog notch filtering to minimize 50/60 Hz electrical noise, one should recognize that some analog filtering creates problems with ERP measures because excessive filtering can alter the latency, amplitude, and morphology of ERP components. In addition, a 60 Hz notch filter can ring in response to sudden transient events such as an auditory stimulus. When electrical noise overlaps with the target signal frequency, we recommend shielding or eliminating the electrical noise source. If 50/60 Hz noise cannot be eliminated, one can carefully avoid signals in the vicinity and adjust the analysis accordingly. For example, EMG above 65 Hz still reflects an adequate signal for most purposes, and EEG gamma outside the 50/60 range still has research potential. In general, investigators should routinely quantify the 50/60 Hz power in their data as well as examine potential harmonic and intermodulation distortions as artifact sources.

Second, physiological artifacts arise from bodily processes such as gross movements, muscle twitches, eye movements, tongue movements, heartbeats, and respiration (see Fisch, 1991). Physiological artifact contamination tends to be one of degree. For example, extreme movements may result in amplitude shifts that exceed the range of the bioamplifier or the A/D converter, making all electrophysiological data unresolvable (depending on the system's dynamic range). Smaller muscular or ocular movements can produce more minor amplitude and frequency changes. Tongue movement can create EEG artifacts, which can be minimized by instructing participants not to talk, chew gum, or move the tongue during data collection. In addition, cardiopulmonary phenomenon can influence EEG signals, which can be examined with ECG and respiration measures. Most artifact-removal methods apply to circumscribed situations rather than as an all-purpose application because computational models tend to focus on a particular phenomenon.

Movement is a pervasive physiological artifact, particularly with children. Investigators can automate amplitude threshold detection algorithms for major movement artifacts in some measures such as EEG. In addition, auto-mated routines can reliably identify some smaller movements such as eye blinks in the EEG, because they produce specific and well-characterized sig-nal deflections. EEG with ocular artifacts can either be excluded or corrected for analyses. Other movements can require manually inspecting physiology and video records. In general, participants cannot freely move about the room while recording physiology without compromising the signal quality to some degree. Data quality improve when participants are seated, still, and quiet. Notably, however, electrophysiology measures can withstand consider-ably more motion artifact relative to neuroimaging procedures such as func-tional magnetic resonance imaging, where the participant must be supine with the head restrained in order to generate usable data. This fact makes electrophysiological measures attractive, particularly in pediatric samples in which some degree of movement is inevitable (Davidson, Jackson, & Larson, 2000).

Indeed, psychophysiology data may not invariably need to be absolutely artifact free, particularly when artifacts' frequency characteristics do not over-lap with or alias into the target phenomenon. Under such circumstances, minor artifacts tend not to affect results, and excessive artifact rejection lim-its the amount of usable data. However, if artifacts do overlap with the signal of interest (e.g., electrical noise in the EMG) or if excessive data extrapola-tion occurs (e.g., altering heart rate data without a clear ECG signal), then artifacts either overpower the signal of interest, or worse, confound results and bias interpretation. We recommend implementing reliable procedures that preserve a robust signal-to-noise ratio for the target phenomena. Doing so requires understanding, measuring, and quantifying each measure's core features and relevant vulnerabilities to interference and distortion.

Consider the example of recording EEG from infants and young children. If investigators study EEG power in the dominant frequency band as an index of resting brain activity, then they must recognize that such activity changes with development. Generally, EEG spectral power peaks between 8 and 12 Hz in adults and adolescents and between 6 and 9 Hz in young children. However, the dominant frequency during the first year after birth can be below 6 Hz. EEG power at these lower frequencies can overlap with that of eye movements and blinks. This overlap creates an essential conundrum with infant data: a general ocular artifact correction procedure risks reducing EEG activity, but ignoring ocular artifacts can distort the data as well (Somsen & van Beek, 1998). One approach to addressing such tradeoffs is to maximize the number of trials, collect high-quality EOG signals, visually inspect the data, and reject those epochs containing substantial artifact. Thus, in many circumstances, manual artifact editing remains essential. EEG protocols with older children and adults may benefit from additional artifact correction routines.

A number of papers document procedures for ocular artifact correction using regression, principal component analysis, or independent component analysis (e.g., Croft & Barry, 2000; Elbert et al., 1985; Gratton, Coles, & Donchin, 1983; Jung et al., 2000; Lins et al., 1993a, 1993b; Miller, Gratton, & Yee, 1988; Picton et al., 2000c; Wallstrom et al., 2004). Given that ocular signals propagate across the skull by volume conduction, one straightforward approach involves correcting the EEG data using site-specific EOG propagation factors computed with regression techniques (e.g., Miller & Tomarken, 2001). This approach typically involves three steps. First, a temporary dataset is created that contains epochs with ocular artifact exemplars (identified with pattern recognition algorithms) and that minimizes EEG alpha activity and muscle contamination (e.g., with a 7 Hz digital lowpass filter). Second, using this temporary dataset, the EOG data are regressed on each EEG site to compute propagation factors (i.e., beta weights) that characterize the linear relations between the EOG and the ocular artifact at each EEG site. The temporary dataset is then discarded. Third, the correction is applied to the entire original, unfiltered dataset by (a) generating an identity matrix with the negative value of each propagation factor and (b) performing a linear transformation for every data point (i.e., residualizing the EEG from the blink-contaminated signal by computing $[EEG-\beta(EOG]$ for each EEG sample). This approach ensures that the data remain continuous and continuously differentiable, which is a prerequisite for Fourier analyses.

In general, a robust signal-to-noise ratio is critical for most psychophysiology measures. Consider ECG. ECG artifacts exist when R-waves are spuriously detected or missed, and investigators cannot delete unusual R-wave periods without disrupting data continuity. Rather, aberrant R-R intervals should be identified and visually inspected using an artifact-detection algorithm (e.g., Berntson, Quigley, Jang, & Boysen, 1990). For example, a program can automatically identify outliers in the R-R interval distribution, and then an experimenter can manually inspect the ECG record to correct the R-wave onset times. Such manual inspection should be blind to experimental hypotheses or group membership. The task requires distinguishing between genuinely abnormal beats (requiring no correction) and artifact-laden data (requiring editing R-wave onset times). In most cases, visually inspecting correctly acquired ECG data enables unambiguous distinctions. Without raw ECG data, heart period outliers cannot be edited adequately, and failing to inspect raw data substantially increases risks of spurious or biased results.

Artifacts can also plague skin conductance measures. This issue was discussed above because skin conductance artifacts can be minimized substantially during data acquisition. In particular, investigators should systematically control the gel-skin contact area, room temperature, hand movement, and noncompliance. In addition, a video record time-locked with physiology can be used to identify and eliminate epochs when participants move their hands, press the electrodes, or pull the leads, because such events can produce signal changes that mimic genuine skin conductance effects.

Electrophysiological Analysis Techniques

EEG Power, Asymmetry, and Coherence
The EEG's sinusoidal fluctuations (see Figure 13.2) are described in terms of two characteristic parameters: frequency and voltage (Duffy et al., 1989). The frequency reflects how many oscillations or cycles occur per second, and the unit is hertz (Hz). Voltage is described as the magnitude or amplitude, and the unit is microvolts (μV).

Standard methods of Fourier analysis are used to compute spectral power, typically using the Fast Fourier Transform (FFT; Cooley & Tukey, 1965; Dumermuth & Molinari, 1987). Fourier analysis separates a waveform into specific frequency components. Before applying the FFT, the mean voltage may be subtracted to reduce DC offset in the data series. The FFT algorithm is usually applied to short, stable data periods (e.g., one second in duration). A Hanning window is often used to taper the ends of selected epochs, eliminating spurious end effects. If consecutive Hanning windows are overlapped by 50 percent, then uniform weight is given to each sample. When one-second windows are used, the FFT gives spectral power for one Hz bins (traditionally expressed as mean square volts), and the bins are centered on integer numbers (i.e., the bin centered at 10 Hz is defined as power from 9.5 to 10.5 Hz).

Fourier analysis results can be grouped into components, or broad bands, by summing power across individual frequency bins. (Power density is power divided by the number of bins.) Bands are identified by the Greek letters delta (δ), theta (θ), alpha (α), beta (β), and gamma (γ). Delta activity (1–3 Hz bins) is common in the deep sleep of adults and older children; neonatal EEG is less clearly related to sleep-wake states (Niedermeyer, 1993). Theta activity (4–7 Hz bins) is normally seen in drowsiness and light sleep but is also present during wakefulness. Alpha is the dominant rhythm (8–12 Hz bins for adults and older children; 6–9 Hz bins for infants and younger children). Beginning during late childhood, alpha power decreases with eye opening, attention, and mental effort. During infancy, power in the peak 6–9 Hz band tends to increase with task performance (Bell, 2002; Bell & Fox, 1992). Given the developmental changes in theta and alpha activity (Yordanova & Kolev, 1996), pediatric studies should include multiple bands in this range (e.g., 3–5, 6–9, and 10–12 Hz bins; Marshall et al., 2002). Beta activity (13–30 Hz bins) generally increases during task performance in adults and is often separated into low and high subcomponents (e.g., at 20 Hz). Gamma activity includes higher frequency power, typically in the 31 to 45 Hz range and higher. Although evidence supports the independence of EEG spectral bands, their boundaries can vary among individuals and across development. Such individual differences and developmental changes underscore the value of examining EEG power distributions and peaks for individual and group data. Normative data can aid interpretation (John et al., 1980, 1987).

Spectral coherence also can be computed with Fourier analysis (e.g., Als et al., 2004). Coherence analyses focus on selected electrode pairs in selected spectral bands across a time period, and results document the dependence relations between target brain waves or the degree of regional neural interactive coupling (Saltzberg et al., 1986). Coherence values range from zero to one, and phase can be measured in degrees as well as a lag time in seconds, with a positive lag time implying that the second channel lags the first channel.

In order to prepare for statistical hypothesis testing, investigators often transform Fourier results and compute summary indexes (see Allen, Coan, & Nazarian, 2004). For example, because the distributional characteristics of spectral power and asymmetry values may not meet the assumptions of parametric statistical analyses, a natural log transformation is often used to normalize the distribution (Gasser, Bacher, & Mocks, 1982; Wackermann & Matousek, 1998). A frequently used summary statistic is the asymmetry metric, defined as the ratio of power for homologous left- and right-hemisphere sites (Davidson & Tomarken, 1989). Log ratios of raw power are mathematically equivalent to differences between log-transformed power values. When using EEG asymmetry as an individual difference measure, investigators should address its reliability and stability (Tomarken, 1995; Tomarken, Davidson, Wheeler, & Kinney, 1992). Notably, extraneous variables such as individual variability in skull thickness and conductivity can differentially attenuate EEG power (Tomarken, 1999). This confound for group comparisons should inform hypothesis testing and statistical modeling. Constant skull-related variance is factored out of within-participant ratio scores such as asymmetry metrics. Likewise, repeated measures designs use within-participant comparisons, so analysis of variance results with hemisphere as a repeated measure and power as the dependent variable are equivalent to results with asymmetry as the dependent measure. Investigators can increase the signal-to-noise of EEG alpha measures by focusing on relative power between recording sites or time points.

For many psychophysiology measures, relative changes have greater validity and reliability than absolute values. Thus, within-participant repeated measures designs often provide more powerful tests than between-participant comparisons. However, investigators should be aware of issues that complicate repeated measures analysis of variance (ANOVA) designs, particularly when a variable includes three or more levels (Jennings, Cohen, Ruchkin, & Fridlund, 1987; Rogan, Keselman, & Mendoza, 1979). Traditional ANOVAs assume sphericity (i.e., constant variance of all pairwise difference), and violations of this statistical assumption increase the Type I (false positive) error rates (Boik, 1981). Thus, repeated-measures ANOVAs often require standard adjustments of the degrees of freedom to compensate for positive biases. In many circumstances, a multivariate analysis of variance (MANOVA) approach using the Pillai's Trace statistic, which does not assume sphericity, allows for more valid, accurate, and powerful tests of small but reliable effects within a repeated measures design (Vasey & Thayer, 1987). We recommend the MANOVA approach for most repeated measure designs with three or more levels.

ERP Waveforms, Components, and Sources

Event-related potentials (ERPs) reflect brain electrical responses to specific sensory stimuli (e.g., brainstem auditory evoked potentials or BAEPs; Markand, 1994), cognitive events (e.g., mismatch negativity or MMN, Näätänen, 2003; Picton et al., 2000a; P300, Cycowicz & Friedman, 1997; Fabiani, Gratton, Karis, & Donchin, 1987; Howard & Polich, 1985; Pritchard, 1981), or motor responses (e.g., contingent negative variation or CNV, Walter et al., 1964; error related negativity or ERN, Falkenstein et al., 1990). ERP data typically are plotted as voltage changes at particular spatial locations as a function of time. The excellent timing precision of ERPs provides a unique view of the temporal patterns of brain activity (Picton et al., 2000b).

Scalp-recorded ERPs are signal changes of a few microvolts, occurring within ongoing EEG oscillations of up to 50 µV. ERP analyses involve procedures to resolve the ERP waveform relative to the background EEG oscillations. One approach to increasing the signal-to-noise ratio is with digital filtering (Cook & Miller, 1992; Nitschke, Miller, & Cook, 1998). Another classic technique is signal averaging (see Fabiani et al., 2000). Based on the central limit theorem, signal averaging provides an estimate of the central tendency across multiple trial epochs that are time-locked to a target event. Random EEG oscillations that are not time-locked to the target event will approach zero in the averaged waveform. To the extent that ERP signals are constant and background noise is random across trials, then the signal-to-noise ratio will increase by the square root of the number of trials included in the average. ERPs also can be identified with statistical pattern recognition techniques such as discriminant analysis (DA; Donchin & Herning, 1975; Gevins, 1984; Horst & Donchin, 1980; Squires & Donchin, 1976) or cosinusoidal functions (Fabiani et al., 1987; Gratton et al., 1989). This approach involves quantifying individual waveform's relation to a standard or "ideal" waveform generated from a sizeable, controlled training dataset (Fabiani et al., 1987; Glaser & Ruchkin, 1976).

ERP waveforms are generally interpreted as aggregates of multiple components. Such components are classically defined in terms of the waveform's peaks and troughs, or the voltage maxima and minima within particular latency ranges (e.g., see Figure 13.3). The earliest components, beginning milliseconds after stimulus onset, vary in relation to the physical properties of external auditory or visual events and reflect basic sensory and perceptual processes. Peaks and troughs with longer latencies are more sensitive to psychological processes related to interactions between the participant and eliciting events such as selective attention, feature discrimination, novelty orienting, pattern recognition, decision making, mnemonic mechanisms, language processing, motor preparation, and error detection. Such early and late potentials have been referred to traditionally as "exogenous" and "endogenous" potentials, respectively (Donchin, Ritter, & McCallum, 1978), although the distinction has been difficult to support in more recent times.

ERP components can be quantified in different ways (see Fabiani et al., 2000). One approach defines peak latencies within selected time windows. Such "peak picking" involves choosing time windows for expected components (e.g., 50 to 150, 150 to 300, and 300 to 700 ms), examining the mean voltage within each window, and then defining latencies by the time points of the maximum and minimum voltages within each window (Luck & Hillyard, 1994). Usually, peak amplitudes are defined in relation to a baseline voltage level before the target event (base-to-peak amplitude) or to another voltage peak in the waveform (peak-to-peak amplitude). If a component does not have a definite peak, then one can quantify the integrated activity with an area measure, or the average activity across a specific time range with a mean amplitude measure. Notably, ERP components observed in infants tend to be delayed relative to those in adults. For example, early P1 and N1 components related to perception and attention may occur as late as 200 to 300 ms at the youngest ages (Thomas & Crow, 1994), but by 6 months such latencies usually begin to decrease (McIsaac & Polich, 1992; Richards, 2000).

Another approach to ERP quantification involves identifying latent components with multivariate statistical procedures such as principal components analysis (PCA; Alexander & Moeller, 1994; Donchin & Heffley, 1978; Kayser & Tenke, 2003; Richards, 2004) or independent component analysis (ICA; Delorme & Makeig, 2004; Makeig et al., 1997). PCA decomposes the data into orthogonal components that account for maximal variance. In practice, orthogonal components are computed from the sample covariance matrix, and the components are defined by the weights of the eigenvectors that correspond to the largest eigenvalues (Möcks & Verleger, 1991). The raw component solution is generally rotated, or transformed, to fulfill specific criteria for component loadings (e.g., maximizing sample variance with a Varimax rotation). Such PCA computations can be implemented with commercial statistical software packages. ICA functions much like an oblique rotation of a spatial PCA solution. ICA decomposes the data into latent components that are as independent from each other as possible. The independence criterion implies not simply that components are uncorrelated (a condition of the second-order moments), but that all of the higher-order moments are zero. ICA algorithms can be implemented with MATLAB routines available in the public domain (see Delorme & Makeig, 2004). Such routines for separating independent components are best applied to data containing distinct target phenomena. ICA may distort the spectral characteristics of EEG data (Wallstrom et al., 2004). Ultimately, the value of latent ERP component structures depends on their validity, replicability, and interpretability.

ERP components also can be defined in terms of neural source generators. Algorithms exist for dipole source analysis (e.g., Brain Electrical Source Analysis; BESA, Scherg, Ille, Bornfleth, & Berg, 2002) and distributed source analysis (Low Resolution Brain Electromagnetic Tomography Analysis, LORETA; Pascual-Marqui et al., 2002, 1994). Spatiotemporal dipole models represent variance in surface activity in terms of individual point source dipoles. In these models, amplitude and polarity vary over time, while location and orientation can be fixed based on an assumed head model. Distributed source models assume that extended areas are simultaneously active. To explain variance in the distribution of surface activity, source analysis models allow the relative contribution of different brain areas to vary over time. A core problem with such models that attempt to solve the "inverse problem" is that they tend to include more free parameters than data points. In addition to the electrical activity data, other observations are generally needed to constrain the number of solutions, even with large electrode arrays. Thus, source models of brain activity should be guided and constrained by anatomical and functional data obtained with other methods such as functional magnetic resonance imaging (fMRI). Evidence suggests good correspondence between ERP sources and fMRI patterns for some tasks (e.g., sensorimotor, face perception, and target detection tasks) but not others (e.g., somatosensory and hippocampal activation tasks), and so one cannot assume a one-to-one correspondence between ERP generators and fMRI activations under all conditions (Huettel et al., 2004; McCarthy, 1999).

Some ERP quantification does not require the classic concept of ERP components. By subtracting waveforms from different conditions, investigators focus more on understanding the way stimuli are processed than on describing the functional significance or the source localization of ERP components, e.g., the repetition effect contrasts ERPs during previously viewed versus new stimuli (Friedman, 2000), and the attention effect contrasts items to which attention is or is not directed (Näätänen & Teder, 1991). Such subtraction techniques generally assume that variation is selective to one component and that only amplitude, and not latency, varies across conditions.

Results from different ERP analytic approaches may converge or diverge. Interpretation is complicated by factors such as the overlap of multiple components. Indeed some ERP peaks (e.g., N1) may represent the summation of multiple functionally and structurally distinct components (Näätänen & Picton, 1987). In addition, components may not appear in isolation, but several may be active at the same time, reflecting parallel processing in the brain. Some brain structures may contribute to multiple ERP peaks, and different brain structures may produce similar activity (e.g., homologous left and right cortical areas). The fact that ERPs tend to be multiply determined underscores the importance of well-designed and focused analytic strategies.

Heart Period and Heart Period Variability

Heart period, or the time between successive R-wave onsets, is a robust measure with limited dynamic range (Jennings et al., 1981). For example, adult resting heart period (or interbeat interval, IBI) typically ranges from 500 ms to 2 s (i.e., heart rates between 120 and 30 beats per minute). Pediatric heart period tends to have a range of 400 ms to 1.2 s (i.e., heart rates between 150 and 50 beats per minute). With ECG recordings, heart period can be quantified reliably using automated algorithms for detecting R-waves. Visually inspecting the raw ECG signal facilitates correction of missed or misidentified R-waves. The R-wave onset times are converted to IBIs, or the time periods between successive R-wave onsets. The IBIs are sampled on an equal time interval basis using proration, and the mean and variance are computed. In the absence of an intact ECG signal, investigators are left to guess about the time of missed or misidentified heartbeats. In addition, other methods for deriving IBIs such as cardiotachometers can introduce random errors and nonlinearities to the time series (Berntson et al., 1997).

Given that cardiac rhythms are continuously modified by the autonomic nervous system, heart period variability is a widely used measure of cardiac autonomic regulation (Berntson et al., 1997). Beat-to-beat fluctuations include multiple components. Global heart period variability is a composite of several periodic oscillations and some aperiodic noise (Akselrod et al., 1981). The global heart period standard deviation includes all such components and does not distinguish among them. In addition to effects from thermoregulation, sympathetic arousal, and hormonal influences, perhaps the most pronounced influence on heart period variability is from the respiratory cycle. Typically, the relative heart period is shorter during inspiration and longer during expiration. In other words, when a person inhales, the heart speeds up, with less time between successive beats; when a person exhales, the heart slows down, with more time between beats (Hirsch & Bishop, 1981). Laboratory studies have established that pharmacological blockade of vagal or parasympathetic activity reduces high-frequency heart rate variability in the respiratory range, while total autonomic blockade essentially eliminates all heart period variability (Akselrod et al., 1981). Thus, measures of high-frequency heart period variability, or respiratory sinus arrhythmia (RSA), are often said to index individual differences in parasympathetic control or "vagal tone" (Eckberg, 1983; Porges, 1986).

RSA can be quantified in multiple ways from the ECG-derived heart period (IBI) or heart rate (HR) time series, including a spectral analysis method and a peak-valley technique (Grossman, van Beek, & Wientjes, 1990; Porges & Byrne, 1992). A spectral analysis approach applies Fourier analyses to extract power within a target respiratory frequency band (in mean square seconds for IBI data, or mean square hertz for HR data). The procedure uses the IBI or HR time series for equal sampling intervals, and the time series is often detrended to minimize variability from aperiodic shifts in tonic heart period. The remaining variance is then computed for a respiratory band, typically defined for adults as 0.12–0.4 Hz, or approximately 7–24 breaths per minute (Berntson et al., 1997). A higher frequency band is used for infants and children. For example, a band from 0.24–1.04 Hz is appropriate from infancy to 4 years of age (Bar-Haim et al., 2000). Given that the RSA distribution may not meet assumptions for parametric statistics, a natural log transformation of variance estimates is commonly used.

Peak-valley estimation uses temporally synchronized heart period duration and respiration data. The respiration signal is used to identify inspiration and expiration onset times and relative tidal volume. Next, heart period differences are computed for each inspiration and expiration cycle. Grossman et al., (1990) documented similar RSA results from the different quantification methods, with interindividual correlations between measures above 0.92 and a mean within-participant correlation of 0.96 (see also Galles, Miller, Cohn, & Fox, 2002). Convergent results across methods depend on the particular parameters selected for analyses, emphasizing the need to specify detailed analytic procedures in order to facilitate comparison across studies.

Given that the peak-valley method is computed breath-by-breath, rather than across a 32-s or 64-s window needed for reliable spectral results, the peak-valley method allows greater temporal resolution than can be obtained with spectral analysis. In addition, respiration data are important because RSA can be confounded by respiratory parameters (Grossman et al., 1991). Although RSA itself is parasympathetically mediated, the breathing that induces RSA has both voluntary and sympathetic influences. Although respiratory parameters tend to be relatively stable during resting baseline conditions, they may be less so during experimental conditions that induce sympathetic arousal or voluntary breathing changes. In such case, RSA may need to be corrected via a transfer function for changes in respiration across experimental conditions (Wilhelm et al., 2004).

Developmental influences are an important factor in interpreting RSA. In neonates, sharp drops in high-frequency heart period variability reliably index fetal distress and risk (DiPietro, Caughy, Cusson, & Fox, 1994). In infants, low heart period variability tends to predict decreased adaptation and emotional expressiveness, but effects in older children can be more difficult to interpret, in part due to greater voluntary control of respiration (Fox & Porges, 1985; Bar-Haim et al., 2000). Methodological studies also emphasize measures of temporal stability, documenting that resting baseline heart period variability has high reliability (with intraclass correlation coefficients of 0.68 to 0.86) but task-related reactivity is less stable (0.17 to 0.73) (Sloan et al., 1995; see also El-Sheikh, 2005).

Impedance Cardiography

When measuring impedance cardiography, we recommend digitizing signals for Z_0 (basal thoracic impedance), ΔZ (time-varying thoracic impedance), and dZ/dt (the first derivative of impedance with respect to time), along with a separate ECG signal. The phonocardiogram (i.e., heart sounds) also can be useful in studies of stroke volume and cardiac output but are not necessary for quantifying preejection period (PEP). Some impedance cardiographs incorporate on-line microprocessing for real-time computations. Applications generally do not require such automatic processing, which precludes most artifact rejection procedures. As with other psychophysiological measures, off-line processing facilitates essential visual inspection of raw data for artifacts. Although impedance cardiograph measures are fairly robust, the signal can be compromised significantly by factors such as extreme obesity and physical activity. With an eye for valid and reliable measures, we recommend acquiring high-quality raw data, visually inspecting the data, eliminating artifact-laden epochs (i.e., those periods where one cannot extract the target phenomenon's essential components such as the β-point for PEP), and quantifying measures with off-line analysis routines.

Off-line digital processing also facilitates ensemble averaging of multiple cardiac cycles by using R-wave peaks as references (see Sherwood et al., 1990). Such ensemble averaging works much like ERP averaging to improve the signal-to-noise ratio and resolves waveform components. Specific dZ/dt waveform components can be identified with interactive graphics editing software. For example, the β-point corresponds to the onset of left-ventricular ejection and is defined by the initiation of the rapid upslope in the dZ/dt signal as it rises to its peak value within the cardiac cycle, $dZ/dt_{(max)}$ (Kubicek et al., 1970; Martin et al., 1971). The X-point is the lowest point of a sharp notch in the dZ/dt waveform, representing aortic valve closure at the end of left-ventricular ejection. The left-ventricular ejection period (LVET) is the dZ/dt β-point to the X-point. Cardiac output is computed as the product of stroke volume (SV) and heart rate. A commonly used equation for estimating left-ventricular stroke volume was first suggested by Kubicek and colleagues (1966):

$$SV = rho * (L/Z_0)^2 * LVET * dZ/dt_{(max)}$$

where, SV is stroke volume (ml), rho is the resistivity of blood (often defined as 135 Ωcm), L is the distance between recording electrodes (cm), Z_0 is the basal thoracic impedance (Ω), LVET is the left-ventricular ejection time (s), and $dZ/dt_{(max)}$ is the absolute value of the maximum rate of change (slope) in the impedance waveform on a given beat (Ω/s). According to Mohapatra (1981), the Kubicek SV computation should consider the blood hematocrit level to define rho, as 67.919 exp(0.0247 hematocrit level), particularly when hematocrit may be abnormal (e.g., from anemia, iron deficiency, cardiac abnormalities). Interpretation of volume-based indices, including cardiac output and stroke volume, is based on assumptions about body conductivity

(Sherwood et al., 1990). Cardiac index (CI, liter/min/m²) and stroke volume index (SVI, ml/m²) are computed by dividing individual cardiac output and stroke volume measures by body surface areas (BSA), estimated on the basis of height and weight:

$$BSA(m^2) = Weight(kg)^{0.425} * Height(cm)^{0.725} * 0.007184$$

Computational details reveal that volume-based measures are sensitive to blood resistivity, electrode distance, and body conductivity. Investigators should ensure that their computational constants and assumptions reflect the actual variability within their sample, because uncontrolled variability decreases reliability and validity.

Preejection period (PEP), an index of myocardial contractility and sympathetic cardiac control, is a robust time-based measure extracted from the impedance cardiogram (see Berntson et al., 1994; Harris et al., 1967; McCubbin et al., 1983; Newlin & Levenson, 1979; Obrist et al., 1987; Schachinger et al., 2001). PEP computation requires fewer assumptions than volume-based measures. PEP is defined as the time period from the onset of ventricular depolarization to the start of left-ventricular ejection of blood into the aorta. Operationally, PEP is the time interval from the ECG Q wave (see Figure 13.6) to the dZ/dt β-point. Traditionally, ventricular depolarization is marked by the Q onset, but small or absent Q expression can introduce spurious variance for many participants. Thus, Berntson and his colleagues (2004) provided conceptual, physiological, and empirical support for using the Q peak (i.e., the R-wave onset) as the fiducial point for PEP in order to maximize its reliability and validity. For clarity, investigators can designate pre-ejection period measures derived from R-onset or Q-onset as PEP_r or PEP_q, respectively, and provide explicit descriptions of their methodology.

Investigators should be aware of possible interpretation errors for PEP. For example, increased preload raises myocardial contractility via autoregulatory mechanisms and decreases PEP independent of sympathetic influences. Whereas, increased peripheral vascular resistance raises afterload and tends to lengthen PEP. Generally, such effects are minor, but investigators can inform their interpretations of sympathetic arousal by assessing multiple measures. For example, sympathetic arousal can be interpreted from PEP decreases in the context of concurrent heart rate increases, blood pressure elevations, and other electromechanical systole decreases (McCubbin et al., 1983; Obrist et al., 1987). Some investigators have proposed that the ratio of pre-ejection period to left-ventricular ejection time (PEP/LVET ratio) is an index of left-ventricular function that corrects for heart rate dependencies (i.e., PEP/LVET ratio). However, rather than using such formulas as standard corrections, Sherwood recommends that investigators evaluate the incremental contributions or redundancy of specific measures in order to address interpretation in a "physiologically and conceptually explicit manner" (Sherwood et al., 1990, p. 13).

EMG Amplitude

The surface EMG signal from the muscles has a broad frequency range (several Hz to over 500 Hz) and amplitude range (μV to mV). Typically, a bipolar surface EMG signal peaks near 90 Hz, with most of the activity between 30 and 200 Hz (Tassinary & Cacioppo, 2000).

Traditionally, EMG signal conditioning was performed during acquisition, such as with a contour following integrator (a misnamed electronic device comprising mainly a precision rectifier connected to a simple first-order low-pass filter), resulting in a running average of ongoing EMG amplitude. However, such devices can distort the signal. In order to preserve the frequency and time components of the raw signal, we recommend off-line techniques for digital filtering, amplitude computation, and latency measurement.

Orbicularis oculi EMG startle magnitude and latency are commonly computed off-line from digitized signals (e.g., Schmidt et al., 1998). Epoching software is used to identify and resolve peak latency and amplitude. Thirty-two ms windows (effectively 16 ms after Hanning taper) are 93 percent overlapped (with 2 ms increments). Each baseline epoch is usually defined as the 200 ms period prior to the onset of the acoustic startle probe, and trials are eliminated if pre-stimulus ocular muscle artifact is detected that interferes with startle blink responses. Target startle response epochs tend to be the 20 to 200 ms interval following the acoustic stimulus onset. EMG responses can be quantified using several different methods. The first approach is a bandpass-filter and rectification method. After filtering the raw EMG signal by convolving with a truncated sinc function, the data are rectified to make all values positive, and the peak EMG amplitude is computed. Alternatively, the data can be squared before computing amplitude values. A second approach uses spectral analysis. Using the same aforementioned sampling windows, the Fast Fourier Transform (FFT) is applied to compute spectral power in particular frequency bands. A band from 80 to 240 Hz identifies the bulk of the startle EMG activity while maintaining temporal precision appropriate for responses with a latency of approximately 50 ms. Resolving lower frequencies with FFT compromises timing precision, and the 80 to 240 Hz band avoids 50/60 Hz noise confounds. Root mean square amplitude is computed by taking the square root of spectral power values. As in the rectification method, the peak EMG amplitude can then be identified within each target startle epoch. Within-participant standardized scores (e.g., Z transformations) are often used to minimize error variance and outliers in the distribution.

Techniques for rectification and filtering as well as spectral analysis can be applied to other EMG signals and conditions such as corrugator and zygomaticus regional facial muscle activity during emotion challenges (Dimberg, 1990). These techniques typically focus on some variation of EMG signal amplitude as a function of time. However, simple averaging of EMG amplitudes is not informative because the nature of the signal suggests that the expected average value will be zero. Common dependent measures include the average of EMG peaks, the average of the rectified and filtered EMG activity, or the root mean square of the EMG signal (i.e., the square root of the sum of squared amplitudes within an epoch). Standardizing EMG scores within sites and participants is widely used to reduce site and participant variability. As discussed by Tassinary and Cacioppo (2000), the Z-score metric performed better than other common transformations regarding both consistency with the raw data and ability to detect true differences (Bush, Hess, & Wolford, 1993). However, such transformations should not be applied blindly. In general, they should have an explicit justification, and investigators should report any differences between the ordering of untransformed versus transformed means.

Skin Conductance Response and Level

Electrodermal activity or skin conductance differs from other electrophysiological measures in its large dynamic range (see above EDA discussion), and this fact presents challenges for analysis (Fowles et al., 1981). As noted earlier, recording separate SCR and SCL signals facilitates accurate computations of both small SCRs and mean SCLs.

SCRs have a characteristic saw-tooth pattern. Sympathetic responses induce a sharp peak of 0.01 to 1.0 $\mu S/cm^2$ within 1 to 3 s, and each peak is followed by a slow recovery. During resting periods, the skin conductance signal commonly trends downward. SCRs can be either event related or spontaneous. For example, skin conductance orienting responses can be induced with high sound pressure level white noise probes as well as other novel or unexpected stimuli (see above laboratory stimulation discussion). Automated algorithms can identify SCRs from the digitized signal. Methods that extract SCRs without regard to the underlying trend in SC often miss small responses. Techniques that use a regression baseline or slope projected out in time enable more sensitive and accurate measurement. This approach becomes progressively more valuable with shorter inter-stimulus-intervals because the responses are still recovering from one stimulus during the presentation of the next stimulus (i.e., significant down slopes often occur at stimulus onset). Commonly quantified event-related SCR parameters include latency to onset, latency to peak, response slope, peak height, quarter recovery time, and half recovery time. Another phenomenon of interest is the spontaneous or nonspecific SCR, which is thought to be like the event related SCR but is asynchronous to any stimuli. The most widely used measure of the spontaneous SCR is the rate per minute (typically between 1 and 3 per minute).

Mean SCL within epochs has been used as an index of general arousal, which varies across individuals, beginning during infancy (Hernes et al., 2002). However, direct comparisons of SCL across participants are confounded by large individual differences in the thickness of the stratum corneum, the density of the sweat glands, and other extraneous factors. Age, gender, and race effects are also common. The sizeable individual differences suggest caution with threshold based analysis methods for SCL or SCR because the degree of change may itself vary among people (see studies of electrodermal lability, e.g., Crider, 1993). Likewise, extreme outliers in the distribution can bias group means. In addition, difference or change scores from baseline to experimental conditions may be greater for participants with a high tonic SCL than those with a low tonic SCL.

Analytic strategies entail computing dimensionless skin conductance measures in order to reduce error variance. For example, Lykken and his colleagues (1966) proposed computing individual range scores and expressing momentary values as a proportion of this range. For example, a minimum SCL can be computed during a resting baseline epoch, and a maximum SCL can be computed during an epoch in which a balloon is blown to bursting. The target SCL can then be expressed as: $(SCL - SCL_{min})/(SCL_{max} - SCL_{min})$. The minimum SCR can be assumed to be zero, and the maximum SCR can be estimated from a response to an alarming or startling stimulus. The target SCR can then be computed by dividing each SCR by the participant's maximum SCR. Such an approach is inappropriate when the ranges differ between compared groups or when range values cannot reliably be assessed (Lykken & Venables, 1971). Alternatively, investigators can compute within-participant standardized scores (Ben-Shakhar, 1985). For example, Z scores express the deviation from the mean in standard deviation units. As emphasized above, such transformations should be accompanied by explicit statements about their effects on observed distributions.

SUMMARY AND CLOSING REMARKS

Psychophysiology is a multidisciplinary science focused on psychological-physiological relations in people across the lifespan (Stern, 1964, 1968). The current chapter described basic principles, pointers, and pitfalls for conducting psychophysiology assessments, with emphasis on physiological signal acquisition, off-line digital processing, and experimental design issues. As W. A. McCall (1923) once wrote about experimenting in education, "There are excellent books and courses of instruction dealing with the statistical manipulation of experimental data, but there is little help to be found on the methods of securing adequate and proper data to which to apply statistical procedures" (Campbell & Stanley, 1963, p. 1). McCall's words capture an essential theme of this chapter. Just as educational research requires attention to experimental complexities and subtleties, so does psychophysiology research.

Securing adequate and proper psychophysiology data has inherent challenges. As we emphasized throughout this chapter, one of the most fundamental challenges is that psychophysiological measures are multiply determined. By nature, such measures are difficult to control and manipulate for optimal statistical efficiency. They are complex phenomena related to various psychological and developmental processes as well as electrical and physiological factors. This review provided concrete examples of some of the most basic contributions and confounds of psychophysiological measures and offered practical ways to address such factors.

Given the inherent challenges of psychophysiology assessment, we advocated a multifaceted methodological approach that emphasized both practical and conceptual rigor. Psychophysiologists must ensure the technical quality and high signal-to-noise ratios of their target physiological measures. The work also demands carefully controlled and designed experiments that address interpretative confounds. Such methodological issues inform and are informed by the conceptual context that guides individual research programs. Ultimately, the multiple determinants of psychophysiological processes reflect the complexities of human nature itself. Testing and refining psychophysiological models involves assessing multiple measures in order to identify convergent and divergent observations over time.

References

Ahmed, S. S., Levinson, G. E., Schwartz, C. J., & Ettinger, P. O. (1972). Systolic time intervals as measures of the contractile state of the left ventricular myocardium in man. *Circulation, 46*, 559–571.

Akselrod, S., Gordon, D., Ubel, F. A., Shannon, D. C., Barger, A. C., & Cohen, R. J. (1981). Power spectrum analysis of heart rate fluctuations: A quantitative probe of beat-to-beat cardiovascular control. *Science, 213,* 220–222.

Alexander, G. E., & Moeller, J. R. (1994). Application of the scaled subprofile model to functional imaging in neuropsychiatric disorders: A principal component approach to modeling brain function and disease. *Human Brain Mapping, 2,* 79–94.

Allen, J. J. B., Coan, J. A., & Nazarian, M. (2004). Issues and assumptions on the road from raw signals to metrics of frontal EEG asymmetry in emotion. *Biological Psychology, 67,* 183–218.

Als, H., Duffy, F. H., McAnulty, G. B., Rivkin, M. J., Vajapeyam, S., Mulkern, R. V., Warfield, S. K., Huppi, P. S., Butler, S. C., Conneman, N., Fischer, C., & Eichenwald, E. C. (2004). Early experience alters brain function and structure. *Pediatrics, 113,* 846–857.

American Electroencephalographic Society. (1994). Guideline thirteen: Guidelines for standard electrode position nomenclature. *Journal of Clinical Neurophysiology, 11,* 111–113.

Artman, M., Mahoney, L., & Teitel, D. F. (2002). *Neonatal cardiology.* New York: McGraw-Hill.

Attuel, P., Leporho, M. A., Ruta, J., Lucet, V., Steinberg, C., Azancot, A., & Coumel, P. (1986). The evolution of the sinus heart rate and variability as a function of age from birth to 16 years. In E. F. Doyle (Ed.), *Pediatric cardiology: Proceeding of the Second World Congress 1985.* New York: Springer-Verlag.

Bakeman, R., & Gottman, J. M. (1997). *Observing interaction: An introduction to sequential analysis* (2nd ed.). New York: Cambridge University Press.

Balaban, M. T. (1995). Affective influences on startle in five-month-old infants: Reactions to facial expressions of emotion. *Child Development, 66,* 28–36.

Bar-Haim, Y., Marshall, P. J., & Fox, N. A. (2000). Developmental changes in heart period and high-frequency heart period variability from 4 months to 4 years of age. *Developmental Psychobiology, 37,* 44–56.

Basar, E. (1980). *EEG brain dynamics: Relations between EEG and brain evoked potentials.* Amsterdam, Netherlands: Elsevier.

Basar, E. (1998). *Brain oscillations: Principles and approaches.* Berlin, Germany: Elsevier.

Belik, J., & Pelech, A. (1988). Thoracic electric bioimpedance measurement of cardiac output in the newborn infant. *Journal of Pediatrics, 113,* 890–895.

Bell, M. A. (2002). Power changes in infant EEG frequency bands during a spatial working memory task. *Psychophysiology, 39,* 450–458.

Bell, M. A. & Fox, N. A. (1992). The relations between frontal brain electrical activity and cognitive development during infancy. *Child Development, 63,* 1142–1163.

Ben-Shakhar, G. (1985). Standardization within individuals: Simple method to neutralize individual differences in skin conductance. *Psychophysiology, 22,* 292–299.

Berger, H. (1929). On the electroencephalogram of man. I. *Archives Psychiatry Nervenkr, 87,* 527–570.

Berne, R. M., & Levy, M. N. (2001). *Cardiovascular physiology* (8th ed.). London: Mosby.

Berntson, G. G., Bigger, J. T., Eckberg, D. L., Grossman, P., Kaufmann, P. G., Malik, M., Nagaraja, H. N., Porges, S. W., Saul, J. P., Stone, P. H., & Van Der Molen, M. W. (1997). Heart rate variability: Origins, methods, and interpretive caveats. *Psychophysiology, 34,* 623–648.

Berntson, G. G., & Cacioppo, J. T. (2002). Psychophysiology. In H. D'Haenen, J. A. Den Boer, & P. Willner (Eds.), *Biological psychiatry* (Vol. 1, pp. 123–138). West Sussex, UK: John Wiley & Sons.

Berntson, G. G., Cacioppo, J. T., Binkley, P. F., Uchino, B. N., Quigley, K. S., & Fieldstone, A. (1994). Autonomic cardiac control:III. Psychological stress and cardiac response in autonomic space as revealed by pharmacological blockades. *Psychophysiology, 31,* 599–608.

Berntson, G. G., Lozano, D. L., Chen, Y. J., & Cacioppo, J. T. (2004). Where to Q in PEP. *Psychophysiology, 41,* 333–337.

Berntson, G. G., Quigley, K. S., Jang, J. F., & Boysen, S. T. (1990). An approach to artifact identification: Applications to heart period data. *Psychophysiology, 27,* 586–598.

Bertrand, O., Perrin, F., & Pernier, J. (1985). A theoretical justification of the average reference in topographic evoked potential studies. *Electroencephalography and Clinical Neurophysiology, 62,* 462–464.

Blumenthal, T. D., Cuthbert, B. N., Filion, D., Hackley, S., Lipp, O. V., & Van Boxtel, A. (2005). Committee report: Guidelines for human startle eyeblink electromyographic studies. *Psychophysiology, 42,* 1–15.

Boik, R. J. (1981). A priori tests in repeated measures designs: Effects of nonsphericity. *Psychometrika, 46,* 241–255.

Boucsein, W. (1992). *Electrodermal activity.* New York: Plenum.

Bradley, M. M. (2000). Emotion and motivation. In J. T. Cacioppo, L. G. Tassinary, & G. G. Berntson (Eds.), *Handbook of psychophysiology* (2nd ed., pp. 602–642). New York: Cambridge University Press.

Brunia, C. H. M. (1997). Gaiting in readiness. In P. J. Lang & R. F. Simons. *Attention and orienting: Sensory and motivational processes* (pp. 281–306). Mahwah, NJ: Lawrence Erlbaum Associates.

Bush, L. K., Hess, U., & Wolford, G. (1993). Transformations for within-subject designs: A Monte Carlo investigation. *Psychological Bulletin, 101,* 147–158.

Cacioppo, J. T., Tassinary, L. G., & Berntson, G. G. (Eds.) (2000). *Handbook of psychophysiology* (2nd ed.), New York: Cambridge University Press.

Campbell, D. T., & Stanley, J. C. (1963). *Experimental and quasi-experimental designs for research.* Boston: Houghton Mifflin Company.

Chapman, L. J., & Chapman, J. P. (2001). Commentary on two articles concerning generalized and specific cognitive deficits. *Journal of Abnormal Psychology, 110,* 31–39.

Chiarenza, G. A. (1998). Editorial: The richness of developmental psychophysiology. *Journal of Psychophysiology, 12,* 220–222.

Cohen, J. (1960). Coefficient of agreement for nominal scales. *Educational and Psychological Measurement, 20,* 37–46.

Cohen, J. (1968). Weighted kappa: Nominal scale agreement with provision for scaled disagreement or partial credit. *Psychological Bulletin, 70,* 213–220.

Coles, M. G. H., Donchin, E., & Porges, S. W. (1986). *Psychophysiology: Systems, processes, and applications.* New York: Guilford.

Cook, E. W., & Miller, G. A. (1992). Digital filtering: Background and tutorial for psychophysiologists. *Psychophysiology, 29*, 350–367.

Cooley, J. W., & Tukey, J. W. (1965). An algorithm for the machine calculation of complex Fourier series. *Mathematics of Computation, 19*, 297–301.

Crider, A. (1993) Electrodermal response lability-stability: Individual difference correlates. In J. C. Roy, W. Boucsein, D. C. Fowles, & J. H. Gruzelier (Eds.), *Progress in electrodermal research* (pp. 173–186). New York: Plenum.

Croft, R. J., & Barry, R. J. (2000). Removal of ocular artifact from the EEG: A review. *Neurophysiologie Clinique, 30*, 5–19.

Cycowicz, Y. M., & Friedman, D. (1997). A developmental study of the effect of temporal order on the ERPs elicited by novel environmental sounds. *Electroencephalography and Clinical Neurophysiology, 103*, 304–318.

Davidson, R. J., Jackson, D. C., & Larson, C. L. (2000). Human electroencephalography. In J. T. Cacioppo, L. G. Tassinary, & G. G. Berntson (Eds.), *Handbook of psychophysiology* (2nd ed., pp. 27–52). New York: Cambridge University Press.

Davidson, R. J. & Tomarken, A. J. (1989). Laterality and emotion: An electrophysiological approach. In F. Boller & J. Grafman (Eds.), *Handbook of neuropsychology* (Vol. 3, pp. 419–441). Amsterdam, Netherlands: Elsevier Science.

Dawson, M. E., Schell, A. M., & Filion, D. L. (2000). The electrodermal system. In J. T. Cacioppo, L. G. Tassinary, & G. G. Berntson (Eds.), *Handbook of psychophysiology* (2nd Ed., pp. 200–223). New York: Cambridge University Press.

Delorme, A., & Makeig, S. (2004). EEGLAB: An open source toolbox for analysis of single-trial EEG dynamics including independent component analysis. *Journal of Neuroscience Methods, 15*, 9–21.

Dien, J. (1998). Issues in the application of the average reference: Review, critiques, and recommendations. *Behavior Research Methods, Instruments, and Computers, 30*, 34–43.

Dimberg, U. (1990). Facial electromyography and emotional reactions. *Psychophysiology, 27*, 481–494.

DiPietro, J. A., Caughy, M. O., Cusson, R., & Fox, N. A. (1994). Cardiorespiratory functioning of preterm infants: Stability and risk associations for measures of heart rate variability and oxygen saturation. *Developmental Psychobiology, 27*, 137–152.

Donchin, E., & Heffley, E. (1978). Multivariate analysis of event-related potential data: A tutorial review. In D. Otto (Ed.), *Multidisciplinary perspectives in event-related brain potential research* (EPA-600/9-77043, pp. 555–572). Washington, DC: U.S. Government Printing Office.

Donchin, E., & Herning, R. I. (1975). A simulation study of the efficacy of step-wise discriminant analysis in the detection and comparison of event-related potentials. *Electroencephalography and Clinical Neurophysiology, 38*, 51–68.

Donchin, E., Ritter, W., & McCallum, C. (1978). Cognitive psychophysiology: The endogenous components of the ERP. In E. Callaway, P. Tueting, & S. H. Koslow (Eds.), *Event-related brain potentials in man* (pp. 349–411). New York: Academic Press.

Duffy, F. H., Iyer, V. G., & Surwillo, W. W. (1989). *Clinical electroencephalography and topographic brain mapping: Technology and practice.* New York: Springer-Verlag.

Dumermuth, G., & Molinari, L. (1987). Spectral analysis of the EEG: Some fundamentals revisited and some open problems. *Neuropsychobiology, 17*, 85–99.

Eckberg, D. L. (1983). Human sinus arrhythmia as an index of vagal cardiac outflow. *Journal of Applied Physiology, 54*, 961–966.

Edelberg, R. (1972). Electrical activity of the skin: Its measurement and uses in psychophysiology. In N. S. Greenfield & R. A. Sternbach (Eds.), *Handbook of psychophysiology* (pp. 367–418). New York: Holt.

Elbert, T., Lutzenberger, W., Rockstroh, B., & Birbaumer, N. (1985). Removal of ocular artifacts from the EEG – A biophysical approach to the EOG. *Electroencephalography and Clinical Neurophysiology, 60*, 455–463.

El-Sheikh, M. (2005). Stability of respiratory sinus arrhythmia in children and young adolescents: A longitudinal examination. *Developmental Psychobiology, 46*, 66–74.

Fabiani, M., Gratton, G., & Coles, M. G. H. (2000). Event-related brain potentials: Methods, theory, and applications. In J. T. Cacioppo, L. G. Tassinary, & G. G. Berntson (Eds.), *Handbook of psychophysiology* (2nd ed., pp. 53–84). New York: Cambridge University Press.

Fabiani, M., Gratton, G., Karis, D., & Donchin, E. (1987). The definition, identification, and reliability of measurement of the P300 component of the event-related brain potential. In P. K. Ackles, J. R. Jennings, & M. G. H. Coles (Eds.), *Advances in psychophysiology* (Vol. 1, pp. 1–78). Greenwich, CT: JAI.

Falkenstein, M., Hohnsbein, J., Hoormann, J., & Blanke, L. (1990). Effects of errors in choice reaction tasks on the ERP under focused and divided attention. In C. H. M. Brunia, A. W. K. Gaillard, & A. Kok (Eds.), *Psychophysiological brain research* (pp. 192–195). Tilburg, The Netherlands: Tilburg University Press.

Ferree, T. C., Luu, P., Russell, G. S., & Tucker, D. M. (2001). Scalp electrode impedance, infection risk, and EEG data quality. *Clinical Neurophysiology, 112*, 536–544.

Fisch, B. J. (1991). Artifacts. In B. J. Fisch (Ed.), *Spehlmann's EEG Primer* (2nd Ed., pp. 107–126). New York: Elsevier.

Fowles, D. C. (1986). The eccrine system and electrodermal activity. In M. G. H. Coles, E. Donchin, & S. W. Porges (Eds.), *Psychophysiology: Systems, processes, and applications* (pp. 51–96). New York: Guilford.

Fowles, D. C., Christie, M. J., Edelberg, R., Grings, W. W., Lykken, D. T., & Venables, P. H. (1981). Publication recommendations for electrodermal measurements. *Psychophysiology, 18*, 232–239.

Fox, N. A., & Calkins, S. D. (1993). Multiple-measure approaches to the study of infant emotion. In M. Lewis & J. M. Haviland (Eds.), *Handbook of emotions* (pp. 203–219). New York: Guilford.

Fox, N. A., & Porges, S. W. (1985). The relation between neonatal heart period patterns and developmental outcome. *Child Development, 56*, 28–37.

Fox, N. A., Schmidt, L. A., & Henderson, H. A. (2000). Developmental psychophysiology: Conceptual and methodological perspectives. In J. T. Cacioppo, L. G. Tassinary, & G. G. Berntson (Eds.), *Handbook of psychophysiology* (2nd ed., pp. 665–686). New York: Cambridge University Press.

Fridlund, A. J., & Cacioppo, J. T. (1986). Guidelines for human electromyographic research. *Psychophysiology, 23*, 567–589.

Friedman, D. (2000). Event-related brain potential investigations of memory and aging. *Biological Psychology, 54*, 175–206.

Galles, S. J., Miller, A., Cohn, J. F., & Fox, N. A. (2002). Estimating parasympathetic control of heart rate variability: Two approaches to quantifying vagal tone. *Psychophysiology, 39*, S37.

Gasser, T., Bacher, P., & Mocks, J. (1982). Transformations towards the normal distribution of broad band spectral parameters of the EEG. *Electroencephalography and Clinical Neurophysiology, 53*, 119–124.

Gevins, A. S. (1984). Analysis of the electromagnetic signals of the human brain: Milestones, obstacles, and goals. *IEEE Transactions in Biomedical Engineering, 31*, 833–850.

Gevins, A., Le, J., Martin, N. K., Brickett, P., Desmond, J., & Reutter, B. (1994). High resolution EEG: 124–channel recording, spatial deblurring and MRI integration methods. *Electroencephalography and Clinical Neurophysiology, 90*, 337–358.

Glaser, E. M., & Ruchkin, D. S. (1976). *Principles of neurobiological signal analysis.* New York: Academic Press.

Graham, F. K. (1979). Distinguishing among orienting, defense, and startle reflexes. In H. D. Kimmel, E. H. van Olst, & J. F. Orlebeke (Eds.), *The orienting reflex in humans* (pp. 137–167). Hillsdale, NJ: Lawrence Erlbaum Associates.

Graham, F. K. (1992). Attention: The heartbeat, the blink, and the brain. In B. A. Campbell, H. Hayne, & R. Richardson (Eds.), *Attention and information processing in infants and adults: Perspectives from human and animal research* (pp. 3–29). Hillsdale, NJ: Lawrence Erlbaum Associates.

Graham, F. K., Anthony, B. J., & Zeigler, B. L. (1983). The orienting response and development processes. In D. Siddle (Ed.), *Orienting and habituation: Perspectives in human research* (pp. 371–430). Sussex, UK: John Wiley & Sons.

Gratton, G., Coles, M. G. H., & Donchin, E. (1983). A new method for off-line removal of ocular artifact. *Electroencephalography and Clinical Neurophysiology, 55*, 468–484.

Gratton, G., Kramer, A. F., Coles, M. G., & Donchin, E. (1989). Simulation studies of latency measures of components of the event-related brain potential. *Psychophysiology, 26*, 233–248.

Greene, W. A., Turetsky, B., & Kohler, C. (2000). General laboratory safety. In J. T. Cacioppo, L. G. Tassinary, & G. G. Berntson (Eds.), *Handbook of psychophysiology* (2nd ed., pp. 951–977). New York: Cambridge University Press.

Grossman, P., Karemaker, J., & Wieling, W. (1991). Prediction of tonic parasympathetic cardiac control using respiratory sinus arrhythmia: The need for respiratory control. *Psychophysiology, 28*, 201–216.

Grossman, P., van Beek, J., & Wientjes, C. (1990). A comparison of three quantification methods for estimation of respiratory sinus arrhythmia. *Psychophysiology, 27*, 702–714.

Gunnar, M. R. (2003). Integrating neuroscience and psychological approaches in the study of early experiences. *Annals of the New York Academy of Science, 1008*, 238–247.

Harris, W. S., Schoenfeld, C. D., & Weissler, A. M. (1967). Effects of adrenergic receptor activation and blockade of the systolic pre-ejection period, heart rate, and arterial pressure in man. *The Journal of Clinical Investigation, 46*, 1704–1714.

Harver, A., & Lorig, T. S. (2000). Respiration. In J. T. Cacioppo, L. G. Tassinary, & G. G. Berntson (Eds.), *Handbook of psychophysiology* (2nd ed., pp. 265–293). New York: Cambridge.

Hernes, K. G., Morkrid, L., Fremming, A., Odegarden, S., Martinsen, O. G., & Storm, H. (2002). Skin conductance changes during the first year of life in full-term infants. *Pediatric Research, 52,* 837–843.

Hirsch, J. A., & Bishop, B. (1981). Respiratory sinus arrhythmia: How breathing patterns modulates heart rate. *American Journal of Physiology, 241,* 620–629.

Horowitz, P., & Hill, W. (1989). *The art of electronics (2nd ed.).* New York: Cambridge University Press.

Horst, R. L., & Donchin, E. (1980). Beyond averaging II: Single trial classification of exogenous event-related potentials using step-wise discriminant analysis. *Electroencephalography and Clinical Neurophysiology, 48,* 113–126.

Howard, L., & Polich, J. (1985). P300 latency and memory span development. *Developmental Psychology, 21,* 283–289.

Huettel, S. A., McKeown, M. J., Song, A. W., Hart, S., Spencer, D. D., Allison, T., & McCarthy, G. (2004). Linking hemodynamic and electrophysiological measures of brain activity: Evidence from functional MRI and intracranial field potentials. *Cerebral Cortex, 14,* 165–173.

Hugdahl, K. (1995). *Psychophysiology: The mind-body perspective.* Cambridge, MA: Harvard University Press.

Jacobson, L., & Sapolsky, R. (1991). The role of the hippocampus in feedback regulation of the hypothalamic-pituitary-adrenocortical axis. *Endocrinology Review, 12,* 118–134.

Jennings, J. R., Berg, W. K., Hutcheson, J. S., Obrist, P., Porges, S., & Turpin, G. (1981). Publication guidelines for heart rate studies in man. *Psychophysiology, 18,* 226–231.

Jennings, J. R., Cohen, M. J., Ruchkin, D. S., & Fridlund, A. J. (1987). Editorial policy on analysis of variance with repeated measures. *Psychophysiology, 24,* 474–478.

Jennings, J. R. & van der Molen, M. W. (2002). Cardiac timing and the central regulation of action. *Psychology Research, 66,* 337–349.

John, E. R., Ahn, H., Prichep, L. S., Trepetin, M., Brown, D., & Kaye, H. (1980). Development equations for the electroencephalogram. *Science, 210,* 1255–1258.

John, E. R., Prichep, L. S., & Easton, P. (1987). Normative data banks and neurometrics. Basic concepts, methods, and results of norm constructions. In A. S. Gevins & A. Remond (Eds.), *Methods of analysis of brain electrical and magnetic signals* (pp. 449–495). Amsterdam, Netherlands: Elsevier Science.

John, M. S., Brown, D. K., Muir, P. J., & Picton, T. W. (2004). Recording auditory steady-state responses in young infants. *Ear and Hearing, 25,* 539–553.

Jung, T. P., Makeig, S., Humphries, C., Lee, T. W., McKeown, M. J., Iragui, V., & Sejnowski, T. J. (2000). Removing electroencephalographic artifacts by blind source separation. *Psychophysiology, 37,* 163–178.

Kayser, J., & Tenke, C. E. (2003). Optimizing PCA methodology for ERP component identification and measurement: Theoretical rational and empirical evaluation. *Clinical Neurophysiology, 114,* 2307–2325.

Kendall, P. T., & McCreary, E. K. (1980). *Muscles: Testing and function* (3rd ed.). Baltimore: Williams & Wilkins.

Kirschbaum, C., & Hellhammer, D. H. (1989). Salivary cortisol in psychobiological research: An overview. *Neuropsychobiology, 22,* 150–169.

Kubicek, W. G., Karnegis, J. N., Patterson, R. P., Witsoe, D. A., & Mattson, R. H. (1966). Development and evaluation of an impedance cardiograph system. *Aerospace Medicine, 37,* 1208–1212.

Kubicek, W. G., Patterson, R. P., & Witsoe, D. A. (1970). Impedance cardiography as a noninvasive method of monitoring cardiac function and other parameters of the cardiovascular system. *Annals of the New York Academy of Science, 170,* 724–732.

Lagercrantz, H., Hanson, M., Evrard, P., & Rodeck, C. (Eds.) (2002). *The newborn brain: Neuroscience and clinical applications.* Cambridge, UK: Cambridge University Press.

Lamberts, R., Visser, K. R., & Zijlstra, W. G. (1984). *Impedance cardiography.* Assen, The Netherlands: Van Gorcum.

Lang, P. J., Bradley, M. M., & Cuthbert, B. N. (1990). Emotion, attention, and the startle reflex. *Psychological Review, 97,* 377–398.

Lang, P. J., Bradley, M. M., & Cuthbert, B. N. (2005). *International affective picture system (IAPS): Affective ratings of pictures and instruction manual. Technical Report A-6.* University of Florida, Gainesville, FL.

Lins, O. G., Picton, T. W., Berg, P. & Scherg, M. (1993a). Ocular artifacts in EEG and event-related potentials: II. Scalp topography. *Brain Topography, 6,* 51–63.

Lins, O. G., Picton, T. W., Berg, P., & Scherg, M. (1993b). Ocular artifacts in recording EEGs and event-related potentials: II. Source dipoles and source components. *Brain Topography, 6,* 65–78.

Lovallo, W. R. &,Thomas, T. L. (2000). Stress hormones in psychophysiological research: Emotional, behavioral, and cognitive interpretations. In J. T. Cacioppo, L. G. Tassinary, & G. G. Berntson (Eds.), *Handbook of psychophysiology* (2nd ed., pp. 342–367). New York: Cambridge University Press.

Luck, S. J., & Hillyard, S. A. (1994). Electrophysiological correlates of feature analysis during visual search. *Psychophysiology, 31,* 291–308.

Lykken, D. T., Rose, R. J., Luther, B., & Maley, M. (1966). Correcting psychophysiological measures for individual differences in range. *Psychological Bulletin, 66,* 481–484.

Lykken, D. T., & Venables, P. H. (1971). Direct measurement of skin conductance: A proposal for standardization. *Psychophysiology, 8,* 656–672.

MacGregor, J. (2000). *Introduction to the anatomy and physiology of children.* Oxford, UK: Routledge.

Makeig, S., Jung, T. P., Bell, A. J., Ghahremani, D., & Sejnowski, T. J. (1997). Blind separation of auditory event-related brain responses into independent components. *Proceedings of the National Academy of Science, 94,* 10979–10984.

Markand, O. N. (1994). Brainstem auditory evoked potentials. *Journal of Clinical Neurophysiology, 11,* 319–342.

Marshall, P. J., Bar-Haim, Y., & Fox, N. A. (2002). Development of the EEG from 5 months to 4 years of age. *Clinical Neurophysiology, 113,* 1199–1208.

Martin, C. E., Shaver, J. A., Thompson, M. E., Reddy, P. S., & Leonard, J. J. (1971). Direct correlation of external systolic time intervals with internal indices of left ventricular function in man. *Circulation, 44,* 419–431.

Matthews, K. A., Salomon, K., Kenyon, K., & Allen, M. T. (2002). Stability of children's and adolescents' hemodynamic responses to psychological challenge: A three-year longitudinal study of a multiethnic cohort of boys and girls. *Psychophysiology, 39*, 826–834.

McCall, W. A. (1923). *How to experiment in education.* New York: Macmillan.

McCarthy, G. (1999). Event-related potentials and functional MRI: A comparison of localization in sensory, perceptual, and cognitive tasks. *Electroencephalography and Clinical Neurophysiology Supplement, 49*, 3–12.

McCubbin, J. A., Richardson, J. E., Langer, A. W., Kizer, J. S., & Obrist, P. A. (1983). Sympathetic neuronal function and left ventricular performance during behavioral stress in humans: The relationship between plasma catecholamines and systolic time intervals. *Psychophysiology, 20*, 102–110.

McGrath, J. J., & O'Brien, W. H. (2001). Pediatric impedance cardiography: Temporal stability and intertask consistency. *Psychophysiology, 38*, 479–484.

McIsaac, H., & Polich, J. (1992). Comparison of infant and adult P300 from auditory stimuli. *Journal of Experimental Child Psychology, 53*, 115–128.

Miller, A., & Tomarken, A. J. (2001). Task-dependent changes in frontal brain asymmetry: Effects of incentive cues, outcome expectancies, and motor responses. *Psychophysiology, 38*, 500–511.

Miller, G. A., Gratton, G., & Yee, C. M. (1988). Generalized implementation of an eye movement correction procedure. *Psychophysiology, 25*, 241–243.

Möcks, J., & Verleger, R. (1991). Multivariate methods in biosignal analysis: Application of principal component analysis to event-related potentials. In R. Weitkunat (Ed.), *Digital biosignal processing* (pp. 399–458). Amsterdam, Netherlands: Elsevier Science.

Mohapatra, S. N. (1981). *Non-invasive cardiovascular monitoring by electrical impedance technique.* London: Pittman Medical Ltd.

Näätänen, R. (2003). Mismatch negativity: Clinical research and possible applications. *International Journal of Psychophysiology, 48*, 179–188.

Näätänen, R., & Picton, T. (1987). The N1 wave of the human electric and magnetic response to sound: A review and an analysis of the component structure. *Psychophysiology, 24*, 375–425.

Näätänen, R., & Teder, W. (1991). Attention effects on the auditory event-related potential. *Acta Otolaryngology Supplement, 491*, 161–167.

Nelson, C. A. (1994). Neural correlates of recognition memory in the first postnatal year. In G. Dawson & K. W. Fischer (Eds.), *Human behavior and the developing brain* (pp. 269–313). New York: Guilford.

Nelson, C. A., & Monk, C. S. (2001). The use of the event-related potentials in the study of cognitive development. In C. A. Nelson & M. Luciana (Eds.), *Handbook of developmental cognitive neuroscience* (pp. 125–136). Cambridge, MA: MIT Press.

Newlin, D. B., & Levenson, R. W. (1979). Pre-ejection period: Measuring beta-adrenergic influences upon the heart. *Psychophysiology, 16*, 546–553.

Niedermeyer, E. (1993). Maturation of the EEG: Development of waking and sleep patterns. In E. Niedermeyer & F. H. Lopes da Silva (Eds.), *Electroencephalography: Basic principles, clinical applications, and related fields* (pp. 167–191). Baltimore, MD: Williams & Wilkins.

Nitschke, J. B., Miller, G. A., & Cook, E. W. (1998). Digital filtering in EEG/ERP analysis: Some technical and empirical comparisons. *Behavior Research Methods, Instruments, and Computers, 30,* 54–67.

Nuñez, P. L. (1981). *Electrical fields of the brain: The neurophysics of EEG.* New York: Oxford University Press.

Obrist, P. A., Light, K. C., James, S. A., & Strogatz, D. S. (1987). Cardiovascular responses to stress: I. Measures of myocardial response and relationships to high resting systolic pressure and parental hypertension. *Psychophysiology, 24,* 65–78.

Pascual-Marqui, R. D., Esslen, M., Kochi, K., & Lehmann, D. (2002). Functional imaging with low-resolution brain electromagnetic tomography (LORETA): A review. *Methods, Findings, and Experiments in Clinical Pharmacology, 24 Supplement,* 91–95.

Pascual-Marqui, R. D., Michel, C. M., & Lehmann, D. (1994). Low resolution electromagnetic tomography: A new method for localizing electrical activity in the brain. *International Journal of Psychophysiology, 18,* 49–65.

Penney, B. C., Patwardhan, N. A., & Wheeler, H. B. (1985). Simplified electrode array for impedance cardiography. *Medical and Biological Engineering and Computing, 23,* 1–7.

Pernier, J., Perrin, F., & Bertrand, O. (1988). Scalp current density fields: Concept and properties. *Electroencephalography and Clinical Neurophysiology, 69,* 385–389.

Perrin, F., Bertrand, O., & Pernier, J. (1987). Scalp current density mapping: Value and estimation from potential data. *IEEE Transactions in Biomedical Engineering, 34,* 283–288.

Picton, T. W., Alain, C., Otten, L., Ritter, W., & Achim, A. (2000a). Mismatch negativity: Different water in the same river. *Audiology and Neuro-Otology, 5,* 111–139.

Picton, T. W., Bentin, S., Berg, P., Donchin, E., Hillyard, S. A., Johnson, R., Miller, G. A., Ritter, W., Ruchkin, D. S., Rugg, M. D., & Taylor, M. J. (2000b). Guidelines for using human event-related potentials to study cognition: Recording standards and publication criteria. *Psychophysiology, 37,* 127–152.

Picton, T. W., John, M. S., Dimitrijevic, A., & Purcell, D. (2003). Human auditory steady-state responses. *International Journal of Audiology, 42,* 177–219.

Picton, T. W., van Roon, P., Armilio, M. L., Berg, P., Ille, N., & Scherg, M. (2000c). The correction of ocular artifacts: A topographic perspective. *Clinical Neurophysiology, 111,* 53–65.

Pivik, R. T., Broughton, R. J., Coppola, R., Davidson, R. J., Fox, N., & Nuwer, M. R. (1993). Guidelines for the recording and quantitative analysis of electroencephalographic activity in research contexts. *Psychophysiology, 30,* 547–558.

Porges, S. W., & Byrne, E. A. (1992). Research methods for measurement of heart rate and respiration. *Biological Psychology, 34,* 93–130.

Porges, S. W. (1986). Respiratory sinus arrhythmia: Physiological basis, quantitative methods, and clinical implications. In P. Grossman, K. Janssen, & D. Vaitl (Eds.), *Cardiorespiratory and cardiosomatic psychophysiology* (pp. 101–115). New York: Plenum.

Pritchard, W. S. (1981). Psychophysiology of P300. *Psychological Bulletin, 89,* 506–540.

Raine, A. (2002). Biosocial studies of antisocial and violent behavior in children and adults: A review. *Journal of Abnormal Child Psychology, 30,* 311–326.

Richards, J. E. (2000). Localizing the development of covert attention in infants using scalp event-related-potentials. *Developmental Psychology, 36,* 91–108.

Richards, J. E. (2004). Recovering dipole sources from scalp-recorded event-related-potentials using component analysis: Principal component analysis and independent component analysis. *International Journal of Psychophysiology, 54*, 201–220.

Riniolo, T., & Porges, S. W. (1997). Inferential and descriptive influences on measures of respiratory sinus arrhythmia: Sampling rate, R-wave trigger accuracy, and variance estimates. *Psychophysiology, 34*, 613–621.

Rogan, J. C., Keselman, H. J., & Mendoza, J. L. (1979). Analysis of repeated measurements. *British Journal of Mathematical and Statistical Psychology, 32*, 269–286.

Saltzberg, B., Burton, W. D., Burch, N. R., Fletcher, J., & Michaels, R. (1986). Electrophysiological measures of regional neural interactive coupling. Linear and non-linear dependence relationships among multiple channel electroencephalographic recordings. *International Journal of Biomedical Computation, 18*, 77–87.

Scerbo, A., Freedman, L. W., Raine, A., Dawson, M. E., & Venables, P. H. (1992). A major effect of recording site on measurement of electrodermal activity. *Psychophysiology, 29*, 241–246.

Schachinger, H., Weinbacher, M., Kiss, A., Ritz, R., & Langewitz, W. (2001). Cardiovascular indices of peripheral and central sympathetic activation. *Psychosomatic Medicine, 63*, 788–796.

Scherg, M., & Berg, P. (1991). Use of prior knowledge in brain electromagnetic source analysis. *Brain Topography* 4:143–150.

Scherg, M., Ille, N., Bornfleth, H., & Berg, P. (2002). Advanced tools for digital EEG review: Virtual source montages, whole-head mapping, correlation, and phase analysis. *Journal of Clinical Neurophysiology, 19*, 91–112.

Schmidt, L. A., & Fox, N. A. (1998). Fear-potentiated startle responses in temperamentally different human infants. *Developmental Psychobiology, 32*, 113–120.

Schmidt, L. A., Fox, N. A., & Long, J. M. (1998). Acoustic startle electromyographic (EMG) activity indexed from an electrooculargraphic (EOG) electrode placement: A methodological note. *International Journal of Neuroscience, 93*, 185–188.

Segalowitz, S. J., & Davies, P. L. (2004). Charting the maturation of the frontal lobe: An electrophysiological strategy. *Brain and Cognition, 55*, 116–133.

Segalowitz, S. J. & Graves, R. (1990). Suitability of the IBM PC/AT/PS2 keyboard, mouse and game port as response devices in reaction time paradigms. *Behavior Research Methods, Instruments, & Computers, 22*, 283–289.

Sherwood, A., Allen, M. T., Fahrenberg, J., Kelsey, R. M., Lovallo, W. R., & van Doornen, L. J. P. (1990). Methodological guidelines for impedance cardiography. *Psychophysiology, 27*, 1–23.

Simons, R. F., & Zelson, M. F. (1985). Engaging visual stimuli and blink modification. *Psychophysiology, 22*, 44–49.

Sloan, R. P., Shapiro, P. A., Bagiella, E., Gorman, J. M., & Bigger, J. T. (1995). Temporal stability of heart period variability during a resting baseline and in response to psychological challenge. *Psychophysiology, 32*, 191–196.

Sokolov, E. N. (1990). The orienting response and future directions of its development. *Pavlovian Journal of Biological Science, 25*, 142–150.

Somsen, R. J. & van Beek, B. (1998). Ocular artifacts in children's EEG: Selection is better than correction. *Biological Psychology, 48*, 281–300.

Sonin, A. A. (2001). *The physical basis of dimensional analysis.* Cambridge, MA: MIT.

Spangler, G. (1991). The emergence of adrenocortical circadian function in newborns and infants and its relationship to sleep, feeding, and maternal adrenocortical activity. *Early Human Development, 25*, 197–208.

Squires, K. C., & Donchin, E. (1976). Beyond averaging: The use of discriminant functions to recognize event related potentials elicited by single auditory stimuli. *Electroencephalography and Clinical Neurophysiology, 41*, 449–459.

Stern, J. A. (1964). Toward a definition of psychophysiology. *Psychophysiology, 1*, 90–91.

Stern, J. A. (1968). Toward a developmental psychophysiology: My look into the crystal ball. *Psychophysiology, 4*, 403–420.

Strauss, M. E. (2001). Demonstrating specific cognitive deficits: A psychometric perspective. *Journal of Abnormal Psychology, 110*, 6–14.

Tassinary, L. G. & Cacioppo, J. T. (2000). The skeletomotor system: Surface electromyography. In J. T. Cacioppo, L. G. Tassinary, & G. G. Berntson (Eds.), *Handbook of psychophysiology* (2nd ed., pp. 163–199). New York: Cambridge.

Taylor, M. J., McCarthy, G., Saliba, E., & Degiovanni, E. (1999). ERP evidence of developmental changes in processing of faces. *Clinical Neurophysiology, 110*, 910–915.

Thomas, D. G., & Crow, C. D. (1994). Development of evoked electrical brain activity in infancy. In G. Dawson & K. W. Fischer (Eds.), *Human behavior and the developing brain* (pp. 207–231). New York: Guilford.

Tomarken, A. J. (1995). A psychometric perspective on psychophysiological measures. *Psychological Assessment, 7*, 387–395.

Tomarken, A. J. (1999). Methodological issues in psychophysiological research. In P. C. Kendall, J. N. Butcher, & G. N. Holmbeck (Eds.), *Handbook of research methods in clinical psychology* (2nd ed., pp. 251–275). New York: John Wiley & Sons.

Tomarken, A. J., Davidson, R. J., Wheeler, R. E., & Kinney, L. (1992). Psychometric properties of resting anterior EEG asymmetry: Temporal stability and internal consistency. *Psychophysiology, 29*, 576–592.

van der Molen, M. W., & Ridderinkhof, K. R. (1998). Chronopsychophysiology of developmental changes in selective attention and processing speed: A selective review and re-analysis. *Journal of Psychophysiology, 12*, 223–235.

Vasey, M., & Thayer, J. F. (1987). The continuing problem of false positives in repeated measures ANOVA in psychophysiology: A multivariate solution. *Psychophysiology, 24*, 479–486.

Wackermann, J., & Matousek, M. (1998). From the 'EEG age' to a rational scale of brain electric maturation. *Electroencephalography and Clinical Neurophysiology, 107*, 415–421.

Wallstrom, G. L., Kass, R. E., Miller, A., Cohn, J. F., & Fox, N. A. (2004). Automatic correction of ocular artifacts in the EEG: A comparison of regression-based and component-based methods. *International Journal of Psychophysiology, 53*, 105–119.

Walter, W. G., Cooper, R., Aldridge, V. J., McCallum, W. C., & Winter, A. L. (1964). Contingent negative variation: An electrical sign of sensorimotor association and expectancy in the human brain. *Nature, 203*, 380–384.

Watamura, S. E., Donzella, B., Kertes, D. A., & Gunnar, M. R. (2004). Developmental changes in baseline cortisol activity in early childhood: Relations with napping and effortful control. *Developmental Psychobiology, 45*, 125–133.

West, J. B. (2000). *Respiratory physiology: The essentials.* (6th ed.). Philadelphia: Lippincott Williams & Wilkins.

Wientjes, C. J. E. (1992). Respiration in psychophysiology: Methods and application. *Biological Psychology, 34*, 179–203.

Wilhelm, F. H., Grossman, P., & Coyle, M. A. (2004). Improving estimation of cardiac vagal tone during spontaneous breathing using a paced breathing calibration. *Biomedical Science Instrumentation, 40*, 317–324.

Yao, D., Wang, L., Oostenveld, R., Nielsen, K. D., Arendt-Nielsen, L., & Chen, A. C. N. (2005). A comparative study of different references for EEG spectral mapping: The issue of neutral reference and the use of the infinity reference. *Physiological Measurement, 26*, 173–184.

Yordanova, J., & Kolev, V. (1996). Developmental changes in the alpha response system. *Electroencephalography and Clinical Neurophysiology, 99*, 527–538.

14   Obtaining Reliable Psychophysiological Data with Child Participants

Methodological Considerations

William J. Gavin and Patricia L. Davies

INTRODUCTION

Developmental psychophysiological research is a relatively young field that is rapidly expanding partly because sophisticated, cost-effective technology now allows researchers to collect physiological data much more efficiently and effectively. This volume of developmental psychophysiology reflects both the newness as well as the growth of the field. As alluded to by many of the authors included in this volume, researchers collecting valid psychophysiological data in children face challenges that are magnified when compared to the collection of these same data in adults. However, developmental psychophysiologists are not alone in addressing these challenges as we can readily draw upon the experiences from specialists working in other related fields.

The fields of psychology and education have also contributed to our general knowledge about effective methods of assessing children. Notably, the number of texts written on behavioral and neuropsychological assessment of children is plentiful, and we can apply this knowledge to assessment of psychophysiological information as well. For example, the recent editions of assessment of children (Sattler 2001, 2002) comprehensively discuss skills necessary for test administrators to have in order to successfully assess children. Some of these skills include effective listening, building rapport with the child, and how to handle difficult behaviors and individual temperaments. A researcher who develops these assessment skills discussed by psychologists, neuropsychologists, and education professionals, along with the technical skills necessary for obtaining the desired psychophysiological measurements will be much more successful in obtaining reliable and valid research data.

The purpose of this chapter was to highlight some of the important assessment skills advocated by specialists in related fields while bringing together and further exploring the insights learned through the trial and error experiences of experts in developmental psychophysiology, that is, the authors of the previous chapters. In addition to summarizing commentary taken from these authors, we introduce a conceptual framework to aid in the discussion of the relevancy of their experiences in terms of conducting successful research. Through this discussion of the collected shared experiences of these researchers, we hope that investigators who are relatively new to the field will be able to avoid the time-consuming learning curve based on trial and error experiences as one attempts to prevail over the challenges of collecting valid psychophysiological data in children.

CHARACTERIZING INDIVIDUAL DIFFERENCES AS A PRODUCT OF EXPERIMENTAL, STATE, AND TRAIT EFFECTS

The difficulties in obtaining meaningful psychophysiological data in studies involving infants and young children were eloquently discussed by several authors in this volume. At various points in their chapters, they highlight the difficulties researchers might encounter in collecting, analyzing, and interpreting psychophysiological measures obtained as responses to the presentation of discrete auditory, visual, somatosensory, or cognitive/affective stimuli. These difficulties can be roughly catalogued as (1) issues regarding variability in the psychological and physiological state of the participant, (2) issues involved in standardizing (i.e., controlling for) the influences of trait characteristics across the participants, and (3) issues concerning data distortion that may result from the procedural steps used to address artifact removal during data reduction.

As an example of issues pertaining to variability in psychological and physiological state, Berg and Byrd (Chapter 8) point out that developmental psychophysiologists need to consider the infants' behavioral manifestations of physical and psychological needs in order to minimize difficulties in interacting with the infant to both properly prepare the infant for electrophysiological measurements and to successfully complete the testing session. These needs include infants' frequent sleeping periods, periodic hunger, their fear of strangers and strange environments, and their parental attachment. Failure to consider managing these needs across infants within a study will not only lead to increased participant attrition rates but, more importantly, will contribute to variations in arousal states which may directly affect the variability seen in the psychophysiological measures within and between participants. For example, an infant who is in a fearful state is likely to have an accelerated heart rate compared to an infant in a contented state. Failure to manage these needs in young children will also influence their psychophysiological states as well, though not necessarily to the degree found in infants.

Berg and Byrd also addressed the need for researchers to recognize influences of trait characteristics when attempting to measure psychophysiological responses to presentations of discrete stimuli. They cautioned researchers that large differences in resting heart rate exist among infants, children of different ages, and adults. They suggested that these maturational effects must be taken into account in age comparisons of heart rate because the magnitude of the responses to interesting stimuli depends on the resting heart rate. As they note, this issue has serious implications for the interpretation of heart rate changes obtained in response to stimulus events.

The issues concerning data distortion that occur post data collection during the artifact removal steps in processing the electrophysiological recordings were discussed by Berg and Byrd several times in their chapter. Artifacts are inevitable to some degree whenever electrophysiological recordings are made but are more likely to occur when recording infants and young children. While verbal instructions are often sufficient for effectively reducing movement and muscle activity artifacts in adults, movement and muscle activity artifacts are more pronounced in developmental psychophysiological studies partly because infants and young children are less effective in minimizing movement artifacts even when given verbal instructions to do so. Wire movement (e.g., which when recording EEG induces slow potential shifts) and muscle activity are more likely to occur in infants when they exhibit the extremes of their psychophysiological states; that is, an angry baby or a baby who is excessively happy may manifest their state by increased movements of arms and legs introducing artifacts to the electrophysiological recordings. Thus, as several authors acknowledge, movement and muscle activity artifacts will always be present in the electrophysiological recordings and developmental researchers must contend with them by deleting segments of the recording containing the artifacts or by applying mathematically routines to isolate or remove the artifact contamination. Invoking the former approach results in loss of data and invoking the later approach may result in some distortion of the data (see Somsen & van Beek, 1998). This issue remains a difficult problem and needs to be anticipated when designing a research project.

In their chapter on neuroendocrine measures, Gunnar and Talge (Chapter 12) further highlight the fact that analyzing and interpreting cortisol measures is complicated due to both the variability of the physiological state and differing levels of trait characteristics often found in children. They point out that pre-stress manipulation samples taken when children arrive at the laboratory do not necessarily reflect the child's typical cortisol levels at that time of day; that is, they may not reflect a true basal level. They argue that when compared to multiple baseline samples taken in the home for infants, the lab cortisol level will be lower, and for children 9 and older the lab samples will be greater. They suggest that these differences between home cortisol levels and those obtained in the initial lab sample may reflect a response to coming to the lab, that is, a temporary change in the child's anxiety level, reflecting a change in the individual's state resulting in cortisol levels below or above the individual's trait level. Furthermore, the authors suggest that given the constraints of the glucocorticoid system itself, the degree of state change due to "visiting the lab" may influence the cortisol levels obtained in samples after the stressor event is presented; that is, the state change due to visiting the lab, may accentuate or suppress the response to the experimental manipulation being studied. Gunnar and Talge also note the difficulty they and others have had in obtaining reliable estimates of true basal levels of cortisol.

The issues of variability of physiological state, differing levels of trait characteristics, and artifact reduction affect more than just heart rate and neuroendocrine measures. Difficulties in analyzing and interpreting EEG measures were also address by Trainor (Chapter 3) in her discussion of ERP measures of auditory development. She noted that developmental researchers face a significant problem analyzing infant data due to the large variation from infant to infant. She attributes this variability to several factors such as increased biological noise in the data due to movement artifacts, individual differences in rates of cortical maturation, and the small number of trials from which data can be obtained due to short attention spans and frequent changes in emotional or physical states (e.g., hunger). Thus, variability of physiological state, differing levels of trait characteristics, and methods used to process the raw physiological response that might affect the outcome measures should be considered in advance when designing developmental psychophysiological studies.

A MODEL FOR ADDRESSING INDIVIDUAL DIFFERENCES

In our laboratory, we use a simple basic additive model to provide a framework for conceptualizing the need to manage these issues of variability either methodologically or statistically. Briefly stated, the model assumes that any given psychophysiological measurement (PM) obtained from an individual reflects the contributions of the elicited neurobiological response that is related to (1) the degree and modality of the stimulus being presented, (2) the physiological and emotional state of the individual at the time of testing,

(3) the current developmental status of the trait or traits being studied, and (4) the manner in which the raw physiological response is obtained and processed. Furthermore, borrowing from test and measurement theory, we also recognize that because we can never obtain true scores for each these four components, we introduce measurement error to some degree or another when deriving obtained scores for one or more these components. Collectively, measurement error from one or more these components contributes to the overall measurement error (ME) of the obtained psychophysiological measurement. Thus, the model states that a given psychophysiological measurement (PM) of an individual represents the sum of the effects of the four components listed above along with measurement error and can be expressed as:

$$PM = Effect_{STIMULUS} + Effect_{STATE} + Effect_{TRAIT}$$
$$+ Effect_{PM\_PROCESSING} + ME \tag{1}$$

We present this base model in its simplistic form for the sake of brevity. However, the model can be expanded to acknowledge possible interactions between components or non-linear contributions such as quadratic or cubic effects for each component.

When we design our developmental ERP studies, this model directs our focus on how best to maximize our ability to measure psychophysiological responses of interest while minimizing or controlling for measurement error that is inherent in all psychophysiological measurements. For instance, if we measured cortisol in response to a challenge stimulus without first measuring pre-challenge levels (state) or without knowing the participants basal levels (trait) then the psychophysiological measurement (PM) of each participant would be represented as:

$$PM = Effect_{STIMULUS} + ME_{Total} \tag{2}$$

where

$$ME_{Total} = Effect_{STATE} + Effect_{TRAIT} + Effect_{PM\_PROCESSING} + ME \tag{3}$$

In equation 2, the psychophysiological measurement (PM) of interest is any obtained measure and consists of both the $Effect_{STIMULUS}$ and ME_{Total}. Basic statistical theory allows one to derive estimates of these two terms. Two methodological approaches are used to estimate the $Effect_{STIMULUS}$, a between-groups approach and a within-participants approach. The between-groups approach averages multiple PM values acquired by presenting the stimulus to each member of a specified homogeneous group of participants. The within-participants approach averages multiple PM values obtained from repeated presentations of the stimulus to the same individual. An estimate of the ME_{Total} component is obtained by computing the standard deviation of PM values used to estimate the value for the $Effect_{STIMULUS}$ component. Thus, the variability in any set of scores used to estimate the effect ($Effect_{STIMULUS}$) defines the ME_{Total} component and represents the portion of the PM that is not attributed to the stimulus itself. Therefore, ME_{Total} is considered variance unaccounted for, that is, from an unknown source or sources. However, as shown in equation 3, it is possible to identify and measure some sources within the ME_{Total}.

While the above is standard statistical theory, we wish to emphasize its implications. In the example above, the uncontrolled effects of state, trait, and assay processing procedures for each participant's PM contributes to the inflation of the measurement error term in any statistical analyses. Consequently, any statistical evaluation would be highly prone to Type II error, that is, failing to demonstrate significant differences when the differences are due to real and meaningful effects. However, one can minimize the effects of the other components within the ME_{Total} by either standardizing their values such that they become a constant (i.e., holding them constant by choosing participants with the same trait or state measurements) or measuring one or more of the other components in each participant and removing their contribution to the PM leaving the residual to represent the effect being investigated. Regarding the former approach, some of the methods commonly used to standardize state variables across participants are discussed later in this chapter. The latter approach can be accomplished using either linear or non-linear multivariate regression analyses and is appropriate for studying how individuals differ from one another.

To illustrate how the basic model can be used to study individual differences, we introduce a slight modification in the notation to indicate a shift in focus from estimating a single effect to understanding the interrelation of variability across the measures. For example, Segalowitz and Barnes (1993) provide a version of the model for conceptualizing the relation between possible sources contributing to the variability of event-related potentials (ERP) measures within a data set. Extending the general concepts of the standard Linear Effect Model, the authors conceptualize the variance (Var) in an ERP measure as a function of four terms. In Davies, Segalowitz, and Gavin (2004), we expanded the model to include a fifth term (Var_{WAVE}), the variance attributed to parameters creating the waveform from which ERP component measures are extracted, and demonstrated the validity of this new term within a regression analysis. Thus, our expanded model for analysis of ERP measures is expressed as:

$$\text{Var}_{\text{ERP}} = \text{Var}_{\text{STIM}} + \text{Var}_{\text{STATE}} + \text{Var}_{\text{TRAIT}} + \text{Var}_{\text{WAVE}} + \text{Var}_{\text{ME}} \qquad (4)$$

where

- Var_{ERP} is the variance in the measurement of an ERP component of interest, such as ERN or Pe amplitude;
- Var_{STIM} represents the various stimulus factors used to elicit the ERP in a given paradigm such as the modality and duration of stimulus or the inter-stimulus interval;
- $\text{Var}_{\text{STATE}}$ represents aspects of the participant's psychological or physiological state that may affect the ERP, independent of any manipulations in the experimental paradigm, that the participant may bring to the testing session such as degree of fatigue or test anxiety;
- $\text{Var}_{\text{TRAIT}}$ represents stable characteristics of the participant that may affect the ERP outcome such as age (a measure of maturation) or the gender of the participant;
- Var_{WAVE} represents the variance attributed to parameters creating the waveform from which ERP component measures are extracted (e.g., number of trials in the averaged waveform); and
- Var_{ME} represents the variability of Var_{ERP} not accounted for by the other components; in other words, measurement error.

Using this model as a framework in a study of error-related negativity (ERN), we used a series of multiple regression analyses to determine the degree to which the ERN amplitude is a result of the interrelations between the $\text{Var}_{\text{TRAIT}}$ components represented by the variables of age and gender (Davies et al., 2004). Initial regression analyses revealed a significant relation between ERN amplitude and age as well as a significant age by gender interaction effect. However, zero order correlations also showed a significant relation between age and the number of trials in the averaged waveform, possibly confounding the interpretation of the age effects on ERN amplitude. To control for this possible confound, we conducted a second regression analyses incorporating the Var_{WAVE} component of the model. This component was represented by the combination of two variables, one denoting the number of trials in the average waveform, and another indicating whether an eye blink removal method was used to increase the number of trials in the averaged waveform. The subsequent analysis revealed a significant amount of the variance in the ERP measures such as the ERN amplitude can be accounted for by the number of trials in the averaged waveform and whether an eye blink removal method was used. Furthermore, after controlling for the effects these variables representing the methods for dealing with eye blink artifacts, a significant age effect still accounted for 17% of the variance in the ERN amplitude.

The remainder of the chapter will discuss the ways that researchers can control some of the unintentional state variables. These suggestions are based on our experiences in our lab and the experiences of the other authors who have shared some "gems" in their chapters.

CREATING A POSITIVE ENVIRONMENT DESIGNED TO MINIMIZE ANXIETY AND FEAR IN CHILDREN

Numerous studies have shown that anxiety and stress levels can affect psychophysiological data such as EDA (e.g., Gilbert, & Gilbert, 1991; Naveteur, Buisine, & Gruzelier, 2005; Wilken, Smith, Tola, & Mann, 2000), ERP waveforms (e.g., Johnson & Adler, 1993; Waldo et al., 1992; White & Yee, 1997), EEG spectral data (e.g., Umrymkhin, Dzebrailova, & Korobeinikova, 2004), and cortisol measurements (see Gunnar & Talge, Chapter 12). Adults and children, particularly young children, are naturally anxious when placed in novel environments and asked to perform unusual tasks. Slatter (2002) suggests that reducing anxiety is an important aspect of developing rapport and creating a successful testing environment. Our methodological approach to control unwanted anxiety effects, a possible confounding variable inflating the error term of our statistical analyses, is one of trying to minimize anxiety levels whenever possible. The following paragraphs outline some strategies that have been used by various experimenters in developmental psychophysiological labs to create a positive environment.

Because many children and even some adults have fears associated with visiting doctors and hospitals, whenever possible, it is best to avoid the appearance of being a medical facility where a medical procedure is about to be employed. Fox and colleagues (1995) and the authors of several chapters in this volume (e.g., Berg & Byrd, Chapter 8; Marshall & Fox, Chapter 5) have had success decorating the lab environment with child friendly themes consistent with the technology, such as astronauts in space. Conversely, de Haan (Chapter 4) recommends that for infants participating in studies that require their attention to be focused on a monitor, it may be best for the lab to have minimal enticing decorations. Instead, one should use monochrome screens or curtains or blinds to cover windows, and display minimal items on the walls, as infants may be distracted away from the monitor to the attractive decorations.

This strategy of creating a positive environment obviously goes beyond just the appearance of the testing suite itself. How the research staff behaves and what they say to children can also alleviate anxieties associated with medical-like procedures. Berg and Byrd (Chapter 8) recommend avoiding wearing white lab coats or scrubs and hiding equipment so it is not prominent when the family enters the laboratory. They suggest having the participants enter the laboratory through a "play room" for a more comfortable and familiar setting in which to develop initial rapport with the child before entering the laboratory room. When a family visits our laboratory, we strive for having an attitude that is informal and playful with an element of "teacher" thrown in, and we purposefully choose not to use the titles of "Doctor" when introducing ourselves to parents or the children.

Rapport is often defined as establishing a relationship with mutual trust. Thus, in establishing a positive rapport with a child, a goal of every interaction should be that of building a high level of trust in the child. This procedure involves making sure the child understands what the experiment will entail by allowing not only the parent but also the child to have informed consent at the level he or she is capable. Trust is further established by ensuring the child that he or she can ask questions at any time and if he or she decides not to continue participating at any point, it is okay to ask to terminate the experiment. Introducing the equipment with sensitivity will not only help develop trust but also help minimize anxiety. When applying an electrode cap for recording EEG, Berg and Byrd (Chapter 8) recommend showing the children and letting them handle and touch a no longer used set of electrodes and to call them "sensors" instead of electrodes. We, like Berg and Byrd, take time to explain how the sensors work (see Berg & Bryd for some creative illustrations). For instance, we introduce the need to use the gel by saying it "makes a liquid wire" between the scalp and sensor. When showing the syringe which we refer to as an "applicator," we first cover the blunt tip so they only see the plastic tube, then explain how the gel is applied after the cap is placed on the head using this special "applicator." Then we let the child feel the blunt tip of the applicator. Also during this interaction, we take time to assure the child that the procedures are very safe and that they should not feel any discomfort (e.g., "Wearing the sensors should not hurt at all") but if they become uncomfortable, they should let us know right away so we can fix it. Fears of the equipment in young children seem to dissipate quickly when we tell them that the cap and sensors are safe enough for infants to wear to show us their brainwaves.

Not only may the children have some anxiety or fear associated with medical-like equipment, studies in developmental trends of fear and anxiety in children suggest that different types of situations cause more fear at different ages (e.g., Eme & Schmidt, 1978; Kashani & Orvaschel, 1990). For instance, infants, toddlers, and preschoolers may have more anxiety related to separation from parents and children 9 years of age or older may have more anxiety related to school performance, being evaluated by others, and social flaws (Albano, Causey, & Carter, 2001). Thus, in terms of the above statistical model, not diminishing sources of anxiety contributes unmeasured variability. With infants and young children, another step that can be used to diminish anxiety is to capitalize on the parent's presence, which can serve as a bridge as one strives for establishing a positive rapport with the child. The authors of the chapters in this volume who discussed data collection with infants and toddlers consistently suggest that an infant or toddler can sit on the parent's lap or the parent can help entertain and encourage a positive mood in the infant or young child. Children around 8 or 9 years and older seem to be quite comfortable participating in our studies without having their parents present the whole time, though often parents will stay and observe a data collection session related to the parent's own curiosity and interest. Nevertheless, these older children may show some anxiousness related to performance or being evaluated.

MAINTAINING CHILD COOPERATION AND ATTENTION WHILE CURTAILING FATIGUE

Besides developing a rapport, experimenters should always consider addressing a second goal when collecting data from children, namely maintaining child cooperation (Querido, Eyber, Kanfer, & Krahn, 2001), which will be addressed in this section. Authors of most of chapters in this volume mention the criticality of quickness (swiftness) in preparing for the experiment and applying the electrodes on an infant or young child. We concur with Berg and Bryd (Chapter 8) that experimenters planning to test infants and children should be well practiced with adults before employing their methods with children so that the process is completed quickly and accurately as possible. As noted by Bell and Wolfe (Chapter 6) application of an EEG cap on an infant's or child's head "requires much patience and planning." It is very time consuming to have to reapply electrodes that are either not correctly placed or are pulled off by the participant. Marshall and Fox (Chapter 5) propose that the duration of cap application depends on efficiency of experimenter, the number of electrodes, and the desired impedance threshold. We have found that the number of experimenters assisting in the application of the cap can also factor into the total time required. Infants and young children will only be cooperative for a short while; accordingly, the longer it takes to apply the electrodes, the less time will remain for the experiment.

Keeping the infant or child in a happy mood during the application process is critical to ensure cooperativeness during the pursuing experiment. The authors of the chapters in this volume propose a number of suggestions for keeping the infant and young child content and cooperative through the preparation phase, such as having a second experimenter or parent entertain the infant or child (e.g., chapters by de Haan; Marshall & Fox), blowing soap bubbles and playing peek-a-boo games (de Haan; Trainor), and using electronic games or showing short cartoons or movie clips (Bell & Wolfe; Berg & Bryd; Marshall & Fox). Berg and Byrd suggest that the movie or cartoon be a short clip given that stopping an ongoing movie or cartoon in itself can upset the infant or young child. Infants and toddlers can be even more of a challenge because they have the propensity to pull at the wires or pull off the applied electrodes. In this case, de Haan and Trainor offer some creative suggestions in their chapters, which include having the infant wear mitts, keeping the infant's hands busy with a cracker, or having the individual that is holding the infant keep the infant's hands controlled. Also placing the wires to the infant's back may help.

To keep an infant's or child's attention on the screen, de Haan (Chapter 4) recommends displaying brief sounds or calling the infant's name in the direction of the screen. Some creative methods of keeping an infant's or child's attention to the essential task is to intermingle the imperative visual stimuli with an interesting movie like Sesame Street (Richards, 2000) and presenting auditory stimuli to the right ear through ear inserts and leaving the left ear unoccluded in order to allow the participant to hear a movie soundtrack at a low volume (Kraus & Nicol, 2003). Another solution to keep alertness in participants during a passive auditory paradigm is to use a silent movie (Davies & Gavin, 2007; Marshall, Bar-Haim, & Fox, 2004). Another approach might be to present stimuli of interest for the duration of the trial (e.g., Gliga & Dehaene-Lambertz, 2005; Grunewald-Zuberbier, Grunewald, Resche, & Netz, 1978; Prevec, Ribaric, & Butinar, 1984).

Berg and Byrd (Chapter 8) mention that participants vary in the degree to which they tolerate wearing an electrode cap, or electrodes or wires on other parts of the body. However, from our experience it is rare that a typically developing child does not tolerate wearing an EEG cap. When working with children with disabilities some of whom may be particularly more sensitive to sensory input (especially tactile stimuli), taking extra time for desensitizing the child to the experience of wearing electrodes and a cap may increase their ability to tolerate the cap. Berg and Byrd offer several suggestions to help train the children so that they will tolerate the cap, ranging from letting the child see the parent wearing the cap to sending home a mock cap and for the parent to work daily with the child wearing the cap.

Using photos with the children smiling and appearing to be enjoying the experience are especially helpful to increase child cooperation in the application of the electrodes. Many of the authors in this volume use photos of other happy children participating in a similar experiment that uses the same equipment or techniques. Marshall and Fox mention that they framed photos of children wearing EEG caps and hung them around their lab. Berg and Bryd suggest providing photos of other children wearing a cap to the parent to use when explaining the experiment to the child. A website with photos can also be helpful. We keep a folder of photos of children wearing EEG caps and electrodes that are applied to the face and ears to illustrate where the sensors will be placed, and this approach seems to reduce the child's anxiety.

Berg and Bryd note that children can be markedly sensitive and anxious about having items affixed to their faces, especially around their eyes (see Berg & Bryd's chapter for suggestions and how to make the child more comfortable with having items affixed to their face). Given that children seem to be sensitive to having things around their face, we also try to avoid moving one's hands across the child's face or blocking his or her vision when reaching for items or affixing electrodes; a better approach is to stand on the side where the action is occurring. One other suggestion made in several chapters included using a cap with electrodes imbedded, rather than placing individual electrodes, or using a high impedance EEG system as the application, because this equipment is usually much quicker than low impedance systems. However, as noted in two chapters (Berg & Bryd; Trainor), while the use of high impedance systems have advanced developmental neuroscience, these systems also are more vulnerable to movement of electrodes, bridging across electrodes, and electrical noise. Decisions on choosing equipment depend on the goals of the research.

CONTROLLING FOR ARTIFACTS IN THE RECORDINGS OF ELECTROPHYSIOLOGICAL DATA

All researchers who routinely collect psychophysiological data understand the need to incorporate into their experimental methodologies procedures that minimize, if not eliminate, artifacts in the electronic signals they record. The term "artifact" here refers to any components in the electronic signal that are not being generated by the physiological processes of interest. Artifacts can be generated from two sources, physiological sources or sources that are not physiological. An example of a non-physiological artifact is 60-cycle noise that can be introduced to the signals being recorded if the participant is sitting too close to an unshielded transformer. Miller and Long (Chapter 13) discuss the sources of non-physiological artifacts and offer some suggestions to minimize these artifacts.

A second type of artifacts is movement or motor artifacts. A common theme addressed by the authors in this volume is that movement artifacts are more pronounced in infants and children than in adults. Berg and Bryd (Chapter 8) suggest that there are two sources of movement artifact, those caused by internal origin generated by muscles (physiological), and those caused by external sources such as movement of electrodes against skin or movement of wires (non-physiological). Berg and Byrd offer several suggestions on how to reduce the non-physiological movement artifacts such as taping electrodes to skin, placing wires behind the child's back out of reach, and to lightly twist the lead wires together between the child and the amplifier or A/D boards. In addition, we tape the wires to the child's shirt at the top of the shoulder to help contain the wires and keep them out of reach and less likely to move, while ensuring that there is enough slack in the wires to allow natural head movements.

Blinking, eye movements, and moving the head or other parts of the body are examples of internal sources of movement artifacts. Reducing the artifacts caused by internal sources can be more challenging. Because infants and toddlers have minimal ability to carry out verbal requests to control their bodies, movement artifacts can be a large contributor to attrition in infant and toddler studies (de Haan, Chapter 4) emphasizing the importance of attending to this type of artifact.

Artifact Reduction Training

When recording EEG signals, movements such as eye blinks and contractions of the muscles in the face and jaw introduce artifacts, severe perturbations of the recorded signal, which can be particularly troublesome. While verbal requests to not blink or move is usually an effective means of decreasing movement artifacts in adults, this method does not provide adequate control over these sources of artifacts when used with children. Indeed, merely asking a young child not to blink often leads to increased blinking. We have found that providing a brief "show and tell" training period before the onset of data collection can serve as an effective strategy to minimize these movement artifacts in children. This procedural step has been helpful with adult participants as well. "Show and tell" training allows the participant to associate these artifacts with their muscle movements as they are generated, and more importantly, allows the participant to understand *why* we want them to remain relaxed and not blink.

This training involves showing the participant his or her brainwaves immediately after finishing prepping the EEG cap on the participant. Upon directing the participant's attention to the computer monitor displaying the EEG tracings in real time, we ask the participant to blink several times pointing out the resulting large jumps in some of the signal tracings. We explain that these distortions are called artifacts. We then ask the participant to "stare" at the monitor screen and notice how the tracings contain only the smaller signals that come from the brain. We describe the smaller signals as "quiet" brainwaves. We then have the participant blink several times to see the artifact effects again. Next we have the participant smile and grit his or her teeth to demonstrate what muscle artifacts look like on the monitor screen. We ask the participant to note how blinking and using his or her face muscles hide the brainwaves so we cannot see them. If the child shows interest, we allow the child to play with the signals for a brief period.

We finish off our training by again asking the participant to sit quietly, to not move, and to stare at the EEG monitor screen to produce the quiet brainwaves. We remind the participant that we are interested in recording the brainwaves and not muscle activity during the tasks and that to get good and accurate brainwave recordings we need him or her to sit as still as possible keeping his or her face relaxed while trying to minimize the number of blinks. We suggest that one way to keep the blinking to a minimum is for the child to pretend having a staring contest with a friend during the experiment, noting that the "friend" will be the computer monitor that is used to present stimuli. We also make sure the participant understands that blinking is necessary to keep the eyes from drying out and becoming irritated so we expect him or her to blink now and then. We end our artifact training by having the participant practice staring at the EEG monitor for a full pass of the line cursor across the screen to give the participant an idea of what a good period (i.e., 8 to 10 seconds) of "quiet brainwaves" *feels* like rather than specifying a number of seconds we expect between blinks.

Frequent Breaks

To reduce movement artifacts from the children fidgeting in their chairs, we organize our testing procedures such that children are given a break every 8 to 10 minutes to stretch arms and legs usually while sitting. During these break periods between tasks we ask the child to rest the eyes by closing them for a few seconds as well as having him or her stretch. If the fidgeting becomes extreme we have the child stand up to stretch. Special attention to the placement of equipment and cabling is needed to accommodate the possibility of the participant stretching while standing.

Motor Movements and Associated Movements

As highlighted by Berg and Bryd, during reaction time tasks children often display associated movements or motor overflow prior to a motor action (e.g., quickly pressing a button). Associated movements decrease with age especially between 6 and 9 years of age (Cohen, Taft, Mahadeviah, & Birch, 1967; Lazarus & Todor, 1987). However, a few studies indicated that some level of associated reactions may be present through adolescence (Connolly & Stratton, 1968; Fog & Fog, 1967; Warren & Karrer, 1984). Thus, body movement artifacts may increase by requiring a child, especially a young child, to press a button during an experiment. In some children, these associated movements can be so severe that they will involve a full body forward motion while pressing buttons creating sizable movement artifacts. In addition to the movement artifact, it is possible when collecting EEG data in children that motor actions may inadvertently produce a positive slow wave prior to the button press, which may be related to neural inhibition of associated reactions (Warren & Karrer, 1984). With a button press, another type of artifact may result because some children look down at their hand and the button causing a downward eye movement artifact (de Haan, Chapter 4; Berg, personal communication).

Positioning

Positioning is an essential consideration that researchers should take into account when collecting any type of psychophysiological data. In the discussion of placement of electrodes for heart rate, Berg and Byrd recommend seating the child in a child seat so that feet are solidly placed on the floor to minimize motor artifacts that may be caused by leg swinging. Appropriate positioning is often considered only necessary for children with disabilities, but even for children without motor disabilities, good positioning stabilizes the trunk and helps prevent extraneous movements and appropriate positioning facilitates better hand manipulations (Smith-Zuzovsky & Exner, 2004). Even more convincing, fourth grade students in general education displayed better on-task behaviors such as eye contact, attention to task, and following directions when seated in appropriate sized chairs and at the correct height of table when compared to the same children who were seated in chairs and at tables that were too large (Wingrat & Exner, 2005). There-fore, appropriate positioning decreases extraneous movements and may even increase a child's ability to stay on task.

One obstacle in using a child-sized chair as mentioned by Berg and Bryd is that many labs are set up with tables at the standard adult height to accom-modate adult participants. In this case, a child-sized seat is not optimal, especially if the child is required to make responses on a keyboard or key-pad or attend to a monitor unless that lab also has a child-sized table. One solution to this situation is having a set of nesting footstools or footrests that can be used so that the child's feet can be placed on a solid surface while using an adjustable adult-sized chair and standard table. In our lab, we have a standard-sized table, an adjustable adult-sized chair so that children can be raised so that the table is a correct height for them and their elbows can easily rest on the table, and a set of five footstools ranging from 2 inches to 12 inches to provide a stable surface for feet for any sized child. At times for the young children, we place a large firm pillow (that extends from the seat to the top of the back rest) in the chair between the child and the back of the chair to bring the child closer to the table while giving them a surface to lean his or her back against. This arrangement and choices of "positioning" equipment has worked splendidly for children ages 4 up through adolescence.

With infants and toddlers, other positioning options should be considered. With infants, having a parent or another adult hold the infant may seem to be the best choice. Although, de Haan (Chapter 4) cautions that an adult holding a child may change how the infant responds and an adult may introduce additional unintended artifacts (e.g., inadvertently bouncing the baby or causing the baby to turn his or her head to look at the adult). If these items are a concern and the lab is equipped with infant and child furniture, a child-sized chair and table or an infant seat may be the best positioning choice.

Head control is another issue that should be considered. This issue may be particularly important with infants or for participants of all ages in long paradigms to keep the neck muscles relaxed (de Haan). In EEG studies, when using electrode caps, leaning the head back on the chair can produce artifacts in the occipital region, which can be especially problematic in studies examining visual processing.

Encourage Use of Lavatory

Another source of motor artifacts occurs when children move about in their chair because they need to use the lavatory. This behavior can be partially avoided by strongly encouraging child participants to use the lavatory before beginning the preparation phase of a recording session. This procedure is particularly important for young children as they will have difficulty sitting still even when their bladder is empty. We have also observed that children are not always comfortable asking to use the lavatory once they are wired for data recording. Therefore, even if the child uses the lavatory before the session, it is still wise to watch for fidgeting behaviors such as leg swinging and rocking back and forth in the chair, because these behaviors increase as the urge to relieve himself or herself increases often before the participant is conscious of having such urges.

Artifact Removal

Authors of several chapters in this volume address the computational methods for removing or reducing recorded artifacts (Trainor; Berg, & Byrd; de Haan; Marshall, & Fox; Miller, & Long). Somsen and van Beek (1998) state that rejection is better than correction algorithms in ages 5 to 12 years of age. Nonetheless, Marshall and Fox (Chapter 5) argue that in order to have enough trials it may be necessary to use eye blink correction strategies. Although conclusive recommendations have not been drawn in this volume as to the best way to handle the elimination of movement artifacts in child data, Miller and Long offer a few suggestions to handle artifact elimination, which include increasing the number of trials collected, collecting high-quality EOG signals, and using visual inspection to reject segments that contain sizeable artifacts.

GIVING AND EXPLAINING TASK INSTRUCTIONS

Just as it is important to consider modifying one's experimental methodologies to include training procedures designed to minimize artifacts in the electrophysiological data, when working with children, particularly young children, extra consideration is needed for providing task instructions to the participant. Two principles should guide one when providing instructions to children. First, the younger the child, the more literal he or she will be in their interpretation of instructions; and second, the younger the child, the more likely he or she is to show perseverating behaviors. Indeed, we have observed that even for the simplest of tasks where brief straightforward instructions work for adults, children often interpret the instructions differently than intended. The following describes several steps we take to insure children perform the tasks as expected.

First, as with our studies with adults, we provide instructions to a child by reading from a prepared script to insure that the same basic information and instructions are given to each participant. The script is written at a cognitive and language level appropriate for our youngest participants in the study. A second element of our written instructions is the repetition of key concepts we wish to impart on the participant. After reading the scripted instructions, we assess the understanding of the younger children (especially those under the ages of nine years) by engaging them in a short dialogue by asking them to tell us in their own words what they are expected to do. For studies that include young children, we also run a few practice trials. The practice trials ensure that the participant understands the instructions and is responding as expected.

The tendency for young children to perseverate in their behaviors has implications for studies in which young children are asked to do a second task that has some but not all elements similar to the first task. In this situation, the children often will carry over their behaviors and expectations from the previous task. With young children we found we had to emphasize what is different in the task, for example, by physically removing the mouse or response pad if button presses are no longer needed.

Even with well-prepared and delivered instructions at the beginning of the task, children may lose interest or forget what they were asked to do as the task continues. Thus, monitoring participants' performance throughout the data collection period is critical to insure that the children stay on task. If the protocols place heavy demands on their cognitive abilities or lead to increases in anxiety levels, the children's attention can easily wander which may result in becoming confused or even forgetting specific instructions. Often, not wanting to become embarrassed, children will not ask for help. When we observe that children are deviating from the desired task behaviors, we provide gentle reminders to guide them back to performing appropriate behaviors. However, one does need to be judicious in providing reminders as we have noted that these reminders are perceived by some children as additional demands provoking increased anxiety and even worse behavioral outcomes.

SPECIAL POPULATIONS

When involving children with special needs in psychophysiological research, whether the special needs relate to cognitive, physical, or emotional disabilities, we have found that building a trusting relationship with the child and parent is often the most critical factor in being able to complete a research protocol and obtaining usable data. The key to building the trusting relations is to assure that the child is physically comfortable and that both the parent and child feel emotionally safe. From our experience, some parents of children with special needs are more protective of their children and may want to intervene more often in the session so it is especially important to assure that both the child and parent are comfortable with the process.

The technique that we have used to increase the physical comfort of the child with special needs primarily involves positioning (i.e., chair height, footstool to place feet) as discussed previously. In addition to reducing artifacts, good positioning for a child with special needs will help the child feel secure and will allow the child to have more control over movements. If the child feels lost in a large chair and is not able to put his or her feet on a stable surface (floor or footstool), he or she may be less able to attend and participate.

Promoting emotional security is a more complex issue. First, we always have the parent(s) in the room with the child at the beginning of the experiment while explaining the process and preparing for data collection (e.g., putting on electrodes). Second, we have one experimenter designated to build a rapport with the child, as discussed in a previous section, but this is particularly important with children with disabilities as they may have more difficulty building trust. This experimenter, often a third member to the research team, devotes his or her full attention to the child's comfort and does not engage in any other preparation activity. When the child is prepped in this manner, often the parents and an experimenter are able to leave the room once the child feels emotionally secure with the experimenter(s) collecting the psychophysiological data.

For some special populations, be prepared to engage in prepping procedures at a slower pace and with additional sensitivity to child's needs. Children with special needs often feel anxious in a novel setting, much more so than children without disabilities. Working with children with special needs requires proactive warding off anxiety-provoking incidents that may be more salient for the children with special needs. For example, many children with disabilities have had more encounters with medical procedures, and thus, may have more anxiety related to them. Consequently, we have found that it is even more important to make the environment as non-medical as possible for children with special needs. Supplies and instrumentation used in psychophysiological research that may be seen as medical instruments or materials such as the applicator (i.e., syringe, as indicated earlier) used to insert gel into the electrodes on an electrode cap, alcohol used to clean skin, medical tape, and gauze or cotton should all be used cautiously. Thus, we do not have these materials in the child's viewing range when he or she enters the laboratory area and always introduce the materials very carefully.

When we are faced with a more challenging preparation, we have found that providing the child with small electronic games and fidget toys to occupy the child's hands and dissipate energy often help. In certain cases, we have encouraged parents to have their child bring his or her "security toy" as an additional comfort. A familiar toy brought from home may also be beneficial for young children without disabilities. However, we have found that for children without disabilities who are 5 years of age and older usually do not require this type of prop. With children with disabilities we often use either a security toy or electronic games for children as old as 10 to 12 years of age.

Many children with special needs, especially those children with autism, attention deficit hyperactive disorder (ADHD), and learning disabilities may have difficulty processing sensory information. In other words, children with sensory processing disorders are very sensitive to certain sensory experiences. These sensory sensitivities are more subtle deficits than primary sensory impairments such as deafness and blindness. We have found that it is important at the beginning of the session to determine if the child is sensitive. If the child is sensitive to touch, he or she may not like things touching his or her skin. If this is the case, activities such as cleaning areas on the child's face, placing electrodes on the face, arms, or hands, squirting gel into electrodes in an electrode cap, water or other liquid dripping onto the child's face, or even the pressure of an electrode cap on the child's head may become so annoying to the child that he or she may refuse to complete the experiment or may pull off electrodes or caps in the middle of the experiment. A child may also be sensitive to auditory, visual, or movement sensation. Thus, we introduce the items that may precipitate an unpleasant experience very slowly and allow the child to experience the event on his or her own terms. For example, we ask the child if he or she would like to feel the gel on his or her fingers before inserting the gel into the electrode sites in the cap. In addition, we never move ahead with a new step in the preparation until the child has given us verbal or nonverbal permission, which can be a head nod, eye contact or a smile. By using these procedures with children that we suspect may be sensitive to sensory stimuli, we have been extremely successful in getting the children to complete the experiment even though in many other situations the child might refuse to participate. Our attrition rate for children with disabilities is less than 1% once they visit our laboratory.

DEVELOPING A COMMUNITY PRESENCE EASES THE BURDEN OF RECRUITING CHILD PARTICIPANTS

A major consideration of any research program involving children is finding enough children to participate in the planned project. Word of mouth and advertisements in local media often suffice for a one time study involving small sample sizes. However, for projects that involve a series of studies to be conducted over several years and require a large number of children as participants, a more global approach to solicitation of participants may be warranted at the outset of the project. This approach is analogous to the concept found in the commercial sector of our society, namely, that a positive corporate image is essential to a consumer's confidence in a product when he or she is considering a purchase. Obvious factors that help create a positive reputation for a psychophysiological laboratory studying children include making the family feel they are always the focus of your attention, acknowledging that the family's participation is essential to the success of the project since without their help the study cannot be done, always being considerate of the family's time and effort needed to participate, taking time to answer questions, and explaining how this particular research contributes to our knowledge about children and development, and insuring nothing less than professional behavior by all research staff when interacting with family members. The following paragraphs outline the procedures we use to solicit participants and ensure that their experiences before, during, and after visiting the laboratory are positive ones.

Many of us who begin planning research projects involving child participants immediately think of the schools as a potential source for obtaining volunteers. Indeed, schools can provide a large number of children that can be contacted and their participation solicited. Some researchers have reported great success in recruiting participants through the school system and develop collaborations with the school administration and teachers. However, from our experience, most often the actual participation rate in return for the time and effort involved in this solicitation process is often low, especially for elementary school-aged children. The process of obtaining permission from school principals and sometimes the school district review panels often results in the solicitation process being reduced to flyers being handed out to children in a classroom by the teacher who consents to the request. If the flyers are to be effective, they must actually make it home and be seen by the parents at a time that is conducive to their being able to contact a project representative in a timely manner to volunteer for the research study.

An alternative to focusing on the schools as a source of participants is to solicit volunteers at community and social group meetings where children and their parents are both present. For instance, we have had good success in obtaining volunteers by attending Cub Scout Pack meetings where we give a brief "show and tell" presentation about our research and then ask for volunteers to help us in our studies. We have also obtain volunteers by giving presentations at the meetings of the Boy Scouts, Brownies and Girl Scouts, associations for home schooling, parent organizations for children with disabilities, and church socials or other community family gatherings. By showing photos of other children engaged in the activities of the study, discussing how the brain produces electricity, and letting the audience see and try on an EEG cap in these live presentations, we have the opportunity to build a rapport with the children and their parents. A great advantage to these meetings is that we often talk with both the children and the parents all together increasing the probability that the children and parent both become committed to volunteering. Besides soliciting volunteers at community and social group meetings, we have successfully recruited adolescents in junior and senior high schools by participating in our local presentations of Brain Awareness Week sponsored by the Society for Neuroscience (for more information, see http://web.sfn.org/baw/).

Our communication with families begins before they come to the laboratory when we send them a packet of information with the consent forms, maps to the laboratory, and a parking permit. In this packet we include a "Tip Sheet." The items we list on the tip sheet are selected because having the participant know about these things will make the data collection go smoother when they arrive. The tip sheet includes information about dressing in layers of clothing so that participants can be comfortable in warm or cool rooms. We suggest the family bring snacks and a drink for the participant to have during breaks. We also remind them, for the EEG studies that we will be placing gel in the participant's hair and they may want to bring a cap to wear afterwards or a brush or comb to use after we wash out the gel with a wet towel. The last suggestion we put on the tip sheet is for participants who wear contact lenses. Since contacts tend to require more moisture to keep the eyes from being irritated, an individual wearing contacts will blink more frequently. On the tip sheet we ask the participant to consider wearing glasses during the recording session instead of contacts. We also request the older children to not bring chewing gum.

FINAL REMARKS

We acknowledge that many of the guidelines and suggestions outlined in this chapter are self-evident, especially after the fact and to the experienced researcher. The authors in this book have offered many good pointers. We have added our own lessons learned from having had in our laboratory hundreds of participants from early childhood to late adolescence. By gathering these ideas together, we hope our collective wisdom will be useful to new researchers in the field. We welcome further suggestions as we build a collective wisdom in our growing community of developmental psychophysiologists.

References

Albano, A. M., Causey, D., & Carter, B. D. (2001). Fear and anxiety in children. In C. E. Walker & M. C. Roberts (Eds.), *Handbook of clinical child psychology* (3rd ed., pp. 291–316). New York: John Wiley & Sons.

Cohen, H. J., Taft, L. T., Mahadeviah, M. S., & Birch, H. G. (1967). Developmental changes in overflow in normal and aberrantly functioning children. *Journal of Pediatrics, 71*, 39–47.

Connolly, K. J., & Stratton, P. (1968). Developmental changes in associated movements. *Developmental Medicine and Child Neurology, 10*, 49–56.

Davies P. L., & Gavin, W. J. (2007). Validating the diagnosis of sensory processing disorders using EEG technology. *American Journal of Occupational Therapy, 61*, 176–189.

Davies, P. L., Segalowitz, S. J., & Gavin, W. J. (2004). Development of response-monitoring ERPs in participants 7- to 25-year olds. *Developmental Neuropsychology, 25*, 355–376.

Eme, R., & Schmidt, D. (1978). The stability of children's reas. *Child Development, 49*, 1277–1279.

Fog, E., & Fog, M. (1967). Cerebral inhibition examined by associated movements. In M. Bax & R. C. Mac Keith (Eds.), *Minimal cerebral dysfunction: Clinics in developmental medicine* (No. 10, pp. 52–57). London: Spastics Society with Heinemann.

Fox, N. A., Rubin, K. H., Calkins, S. D., Marshall, T. R., Coplan, R. J., Porges, S. W., Long, J. M., & Stewart, S. (1995). Frontal activation asymmetry and social competence at four years of age. *Child Development, 66*, 1770–1784.

Gilbert, B. O., & Gilbert, D. G. (1991). Electrodermal responses to movie-induced stress as a function of EPI and MMPI scale scores. *Journal of Social Behavior and Personality. 6*, 903–914.

Gliga, T., & Dehaene-Lambertz, G. (2005). Structural encoding of body and face in human infants and adult. *Journal of Cognitive Neuroscience, 17*, 1328–1340.

Grunewald-Zuberbier, E., Grunewald, G., Resche, A., & Netz, J. (1978). Contingent negative variation and alpha attenuation responses in children with different abilities to concentrate. *Electroencephalography and Clinical Neurophysiology, 44*, 37–47.

Johnson, M. R., & Adler, L. E. (1993). Transient impairment in P50 auditory sensory gating induced by a cold-pressor test. *Biological Psychiatry, 33*, 380–387.

Kashani, J. H., & Orvaschel, H. (1990). A community study of anxiety in children and adolescents. *American Journal of Psychiatry, 147*, 313–318.

Kraus, N., & Nicol, T. (2003). Aggregate neural responses to speech sounds in the central auditory system. *Speech Communication, 41*, 35–47.

Lazarus, J. C., & Todor, J. I. (1987). Age differences in the magnitude of associated movement. *Developmental Medicine and Child Neurology, 29*, 726–733.

Marshall, P. J., Bar-Haim, Y., & Fox, N. A. (2004). Development of P50 gating in the auditory event-related potential. *International Journal of Psychophysiology, 51*, 135–141.

Naveteur, J., Buisine, S., & Gruzelier, J. H. (2005). The influence of anxiety on electrodermal responses to distractors. *International Journal of Psychophysiology, 56*, 261–269.

Prevec, T. S., Ribaric, K., & Butinar, D. (1984). Contingent negative variation audiometry in children. *Audiology, 23*, 114–126.

Querido, J., Eyber, S., Kanfer, R. & Krahn, G. (2001). The process of the clinical child assessment interview. In C. E. Walker & M. C. Roberts (Eds.) *Handbook of clinical child psychology* (3rd ed., pp. 74–89). New York: John Wiley & Sons.

Richards, J. E. (2003). Attention affects the recognition of briefly presented visual stimuli in infants: An ERP study. *Developmental Science 6*, 312–328.

Sattler, J. M. (2001). *Assessment of children: Cognitive applications* (4th ed.). San Diego: Jerome M. Sattler.

Sattler, J. M. (2002). *Assessment of children: Behavioral and clinical applications* (4th ed.). San Diego: Jerome M. Sattler.

Segalowitz, S. J., & Barnes, K. L. (1993). The reliability of ERP components in the auditory oddball paradigm. *Psychophysiology, 30*, 451–459.

Smith-Zuzovsky, N., & Exner, C. E. (2004). The effect of seated positioning quality on typical 6- and 7-year old children's object manipulation skills. *American Journal of Occupational Therapy, 58*, 380–388.

Somsen, R. J., & van Beek, B. (1998). Ocular artifacts in children's EEG: Selection is better than correction. *Biological Psychology, 48*, 281–300.

Umrymkhin, E. A., Dzebrailova, T. D., & Korobeinikova, I. I. (2004). Spectral characteristics of the EEG in students with different levels of result achievement under the conditions of examination stress. *Human Physiology, 30*, 28–35.

Waldo, M., Gerhardt, G., Baker, N., Drebing, C., Adler, L., & Freedman, R. (1992). Auditory sensory gating and catecholamine metabolism in schizophrenic and normal subjects. *Psychiatry Research, 44*, 21–32.

Warren, C., & Karrer, R. (1984). Movement-related potentials in children: A replication of waveforms, and their relationships to age, performance and cognitive development. *Annals of the New York Academy of Sciences, 425*, 489–495.

White, P. M., & Yee, C. M. (1997). Effects of attentional and stressor manipulations on the P50 gating response. *Psychophysiology, 34*, 703–711.

Wilken, J. A., Smith, B. D., Tola, K., & Mann, M. (2000). Trait anxiety and prior exposure to non-stressful stimuli: Effects on psychophysiological arousal and anxiety. *International Journal of Psychophysiology, 37*, 233–242.

Wingrat, J., & Exner, C. E. (2005). The impact of school furniture on fourth grade children's on-task and sitting behavior in the classroom: A pilot study. *Work, 25*, 263–272.

Index